FinancialHistory class protocol

class initialization

initialBalance: amount	Begin a financial history with amount as the amount of money on hand.
new	Begin a financial history with 0 as the amount of money on hand.

FinancialHistory instance protocol

transaction recording

receive: amount from: source	Remember that an amount of money, amount, has been received from source.
spend: amount for: reason	Remember that an amount of money, amount, has been spent for reason.

inquiries

cashOnHand	Answer the total amount of money currently on hand.
totalReceivedFrom: source	Answer the total amount received from source, so far.
totalSpentFor: reason	Answer the total amount spent for reason, so far.

Smalltalk-80

Smalltalk–80

The Language and its Implementation

Adele Goldberg and David Robson

Xerox Palo Alto Research Center

Addison-Wesley Publishing Company
Reading, Massachusetts • Menlo Park, California
London • Amsterdam • Don Mills, Ontario • Sydney

This book is in the
Addison-Wesley series in Computer Science
MICHAEL A. HARRISON
CONSULTING EDITOR

Library of Congress Cataloging in Publication Data

Goldberg, Adele.
  Smalltalk-80: the language and its implementation.

  1. Smalltalk-80 (Computer system) I. Robson, David.
II. Title.
QA76.8.S635G64 1983   001.64'2   82-13741
ISBN 0-201-11371-6

Smalltalk-80 is a trademark of Xerox Corporation.

Reprinted with corrections, May 1983

ISBN 0-201-11371-6

BCDEFGHIJ-HA-89876543

Preface

Advances in the design and production of computer hardware have brought many more people into direct contact with computers. Similar advances in the design and production of computer software are required in order that this increased contact be as rewarding as possible. The Smalltalk-80 system is a result of a decade of research into creating computer software that is appropriate for producing highly functional and interactive contact with personal computer systems.

This book is the first detailed account of the Smalltalk-80 system. It is divided into four major parts:

Part One — an overview of the concepts and syntax of the programming language.

Part Two — an annotated and illustrated specification of the system's functionality.

Part Three — an example of the design and implementation of a moderate-size application.

Part Four — a specification of the Smalltalk-80 virtual machine.

The first part introduces the Smalltalk approach to information representation and manipulation. Five words—*object, message, class, instance,* and *method*—make up the vocabulary with which Smalltalk is discussed. These terms are defined and the syntax of the Smalltalk-80 programming language is introduced.

The second part of the book contains specifications of the kinds of objects already present in the Smalltalk-80 programming environment. New kinds of objects can be added by a programmer, but a wide variety of objects come with the standard system. The messages that can be sent to each kind of object are listed, commented upon, and illustrated.

The third part of the book is an example of adding new kinds of objects to the system. It describes the addition of an application to model discrete, event-driven simulations such as car washes, banks, or information systems. Some readers may find it useful to read the third part of the book immediately after reading the first part, referring to the specifications in the second part whenever the meaning of a Smalltalk-80 expression is not clear.

The fourth part of the book specifies how the Smalltalk-80 virtual machine can be implemented. This virtual machine provides object-oriented storage, message-oriented processing and graphically-oriented interaction. It is primarily of interest to readers who wish to implement a Smalltalk-80 system, or to readers who wish to understand the implementation of a message-oriented system in detail.

The Task of Book-Writing

Writing this first book about the Smalltalk-80 system was a complex task, partially due to the sociology of the system's creation, and partially due to the diverse kinds of information people require about such a system. We can divide the different reasons for the complexity of this task into four categories:

- Smalltalk is a vision.
- Smalltalk is based on a small number of concepts, but defined by unusual terminology.
- Smalltalk is a graphical, interactive programming environment.
- Smalltalk is a big system.

Smalltalk is a vision

In the early 1970's, the Xerox Palo Alto Research Center Learning Research Group began work on a vision of the ways different people might effectively and joyfully use computing power. In 1981 the name of the group was changed to the Software Concepts Group or SCG. The goal of SCG is to create a powerful information system, one in which the user can store, access and manipulate information so that the system can grow as the user's ideas grow. Both the number and kinds of system components should grow in proportion to the growth of the user's awareness of how to effectively use the system.

SCG's strategy for realizing this vision has been to concentrate on two principal areas of research: a language of description (a programming language) which serves as an interface between the models in the human mind and those in computing hardware, and a language of interaction (a user interface) which matches the human communication system to that of the computer. Smalltalk research has followed a two- to four-year cycle: create a system embodying current understanding of the software needs; implement applications that test the system's ability to support these applications; and finally, based on the resulting experience, reformulate the understanding of software needs and redesign the programming language and/or the user interface.

The Smalltalk-80 system marks the fifth time through this cycle. The research is still in progress. We hope that presenting a detailed description of the current research results will contribute to the community working towards SCG's vision. The continued unfolding of the research means that the software system described in this book is literally a "moving target" and the information in this book represents only one station on a long track. Holding the train in the station long enough to write about it made the writing task complex.

Smalltalk has few concepts

Smalltalk is based on a small number of concepts, but defined by unusual terminology. Due to the uniformity with which the object-message orientation is carried out in the system, there are very few new programming concepts to learn in order to understand Smalltalk. On the one hand, this means that the reader can be told all the concepts quickly and then explore the various ways in which these concepts are applied in the system. These concepts are presented by defining the five words mentioned earlier that make up the vocabulary of Smalltalk—object, message, class, instance, and method. These five words are defined in terms of each other, so it is almost as though the reader must know everything before knowing anything.

Smalltalk is an environment

Smalltalk is a graphical, interactive programming environment. As suggested by the personal computing vision, Smalltalk is designed so that every component in the system that is accessible to the user can be presented in a meaningful way for observation and manipulation. The user interface issues in Smalltalk revolve around the attempt to create a visual language for each object. The preferred hardware system for Smalltalk includes a high-resolution graphical display screen and a pointing device such as a graphics pen or a mouse. With these devices, the user can select information viewed on the screen and invoke messages in order to interact with that information.

One way to present the details of the Smalltalk-80 system would be to start with the user interface and to describe each facility for accessing objects. Such a presentation might begin with scenarios of the ways in which the programmer might interact with the system. Each scenario would be a snapshot of a dynamic system. In a linear, static way, the book would try to convey the dynamics of multiple access paths to a large and diverse amount of information.

These aspects of the system are an important part of what Smalltalk provides as an applications development environment. However, in order to explain how this graphical user interface really works, the reader first has to understand the programming language. Thus, this book inverts the presentation of the system by starting with the language itself. Information about the system objects that support the user interface has been separated out and, except for the kernel graphics classes, is not presented in this book. Another book on the Smalltalk-80 user interface presents a detailed treatment of the implementation of these system objects (*Smalltalk-80: The Interactive Programming Environment* by Adele Goldberg).

Smalltalk is a big system

The Smalltalk-80 system is made up of many components. It includes objects that provide the functions usually attributed to a computer operating system: automatic storage management, a file system, display handling, text and picture editing, keyboard and pointing device input, a debugger, a performance spy, processor scheduling, compilation and decompilation. There are a lot of kinds of objects to learn about.

Smalltalk is built on the model of communicating objects. Large applications are viewed in the same way as the fundamental units from which the system is built. The interaction between the most primitive objects is viewed in the same way as the highest-level interaction between the computer and the user. Objects support modularity—the functioning of any object does not depend on the internal details of other objects. The complexity of the system is reduced by this minimization of interdependencies of system components. Complexity is further reduced by grouping together similar components; this is achieved through classes in Smalltalk. Classes are the chief mechanism for extension in Smalltalk. User-defined classes become a part of the system on an equal footing with the kernel classes of the system. Subclasses support the ability to factor the system in order to avoid repetitions of the same concepts in many different places.

Managing complexity is a key contribution of the Smalltalk approach to software. The early examples of the language are very simple, taken from the kinds of programming exercises common in many programming language books. This is so examples can be short, illustrating one or two points. The value of Smalltalk may not be apparent in these examples. After all, they can be done in other languages, and probably just as well. The value of Smalltalk becomes apparent when designing and implementing large applications, or when trying to make a modification to the system itself. For example, consider a dictionary, a frequently-used data structure in the Smalltalk-80 system. It is possible to design, implement, test, and install a new representation for dictionaries without in any way disrupting the running system. This is possible as long as the message interface upon which the functioning of other system objects depends is not destroyed.

The Smalltalk-80 system supports a number of interesting design tools, notably classes and instances as units for organizing and sharing information, and subclassing as a means to inherit and to refine existing capability. Combined with the interactive way in which the program development process is carried out, the Smalltalk-80 system provides a rich environment for prototyping new applications and refining old ones.

Writing a book about such a rich system means that some things must be left out. Again, we chose to omit in this first book the details of the programming interface and the way in which interactive graphical applications can be created. We focus on the language and the kernel classes of the system.

The Task of Book-Reading

This book takes for granted a certain amount of computer literacy on the part of its reader. We assume that the reader

- knows why software systems are a good idea;
- is a programmer or programming-language designer who knows at least one language well;
- is familiar with the idea of expression syntax and of evaluation of expressions by an interpreter;
- is familiar with sequencing of instructions in a computer, control structures such as iteration and recursion, and the role of data structures;
- is concerned with the need to have better control of the representation and manipulation of information in a computing system; and
- is seeking new ideas for how to create a software (application) system that supports the ability to express a software solution in a way that is closely associated with the natural expression of the solution.

Part of this book is for programmers interested in how to implement the language and its development environment on a particular kind of hardware system. Because of the variety of hardware systems on the market, the issue of "portability" has been emphasized. Portability means that only a small kernel of functionality must actually be created for each hardware system in order to realize a running system. This book provides an example of how to attain such portability.

Sharing the Credit

The Smalltalk-80 system is based on ideas gleaned from the Simula language and from the visions of Alan Kay, who first encouraged us to try to create a uniformly object-oriented system. The current embodiment of these ideas is the result of two related activities: research carried out at the Xerox Palo Alto Research Center, and cooperation with a group of stalwart participants in a project to review the research results.

In August, 1980, several hardware manufacturers were invited to review the pages of our second attempt to write a book about Smalltalk and its latest realization. Our first attempt described the Smalltalk-76 system and was abandoned in response to our desire to create a more portable system for distribution outside the Xerox research centers. Our second attempt was a book that was partially historical in nature, partially statements about a vision for personal computing, and partially functional specification for a new Smalltalk system. We thought we would entitle it *Smalltalk Dreams and Schemes* as a reflection of the dual purpose of our writing. The manufacturers who patiently reviewed our material were from Apple Computer, Digital Equipment Corporation, Hewlett-Packard, and Tektronix. These companies were chosen because they designed hardware systems. We hoped that, in reviewing the material, they would learn about our unusual software goals and would devote some time to the problem of creating hardware systems specifically for Smalltalk-like systems. We knew that hardware systems currently on the market, and even ones planned for the near future, would have insufficient power to support our goals. Instead of designing software to fit the hardware we could buy, we decided to try to get the hardware designed to fit the software we wanted.

The manufacturers assigned personnel from their research laboratories to the task of reading the second version of the book. This book has benefited from much discussion and hard work on the part of these reviewers. The early part of the book was completely rewritten as a result of their constructive criticism. The reviewers are responsible for our continuing to try to complete the distribution process and for our completing this book, but not for any faults in its ultimate form. Each set of reviewers implemented the system at least once in order to test our specification of the Smalltalk-80 virtual machine. The current specification reflects their careful review.

As authors of this book, we took responsibility for creating the written description of the Smalltalk-80 system. But credit for the creation of the system goes to all the members of the Software Concepts Group. To these people, we state our debt, our thanks, and our love. Dan Ingalls manages the overall systems design and development effort. Peter Deutsch on the Dorado, Glenn Krasner on the Alto, and Kim McCall on the Dolphin (also called the Xerox 1100 Scientific Information Processor), contributed expertise to the virtual machine implementations on the Xerox computers. User interface ideas, implementations, and management of the release process were carried out by James Althoff (user interface development), Robert Flegal (design of the graphics editor), Ted Kaehler (while laboring over virtual memory problems), Diana Merry (our text guru), and Steve Putz (version management). Peggy Asprey, Marc Meyer, Bill Finzer, and Laura Gould, in trying to keep their applications studies in pace with the system development, tested major changes. Copious reading of the manuscript at various stages of inception was done by Michael Rutenberg, Michael Madsen, Susanne Bodker, and Jay Trow. Editing assistance was given by Rachel Rutherford and Janet Moreland.

Chapter 18 on the Smalltalk-80 graphics kernel was revised from a paper written by Dan Ingalls for *Byte* magazine; Chapter 30 was initially written by Larry Tesler. Graphical images in Chapters 18, 19, and 20, were created by Robert Flegal (especially Figures 18.1 and 20.1), Dan Ingalls, and Adele Goldberg (especially Figures 20.2 and 20.3). Steve Putz offered valuable assistance in creating the images for Chapter 17. Images for the openings to Parts One and Two, and all images for the opening pages of Chapters 1 through 20, were created by Adele Goldberg. Images for Parts Three and Four, and all images for the opening pages of Chapters 21 through 30, were created by Robert Flegal. These images were created using the Smalltalk-80 graphics editor in combination with a low-resolution image scanner designed by Joseph Maleson.

To the participants in the review process, we also give our thanks. With them we have set an example of cooperative scientific exchange that we hope will evolve and continue to grow. Encouragement to begin this project came from our laboratory manager, Bert Sutherland. Reviewers and implementors were: from Apple, Rick Meyers and David Casseres; from Digital Equipment Corporation, Stoney Ballard, Eric Osman, and Steve Shirron; from Hewlett-Packard, Alec Dara-Abrams, Joe Falcone, Jim Stinger, Bert Speelpenning, and Jeff Eastman; and from Tektronix, Paul McCullough, Allen Wirfs-Brock, D. Jason Penney, Larry Katz, Robert Reed, and Rick Samco. We thank their companies and administrators for their patience and willingness to depart from industry standards, at least for one brief moment—at Apple, Steve Jobs and Bruce Daniels; at Digital, Larry Samburg; at Hewlett-Packard, Paul Stoft, Jim Duley, and Ted Laliotis; and at Tektronix, Jack Grimes, and George Rhine. The folks from Tektronix prepared detailed reviews on audiotape, so we could not only see the errors of our ways, but hear them as well!

It is our hope that this book and its companion will facilitate the distribution of the Smalltalk concepts in the computer community. If it succeeds, then that success is shared by us with our colleagues at the Xerox Palo Alto Research Center.

Postscript on the Production of This Book

The original text for this book was supplied to the publisher on magnetic tape. The tape included formatting codes identifying the various types of textual entity in the manuscript. The actual format of each type of entity was supplied by the publisher. This process worked smoothly thanks in large part to the efforts and patience of Eileen Colahan of the International Computaprint Corporation and Fran Fulton, our production editor, as well as the cooperation of Sue Zorn, Marshall Henrichs, and Jim DeWolf of Addison-Wesley.

Many of the graphical images that represent Smalltalk-80 screen graphics and the Part and Chapter artwork were printed on the Platemaker system developed by Gary Starkweather and the Imaging Sciences Laboratory of PARC. We would like to thank Gary, Eric Larson, and Julian Orr for making the Platemaker available to us.

Adele Goldberg
David Robson
Palo Alto, California
January, 1983

Contents

PARTFOUR

Smalltalk-80

PART ONE

Part One of this book provides an overview of the Smalltalk-80 programming language. Chapter 1 introduces the basic concepts and vocabulary of the Smalltalk-80 programming language without introducing its syntax. It describes objects, messages, classes, instances, and methods. These concepts are discussed in greater detail in the next four chapters as the relevant parts of the programming language syntax are described. Chapter 2 describes the syntax of expressions. Expressions allow objects to be referred to and messages to be described. Chapter 3 describes the basic syntax for classes and methods. Classes and methods allow new kinds of objects to be created and existing kinds to be modified. The final two chapters describe two important refinements to the role of classes in the Smalltalk-80 system. These refinements allow subclasses and metaclasses.

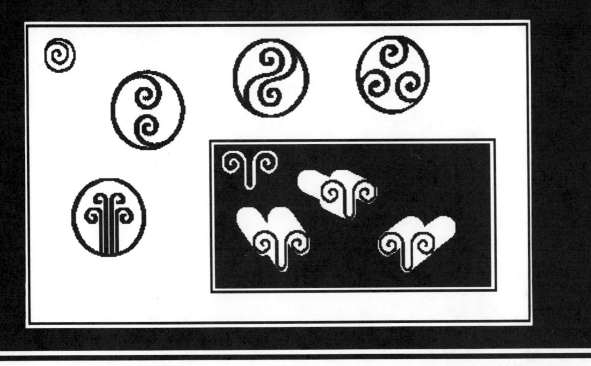

1

Objects and Messages

An *object* represents a component of the Smalltalk-80 software system. For example, objects represent

- numbers
- character strings
- queues
- dictionaries
- rectangles
- file directories
- text editors
- programs
- compilers
- computational processes
- financial histories
- views of information

An object consists of some private memory and a set of operations. The nature of an object's operations depends on the type of component it represents. Objects representing numbers compute arithmetic functions. Objects representing data structures store and retrieve information. Objects representing positions and areas answer inquiries about their relation to other positions and areas.

A *message* is a request for an object to carry out one of its operations. A message specifies which operation is desired, but not how that operation should be carried out. The *receiver*, the object to which the message was sent, determines how to carry out the requested operation. For example, addition is performed by sending a message to an object representing a number. The message specifies that the desired operation is addition and also specifies what number should be added to the receiver. The message does not specify how the addition will be performed. The receiver determines how to accomplish the addition. Computing is viewed as an intrinsic capability of objects that can be uniformly invoked by sending messages.

The set of messages to which an object can respond is called its *interface* with the rest of the system. The only way to interact with an object is through its interface. A crucial property of an object is that its private memory can be manipulated only by its own operations. A crucial property of messages is that they are the only way to invoke an object's operations. These properties insure that the implementation of one object cannot depend on the internal details of other objects, only on the messages to which they respond.

Messages insure the modularity of the system because they specify the type of operation desired, but not how that operation should be accomplished. For example, there are several representations of numerical values in the Smalltalk-80 system. Fractions, small integers, large integers, and floating point numbers are represented in different ways. They all understand the same message requesting the computation of their sum with another number, but each representation implies a different way to compute that sum. To interact with a number or any object, one need only know what messages it responds to, not how it is represented.

Other programming environments also use objects and messages to facilitate modular design. For example, Simula uses them for describing simulations and Hydra uses them for describing operating system facilities in a distributed system. In the Smalltalk-80 system, objects and messages are used to implement the entire programming environment. Once objects and messages are understood, the entire system becomes accessible.

An example of a commonly-used data structure in programming is a dictionary, which associates names and values. In the Smalltalk-80 system, a dictionary is represented by an object that can perform two operations: associate a name with a new value, and find the value last associated with a particular name. A programmer using a dictionary must know how to specify these two operations with messages. Dictionary objects understand messages that make requests like "associate the name *Brett* with the value *3*" and "what is the value associated with the name *Dave?*" Since everything is an object, the names, such as *Brett* or *Dave*, and the values, such as *3* or *30*, are also represented by objects. Although a curious programmer may want to know how associations are represented in a dictionary, this internal implementation information is unnecessary for successful use of a dictionary. Knowledge of a dictionary's implementation is of interest only to the programmer who works on the definition of the dictionary object itself.

An important part of designing Smalltalk-80 programs is determining which kinds of objects should be described and which message names provide a useful vocabulary of interaction among these objects. A language is designed whenever the programmer specifies the messages that can be sent to an object. Appropriate choice of objects depends, of course, on the purposes to which the object will be put and the granularity of information to be manipulated. For example, if a simulation of an amusement park is to be created for the purpose of collecting data on queues at the various rides, then it would be useful to describe objects representing the rides, workers who control the rides, the waiting lines, and the people visiting the park. If the purpose of the simulation includes monitoring the consumption of food in the park, then objects representing these consumable resources are required. If the amount of money exchanged in the park is to be monitored, then details about the cost of rides have to be represented.

In designing a Smalltalk-80 application, then, choice of objects is the first key step. There really is nothing definitive to say about the "right way" to choose objects. As in any design process, this is an acquired skill. Different choices provide different bases for extending an application or for using the objects for other purposes. The skilled Smalltalk-80 programmer is mindful that the objects created for an application might prove more useful for other applications if a semantically complete set of functions for an object is specified. For example, a dictionary whose associations can be removed as well as added is generally more useful than an add-only version.

Classes and Instances

A *class* describes the implementation of a set of objects that all represent the same kind of system component. The individual objects described by a class are called its *instances*. A class describes the form of its instances' private memories and it describes how they carry out their operations. For example, there is a system class that describes the implementation of objects representing rectangular areas. This class describes how the individual instances remember the locations of their areas and also how the instances carry out the operations that rectangular areas perform. Every object in the Smalltalk-80 system is an instance of a class. Even an object that represents a unique system component is implemented as the single instance of a class. Programming in the Smalltalk-80 system consists of creating classes, creating instances of classes, and specifying sequences of message exchanges among these objects.

The instances of a class are similar in both their public and private properties. An object's public properties are the messages that make up its interface. All instances of a class have the same message interface since they represent the same kind of component. An object's private properties are a set of *instance variables* that make up its private memory and a set of *methods* that describe how to carry out its operations. The instance variables and methods are not directly available to other objects. The instances of a class all use the same set of methods to describe their operations. For example, the instances that represent rectangles all respond to the same set of messages and they all use the same methods to determine how to respond. Each instance has its own set of instance variables, but they generally all have the same number of instance variables. For example, the instances that represent rectangles all have two instance variables.

Each class has a name that describes the type of component its instances represent. Class names will appear in a special font because they are part of the programming language. The same font will be used for all text that represents Smalltalk-80 expressions. The class whose instances represent character sequences is named String. The class whose instances represent spatial locations is named Point. The class whose instances represent rectangular areas is named Rectangle. The class whose instances represent computational processes is named Process.

Each instance variable in an object's private memory refers to one object, called its value. The values of a Rectangle's two instance variables are instances of Point that represent opposing corners of its rectangular area. The fact that Rectangles have two instance variables, or that those instance variables refer to Points is strictly internal information, unavailable outside the individual Rectangle.

Each method in a class tells how to perform the operation requested by a particular type of message. When that type of message is sent to any instance of the class, the method is executed. The methods used by all Rectangles describe how to perform their operations in terms of the two Points representing opposing corners. For example, one message asks a Rectangle for the location of its center. The corresponding method tells how to calculate the center by finding the point halfway between the opposing corners.

A class includes a method for each type of operation its instances can perform. A method may specify some changes to the object's private memory and/or some other messages to be sent. A method also specifies an object that should be returned as the value of the invoking message. An object's methods can access the object's own instance variables, but not those of any other objects. For example, the method a Rectangle uses to compute its center has access to the two Points referred to by its instance variables; however, the method cannot access the instance variables of those Points. The method specifies messages to be sent to the Points asking them to perform the required calculations.

A small subset of the methods in the Smalltalk-80 system are not expressed in the Smalltalk-80 programming language. These are called *primitive* methods. The primitive methods are built into the virtual machine and cannot be changed by the Smalltalk-80 programmer. They are invoked with messages in exactly the same way that other methods are. Primitive methods allow the underlying hardware and virtual machine structures to be accessed. For example, instances of Integer use a primitive method to respond to the message +. Other primitive methods perform disk and terminal interactions.

An Example Application

Examples are an important part of the description of a programming language and environment. Many of the examples used in this book are taken from the classes found in the standard Smalltalk-80 system. Other examples are taken from classes that might be added to the system to enhance its functionality. The first part of the book draws examples from an application that might be added to the system to maintain simple financial histories for individuals, households, clubs, or small businesses. The full application allows information about financial transactions to be entered and views of that information to be displayed. Figure 1.1 shows a view of a financial history as it might appear on a Smalltalk-80 display screen. The top two parts of the view show two views of the amount of money spent for various reasons. The next view down shows how the cash-on-hand fluctuated over time as transactions were made.

At the bottom of the picture are two areas in which the user can type in order to add new expenditures and incomes to the history. When new information is added, the three views are automatically updated. In Figure 1.2, a new expenditure for food has been added.

This application requires the addition of several classes to the system. These new classes describe the different kinds of view as well as the underlying financial history information. The class that actually records the financial information is named FinancialHistory and will be used as an example in the next four chapters. This example application will make use of several classes already in the system; it will use numbers to represent amounts of money and strings to represent the reasons for expenditures and the sources of income.

FinancialHistory is used to introduce the basic concepts of the Smalltalk-80 programming language because its functionality and implementation are easy to describe. The functionality of a class can be specified by listing the operations available through its message interface. FinancialHistory provides six operations:

1. Create a new financial history object with a certain initial amount of money available.

2. Remember that a certain amount was spent for a particular reason.

3. Remember that a certain amount was received from a particular source.

4. Find out how much money is available.

5. Find out how much has been spent for a particular reason.

6. Find out how much has been received from a particular source.

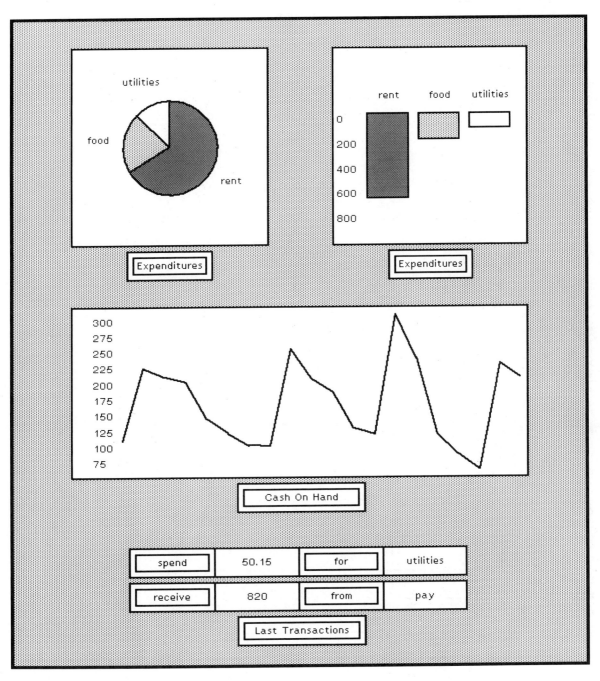

Figure 1.1

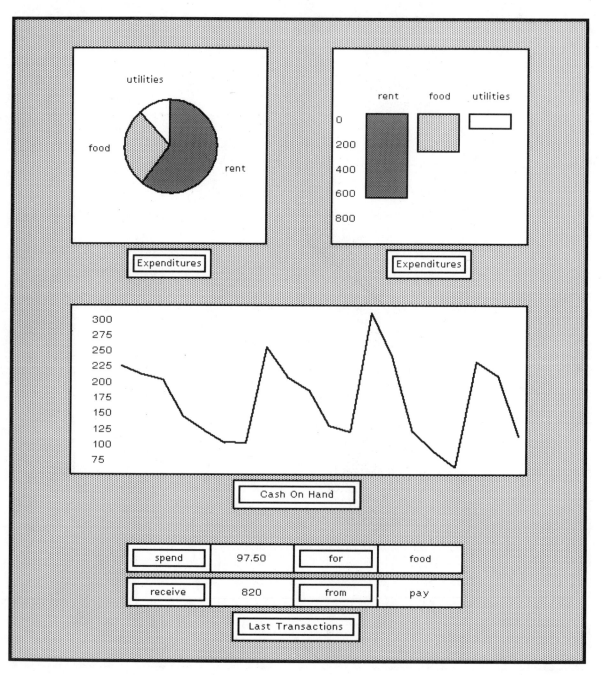

Figure 1.2

An implementation of these operations is specified in the class description shown inside the front cover of this book. The form of class descriptions will be described in Chapters 3, 4, and 5.

System Classes

The Smalltalk-80 system includes a set of classes that provides the standard functionality of a programming language and environment: arithmetic, data structures, control structures, and input/output facilities. The functionality of these classes will be specified in detail in Part Two of this book. Figure 1.3 is a diagram of the system classes presented in Part Two. Lines are drawn around groups of related classes; the groups are labeled to indicate the chapters in which the specifications of the classes can be found.

Arithmetic

The Smalltalk-80 system includes objects representing both real and rational numbers. Real numbers can be represented with an accuracy of about six digits. Integers with absolute value less than 2^{524288} can be represented exactly. Rational numbers can be represented using these integers. There are also classes for representing linear magnitudes (like dates and times) and random number generators.

Data Structures

Most of the objects in the Smalltalk-80 system function as data structures of some kind. However, while most objects also have other functionality, there is a set of classes representing more or less pure data structures. These classes represent different types of collections. The elements of some collections are unordered while the elements of others are ordered. Of the collections with unordered elements, there are bags that allow duplicate elements and sets that don't allow duplication. There are also dictionaries that associate pairs of objects. Of the collections with ordered elements, some have the order specified externally when elements are added and others determine the order based on properties of the elements themselves. The common data structures of arrays and strings are provided by classes that have associative behavior (associating indices and elements) and external ordering (corresponding to the inherent ordering of the indices).

Control Structures

The Smalltalk-80 system includes objects and messages that implement the standard control structures found in most programming languages. They provide conditional selection similar to the if-then-else statements of Algol and conditional repetition similar to its while and until state-

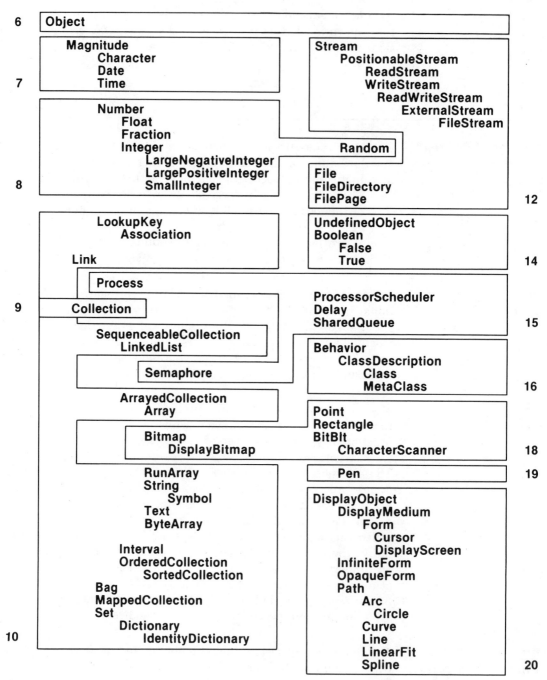

6 Object

7 Magnitude
   Character
   Date
   Time

Stream
   PositionableStream
      ReadStream
      WriteStream
         ReadWriteStream
      ExternalStream
         FileStream

8 Number
   Float
   Fraction
   Integer
      LargeNegativeInteger
      LargePositiveInteger
      SmallInteger

Random

File
FileDirectory
FilePage **12**

9 LookupKey
   Association

Link

UndefinedObject
Boolean
   False
   True **14**

Process

ProcessorScheduler
Delay
SharedQueue **15**

Collection

SequenceableCollection
LinkedList

Semaphore

Behavior
   ClassDescription
      Class
      MetaClass **16**

ArrayedCollection
Array

Bitmap
   DisplayBitmap

Point
Rectangle
BitBlt
      CharacterScanner **18**

RunArray
String
   Symbol
Text
ByteArray

Interval
OrderedCollection
   SortedCollection
Bag
MappedCollection
Set
Dictionary
   IdentityDictionary

Pen **19**

DisplayObject
   DisplayMedium
      Form
         Cursor
         DisplayScreen
   InfiniteForm
   OpaqueForm
   Path
      Arc
         Circle
      Curve
      Line
      LinearFit
      Spline **20**

10

Figure 1.3

ments. Objects representing independent processes and mechanisms for scheduling and synchronous interaction are also provided. Two classes are provided to support these control structures. Booleans represent the two truth values and blocks represent sequences of actions. Booleans and blocks can also be used to create new kinds of control structures.

Programming Environment

There are several classes in the Smalltalk-80 system that assist in the programming process. There are separate classes representing the source (human-readable) form and the compiled (machine-executable) form of methods. Objects representing parsers, compilers, and decompilers translate between the two forms of method. Objects representing classes connect methods with the objects that use them (the instances of the classes).

Objects representing organizational structures for classes and methods help the programmer keep track of the system, and objects representing histories of software modification help interface with the efforts of other programmers. Even the execution state of a method is represented by an object. These objects are called *contexts* and are analogous to stack frames or activation records of other systems.

Viewing and Interacting

The Smalltalk-80 system includes classes of objects that can be used to view and edit information. Classes helpful for presenting graphical views represent points, lines, rectangles, and arcs. Since the Smalltalk-80 system is oriented toward a bitmap display, there are classes for representing and manipulating bitmap images. There are also classes for representing and manipulating the more specific use of bitmap images for character fonts, text, and cursors.

Built from these graphical objects are other objects representing rectangular windows, command menus, and content selections. There are also objects that represent the user's actions on the input devices and how these relate to the information being viewed. Classes representing specific viewing and editing mechanisms constructed from these components provide views for classes, contexts, and documents containing text and graphics. The views of classes provide the fundamental mechanism to interact with the software in the system. Smalltalk-80 views and editors are presented in a separate book.

Communication

The Smalltalk-80 system allows communication with external media. The standard external medium is a disk file system. Objects represent individual files as well as directories. If a connection to a communications network is available, it can be accessed through objects as well.

Summary of Terminology

object	A component of the Smalltalk-80 system represented by some private memory and a set of operations.
message	A request for an object to carry out one of its operations.
receiver	The object to which a message is sent.
interface	The messages to which an object can respond.
class	A description of a group of similar objects.
instance	One of the objects described by a class.
instance variable	A part of an object's private memory.
method	A description of how to perform one of an object's operations.
primitive method	An operation performed directly by the Smalltalk-80 virtual machine.
FinancialHistory	The name of a class used as an example in this book.
system classes	The set of classes that come with the Smalltalk-80 system.

2

Expression Syntax

Chapter 1 introduced the fundamental concepts of the Smalltalk-80 system. System components are represented by *objects*. Objects are *instances* of *classes*. Objects interact by sending *messages*. Messages cause *methods* to be executed. This chapter introduces an expression syntax for describing objects and messages. The next chapter introduces a syntax for describing classes and methods.

An *expression* is a sequence of characters that describes an object called the value of the expression. The syntax presented in this chapter explains which sequences of characters form legal expressions. There are four types of expression in the Smalltalk-80 programming language.

1. *Literals* describe certain constant objects, such as numbers and character strings.

2. *Variable names* describe the accessible variables. The value of a variable name is the current value of the variable with that name.

3. *Message expressions* describe messages to receivers. The value of a message expression is determined by the method the message invokes. That method is found in the class of the receiver.

4. *Block expressions* describe objects representing deferred activities. Blocks are used to implement control structures.

Expressions are found in two places, in methods and in text displayed on the screen. When a message is sent, a method from the receiver's class is selected and its expressions are evaluated. Part of the user interface allows expressions to be selected on the screen and evaluated. The details of selecting and evaluating expressions on the screen fall outside the scope of this book, since they are part of the user interface. Some examples, however, are given in Chapter 17.

Of the four types of expression listed above, only the variable names are context-dependent. An expression's location in the system determines which character sequences are legal variable names. The set of variable names available in a method's expressions depends on the class in which the method is found. For example, methods in class Rectangle and methods in class Point have access to different sets of variable names. The variables available in a class's methods will be fully described in Chapters 3, 4, and 5. The variable names available for use in expressions on the screen depend on where the expressions are displayed on the screen. All other aspects of the expression syntax are independent of the expression's location.

The syntax for expressions is summarized in the diagram that appears inside the back cover of this book. The rest of this chapter describes the four types of expression.

Literals

Five kinds of objects can be referred to by literal expressions. Since the value of a literal expression is always the same object, these expressions are also called *literal constants*. The five types of literal constant are:

1. numbers

2. individual characters

3. strings of characters

4. symbols

5. arrays of other literal constants

Numbers

Numbers are objects that represent numerical values and respond to messages that compute mathematical results. The literal representation of a number is a sequence of digits that may be preceded by a minus sign and/or followed by a decimal point and another sequence of digits. For example,

```
3
30.45
−3
0.005
−14.0
13772
```

Number literals can also be expressed in a nondecimal base by preceding the digits with a radix prefix. The radix prefix includes the value of the digit radix (always expressed in decimal) followed by the letter "r". The following examples specify numbers in octal with their corresponding decimal values.

octal	decimal
8r377	255
8r153	107
8r34.1	28.125
8r−37	−31

When the base is greater than ten, the capital letters starting with "A" are used for digits greater than nine. The following examples specify numbers in hexadecimal with their corresponding decimal values.

hexadecimal	decimal
16r106	262
16rFF	255
16rAC.DC	172.859
16r−1.C	−1.75

Number literals can also be expressed in scientific notation by following the digits of the value with an exponent suffix. The exponent suffix includes the letter "e" followed by the exponent (expressed in decimal). The number specified before the exponent suffix is multiplied by the radix raised to the power specified by the exponent.

scientific notation	decimal
1.586e5	158600.0
1.586e−3	0.001586
8r3e2	192
2r11e6	192

Characters

Characters are objects that represent the individual symbols of an alphabet. A character literal expression consists of a dollar sign followed by any character, for example,

```
$a
$M
$−
$$
$1
```

Strings

Strings are objects that represent sequences of characters. Strings respond to messages that access individual characters, replace substrings, and perform comparisons with other strings. The literal representation of a string is a sequence of characters delimited by single quotes, for example,

```
'hi'
'food'
'the Smalltalk-80 system'
```

Any character may be included in a string literal. If a single quote is to be included in a string, it must be duplicated to avoid confusion with the delimiters. For example, the string literal 'can"t'

refers to a string of the five characters $c, $a, $n, $ ', and $t.

Symbols

Symbols are objects that represent strings used for names in the system. The literal representation of a symbol is a sequence of alphanumeric characters preceded by a pound sign, for example,

```
#bill
#M63
```

There will never be two symbols with the same characters; each symbol is unique. This makes it possible to compare symbols efficiently.

Arrays

An array is a simple data structure object whose contents can be referenced by an integer index from one to a number that is the size of the array. Arrays respond to messages requesting access to their contents. The literal representation of an array is a sequence of other literals—numbers, characters, strings, symbols, and arrays—delimited by parentheses and preceded by a pound sign. The other literals are separated by spaces. Embedded symbols and arrays are not preceded by pound signs. An array of three numbers is described by the expression

```
#(1 2 3)
```

An array of seven strings is described by the expression

```
#('food' 'utilities' 'rent' 'household' 'transportation' 'taxes' 'recreation')
```

An array of two arrays and two numbers is described by the expression

```
#(('one' 1) ('not' 'negative') 0 −1)
```

And an array of a number, a string, a character, a symbol, and another array is described by the expression

```
#(9 'nine' $9 nine (0 'zero' $0 ( ) 'e' $f 'g' $h 'i'))
```

Variables

The memory available to an object is made up of variables. Most of these variables have names. Each variable remembers a single object and the variable's name can be used as an expression referring to that object. The objects that can be accessed from a particular place are determined by which variable names are available. For example, the contents of an object's instance variables are unavailable to other objects because the names of those variables can be used only in the methods of the object's class.

A variable name is a simple identifier, a sequence of letters and digits beginning with a letter. Some examples of variable names are:

```
index
initialIndex
textEditor
bin14
bin14Total
HouseholdFinances
Rectangle
IncomeReasons
```

There are two kinds of variables in the system, distinguished by how widely they are accessible. Private variables are accessible only to a single object. Instance variables are private. Shared variables can be accessed by more than one object. Private variable names are required to have lowercase initial letters; shared variable names are required to have uppercase initial letters. The first five example identifiers shown above refer to private variables and the last three refer to shared variables.

Another capitalization convention evident in the examples above is that identifiers formed by concatenating several words capitalize each word following the first one. This convention is not enforced by the system.

Assignments

A literal constant will always refer to the same object, but a variable name may refer to different objects at different times. The object referred to by a variable is changed when an assignment expression is evaluated. Assignments were not listed earlier as a type of expression since any expression can become an assignment by including an assignment prefix.

An assignment prefix is composed of the name of the variable whose value will be changed followed by a left arrow ($\leftarrow$). The following example is a literal expression that has an assignment prefix. It indicates that the variable named quantity should now refer to the object representing the number 19.

```
quantity ← 19
```

The following example is a variable-name expression with an assignment prefix. It indicates that the variable named index should refer to the same object as does the variable named initialIndex.

index ← initialIndex

Other examples of assignment expressions are:

chapterName ← 'Expression Syntax'
flavors ← #('vanilla' 'chocolate' 'butter pecan' 'garlic')

More than one assignment prefix can be included, indicating that the values of several variables are changed.

index ← initialIndex ← 1

This expression indicates that both the variables named index and initialIndex should refer to the number 1. Message expressions and block expressions can also have assignment prefixes, as will be seen in the following sections.

Pseudo-variable Names

A pseudo-variable name is an identifier that refers to an object. In this way, it is similar to a variable name. A pseudo-variable name is different from a variable name in that its value cannot be changed with an assignment expression. Some of the pseudo-variables in the system are constants; they always refer to the same objects. Three important pseudo-variable names are nil, true, and false.

nil	refers to an object used as the value of a variable when no other object is appropriate. Variables that have not been otherwise initialized refer to nil.
true	refers to an object that represents logical accuracy. It is used as an affirmative response to a message making a simple yes-no inquiry.
false	refers to an object that represents logical inaccuracy. It is used as a negative response to a message making a simple yes-no inquiry.

The objects named true and false are called *Boolean* objects. They represent the answers to yes-no questions. For example, a number will respond with true or false to a message asking whether or not the number is greater than another number. Boolean objects respond to messages that compute logical functions and perform conditional control structures.

There are other pseudo-variables in the system (for example, self and super) whose values are different depending on where they are used. These will be described in the next three chapters.

Messages

Messages represent the interactions between the components of the Smalltalk-80 system. A message requests an operation on the part of the receiver. Some examples of message expressions and the interactions they represent follow.

Messages to numbers representing arithmetic operations

3 + 4	computes the sum of three and four.
index + 1	adds one to the number named index.
index > limit	inquires whether or not the number named index is greater than the number named limit.
theta sin	computes the sine of the number named theta.
quantity sqrt	computes the positive square root of the number named quantity.

Messages to linear data structures representing the addition or removal of information

list addFirst: newComponent

adds the object named newComponent as the first element of the linear data structure named list.

list removeLast

removes and returns the last element in list.

Messages to associative data structures (such as dictionaries) representing the addition or removal of information

ages at: 'Brett Jorgensen' put: 3

associates the string 'Brett Jorgensen' with the number 3 in the dictionary named ages.

addresses at: 'Peggy Jorgensen'

looks up the object associated with the string 'Peggy Jorgensen' in the dictionary named addresses.

Messages to rectangles representing graphical inquiries and calculations

frame center

answers the position of the center of the rectangle named frame.

frame containsPoint: cursorLocation

answers true if the position named cursorLocation is inside the rectangle named frame, and false otherwise.

frame intersect: clippingBox
> computes the rectangle that represents the intersection of the two rectangles named frame and clippingBox.

Messages to financial history records representing transactions and inquiries

HouseholdFinances spend: 32.50 on: 'utilities'
> informs the financial history named HouseholdFinances that $32.50 has been spent on utility bills.

HouseholdFinances totalSpentFor: 'food'
> asks HouseholdFinances how much money has been spent for food.

Selectors and Arguments

A message expression describes a receiver, *selector,* and possibly some *arguments.* The receiver and arguments are described by other expressions. The selector is specified literally.

A message's selector is a name for the type of interaction the sender desires with the receiver. For example, in the message

theta sin

the receiver is a number referred to by the variable named theta and the selector is sin. It is up to the receiver to decide how to respond to the message (in this case, how to compute the sine function of its value).

In the two message expressions

3 + 4

and

previousTotal + increment

the selectors are +. Both messages ask the receiver to calculate and return a sum. These messages each contain an object in addition to the selector (4 in the first expression and increment in the second). The additional objects in the message are arguments that specify the amount to be added.

The following two message expressions describe the same kind of operation. The receiver is an instance of FinancialHistory and will return the amount of money spent for a particular reason. The argument indicates the reason of interest. The first expression requests the amount spent for utility bills.

HouseholdFinances totalSpentOn: 'utilities'

The amount spent for food can be found by sending a message with the same selector, but with a different argument.

HouseholdFinances totalSpentOn: 'food'

The selector of a message determines which of the receiver's operations will be invoked. The arguments are other objects that are involved in the selected operation.

☐ *Unary Messages*   Messages without arguments are called *unary messages*. For example, the money currently available according to HouseholdFinances is the value of the unary message expression

HouseholdFinances cashOnHand

These messages are called unary because only one object, the receiver, is involved. A unary message selector can be any simple identifier. Other examples of unary message expressions are

theta sin
quantity sqrt
nameString size

☐ *Keyword Messages*   The general type of message with one or more arguments is the *keyword message*. The selector of a keyword message is composed of one or more keywords, one preceding each argument. A keyword is a simple identifier with a trailing colon. Examples of expressions describing single keyword messages are

HouseholdFinances totalSpentOn: 'utilities'
index max: limit

A message with two arguments will have a selector with two keywords. Examples of expressions describing double keyword messages are

HouseholdFinances spend: 30.45 on: 'food'
ages at: 'Brett Jorgensen' put: 3

When the selector of a multiple keyword message is referred to independently, the keywords are concatenated. The selectors of the last two message expressions are spend:on: and at:put:. There can be any number of keywords in a message, but most messages in the system have fewer than three.

☐ *Binary Messages*   There is one other type of message expression that takes a single argument, the *binary message*. A binary message selector is composed of one or two nonalphanumeric characters. The only restriction is that the second character cannot be a minus sign. Binary selectors tend to be used for arithmetic messages. Examples of binary message expressions are

```
3 + 4
total − 1
total < = max
```

Returning Values

Smalltalk-80 messages provide two-way communication. The selector and arguments transmit information to the receiver about what type of response to make. The receiver transmits information back by returning an object that becomes the value of the message expression. If a message expression includes an assignment prefix, the object returned by the receiver will become the new object referred to by the variable. For example, the expression

```
sum ← 3 + 4
```

makes 7 be the new value of the variable named sum. The expression

```
x ← theta sin
```

makes the sine of theta be the new value of the variable named x. If the value of theta is 1, the new value of x becomes 0.841471. If the value of theta is 1.5, the new value of x becomes 0.997495.

The number referred to by index can be incremented by the expression

```
index ← index + 1
```

Even if no information needs to be communicated back to the sender, a receiver *always* returns a value for the message expression. Returning a value indicates that the response to the message is complete. Some messages are meant only to inform the receiver of something. Examples are the messages to record financial transactions described by the following expressions.

```
HouseholdFinances spend: 32.50 on: 'utilities'
HouseholdFinances receive: 1000 from: 'pay'
```

The receiver of these messages informs the sender only that it is finished recording the transaction. The default value returned in such cases is usually the receiver itself. So, the expression

var ← HouseholdFinances spend: 32.50 on: 'utilities'

results in var referring to the same financial history as HouseholdFinances.

Parsing

All of the message expressions shown thus far have described the receiver and arguments with literals or variable names. When the receiver or argument of a message expression is described by another message expression, the issue of how the expression is parsed arises. An example of a unary message describing the receiver of another unary message is

1.5 tan rounded

Unary messages are parsed left to right. The first message in the example is the unary selector tan sent to 1.5. The value of that message expression (a number around 14.1014) receives the unary message rounded and returns the nearest integer, 14. The number 14 is the value of the whole expression.

Binary messages are also parsed left to right. An example of a binary message describing the receiver of another binary message is

index + offset * 2

The value returned by index from the message + offset is the receiver for the binary message * 2.

All binary selectors have the same precedence; only the order in which they are written matters. Note that this makes mathematical expressions in the Smalltalk-80 language different from those in many other languages in which multiplication and division take precedence over addition and subtraction.

Parentheses can be used to change the order of evaluation. A message within parentheses is sent before any messages outside the parentheses. If the previous example were written as

index + (offset * 2)

the multiplication would be performed before the addition.

Unary messages take precedence over binary messages. If unary messages and binary messages appear together, the unary messages will all be sent first. In the example frame width + border width * 2

the value of frame width is the receiver of the binary message whose selector is + and whose argument is the value of border width. The value of the + message is, in turn, the receiver of the binary message * 2. The expression parses as if it had been parenthesized as follows:

((frame width) + (border width)) * 2

Parentheses can be used to send binary messages before unary messages. The expression

2 * theta sin

calculates twice the sine of theta, while the expression

(2 * theta) sin .

calculates the sine of twice theta.

Whenever keywords appear in an unparenthesized message, they compose a single selector. Because of this concatenation, there is no left-to-right parsing rule for keyword messages. If a keyword message is to be used as a receiver or argument of another keyword message, it must be parenthesized. The expression

frame scale: factor max: 5

describes a single two-argument keyword message whose selector is scale:max:. The expression

frame scale: (factor max: 5)

describes two single keyword messages whose selectors are scale: and max:. The value of the expression factor max: 5 is the argument for the scale: message to frame.

Binary messages take precedence over keyword messages. When unary, binary, and keyword messages appear in the same expression without parentheses, the unaries are sent first, the binaries next, and the keyword last. The example

bigFrame width: smallFrame width * 2

is evaluated as if it had been parenthesized as follows:

bigFrame width: ((smallFrame width) * 2)

In the following example, a unary message describes the receiver of a keyword message and a binary message describes the argument.

OrderedCollection new add: value * rate

To summarize the parsing rules:

1. Unary expressions parse left to right.

2. Binary expressions parse left to right.

3. Binary expressions take precedence over keyword expressions.

4. Unary expressions take precedence over binary expressions.

5. Parenthesized expressions take precedence over unary expressions.

Formatting Conventions

A programmer is free to format expressions in various ways using spaces, tabs, and carriage returns. For example, multiple keyword messages are often written with each keyword-argument pair on a different line, as in

ages at: 'Brett Jorgensen'
    put: 3

or

HouseholdFinances
        spend: 30.45
        on: 'food'

The only time that a space, tab, or carriage return affects the meaning of an expression is when its absence would cause two letters or two numbers to fall next to each other.

Cascading

There is one special syntactic form called *cascading* that specifies multiple messages to the same object. Any sequence of messages can be expressed without cascading. However, cascading often reduces the need for using variables. A cascaded message expression consists of one description of the receiver followed by several messages separated by semicolons. For example,

OrderedCollection new add: 1; add: 2; add: 3

Three add: messages are sent to the result of OrderedCollection new. Without cascading, this would have required four expressions and a variable. For example, the following four expressions, separated by periods, have the same result as the cascaded expression above.

```
temp ← OrderedCollection new.
temp add: 1.
temp add: 2.
temp add: 3
```

Blocks

Blocks are objects used in many of the control structures in the Smalltalk-80 system. A block represents a deferred sequence of actions. A block expression consists of a sequence of expressions separated by periods and delimited by square brackets. For example,

```
[index ← index + 1]
```

or

```
[index ← index + 1.
 array at: index put: 0]
```

If a period follows the last expression, it is ignored, as in

```
[expenditures at: reason.]
```

When a block expression is encountered, the statements enclosed in the brackets are not executed immediately. The value of a block expression is an object that can execute these enclosed expressions at a later time, when requested to do so. For example, the expression

```
actions at: 'monthly payments'
        put: [HouseholdFinances spend: 650 on: 'rent'.
              HouseholdFinances spend: 7.25 on: 'newspaper'.
              HouseholdFinances spend: 225.50 on: 'car payment']
```

does not actually send any spend:on: messages to HouseholdFinances. It simply associates a block with the string 'monthly payments'.

The sequence of actions a block describes will take place when the block receives the unary message value. For example, the following two expressions have identical effects.

$$index \leftarrow index + 1$$

and

$$[index \leftarrow index + 1] \ value$$

The object referred to by the expression

actions at: 'monthly payments'

is the block containing three spend:on: messages. The execution of the
expression

(actions at: 'monthly payments') value

results in those three spend:on: messages being sent to
HouseholdFinances.

A block can also be assigned to a variable. So if the expression

$$incrementBlock \leftarrow [index \leftarrow index + 1]$$

is executed, then the expression

incrementBlock value

increments index.

The object returned after a value message is sent to a block is the
value of the last expression in the sequence. So if the expression

$$addBlock \leftarrow [index + 1]$$

is executed, then another way to increment index is to evaluate

$$index \leftarrow addBlock \ value$$

A block that contains no expressions returns nil when sent the message
value. The expression

[] value

has the value nil.

Control Structures

A control structure determines the order of some activities. The fundamental control structure in the Smalltalk-80 language provides that a
sequence of expressions will be evaluated sequentially. Many

nonsequential control structures can be implemented with blocks. These control structures are invoked either by sending a message to a block or by sending a message with one or more blocks as arguments. The response to one of these control structure messages determines the order of activities with the pattern of value messages it sends to the block(s).

Examining the evaluation of the following sequence of expressions gives an example of the way blocks work.

```
incrementBlock ← [index ← index + 1].
sumBlock ← [sum + (index * index)].
sum ← 0.
index ← 1.
sum ← sumBlock value.
incrementBlock value.
sum ← sumBlock value
```

The 15 actions taken as a result of evaluating this sequence of expressions are

1. *Assign* a block to incrementBlock.
2. *Assign* a block to sumBlock.
3. *Assign* the number 0 to sum.
4. *Assign* the number 1 to index.
5. *Send* the message value to the block sumBlock.
6. *Send* the message * 1 to the number 1.
7. *Send* the message + 1 to the number 0.
8. *Assign* the number 1 to sum.
9. *Send* the message value to the block IncrementBlock.
10. *Send* the message + 1 to the number 1.
11. *Assign* the number 2 to index.
12. *Send* the message value to the block sumBlock.
13. *Send* the message * 2 to the number 2.
14. *Send* the message + 4 to the number 1.
15. *Assign* the number 5 to sum.

An example of a control structure implemented with blocks is simple repetition, represented by a message to an integer with timesRepeat: as the selector and a block as the argument. The integer will respond by sending the block as many value messages as its own value indicates. For example, the following expression doubles the value of the variable named amount four times.

```
4 timesRepeat: [amount ← amount + amount]
```

Conditionals

Two common control structures implemented with blocks are *conditional selection* and *conditional repetition*. Conditional selection is similar to the if-then-else statements in Algol-like languages and conditional repetition is similar to the while and until statements in those languages. These conditional control structures use the two Boolean objects named true and false described in the section on pseudo-variables. Booleans are returned from messages that ask simple yes-no questions (for example, the magnitude comparison messages: $<$, $=$, $<=$, $>$, $>=$, $\sim=$).

☐ *Conditional Selection* The conditional selection of an activity is provided by a message to a Boolean with the selector ifTrue:ifFalse: and two blocks as arguments. The only objects that understand ifTrue:ifFalse: messages are true and false. They have opposite responses: true sends value to the first argument block and ignores the second; false sends value to the second argument block and ignores the first. For example, the following expression assigns 0 or 1 to the variable parity depending on whether or not the value of the variable number is divisible by 2. The binary message $\backslash\backslash$ computes the modulus or remainder function.

```
(number \\ 2) = 0
        ifTrue: [parity ← 0]
        ifFalse: [parity ← 1]
```

The value returned from ifTrue:ifFalse: is the value of the block that was executed. The previous example could also be written

```
parity ← (number \\ 2) = 0 ifTrue: [0] ifFalse: [1]
```

In addition to ifTrue:ifFalse:, there are two single-keyword messages that specify only one conditional consequent. The selectors of these messages are ifTrue: and ifFalse:. These messages have the same effect as the ifTrue:ifFalse: message when one argument is an empty block. For example, these two expressions have the same effect.

```
index <= limit
        ifTrue: [total ← total + (list at: index)]
```

and

```
index <= limit
        ifTrue: [total ← total + (list at: index)]
        ifFalse: []
```

Since the value of an empty block is nil, the following expression would set lastElement to nil if index is greater than limit.

lastElement ← index > limit ifFalse: [list at: index]

☐ *Conditional Repetition*　The conditional repetition of an activity is provided by a message to a block with the selector whileTrue: and another block as an argument. The receiver block sends itself the message value and, if the response is true, it sends the other block value and then starts over, sending itself value again. When the receiver's response to value becomes false, it stops the repetition and returns from the whileTrue: message. For example, conditional repetition could be used to initialize all of the elements of an array named list.

```
index ← 1.
[index < = list size]
        whileTrue: [list at: index put: 0.
                        index ← index + 1]
```

Blocks also understand a message with selector whileFalse: that repeats the execution of the argument block as long as the value of the receiver is false. So, the following expressions are equivalent to the one above.

```
index ← 1.
[index > list size]
        whileFalse: [list at: index put: 0.
                        index ← index + 1]
```

The programmer is free to choose whichever message makes the intent of the repetition clearest. The value returned by both whileTrue: and whileFalse: is always nil.

Block Arguments

In order to make some nonsequential control structures easy to express, blocks may take one or more arguments. Block arguments are specified by including identifiers preceded by colons at the beginning of a block. The block arguments are separated from the expressions that make up the block by a vertical bar. The following two examples describe blocks with one argument.

```
[ :array |  total ← total + array size]
```

and

```
[ :newElement |
  index ← index + 1.
  list at: index put: newElement]
```

A common use of blocks with arguments is to implement functions to be applied to all elements of a data structure. For example, many objects representing different kinds of data structures respond to the message do:, which takes a single-argument block as its argument. The object that receives a do: message evaluates the block once for each of the elements contained in the data structure. Each element is made the value of the block argument for one evaluation of the block. The following example calculates the sum of the squares of the first five primes. The result is the value of sum.

```
sum ← 0.
#(2 3 5 7 11) do: [ :prime |   sum ← sum + (prime * prime)]
```

The message collect: creates a collection of the values produced by the block when supplied with the elements of the receiver. The value of the following expression is an array of the squares of the first five primes.

```
#(2 3 5 7 11) collect: [ :prime |   prime * prime]
```

The objects that implement these control structures supply the values of the block arguments by sending the block the message value:. A block with one block argument responds to value: by setting the block argument to the argument of value: and then executing the expressions in the block. For example, evaluating the following expressions results in the variable total having the value 7.

```
sizeAdder ← [ :array |   total ← total + array size].
total ← 0.
sizeAdder value: #(a b c).
sizeAdder value: #(1 2).
sizeAdder value: #(e f)
```

Blocks can take more than one argument. For example

```
[ :x :y |   (x * x) + (y * y)]
```

or

```
[ :frame :clippingBox |   frame intersect: clippingBox]
```

A block must have the same number of block arguments as the number of value: keywords in the message to evaluate it. The two blocks above would be evaluated by means of a two-keyword message with selector value:value:. The two arguments of the message specify the values of the two block arguments, in order. If a block receives an evaluation message with a different number of arguments from the number of block arguments it takes, an error will be reported.

Summary of Terminology

The syntax of expressions is summarized inside the back cover of this book.

expression	A sequence of characters that describes an object.
literal	An expression describing a constant, such as a number or a string.
symbol	A string whose sequence of characters is guaranteed to be different from that of any other symbol.
array	A data structure whose elements are associated with integer indices.
variable name	An expression describing the current value of a variable.
assignment	An expression describing a change of a variable's value.
pseudo-variable name	An expression similar to a variable name. However, unlike a variable name, the value of a pseudo-variable name cannot be changed by an assignment.
receiver	The object to which a message is sent.
message selector	The name of the type of operation a message requests of its receiver.
message argument	An object that specifies additional information for an operation.
unary message	A message without arguments.
keyword	An identifier with a trailing colon.
keyword message	A message with one or more arguments whose selector is made up of one or more keywords.
binary message	A message with one argument whose selector is made up of one or two special characters.
cascading	A description of several messages to one object in a single expression.
block	A description of a deferred sequence of actions.
block argument	A parameter that must be supplied when certain blocks are evaluated.
value	A message to a block asking it to carry out the set of actions it represents.
value:	A keyword used in a message to a block that has block arguments; the corresponding message asks the block to carry out its set of actions.
ifTrue:ifFalse:	Message to a Boolean requesting conditional selection.
ifFalse:ifTrue:	Message to a Boolean requesting conditional selection.
ifTrue:	Message to a Boolean requesting conditional selection.
ifFalse:	Message to a Boolean requesting conditional selection.
whileTrue:	Message to a block requesting conditional repetition.

whileFalse:	Message to a block requesting conditional repetition.
do:	A message to a collection requesting enumeration of its elements.
collect:	A message to a collection requesting transformation of its elements.

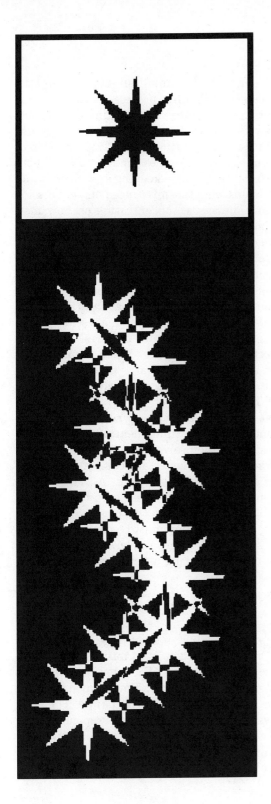

3

Classes and Instances

Objects represent the components of the Smalltalk-80 system—the numbers, data structures, processes, disk files, process schedulers, text editors, compilers, and applications. Messages represent interactions between the components of the Smalltalk-80 system—the arithmetic, data accesses, control structures, file creations, text manipulations, compilations, and application uses. Messages make an object's functionality available to other objects, while keeping the object's implementation hidden. The previous chapter introduced an expression syntax for describing objects and messages, concentrating on how messages are used to access an object's functionality. This chapter introduces the syntax for describing methods and classes in order to show how the functionality of objects is implemented.

Every Smalltalk-80 object is an *instance* of a *class*. The instances of a class all have the same message interface; the class describes how to carry out each of the operations available through that interface. Each operation is described by a *method*. The selector of a message determines what type of operation the receiver should perform, so a class has one method for each selector in its interface. When a message is sent to an object, the method associated with that type of message in the receiver's class is executed. A class also describes what type of private memory its instances will have.

Each class has a name that describes the type of component its instances represent. A class name serves two fundamental purposes; it is a simple way for instances to identify themselves, and it provides a way to refer to the class in expressions. Since classes are components of the Smalltalk-80 system, they are represented by objects. A class's name automatically becomes the name of a globally shared variable. The value of that variable is the object representing the class. Since class names are the names of shared variables, they must be capitalized.

New objects are created by sending messages to classes. Most classes respond to the unary message new by creating a new instance of themselves. For example,

OrderedCollection new

returns a new collection that is an instance of the system class OrderedCollection. The new OrderedCollection is empty. Some classes create instances in response to other messages. For example, the class whose instances represent times in a day is Time; Time responds to the message now with an instance representing the current time. The class whose instances represent days in a year is Date; Date responds to the message today with an instance representing the current day. When a new instance is created, it automatically shares the methods of the class that received the instance creation message.

This chapter introduces two ways to present a class, one describing the functionality of the instances and the other describing the implementation of that functionality.

1. A *protocol description* lists the messages in the instances' message interface. Each message is accompanied by a comment describing the operation an instance will perform when it receives that type of message.

2. An *implementation description* shows how the functionality described in the protocol description is implemented. An implementation description gives the form of the instances' private memory and the set of methods that describe how instances perform their operations.

A third way to present classes is an interactive view called a *system browser*. The browser is part of the programming interface and is used in a running Smalltalk-80 system. Protocol descriptions and implementation descriptions are designed for noninteractive documentation like this book. The browser will be described briefly in Chapter 17.

Protocol Descriptions

A protocol description lists the messages understood by instances of a particular class. Each message is listed with a comment about its functionality. The comment describes the operation that will be performed when the message is received and what value will be returned. The comment describes *what* will happen, not *how* the operation will be performed. If the comment gives no indication of the value to be returned, then the value is assumed to be the receiver of the message.

For example, a protocol description entry for the message to a FinancialHistory with the selector spend:for: is

spend: amount for: reason   Remember that an amount of money, amount, has been spent for reason.

Messages in a protocol description are described in the form of *message patterns*. A message pattern contains a message selector and a set of argument names, one name for each argument that a message with that selector would have. For example, the message pattern

spend: amount for: reason

matches the messages described by each of the following three expressions.

HouseholdFinances spend: 32.50 for: 'utilities'
HouseholdFinances spend: cost+ tax for: 'food'
HouseholdFinances spend: 100 for: usualReason

The argument names are used in the comment to refer to the arguments. The comment in the example above indicates that the first argument represents the amount of money spent and the second argument represents what the money was spent for.

Message Categories

Messages that invoke similar operations are grouped together in *categories*. The categories have names that indicate the common functionality of the messages in the group. For example, the messages to FinancialHistory are grouped into three categories named transaction recording, inquiries, and initialization. This categorization is intended to make the protocol more readable to the user; it does not affect the operation of the class.

The complete protocol description for FinancialHistory is shown next.

FinancialHistory protocol

transaction recording

receive: amount from: source	Remember that an amount of money, amount, has been received from source.
spend: amount for: reason	Remember that an amount of money, amount, has been spent for reason.

inquiries

cashOnHand	Answer the total amount of money currently on hand.
totalReceivedFrom: source	Answer the total amount received from source, so far.
totalSpentFor: reason	Answer the total amount spent for reason, so far.

initialization

initialBalance: amount	Begin a financial history with amount as the amount of money on hand.

A protocol description provides sufficient information for a programmer to know how to use instances of the class. From the above protocol description, we know that any instance of FinancialHistory should respond to the messages whose selectors are receive:from:, spend:for:, cashOnHand, totalReceivedFrom:, totalSpentFor:, and initialBalance:. We can guess that when we first create an instance of a FinancialHistory, the message initialBalance: should be sent to the instance in order to set values for its variables.

Implementation Descriptions

An implementation description has three parts.

1. a class name

2. a declaration of the variables available to the instances

3. the methods used by instances to respond to messages

An example of a complete implementation description for FinancialHistory is given next. The methods in an implementation description are divided into the same categories used in the protocol description. In the interactive system browser, categories are used to provide a hierarchical query path for accessing the parts of a class description. There are no special character delimiters separating the various parts of implementation descriptions. Changes in character font and emphasis indicate the different parts. In the interactive system browser, the parts are stored independently and the system browser provides a structured editor for accessing them.

```
class name                          FinancialHistory
instance variable names             cashOnHand
                                    incomes
                                    expenditures

instance methods

transaction recording

    receive: amount from: source
        incomes at: source
                put: (self totalReceivedFrom: source) + amount.
        cashOnHand ← cashOnHand + amount
    spend: amount for: reason
        expenditures at: reason
                put: (self totalSpentFor: reason) + amount.
        cashOnHand ← cashOnHand − amount

inquiries

    cashOnHand
        ↑cashOnHand
    totalReceivedFrom: source
        (incomes includesKey: source)
            ifTrue: [↑incomes at: source]
            ifFalse: [↑0]
    totalSpentFor: reason
        (expenditures includesKey: reason)
            ifTrue: [↑expenditures at: reason]
            ifFalse: [↑0]
```

initialization

initialBalance: amount
cashOnHand ← amount.
incomes ← Dictionary new.
expenditures ← Dictionary new

This implementation description is different from the one presented for FinancialHistory on the inside front cover of this book. The one on the inside front cover has an additional part labeled "class methods" that will be explained in Chapter 5; also, it omits the initialization method shown here.

Variable Declarations

The methods in a class have access to five different kinds of variables. These kinds of variables differ in terms of how widely they are available (their scope) and how long they persist.

There are two kinds of private variables available only to a single object.

1. *Instance variables* exist for the entire lifetime of the object.

2. *Temporary variables* are created for a specific activity and are available only for the duration of the activity.

Instance variables represent the current state of an object. Temporary variables represent the transitory state necessary to carry out some activity. Temporary variables are typically associated with a single execution of a method: they are created when a message causes the method to be executed and are discarded when the method completes by returning a value.

The three other kinds of variables can be accessed by more than one object. They are distinguished by how widely they are shared.

3. *Class variables* are shared by all the instances of a single class.

4. *Global variables* are shared by all the instances of all classes (that is, by all objects).

5. *Pool variables* are shared by the instances of a subset of the classes in the system.

The majority of shared variables in the system are either class variables or global variables. The majority of global variables refer to the classes in the system. An instance of FinancialHistory named

HouseholdFinances was used in several of the examples in the previous chapters. We used HouseholdFinances as if it were defined as a global variable name. Global variables are used to refer to objects that are not parts of other objects.

Recall that the names of shared variables (3-5) are capitalized, while the names of private variables (1-2) are not. The value of a shared variable will be independent of which instance is using the method in which its name appears. The value of instance variables and temporaries will depend on the instance using the method, that is, the instance that received a message.

Instance Variables

There are two types of instance variables, named and indexed. They differ in terms of how they are declared and how they are accessed. A class may have only named instance variables, only indexed variables, or some of each.

☐ *Named Instance Variables* An implementation description includes a set of names for the instance variables that make up the individual instances. Each instance has one variable corresponding to each instance variable name. The variable declaration in the implementation description of FinancialHistory specified three instance variable names.

instance variable names	cashOnHand
	incomes
	expenditures

An instance of FinancialHistory uses two dictionaries to store the total amounts spent and received for various reasons, and uses another variable to keep track of the cash on hand.

- expenditures refers to a dictionary that associates spending reasons with amounts spent.

- incomes refers to a dictionary that associates income sources with amounts received.

- cashOnHand refers to a number representing the amount of money available.

When expressions in the methods of the class use one of the variable names incomes, expenditures, or cashOnHand, these expressions refer to the value of the corresponding instance variable in the instance that received the message.

When a new instance is created by sending a message to a class, it has a new set of instance variables. The instance variables are initialized as specified in the method associated with the instance creation message. The default initialization method gives each instance variable a value of nil.

For example, in order for the previous example messages to HouseholdFinances to work, an expression such as the following must have been evaluated.

HouseholdFinances ← FinancialHistory new initialBalance: 350

FinancialHistory new creates a new object whose three instance variables all refer to nil. The initialBalance: message to that new instance gives the three instance variables more appropriate initial values.

☐ *Indexed Instance Variables* Instances of some classes can have instance variables that are not accessed by names. These are called *indexed instance variables*. Instead of being referred to by name, indexed instance variables are referred to by messages that include integers, called indices, as arguments. Since indexing is a form of association, the two fundamental indexing messages have the same selectors as the association messages to dictionaries—at: and at:put:. For example, instances of Array have indexed variables. If names is an instance of Array, the expression

names at: 1

returns the value of its first indexed instance variable. The expression

names at: 4 put: 'Adele'

stores the string 'Adele' as the value of the fourth indexed instance variable of names. The legal indices run from one to the number of indexed variables in the instance.

If the instances of a class have indexed instance variables, its variable declaration will include the line indexed instance variables. For example, part of the implementation description for the system class Array is

class name   Array
indexed instance variables

Each instance of a class that allows indexed instance variables may have a different number of them. All instances of FinancialHistory have three instance variables, but instances of Array may have any number of instance variables.

A class whose instances have indexed instance variables can also have named instance variables. All instances of such a class will have the same number of named instance variables, but may have different numbers of indexed variables. For example, a system class representing a collection whose elements are ordered, OrderedCollection, has indexed instance variables to hold its contents. An OrderedCollection might have more space for storing elements than is currently being used. The two named instance variables remember the indices of the first and last element of the contents.

class name	OrderedCollection
instance variable names	firstIndex
	lastIndex
indexed instance variables	

All instances of OrderedCollection will have two named variables, but one may have five indexed instance variables, another 15, another 18, and so on.

The named instance variables of an instance of FinancialHistory are private in the sense that access to the values of the variables is controlled by the instance. A class may or may not include messages giving direct access to the instance variables. Indexed instance variables are not private in this sense, since direct access to the values of the variables is available by sending messages with selectors at: and at:put:. Since these messages are the only way to access indexed instance variables, they must be provided.

Classes with indexed instance variables create new instances with the message new: instead of the usual message new. The argument of new: tells the number of indexed variables to be provided.

    list ← Array new: 10

creates an Array of 10 elements, each of which is initially the special object nil. The number of indexed instance variables of an instance can be found by sending it the message size. The response to the message size

    list size

is, for this example, the integer 10.

Evaluating each of the following expressions, in order,

    list ← Array new: 3.
    list at: 1 put: 'one'.
    list at: 2 put: 'two'.
    list at: 3 put: 'three'

is equivalent to the single expression

    list ← #('one' 'two' 'three')

Shared Variables

Variables that are shared by more than one object come in groups called *pools*. Each class has two or more pools whose variables can be accessed by its instances. One pool is shared by all classes and contains the global variables; this pool is named Smalltalk. Each class also has a pool which is only available to its instances and contains the class variables.

Besides these two mandatory pools, a class may access some other special purpose pools shared by several classes. For example, there are several classes in the system that represent textual information; these classes need to share the ASCII character codes for characters that are not easily indicated visually, such as a carriage return, tab, or space. These numbers are included as variables in a pool named TextConstants that is shared by the classes implementing text display and text editing.

If FinancialHistory had a class variable named SalesTaxRate and shared a pool dictionary whose name is FinancialConstants, the declaration would be expressed as follows.

instance variable names	cashOnHand
	incomes
	expenditures
class variable names	SalesTaxRate
shared pools	FinancialConstants

SalesTaxRate is the name of a class variable, so it can be used in any methods in the class. FinancialConstants, on the other hand, is the name of a pool; it is the variables *in* the pool that can be used in expressions.

In order to declare a variable to be global (known to all classes and to the user's interactive system), the variable name must be inserted as a key in the dictionary Smalltalk. For example, to make AllHistories global, evaluate the expression

    Smalltalk at: #AllHistories put: nil

Then use an assignment statement to set the value of AllHistories.

Methods

A method describes how an object will perform one of its operations. A method is made up of a message pattern and a sequence of expressions separated by periods. The example method shown below describes the response of a FinancialHistory to messages informing it of expenditures.

```
spend: amount for: reason
    expenditures at: reason
            put: (self totalSpentFor: reason) + amount.
    cashOnHand ← cashOnHand − amount
```

The message pattern, **spend: amount for: reason**, indicates that this method will be used in response to all messages with selector spend:for:.

The first expression in the body of this method adds the new amount to the amount already spent for the reason indicated. The second expression is an assignment that decrements the value of cashOnHand by the new amount.

Message patterns were introduced earlier in this chapter. A message pattern contains a message selector and a set of argument names, one for each argument that a message with that selector would have. A message pattern matches any messages that have the same selector. A class will have only one method with a given selector in its message pattern. When a message is sent, the method with matching message pattern is selected from the class of the receiver. The expressions in the selected method are evaluated one after another. After all the expressions are evaluated, a value is returned to the sender of the message.

The argument names found in a method's message pattern are pseudo-variable names referring to the arguments of the actual message. If the method shown above were invoked by the expression

HouseholdFinances spend: 30.45 for: 'food'

the pseudo-variable name amount would refer to the number 30.45 and the pseudo-variable name reason would refer to the string 'food' during the evaluation of the expressions in the method. If the same method were invoked by the expression

HouseholdFinances spend: cost + tax for: 'food'

cost would be sent the message + tax and the value it returned would be referred to as amount in the method. If cost referred to 100 and tax to 6.5, the value of amount would be 106.5.

Since argument names are pseudo-variable names, they can be used to access values like variable names, but their values cannot be changed by assignment. In the method for spend:for:, a statement of the form

amount ← amount * taxRate

would be syntactically illegal since the value of amount cannot be reassigned.

The method for spend:for: does not specify what the value of the message should be. Therefore, the default value, the receiver itself, will be returned. When another value is to be specified, one or more return expressions are included in the method. Any expression can be turned into a return expression by preceding it with an uparrow (↑). The value of a variable may be returned as in

↑cashOnHand

The value of another message can be returned as in

↑expenditures at: reason

A literal object can be returned as in

↑0

Even an assignment statement can be turned into a return expression, as in

↑initialIndex ← 0

The assignment is performed first. The new value of the variable is then returned.

An example of the use of a return expression is the following implementation of totalSpentFor:.

totalSpentFor: reason
    (expenditures includesKey: reason)
        ifTrue: [↑expenditures at: reason]
        ifFalse: [↑0]

This method consists of a single conditional expression. If the expenditure reason is in expenditures, the associated value is returned; otherwise, zero is returned.

The Pseudo-variable self

Along with the pseudo-variables used to refer to the arguments of a message, all methods have access to a pseudo-variable named self that refers to the message receiver itself. For example, in the method for spend:for:, the message totalSpentFor: is sent to the receiver of the spend:for: message.

spend: amount for: reason
    expenditures at: reason
                put: (self totalSpentFor: reason) + amount.
    cashOnHand ← cashOnHand - amount

When this method is executed, the first thing that happens is that totalSpentFor: is sent to the same object (self) that received spend:for:. The result of that message is sent the message + amount, and the result of that message is used as the second argument to at:put:.

The pseudo-variable self can be used to implement recursive functions. For example, the message factorial is understood by integers in order to compute the appropriate function. The method associated with factorial is

factorial

    self = 0 ifTrue: [↑1].

    self < 0

        ifTrue: [self error: 'factorial invalid']

        ifFalse: [↑self * (self − 1) factorial]

The receiver is an Integer. The first expression tests to see if the receiver is 0 and, if it is, returns 1. The second expression tests the sign of the receiver because, if it is less than 0, the programmer should be notified of an error (all objects respond to the message error: with a report that an error has been encountered). If the receiver is greater than 0, then the value to be returned is

    self * (self − 1) factorial

The value returned is the receiver multiplied by the factorial of one less than the receiver.

Temporary Variables

The argument names and self are available only during a single execution of a method. In addition to these pseudo-variable names, a method may obtain some other variables for use during its execution. These are called *temporary variables*. Temporary variables are indicated by including a temporary variable declaration between the message pattern and the expressions of a method. A temporary declaration consists of a set of variable names between vertical bars. The method for spend:for: could be rewritten to use a temporary variable to hold the previous expenditures.

spend: amount for: reason

    | previousExpenditures |

    previousExpenditures ← self totalSpentFor: reason.

    expenditures at: reason

              put: previousExpenditures + amount.

    cashOnHand ← cashOnHand − amount

The values of temporary variables are accessible only to statements in the method and are forgotten when the method completes execution. All temporary variables initially refer to nil.

In the interactive Smalltalk-80 system, the programmer can test algorithms that make use of temporary variables. The test can be carried out by using the vertical bar notation to declare the variables for the duration of the immediate evaluation only. Suppose the expressions to be tried out include reference to the variable list. If the variable list is undeclared, an attempt to evaluate the expressions will create a syntax error message. Instead, the programmer can declare list as a temporary variable by prefixing the expressions with the declaration | list |. The expressions are separated by periods, as in the syntax of a method.

```
| list |
list ← Array new: 3.
list at: 1 put: 'one'.
list at: 2 put: 'four'.
list printString
```

The programmer interactively selects all five lines—the declaration and the expressions—and requests evaluation. The variable list is available only during the single execution of the selection.

Primitive Methods

When an object receives a message, it typically just sends other messages, so where does something *really* happen? An object may change the value of its instance variables when it receives a message, which certainly qualifies as "something happening." But this hardly seems enough. In fact, it is not enough. All behavior in the system *is* invoked by messages, however, all messages are *not* responded to by executing Smalltalk-80 methods. There are about one hundred *primitive methods* that the Smalltalk-80 virtual machine knows how to perform. Examples of messages that invoke primitives are the + message to small integers, the at: message to objects with indexed instance variables, and the new and new: messages to classes. When 3 gets the message + 4, it does not execute a Smalltalk-80 method. A primitive method returns 7 as the value of the message. The complete set of primitive methods is included in the fourth part of this book, which describes the virtual machine.

Methods that are implemented as primitive methods begin with an expression of the form

```
<primitive # >
```

where # is an integer indicating which primitive method will be followed. If the primitive fails to perform correctly, execution continues in the Smalltalk-80 method. The expression < primitive # > is followed by Smalltalk-80 expressions that handle failure situations.

Summary of Terminology

class

An object that describes the implementation of a set of similar objects.

instance

One of the objects described by a class; it has memory and responds to messages.

instance variable

A variable available to a single object for the entire lifetime of the object; instance variables can be named or indexed.

protocol description

A description of a class in terms of its instances' public message protocol.

implementation description

A description of a class in terms of its instances' private memory and the set of methods that describe how instances perform their operations.

message pattern

A message selector and a set of argument names, one for each argument that a message with this selector must have.

temporary variable

A variable created for a specific activity and available only for the duration of that activity.

class variable

A variable shared by all the instances of a single class.

global variable

A variable shared by all the instances of all classes.

pool variable

A variable shared by the instances of a set of classes.

Smalltalk

A pool shared by all classes that contains the global variables.

method

A procedure describing how to perform one of an object's operations; it is made up of a message pattern, temporary variable declaration, and a sequence of expressions. A method is executed when a message matching its message pattern is sent to an instance of the class in which the method is found

argument name

Name of a pseudo-variable available to a method only for the duration of that method's execution; the value of the argument names are the arguments of the message that invoked the method.

↑

When used in a method, indicates that the value of the next expression is to be the value of the method.

self

A pseudo-variable referring to the receiver of a message.

message category

A group of methods in a class description.

primitive method

An operation performed directly by the Smalltalk-80 virtual machine; it is not described as a sequence of Smalltalk-80 expressions.

4

Subclasses

Every object in the Smalltalk-80 system is an instance of a class. All instances of a class represent the same kind of system component. For example, each instance of Rectangle represents a rectangular area and each instance of Dictionary represents a set of associations between names and values. The fact that the instances of a class all represent the same kind of component is reflected both in the way the instances respond to messages and in the form of their instance variables.

- All instances of a class respond to the same set of messages and use the same set of methods to do so.

- All instances of a class have the same number of named instance variables and use the same names to refer to them.

- An object can have indexed instance variables only if all instances of its class can have indexed instance variables.

The class structure as described so far does not explicitly provide for any intersection in class membership. Each object is an instance of exactly one class. This structure is illustrated in Figure 4.1. In the figure, the small circles represent instances and the boxes represent classes. If a circle is within a box, then it represents an instance of the class represented by the box.

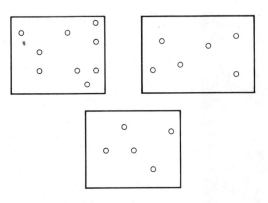

Figure 4.1

Lack of intersection in class membership is a limitation on design in an object-oriented system since it does not allow any sharing between class descriptions. We might want two objects to be substantially similar, but to differ in some particular way. For example, a floating-point number and an integer are similar in their ability to respond to arithmetic messages, but are different in the way they represent numeric values. An ordered collection and a bag are similar in that they are containers to which elements can be added and from which elements can be removed, but they are different in the precise way in which individual elements are accessed. The difference between otherwise similar objects may be externally visible, such as responding to some different messages, or it may be purely internal, such as responding to the same message by executing different methods. If class memberships are not allowed to overlap, this type of partial similarity between two objects cannot be guaranteed by the system.

The most general way to overcome this limitation is to allow arbitrary intersection of class boundaries (Figure 4.2).

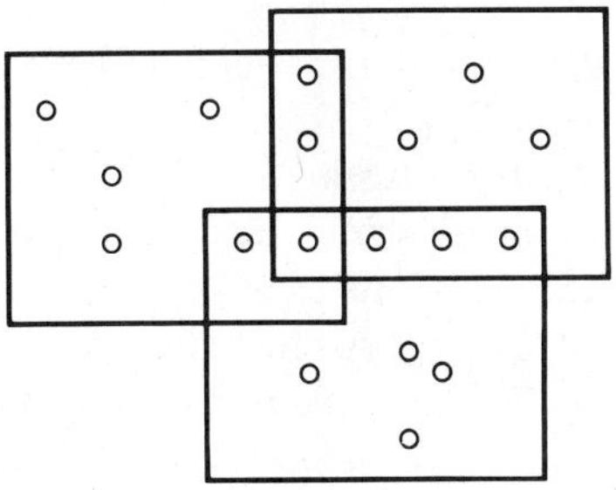

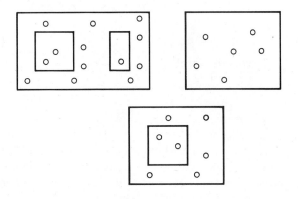

Figure 4.2

We call this approach *multiple inheritance*. Multiple inheritance allows a situation in which some objects are instances of two classes, while other objects are instances of only one class or the other. A less general relaxation of the nonintersection limitation on classes is to allow a class to include all instances of another class, but not to allow more general sharing (Figure 4.3).

Figure 4.3

We call this approach *subclassing*. This follows the terminology of the programming language Simula, which includes a similar concept. Subclassing is strictly hierarchical; if any instances of a class are also instances of another class, then all instances of that class must also be instances of the other class.

The Smalltalk-80 system provides the subclassing form of inheritance for its classes. This chapter describes how subclasses modify their superclasses, how this affects the association of messages and methods, and how the subclass mechanism provides a framework for the classes in the system.

Subclass Descriptions

A subclass specifies that its instances will be the same as instances of another class, called its *superclass*, except for the differences that are explicitly stated. The Smalltalk-80 programmer always creates a new class as a subclass of an existing class. A system class named Object describes the similarities of *all* objects in the system, so every class will at least be a subclass of Object. A class description (protocol or implementation) specifies how its instances differ from the instances of its superclass. The instances of a superclass can not be affected by the existence of subclasses.

A subclass is in all respects a class and can therefore have subclasses itself. Each class has one superclass, although many classes may share the same superclass, so the classes form a tree structure. A class has a sequence of classes from which it inherits both variables and methods. This sequence begins with its superclass and continues with its superclass's superclass, and so on. The inheritance chain continues through the superclass relationship until Object is encountered. Object is the single root class; it is the only class without a superclass.

Recall that an implementation description has three basic parts:

1. A class name

2. A variable declaration

3. A set of methods

A subclass must provide a new class name for itself, but it inherits both the variable declaration and methods of its superclass. New variables may be declared and new methods may be added by the subclass. If instance variable names are added in the subclass variable declaration, instances of the subclass will have more instance variables than instances of the superclass. If shared variables are added, they will be accessible to the instances of the subclass, but not to instances of the superclass. All variable names added must be different from any declared in the superclass.

If a class does not have indexed instance variables, a subclass can declare that its instances will have indexed variables; these indexed variables will be in addition to any inherited named instance variables. If a class has indexed instance variables, its subclasses *must* also have indexed instance variables; a subclass can also declare new named instance variables.

If a subclass adds a method whose message pattern has the same selector as a method in the superclass, its instances will respond to messages with that selector by executing the new method. This is called *overriding* a method. If a subclass adds a method with a selector not found in the methods of the superclass, the instances of the subclass will respond to messages not understood by instances of the superclass.

To summarize, each part of an implementation description can be modified by a subclass in a different way:

1. The class name *must* be overridden.

2. Variables *may* be added.

3. Methods *may* be added or overridden.

An Example Subclass

An implementation description includes an entry, not shown in the previous chapter, that specifies its superclass. The following example is a class created as a subclass of the FinancialHistory class introduced in Chapter 3. Instances of the subclass share the function of FinancialHistory for storing information about monetary expenditures and receipts. They have the additional function of keeping track of the expenditures that are tax deductible. The subclass provides the mandatory new class name (DeductibleHistory), and adds one instance variable and four methods. One of these methods (initialBalance:) overrides a method in the superclass.

The class description for DeductibleHistory follows.

class name	DeductibleHistory
superclass	FinancialHistory
instance variable names	deductibleExpenditures
instance methods	

transaction recording

spendDeductible: amount for: reason
    self spend: amount for: reason.
    deductibleExpenditures ←
        deductibleExpenditures + amount

spend: amount for: reason deducting: deductibleAmount

self spend: amount for: reason.

deductibleExpenditures ←

deductibleExpenditures + deductibleAmount

inquiries

totalDeductions

↑deductibleExpenditures

initialization

initialBalance: amount

super initialBalance: amount.

deductibleExpenditures ← 0

In order to know all the messages understood by an instance of DeductibleHistory, it is necessary to examine the protocols of DeductibleHistory, FinancialHistory, and Object. Instances of DeductibleHistory have four variables—three inherited from the superclass FinancialHistory, and one specified in the class DeductibleHistory. Class Object declares no instance variables.

Figure 4.4 indicates that DeductibleHistory is a subclass of FinancialHistory. Each box in this diagram is labeled in the upper left corner with the name of class it represents.

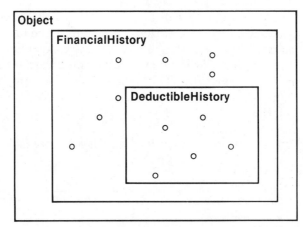

Figure 4.4

Instances of DeductibleHistory can be used to record the history of entities that pay taxes (people, households, businesses). Instances of FinancialHistory can be used to record the history of entities that do not pay taxes (charitable organizations, religious organizations). Actually, an instance of DeductibleHistory could be used in place of an instance of FinancialHistory without detection since it responds to the same messages in the same way. In addition to the messages and methods inherited from FinancialHistory, an instance of DeductibleHistory can respond to messages indicating that all or part of an expenditure is deductible. The new messages available are spendDeductible:for:, which is used if the total amount is deductible; and spend:for:deducting:, which is used if only part of the expenditure is deductible. The total tax deduction can be found by sending a DeductibleHistory the message totalDeductions.

Method Determination

When a message is sent, the methods in the receiver's class are searched for one with a matching selector. If none is found, the methods in that class's superclass are searched next. The search continues up the superclass chain until a matching method is found. Suppose we send an instance of DeductibleHistory a message with selector cashOnHand. The search for the appropriate method to execute begins in the class of the receiver, DeductibleHistory. When it is not found, the search continues by looking at DeductibleHistory's superclass, FinancialHistory. When a method with the selector cashOnHand is found there, that method is executed as the response to the message. The response to this message is to return the value of the instance variable cashOnHand. This value is found in the receiver of the message, that is, in the instance of DeductibleHistory.

The search for a matching method follows the superclass chain, terminating at class Object. If no matching method is found in any class in the superclass chain, the receiver is sent the message doesNotUnderstand:; the argument is the offending message. There is a method for the selector doesNotUnderstand: in Object that reports the error to the programmer.

Suppose we send an instance of DeductibleHistory a message with selector spend:for:. This method is found in the superclass FinancialHistory. The method, as given in Chapter 3, is

spend: amount for: reason
```
    expenditures at: reason
              put: (self totalSpentFor: reason) + amount.
    cashOnHand ← cashOnHand − amount
```

The values of the instance variables (expenditures and cashOnHand) are found in the receiver of the message, the instance of DeductibleHistory.

The pseudo-variable self is also referenced in this method; self represents the DeductibleHistory instance that was the receiver of the message.

When a method contains a message whose receiver is self, the search for the method for that message begins in the instance's class, regardless of which class contains the method containing self. Thus, when the expression self totalSpentFor: reason is evaluated in the method for spend:for: found in FinancialHistory, the search for the method associated with the message selector totalSpentFor: begins in the class of self, i.e., in DeductibleHistory.

Messages to self will be explained using two example classes named One and Two. Two is a subclass of One and One is a subclass of Object. Both classes include a method for the message test. Class One also includes a method for the message result1 that returns the result of the expression self test.

class name	One
superclass	Object
instance methods	

   test
      ↑1
   result1
      ↑self test

class name	Two
superclass	One
instance methods	

   test
      ↑2

An instance of each class will be used to demonstrate the method determination for messages to self. example1 is an instance of class One and example2 is an instance of class Two.

example1 ← One new.
example2 ← Two new

The relationship between One and Two is shown in Figure 4.5. In addition to labeling the boxes in order to indicate class names, several of the circles are also labeled in order to indicate a name referring to the corresponding instance.

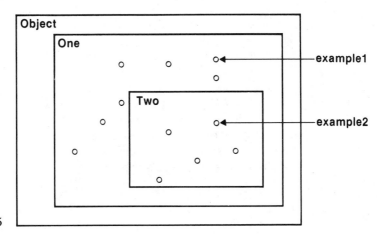

Figure 4.5

The following table shows the results of evaluating various expressions.

expression	result
example1 test	1
example1 result1	1
example2 test	2
example2 result1	2

The two result1 messages both invoke the same method, which is found in class One. They produce different results because of the message to self contained in that method. When result1 is sent to example2, the search for a matching method begins in Two. A method is not found in Two, so the search continues by looking in the superclass, One. A method for result1 is found in One, which consists of one expression, ↑self test. The pseudo-variable self refers to the receiver, example2. The search for the response to test, therefore, begins in class Two. A method for test is found in Two, which returns 2.

Messages to super

An additional pseudo-variable named super is available for use in a method's expressions. The pseudo-variable super refers to the receiver of the message, just as self does. However, when a message is sent to super, the search for a method does not begin in the receiver's class. Instead, the search begins in the superclass of the class containing the method. The use of super allows a method to access methods defined in a superclass even if the methods have been overridden in subclasses. The use of super as other than a receiver (for example, as an argument), has no different effect from using self; the use of super only affects the initial class in which messages are looked up.

Messages to super will be explained using two more example classes named Three and Four. Four is a subclass of Three, Three is a subclass of the previous example Two. Four overrides the method for the message test. Three contains methods for two new messages—result2 returns the result of the expression self result1, and result3 returns the result of the expression super test.

class name	Three
superclass	Two
instance methods	

result2
  ↑self result1
result3
  ↑super test

class name	Four
superclass	Three
instance methods	

test
  ↑4

Instances of One, Two, Three, and Four can all respond to the messages test and result1. The response of instances of Three and Four to messages illustrates the effect of super (Figure 4.6).

example3 ← Three new.
example4 ← Four new

An attempt to send the messages result2 or result3 to example1 or example2 is an error since instances of One or Two do not understand the messages result2 or result3.

The following table shows the results of sending various messages.

expression	result
example3 test	2
example4 result1	4
example3 result2	2
example4 result2	4
example3 result3	2
example4 result3	2

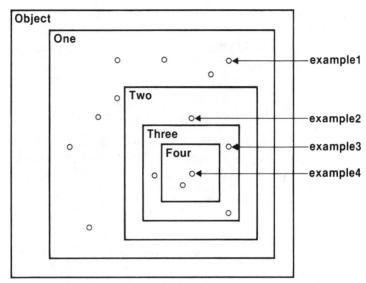

Figure 4.6

When test is sent to example3, the method in Two is used, since Three doesn't override the method. example4 responds to result1 with a 4 for the same reason that example2 responded with a 2. When result2 is sent to example3, the search for a matching method begins in Three. The method found there returns the result of the expression self result1. The search for the response to result1 also begins in class Three. A matching method is not found in Three or its superclass, Two. The method for result1 is found in One and returns the result of self test. The search for the response to test once more begins in class Three. This time, the matching method is found in Three's superclass Two.

The effect of sending messages to super will be illustrated by the responses of example3 and example4 to the message result3. When result3 is sent to example3, the search for a matching method begins in Three. The method found there returns the result of the expression super test. Since test is sent to super, the search for a matching method begins not in class Three, but in its superclass, Two. The method for test in Two returns a 2. When result3 is sent to example4, the result is still 2, even though Four overrides the message for test.

This example highlights a potential confusion: super does not mean start the search in the superclass of the receiver, which, in the last example, would have been class Three. It means start the search in the superclass of the class containing the method in which super was used, which, in the last example, was class Two. Even if Three had overridden the method for test by returning 3, the result of example4 result3 would still be 2. Sometimes, of course, the superclass of the class in which the method containing super is found is the same as the superclass of the receiver.

Another example of the use of super is in the method for initialBalance: in DeductibleHistory.

initialBalance: amount
    super initialBalance: amount.
    deductibleExpenditures ← 0

This method overrides a method in the superclass FinancialHistory. The method in DeductibleHistory consists of two expressions. The first expression passes control to the superclass in order to process the initialization of the balance.

    super initialBalance: amount

The pseudo-variable super refers to the receiver of the message, but indicates that the search for the method should skip DeductibleHistory and begin in FinancialHistory. In this way, the expressions from FinancialHistory do not have to be duplicated in DeductibleHistory. The second expression in the method does the subclass-specific initialization.

    deductibleExpenditures ← 0

If self were substituted for super in the initialBalance: method, it would result in an infinite recursion, since every time initialBalance: is sent, it will be sent again.

Abstract Superclasses

Abstract superclasses are created when two classes share a part of their descriptions and yet neither one is properly a subclass of the other. A mutual superclass is created for the two classes which contains their shared aspects. This type of superclass is called *abstract* because it was not created in order to have instances. In terms of the figures shown earlier, an abstract superclass represents the situation illustrated in Figure 4.7. Notice that the abstract class does not directly contain instances.

As an example of the use of an abstract superclass, consider two classes whose instances represent dictionaries. One class, named SmallDictionary, minimizes the space needed to store its contents; the other, named FastDictionary, stores names and values sparsely and uses a hashing technique to locate names. Both classes use two parallel lists

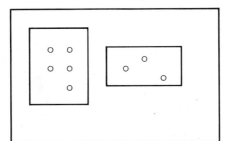

Figure 4.7

that contain names and associated values. SmallDictionary stores the names and values contiguously and uses a simple linear search to locate a name. FastDictionary stores names and values sparsely and uses a hashing technique to locate a name. Other than the difference in how names are located, these two classes are very similar: they share identical protocol and they both use parallel lists to store their contents. These similarities are represented in an abstract superclass named DualListDictionary. The relationships among these three classes is shown in Figure 4.8.

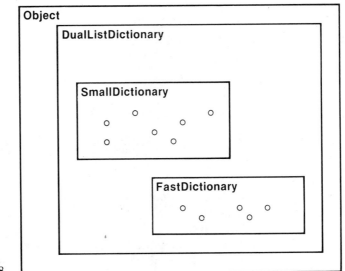

Figure 4.8

The implementation description for the abstract class, DualListDictionary is shown next.

class name	DualListDictionary
superclass	Object
instance variable names	names
	values

instance methods

accessing

at: name
    | index |
    index ← self indexOf: name.
    index = 0
        ifTrue: [self error: 'Name not found']
        ifFalse: [↑values at: index]

at: name put: value
    | index |
    index ← self indexOf: name.
    index = 0
        ifTrue: [index ← self newIndexOf: name].
    ↑values at: index put: value

testing

includes: name
    ↑(self indexOf: name) ~= 0
isEmpty
    ↑self size = 0

initialization

initialize
    names ← Array new: 0.
    values ← Array new: 0

This description of DualListDictionary uses only messages defined in DualListDictionary itself or ones already described in this or in the previous chapters. The external protocol for a DualListDictionary consists of messages at:, at:put:, includes:, isEmpty, and initialize. A new DualListDictionary (actually an instance of a subclass of DualListDictionary) is created by sending it the message new. It is then sent the message initialize so that assignments can be made to the two instance variables. The two variables are initially empty arrays (Array new: 0).

Three messages to self used in its methods are not implemented in DualListDictionary—size, indexOf:, and newIndexOf:. This is the reason that DualListDictionary is called abstract. If an instance were created, it would not be able to respond successfully to all of the necessary messages. The two subclasses, SmallDictionary and FastDictionary, must implement the three missing messages. The fact that the search always starts at the class of the instance referred to by self means that a method in a superclass can be specified in which messages are sent to self, but the corresponding methods are found in the subclass. In this way, a superclass can provide a framework for a method that is refined or actually implemented by the subclass.

SmallDictionary is a subclass of DualListDictionary that uses a minimal amount of space to represent the associations, but may take a long time to find an association. It provides methods for the three messages that were not implemented in DualListDictionary—size, indexOf:, and newIndexOf:. It does not add variables.

class name	SmallDictionary
superclass	DualListDictionary
instance methods	

accessing

size
    ↑names size

private

indexOf: name
    1 to: names size do:
      [:index | (names at: index) = name ifTrue: [↑index]].
    ↑0

newIndexOf: name
    self grow.
    names at: names size put: name.
    ↑names size

grow
    | oldNames oldValues |
    oldNames ← names.
    oldValues ← values.
    names ← Array new: names size + 1.
    values ← Array new: values size + 1.
    names replaceFrom: 1 to: oldNames size with: oldNames.
    values replaceFrom: 1 to: oldValues size with: oldValues

Since names are stored contiguously, the size of a SmallDictionary is the size of its array of names, names. The index of a particular name is determined by a linear search of the array names. If no match is found, the index is 0, signalling failure in the search. Whenever a new association is to be added to the dictionary, the method for newIndexOf: is used to find the appropriate index. It assumes that the sizes of names and values are exactly the sizes needed to store their current elements. This means no space is available for adding a new element. The message grow creates two new Arrays that are copies of the previous ones, with one more element at the end. In the method for newIndexOf:, first the sizes of names and values are increased and then the new name is stored in the new empty position (the last one). The method that called on newIndexOf: has the responsibility for storing the value.

We could evaluate the following example expressions.

expression	result
ages ← SmallDictionary new	a new, uninitialized instance
ages initialize	instance variables initialized
ages isEmpty	true
ages at: 'Brett' put: 3	3
ages at: 'Dave' put: 30	30
ages includes: 'Sam'	false
ages includes: 'Brett'	true
ages size	2
ages at: 'Dave'	30

For each of the above example expressions, we indicate in which class the message is found and in which class any messages sent to self are found.

message selector	message to self	class of method
initialize		DualListDictionary
at:put:		DualListDictionary
	indexOf:	SmallDictionary
	newIndexOf:	SmallDictionary
includes:		DualListDictionary
	indexOf:	SmallDictionary
size		SmallDictionary
at:		DualListDictionary
	indexOf:	SmallDictionary
	error:	Object

FastDictionary is another subclass of DualListDictionary. It uses a hashing technique to locate names. Hashing requires more space, but takes less time than a linear search. All objects respond to the hash message by returning a number. Numbers respond to the \ \ message by returning their value in the modulus of the argument.

class name	FastDictionary
superclass	DualListDictionary
instance methods	

accessing

size
```
| size |
size ← 0.
names do: [ :name | name notNil ifTrue: [size ← size + 1]].
↑size
```

initialization

initialize
```
names ← Array new: 4.
values ← Array new: 4
```

private

indexOf: name
```
| index |
index ← name hash \ \ names size + 1.
[(names at: index) = name]
    whileFalse: [(names at: index) isNil
                        ifTrue: [↑0]
                        ifFalse: [index ← index \ \ names size + 1]].
↑index
```

newIndexOf: name
```
| index |
names size - self size  < = (names size / 4)
    ifTrue: [self grow].
index ← name hash \ \ names size + 1.
[(names at: index) isNil]
    whileFalse: [index ← index \ \ names size + 1].
names at: index put: name.
↑index
```

grow
```
| oldNames oldValues |
oldNames ← names.
oldValues ← values.
names ← Array new: names size * 2.
values ← Array new: values size * 2.
1 to: oldNames size do:
    [ :index |
    (oldNames at: index) isNil
            ifFalse: [self at: (oldNames at: index)
                            put: (oldValues at: index)]]
```

FastDictionary overrides DualListDictionary's implementation of initialize in order to create Arrays that already have some space allocated (Array new: 4). The size of a FastDictionary is not simply the size of one of its variables since the Arrays always have empty entries. So the size is determined by examining each element in the Array and counting the number that are not nil.

The implementation of newIndexOf: follows basically the same idea as that used for SmallDictionary except that when the size of an Array is changed (doubled in this case in the method for grow), each element is explicitly copied from the old Arrays into the new ones so that elements are rehashed. The size does not always have to be changed as is necessary in SmallDictionary. The size of a FastDictionary is changed only when the number of empty locations in names falls below a minimum. The minimum is equal to 25% of the elements.

names size − self size < = (names size / 4)

Subclass Framework Messages

As a matter of programming style, a method should not include messages to self if the messages are neither implemented by the class nor inherited from a superclass. In the description of DualListDictionary, three such messages exist—size, indexOf:, and newIndexOf:. As we shall see in subsequent chapters, the ability to respond to size is inherited from Object; the response is the number of indexed instance variables. A subclass of DualListDictionary is supposed to override this method in order to return the number of names in the dictionary.

A special message, subclassResponsibility, is specified in Object. It is to be used in the implementation of messages that cannot be properly implemented in an abstract class. That is, the implementation of size and indexOf: and newIndexOf:, by Smalltalk-80 convention, should be

self subclassResponsibility

The response to this message is to invoke the following method defined in class Object.

subclassResponsibility
self error: 'My subclass should have overridden one of my messages.'

In this way, if a method should have been implemented in a subclass of an abstract class, the error reported is an indication to the programmer of how to fix the problem. Moreover, using this message, the programmer creates abstract classes in which all messages sent to self are implemented, and in which the implementation is an indication to the programmer of which methods must be overridden in the subclass.

By convention, if the programmer decides that a message inherited from an abstract superclass should actually *not* be implemented, the appropriate way to override the inherited method is

    self shouldNotImplement

The response to this message is to invoke the following method defined in class Object.

shouldNotImplement
    self error: 'This message is not appropriate for this object.

There are several major subclass hierarchies in the Smalltalk-80 system that make use of the idea of creating a framework of messages whose implementations must be completed in subclasses. There are classes describing various kinds of collections (see Chapters 9 and 10). The collection classes are arranged hierarchically in order to share as much as possible among classes describing similar kinds of collections. They make use of the messages subclassResponsibility and shouldNotImplement. Another example of the use of subclasses is the hierarchy of linear measures and number classes (see Chapters 7 and 8).

Summary of Terminology	**subclass**	A class that inherits variables and methods from an existing class.
	superclass	The class from which variables and methods are inherited.
	Object	The class that is the root of the tree-structured class hierarchy.
	overriding a method	Specifying a method in a subclass for the same message as a method in a superclass.
	super	A pseudo-variable that refers to the receiver of a message; differs from self in where to start the search for methods.
	abstract class	A class that specifies protocol, but is not able to fully implement it; by convention, instances are not created of this kind of class.
	subclassResponsibility	A message to report the error that a subclass should have implemented one of the superclass's messages.
	shouldNotImplement	A message to report the error that this is a message inherited from a superclass but explicitly not available to instances of the subclass.

5

Metaclasses

Since all Smalltalk-80 system components are represented by objects and all objects are instances of a class, the classes themselves must be represented by instances of a class. A class whose instances are themselves classes is called a *metaclass*. This chapter describes the special properties of metaclasses. Examples illustrate how metaclasses are used to support instance creation and general class inquiries.

In earlier versions of the Smalltalk system, there was only one metaclass, named Class. It corresponded to the class organization depicted in Figure 5.1. As used in Chapter 4, a box denotes a class and a circle denotes an instance of the class in which it is contained. Where possible, the box is labeled with the name of the class it represents. Note that there is one circle in the box labeled Class for each box in the diagram.

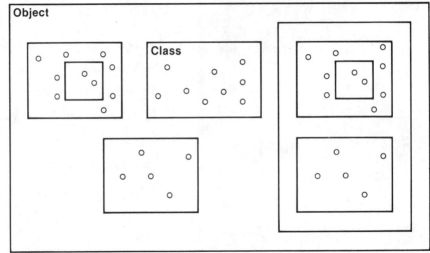

 Figure 5.1

This approach had the difficulty that the message protocol of all classes was constrained to be the same since it was specified in one place. In particular, the messages used to create new instances were the same for all classes and could not take any special initialization requirements into account. With a single metaclass, all classes respond to the message new or new: by returning an instance whose instance variables all refer to nil. For most objects, nil is not a reasonable instance variable value, so new instances have to be initialized by sending another message. The programmer must ensure that every time a new or new: is sent, another message is sent to the new object so that it will be properly initialized. Examples of this kind of initialization were shown in Chapter 4 for SmallDictionary and FinancialHistory.

The Smalltalk-80 system removes the restriction that all classes have the same message protocol by making each class an instance of its own metaclass. Whenever a new class is created, a new metaclass is created for it automatically. Metaclasses are similar to other classes because they contain the methods used by their instances. Metaclasses are different from other classes because they are not themselves instances of metaclasses. Instead, they are all instances of a class called Metaclass. Also, metaclasses do not have class names. A metaclass can be accessed by sending its instance the unary message class. For example, Rectangle's metaclass can be referred to with the expression Rectangle class.

The messages of a metaclass typically support creation and initialization of instances, and initialization of class variables.

Initialization of Instances

Each class can respond to messages that request properly initialized new instances. Multiple metaclasses are needed because the initialization messages are different for different classes. For example, we have already seen that Time creates new instances in response to the message now and Date creates new instances in response to the message today.

Time now
Date today

These messages are meaningless to Point, the class whose instances represent two-dimensional locations. Point creates a new instance in response to a message with selector x:y: and two arguments specifying the coordinates. This message is, in turn, meaningless to Time or Date.

Point x: 100 y: 150

Class Rectangle understands several messages that create new instances. A message with the selector origin:corner: takes Points representing the upper left and lower right corners as arguments.

Rectangle
        origin: (Point x: 50 y: 50)
        corner: (Point x: 250 y: 300)

A message with the selector origin:extent: takes as arguments the upper left corner and a Point representing the width and height. The same rectangle could have been created by the following expression.

Rectangle
       origin: (Point x: 50 y: 50)
       extent: (Point x: 200 y: 250)

In the Smalltalk-80 system, Class is an abstract superclass for all of the metaclasses. Class describes the general nature of classes. Each metaclass adds the behavior specific to its single instance. Metaclasses may add new instance creation messages like those of Date, Time, Point, and Rectangle mentioned above, or they may redefine the fundamental new and new: messages in order to perform some default initialization.

The organization of classes and instances in the system, as described so far, is illustrated in Figure 5.2.

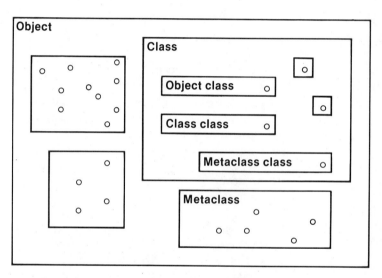

Figure 5.2

In this figure, we indicate classes Object, Metaclass, and Class, and metaclasses for each. Each circle within the box labeled Metaclass denotes a metaclass. Each box within the box labeled Class denotes a subclass of Class. There is one such box for each circle within the box labeled Metaclass. Each of these boxes contains a circle denoting its instance; these instances refer to Object or one of the subclasses of Object, but not to metaclasses.

An Example Metaclass

Since there is a one-to-one correspondence between a class and its metaclass, their descriptions are presented together. An implementation description includes a part entitled "class methods" that shows the methods added by the metaclass. The protocol for the metaclass is always found by looking at the class methods part of the implementation description of its single instance. In this way, messages sent to the class (class methods) and messages sent to instances of the class (instance methods) are listed together as part of the complete implementation description.

The following new version of the implementation description for FinancialHistory includes class methods.

class name	FinancialHistory
superclass	Object
instance variable names	cashOnHand
	incomes
	expenditures

class methods

instance creation

initialBalance: amount
    ↑super new setInitialBalance: amount
new
    ↑super new setInitialBalance: 0

instance methods

transaction recording

receive: amount from: source
    incomes at: source
        put: (self totalReceivedFrom: source) + amount.
    cashOnHand ← cashOnHand + amount
spend: amount for: reason
    expenditures at: reason
        put: (self totalSpentFor: reason) + amount.
    cashOnHand ← cashOnHand — amount

inquiries

cashOnHand
    ↑cashOnHand
totalReceivedFrom: source
    (incomes includesKey: source)
        ifTrue: [↑incomes at: source]
        ifFalse: [↑0]
totalSpentFor: reason
    (expenditures includesKey: reason)
        ifTrue: [↑expenditures at: reason]
        ifFalse: [↑0]

private

setInitialBalance: amount
cashOnHand ← amount.
incomes ← Dictionary new.
expenditures ← Dictionary new

Three changes have been made to the implementation description.

1. One category of class methods named instance creation has been added. The category contains methods for initialBalance: and new. By convention, the category instance creation is used for class methods that return new instances.

2. The category of instance methods named initialization has been deleted. It had included a method for initialBalance:.

3. A category of instance methods named private has been added. The category contains one method for setInitialBalance:; this method contains the same expressions that were in the deleted method for initialBalance:.

This example illustrates how metaclasses create initialized instances. The instance creation methods for initialBalance: and new do not have direct access to the instance variables of the new instance (cashOnHand, incomes, and expenses). This is because the methods are not a part of the class of the new instance, but rather of the class's class. Therefore, the instance creation methods first create uninitialized instances and then send an initialization message, setInitialBalance:, to the new instance. The method for this message is found in the instance methods part of FinancialHistory's implementation description; it can assign appropriate values to the instance variables. The initialization message is not considered part of the external protocol of FinancialHistory so it is categorized as private. It is typically only sent once and only by a class method.

The old initialization message initialBalance: was deleted because the proper way to create a FinancialHistory is to use an expression such as

FinancialHistory initialBalance: 350

not

FinancialHistory new initialBalance: 350

Indeed, this second expression would now create an error since instances of FinancialHistory are no longer described as responding to initialBalance:. We could have maintained the instance method initialBalance: and implemented the class method for initialBalance: to call on it, but we try not to use the same selectors for both instance and class methods in order to improve the readability of the implementation description. However, there would be no ambiguity if the same selector were used.

Metaclass Inheritance

Like other classes, a metaclass inherits from a superclass. The simplest way to structure the inheritance of metaclasses would be to make each one a subclass of Class. This organization was shown in Figure 5.2. Class describes the general nature of classes. Each metaclass adds behavior specific to its instance. Metaclasses may add new instance creation messages or they may redefine the fundamental new and new: messages to perform some default initialization.

When metaclasses were added to the Smalltalk-80 system, one further step in class organization was taken. The metaclass subclass hierarchy was constrained to be parallel to the subclass hierarchy of the classes that are their instances. Therefore, if DeductibleHistory is a subclass of FinancialHistory, then DeductibleHistory's metaclass must be a subclass of FinancialHistory's metaclass. A metaclass typically has only one instance.

An abstract class named ClassDescription was provided to describe classes and their instances. Class and Metaclass are subclasses of ClassDescription. Since the superclass chain of all objects ends at Object and Object has no superclass, the superclass of Object's metaclass is Class. From Class, the metaclasses inherit messages that provide protocol for the creation of instances (Figure 5.3).

The superclass chain from Class leads eventually to class Object. Notice that the hierarchy of boxes with the box labeled Object class is like that of the hierarchy of boxes within the box labeled Object; this similarity illustrates the parallel hierarchies. A full description of this part of the system, including the relationship between Metaclass and its metaclass, is provided in Chapter 16.

As an example of the metaclass inheritance hierarchy, consider the implementation of initialBalance: in FinancialHistory class.

initialBalance: amount
   ↑super new setInitialBalance: amount

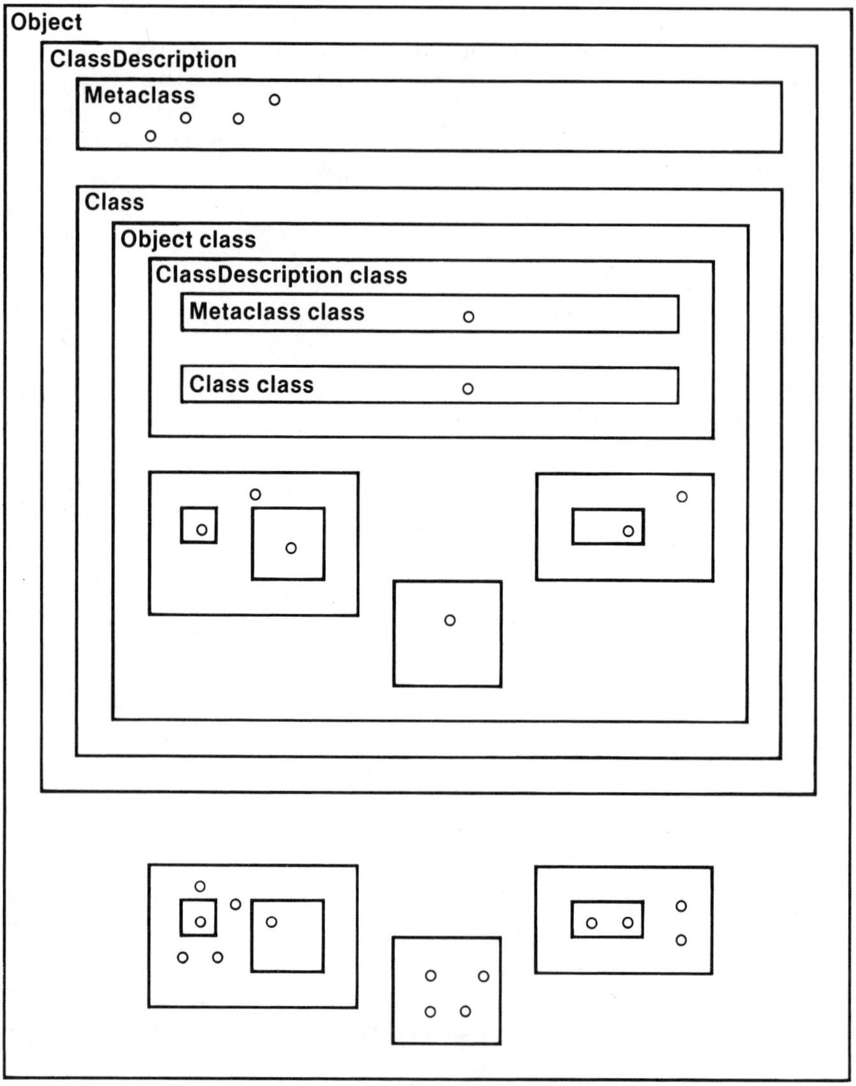

Figure 5.3

This method creates a new instance by evaluating the expression super new; it uses the method for new found in the class methods of the superclass, not the class methods found in this class. It then sends the new instance the message setInitialBalance: with the initial amount of the balance as the argument. Similarly, new is reimplemented as creating an instance using super new followed by setInitialBalance:.

new
    ↑super new setInitialBalance: 0

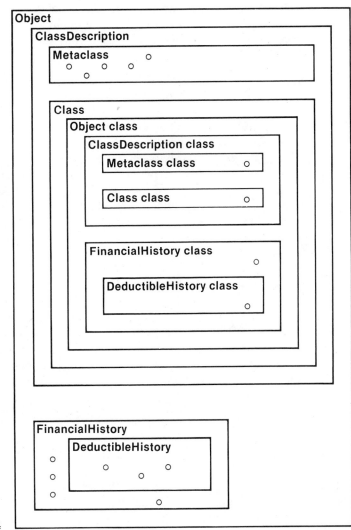

Figure 5.4

Where is the method for the message new sent to super actually found? The subclass hierarchy of the metaclasses parallels the hierarchy of their instances. If one class is a subclass of another, its metaclass will be a subclass of the other's metaclass, as indicated in Figure 5.3. The parallel class and metaclass hierarchies for the FinancialHistory application are shown in Figure 5.4.

If we evaluate the expression

FinancialHistory initialBalance: 350

the search for the response to initialBalance: begins in FinancialHistory class, i.e., in the class methods for FinancialHistory. A method for that selector is found there. The method consists of two messages:

1. Send super the message new.

2. Send the result of 1 the message setInitialBalance: 0.

The search for new begins in the superclass of FinancialHistory class, that is, in Object class. A method is not found there, so the search continues up the superclass chain to Class. The message selector new is found in Class, and a primitive method is executed. The result is an uninitialized instance of FinancialHistory. This instance is then sent the message setInitialBalance:. The search for the response begins in the class of the instance, i.e., in FinancialHistory (in the instance methods). A method is found there which assigns a value to each instance variable.

The evaluation of

FinancialHistory new

is carried out in a similar way. The response to new is found in FinancialHistory class (i.e., in the class methods of FinancialHistory). The remaining actions are the same as for initialBalance: with the exception of the value of the argument to setInitialBalance:. The instance creation methods must use super new in order to avoid invoking the same method recursively.

Initialization of Class Variables

The main use of messages to classes other than creation of instances is the initialization of class variables. The implementation description's variable declaration gives the names of the class variables only, not their values. When a class is created, the named class variables are created, but they all have a value of nil. The metaclass typically defines a method that initializes the class variables. By convention, the class-variable initialization method is usually associated with the unary message initialize, categorized as class initialization.

Class variables are accessible to both the class and its metaclass. The assignment of values to class variables can be done in the class methods, rather than indirectly via a private message in the instance methods (as was necessary for instance variables).

The example DeductibleHistory, this time with a class variable that needs to be initialized, is shown next. DeductibleHistory is a subclass of FinancialHistory. It declares one class variable, MinimumDeductions.

class name	DeductibleHistory
superclass	FinancialHistory
instance variable names	deductibleExpenditures
class variable names	MinimumDeductions
class methods	

instance creation

initialBalance: amount
    | newHistory |
    newHistory ← super initialBalance: amount.
    newHistory initializeDeductions.
    ↑newHistory

new
    | newHistory |
    newHistory ← super initialBalance: 0.
    newHistory initializeDeductions.
    ↑newHistory

class initialization

initialize
    MinimumDeductions ← 2300

instance methods

transaction recording

spendDeductible: amount for: reason
    self spend: amount for: reason.
    deductibleExpenditures ←
        deductibleExpenditures + amount
spend: amount for: reason deducting: deductibleAmount
    self spend: amount for: reason.
    deductibleExpenditures ←
        deductibleExpenditures + deductibleAmount

inquiries

isItemizable
    ↑deductibleExpenditures > = MinimumDeductions
totalDeductions
    ↑deductibleExpenditures

private

initializeDeductions
    deductibleExpenditures ← 0

This version of DeductibleHistory adds five instance methods, one of which is isItemizable. The response to this message is true or false depending on whether enough deductions have been accumulated in order to itemize deductions on a tax report. The tax law specifies that a minimum deduction of 2300 can be taken, so if the accumulation is less, the standard deduction should be used. The constant, 2300, is referred to by the class variable MinimumDeductions. In order to successfully send an instance of DeductibleHistory the message isItemizable, the class variable MinimumDeductions must be assigned its numeric value. This is done by sending the class the message initialize before any instances are created.

DeductibleHistory initialize

This message only has to be sent once, after the class initialization message is first defined. The variable is shared by each new instance of the class.

According to the above class description, a new instance of DeductibleHistory can be created by sending the class the messages initialBalance: or new, just as for the superclass FinancialHistory. Suppose we evaluate the expression

DeductibleHistory initialBalance: 100

The determination of which methods are actually followed in order to evaluate the expression depends on the class/superclass chain for DeductibleHistory. The method for initialBalance: is found in the class methods of DeductibleHistory.

initialBalance: amount
  | newHistory |
  newHistory ← super initialBalance: amount.
  newHistory initializeDeductions.
  ↑newHistory

This method declares newHistory as a temporary variable. The first expression of the method is an assignment to the temporary variable.

newHistory ← super initialBalance: amount

The pseudo-variable super refers to the receiver. The receiver is the class DeductibleHistory; its class is its metaclass. The superclass of the metaclass is the metaclass for FinancialHistory. Thus we can find the method that will be followed by looking in the class methods of FinancialHistory. The method is

initialBalance: amount
  ↑super new setInitialBalance: amount

We have already followed evaluation of this method. The response to new is found in Class. A new instance of the original receiver, DeductibleHistory, is created and sent the message setInitialBalance:. The search for setInitialBalance: begins in the class of the new instance, i.e., in DeductibleHistory. It is not found. The search proceeds to the superclass FinancialHistory. It is found and evaluated. Instance variables declared in FinancialHistory are assigned values. The value of the first expression of the class method for initialBalance: in DeductibleHistory, then, is a partially initialized new instance. This new instance is assigned to the temporary variable newHistory.

newHistory is then sent the message initializeDeductions. The search begins in the class of the receiver, newHistory; the class is DeductibleHistory. The method is found. It assigns the value of the fourth instance variable to be 0.

The third expression of the instance creation message returns the new instance.

An alternative way to implement the class DeductibleHistory is presented next. In this alternative class description, the instance-creation class methods of FinancialHistory are not reimplemented. Rather, the private instance-method message setInitialBalance: is overridden in order to account for the additional instance variable.

class name	DeductibleHistory
superclass	FinancialHistory
instance variable names	deductibleExpenditures
class variable names	MinimumDeductions
class methods	

class initialization

initialize
    MinimumDeductions ← 2300

instance methods

transaction recording

spendDeductible: amount for: reason
    self spend: amount for: reason.
    deductibleExpenditures ←
        deductibleExpenditures + amount

spend: amount for: reason deducting: deductibleAmount
    self spend: amount for: reason.
    deductibleExpenditures ←
        deductibleExpenditures + deductibleAmount

inquiries

isItemizable
    ↑deductibleExpenditures > = MinimumDeductions

totalDeductions
    ↑deductibleExpenditures

private

setInitialBalance: amount
    super setInitialBalance: amount.
    deductibleExpenditures ← 0

Using this alternative class description for DeductibleHistory, the evaluation of the response to initialBalance: in

    DeductibleHistory initialBalance: 350

is to search in DeductibleHistory class for initialBalance:. It is not found. Continue the search in the superclass, FinancialHistory class. It is found. The method evaluated consists of the expression

    super new setInitialBalance: amount

The method for new is found in Class. Search for setInitialBalance: beginning in the class of the new instance, a DeductibleHistory. The method for setInitialBalance: is found in DeductibleHistory. The response of setInitialBalance: in DeductibleHistory is to send the same message to super so that the search for the method begins in FinancialHistory. It is found and three instance variables are assigned values. The second expression of setInitialBalance: in DeductibleHistory sets the fourth variable to 0. The result of the original message is a fully initialized instance of DeductibleHistory.

Summary of Method Determination

Determining the actual actions taken when a message is sent involves searching the methods in the class hierarchy of the receiver. The search begins with the class of the receiver and follows the superclass chain. If not found after searching the last superclass, Object, an error is reported. If the receiver is a class, its class is a metaclass. The messages to which a class can respond are listed in the implementation description in the part entitled "class methods." If the receiver is not a class, then the messages to which it can respond are listed in its implementation description in the part entitled "instance methods."

The pseudo-variable self refers to the receiver of the message that invoked the executing method. The search for a method corresponding to a message to self begins in the class of self. The pseudo-variable super also refers to the receiver of the message. The search for a method corresponding to a message to super begins in the superclass of the class in which the executing method was found.

This ends the description of the Smalltalk-80 programming language. To use the system, the programmer must have general knowledge of the system classes. Part Two gives detailed accounts of the protocol descriptions for each of the system classes and provides examples, often by presenting the implementation descriptions of system classes. Part Three introduces a moderate-size application. Before delving into the details of the actual system classes, the reader might want to skip to Part Three to get a sense of what it is like to define a larger application.

Summary of Terminology

metaclass	The class of a class.
Class	An abstract superclass of all classes other than metaclasses.
Metaclass	A class whose instances are classes of classes.

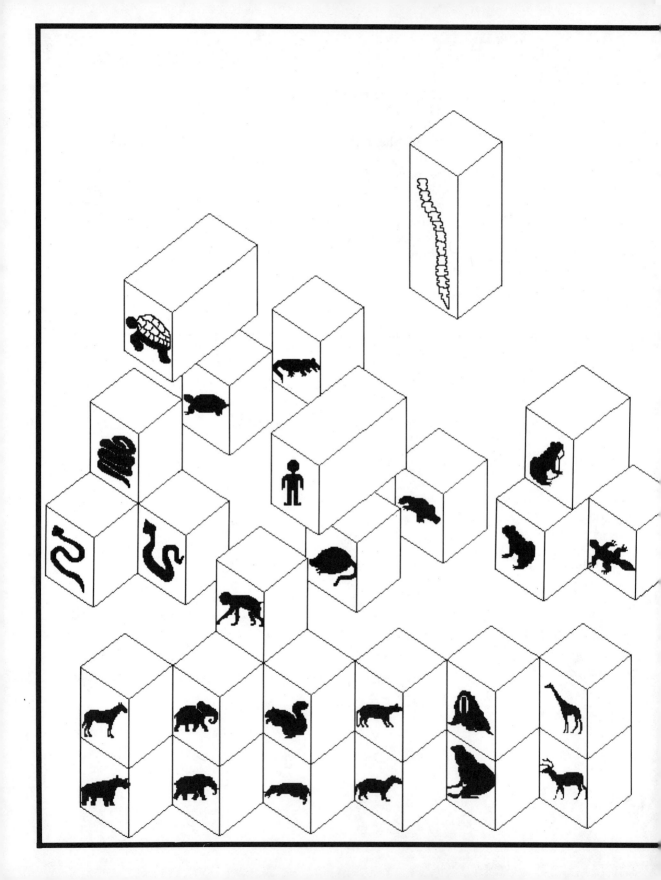

PART TWO

Part One provided an overview of the Smalltalk-80 language both from the semantic view of objects and message sending and from the syntactic view of the form that expressions take. The Smalltalk-80 programmer must first understand the semantics of the language: that all information is represented in the form of objects and that all processing is done by sending messages to objects. Every object is described by a class; every class, with the exception of class Object, is a subclass of another class. Programming in the Smalltalk-80 system involves the description of new classes of objects, the creation of instances of classes, and the sequencing of messages to the instances. The Smalltalk-80 syntax defines three forms that messages can take: unary, binary, and keyword messages. Successful use of the language requires that the programmer have a general knowledge of each of the basic kinds of objects in the system and of the messages that can be sent to them.

The semantics and syntax of the language are relatively simple. Yet the system is large and powerful due to the numbers of and kinds of available objects. There are eight significant categories of classes in the Smalltalk-80 system: kernel and kernel support, linear measures, numbers, collections, streams, classes, independent processes, and graphics. The protocol of these kinds of objects is reviewed in 12 chapters of Part Two. In each of these chapters, the diagram of the class hierarchy given in Chapter 1 is re-presented in order to highlight the portion of the hierarchy discussed in that chapter. Three additional chapters in Part Two provide examples of Smalltalk-80 expressions and class descriptions.

The classes in the Smalltalk-80 system are defined in a linear hierarchy. The chapters in Part Two take an encyclopedic approach to reviewing class protocol: categories of messages are defined, each message is annotated, and examples are given. In presenting the protocol of a class, however, only those messages added by the class are described. The complete message protocol is determined by examining the protocol specified in the class and in each of its superclasses. Thus it is useful to present the classes starting with a description of class Object and to proceed in a mostly depth-first manner so that inherited protocol can be understood in conjunction with the new protocol.

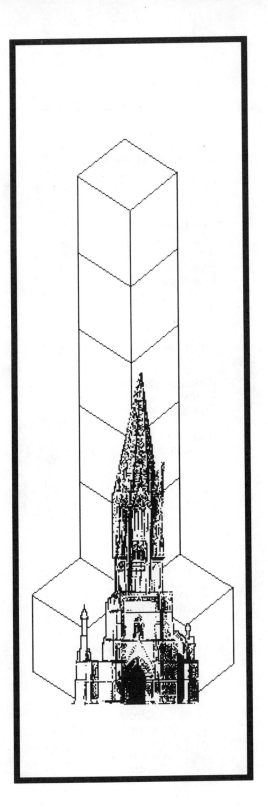

6

Protocol for All Objects

Object

    Magnitude
        Character
        Date
        Time

        Number
            Float
            Fraction
            Integer
                LargeNegativeInteger
                LargePositiveInteger
                SmallInteger

        LookupKey
            Association

    Link

        Process

    Collection

        SequenceableCollection
            LinkedList

                Semaphore

            ArrayedCollection
                Array

                Bitmap
                    DisplayBitmap

                RunArray
                String
                    Symbol
                Text
                ByteArray

            Interval
            OrderedCollection
                SortedCollection
        Bag
        MappedCollection
        Set
            Dictionary
                IdentityDictionary

    Stream
        PositionableStream
            ReadStream
            WriteStream
                ReadWriteStream
                  ExternalStream
                    FileStream

        Random

    File
    FileDirectory
    FilePage

    UndefinedObject
    Boolean
        False
        True

    ProcessorScheduler
    Delay
    SharedQueue

    Behavior
        ClassDescription
            Class
            MetaClass

    Point
    Rectangle
    BitBlt
        CharacterScanner

        Pen

    DisplayObject
        DisplayMedium
            Form
                Cursor
                DisplayScreen
        InfiniteForm
        OpaqueForm
        Path
            Arc
                Circle
            Curve
            Line
            LinearFit
            Spline

Everything in the system is an object. The protocol common to all objects in the system is provided in the description of class Object. This means that any and every object created in the system can respond to the messages defined by class Object. These are typically messages that support reasonable default behavior in order to provide a starting place from which to develop new kinds of objects, either by adding new messages or by modifying the response to existing messages. Examples to consider when examining Object's protocol are numeric objects such as 3 or 16.23, collections such as 'this is a string' or #(this is an array), nil or true, and class-describing objects such as Collection or SmallInteger or, indeed, Object itself.

The specification of protocol for class Object given in this chapter is incomplete. We have omitted messages pertaining to message handling, special dependency relationships, and system primitives. These are presented in Chapter 14.

Testing the Functionality of an Object

Every object is an instance of a class. An object's functionality is determined by its class. This functionality is tested in two ways: explicit naming of a class to determine whether it is the class or the superclass of the object, and naming of a message selector to determine whether the object can respond to it. These reflect two ways of thinking about the relationship among instances of different classes: in terms of the class/subclass hierarchy, or in terms of shared message protocols.

Object instance protocol

testing functionality	
class	Answer the object which is the receiver's class.
isKindOf: aClass	Answer whether the argument, aClass, is a superclass or class of the receiver.
isMemberOf: aClass	Answer whether the receiver is a direct instance of the argument, aClass. This is the same as testing whether the response to sending the receiver the message class is the same as (==) aClass.
respondsTo: aSymbol	Answer whether the method dictionary of the receiver's class or one of its superclasses contains the argument, aSymbol, as a message selector.

Example messages and their corresponding results are

expression	*result*
3 class	SmallInteger
#(this is an array) isKindOf: Collection	true

#(this is an array) isMemberOf: Collection	false
#(this is an array) class	Array
3 respondsTo: #isKindOf:	true
#(1 2 3) isMemberOf: Array	true
Object class	Object class

Comparing Objects

Since all information in the system is represented as objects, there is a basic protocol provided for testing the identity of an object and for copying objects. The important comparisons specified in class Object are equivalence and equality testing. Equivalence (==) is the test of whether two objects are the same object. Equality (=) is the test of whether two objects represent the same component. The decision as to what it means to be "represent the same component" is made by the receiver of the message; each new kind of object that adds new instance variables typically must reimplement the = message in order to specify which of its instance variables should enter into the test of equality. For example, equality of two arrays is determined by checking the size of the arrays and then the equality of each of the elements of the arrays; equality of two numbers is determined by testing whether the two numbers represent the same value; and equality of two bank accounts might rest solely on the equality of each account identification number.

The message hash is a special part of the comparing protocol. The response to hash is an integer. Any two objects that are equal must return the same value for hash. Unequal objects may or may not return equal values for hash. Typically, this integer is used as an index to locate the object in an indexed collection (as illustrated in Chapter 3). Any time = is redefined, hash may also have to be redefined in order to preserve the property that any two objects that are equal return equal values for hash.

Object instance protocol

comparing

== anObject	Answer whether the receiver and the argument are the same object.
= anObject	Answer whether the receiver and the argument represent the same component.
~= anObject	Answer whether the receiver and the argument do not represent the same component.
~~ anObject	Answer whether the receiver and the argument are not the same object.
hash	Answer an Integer computed with respect to the representation of the receiver.

The default implementation of = is the same as that of ==.

Some specialized comparison protocol provides a concise way to test for identity with the object nil.

testing

  isNil   Answer whether the receiver is nil.

  notNil   Answer whether the receiver is not nil.

These messages are identical to == nil and ~~ nil, respectively. Choice of which to use is a matter of personal style.

Some obvious examples are

expression	result
nil isNil	true
true notNil	true
3 isNil	false
#(a b c) = #(a b c)	true
3 = (6/2)	true
#(1 2 3) class == Array	true

Copying Objects

There are two ways to make copies of an object. The distinction is whether or not the values of the object's variables are copied. If the values are not copied, then they are shared (shallowCopy); if the values are copied, then they are not shared (deepCopy).

copying

  copy   Answer another instance just like the receiver.

  shallowCopy   Answer a copy of the receiver which shares the receiver's instance variables.

  deepCopy   Answer a copy of the receiver with its own copy of each instance variable.

The default implementation of copy is shallowCopy. In subclasses in which copying must result in a special combination of shared and unshared variables, the method associated with copy is usually re-implemented, rather than the method associated with shallowCopy or deepCopy.

As an example, a copy (a shallow copy) of an Array refers to the same elements as in the original Array, but the copy is a different object. Replacing an element in the copy does not change the original. Thus

expression	result
a ← #('first' 'second' 'third')	('first' 'second' 'third')
b ← a copy	('first' 'second' 'third')
a = b	true
a == b	false
(a at: 1) == (b at: 1)	true
b at: 1 put: 'newFirst'	'newFirst'
a = b	false
a ← 'hello'	'hello'
b ← a copy	'hello'
a = b	true
a == b	false

Figure 6.1 shows the relationship between shallow and deep copying. To further illustrate the distinction between shallowCopy and deepCopy, take as an example a PersonnelRecord. Suppose it is defined to include the variable insurancePlan, an instance of class Insurance. Suppose further that each instance of Insurance has a value associated with it representing the limit on medical coverage. Now suppose we have created employeeRecord as a prototypical instance of a PersonnelRecord. By "prototypical" we mean that the object has all of the initial attributes of any new instance of its class, so that instances can be created by simply copying it rather than sending a sequence of initialization messages. Suppose further that this prototypical instance is a class variable of PersonnelRecord and that the response to creating a new PersonnelRecord is to make a shallow copy of it; that is, the method associated with the message new is ↑employeeRecord copy.

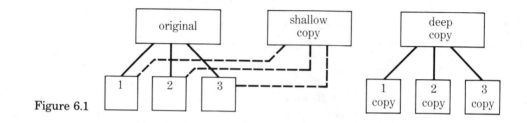

Figure 6.1

As a result of evaluating the expression

joeSmithRecord ← PersonnelRecord new

joeSmithRecord refers to a copy (in particular, a shallow copy) of employeeRecord.

The prototype employeeRecord and the actual record joeSmithRecord share a reference to the same insurance plan. Company policy may change. Suppose PersonnelRecord understands the message changeInsuranceLimit: aNumber, which is implemented by having the prototypical instance of PersonnelRecord, employeeRecord, reset its insurance plan limit on medical coverage. Since this insurance plan is shared, the result of evaluating the expression

PersonnelRecord changeInsuranceLimit: 4000

is to change the medical coverage of all employees. In the example, both the medical coverage referenced by employeeRecord and that referenced by its copy, joeSmithRecord, is changed. The message changeInsuranceLimit: is sent to the class PersonnelRecord because it is the appropriate object to broadcast a change to all of its instances.

Accessing the Parts of an Object

There are two kinds of objects in the Smalltalk-80 system, objects with named variables and objects with indexed variables. Objects with indexed variables may also have named instance variables. This distinction is explained in Chapter 3. Class Object supports six messages intended to access the indexed variables of an object. These are

Object instance protocol

accessing

at: index	Answer the value of the indexed instance variable of the receiver whose index is the argument, index. If the receiver does not have indexed variables, or if the argument is greater than the number of indexed variables, then report an error.
at: index put: anObject	Store the argument, anObject, as the value of the indexed instance variable of the receiver whose index is the argument, index. If the receiver does not have indexed variables, or if the argument is greater than the number of indexed variables, then report an error. Answer anObject.
basicAt: index	Same as at: index. The method associated with this message, however, cannot be modified in any subclass.

basicAt: index put: anObject	Same as at: index put: anObject. The method associated with this message, however, cannot be modified in any subclass.
size	Answer the receiver's number of indexed variables. This value is the same as the largest legal index.
basicSize	Same as size. The method associated with this message, however, cannot be modified in any subclass.

Notice that the accessing messages come in pairs; one message in each pair is prefixed by the word basic meaning that it is a fundamental system message whose implementation should not be modified in any subclass. The purpose of providing pairs is so that the external protocol, at:, at:put:, and size, can be overridden to handle special cases, while still maintaining a way to get at the primitive methods. (Chapter 4 includes an explanation of "primitive" methods, which are methods implemented in the virtual machine for the system.) Thus in any method in a hierarchy of class descriptions, the messages, basicAt:, basicAt:put:, and basicSize, can always be used to obtain the primitive implementations. The message basicSize can be sent to any object; if the object is not variable length, then the response is 0.

Instances of class Array are variable-length objects. Suppose letters is the Array #(a b d f j m p s). Then

expression	result
letters size	8
letters at: 3	d
letters at: 3 put: #c	c
letters	(a b c f j m p s)

Printing and Storing Objects

There are various ways to create a sequence of characters that provides a description of an object. The description might give only a clue as to the identity of an object. Or the description might provide enough information so that a similar object can be constructed. In the first case (printing), the description may or may not be in a well-formatted, visually pleasing style, such as that provided by a Lisp pretty-printing routine. In the second case (storing), the description might preserve information shared with other objects.

The message protocol of the classes in the Smalltalk-80 system support printing and storing. The implementation of these messages in class Object provides minimal capability; most subclasses override the messages in order to enhance the descriptions created. The arguments to two of the messages are instances of a kind of Stream; Streams are presented in Chapter 12.

Object instance protocol
_____

printing

printString | Answer a String whose characters are a description of the receiver.

printOn: aStream | Append to the argument, aStream, a String whose characters are a description of the receiver.

storing

storeString | Answer a String representation of the receiver from which the receiver can be reconstructed.

storeOn: aStream | Append to the argument, aStream, a String representation of the receiver from which the receiver can be reconstructed.

Each of the two kinds of printing is based on producing a sequence of characters that may be shown on a display screen, written on a file, or transferred over a network. The sequence created by storeString or storeOn: should be interpretable as one or more expressions that can be evaluated in order to reconstruct the object. Thus, for example, a Set of three elements, $a, $b, and $c, might print as

Set ($a $b $c)

while it might store as

(Set new add: $a; add: $b; add: $c)

Literals can use the same representation for printing and storing. Thus the String 'hello' would print and store as 'hello'. The Symbol #name prints as name, but stores as #name.

For lack of more information, the default implementation of printString is the object's class name; the default implementation of storeString is the class name followed by the instance creation message basicNew, followed by a sequence of messages to store each instance variable. For example, if a subclass of Object, say class Example, demonstrated the default behavior, then, for eg, an instance of Example with no instance variables, we would have

expression	*result*
eg printString	'an Example'
eg storeString	'(Example basicNew)'

Error Handling   The fact that all processing is carried out by sending messages to objects means that there is one basic error condition that must be handled by the system: a message is sent to an object, but the message is not specified in any class in the object's superclass chain. This error is determined by the interpreter whose reaction is to send the original object the message doesNotUnderstand: aMessage. The argument, aMessage, represents the failed message selector and its associated arguments, if any. The method associated with doesNotUnderstand: gives the user a report that the error occurred. How the report is presented to the user is a function of the (graphical) interface supported by the system and is not specified here; a minimum requirement of an interactive system is that the error message be printed on the user's output device and then the user be given the opportunity to correct the erroneous situation. Chapter 17 illustrates the Smalltalk-80 system error notification and debugging mechanisms.

In addition to the basic error condition, methods might explicitly want to use the system error handling mechanism for cases in which a test determines that the user program is about to do something unacceptable. In such cases, the method might want to specify an error comment that should be presented to the user. A typical thing to do is to send the active instance the message error: aString, where the argument represents the desired comment. The default implementation is to invoke the system notification mechanism. The programmer can provide an alternative implementation for error: that uses application-dependent error reporting.

Common error messages are supported in the protocol of class Object. An error message might report that a system primitive failed, or that a subclass is overriding an inherited message which it can not support and therefore the user should not call upon it, or that a superclass specifies a message that must be implemented in a subclass.

Object instance protocol

error handling

doesNotUnderstand: aMessage	Report to the user that the receiver does not understand the argument, aMessage, as a message.
error: aString	Report to the user that an error occurred in the context of responding to a message to the receiver. The report uses the argument, aString, as part of the error notification comment.
primitiveFailed	Report to the user that a method implemented as a system primitive has failed.

shouldNotImplement   Report to the user that, although the super-
                              class of the receiver specifies that a message
                              should be implemented by subclasses, the
                              class of the receiver cannot provide an appro-
                              priate implementation.

subclassResponsibility   Report to the user that a method specified in
                              the superclass of the receiver should have
                              been implemented in the receiver's class.

A subclass can choose to override the error-handling messages in order
to provide special support for correcting the erroneous situation. Chapter 13, which is about the implementation of the collection classes, provides examples of the use of the last two messages.

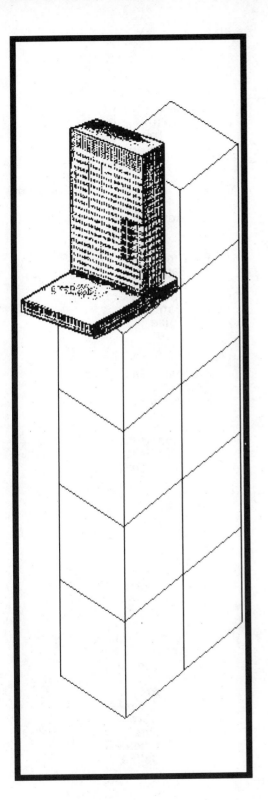

7

Linear Measures

Class Magnitude
Class Date
Class Time
Class Character

Object

Magnitude
    Character
    Date
    Time

    Number
        Float
        Fraction
        Integer
            LargeNegativeInteger
            LargePositiveInteger
            SmallInteger

    LookupKey
        Association

Link

    Process

Collection

    SequenceableCollection
        LinkedList

           Semaphore

        ArrayedCollection
           Array

           Bitmap
               DisplayBitmap

           RunArray
           String
               Symbol
           Text
           ByteArray

        Interval
        OrderedCollection
           SortedCollection
    Bag
    MappedCollection
    Set
        Dictionary
           IdentityDictionary

Stream
    PositionableStream
        ReadStream
        WriteStream
            ReadWriteStream
               ExternalStream
                   FileStream

    Random

File
FileDirectory
FilePage

UndefinedObject
Boolean
    False
    True

ProcessorScheduler
Delay
SharedQueue

Behavior
    ClassDescription
        Class
        MetaClass

Point
Rectangle
BitBlt
    CharacterScanner

    Pen

DisplayObject
    DisplayMedium
        Form
           Cursor
           DisplayScreen
    InfiniteForm
    OpaqueForm
    Path
        Arc
           Circle
        Curve
        Line
        LinearFit
        Spline

The Smalltalk-80 system provides several classes representing objects that measure something with linear ordering. Real world examples of such measurable quantities are (1) temporal quantities such as dates and time, (2) spatial quantities such as distance, and (3) numerical quantities such as reals and rationals.

Class Magnitude

Is one number less than another number? Does one date come after another date? Does one time precede another time? Does a character come after another one in the alphabet? Is one distance the same or less than another distance?

The common protocol for answering these queries is provided in the class Magnitude. Magnitude provides the protocol for objects that have the ability to be compared along a linear dimension. Subclasses of class Magnitude include Date, Time, and Number. Classes Character (an element of a string) and LookupKey (a key in a dictionary association) are also implemented as subclasses of class Magnitude. Character is interesting as an example of immutable objects in the system and so is introduced in this chapter; LookupKey is less interesting and is deferred until needed in the chapter on collections. A class Distance is not provided in the actual Smalltalk-80 system.

Magnitude instance protocol

comparing

< aMagnitude	Answer whether the receiver is less than the argument.
< = aMagnitude	Answer whether the receiver is less than or equal to the argument.
> aMagnitude	Answer whether the receiver is greater than the argument.
> = aMagnitude	Answer whether the receiver is greater than or equal to the argument.
between: min and: max	Answer whether the receiver is greater than or equal to the argument, min, and less than or equal to the argument, max.

Although Magnitude inherits from its superclass, Object, the message = for comparing the equality of two quantifiable objects, every kind of Magnitude must redefine this message. The method associated with = in class Magnitude is

self subclassResponsibility

If a subclass of Magnitude does not implement =, then an attempt to send the message to an instance of the subclass results in the special error message that a subclass should have implemented the message, as specified in its superclass.

An instance of a kind of Magnitude can also respond to messages that determine which of two objects that can be linearly measured is the larger or the smaller.

Magnitude instance protocol

testing

min: aMagnitude	Answer the receiver or the argument, whichever has the lesser magnitude.
max: aMagnitude	Answer the receiver or the argument, whichever has the greater magnitude.

Note that protocol for the equality comparisons $==$, $\sim=$, and $\sim\sim$ is inherited from class Object. Using Integers as the example kinds of Magnitudes, we have

expression	result
3 < = 4	true
3 > 4	false
5 between: 2 and: 6	true
5 between: 2 and: 4	false
34 min: 45	34
34 max: 45	45

The programmer does not create instances of Magnitude, but only of its subclasses. This is due to the fact that Magnitude is not able to implement all of the messages it specifies, indeed, that it implements one or more of these messages by the expression self subclassResponsibility.

Class Date

Now that we have defined the general protocol of Magnitudes, it is possible to add additional protocol that supports arithmetic and inquiries about specific linear measurements. The first refinement we will examine is the subclass Date.

An instance of Date represents a specific day since the start of the Julian calendar. A day exists in a particular month and year. Class Date knows about some obvious information: (1) there are seven days in a week, each day having a symbolic name and an index 1, 2, ..., or 7; (2) there are 12 months in a year, each having a symbolic name and an index, 1, 2, ..., or 12; (3) months have 28, 29, 30, or 31 days; and (4) a particular year might be a leap year.

Protocol provided for the object, Date, supports inquiries about Dates in general as well as about a specific Date. Both Date and Time provide interesting examples of classes in the system for which special knowledge is attributed to and accessible from the class itself, rather than from its instances. This "class protocol" is specified in the metaclass of the class. Let's first look at the class protocol of Date supporting general inquiries.

Date class protocol

general inquiries

dayOfWeek: dayName — Answer the index in a week, 1, 2, .., or 7, of the day named as the argument, dayName.

nameOfDay: dayIndex — Answer a Symbol that represents the name of the day whose index is the argument, dayIndex, where 1 is Monday, 2, is Tuesday, and so on.

indexOfMonth: monthName — Answer the index in a year, 1, 2, .., or 12, of the month named as the argument, monthName.

nameOfMonth: monthIndex — Answer a Symbol that represents the name of the month whose index is the argument, monthIndex, where 1 is January, 2, is February, and so on.

daysInMonth: monthName forYear: yearInteger — Answer the number of days in the month whose name is monthName in the year yearInteger (the year must be known in order to account for a leap year).

daysInYear: yearInteger — Answer the number of days in the year, yearInteger.

leapYear: yearInteger — Answer 1 if the year yearInteger is a leap year; answer 0 otherwise.

dateAndTimeNow — Answer an Array whose first element is the current date (an instance of class Date representing today's date) and whose second element is the current time (an instance of class Time representing the time right now).

Thus we can send the following messages.

expression	result
Date daysInYear: 1982	365
Date dayOfWeek: #Wednesday	3
Date nameOfMonth: 10	October
Date leapYear: 1972	1 (meaning it is a leap year)
Date daysInMonth: #February forYear: 1972	29
Date daysInMonth: #Feb forYear: 1971	28

Date is familar with the common abbreviations for names of months.

There are four messages that can be used to create an instance of class Date. The one commonly used in the Smalltalk-80 system, notably for marking the creation date of a file, is Date today.

Date class protocol

instance creation

today — Answer an instance of Date representing the day the message is sent.

fromDays: dayCount — Answer an instance of Date that is dayCount number of days before or after January 1, 1901 (depending on the sign of the argument).

newDay: day month: monthName year: yearInteger — Answer an instance of Date that is day number of days into the month named monthName in the year yearInteger.

newDay: dayCount year: yearInteger — Answer an instance of Date that is dayCount number of days after the beginning of the year yearInteger.

Four examples of instance creation messages are

expression	result
Date today	3 February 1982
Date fromDays: 200	20 July 1901
Date newDay: 6 month: #Feb year: 82	6 February 1982
Date newDay: 3 year: 82	3 January 1982

Messages that can be sent to an instance of Date are categorized as accessing, inquiries, arithmetic, and printing messages. Accessing and inquiries about a particular day consist of

- the day index, month index, or year
- the number of seconds, days, or months since some other date
- the total days in the date's month or year
- the days left in the date's month or year
- the first day of the date's month
- the name of the date's weekday or month
- the date of a particular weekday previous to the instance

Simple arithmetic is supported in the protocol of class Date.

Date instance protocol

arithmetic

addDays: dayCount	Answer a Date that is dayCount number of days after the receiver.
subtractDays: dayCount	Answer a Date that is dayCount number of days before the receiver.
subtractDate: aDate	Answer an Integer that represents the number of days between the receiver and the argument, aDate.

Such arithmetic is useful, for example, in order to compute due dates for books in a library or fines for late books. Suppose dueDate is an instance of Date denoting the day a book was supposed to be returned to the library. Then

Date today subtractDate: dueDate

computes the number of days for which the borrower should be fined. If a book is being borrowed today and it can be kept out for two weeks, then

Date today addDays: 14

is the due date for the book. If the librarian wants to quit work 16 days before Christmas day, then the date of the last day at work is

(Date newDay: 25 month: #December year: 1982) subtractDays: 16

An algorithm to determine the fine a borrower must pay might first compare today's date with the due date and then, if the due date has past, determine the fine as a 10-cent multiple of the number of days overdue.

```
Date today < dueDate
    ifTrue: [fine ← 0]
    ifFalse: [fine ← 0.10 * (Date today subtractDate: dueDate)]
```

Class Time

An instance of class Time represents a particular second in a day. Days start at midnight. Time is a subclass of Magnitude. Like class Date, Time can respond to general inquiry messages that are specified in the class protocol.

Time class protocol

general inquiries

millisecondClockValue	Answer the number of milliseconds since the millisecond clock was last reset or rolled over to 0.
millisecondsToRun: timedBlock	Answer the number of milliseconds timedBlock takes to return its value.
timeWords	Answer the seconds (in Greenwich Mean Time) since Jan. 1, 1901. The answer is a four-element ByteArray (ByteArray is described in Chapter 10).
totalSeconds	Answer the total seconds from Jan. 1, 1901, corrected for time zone and daylight savings time.
dateAndTimeNow	Answer an Array whose first element is the current date (an instance of class Date that represents today's date) and whose second element is the current time (an instance of class Time that represents the time right now). The result of sending this message to Time is identical to the result of sending it to Date.

The only non-obvious inquiry is millisecondsToRun: timedBlock. An example is

Time millisecondsToRun: [Date today]

where the result is the number of milliseconds it took the system to compute today's date. Because there is some overhead in responding to this message, and because the resolution of the clock affects the result, the careful programmer should determine the machine-dependent uncertainties associated with selecting reasonable arguments to this message.

A new instance of Time can be created by sending Time the message now; the corresponding method reads the current time from a system clock. Alternatively, an instance of Time can be created by sending the message fromSeconds: secondCount, where secondCount is the number of seconds since midnight.

Time class protocol

instance creation

now	Answer an instance of Time representing the second the message is sent.
fromSeconds: secondCount	Answer an instance of Time that is secondCount number of seconds since midnight.

Accessing protocol for instances of class Time provide information as to the number of hours (hours), minutes (minutes) and seconds (seconds) that the instance represents.

Arithmetic is also supported.

Time instance protocol
_____

arithmetic
    addTime: timeAmount   Answer an instance of Time that is the argu-
                                        ment, timeAmount, after the receiver.
    subtractTime: timeAmount   Answer an instance of Time that is the argu-
                                        ment, timeAmount, before the receiver.

In the messages given above, the arguments (timeAmount) may be either Dates or Times. For this to be possible, the system must be able to convert a Date and a Time to a common unit of measurement; it converts them to seconds. In the case of Time, the conversion is to the number of seconds since midnight; in the case of Date, the conversion is to the number of seconds between a time on January 1, 1901, and the same time in the receiver's day. To support these methods, instances of each class respond to the conversion message asSeconds.

Time instance protocol
_____

converting
    asSeconds   Answer the number of seconds since midnight
                                        that the receiver represents.

Date instance protocol
_____

converting
    asSeconds   Answer the number of seconds between a time
                                        on January 1, 1901, and the same time in the
                                        receiver's day.

Arithmetic for Time can be used in ways analogous to that for Date. Suppose the amount of time a person spends working on a particular project is to be logged so that a customer can be charged an hourly fee. Suppose the person started work at startTime and worked continuously during the day until right now; the phone rings and the customer wants to know today's charges. At that moment, the bill at $5.00 an hour is

(Time now subtractTime: startTime) hours * 5

ignoring any additional minutes or seconds. If a charge for any fraction of an hour over 30 minutes is to be charged as a full hour then an additional $5.00 is added if

(Time now subtractTime: startTime) minutes > 30

Who is more productive, the worker who finished the job with time logged at timeA or the worker with time timeB? The answer is the first worker if timeA < timeB. Comparing protocol is inherited from the superclasses Magnitude and Object.

Suppose times are computed across days, for example, in computing the time of a car in a four-day rally. If the first day of the rally started at startTime on day startDate, then the time for a car arriving at the finish line right now is computed as follows.

Let the start time be 6:00 a.m.

    startTime ← Time fromSeconds: (60*60*6).

on February 2, 1982

    startDate ← Date newDay: 2 month: #Feb year: 82.

The time that has passed up to the start of the current day is

    todayStart ← (((Time fromSeconds: 0) addTime: Date today)
                    subtractTime: startDate)
                        subtractTime: startTime

That is, add all the seconds since Jan. 1, 1901, up to the start of today and then subtract all the seconds since Jan. 1, 1901, up to the start of the start date. This is equivalent to adding the number of seconds in the number of elapsed days, but then the programmer would have to do all the conversions.

    (Date today subtractDate: startDate) * 24*60*60)

By adding the current time, we have the elapsed rally time for the car.

    todayStart addTime: Time now

Class Character

Class Character is the third subclass of class Magnitude we shall examine. It is a kind of Magnitude because instances of class Character form an ordered sequence about which we can make inquiries such as whether one character precedes (<) or succeeds (>) another character alphabetically. There are 256 instances of class Character in the system. Each one is associated with a code in an extended ASCII character set.

Characters can be expressed literally by preceding the alphabetic character by a dollar sign ($); thus, $A is the Character representing the capital letter "A". Protocol for creating instances of class Character consists of

instance creation

value: anInteger
 Answer an instance of Character whose value is the argument, anInteger. The value is associated with an element of the ASCII character set. For example, Character value: 65 is a capital "A".

digitValue: anInteger
 Answer an instance of Character whose digit value is the argument, anInteger. For example, answer $9 if the argument is 9; answer $0 for 0; answer $A for 10, and $Z for 35. This method is useful in parsing numbers into strings. Typically, only Characters up to $F are useful (for base 16 numbers).

Class protocol, that is, the set of messages to the object Character, provides a vocabulary for accessing characters that are not easy to distinguish when printed: backspace, cr, esc, newPage (that is, form feed), space, and tab.

Messages to instances of Character support accessing the ASCII value and the digit value of the instance and testing the type of character. The only state of a Character is its value which can never change. Objects that can not change their internal state are called *immutable objects*. This means that, once created, they are not destroyed and then recreated when they are needed again. Rather, the 256 instances of Character are created at the time the system is initialized and remain in the system. Whenever a new Character whose code is between 0 and 255 is requested, a reference is provided to an already existing Character. In this way the 256 Characters are unique. Besides Characters, the Smalltalk-80 system includes SmallIntegers and Symbols as immutable objects.

accessing

asciiValue
 Answer the number corresponding to the ASCII encoding for the receiver.

digitValue
 Answer the number corresponding to the numerical radix represented by the receiver (see the instance creation message digitValue: for the correspondences).

testing

isAlphaNumeric
 Answer true if the receiver is a letter or a digit.

isDigit
 Answer whether the receiver is a digit.

isLetter
 Answer whether the receiver is a letter.

isLowercase
 Answer whether the receiver is a lowercase letter.

isUppercase
 Answer whether the receiver is an uppercase letter.

isSeparator	Answer whether the receiver is one of the separator characters in the expression syntax: space, cr, tab, line feed, or form feed.
isVowel	Answer whether the receiver is one of the vowels: a, e, i, o, or u, in upper or lowercase.

Instance protocol also provides conversion of a character into upper- or lowercase (asLowercase and asUppercase) and into a symbol (asSymbol).

A simple alphabetic comparison demonstrates the use of comparing protocol for instances of Character. Suppose we wish to know if one string of characters precedes another string in the telephone book. Strings respond to the message at: to retrieve the element whose index is the argument; elements of Strings are Characters. Thus ′abc′ at: 2 is $b. In the following we assume we are specifying a method in class String whose message selector is min:. The method returns a String, either the receiver of the message min: or its argument, whichever is collated first alphabetically.

min: aString

```
1 to: self size do:
    [ :index |
        (index > aString size) ifTrue: [↑aString].
        (self at: index) > (aString at: index) ifTrue: [↑aString].
        (self at: index) < (aString at: index) ifTrue: [↑self]].
↑self
```

The algorithm consists of two statements. The first is an iteration over each element of the receiver. The iteration stops when either (1) the argument, aString, no longer has a character with which to compare the next character in the receiver (i.e., index > aString size); (2) the next character in self comes after the next character in aString (i.e., (self at: index) > (aString at: index)); or (3) the next character in self comes before the next character in aString. As an example of (1), take the comparison of ′abcd′ and ′abc′ which terminates when index = 4; the answer is that ′abc′ is first alphabetically. For (2), suppose we compare ′abde′ with ′abce′. When index = 3, $d > $c is true; the answer is ′abce′. For (3), compare ′az′ with ′by′ which terminates when index = 1; the answer is ′az′. In the case that the receiver has fewer characters than the argument, even when the receiver is the initial substring of the argument, the first statement will complete and the second statement is evaluated; the result is the receiver. An example is the comparison of ′abc′ and ′abcd′.

Note that arithmetic on characters is not supported. For example, the following expression is incorrect.

a ← $A + 1

The error occurs because a Character does not understand the message +.

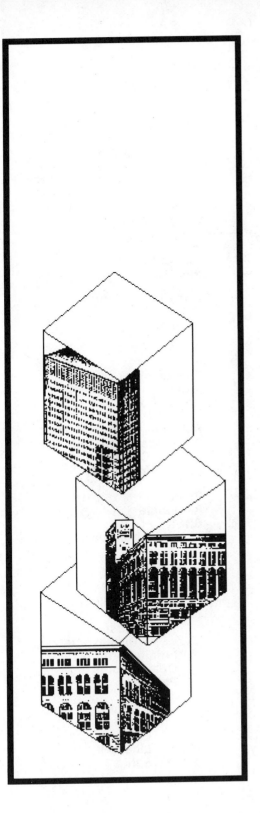

8

Numerical Classes

Object

Magnitude
   Character
   Date
   Time

Number
   Float
   Fraction
   Integer
     LargeNegativeInteger
     LargePositiveInteger
     SmallInteger

LookupKey
   Association

Link

   Process

Collection

   SequenceableCollection
     LinkedList

       Semaphore

     ArrayedCollection
     Array

     Bitmap
       DisplayBitmap

     RunArray
     String
       Symbol
     Text
     ByteArray

     Interval
     OrderedCollection
       SortedCollection
   Bag
   MappedCollection
   Set
     Dictionary
       IdentityDictionary

Stream
   PositionableStream
     ReadStream
     WriteStream
       ReadWriteStream
         ExternalStream
           FileStream

       Random

File
FileDirectory
FilePage

UndefinedObject
Boolean
   False
   True

ProcessorScheduler
Delay
SharedQueue

Behavior
   ClassDescription
     Class
     MetaClass

Point
Rectangle
BitBlt
   CharacterScanner

   Pen

DisplayObject
   DisplayMedium
     Form
       Cursor
       DisplayScreen
   InfiniteForm
   OpaqueForm
   Path
     Arc
       Circle
     Curve
     Line
     LinearFit
     Spline

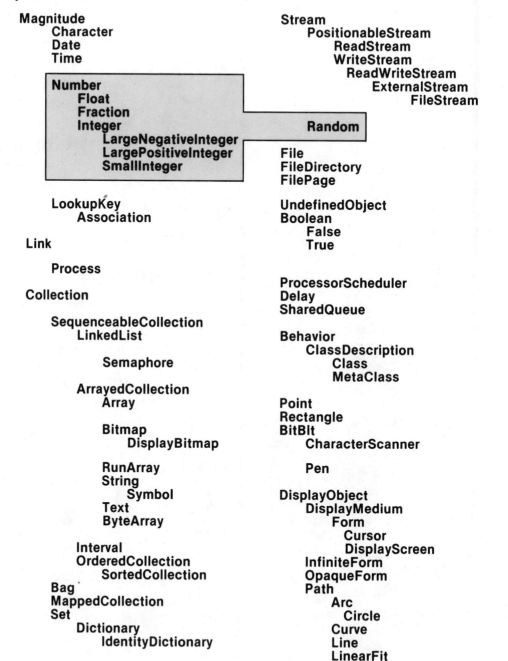

One of the major goals of the Smalltalk programming system is to apply a single metaphor for information processing as uniformly as possible. The Smalltalk metaphor, as described in earlier chapters, is one of objects that communicate by sending messages. This metaphor is very similar to the one used in Simula for implementing simulation systems. One of the greatest challenges to the application of the Smalltalk metaphor to all aspects of a programming system has been in the area of arithmetic. Simula used the object/message metaphor only for the higher level interactions in the simulations it implemented. For arithmetic, as well as most algorithmic control structures, Simula relied on the embedded Algol programming language with its built-in number representations, operations, and syntax. The contention that even the addition of two integers should be interpreted as message-sending met with a certain amount of resistance in the early days of Smalltalk. Experience has demonstrated that the benefits of this extreme uniformity in the programming language outweigh any inconvenience in its implementation. Over several versions of Smalltalk, implementation techniques have been developed to reduce the message-sending overhead for the most common arithmetic operations so that there is now almost no cost for the benefits of uniformity.

Objects that represent numerical values are used in most systems done in Smalltalk (as with most other programming languages). Numbers are naturally used to perform mathematical computations; they are also used in algorithms as indices, counters, and encodings of states or conditions (often called flags). Integral numbers are also used as collections of binary digits (bits) that perform boolean masking operations with each other.

Each different kind of numerical value is represented by a class. The number classes have been implemented so that all numbers behave as if they were of the most general type. The actual class of a particular number object is determined by how much of the full generality is needed to represent its value. Therefore the external protocol of all number objects is inherited from the class Number. Number has three subclasses: Float, Fraction, and Integer. Integer has three subclasses: SmallInteger, LargePositiveInteger, and LargeNegativeInteger. Integral numbers provide further protocol to support treating the number as a sequence of bits. This protocol is specified in the class Integer. Numbers in the system are instances of Float, Fraction, SmallInteger, LargePositiveInteger, or LargeNegativeInteger. Classes Number and Integer specify shared protocol, but they do not specify particular representations for numeric values. Therefore no instances of Number or Integer are created.

Unlike other objects that may change their internal state, the only state of a number is its value, which should never change. The object 3, for example, should never change its state to 4, or disastrous effects could occur.

Protocol of the Number Classes

Number defines the protocol of all numeric objects. Its messages support standard arithmetic operations and comparisons. Most of these must be implemented by subclasses of Number since they depend on the actual representation of values.

The protocol of arithmetic messages consists of the usual binary operators such as $+$, $-$, $*$ and $/$, and several unary and keyword messages for computing the absolute value of a number, the negation of a number, or the integer quotient or remainder of a number. The category for arithmetic messages is as follows.

Number instance protocol

arithmetic

$+$ aNumber	Answer the sum of the receiver and the argument, aNumber.
$-$ aNumber	Answer the difference between the receiver and the argument, aNumber.
$*$ aNumber	Answer the result of multiplying the receiver by the argument, aNumber.
/ aNumber	Answer the result of dividing the receiver by the argument, aNumber. Note that since as much precision as possible is retained, if the division is not exact, the result will be an instance of Fraction.
// aNumber	Answer the integer quotient defined by division with truncation toward negative infinity.
\\ aNumber	Answer the integer remainder defined by division with truncation toward negative infinity. This is the modulo operation.
abs	Answer a Number that is the absolute value (positive magnitude) of the receiver.
negated	Answer a Number that is the negation of the receiver.
quo: aNumber	Answer the integer quotient defined by division with truncation toward zero.
rem: aNumber	Answer the integer remainder defined by division with truncation toward zero.
reciprocal	Answer 1 divided by the receiver. Report an error to the user if the receiver is 0.

Some examples follow.

expression	result
1 + 10	11
5.6 − 3	2.6
5 − 2.6	2.4
(−4) abs	4
6 / 2	3

7 / 2	(7/2), a Fraction with numerator 7 and denominator 2
7 reciprocal	(1/7), a Fraction with numerator 1 and denominator 7

Arithmetic messages that return integral quotients and remainders from a division operation follow two conventions. One convention truncates the resulting number toward zero, the other toward negative infinity. These are the same for positive results since zero and negative infinity are in the same direction. For negative results, the two conventions round in different directions. The protocol for Number provides for both conventions.

The following table shows the relationships among the selectors.

result	truncate toward negative infinity	truncate toward zero
quotient	//	quo:
remainder	\\	rem:

Examples include:

expression	result
6 quo: 2	3
7 quo: 2	3
(7 quo: 2) + 1	4
7 quo: 2 + 1	2
7 rem: 2	1
7 // 2	3
7 \\ 2	1
7 \\ 2 +1	2
−7 quo: 2	−3
−7 rem: 2	−1
−7 // 2	−4
−7 \\ 2	1

The result of quo:, rem:, or // is always to return a value whose sign is positive if the receiver and argument have the same sign, and negative if their signs are different. \\ always produces a positive result.

Additional mathematical functions are

mathematical functions

exp	Answer a floating point number that is the exponential of the receiver.
ln	Answer the natural log of the receiver.
log: aNumber	Answer the log base aNumber of the receiver.
floorLog: radix	Answer the floor of the log base radix of the receiver, where the floor is the integer nearest the receiver toward negative infinity.
raisedTo: aNumber	Answer the receiver raised to the power of the argument, aNumber.
raisedToInteger: anInteger	Answer the receiver raised to the power of the argument, anInteger, where the argument must be a kind of Integer.
sqrt	Answer a floating point number that is the positive square root of the receiver.
squared	Answer the receiver multiplied by itself.

Some examples are

expression	result
2.718284 ln	1.0
6 exp	403.429
2 exp	7.38906
7.38906 ln	1.99998 (that is, 2)
2 log: 2	1.0
2 floorLog: 2	1
6 log: 2	2.58496
6 floorLog: 2	2
6 raisedTo: 1.2	8.58579
6 raisedToInteger: 2	36
64 sqrt	8.0
8 squared	64

Properties of numbers that deal with whether a number is even or odd and negative or positive can be tested with the following messages.

testing

even	Answer whether the receiver is an even number.
odd	Answer whether the receiver is an odd number.
negative	Answer whether the receiver is less than 0.
positive	Answer whether the receiver is greater than or equal to 0.
strictlyPositive	Answer whether the receiver is greater than 0.
sign	Answer 1 if the receiver is greater than 0, answer -1 if less than 0, else answer 0.

Properties of numbers that deal with truncation and round off are supplied by the following protocol.

Number instance protocol

truncation and round off	
ceiling	Answer the integer nearest the receiver toward positive infinity.
floor	Answer the integer nearest the receiver toward negative infinity.
truncated	Answer the integer nearest the receiver toward zero.
truncateTo: aNumber	Answer the next multiple of the argument, aNumber, that is nearest the receiver toward zero.
rounded	Answer the integer nearest the receiver.
roundTo: aNumber	Answer the multiple of the argument, aNumber, that is nearest the receiver.

Whenever a Number must be converted to an Integer, the message truncated can be used. So we have

expression	*result*
16.32 ceiling	17
16.32 floor	16
−16.32 floor	−17
−16.32 truncated	−16
16.32 truncated	16
16.32 truncateTo: 5	15
16.32 truncateTo: 5.1	15.3
16.32 rounded	16
16.32 roundTo: 6	18
16.32 roundTo: 6.3	18.9

The protocol provided in class Number includes various messages for converting a number into another kind of object or a different unit of representation. Numbers can represent various unit measurements such as degrees and radians. The following two messages perform conversions.

Number instance protocol

converting	
degreesToRadians	The receiver is assumed to represent degrees. Answer the conversion to radians.
radiansToDegrees	The receiver is assumed to represent radians. Answer the conversion to degrees.

So that

    30 degreesToRadians = 0.523599
    90 degreesToRadians = 1.5708

Trigonometric and logarithmic functions are included in the protocol for mathematical functions. The receiver for the trigonometric functions cos, sin, and tan is an angle measured in radians; the result of the functions arcCos, arcSin and arcTan is the angle measured in radians.

In the following examples, 30 degrees is given as 0.523599 radians; 90 degrees is 1.5708 radians.

expression	result
0.523599 sin	0.5
0.523599 cos	0.866025
0.523599 tan	0.57735
1.5708 sin	1.0
0.57735 arcTan	0.523551
1.0 arcSin	1.5708

When a kind of Integer is asked to add itself to another kind of Integer, the result returned will naturally also be a kind of Integer. The same is true for the sum of two Floats; the class of the result will be the same as the class of the operands. If the two operands are SmallIntegers and the absolute value of their sum is too large to be represented as a SmallInteger, the result will be a LargePositiveInteger or a LargeNegativeInteger. The determination of the appropriate class of result when the operands are of different classes is somewhat more complicated. Two design criteria are that there be as little loss of information as possible and that commutative operations produce the same result regardless of which operand is the receiver of the message and which is the argument. So for example, 3.1 * 4 will return the same result as 4 * 3.1.

The appropriate representation for the result of operations on numbers of different classes is determined by a numerical measure of generality assigned to each class. Classes said to have more generality will have a larger number for this generality measure. Each class must be able to convert its instances into equal-valued instances of more general classes. The measure of generality is used to decide which of the operands should be converted. In this way, the arithmetic operations obey the law of commutativity with no loss of numerical information. When the differences between two classes of numbers are only a matter of precision (where "precision" is a measure of the information provided in a number), the more precise class is assigned a higher degree of generality. We have arbitrarily assigned approximate numbers a higher generality in cases where precision was not the issue (so, Float is more general than Fraction).

The generality hierarchy for the kinds of numbers in the Smalltalk-80 system, with most general listed first, is

Float
Fraction
LargePositiveInteger, LargeNegativeInteger
SmallInteger

The messages in the Number protocol designed to support the necessary coercions are categorized as "coercing" messages.

Number instance protocol

---

coercing

coerce: aNumber

Answer a number representing the argument, aNumber, that is the same kind of Number as the receiver. This method must be defined by all subclasses of Number.

generality

Answer the number representing the ordering of the receiver in the generality hierarchy.

retry: aSymbol coercing: aNumber

An arithmetic operation denoted by the symbol, aSymbol, could not be performed with the receiver and the argument, aNumber, as the operands because of the difference in representation. Coerce either the receiver or the argument, depending on which has the lower generality, and then try the arithmetic operation again. If the symbol is the equals sign, answer false if the argument is not a Number. If the generalities are the same, then retry:coercing: should not have been sent, so report an error to the user.

Thus if we try to evaluate 32.45 * 4, the multiplication of a Float by a SmallInteger will result in evaluating the expression

    32.45 retry: # * coercing: 4

and the argument 4 will be coerced to 4.0 (Float has higher generality than SmallInteger). Then the multiplication will be carried out successfully.

Defining a hierarchy of the numbers in terms of a numerical measure of generality works for the kinds of numbers provided in the basic Smalltalk-80 system because the generality is transitive for these kinds of numbers. However, it does not provide a technique that can be used for all kinds of numbers.

Intervals (described in detail in Chapter 10) can be created by sending one of two messages to a number. For each element of such an interval, a block can be evaluated with the element as the block value.

Number instance protocol

intervals

to: stop	Answer an Interval from the receiver up to the argument, stop, with each next element computed by incrementing the previous one by 1.
to: stop by: step	Answer an Interval from the receiver up to the argument, stop, with each next element computed by incrementing the previous one by step.
to: stop do: aBlock	Create an Interval from the receiver up to the argument, stop, incrementing by 1. Evaluate the argument, aBlock, for each element of the Interval.
to: stop by: step do: aBlock	Create an Interval from the receiver up to the argument, stop, incrementing by step. Evaluate the argument, aBlock, for each element of the Interval.

Thus if we evaluate

a ← 0.
10 to: 100 by: 10 do: [:each | a ← a + each]

the final value of a will be 550.

If a is the array #('one' 'two' 'three' 'four' 'five'), then each element of the array can be accessed by indices that are in the interval from 1 to the size of the array. The following expression changes each element so that only the initial characters are kept.

1 to: a size do: [:index | a at: index put: ((a at: index) at: 1)]

The resulting array is #('o' 't' 't' 'f' 'f'). Note that, like an array, elements of a string can be accessed using the messages at: and at:put:. Messages to objects like strings and arrays are detailed in Chapters 9 and 10.

Classes Float **and** Fraction

The classes Float and Fraction provide two representations of non-integral values. Floats are representations of real numbers that may be approximate; they represent about 6 digits of accuracy with a range between plus or minus 10 raised to the power plus or minus 32. Some examples are

8.0
13.3

0.3
2.5e6
1.27e−30
−12.987654e12

Fractions are representations of rational numbers that will always be exact. All arithmetic operations on a Fraction answer a reduced fractional result.

Instances of Float can be created by literal notation in methods (for example, 3.14159) or as the result of an arithmetic operation, one argument of which is another Float.

Instances of Fraction can be created as a result of an arithmetic operation if one of the operands is a Fraction and the other is not a Float. (If it were a Float, the result would be a Float since the generality number of Float is higher than that of Fraction). Instances of Fraction can also be created when the mathematical division operation (/) is performed on two Integers and the result is not integral. In addition, class protocol for Fraction supports sending a message of the form numerator: numInteger denominator: denInteger in order to create an instance.

Float responds to the message pi to return the corresponding constant. It adds truncation and round off protocol to return the fraction and integer parts of the receiver (fractionPart and integerPart), and it adds converting protocol to convert the receiver to a Fraction (asFraction). Similarly class Fraction adds converting protocol to convert the receiver to a Float (asFloat).

Integer Classes

Class Integer adds protocol particular to integral numbers. It has three subclasses. One is class SmallInteger, which provides a space-economical representation for a substantial range of integral values that occur frequently in counting and indexing. The representation limits the range to a little less than the magnitudes representable by a single machine word. Large integers, which are represented by instances of LargePositiveInteger or LargeNegativeInteger depending on the sign of the integer, do not have a limit to their magnitude. The cost in providing the generality of large integers is longer computation time. Thus if the result of an arithmetic operation on a large integer is representable as a small integer, it will in fact be a small integer.

In addition to the messages inherited from the class Number, class Integer adds converting protocol (asCharacter, asFloat and asFraction), further printing (printOn: aStream base: b, radix: baseInteger), and enumerating protocol. Thus 8 radix: 2 is 2r1000.

For enumerating, it is possible to evaluate a block repetitively an integral number of times using the message timesRepeat: aBlock. Take as an example

a ← 1.
10 timesRepeat: [a ← a + a]

where the block has no arguments. The resulting value of a is 2^{10}, or 1024.

Class Integer provides factorization and divisibility protocol not specified for numbers in general.

Integer instance protocol

factorization and divisibility	
factorial	Answer the factorial of the receiver. The receiver must not be less than 0.
gcd: anInteger	Answer the greatest common divisor of the receiver and the argument, anInteger.
lcm: anInteger	Answer the least common multiple of the receiver and the argument, anInteger.

Examples are

expression	result
3 factorial	6
55 gcd: 30	5
6 lcm: 10	30

In addition to the numerical properties of integers, some algorithms make use of the fact that integers can be interpreted as a sequence of bits. Thus protocol for bit manipulation is specified in Integer.

Integer instance protocol

bit manipulation	
allMask: anInteger	Treat the argument anInteger as a bit mask. Answer whether *all* of the bits that are 1 in anInteger are 1 in the receiver.
anyMask: anInteger	Treat the argument anInteger as a bit mask. Answer whether *any* of the bits that are 1 in anInteger are 1 in the receiver.
noMask: anInteger	Treat the argument anInteger as a bit mask. Answer whether *none* of the bits that are 1 in anInteger are 1 in the receiver.
bitAnd: anInteger	Answer an Integer whose bits are the logical *and* of the receiver's bits and those of the argument anInteger.
bitOr: anInteger	Answer an Integer whose bits are the logical *or* of the receiver's bits and those of the argument anInteger.

bitXor: anInteger	Answer an Integer whose bits are the logical *xor* of the receiver's bits and those of the argument anInteger.
bitAt: index	Answer the bit (0 or 1) at position index of the receiver.
bitInvert	Answer an Integer whose bits are the complement of the receiver.
highBit	Answer the index of the high order bit of the binary representation of the receiver.
bitShift: anInteger	Answer an Integer whose value (in two's-complement representation) is the receiver's value (in two's-complement representation) shifted left by the number of bits indicated by the argument, anInteger. Negative arguments shift right. Zeros are shifted in from the right in left shifts. The sign bit is extended in right shifts.

Some examples follow. Note that the default radix for printing an Integer is 10.

expression	result
2r111000111000111	29127
2r101010101010101	21845
2r101000101000101	20805
2r000111000111000	3640
29127 allMask: 20805	true
29127 allMask: 21845	false
29127 anyMask: 21845	true
29127 noMask: 3640	true
29127 bitAnd: 3640	0
29127 bitOr: 3640	32767
32767 radix: 2	2r111111111111111
29127 bitOr: 21845	30167
30167 radix: 2	2r111010111010111
3640 bitShift: 1	7280

Class Random: A Random Number Generator

Many applications require random choices of numbers. Random numbers are useful, for example, in statistical applications and data encryption algorithms. Class Random is a random number generator that is included in the standard Smalltalk-80 system. It provides a simple way of obtaining a sequence of random numbers that will be uniformly distributed over the interval between, but not including, 0.0 and 1.0.

An instance of class Random maintains a seed from which the next random number is generated. The seed is initialized in a pseudo-random way. An instance of Random is sent the message next whenever a new random number is desired.

A random number generator can be created with the expression

rand ← Random new

The expression

rand next

can then be evaluated whenever a new random number is needed. The response is a number (Float) between 0.0 and 1.0.

The implementation of next is based on Lehmer's linear congruential method as presented in Knuth, Volume 1 [D. E. Knuth, *The Art of Computer Programming: Fundamental Algorithms,* Volume 1, Reading, Mass: Addison Wesley, 1968].

next
```
| temp |
"Lehmer's linear congruential method with modulus m = 2 raisedTo: 16,
a = 27181 odd, and 5 = a \\ 8, c = 13849 odd, and c / m approxi-
mately 0.21132"
[seed ← 13849 + (27181 * seed) bitAnd: 8r177777.
 temp ← seed / 65536.0.
 temp = 0] whileTrue.
↑temp
```

It is also possible to send an instance of class Random the messages next: anInteger, to obtain an OrderedCollection of anInteger number of random numbers, and nextMatchFor: aNumber, to determine whether the next random number is equal to aNumber.

Suppose we want to select one of 10 integers, 1, ..., 10, using the random number generator rand. The expression to be evaluated is

(rand next * 10) truncated + 1

That is,

expression	result
rand next	a random number between 0 and 1
rand next * 10	a random number between 0 and 10
(rand next * 10) truncated	an integer $>= 0$ and $<= 9$
(rand next * 10) truncated + 1	an integer $>= 1$ and $<= 10$

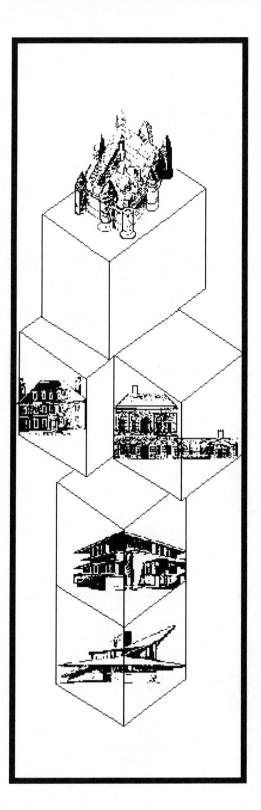

9

Protocol for All Collection Classes

Adding, Removing, and Testing Elements

Enumerating Elements
Selecting and Rejecting
Collecting
Detecting
Injecting

Instance Creation

Conversion Among Collection Classes

Object

    Magnitude
        Character
        Date
        Time

        Number
            Float
            Fraction
            Integer
                LargeNegativeInteger
                LargePositiveInteger
                SmallInteger

        LookupKey
            Association

  Link

    Process

Collection

    SequenceableCollection
        LinkedList

            Semaphore

        ArrayedCollection
        Array

        Bitmap
            DisplayBitmap

        RunArray
        String
            Symbol
        Text
        ByteArray

        Interval
        OrderedCollection
            SortedCollection
    Bag
    MappedCollection
    Set
        Dictionary
            IdentityDictionary

Stream
    PositionableStream
        ReadStream
        WriteStream
            ReadWriteStream
                ExternalStream
                    FileStream

    Random

File
FileDirectory
FilePage

UndefinedObject
Boolean
    False
    True

ProcessorScheduler
Delay
SharedQueue

Behavior
    ClassDescription
        Class
        MetaClass

Point
Rectangle
BitBlt
    CharacterScanner

    Pen

DisplayObject
    DisplayMedium
        Form
            Cursor
            DisplayScreen
    InfiniteForm
    OpaqueForm
    Path
        Arc
            Circle
        Curve
        Line
        LinearFit
        Spline

A collection represents a group of objects. These objects are called the *elements* of the collection. For example, an Array is a collection. The Array

   #('word' 3 5 $G (1 2 3))

is a collection of five elements. The first one is a String, the second and third are SmallIntegers, the fourth element is a Character, and the fifth is itself an Array. The first element, the String, is also a collection; in this case, it is a collection of four Characters.

Collections provide basic data structures for programming in the Smalltalk-80 system. Elements of some of the collections are unordered and elements of other collections are ordered. Of the collections with unordered elements, Bags allow duplicate elements and Sets do not allow duplication. There are also Dictionaries that associate pairs of objects. Of the collections with ordered elements, some have the order specified externally when the elements are added (OrderedCollections, Arrays, Strings) and others determine the order based on the elements themselves (SortedCollections). For example, the common data structures of arrays and strings are provided by classes that associate integer indices and elements and that have external ordering corresponding to the ordering of the indices.

This chapter introduces the protocol shared by all collections. Each message described in this chapter is understood by any kind of collection, unless that collection specifically disallows it. Descriptions of each kind of collection are provided in the next chapter.

Collections support four categories of messages for accessing elements:

- messages for adding new elements
- messages for removing elements
- messages for testing occurrences of elements
- messages for enumerating elements

A single element or several elements can be added or removed from a collection. It is possible to test whether a collection is empty or whether it includes a particular element. It is also possible to determine the number of times a particular element occurs in the collection. Enumeration allows one to access the elements without removing them from the collection.

Adding, Removing, and Testing Elements

The basic protocol for collections is specified by the superclass of all collection classes, named Collection. Class Collection is a subclass of class Object. The protocol for adding, removing, and testing elements follows.

Collection instance protocol	
adding	
add: newObject	Include the argument, newObject, as one of the receiver's elements. Answer newObject.
addAll: aCollection	Include all the elements of the argument, aCollection, as the receiver's elements. Answer aCollection.
removing	
remove: oldObject	Remove the argument, oldObject, from the receiver's elements. Answer oldObject unless no element is equal to oldObject, in which case, report that an error occurred.
remove: oldObject ifAbsent: anExceptionBlock	Remove the argument, oldObject, from the receiver's elements. If several of the elements are equal to oldObject, only one is removed. If no element is equal to oldObject, answer the result of evaluating anExceptionBlock. Otherwise, answer oldObject.
removeAll: aCollection	Remove each element of the argument, aCollection, from the receiver. If successful for each, answer aCollection. Otherwise report that an error occurred.
testing	
includes: anObject	Answer whether the argument, anObject, is equal to one of the receiver's elements.
isEmpty	Answer whether the receiver contains any elements.
occurrencesOf: anObject	Answer how many of the receiver's elements are equal to the argument, anObject.

In order to demonstrate the use of these messages, we introduce the collection lotteryA

(272 572 852 156)

and the collection lotteryB

(572 621 274)

We will assume that these two collections, representing numbers drawn in a lottery, are instances of Bag, a subclass of Collection. Collection itself is abstract in the sense that it describes protocol for all collections. Collection does not provide sufficient representation for storing elements and so it is not possible to provide implementations in Collection of all of its messages. Because of this incompleteness in the definition of Collection, it is not useful to create instances of Collection. Bag is concrete in the sense that it provides a representation for storing elements and implementations of the messages not implementable in its superclass.

All collections respond to size in order to answer the number of their elements. So we can determine that

lotteryA size

is 4 and

lotteryB size

is 3. Then, evaluating the messages in order, we have

expression	result	lotteryA *if it changed*
lotteryA isEmpty	false	
lotteryA includes: 572	true	
lotteryA add: 596	596	Bag (272 572 852 156 596)
lotteryA addAll: lotteryB	Bag (572 621 274)	Bag (272 274 852 156 596 572 572 621)
lotteryA occurrencesOf: 572	2	
lotteryA remove: 572	572	Bag (272 274 852 156 596 572 621)
lotteryA size	7	
lotteryA removeAll: lotteryB	Bag (572 621 274)	Bag (272 852 596 156)
lotteryA size	4	

Note that the add: and remove: messages answer the argument rather than the collection itself so that computed arguments can be accessed. The message remove: deletes only one occurrence of the argument, not all occurrences.

Blocks were introduced in Chapter 2. The message remove: oldObject ifAbsent: anExceptionBlock makes use of a block in order to specify the behavior of the collection if an error should occur. The argument anExceptionBlock is evaluated if the object referred to by oldObject is not an element of the collection. This block can contain code to deal with the error or simply to ignore it. For example, the expression

lotteryA remove: 121 ifAbsent: []

does nothing when it is determined that 121 is not an element of lotteryA.

The default behavior of the message remove: is to report the error by sending the collection the message error: ' object is not in the collection ' . (Recall that the message error: is specified in the protocol for all objects and is therefore understood by any collection.)

Enumerating Elements

Included in the instance protocol of collections are several enumeration messages that support the ability to list the elements of a collection and to supply each element in the evaluation of a block. The basic enumeration message is do: aBlock. It takes a one-argument block as its argument and evaluates the block once for each of the elements of the collection. As an example, suppose letters is a collection of Characters and we want to know how many of the Characters are a or A.

```
count ← 0.
letters do: [ :each | each asLowercase == $a
                ifTrue: [count ← count + 1]]
```

That is, increment the counter, count, by 1 for each element that is an upper- or lowercase a. The desired result is the final value of count. We can use the equivalence test (==) rather than equality since objects representing Characters are unique.

Six enhancements of the basic enumeration messages are specified in the protocol for all collections. The description of these enumeration messages indicates that "a new collection like the receiver" is created for gathering the resulting information. This phrase means that the new collection is an instance of the same class as that of the receiver. For example, if the receiver of the message select: is a Set or an Array, then the response is a new Set or Array, respectively. In the Smalltalk-80 system, the only exception is in the implementation of class Interval, which returns a new OrderedCollection, not a new Interval, from these enumeration messages. The reason for this exception is that the elements of an Interval are created when the Interval is first created; it is not possible to store elements into an existing Interval.

Collection instance protocol

enumerating	
do: aBlock	Evaluate the argument, aBlock, for each of the receiver's elements.
select: aBlock	Evaluate the argument, aBlock, for each of the receiver's elements. Collect into a new collection like that of the receiver, only those elements for which aBlock evaluates to true. Answer the new collection.

reject: aBlock	Evaluate the argument, aBlock, for each of the receiver's elements. Collect into a new collection like that of the receiver only those elements for which aBlock evaluates to false. Answer the new collection.
collect: aBlock	Evaluate the argument, aBlock, for each of the receiver's elements. Answer a new collection like that of the receiver containing the values returned by the block on each evaluation.
detect: aBlock	Evaluate the argument, aBlock, for each of the receiver's elements. Answer the first element for which aBlock evaluates to true. If none evaluates to true, report an error.
detect: aBlock ifNone: exceptionBlock	Evaluate the argument, aBlock, for each of the receiver's elements. Answer the first element for which aBlock evaluates to true. If none evaluates to true, evaluate the argument, exceptionBlock. exceptionBlock must be a block requiring no arguments.
inject: thisValue into: binaryBlock	Evaluate the argument, binaryBlock, once for each element in the receiver. The block has two arguments: the second is an element from the receiver; the first is the value of the previous evaluation of the block, starting with the argument, thisValue. Answer the final value of the block.

Each enumeration message provides a concise way to express a sequence of messages for testing or gathering information about the elements of a collection.

Selecting and Rejecting

We could have determined the number of occurrences of the character a or A using the message select:.

    (letters select: [:each | each asLowercase == $a]) size

That is, create a collection containing only those elements of letters that are a or A, and then answer the size of the resulting collection.

We could also have determined the number of occurrences of the character a or A using the message reject:.

    (letters reject: [:each | each asLowercase ~~ $a]) size

That is, create a collection by eliminating those elements of letters that are not a or A, and then answer the size of the resulting collection.

The choice between select: and reject: should be based on the best expression of the test. If the selection test is best expressed in terms of acceptance, then select: is easier to use; if the selection test is best expressed in terms of rejection, then reject: is easier to use. In this example, select: would be preferred.

As another example, assume employees is a collection of workers, each of whom responds to the message salary with his or her gross earnings. To make a collection of all employees whose salary is at least $10,000, use

employees select: [:each | each salary > = 10000]

or

employees reject: [:each | each salary < 10000]

The resulting collections are the same. The choice of which message to use, select: or reject:, depends on the way the programmer wishes to express the criterion "at least $10,000."

Collecting

Suppose we wish to create a new collection in which each element is the salary of each worker in the collection employees.

employees collect: [:each | each salary]

The resulting collection is the same size as employees. Each of the elements of the new collection is the salary of the corresponding element of employees.

Detecting

Suppose we wish to find one worker in the collection of employees whose salary is greater than $20,000. The expression

employees detect: [:each | each salary > 20000]

will answer with that worker, if one exists. If none exists, then employees will be sent the message error: ' object is not in the collection ' . Just as in the specification of the removing messages, the programmer has the option to specify the exception behavior for an unsuccessful detect:. The next expression answers one worker whose salary exceeds $20,000, or, if none exists, answers nil.

employees detect: [:each | each salary > 20000] ifNone: [nil]

Injecting

In the message inject:into:, the first argument is the initial value that takes part in determining the result; the second argument is a two-argument block. The first block argument names the variable that refers to the result; the second block argument refers to each element of the collection. An example using this message sums the salaries of the workers in the collection employees.

employees
       inject: 0
       into: [:subTotal :nextWorker | subTotal + nextWorker salary]

where the initial value of 0 increases by the value of the salary for each worker in the collection, employees. The result is the final value of sub-Total.

By using the message inject:into:, the programmer can locally specify temporary variable names and can avoid separate initialization of the object into which the result is accumulated. For example, in an earlier expression that counted the number of occurrences of the Characters a and A in the collection letters, we used a counter, count.

```
count ← 0.
letters do: [ :each | each asLowercase = = $a
                 ifTrue: [count ← count + 1]]
```

An alternative approach is to use the message inject:into:. In the example expression, the result is accumulated in count. count starts at 0. If the next character (nextElement) is a or A, then add 1 to count; otherwise add 0.

```
letters inject: 0
        into: [ :count :nextElement |
            count + (nextElement asLowerCase = = $a
                     ifTrue: [1]
                     ifFalse: [0])]
```

Instance Creation

In the beginning of this chapter, examples were given in which new collections were expressed as literals. These collections were Arrays and Strings. For example, an expression for creating an array is

```
#('first' 'second' 'third')
```

where each element is a String expressed literally.

The messages new and new: can be used to create instances of particular kinds of collections. In addition, the class protocol for all collections supports messages for creating instances with one, two, three, or four elements. These messages provide a shorthand notation for creating kinds of collections that are not expressible as literals.

Collection class protocol

instance creation
   with: anObject   Answer an instance of the collection containing anObject.

with: firstObject with: secondObject

> Answer an instance of the collection containing firstObject and secondObject as elements.

with: firstObject with: secondObject with: thirdObject

> Answer an instance of the collection containing firstObject, secondObject, and thirdObject as elements.

with: firstObject with: secondObject with: thirdObject with: fourthObject

> Answer an instance of the collection, containing firstObject, secondObject, thirdObject, and fourthObject as the elements.

For example, Set is a subclass of Collection. To create a new Set with three elements that are the Characters s, e, and t, evaluate the expression

    Set with: $s with: $e with: $t

Note that the rationale for providing these four instance creation messages, no more and no fewer, is that this number satisfies the uses to which collections are put in the system itself.

Conversion Among Collection Classes

A complete description and understanding of the permissible conversions between kinds of collections depends on a presentation of all the subclasses of Collection. Here we simply note that five messages are specified in the converting protocol for all collections in order to convert the receiver to a Bag, a Set, an OrderedCollection, and a SortedCollection. These messages are specified in class Collection because it is possible to convert any collection into any of these kinds of collections. The ordering of elements from any collection whose elements are unordered, when converted to a collection whose elements are ordered, is arbitrary.

Collection instance protocol

converting

    asBag

> Answer a Bag whose elements are those of the receiver.

    asSet

> Answer a Set whose elements are those of the receiver (any duplications are therefore eliminated).

    asOrderedCollection

> Answer an OrderedCollection whose elements are those of the receiver (ordering is possibly arbitrary).

| asSortedCollection | Answer a SortedCollection whose elements are those of the receiver, sorted so that each element is less than or equal to ($<=$) its successors. |
| asSortedCollection: aBlock | Answer a SortedCollection whose elements are those of the receiver, sorted according to the argument aBlock. |

Thus if lotteryA is a Bag containing elements

272 572 852 156 596 272 572

then

lotteryA asSet

is a Set containing elements

852 596 156 572 272

and

lotteryA asSortedCollection

is a SortedCollection containing elements ordered (the first element is listed as the leftmost one)

156 272 272 572 572 596 852

10

Hierarchy of the Collection Classes

Object

Magnitude
    Character
    Date
    Time

    Number
        Float
        Fraction
        Integer
            LargeNegativeInteger
            LargePositiveInteger
            SmallInteger

        LookupKey
            Association

    Link

        Process

    Collection

        SequenceableCollection
            LinkedList

            Semaphore

        ArrayedCollection
            Array

            Bitmap
                DisplayBitmap

            RunArray
            String
                Symbol
            Text
            ByteArray

        Interval
        OrderedCollection
            SortedCollection
        Bag
        MappedCollection
        Set
            Dictionary
                IdentityDictionary

Stream
    PositionableStream
        ReadStream
        WriteStream
            ReadWriteStream
                ExternalStream
                    FileStream

    Random

File
FileDirectory
FilePage

UndefinedObject
Boolean
    False
    True

ProcessorScheduler
Delay
SharedQueue

Behavior
    ClassDescription
        Class
        MetaClass

Point
Rectangle
BitBlt
    CharacterScanner

    Pen

DisplayObject
    DisplayMedium
        Form
            Cursor
            DisplayScreen
    InfiniteForm
    OpaqueForm
    Path
        Arc
            Circle
        Curve
        Line
        LinearFit
        Spline

Figure 10.1 provides a road map for distinguishing among the various collection classes in the system. Following the choices in the figure is a useful way to determine which kind of collection to use in an implementation.

One distinction among the classes is whether or not a collection has a well-defined order associated with its elements. Another distinction is that elements of some collections can be accessed through externally-known names or *keys*. The type of key defines another way of distinguishing among kinds of collections. Some are integer indices, implicitly assigned according to the order of the elements; others are explicitly assigned objects that serve as lookup keys.

One unordered collection with external keys is a Dictionary. Its keys are typically instances of String or LookupKey; the comparison for matching keys is equality (=). Dictionary has a subclass, IdentityDictionary, whose external keys are typically Symbols. Its comparison for matching keys is equivalence (==). Elements of a Bag or a Set are unordered and not accessible through externally-known keys. Duplicates are allowed in a Bag, but not allowed in a Set.

All ordered collections are kinds of SequenceableCollections. Elements of all SequenceableCollections are accessible through keys that are integer indices. Four subclasses of SequenceableCollection support different ways in which to create the ordering of elements. An additional distinction among the SequenceableCollection classes is whether the elements can be any object or whether they are restricted to be instances of a particular kind of object.

The order of elements is determined externally for OrderedCollections, LinkedLists, and ArrayedCollections. For OrderedCollection and LinkedList, the programmer's sequence for adding and removing elements defines the ordering of the elements. An element of an OrderedCollection can be any object, while that of a LinkedList must be a kind of Link. The different ArrayedCollections in the system include Array, String, and ByteArray. The elements of an Array or a RunArray can be any kind of object, elements of a String or of a Text must be Characters, and those of a ByteArray must be SmallIntegers between 0 and 255.

The order of elements is determined internally for Intervals and SortedCollections. For an Interval, the ordering is an arithmetic progression that is specified at the time the instance is created. For a SortedCollection, the ordering is specified by a sorting criterion determined by evaluating a block known to the collection. Elements of an Interval must be Numbers; elements of a SortedCollection can be any kind of object.

In addition to the collection classes already mentioned, MappedCollection is a Collection that represents an indirect access path to a collection whose elements are accessible via external keys. The

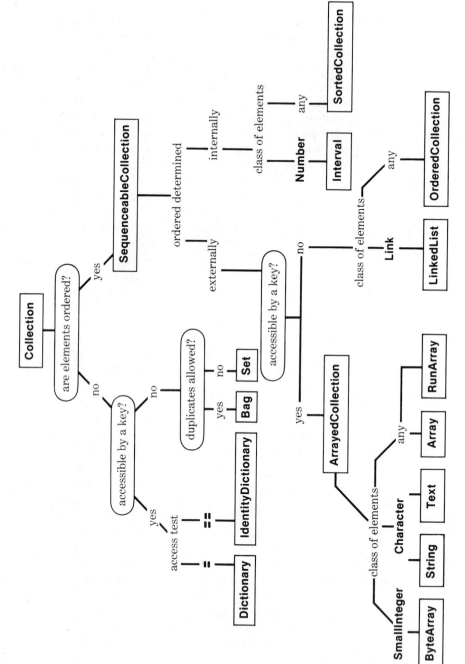

Figure 10.1

mapping from one set of external keys to the collection is determined at the time the MappedCollection is created.

The remainder of this chapter explores each of the collection subclasses, describing any additions to the message protocols and providing simple examples.

Class Bag

A Bag is the simplest kind of collection. It represents collections whose elements are unordered and have no external keys. It is a subclass of Collection. Since its instances do not have external keys, they cannot respond to the messages at: and at:put:. The message size answers the total number of elements in the collection.

A Bag is nothing more than a group of elements that behaves according to the protocol of all collections. The general description of collections does not restrict the number of occurrences of an element in an individual collection. Class Bag emphasizes this generality by specifying an additional message for adding elements.

Bag instance protocol
_____

adding
    add: newObject withOccurrences: anInteger
                Include the argument, newObject, as an element of the receiver, anInteger number of times. Answer the argument, newObject.

Consider the example class Product which represents a grocery item and its price. A new Product may be created using the message of: name at: price, and the price of an instance is accessible by sending it the message price. Filling one's grocery bag may be expressed by

```
sack ← Bag new.
sack add: (Product of: #steak at: 5.80).
sack add: (Product of: #potatoes at: 0.50) withOccurrences: 6.
sack add: (Product of: #carrots at: 0.10) withOccurrences: 4.
sack add: (Product of: #milk at: 2.20)
```

Then the grocery bill is determined by the expression

```
amount ← 0.
sack do: [ :eachProduct | amount ← amount + eachProduct price]
```

or

```
sack inject: 0
    into: [ :amount :eachProduct | amount + eachProduct price]
```

to be $11.40. Note that the messages add:, do:, and inject:into: to a Bag are inherited from its superclass, Collection.

A Bag is unordered, so that, although enumeration messages are supported, the programmer cannot depend on the order in which elements are enumerated.

Class Set

Class Set represents collections whose elements are unordered and have no external keys. Its instances cannot respond to the messages at: and at:put:. A Set is like a Bag except that its elements cannot be duplicated. The adding messages add the element only if it is not already in the collection. Class Set is a subclass of class Collection.

Classes Dictionary and IdentityDictionary

Class Dictionary represents a set of associations between keys and values. The elements of a Dictionary are instances of class Association, a simple data structure for storing and retrieving the members of the key-value pair.

An alternative way of thinking about a Dictionary is that it is a collection whose elements are unordered but have explicitly assigned keys or names. From this perspective, the elements of a Dictionary are arbitrary objects (values) with external keys. These alternative ways of thinking about a Dictionary are reflected in the message protocol of the class. Messages inherited from class Collection—includes:, do:, and other enumeration messages—are applied to the *values* of the Dictionary. That is, these messages refer to the values of each association in the Dictionary, rather than to the keys or to the associations themselves.

Messages inherited from class Object—at: and at:put:—are applied to the keys of the Dictionary. The at: and at:put: paradigm is extended for the associations and the values by adding messages associationAt: and keyAtValue:. In order to provide additional control when looking up elements in a Dictionary, the message at:ifAbsent: is provided; using it, the programmer can specify the action to take if the element whose key is the first argument is not found. The inherited message at: reports an error if the key is not found.

Dictionary instance protocol

accessing

at: key ifAbsent: aBlock	Answer the value named by the argument, key. If key is not found, answer the result of evaluating aBlock.
associationAt: key	Answer the association named by the argument, key. If key is not found, report an error.
associationAt: key ifAbsent: aBlock	Answer the association named by the argument, key. If key is not found, answer the result of evaluating aBlock.
keyAtValue: value	Answer the name for the argument, value. If there is no such value, answer nil. Since values are not necessarily unique, answer the name for the first one encountered in the search.
keyAtValue: value ifAbsent: exceptionBlock	Answer the key for the argument, value. If there is no such value, answer the result of evaluating exceptionBlock.
keys	Answer a Set containing the receiver's keys.
values	Answer a Bag containing the receiver's values (includes any duplications).

As an example of the use of a Dictionary, suppose opposites is a Dictionary of word Symbols and their opposites.

```
opposites ← Dictionary new.
opposites at: #hot put: #cold.
opposites at: #push put: #pull.
opposites at: #stop put: #go.
opposites at: #come put: #go
```

Alternatively, an element can be added using the message add: by creating an Association as the argument.

```
opposites add: (Association key: #front value: #back).
opposites add: (Association key: #top value: #bottom)
```

The Dictionary, opposites, now consists of

key	value
hot	cold
push	pull
stop	go
come	go
front	back
top	bottom

We can use the testing protocol inherited from class Collection to test the values in the Dictionary. Notice that includes: tests the inclusion of a value, not a key.

expression	result
opposites size	6
opposites includes: #cold	true
opposites includes: #hot	false
opposites occurrencesOf: #go	2
opposites at: #stop put: #start	start

The fourth example indicates that, although a key can appear only once in a Dictionary, a value can be associated with any number of keys. The last example re-associates the key #stop with a new value, #start. Additional messages are provided in class Dictionary for testing associations and keys.

Dictionary instance protocol

dictionary testing
   includesAssociation: anAssociation

                                    Answer whether the receiver has an element (association between a key and a value) that is equal to the argument, anAssociation.

   includesKey: key
                                      Answer whether the receiver has a key equal to the argument, key.

Then we can try

expression	result

opposites
   includesAssociation:
     (Association
       key: #come
       value: #go)
	true

opposites includesKey: #hot	true

Similarly, the removing protocol specified in class Collection is extended to provide access by reference to associations and keys, as well as to values. However, the message remove: itself is not appropriate for a Dictionary; in removing an element, mention of the key is required.

Dictionary instance protocol

---

dictionary removing

    removeAssociation: anAssociation

	Remove the key and value association, anAssociation, from the receiver. Answer anAssociation.
removeKey: key	Remove key (and its associated value) from the receiver. If key is not in the receiver, report an error. Otherwise, answer the value associated with key.
removeKey: key ifAbsent: aBlock	Remove key (and its associated value) from the receiver. If key is not in the receiver, answer the result of evaluating aBlock. Otherwise, answer the value named by key.

For example

---

expression	*result*

opposites
  removeAssociation:
    (Association
      key: #top
      value: #bottom)
	The association whose key is #top and value is #bottom. opposites has one less element.

opposites removeKey: #hot	The association whose key is #hot and whose value is #cold. This association is removed from opposites.

opposites
  removeKey: #cold
  ifAbsent: [opposites
      at: #cold
      put: #hot]
	hot

As a result of the last example, the association of #cold with #hot is now an element of opposites.

The message do: evaluates its argument, a block, for each of the Dictionary's values. The collection enumerating protocol, inherited from class Collection, is again extended in order to provide messages for enumerating over the associations and the keys. Messages supporting uses of reject: and inject:into: are not provided.

dictionary enumerating
    associationsDo: aBlock

Evaluate aBlock for each of the receiver's
key/value associations.

    keysDo: aBlock

Evaluate aBlock for each of the receiver's
keys.

We thus have three possible ways of enumerating over a Dictionary.
Suppose newWords is a Set of vocabulary words that a child has not yet
learned. Any word in opposites is now part of the child's repertoire and
can be removed from newWords. Evaluating the following two expressions removes these words (the first removes the values, the second the
keys).

    opposites do: [:word | newWords remove: word ifAbsent: []].
    opposites keysDo: [:word | newWords remove: word ifAbsent: []]

Note that if a word from opposites is not in newWords, then nothing
(no error report) happens. Alternatively, one expression, enumerating
the Associations, can be used.

    opposites associationsDo:
            [:each |
                newWords remove: each key ifAbsent: [].
                newWords remove: each value ifAbsent: []]

The accessing messages keys and values can be used to obtain collections of the words in the opposites dictionary. Assuming the evaluation
of all previous example expressions, then

    opposites keys

returns the Set whose elements are

    push come front stop cold

and

    opposites values

returns the Bag whose elements are

    pull go back start hot

**Class
Sequenceable-
Collection**

Class SequenceableCollection represents collections whose elements are ordered and are externally named by integer indices. SequenceableCollection is a subclass of Collection and provides the protocol for accessing, copying, and enumerating elements of a collection when it is known that there is an ordering associated with the elements. Since the elements are ordered, there is a well-defined first and last element of the collection. It is possible to ask the index of a particular element (indexOf:) and the index of the beginning of a sequence of elements within the collection (indexOfSubCollection:startingAt:). All collections inherit messages from class Object for accessing indexed variables. As described in Chapter 6, these are at:, at:put:, and size. In addition, SequenceableCollections support putting an object at all positions named by the elements of a Collection (atAll:put:), and putting an object at all positions in the sequence (atAllPut:). Sequences of elements within the collection can be replaced by the elements of another collection (replaceFrom:to:with: and replaceFrom:to:with:startingAt:).

SequenceableCollection instance protocol

accessing

    atAll: aCollection put: anObject
        Associate each element of the argument, aCollection (an Integer or other external key), with the second argument, anObject.

    atAllPut: anObject
        Put the argument, anObject, as every one of the receiver's elements.

    first
        Answer the first element of the receiver. Report an error if the receiver contains no elements.

    last
        Answer the last element of the receiver. Report an error if the receiver contains no elements.

    indexOf: anElement
        Answer the first index of the argument, anElement, within the receiver. If the receiver does not contain anElement, answer 0.

    indexOf: anElement ifAbsent: exceptionBlock
        Answer the first index of the argument, anElement, within the receiver. If the receiver does not contain anElement, answer the result of evaluating the argument, exceptionBlock.

    indexOfSubCollection: aSubCollection startingAt: anIndex
        If the elements of the argument, aSubCollection, appear, in order, in the receiver, then answer the index of the first element of the first such occurrence. If no such match is found, answer 0.

    indexOfSubCollection: aSubCollection startingAt: anIndex
        ifAbsent: exceptionBlock
        Answer the index of the receiver's first element, such that that element equals the first

element of the argument, aSubCollection, and the next elements equal the rest of the elements of aSubCollection. Begin the search of the receiver at the element whose index is the argument, anIndex. If no such match is found, answer the result of evaluating the argument, exceptionBlock.

replaceFrom: start to: stop with: replacementCollection

Associate each index between start and stop with the elements of the argument, replacementCollection. Answer the receiver. The number of elements in replacementCollection must equal stop-start+1.

replaceFrom: start to: stop with: replacementCollection startingAt: repStart

Associate each index between start and stop with the elements of the argument, replacementCollection, starting at the element of replacementCollection whose index is repStart. Answer the receiver. No range checks are performed, except if the receiver is the same as replacementCollection but repStart is not 1, then an error reporting that indices are out of range will occur.

Examples of using these accessing messages, using instances of String, are

expression	*result*
' aaaaaaaaaa ' size	10
' aaaaaaaaaa ' atAll: (2 to: 10 by: 2) put: $b	' abababab '
' aaaaaaaaaa ' atAllPut: $b	' bbbbbbbbbb '
' This string ' first	$T
' This string ' last	$g
' ABCDEFGHIJKLMNOP ' indexOf: $F	6
' ABCDEFGHIJKLMNOP ' indexOf: $M ifAbsent: [0]	13
' ABCDEFGHIJKLMNOP ' indexOf: $Z ifAbsent: [0]	0
' The cow jumped ' indexOfSubCollection: ' cow ' startingAt: 1	5
' The cow jumped ' replaceFrom: 5 to: 7 with: ' dog '	' The dog jumped '
' The cow jumped ' replaceFrom: 5 to: 7 with: ' the spoon ran ' startingAt: 5	' The spo jumped '

Any of these examples could be similarly carried out with an instance of any subclass of SequenceableCollection, for example, with an Array. For the Array, #(The brown jug), replacement of brown by black is carried out by evaluating the expression

#(The brown jug) replaceFrom: 2 to: 2 with: #(black)

Notice that the last argument must be an Array as well. And notice that the replacement messages do not change the size of the original collection (the receiver), although they do alter the collection. It may be preferrable to preserve the original by creating a copy. The copying protocol of SequenceableCollections supports copying a sequence of elements in the collection, copying the entire collection with part of it replaced, copying the entire collection with an element deleted, or copying the entire collection with one or more elements concatenated.

SequenceableCollection instance protocol

copying

, aSequenceableCollection	This is the concatenation operation. Answer a copy of the receiver with each element of the argument, aSequenceableCollection, added, in order.
copyFrom: start to: stop	Answer a copy of a subset of the receiver, starting from element at index start until element at index stop.
copyReplaceAll: oldSubCollection with: newSubCollection	
	Answer a copy of the receiver in which all occurrences of oldSubCollection have been replaced by newSubCollection.
copyReplaceFrom: start to: stop with: replacementCollection	
	Answer a copy of the receiver satisfying the following conditions: If stop is less than start, then this is an insertion; stop should be exactly start-1. start = 1 means insert before the first character. start = size + 1 means append after last character. Otherwise, this is a replacement; start and stop have to be within the receiver's bounds.
copyWith: newElement	Answer a copy of the receiver that is 1 bigger than the receiver and has newElement as the last element.
copyWithout: oldElement	Answer a copy of the receiver in which all occurrences of oldElement have been left out.

Using the replace and copy messages, a simple text editor can be devised. The Smalltalk-80 system includes class String as well as class Text, the latter providing support for associating the characters in the String with font or emphasis changes in order to mix character fonts, bold, italic, and underline. The message protocol for Text is that of a SequenceableCollection with additional protocol for setting the emphasis codes. For illustration purposes, we use an instance of class String, but remind the reader of the analogous application of editing messages for an instance of class Text. Assume that line is initially an empty string

    line ← String new: 0

Then

expression	result
line ← line copyReplaceFrom: 1 to: 0 with: ' this is the first line tril '	' this is the first line tril '
line ← line copyReplaceAll: ' tril ' with: ' trial '	' this is the first line trial '
line ← line copyReplaceFrom: (line size+ 1) to: (line size) with: ' and so on '	' this is the first line trialand so on '
line indexOfSubCollection: ' trial ' startingAt: 1	24
line ← line copyReplaceFrom: 29 to: 28 with: ' '	' this is the first line trial and so on '

The last two messages of the copying protocol given above are useful in obtaining copies of an Array with or without an element. For example

expression	result
#(one two three) copyWith: #four	(one two three four)
#(one two three) copyWithout: #two	(one three)

Because the elements of a SequenceableCollection are ordered, enumeration is in order, starting with the first element and taking each successive element until the last. Reverse enumeration is also possible, using the message reverseDo: aBlock. Enumeration of two SequenceableCollections can be done together so that pairs of elements, one from each collection, can be used in evaluating a block.

SequenceableCollection instance protocol

enumerating

findFirst: aBlock

Evaluate aBlock with each of the receiver's elements as the argument. Answer the index of the first element for which the argument, aBlock evaluates to true.

findLast: aBlock   Evaluate aBlock with each of the receiver's elements as the argument. Answer the index of the last element for which the argument, aBlock evaluates to true.

reverseDo: aBlock   Evaluate aBlock with each of the receiver's elements as the argument, starting with the last element and taking each in sequence up to the first. For SequenceableCollections, this is the reverse of the enumeration for do:. aBlock is a one-argument block.

with: aSequenceableCollection do: aBlock

Evaluate aBlock with each of the receiver's elements along with the corresponding element from aSequenceableCollection. aSequenceableCollection must be the same size as the receiver, and aBlock must be a two-argument block.

The following expressions create the Dictionary, opposites, which was introduced in an earlier example.

```
opposites ← Dictionary new.
#(come cold front hot push stop)
        with: #(go hot back cold pull start)
        do: [ :key :value | opposites at: key put: value]
```

The Dictionary now has six associations as its elements.

Any SequenceableCollection can be converted to an Array or a MappedCollection. The messages are asArray and mappedBy: aSequenceableCollection.

Subclasses of
Sequenceable-
Collection

Subclasses of SequenceableCollection are OrderedCollection, LinkedList, Interval, and MappedCollection. ArrayedCollection is a subclass representing a collection of elements with a fixed range of integers as external keys. Subclasses of ArrayedCollection are, for example, Array and String.

Class
OrderedCollection

OrderedCollections are ordered by the sequence in which objects are added and removed from them. The elements are accessible by external keys that are indices. The accessing, adding, and removing protocols are augmented to refer to the first and last elements, and to elements preceding or succeeding other elements.

OrderedCollections can act as *stacks* or *queues*. A stack is a sequential list for which all additions and deletions are made at one end of the list (called either the "rear" or the "front") of the list. It is often called a *last-in first-out* queue.

usual vocabulary	OrderedCollection *message*
push newObject	addLast: newObject
pop	removeLast
top	last
empty	isEmpty

A queue is a sequential list for which all additions are made at one end of the list (the "rear"), but all deletions are made from the other end (the "front"). It is often called a *first-in first-out* queue.

usual vocabulary	OrderedCollection *message*
add newObject	addLast: newObject
delete	removeFirst
front	first
empty	isEmpty

The message add: to an OrderedCollection means "add the element as the last member of the collection" and remove: means "remove the argument as an element." The message protocol for OrderedCollections, in addition to that inherited from classes Collection and SequenceableCollection, follows.

OrderedCollection instance protocol
_____

accessing
    after: oldObject   Answer the element after oldObject in the receiver. If the receiver does not contain oldObject or if the receiver contains no elements after oldObject, report an error.

    before: oldObject   Answer the element before oldObject in the receiver. If the receiver does not contain oldObject or if the receiver contains no elements before oldObject, report an error.

adding
    add: newObject after: oldObject   Add the argument, newObject, as an element of the receiver. Put it in the sequence just succeeding oldObject. Answer newObject. If oldObject is not found, then report an error.

add: newObject before: oldObject	Add the argument, newObject, as an element of the receiver. Put it in the sequence just preceding oldObject. Answer newObject. If oldObject is not found, then report an error.
addAllFirst: anOrderedCollection	Add each element of the argument, anOrderedCollection, at the beginning of the receiver. Answer anOrderedCollection.
addAllLast: anOrderedCollection	Add each element of the argument, anOrderedCollection, to the end of the receiver. Answer anOrderedCollection.
addFirst: newObject	Add the argument, newObject, to the beginning of the receiver. Answer newObject.
addLast: newObject	Add the argument, newObject, to the end of the receiver. Answer newObject.

removing
removeFirst	Remove the first element of the receiver and answer it. If the receiver is empty, report an error.
removeLast	Remove the last element of the receiver and answer it. If the receiver is empty, report an error.

Class
SortedCollection

Class SortedCollection is a subclass of OrderedCollection. The elements in a SortedCollection are ordered by a function of two elements. The function is represented by a two-argument block called the sort block. It is possible to add an element only with the message add:; messages such as addLast: that allow the programmer to specify the order of inserting are disallowed for SortedCollections.

An instance of class SortedCollection can be created by sending SortedCollection the message sortBlock:. The argument to this message is a block with two-arguments, for example,

SortedCollection sortBlock: [:a :b | a <= b]

This particular block is the default sorting function when an instance is created simply by sending SortedCollection the message new. Thus examples of the four ways to create a SortedCollection are

SortedCollection new
SortedCollection sortBlock: [:a :b | a > b]
anyCollection asSortedCollection
anyCollection asSortedCollection: [:a :b | a > b]

It is possible to determine the block and to reset the block using two additional accessing messages to instances of SortedCollection. When the block is changed, the elements of the collection are, of course, re-sorted. Notice that the same message is sent to the class itself (sortBlock:) to create an instance with a particular sorting criterion, and to an instance to change its sorting criterion.

SortedCollection class protocol

instance creation

sortBlock: aBlock — Answer an instance of SortedCollection such that its elements will be sorted according to the criterion specified in the argument, aBlock.

SortedCollection instance protocol

accessing

sortBlock — Answer the block that is the criterion for sorting elements of the receiver.

sortBlock: aBlock — Make the argument, aBlock, be the criterion for ordering elements of the receiver.

Suppose we wish to maintain an alphabetical list of the names of children in a classroom.

children ← SortedCollection new

The initial sorting criterion is the default block [:a :b | a <= b]. The elements of the collection can be Strings or Symbols because, as we shall show presently, these kinds of objects respond to the comparison messages <, >, <=, and >=.

---

expression	result
children add: #Joe	Joe
children add: #Bill	Bill
children add: #Alice	Alice
children	SortedCollection (Alice Bill Joe)
children add: #Sam	Sam
children sortBlock: [:a :b	a < b]	SortedCollection (Sam Joe Bill Alice)
children add: #Henrietta	Henrietta
children	SortedCollection (Sam Joe Henrietta Bill Alice)

The sixth message in the example reversed the order in which elements are stored in the collection, children.

Class LinkedList

LinkedList is another subclass of SequenceableCollection whose elements are explicitly ordered by the sequence in which objects are added and removed from them. Like OrderedCollection, the elements of a LinkedList can be referred to by external keys that are indices. Unlike OrderedCollection, where the elements may be any object, the elements of a LinkedList are homogeneous; each must be an instance of class Link or of a subclass of Link.

A Link is a record of a reference to another Link. Its message protocol consists of three messages. The same message (nextLink:) is used to create an instance of Link with a particular reference, and to change the reference of an instance.

LinkedList class protocol
_____

instance creation
    nextLink: aLink   Create an instance of Link that references the
                               argument, aLink.

LinkedList instance protocol
_____

accessing
    nextLink   Answer the receiver's reference.
    nextLink: aLink   Set the receiver's reference to be the argu-
                               ment, aLink.

Since class Link does not provide a way to record a reference to the actual element of the collection, it is treated as an abstract class. That is, instances of it are not created. Rather, subclasses are defined that provide the mechanisms for storing one or more elements, and instances of the subclasses are created.

Since LinkedList is a subclass of SequenceableCollection, its instances can respond to the accessing, adding, removing, and enumerating messages defined for all collections. Additional protocol for LinkedList consists of

LinkedList instance protocol
_____

adding
    addFirst: aLink   Add aLink to the beginning of the receiver's
                               list. Answer aLink.

    addLast: aLink   Add aLink to the end of the receiver's list. An-
                               swer aLink.

removing
    removeFirst   Remove the receiver's first element and answer
                               it. If the receiver is empty, report an error.

    removeLast   Remove the receiver's last element and answer
                               it. If the receiver is empty, report an error.

An example of a subclass of Link in the Smalltalk-80 system is class Process. Class Semaphore is a subclass of LinkedList. These two classes are discussed in Chapter 15, which is about multiple independent processes in the system.

The following is an example of the use of LinkedList. Link does not provide instance information other than a reference to another Link. So, as an example, assume that there is a subclass of Link named Entry. Entry adds the ability to store one object. The instance creation message for an Entry is for: anObject, and its accessing message is element.

class name	Entry
superclass	Link
instance variable names	element
class methods	

instance creation

for: anObject
↑self new setElement: anObject

instance methods

accessing
element
↑element
printing
printOn: aStream
aStream nextPutAll: ′ Entry for: ′, element printString
private
setElement: anObject
element ← anObject

The classes LinkedList and Entry can then be used as follows.

expression	result
list ← LinkedList new	LinkedList ()
list add: (Entry for: 2)	Entry for: 2
list add: (Entry for: 4)	Entry for: 4
list addLast: (Entry for: 5)	Entry for: 5
list addFirst: (Entry for: 1)	Entry for: 1
list	LinkedList (Entry for: 1 Entry for: 2 Entry for: 4 Entry for: 5)
list isEmpty	false
list size	4

list inject: 0
    into: [:value :each |
        (each element)
            + value]
	12

list last	Entry for: 5
list first	Entry for: 1
list remove: (Entry for: 4)	Entry for: 4
list removeFirst	Entry for: 1
list removeLast	Entry for: 5
list first == list last	true

Class Interval

Another kind of SequenceableCollection is a collection of numbers representing a mathematical progression. For example, the collection might consist of all the integers in the interval from 1 to 100; or it might consist of all even integers in the interval from 1 to 100. Or the collection might consist of a series of numbers where each additional number in the series is computed from the previous one by multiplying it by 2. The series might start with 1 and end with the last number that is less than or equal to 100. This would be the sequence 1, 2, 4, 8, 16, 32, 64.

A mathematical progression is characterized by a first number, a limit (maximum or minimum) for the last computed number, and a method for computing each succeeding number. The limit could be positive or negative infinity. An arithmetic progression is one in which the computation method is simply the addition of an increment. For example, it could be a series of numbers where each additional number in the series is computed from the previous one by adding a negative 20. The series might start with 100 and end with the last number that is greater than or equal to 1. This would be the sequence 100, 80, 60, 40, 20.

In the Smalltalk-80 system, the class of collections called Intervals consists of finite arithmetic progressions. In addition to those messages inherited from its superclasses SequenceableCollection and Collection, class Interval supports messages for initialization and for accessing those values that characterize the instance. New elements cannot be added or removed from an Interval.

The class protocol of Interval consists of the following messages for creating instances.

Interval class protocol

instance creation

from: startInteger to: stopInteger   Answer an instance of class Interval, starting with the number startInteger, ending with the number stopInteger, and using the increment 1 to compute each successive element.

from: startInteger to: stopInteger by: stepInteger

> Answer an instance of Interval, starting with the number startInteger, ending with the number stopInteger, and using the increment stepInteger to compute each successive element.

All messages appropriate to SequenceableCollections can be sent to an Interval. In addition, the instance protocol of Interval provides a message for accessing the increment of the arithmetic progression (increment).

Class Number supports two messages that provide a shorthand for expressing new Intervals—to: stop and to: stop by: step. Thus to create an Interval of all integers from 1 to 10, evaluate either

    Interval from: 1 to: 10

or

    1 to: 10

To create an Interval starting with 100 and ending with 1, adding a negative 20 each time, evaluate either

    Interval from: 100 to: 1 by: −20

or

    100 to: 1 by: −20

This is the sequence 100, 80, 60, 40, 20. The Interval need not consist of Integers—to create an Interval between 10 and 40, incrementing by 0.2, evaluate either

    Interval from: 10 to: 40 by: 0.2

or

    10 to: 40 by: 0.2

This is the sequence 10, 10.2, 10.4, 10.6, 10.8, 11.0, ... and so on.

Note that we could provide the more general case of a progression by replacing the numeric value of step by a block. When a new element is to be computed, it would be done by sending the current value as the argument of the message value: to the block. The computations of size and do: would have to take this method of computation into account.

The message do: to an Interval provides the function of the usual for-loop in a programming language. The Algol statement

for i := 10 **step** 6 **until** 100 **do**
     begin
      <statements>
     end

is represented by

(10 to: 100 by: 6) do: [:i | statements]

Numbers respond to the message to:by:do: as though the expression had been written as given in the example. So that iteration can be written without parentheses as

10 to: 100 by: 6 do: [:i | statements]

To increment by 1 every sixth numeric element of an OrderedCollection, numbers, evaluate

6 to: numbers size
  by: 6
  do: [:index | numbers at: index put: (numbers at: index) + 1]

The Interval created is 6, 12, 18, ..., up to the index of the last element of numbers. If the size of the collection is less than 6 (the supposedly first index), nothing happens. Otherwise elements at position 6, 12, 18, and so on, until the last possible position, are replaced.

Class ArrayedCollection

As stated earlier, class ArrayedCollection is a subclass of Collection. It represents a collection of elements with a fixed range of integers as external keys. ArrayedCollection has five subclasses in the Smalltalk-80 system—Array, String, Text, RunArray, and ByteArray.

An Array is a collection whose elements are any objects. It provides the concrete representation for storing a collection of elements that have integers as external keys. Several examples of the use of Arrays have already been given in this chapter.

A String is a collection whose elements are Characters. Many examples of the use of Strings have been given in this and in previous chapters. Class String provides additional protocol for initializing and comparing its instances.

Text represents a String that has font and emphasis changes. It is used in storing information needed for creating textual documents in the Smalltalk-80 system. An instance of Text has two instance variables, the String and an instance of RunArray in which an encoding of the font and emphasis changes is stored.

Class RunArray provides a space-efficient storage of data that tends to be constant over long runs of the possible indices. It stores repeated elements singly and then associates with each single element a number that denotes the consecutive occurrences of the element. For example, suppose the Text representing the String 'He is a good boy.' is to be displayed with the word "boy" in bold, and further suppose that the code for the font is 1 and for its boldface version is 2. Then the RunArray for the Text that is associated with 'He is a good boy.' (a String of 17 Characters) consists of 1 associated with 13, 2 associated with 3, and 1 associated with 1. That is, the first 13 Characters are in font 1, the next three in font 2, and the last in font 1.

A ByteArray represents an ArrayedCollection whose elements are integers between 0 and 255. The implementation of a ByteArray stores two bytes to a 16-bit word; the class supports additional protocol for word and double-word access. ByteArrays are used in the Smalltalk-80 system for storing time in milliseconds.

Class String

As stated earlier, the class protocol for String adds messages for creating a copy of another String (fromString: aString) or for creating a String from the Characters in a Stream (readFrom: aStream). The main significance of this second message is that pairs of embedded quotes are read and stored as one element, the quote character. In addition, class String adds comparing protocol like that specified in class Magnitude. We introduced some of these messages earlier in the description of class SortedCollection.

String instance protocol

comparing

< aString	Answer whether the receiver collates before the argument, aString. The collation sequence is ASCII with case differences ignored.
< = aString	Answer whether the receiver collates before the argument, aString, or is the same as aString. The collation sequence is ASCII with case differences ignored.
> aString	Answer whether the receiver collates after the argument, aString. The collation sequence is ASCII with case differences ignored.

> = aString	Answer whether the receiver collates after the argument, aString, or is the same as aString. The collation sequence is ASCII with case differences ignored.
match: aString	Treat the receiver as a pattern that can contain characters # and *. Answer whether the argument, aString, matches the pattern in the receiver. Matching ignores upper/lower case differences. Where the receiver contains the character #, aString may contain any single character. Where the receiver contains *, aString may contain any sequence of characters, including no characters.
sameAs: aString	Answer whether the receiver collates precisely with the argument, aString. The collation sequence is ASCII with case differences ignored.

We have not as yet given examples of using the last two messages.

expression	result
'first string' sameAs: 'first string'	true
'First String' sameAs: 'first string'	true
'First String' = 'first string'	false
'#irst string' match: 'first string'	true
'* string' match: 'any string'	true
'*.st' match: 'filename.st'	true
'first string' match: 'first *'	false

Strings can be converted to all lowercase characters or all uppercase characters. They can also be converted to instances of class Symbol.

String instance protocol

converting
asLowercase	Answer a String made up from the receiver whose characters are all lowercase.
asUppercase	Answer a String made up from the receiver whose characters are all uppercase.
asSymbol	Answer the unique Symbol whose characters are the characters of the receiver.

Therefore we have

expression	result
'first string' asUppercase	'FIRST STRING'
'First String' asLowercase	'first string'
'First' asSymbol	First

Class Symbol

Symbols are arrays of Characters that are guaranteed to be unique. Thus

'a string' asSymbol == 'a string' asSymbol

answers true. Class Symbol provides two instance creation messages in its class protocol for this purpose.

Symbol class protocol	
instance creation	
intern: aString	Answer a unique Symbol whose characters are those of aString.
internCharacter: aCharacter	Answer a unique Symbol of one character, the argument, aCharacter.

In addition, Symbols can be expressed literally using the character # as a prefix to a sequence of Characters. For example, #dave is a Symbol of four Characters. Symbols print without this prefix notation.

Class MappedCollection

Class MappedCollection is a subclass of Collection. It represents an access mechanism for referencing a subcollection of a collection whose elements are named. This mapping can determine a reordering or filtering of the elements of the collection. The basic idea is that a MappedCollection refers to a *domain* and a *map*. The domain is a Collection that is to be accessed indirectly through the external keys stored in the map. The map is a Collection that associates a set of external keys with another set of external keys. This second set of keys must be external keys that can be used to access the elements of the domain. The domain and the map, therefore, must be instances of Dictionary or of a subclass of SequenceableCollection.

Take, for example, the Dictionary of word Symbols, opposites, introduced earlier.

key	*value*
come	go
cold	hot
front	back
hot	cold
push	pull
stop	start

Suppose we create another Dictionary of synonym Symbols for some of the keys of the entries in opposites and refer to it by the variable name alternates.

key	value
cease	stop
enter	come
scalding	hot
shove	push

Then we can provide a MappedCollection by evaluating the expression

words ← MappedCollection collection: opposites map: alternates

Through words, we can access the elements of opposites. For example, the value of the expression words at: #cease is start (i.e., the value of the key cease in alternatives is stop; the value of the key stop in opposites is start). We can determine which part of opposites is referenced by words by sending words the message contents.

words contents

The result is a Bag containing the symbols start go cold pull.

The message at:put: is an indirect way to change the domain collection. For example

expression	result
words at: #scalding	cold
words at: #cease	start
words at: #cease put: #continue	continue
opposites at: #stop	continue

Summary of Conversions Among Collections

In the sections describing the various kinds of collections, we have indicated which collections can be converted to which other collections. In summary, any collection can be converted to a Bag, a Set, an OrderedCollection, or a SortedCollection. All collections except Bags and Sets can be converted to an Array or a MappedCollection. Strings and Symbols can be converted into one another; but no collection can be converted into an Interval or a LinkedList.

11

Three Examples That Use Collections

Random Selection and Playing Cards

The Drunken Cockroach Problem

Traversing Binary Trees
A Binary Word Tree

Three examples of class descriptions are given in this chapter. Each example makes use of the numeric and collections objects available in the Smalltalk-80 system; each illustrates a different way to add functionality to the system.

Card games can be created in terms of random selection from a collection representing a deck of cards. The example class Card represents a playing card with a particular suit and rank. CardDeck represents a collection of such Cards; a CardHand is a collection of Cards for an individual player. Selecting cards from a CardDeck or a CardHand is carried out using example classes that represent sampling with replacement, SampleSpaceWithReplacement, and sampling without replacement, SampleSpaceWithoutReplacement. A well-known programming problem, the drunken cockroach problem, involves counting the number of steps it takes a cockroach to randomly travel over all the tiles in a room. The solution given in this chapter represents each tile as an instance of example class Tile and the bug as an instance of DrunkenCockroach. The third example in this chapter is of a tree-like data structure represented by classes Tree and Node; a WordNode illustrates the way trees can be used to store strings representing words.

Random Selection and Playing Cards

The Smalltalk-80 class Random, which acts as a generator for randomly selected numbers between 0 and 1, was described in Chapter 8. Random provides the basis for sampling from a set of possible events; such a set is known as a *sample space*. A simple form of discrete random sampling can be obtained in which a random number is used to to select an element from a sequenceable collection. If the selected element remains in the collection, then the sampling is done "with replacement"—that is, every element of the collection is available each time the collection is sampled. Alternatively, the sampled element can be removed from the collection each time the collection is sampled; this is sampling "without replacement."

Class SampleSpaceWithReplacement represents random selection with replacement from a sequenceable collection of items. An instance of the class is created by specifying the collection of items from which random sampling will be done. This initialization message has selector data:. We then sample from the collection by sending the instance the message next. Or we can obtain anInteger number of samples by sending the message next: anInteger.

For example, suppose we wish to sample from an Array of Symbols representing the names of people.

people ← SampleSpaceWithReplacement
            data: #(sally sam sue sarah steve)

Each time we wish to select a name from the Array, we evaluate the expression

people next

The response is one of the Symbols, sally, sam, sue, sarah, or steve. By evaluating the expression

people next: 5

an OrderedCollection of five samples is selected. Instances of SampleSpaceWithReplacement respond to messages isEmpty and size to test whether any elements exist in the sample space and how many elements exist. Thus the response to

people isEmpty

is false; and the response to

people size

is 5.

An implementation of class SampleSpaceWithReplacement is given next. Comments, delimited by double quotes, are given in each method to indicate its purpose.

class name	SampleSpaceWithReplacement
superclass	Object
instance variable names	data
	rand

class methods

instance creation

data: aSequenceableCollection
    "Create an instance of SampleSpaceWithReplacement such that the argument, aSequenceableCollection, is the sample space."
    ↑self new setData: aSequenceableCollection

instance methods

accessing

next
    "The next element selected is chosen at random from the data collection. The index into the data collection is determined by obtaining a

random number between 0 and 1, and normalizing it to be within the range of the size of the data collection."
self isEmpty
   ifTrue: [self error: ' no values exist in the sample space'].
↑data at: (rand next * data size) truncated + 1

next: anInteger

"Answer an OrderedCollection containing anInteger number of selections from the data collection."
| aCollection |
aCollection ← OrderedCollection new: anInteger.
anInteger timesRepeat: [aCollection addLast: self next].
↑aCollection

testing

isEmpty

"Answer whether any items remain to be sampled."
↑self size = 0

size

"Answer the number of items remaining to be sampled."
↑data size

private

setData: aSequenceableCollection

"The argument, aSequenceableCollection, is the sample space. Create a random number generator for sampling from the space."
data ← aSequenceableCollection.
rand ← Random new

The class description declares that each instance has two variables whose names are data and rand. The initialization message, data:, sends the new instance the message setData: in which data is bound to a SequenceableCollection (the value of the argument of the initialization message) and rand is bound to a new instance of class Random.

SampleSpaceWithReplacement is not a subclass of Collection because it implements only a small subset of the messages to which Collections can respond. In response to the messages next and size to a SampleSpaceWithReplacement, the messages at: and size are sent to the instance variable data. This means that any collection that can respond to at: and size can serve as the data from which elements are sampled. All SequenceableCollections respond to these two messages. So, for example, in addition to an Array as illustrated earlier, the data can be an Interval. Suppose we wish to simulate the throw of a die. Then the elements of the sample space are the positive integers 1 through 6.

die ← SampleSpaceWithReplacement data: (1 to: 6)

A throw of the die is obtained by evaluating

die next

The response from this message is one of the Integers, 1, 2, 3, 4, 5, or 6.

We could select a card from a deck of cards in a similar way if the collection associated with the instance of SampleSpaceWithReplacement consists of elements representing playing cards. In order to play card games, however, we have to be able to deal a card out to a player and remove it from the deck. So, we have to use random selection without replacement.

To implement random selection without replacement, we define the response to the message next as removing the selected element. Since all SequenceableCollections do not respond to the message remove:, (for example, Interval does not) we either must check the argument of the initialization message or we must convert the argument to an acceptable kind of collection. Since all OrderedCollections respond to the two messages, and since all collections can be converted to an OrderedCollection, we can use the conversion approach. The method associated with setData: sends its argument the message asOrderedCollection in order to accomplish the goal.

Class SampleSpaceWithoutReplacement is defined to be a subclass of SampleSpaceWithReplacement. The methods associated with the messages next and setData: are overridden; the remaining messages are inherited without modification.

class name	SampleSpaceWithoutReplacement
superclass	SampleSpaceWithReplacement
instance methods	

accessing

next
    ↑data remove: super next

private

setData: aCollection
    data ← aCollection asOrderedCollection.
    rand ← Random new

Notice that the method for next depends on the method implemented in the superclass (super next). The superclass's method checks to make certain that the sample space is not empty and then randomly selects an element. After determining the selected element, the subclass's method removes the element from data. The result of the remove: message is the argument, so that the result of the message next to a SampleSpaceWithoutReplacement is the selected element.

Now let's implement a simple card game. Suppose the sample space data for the card game are instances of a class Card where each Card knows its suit and rank. An instance of Card is created by sending it the message suit:rank:, specifying the suit (heart, club, spade, or diamond) and its rank (1, 2, ..., 13) as the two arguments. A Card responds to the messages suit and rank with the appropriate information.

class name	Card
superclass	Object
instance variable names	suit
	rank

class methods

instance creation

suit: aSymbol rank: anInteger
    "Create an instance of Card whose suit is the argument, aSymbol, and whose rank is the argument, anInteger."
    ↑self new setSuit: aSymbol rank: anInteger

instance methods

accessing

suit
    "Answer the receiver's suit."
    ↑suit
rank
    "Answer the receiver's rank."
    ↑rank

private

setSuit: aSymbol rank: anInteger
    suit ← aSymbol.
    rank ← anInteger

A deck of cards, cardDeck, is created by the following expressions.

```
cardDeck ← OrderedCollection new: 52.
#(heart club spade diamond) do:
        [ :eachSuit |
            1 to: 13 do: [ :n | cardDeck add: (Card suit: eachSuit rank: n)]]
```

The first expression creates an OrderedCollection for 52 elements. The second expression is an enumeration of the ranks 1 through 13 for each of the four suits: heart, club, spade, and diamond. Each element of the OrderedCollection is set to be a Card with a different suit and rank.

The ability to sample from this deck of cards is obtained by creating an instance of SampleSpaceWithoutReplacement with the card deck as the collection from which samples will be taken

cards ← SampleSpaceWithoutReplacement data: cardDeck

To deal a card, evaluate the expression

cards next

The response to this message is an instance of class Card.

Another way to provide a deck of playing cards is illustrated in the description of example class CardDeck. The basic idea is to store a linear list of cards; next means supply the first card in the list. A card can be returned to the deck by placing it at the end or by inserting it at some random position. The linear list is made random by *shuffling*—that is, randomly ordering the cards.

In the implementation of class CardDeck provided next, we store an initial version of the deck of cards as a class variable. It is created using the expressions given earlier. A copy of this variable is made as an instance variable whenever a new instance is created; it is shuffled before cards are dealt out. Each subsequent shuffle of the deck uses the current state of the instance variable, not of the class variable. Of course, the shuffling process, since it is based on the use of an instance of SampleSpaceWithoutReplacement, is quite uniform. A simulation of real shuffling involves first splitting the deck approximately in half and then interleaving the two halves. The interleaving involves selecting chunks from one half and then the other half. Indeed, such a simulation may be more random than an actual person's shuffling; a person's shuffling ability might be observable and predictable.

Messages to a CardDeck, such as return:, next, and shuffle, are useful in creating card games.

class name	CardDeck
superclass	Object
instance variable names	cards
class variable names	InitialCardDeck
class methods	

class initialization

initialize
    "Create a deck of 52 playing cards."
    InitialCardDeck ← OrderedCollection new: 52.
    #(heart club spade diamond) do:
      [:aSuit |
        1 to: 13
          do: [:n | InitialCardDeck add: (Card suit: aSuit rank: n)]]

instance creation

new

"Create an instance of CardDeck with an initial deck of 52 playing cards."

↑super new cards: InitialCardDeck copy

instance methods

accessing

next

"Deal (give out) the next card."

↑cards removeFirst

return: aCard

"Put the argument, aCard, at the bottom of the deck."

cards addLast: aCard

shuffle

| sample tempDeck |

sample ← SampleSpaceWithoutReplacement data: cards.

tempDeck ← OrderedCollection new: cards size.

cards size timesRepeat: [tempDeck addLast: sample next].

self cards: tempDeck

testing

isEmpty

"Answer whether any more cards remain in the deck."

↑cards isEmpty

private

cards: aCollection

cards ← aCollection

The class CardDeck must be initialized by evaluating the expression

CardDeck initialize

In the implementation of CardDeck, cards is the instance variable and is therefore the deck of cards used in playing a game. To play a game, an instance of CardDeck is created

CardDeck new

and then each card is dealt by sending this new instance the message next. When a card is put back in the deck, the CardDeck is sent the message return:. Shuffling always shuffles whichever cards are currently in the deck. If a full CardDeck is to be reused after a round of play, any cards taken from the deck must be returned.

Note the implementation of the message shuffle. A sample space without replacement, sample, is created for a copy of the current deck of cards. A new OrderedCollection, tempDeck, is created for storing randomly selected cards from this sample space. Sampling is done from sample for each possible card; each selected card is added to the tempDeck. Once all the available cards have been shuffled into it, tempDeck is stored as the current game deck.

Suppose we create a simple card game in which there are four players and a dealer. The dealer deals out cards to each of the players. If at least one of the players has between 18 and 21 points, the game ends with the "prize" divided among each of these players. Points are counted by adding up the ranks of the cards. A player with more than 21 points is not dealt new cards.

Each player is represented by an instance of class CardHand that represents a card hand. A CardHand knows the cards it is dealt and can determine its total point count (in response to the message points).

class name	CardHand
superclass	Object
instance variable names	cards
class methods	

instance creation

new
    ↑super new setCards

instance methods

accessing

take: aCard
    "The argument, aCard, is added to the reciever."
    cards add: aCard

returnAllCardsTo: cardDeck
    "Place all of the receiver's cards into the deck of cards referred to by the argument, cardDeck, and remove these cards from the receiver's hand."
    cards do: [:eachCard | cardDeck return: eachCard].
    self setCards

inquiries

points

"Answer the sum of the ranks of the receiver's cards."
↑cards inject: 0 into: [:value :nextCard | value + nextCard rank]

private

setCards

cards ← OrderedCollection new

We create a Set of four players. Each player is represented by an instance of CardHand. The dealer's cards are the gameCards. The dealer (that is, the programmer) starts by shuffling the deck; there is no winner yet. There may be more than one winner; winners will be listed in the Set, winners.

```
players ← Set new.
4 timesRepeat: [players add: CardHand new].
gameCards ← CardDeck new.
gameCards shuffle
```

As long as there is no winner, each player with less than 21 points is given another card from the gameCards. Before dealing a card to each eligible player, the dealer looks to see if there are any winners by testing the points for each player.

```
[ winners ← players select: [ :each | each points between: 18 and: 21].
  winners isEmpty and: [gameCards isEmpty not]]
    whileTrue:
      [players do:
        [ :each |
          each points < 21 ifTrue: [each take: gameCards next]]
```

The condition for continuing to play is a block with two expressions. The first expression determines the winners, if any. The second expression tests to see if there are any winners yet (winners isEmpty) and, if not, if there are any more cards to deal out (gameCards isEmpty not). If there are no winners and more cards, the game continues. The game consists of an enumeration of each player; each player takes another card (each take: gameCards next) only if the number of card points is less than 21 (each points < 21).

To play again, all cards have to be returned to the game deck, which is then shuffled.

```
players do: [ :each | each returnAllCardsTo: gameCards].
gameCards shuffle
```

The players and dealer are ready to play again.

The Drunken Cockroach Problem

We can use some of the collection classes to solve a well-known programming problem. The problem is to measure how long it takes a drunken cockroach to touch each tile of a floor of square tiles which is N tiles wide and M tiles long. To slightly idealize the problem: in a given "step" the cockroach is equally likely to try to move to any of nine tiles, namely the tile the roach is on before the step and the tiles immediately surrounding it. The cockroach's success in moving to some of these tiles will be limited, of course, if the cockroach is next to a wall of the room. The problem is restated as counting the number of steps it takes the cockroach to land on *all* of the tiles at least once.

One straightforward algorithm to use to solve this problem starts with an empty Set and a counter set to 0. After each step, we add to the Set the tile that the cockroach lands on and increment a counter of the number of steps. Since no duplication is allowed in a Set, we would be done when the number of elements in the Set reaches N*M. The solution would be the value of the counter.

While this solves the simplest version of the problem, we might also like to know some additional information, such as how many times each tile was visited. To record this information, we can use an instance of class Bag. The size of the Bag is the total number of steps the cockroach took; the size of the Bag when it is converted to a Set is the total number of distinct tiles touched by the cockroach. When this number reaches N*M, the problem is solved. The number of occurrences of each tile in the Bag is the same as the number of times the roach visited each tile.

Each tile on the floor can be labeled with respect to its row and its column. The objects representing tiles in the solution we offer are instances of class Tile. A commented implementation of class Tile follows.

class name	Tile
superclass	Object
instance variable names	location
	floorArea

instance methods

accessing

location
    "Answer the location of the receiver on the floor."
    ↑location
location: aPoint
    "Answer the location of the receiver on the floor."
    ↑location
location: aPoint
    "Set the receiver's location on the floor to be the argument, aPoint."
    location ← aPoint

floorArea: aRectangle
"Set the floor area to be the rectangular area represented by the argument, aRectangle."
floorArea ← aRectangle

moving

neighborAt: deltaPoint
"Create and answer a new Tile that is at the location of the receiver changed by the x and y amounts represented by the argument, deltaPoint. Keep the location of the newTile within the boundries of the floor area."
| newTile |
newTile ← Tile new floorArea: floorArea.
newTile location: ((location + deltaPoint max: floorArea origin)
                              min: floorArea corner).
↑newTile

comparing

= aTile
"Answer whether the receiver is equal to the argument, aTile."
↑(aTile isKindOf: Tile) and: [location = aTile location]

hash
↑location hash

A Tile refers to its row and column locations, each of which must be at least 1 and no larger than the width or length of the floor. Therefore, in addition to remembering its location, a Tile must remember the maximum floor space in which it can be placed. A Tile can be sent the message neightborAt: aPoint in order to determine a Tile at one of the locations next to it. This new Tile must be at a location within the boundaries of the floor.

The way we will simulate the cockroach's walk is to select a direction in terms of changes in the x-y coordinates of the cockroach's location. Given the location of the cockroach (tile x,y), there are 9 tiles to which the insect can move unless the tile is along one of the edges. We will store the possible changes of x and y in an OrderedCollection that is the data for random selection. The OrderedCollection will contain Points as elements; the Points are direction vectors representing all the possible combinations of moves. We create this collection by the expressions

Directions ← OrderedCollection new: 9.
(−1 to: 1) do: [:x | (−1 to: 1) do: [:y | Directions add: x@y]]

Directions, then, is a collection with elements

   −1@−1, −1@0, −1@1, 0@−1, 0@0, 0@1, 1@−1, 1@0, 1@1

As part of the drunken walk simulation, we will generate a random number for selecting an element from this OrderedCollection of possible moves. As an alternative to using a random number generator directly, we could use the previous example's SampleSpaceWithReplacement with Directions as the sample space.

Suppose the cockroach starts on the Tile that is at location 1@1. Each time the cockroach is supposed to take a step, we obtain an element from the collection, Directions. This element is then the argument of the message neighborAt: to the Tile. In the following, assume Rand is an instance of class Random.

```
tile neighborAt:
        (Directions at: ((Rand next * Directions size) truncated + 1)).
```

The resulting new tile location is the place where the cockroach landed.

Each tile position has to be remembered in order to be able to report on whether every location has been touched and how many steps were required. By storing each tile in a Bag, a tally is kept of the number of times the cockroach landed in each location. So at each step, a new tile is created that is a copy of the previous tile. This new tile is changed according to the randomly selected direction and is added to the Bag. When the number of unique elements of the Bag equals the total number of tiles, the cockroach is done.

Only two messages are needed in class DrunkenCockroach. One is a command to have the cockroach take a walk around a specific floor area until every tile on the floor has been touched. This is the message walkWithin:startingAt:. The second is an inquiry as to the number of steps the cockroach has taken so far; this is the message numberOfSteps. We can also inquire about the number of times the roach stepped on a particular tile by sending the DrunkenCockroach the message timesSteppedOn:. The collection of direction vectors (as described earlier) is created as a class variable of DrunkenCockroach; the random number generator Rand is also a class variable of DrunkenCockroach.

class name	DrunkenCockroach
superclass	Object
instance variable names	currentTile
	tilesVisited
class variable names	Directions
	Rand
class methods	
class initialization	

initialize
"Create the collection of direction vectors and the random number generator."

```
Directions ← OrderedCollection new: 9.
(−1 to: 1) do: [ :x | (−1 to: 1) do: [ :y | Directions add: x@y]].
Rand ← Random new
```

instance creation

new

```
    ↑super new setVariables
```

instance methods

simulation

walkWithin: aRectangle startingAt: aPoint

```
| numberTiles |
tilesVisited ← Bag new.
currentTile location: aPoint.
currentTile floorArea: aRectangle.
numberTiles ← (aRectangle width + 1) * (aRectangle height + 1).
tilesVisited add: currentTile.
[tilesVisited asSet size < numberTiles] whileTrue:
    [currentTile ← currentTile neighborAt:
        (Directions at: (Rand next * Directions size) truncated + 1).
    tilesVisited add: currentTile]
```

data

numberOfSteps

```
    ↑tilesVisited size
```

timesSteppedOn: aTile

```
    ↑tilesVisited occurrencesOf: aTile
```

private

setVariables

```
    currentTile ← Tile new.
    tilesVisited ← Bag new
```

We can now send the following messages in order to experiment with a
drunken cockroach. Initialize the class and create an instance.

```
DrunkenCockroach initialize.
cockroach ← DrunkenCockroach new
```

Obtain the results of 10 experiments with a 5 by 5 room.

```
results ← OrderedCollection new: 10.
10 timesRepeat:
    [cockroach walkWithin: (1@1 corner: 5@5) startingAt: (1@1).
    results add: cockroach numberOfSteps]
```

The average of the 10 results is the average number of steps it took the drunken cockroach to solve the problem.

(results inject: 0 into: [:sum :exp | sum + exp]) / 10

Note that in the implementation of the DrunkenCockroach message walkWithin:startingAt:, the termination condition is whether the Bag, when converted to a Set, has N*M elements. A faster way to make this test would be to add the message uniqueElements to the class Bag so that the conversion to a Set is not done each time through the iteration.
(For those readers wishing to try this change, the method to be added to class Bag is

uniqueElements
   ↑contents size

Then the message walkWithin:startingAt: can be changed so that the termination condition is tilesVisited uniqueElements < numberTiles.)

**Traversing
Binary Trees**

A *tree* is an important nonlinear data structure that is useful in computer algorithms. A tree structure means that there is a branching relationship between elements. There is one element designated as the root of the tree. If there is only one element, then it is the root. If there are more elements, then they are partitioned into disjoint (sub)trees. A *binary tree* is either the root only, the root with one binary (sub)tree, or the root together with two binary (sub)trees. A complete description of the genealogy of tree structures is provided by Knuth in Volume 1 of the *Art of Computer Programming*. Here we assume the reader is familiar with the idea so that we can demonstrate how to specify the data structure as a Smalltalk-80 class.

We will define a class Tree in a way that corresponds to the definition of LinkedList. Elements of a Tree will be Nodes that are like the Links of LinkedLists, able to make connections to other elements. The Tree will reference the root node only.

A node is simple to represent as a Smalltalk-80 object with two instance variables, one refers to the *left* node and another to the *right* node. We choose to treat the order of the nodes to support *in-order traversal*. That is, in enumerating the nodes, visit the left subnode first, the root second, and the right subnode third. If a node has no subnodes, then it is called a *leaf*. We define the *size* of the node to be 1 plus the size of its subnodes, if any. Thus a leaf is a node of size 1, and a node with two leaves as subnodes has size 3. The size of a tree is the size of its root node. This definition of *size* corresponds to the general notion of size for collections.

Messages to a Node give access to the left node, the right node, and the last or end node. It is also possible to remove a subnode (remove:ifAbsent:) and the root (rest).

class name	Node
superclass	Object
instance variable names	leftNode
	rightNode

class methods

instance creation

left: lNode right: rNode
"Create an instance of a Node with the arguments lNode and rNode as the left and right subnodes, respectively."
| newNode |
newNode ← self new.
newNode left: lNode.
newNode right: rNode.
↑newNode

instance methods

testing

isLeaf
"Answer whether the receiver is a leaf, that is, whether it is a node without any subnodes."
↑leftNode isNil & rightNode isNil

accessing

left
↑leftNode

left: aNode
leftNode ← aNode

right
↑rightNode

right: aNode
rightNode ← aNode

size

```
↑1 + (leftNode isNil
            ifTrue: [0]
            ifFalse: [leftNode size])
    + (rightNode isNil
            ifTrue: [0]
            ifFalse: [rightNode size])
```

end

```
| aNode |
aNode ← self.
[aNode right isNil] whileFalse: [aNode ← aNode right].
↑aNode
```

removing

remove: subnode ifAbsent: exceptionBlock

```
"Assumes the root, self, is not the one to remove."
self isLeaf ifTrue: [↑exceptionBlock value].
leftNode = subnode
    ifTrue: [leftNode ← leftNode rest. ↑subnode].
rightNode = subnode
    ifTrue: [rightNode ← rightNode rest. ↑subnode].
leftNode isNil
    ifTrue: [↑rightNode remove: subnode ifAbsent: exceptionBlock].
↑leftNode
    remove: subnode
    ifAbsent:
        [rightNode isNil
            ifTrue: [exceptionBlock value]
            ifFalse:
                [rightNode remove: subnode
                        ifAbsent: exceptionBlock]]
```

rest

```
leftNode isNil
    ifTrue: [↑rightNode]
    ifFalse: [leftNode end right: rightNode.
            ↑leftNode]
```

enumerating

do: aBlock

```
leftNode isNil ifFalse: [leftNode do: aBlock].
aBlock value: self.
rightNode isNil ifFalse: [rightNode do: aBlock]
```

If Node is a leaf, it is denoted by

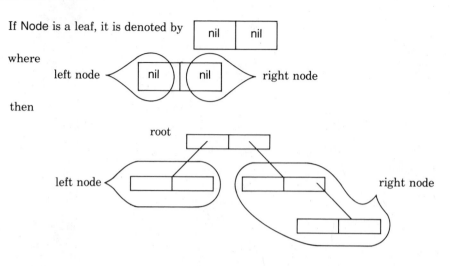

where

then

Enumeration uses in-order traversal, first applying the left subnode as the value of the block, then the root, and third the right subnode. The block must be defined for a block argument that is a Node.

Next we provide a Tree as a kind of SequenceableCollection whose elements are Nodes. A Tree has one instance variable which we name root; root is either nil or it is an instance of Node. As a subclass of SequenceableCollection, class Tree implements messages add: anElement, remove: anElement ifAbsent: exceptionBlock, and do: aBlock. Basically, the methods associated with each of these messages checks to see whether the tree is empty (root isNil) and, if not, passes the appropriate message to root. The check on "empty" is inherited from Collection. The intention is that the programmer who uses a tree structure accesses the elements of that structure only via an instance of class Tree.

class name	Tree
superclass	SequenceableCollection
instance variable names	root
instance methods	

testing

isEmpty
    ↑root isNil

accessing

first
    | save |
    self emptyCheck.
    save ← root.

```
            [save left isNil] whileFalse: [save ← save left].
            ↑save
    last
            self emptyCheck.
            ↑root end
    size
            self isEmpty
                ifTrue: [↑0]
                ifFalse: [↑root size]
    adding

    add: aNode
            ↑self addLast: aNode
    addFirst: aNode
            "If the collection is empty, then the argument, aNode, is the new root;
            otherwise, it is the left node of the current first node."
            self isEmpty
                ifTrue: [↑root ← aNode]
                ifFalse: [self first left: aNode].
            ↑aNode
    addLast: aNode
            "If the collection is empty, then the argument, aNode, is the new root;
            otherwise it is the last element of the current root."
            self isEmpty
                ifTrue: [root ← aNode]
                ifFalse: [self last right: aNode].
            ↑aNode

removing

    remove: aNode ifAbsent: exceptionBlock
            "First check the root. If not found, move down the tree checking each
            node."
            self isEmpty ifTrue: [↑exceptionBlock value].
            root = aNode
                ifTrue: [root ← root rest. ↑aNode]
                ifFalse: [↑root remove: aNode ifAbsent: exceptionBlock]
    removeFirst
            self emptyCheck.
            ↑self remove: self first ifAbsent: []
    removeLast
            self emptyCheck.
            ↑self remove: self last ifAbsent: []

enumerating

    do: aBlock
            self isEmpty ifFalse: [root do: aBlock]
```

Note that the removing messages do not remove the subtree beginning with the node to be removed, only the node itself.

A Binary Word Tree

The definition of a Node, like that of a Link, is all structure without content. We have left the content of each Node to be specified by a subclass. Suppose we wish to use a kind of Node to store words represented as Strings. We call this class WordNode. An instance of WordNode is created by sending WordNode the message for:, if no subnodes are specified, or for:left:right: if the two subnodes are specified. So a WordNode illustrated as

cat

is created by evaluating the expression

WordNode for: ' cat '

A WordNode that looks like

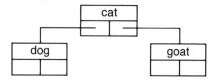

is created by evaluating the expression

WordNode for: ' cat '
         left: (WordNode for: ' dog ')
         right: (WordNode for: ' goat ')

An implementation for the class WordNode follows. Notice that equality (=) is redefined to mean that the words in the Nodes are the same; this means that the inherited removing messages will remove a subnode if its word is the same as the word of the argument.

class name	WordNode
superclass	Node
instance variable names	word
class methods	

instance creation

   for: aString
      ↑self new word: aString

for: aString left: lNode right: rNode
> | newNode |
> newNode ← super left: lNode right: rNode.
> newNode word: aString.
> ↑newNode

instance methods

accessing

> **word**
> > ↑word
> **word: aString**
> > word ← aString

comparing

> **= aWordNode**
> > ↑(aWordNode isKindOf: WordNode) and: [word = aWordNode word]
> **hash**
> > ↑word hash

A sequence of expressions follows to illustrate the use of WordNode. Note that no effort is made in the definition of WordNode to support inserting elements so that each word collates alphabetically when the tree is traversed. An interested reader might add an insert: aWordNode message to WordNode that maintains the alphabetic sort.

tree ← Tree new.

tree add: (WordNode for: 'cat')

tree addFirst: (WordNode for: 'frog')

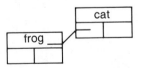

tree addLast: (WordNode for: 'horse' left: (WordNode for: 'monkey') right: nil)

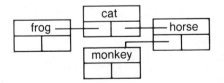

tree addFirst: (WordNode for: 'ape')

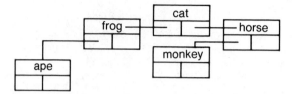

tree remove: (WordNode for: 'horse')

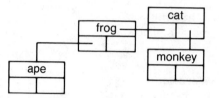

tree remove: (WordNode for: 'frog')

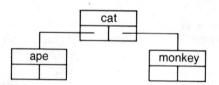

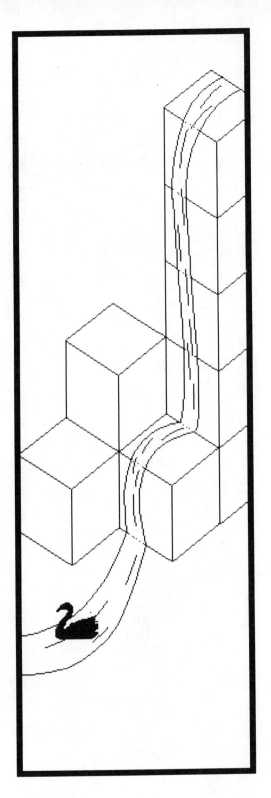

12

Protocol for Streams

Object

Magnitude
    Character
    Date
    Time

    Number
        Float
        Fraction
        Integer
            LargeNegativeInteger
            LargePositiveInteger
            SmallInteger

    LookupKey
        Association

Link

    Process

Collection

    SequenceableCollection
    LinkedList

        Semaphore

    ArrayedCollection
    Array

        Bitmap
            DisplayBitmap

        RunArray
        String
            Symbol
        Text
        ByteArray

    Interval
    OrderedCollection
        SortedCollection
    Bag
    MappedCollection
    Set
        Dictionary
            IdentityDictionary

Stream
    PositionableStream
        ReadStream
        WriteStream
            ReadWriteStream
            ExternalStream
                FileStream

    Random

File
FileDirectory
FilePage

UndefinedObject
Boolean
    False
    True

ProcessorScheduler
Delay
SharedQueue

Behavior
    ClassDescription
        Class
        MetaClass

Point
Rectangle
BitBlt
    CharacterScanner

    Pen

DisplayObject
    DisplayMedium
        Form
            Cursor
            DisplayScreen
    InfiniteForm
    OpaqueForm
    Path
        Arc
            Circle
        Curve
        Line
        LinearFit
        Spline

The collection classes provide the basic data structure for storing objects together as nonlinear and linear groups. The protocol for these classes makes it possible directly to access (store and retrieve) individual elements. It also, through the enumeration messages, supports noninterruptible accessing of all of the elements, in order. However, it does not support intermingling the two kinds of accessing operations—enumerating and storing. Nor does the collection protocol support accessing individual elements, one at a time, unless an external position reference is separately maintained.

Unless an easily computed external name for each element exists, interruptible enumeration of individual elements can not be carried out efficiently. It is possible, for example, sequentially to read elements of an OrderedCollection using a combination of first and after:, as long as the elements of the collection are unique. An alternative approach involves the collection itself remembering, in some way, which element was last accessed. We call this the "position reference" in the discussion that follows. The possibility of shared access to a sequence of elements, however, means that it is necessary to maintain a separate, external memory of the last element accessed.

Class Stream represents the ability to maintain a position reference into a collection of objects. We use the phrase *streaming over a collection* to mean accessing the elements of a collection in such a way that it is possible to enumerate or store each element, one at a time, possibly intermingling these operations. By creating several Streams over the same collection, it is possible to maintain multiple position references into the same collection.

There are a number of ways to maintain a position reference for streaming over a collection. A common one is to use an integer as an index. This approach can be used for any collection whose elements are externally named by an integer. All SequenceableCollections fall into this category. As we shall describe later, such a Stream is represented in the Smalltalk-80 system by the class PositionableStream. A second way to maintain a position reference is to use a *seed* for a generator of objects. An example of this kind of Stream in the Smalltalk-80 system is class Random which was already presented in Chapter 8. And a third way is to maintain a non-numerical position reference, such as a reference to a node in a sequence; this approach is illustrated in this chapter by an example class that supports streaming over a linked list or a tree structure.

Class Stream

Class Stream, a subclass of class Object, is a superclass that specifies the accessing protocol for streaming over collections. Included in this protocol are messages for reading (retrieving) and writing (storing) into the collection, although not all the subclasses of class Stream can support both kinds of accessing operations. The basic reading message is next; its response is the next element in the collection that is referenced by the Stream. Given the ability to access the next element, more general reading messages can be supported. These are next: anInteger, which responds with a collection of anInteger number of elements; nextMatchFor: anObject, which reads the next element and answers whether it is equal to the argument, anObject; and contents, which answers a collection of all of the elements.

Stream instance protocol

accessing — reading	
next	Answer the next object accessible by the receiver.
next: anInteger	Answer the next anInteger number of objects accessible by the receiver. Generally, the answer will be a collection of the same class as the one accessed by the receiver.
nextMatchFor: anObject	Access the next object and answer whether it is equal to the argument, anObject.
contents	Answer all of the objects in the collection accessed by the receiver. Generally, the answer will be a collection of the same class as the one accessed by the receiver.

The basic writing message is nextPut: anObject; this means to store the argument, anObject, as the next element accessible by the receiver. If both read and write messages are possible, a next message following a nextPut: anElement does not read the element just stored, but rather the one after it in the collection. Writing messages also include nextPutAll: aCollection, which stores all of the elements in the argument into the collection accessed by the receiver, and next: anInteger put: anObject, which stores the argument, anObject, as the next anInteger number of elements.

Stream instance protocol

accessing — writing	
nextPut: anObject	Store the argument, anObject, as the next element accessible by the receiver. Answer anObject.
nextPutAll: aCollection	Store the elements in the argument, aCollection, as the next elements accessible by the receiver. Answer aCollection.
next: anInteger put: anObject	Store the argument, anObject, as the next anInteger number of elements accessible by the receiver. Answer anObject.

The reading and writing messages each determine if a next element can be read or written and, if not, an error is reported. The programmer might therefore wish to determine whether accessing is still feasible; this is accomplished by sending the Stream the message atEnd.

Stream instance protocol

testing
    atEnd   Answer whether the receiver cannot access any more objects.

Noninterrupted reading of elements that are applied as arguments to a block can be done by sending the message do: aBlock, similar to the enumerating message supported by the collection classes.

Stream instance protocol

enumerating
    do: aBlock   Evaluate the argument, aBlock, for each of the remaining elements that can be accessed by the receiver.

The implementation of this enumeration message depends on sending the messages atEnd and next to the message receiver. We show this method as an example of the use of these messages.

do: aBlock
    [self atEnd] whileFalse: [aBlock value: self next]

Each kind of Stream must specify its instance creation messages. In general, a Stream can not be created simply by sending the message new because the Stream must be informed of which collection it accesses and what is its initial position reference.

As a simple example, let's assume that the collection accessed by a Stream is an Array and that the Stream is called accessor. The contents of the Array are the Symbols

Bob Dave Earl Frank Harold Jim Kim Mike Peter Rick Sam Tom

and the position reference is such that Bob is the next accessible element. Then

expression	result
accessor next	Bob
accessor next	Dave
accessor nextMatchFor: #Bob	false

accessor nextMatchFor: #Frank	true
accessor next	Harold
accessor nextPut: #James	James

accessor contents	(Bob Dave Earl Frank
	  Harold James Kim
	  Mike Peter Rick
	  Sam Tom)

accessor
    nextPutAll:
      #(Karl Larry Paul)
	(Karl Larry Paul)

accessor contents	(Bob Dave Earl Frank
	  Harold James Karl
	  Larry Paul Rick Sam
	  Tom)

accessor next: 2 put: #John	John

accessor contents	(Bob Dave Earl Frank
	  Harold James Karl
	  Larry Paul John
	  John Tom)

accessor next	Tom
accessor atEnd	true

Positionable Streams

In the introduction to this chapter we indicated three possible approaches that a Stream might use in order to maintain a position reference. The first one we will present uses an integer index which is incremented each time the Stream is accessed. The Stream accesses only those kinds of collections whose elements have integers as external keys; these include all of the subclasses of SequenceableCollection.

Class PositionableStream is a subclass of class Stream. It provides additional protocol appropriate to Streams that can reposition their position references, but, it is an abstract class because it does not provide an implementation of the inherited messages next and nextPut: anObject. The implementation of these messages is left to the subclasses of PositionableStream—ReadStream, WriteStream, and ReadWriteStream.

A PositionableStream is created by sending the class one of two instance creation messages, on: aCollection or on: aCollection from: firstIndex to: lastIndex. The argument, aCollection, is the collection the Stream accesses; in the second case, a copy of a subcollection of aCollection is accessed, i.e., the one delimited by the two arguments firstIndex and lastIndex.

PositionableStream class protocol
_____

instance creation
  on: aCollection   Answer an instance of a kind of
                                     PositionableStream that streams over the ar-
                                     gument, aCollection.
  on: aCollection from: firstIndex to: lastIndex
                                     Answer an instance of a kind of
                                     PositionableStream that streams over a copy of
                                     a subcollection of the argument, aCollection,
                                     from firstIndex to lastIndex.

PositionableStream supports additional protocol for accessing and testing the contents of the collection.

PositionableStream instance protocol
_____

testing
  isEmpty   Answer true if the collection the receiver
                                     accesses has no elements; otherwise, answer
                                     false.

accessing
  peek   Answer the next element in the collection (as
                                     in the message next), but do not change the
                                     position reference. Answer nil if the receiver is
                                     at the end.

  peekFor: anObject   Determine the response to the message peek.
                                     If it is the same as the argument, anObject,
                                     then increment the position reference and an-
                                     swer true. Otherwise answer false and do not
                                     change the position reference.

  upTo: anObject   Answer a collection of elements starting with
                                     the next element accessed by the receiver, and
                                     up to, not inclusive of, the next element that
                                     is equal to anObject. If anObject is not in the
                                     collection, answer the entire rest of the collec-
                                     tion.

  reverseContents   Answer a copy of the receiver's contents in re-
                                     verse order.

Since a PositionableStream is known to store an explicit position reference, protocol for accessing that reference is supported. In particular,
the reference can be reset to access the beginning, the end, or any other
position of the collection.

PositionableStream instance protocol
_____

positioning
  position   Answer the receiver's current position refer-
                                     ence for accessing the collection.

  position: anInteger   Set the receiver's current position reference
                                     for accessing the collection to be the argu-
                                     ment, anInteger. If the argument is not within

	the bounds of the receiver's collection, report an error.
reset	Set the receiver's position reference to the beginning of the collection.
setToEnd	Set the receiver's position reference to the end of the collection.
skip: anInteger	Set the receiver's position reference to be the current position plus the argument, anInteger, possibly adjusting the result so as to remain within the bounds of the collection.
skipTo: anObject	Set the receiver's position reference to be past the next occurrence of the argument, anObject, in the collection. Answer whether such an occurrence existed.

Class ReadStream

Class ReadStream is a concrete subclass of PositionableStream that represents an accessor that can only read elements from its collection. We can create an example similar to the previous one to demonstrate the use of the additional protocol provided in class PositionableStream and inherited by all ReadStreams. None of the nextPut:, next:put:, nor nextPutAll: messages can be successfully sent to a ReadStream.

```
accessor ←
    ReadStream on: #(Bob Dave Earl Frank Harold Jim Kim Mike
                    Peter Rick Sam Tom)
```

expression	result
accessor next	Bob
accessor nextMatchFor: #Dave	true
accessor peek	Earl
accessor next	Earl
accessor peekFor: #Frank	true
accessor next	Harold
accessor upTo: #Rick	(Jim Kim Mike Peter)
accessor position	10
accessor skip: 1	the accessor itself
accessor next	Tom
accessor atEnd	true
accessor reset	the accessor itself
accessor skipTo: #Frank	true
accessor next	Harold

Class WriteStream

Class WriteStream is a subclass of PositionableStream representing accessors for writing elements into a collection. None of the next, next:, nor do: messages can be successfully sent to a WriteStream.

WriteStreams are used throughout the Smalltalk-80 system as a part of the methods for printing or storing a string description of any object. Each object in the system can respond to the messages printOn: aStream and storeOn: aStream. The methods associated with these messages consist of a sequence of messages to the argument, which is a kind of Stream that allows writing elements into the collection it accesses. These messages are nextPut:, where the argument is a Character, and nextPutAll:, where the argument is a String or a Symbol. An example will illustrate this idea.

Class Object printing protocol, as described in Chapter 6, includes the message printString. An implementation of this message is

printString
```
    | aStream |
    aStream ← WriteStream on: (String new: 16).
    self printOn: aStream.
    ↑aStream contents
```

If a collection is sent the message printString, then the answer is a String that is a description of the instance. The method creates a WriteStream that the collection can store into, sends the message printOn: to the collection, and then responds with the contents of the resulting WriteStream. The message storeString to any object is similarly implemented in class Object, the difference being that the second expression consists of the message storeOn: aStream rather than printOn: aStream.

The general way in which collections print a description of themselves is to print their class name followed by a left parenthesis, followed by a description of each element separated by spaces, and terminated by a right parenthesis. So if a Set has four elements—the Symbols one, two, three, and four—then it prints on a Stream as

Set (one two three four)

An OrderedCollection with the same elements prints on a Stream as

OrderedCollection (one two three four)

and so on.

Recall that the definition of printOn: and storeOn: given in Chapter 6 is that any suitable description can be provided for printOn:, but the description created by storeOn: must be a well-formed expression that, when evaluated, re-constructs the object it purports to describe.

Here is an implementation in class Collection for printOn:.

printOn: aStream
```
aStream nextPutAll: self class name.
aStream space.
aStream nextPut: $(.
self do:
    [ :element |
        element printOn: aStream.
        aStream space].
aStream nextPut: $)
```

Notice that the message space is sent to the WriteStream (aStream). It, and a number of other messages are provided in class WriteStream to support concise expressions for storing delimiters into such Streams. They are

WriteStream instance protocol

character writing

cr	Store the return character as the next element of the receiver.
crTab	Store the return character and a single tab character as the next two elements of the receiver.
crTab: anInteger	Store the return character as the next element of the receiver, followed by anInteger number of tab characters.
space	Store the space character as the next element of the receiver.
tab	Store the tab character as the next element of the receiver.

Thus to construct the String

```
' name         city

bob            New York
joe            Chicago
bill           Rochester
```

from two corresponding Arrays,

```
names ← # (bob joe bill)
cities ← # (' New York'  ' Chicago'  ' Rochester')
```

evaluate the expressions

```
aStream ← WriteStream on: (String new: 16).
aStream nextPutAll: ′name′.
aStream tab.
aStream nextPutAll: ′city′.
aStream cr; cr.
names with: cities do:
        [ :name :city |
          aStream nextPutAll: name.
          aStream tab.
          aStream nextPutAll: city.
          aStream cr]
```

then the desired result is obtained by evaluating aStream contents.

Suppose a collection already exists and we wish to append further information into it by using Stream protocol. Class WriteStream supports instance creation protocol that accepts a collection and sets the position reference for writing to the end.

WriteStream class protocol

instance creation

with: aCollection	Answer an instance of WriteStream accessing the argument, aCollection, but positioned to store the next element at the end of it.
with: aCollection from: firstIndex to: lastIndex	Answer an instance of WriteStream accessing the subcollection of the argument, aCollection, from locaton firstIndex to lastIndex, but positioned to store the next element at the end of the subcollection.

Thus if a String referred to as header already existed, containing

```
′name       city
```

then the previous example String would be constructed by

```
aStream ← WriteStream with: header.
names with: cities do:
        [ :name :city |
          aStream nextPutAll: name.
          aStream tab.
          aStream nextPutAll: city.
          aStream cr].
aStream contents
```

Class ReadWriteStream

Class ReadWriteStream is a subclass of WriteStream that represents an accessor that can both read and write elements into its collection. It supports all the protocol of both ReadStream and WriteStream, as given above.

Streams of Generated Elements

Of the three ways to create a position reference for streaming over a collection, the second way cited in the introduction to this chapter was to specify a *seed* by which the next elements of the collection can be generated. This kind of Stream only permits reading the elements, not writing. The reference, however, can be repositioned by resetting the seed.

Class Random, introduced in Chapter 8, is a subclass of Stream that determines its elements based on an algorithm employing a number as a seed. Random provides a concrete implementation for next and atEnd. Because the size of the collection is infinite, it never ends; moreover, Random can not respond to the message contents. It can respond to the message do:, but the method will never end without the programmer's purposeful intervention.

The following is an implementation of class Random; the reader is referred to Chapters 11 and 21 for examples making use of instances of the class. The implementations for do: and nextMatchFor: anObject are inherited from class Stream.

class name	Random
superclass	Stream
instance variable names	seed
class methods	

instance creation

> **new**
> > ↑self basicNew setSeed

instance methods

testing

> **atEnd**
> > ↑false

accessing

> **next**
> > | temp |
> > "Lehmer's linear congruential method with modulus m = 2 raisedTo:

16, a = 27181 odd, and 5 = a \\ 8, c = 13849 odd, and c/m approximately 0.21132"
[seed ← 13849 + (27181 * seed) bitAnd: 8r177777.
 temp ← seed / 65536.0.
 temp = 0] whileTrue.
↑temp

private

setSeed
"For pseudo-random seed, get a time from the system clock. It is a large positive integer; just use the lower 16 bits."
seed ← Time millisecondClockValue bitAnd: 8r177777

Another possible example of a stream of generated elements are the probability distributions that are presented in Chapter 21. The superclass ProbabilityDistribution is implemented as a subclass of Stream. The message next: anInteger is inherited from Stream. Each kind of ProbabilityDistribution determines whether it is "read-only" and, if so, implements nextPut: as self shouldNotImplement. Class SampleSpace, another example in Chapter 21, maintains a collection of data items and implements nextPut: anObject as adding to the collection.

Streams for Collections Without External Keys

The third way to maintain a position reference for streaming over a collection cited in the introduction to this chapter was to maintain a non-numerical reference. This would be useful in cases where the elements of the collection cannot be accessed by external keys or where such access is not the most efficient means to retrieve an element.

Streaming over instances of class LinkedList provides an example in which the elements can be accessed by indexes as the external keys, but each such access requires a search down the chain of linked elements. It is more efficient to maintain a reference to a particular element in the collection (a kind of Link) and then to access the next element by requesting the current elements nextLink. Both reading and writing into the LinkedList can be supported by such a Stream.

Suppose we create a subclass of Stream that we call LinkedListStream. Each instance maintains a reference to a LinkedList and a position reference to an element in the collection. Since both reading and writing are supported, the messages next, nextPut:, atEnd, and contents must be implemented. (Note that these four messages are defined in class Stream as self subclassResponsibility.) A new instance of LinkedListStream is created by sending it the message on: aLinkedList.

class name	LinkedListStream
superclass	Stream
instance variable names	collection
	currentNode

class methods

instance creation

on: aLinkedList

    ↑self basicNew setOn: aLinkedList

instance methods

testing

atEnd

    ↑currentNode isNil

accessing

next

```
| saveCurrentNode |
saveCurrentNode ← currentNode.
self atEnd
    ifFalse: [currentNode ← currentNode nextLink].
↑saveCurrentNode
```

nextPut: aLink

```
| index previousLink |
self atEnd ifTrue: [↑collection addLast: aLink].
index ← collection indexOf: currentNode.
index = 1
    ifTrue: [collection addFirst: aLink]
    ifFalse: [previousLink ← collection at: index - 1.
            previousLink nextLink: aLink].
aLink nextLink: currentNode nextLink.
currentNode ← aLink nextLink.
↑aLink
```

private

setOn: aLinkedList

```
collection ← aLinkedList.
currentNode ← aLinkedList first
```

Now suppose in order to demonstrate the use of this new kind of Stream we make up a LinkedList of nodes that are instances of class WordLink; class WordLink is a subclass of Link that stores a String or a Symbol.

class name	WordLink
superclass	Link
instance variable names	word
class methods	

instance creation

for: aString
    ↑self new word: aString

instance methods

accessing

word
    ↑word
word: aString
    word ← aString

comparing

= aWordLink
    ↑word = aWordLink word

printing

printOn: aStream
    aStream nextPutAll: ' a WordLink for '.
    aStream nextPutAll: word

From the above we can see that an instance of WordLink for the word #one is created by

WordLink for: #one

Its print string is

' a WordLink for one '

We can then create a LinkedList of WordLinks and then a LinkedListStream that accesses this LinkedList.

```
list ← LinkedList new.
list add: (WordLink for: #one).
list add: (WordLink for: #two).
list add: (WordLink for: #three).
list add: (WordLink for: #four).
list add: (WordLink for: #five).
accessor ← LinkedListStream on: list
```

Then an example sequence of messages to accessor is

expression	result
accessor next	a WordLink for one
accessor next	a WordLink for two
accessor nextMatchFor: (WordLink for: #three)	true
accessor nextPut: (WordLink for: #insert)	a WordLink for insert
accessor contents	LinkedList (a WordLink for one a WordLink for two a WordLink for three a WordLink for insert a WordLink for five)
accessor next	a WordLink for five
accessor atEnd	true

Similarly, traversing the nodes of a tree structure, such as that of class Tree given in Chapter 11, can be done by a kind of Stream that maintains a reference to a current node and then accesses the next element by accessing the current node's left tree, root, or right tree. This kind of Stream is slightly more complicated to implement than that for a LinkedList because it is necessary to retain knowledge of whether the left or right tree has been traversed and back references to the *father* of the current node. The order of traversal of the tree structure can be implemented in the Stream, ignoring the method by which subtrees were added to the structure. Thus, although we used in-order traversal in the implementations of class Tree and class Node, we can stream over a Tree with postorder traversal by implementing the messages next and nextPut: appropriately.

External Streams and File Streams

The Streams we have examined so far make the assumption that the elements of the collection can be any objects, independent of representation. For communicating with input/output devices, such as a disk, however, this assumption is not valid. In these cases, the elements are stored as binary, byte-sized elements that may prefer to be accessed as numbers, strings, words (two bytes), or bytes. Thus we have a need to support a mixture of nonhomogeneous accessing messages for reading and writing these different-sized "chunks" of information.

Class ExternalStream is a subclass of class ReadWriteStream. Its purpose is to add the nonhomogeneous accessing protocol. This includes protocol for positioning as well as accessing.

nonhomogeneous accessing

nextNumber: n	Answer the next n bytes of the collection accessed by the receiver as a positive SmallInteger or LargePositiveInteger.
nextNumber: n put: v	Store the argument, v, which is a positive SmallInteger or LargePositiveInteger, as the next n bytes of the collection accessed by the receiver. If necessary, pad with zeros.
nextString	Answer a String made up of the next elements of the collection accessed by the receiver.
nextStringPut: aString	Store the argument, aString, in the collection accessed by the receiver.
nextWord	Answer the next two bytes from the collecton accessed by the receiver as an Integer.
nextWordPut: anInteger	Store the argument, anInteger, as the next two bytes of the collection accessed by the receiver.

nonhomogeneous positioning

padTo: bsize	Skip to the next boundary of bsize characters, and answer how many characters were skipped.
padTo: bsize put: aCharacter	Skip—writing the argument, aCharacter, into the collection accessed by the receiver in order to pad the collection—to the next boundary of bsize characters and answer how many characters were written (padded).
padToNextWord	Make the position reference even (on word boundary), answering the padding character, if any.
padToNextWordPut: aCharacter	Make the position reference even (on word boundary), writing the padding character, aCharacter, if necessary.
skipWords: nWords	Position after nWords number of words.
wordPosition	Answer the current position in words.
wordPosition: wp	Set the current position in words to be the argument, wp.

Class FileStream is a subclass of ExternalStream. All accesses to external files are done using an instance of FileStream. A FileStream acts as though it were accessing a large sequence of bytes or characters; the elements of the sequence are assumed to be Integers or Characters. The protocol for a FileStream is essentially that of class ExternalStream and its superclasses. In addition, protocol is provided to set and to test the status of the sequence the FileStream is streaming over.

Classes ExternalStream and FileStream are provided in the Smalltalk-80 system as the framework in which a file system can be created. Additional protocol in class FileStream assumes that a file system is based on a framework consisting of a directory or dictionary of files, where a file is a sequence of file pages. The Smalltalk-80 system includes classes FileDirectory, File, and FilePage to represent these structural parts of a file system. A FilePage is a record of data that is uniquely identified within its File by a page number. A File is uniquely identified both by an alphanumeric name and a serial number; it maintains a reference to the FileDirectory which contains the File. And the FileDirectory is itself uniquely identified by the device or "server" to which it refers. User programs typically do not access a File or its FilePages directly; rather they access it as a sequence of characters or bytes through a FileStream. Thus the programmer can create a FileStream as an accessor to a file using an expression of the form

Disk file: ' name.smalltalk '

where Disk is an instance of a FileDirectory. The FileStream can then be sent sequences of reading and writing messages as specified in the protocol of this chapter.

13

Implementation of the Basic Collection Protocol

Class Collection

Subclasses of Collection
Class Bag
Class Set
Class Dictionary
SequenceableCollections
Subclasses of SequenceableCollection
Class MappedCollection

The protocol for the classes in the Collection hierarchy was presented in Chapters 9 and 10. This chapter presents the complete implementation of class Collection and the implementation of the basic protocol for instance creation, accessing, testing, adding, removing, and enumerating for each subclass of Collection. These implementations make effective use of a framework in class Collection that is refined in its subclasses. Messages in Collection are implemented in a very general way or as self subclassResponsibility. Messages are implemented as

self subclassResponsibility

if the method depends on the representation of the instances. Each subclass must override such messages to fulfill any "subclass responsibilities." Subclasses may override other messages, for efficiency purposes, with a new method that takes advantage of the representation. A subclass may implement some messages with

self shouldNotImplement

which results in a report that the message should not be sent to instances of the class. For example, SequenceableCollections cannot respond to remove:ifAbsent:; therefore the method is implemented as self shouldNotImplement.

Class Collection ☐ Collection *instance creation protocol* In addition to the messages new and new:, an instance of a Collection can be created by sending any one of four messages made up of one, two, three, or four occurrences of the keyword with:. The messages new and new: are not reimplemented in Collection; they produce an instance that is an empty collection. Each of the other four instance creation methods is specified in Collection in a similar way. First an instance is created (with the expression self new) and then the arguments, in order, are added to the instance. The new instance is returned as the result. The instance is created using self new, rather than super new or self basicNew, because a subclass of Collection might reimplement the message new. Any subclass of Collection that represents fixed-size objects with indexed instance variables must reimplement the following instance creation messages since such a subclass cannot provide an implementation for new.

class name	Collection
superclass	Object
class methods	

instance creation

with: anObject
  | newCollection |
  newCollection ← self new.
  newCollection add: anObject.
  ↑newCollection

with: firstObject with: secondObject
  | newCollection |
  newCollection ← self new.
  newCollection add: firstObject.
  newCollection add: secondObject.
  ↑newCollection

with: firstObject with: secondObject with: thirdObject
  | newCollection |
  newCollection ← self new.
  newCollection add: firstObject.
  newCollection add: secondObject.
  newCollection add: thirdObject.
  ↑newCollection

**with: firstObject with: secondObject with: thirdObject
  with: fourthObject**
  | newCollection |
  newCollection ← self new.
  newCollection add: firstObject.
  newCollection add: secondObject.
  newCollection add: thirdObject.
  newCollection add: fourthObject.
  ↑newCollection

The implementation of each of the instance creation messages depends on the ability of the newly-created instance to respond to the message add:. Class Collection cannot provide implementations of the following messages because they depend on the representation used by a subclass:

  add: anObject
  remove: anObject ifAbsent: aBlock
  do: aBlock

All other messages in the basic collection protocol are implemented in terms of these three messages. Each subclass must implement the three basic messages; each can then reimplement any others in order to improve its performance.

☐ Collection *adding protocol* The protocol for adding elements to a collection is implemented in class Collection as follows.

adding

add: anObject
> self subclassResponsibility

addAll: aCollection
> aCollection do: [:each | self add: each].
> ↑aCollection

Notice that the implementation of addAll: depends on both do: and add:. The order of adding elements from the argument, aCollection, depends on both the order in which the collection enumerates its elements (do:) and the manner in which the elements are included into this collection (add:).

☐ Collection *removing protocol* The messages remove: and removeAll: are implemented in terms of the basic message remove:ifAbsent:, which must be provided in a subclass. These methods report an error if the element to be removed is not in the collection. The method remove:ifAbsent: can be used to specify different exception behavior.

removing

remove: anObject ifAbsent: exceptionBlock
> self subclassResponsibility

remove: anObject
> self remove: anObject ifAbsent: [self errorNotFound]

removeAll: aCollection
> aCollection do: [:each | self remove: each].
> ↑aCollection

private

errorNotFound
> self error: 'Object is not in the collection'

As usual, the category private refers to messages introduced to support the implementations of other messages; it is not to be used by other objects. Most error messages that are used more than once will be specified as private messages in order to create the literal message string once only.

☐ Collection *testing protocol* All the messages in the protocol for testing the status of a collection can be implemented in Collection.

testing

> **isEmpty**
> > ↑self size = 0
>
> **includes: anObject**
> > self do: [:each | anObject = each ifTrue: [↑true]].
> > ↑false
>
> **occurrencesOf: anObject**
> > | tally |
> > tally ← 0.
> > self do: [:each | anObject = each ifTrue: [tally ← tally + 1]].
> > ↑tally

The implementations of includes: and occurrencesOf: depend on the subclass's implementation of the basic enumerating message do:. The block argument of do: in the method for includes: terminates as soon as an element equal to the argument is found. If no such element is found, the last expression (↑false) is evaluated. The response to isEmpty and includes: are Boolean objects, true or false. The message size is inherited from class Object, but is reimplemented in Collection because size, as defined in Object, is only nonzero for variable-length objects.

accessing

> **size**
> > | tally |
> > tally ← 0.
> > self do: [:each | tally ← tally + 1].
> > ↑tally

This is a low-performance approach to computing the size of a collection which, as we shall see, is reimplemented in most of the subclasses.

☐ Collection *enumerating protocol*   An implementation of all of the messages that enumerate the elements of collections, except do:, can be provided in class Collection.

enumerating

> **do: aBlock**
> > self subclassResponsibility
>
> **collect: aBlock**
> > | newCollection |
> > newCollection ← self species new.
> > self do: [:each | newCollection add: (aBlock value: each)].
> > ↑newCollection
>
> **detect: aBlock**
> > ↑self detect: aBlock ifNone: [self errorNotFound]

detect: aBlock ifNone: exceptionBlock
    self do: [:each | (aBlock value: each) ifTrue: [↑each]].
    ↑exceptionBlock value
inject: thisValue into: binaryBlock
    | nextValue |
    nextValue ← thisValue.
    self do: [:each | nextValue ← binaryBlock value: nextValue value: each].
    ↑nextValue
reject: aBlock
    ↑self select: [:element | (aBlock value: element) == false]
select: aBlock
    | newCollection |
    newCollection ← self species new.
    self do: [:each | (aBlock value: each) ifTrue: [newCollection add: each]].
    ↑newCollection

In the methods associated with collect: and select:, the message species is sent to self. This message was not shown in Chapter 9 because it is not part of the external protocol of collections. It is categorized as private to indicate the intention for internal use only. The message is implemented in class Object as returning the class of the receiver.

    private

    species
        ↑self class

Thus the expression

    self species new

means "create a new instance of the same class as that of the receiver."

For some collections, it may not be appropriate to create a "similar" instance in this way; a new collection that is like it may not be an instance of its class. Such a collection will override the message species. In particular, an Interval responds that its species is Array (because it is not possible to modify an Interval); the species of a MappedCollection is the species of the collection it maps (since the MappedCollection is simply acting as an accessor for that collection).

If a collection cannot create an instance by simply sending the class the message new, it must reimplement messages collect: and select:. Since reject: is implemented in terms of select:, it need not be reimplemented.

The method for inject:into: evaluates the block argument once for each element in the receiver. The block is also provided with its own value from each previous evaluation; the initial value is provided as the argument of inject:. The final value of the block is returned as the value of the inject:into: message.

The reason for the introduction of two messages, detect: and detect:ifNone:, is similar to the reason for the two removing messages, remove: and remove:ifAbsent:. The general case (detect:) reports an error if no element meeting the detection criterion is found; the programmer can avoid this error report by specifying an alternative exception (detect:ifNone:).

☐ Collection *converting protocol*   The protocol for converting from any collection into a Bag, Set, OrderedCollection, or SortedCollection is implemented in a straightforward way—create a new instance of the target collection, then add to it each element of the receiver. In most cases, the new instance is the same size as the original collection. In the case of OrderedCollections, elements are added at the end of the sequence (addLast:), regardless of the order of enumerating from the source.

converting

asBag
   | aBag |
   aBag ← Bag new.
   self do: [:each | aBag add: each].
   ↑aBag

asOrderedCollection
   | anOrderedCollection |
   anOrderedCollection ← OrderedCollection new: self size.
   self do: [:each | anOrderedCollection addLast: each].
   ↑anOrderedCollection

asSet
   | aSet |
   aSet ← Set new: self size.
   self do: [:each | aSet add: each].
   ↑aSet

asSortedCollection
   | aSortedCollection |
   aSortedCollection ← SortedCollection new: self size.
   aSortedCollection addAll: self.
   ↑aSortedCollection

asSortedCollection: aBlock
   | aSortedCollection |
   aSortedCollection ← SortedCollection new: self size.
   aSortedCollection sortBlock: aBlock.
   aSortedCollection addAll: self.
   ↑aSortedCollection

☐ Collection *printing protocol* The implementations of the printOn: and storeOn: messages in Object are overridden in Collection. Collections print in the form

className (element element element)

Collections store themselves as an expression from which an equal collection can be constructed. This takes the form of

((className new))

or

((className new) add: element; yourself)

or

((className new) add: element; add: element; yourself)

with the appropriate number of cascaded messages for adding each element, depending on whether the collection has no, one, or more elements. The message yourself returns the receiver of the message. It is used in cascaded messages to guarantee that the result of the cascaded message is the receiver. All objects respond to the message yourself; it is defined in class Object.

The general methods for printing and storing are

printing

printOn: aStream
   | tooMany |
   tooMany ← aStream position + self maxPrint.
   aStream nextPutAll: self class name, ' ('.
   self do: .
     [:element |
      aStream position > tooMany
       ifTrue: [aStream nextPutAll: '...etc...)' . ↑self].
      element printOn: aStream.
      aStream space].
   aStream nextPut: $)

storeOn: aStream
   | noneYet |
   aStream nextPutAll: '(('.
   aStream nextPutAll: self class name.
   aStream nextPutAll: 'new)'.
   noneYet ← true.
   self do:
     [:each |
      noneYet
       ifTrue: [noneYet ← false]

```
            ifFalse: [aStream nextPut: $;].
          aStream nextPutAll: 'add:'.
          aStream store: each].
      noneYet ifFalse: [aStream nextPutAll: '; yourself'].
      aStream nextPut: $)
```

private

maxPrint
↑5000

These methods make use of instances of a kind of Stream that acts as an accessor for a String. The method printOn: sets a threshold for the length of the String to be created; a long collection may print as

className (element element ...etc...)

The threshold is determined as the response to the message maxPrint which is set at 5000 characters. Subclasses can override the private message maxPrint in order to modify the threshold.

Note that this technique of using a method rather than a variable is a way of providing a parameter in a method. A variable cannot be used as the parameter because the variable, to be accessible to all instances, would have to be a class variable. Subclasses cannot specify a class variable whose name is the same as a class variable in one of its superclasses; thus if a subclass wants to change the value of the variable, it will do so for instances of its superclass as well. This is not the desired effect.

The printing format is modified in several subclasses. Array does not print its class name; Intervals print using the shorthand notation of the messages to: and to:by: to a Number. A Symbol prints its characters (without the # prefix of the literal form of a Symbol); a String prints its characters delimited by single quotes.

The storeOn: message is reimplemented in ArrayedCollection and several of its subclasses because instances are created using new: anInteger rather than simply new. Arrays, Strings, and Symbols store in their literal forms. Intervals use the shorthand notation of messages to: and to:by:. MappedCollections store using the converting message mappedBy: that is sent to the collection that is indirectly accessed.

Subclasses of Collection

For each subclass of Collection, we show the methods that implement the three required messages (add:, remove:ifAbsent:, and do:) and the messages in the adding, removing, testing, and enumerating protocols that are reimplemented. New collection protocol for a particular sub-class as specified in Chapter 9 will generally not be presented in this chapter.

Class Bag

Bag represents an unordered collection in which an element can appear more than once. Since the elements of Bags are unordered, the messages at: and at:put: are reimplemented to report an error.

Instances of Bag have an instance of Dictionary as a single instance variable named contents. Each unique element of a Bag is the key of an Association in contents; the value of an Association is an Integer representing the number of times the element appears in the Bag. Removing an element decrements the tally; when the tally falls below 1, the Association is removed from contents. Bag implements new, size, includes:, and occurrencesOf:. A new instance must initialize its instance variable to be a Dictionary. The reimplementation of size is made efficient by summing all the values of elements of contents. The arguments of the testing messages are used as keys of contents. In implementing includes:, the responsibility for checking is passed to contents. In order to answer the query occurrencesOf: anObject, the method checks that anObject is included as a key in contents and then looks up the value (the tally) associated with it.

class name	Bag
superclass	Collection
instance variable names	contents
class methods	

instance creation

new
    ↑super new setDictionary

instance methods

accessing

at: index
    self errorNotKeyed
at: index put: anObject
    self errorNotKeyed
size
    | tally |
    tally ← 0
    contents do: [:each | tally ← tally + each].
    ↑tally

testing

includes: anObject
    ↑contents includesKey: anObject

occurrencesOf: anObject
> (self includes: anObject)
> > ifTrue: [↑contents at: anObject]
> > ifFalse: [↑0]

private

setDictionary
> contents ← Dictionary new

(in Collection)

private

errorNotKeyed
> self error:
> > self class name, 's do not respond to keyed accessing messages'

To add an element is to add it once, but Bags can add multiple times. The implementation of add: calls on add:withOccurrences:. Removing an element checks the number of occurrences, decrementing the tally or removing the element as a key in contents if the tally is less than 1.

adding

add: newObject
> ↑self add: newObject withOccurrences: 1

add: newObject withOccurrences: anInteger
> contents at: newObject
> > put: anInteger + (self occurrencesOf: newObject).
> ↑newObject

removing

remove: oldObject ifAbsent: exceptionBlock
> | count |
> count ← self occurrencesOf: oldObject.
> count = 0 ifTrue: [↑exceptionBlock value].
> count = 1
> > ifTrue: [contents removeKey: oldObject]
> > ifFalse: [contents at: oldObject put: count − 1]].
> ↑oldObject

Enumerating the elements of a Bag means selecting each element of the Dictionary and evaluating a block with the key of that element (i.e., the actual Bag element is the key of the Dictionary). This has to be done multiple times, once for each occurrence of the element, as indicated by the value associated with the key.

enumerating

do: aBlock
 contents associationsDo:
  [:assoc | assoc value timesRepeat: [aBlock value: assoc key]]

Class Set

The elements of Sets are unordered like those of Bags, so the messages at: and at:put: produce an error report. A Set may not contain an element more than once, therefore, every insertion of an element must, in theory, check the entire collection. To avoid searching all elements, a Set determines where in its indexed instance variables to start a search for a particular element by using a hashing technique.

Each Set has an instance variable named tally. Maintaining this tally of the number of elements avoids the inefficiencies involved in determining the size of the Set by counting every non-nil element. Thus new, new:, and size are reimplemented; the first two in order to initialize the variable tally and the last simply to respond with the value of tally.

class name	Set
superclass	Collection
instance variable names	tally
class methods	

instance creation

new
 ↑self new: 2
new: anInteger
 ↑(super new: anInteger) setTally

instance methods

accessing

at: index
 self errorNotKeyed
at: index put: anObject
 self errorNotKeyed
size
 ↑tally

private

setTally
 tally ← 0

In the method for new:, super is used in order to avoid recursion. A private message of Set, findElementOrNil:, hashes the argument to produce the index at which to begin the probe of the Set. The probe proceeds until the argument, anObject, is found, or until nil is encountered. The response is the index of the last position checked. Then the testing messages are implemented as

testing

includes: anObject

↑(self basicAt: (self findElementOrNil: anObject)) ~~ nil

occurrencesOf: anObject

(self includes: anObject)
    ifTrue: [↑1]
    ifFalse: [↑0]

The number of occurrences of any element in the Set is never more than 1. The three basic messages must make use of basicAt: and basicAt:put: because Sets report an error if at: or at:put: is used.

adding

add: newObject

| index |
newObject isNil ifTrue: [↑newObject].
index ← self findElementOrNil: newObject.
(self basicAt: index) isNil
    ifTrue: [self basicAt: index put: newObject. tally ← tally + 1].
↑newObject

removing

remove: oldObject ifAbsent: aBlock

| index |
index ← self find: oldObject ifAbsent: [↑aBlock value].
self basicAt: index put: nil.
tally ← tally − 1.
self fixCollisionsFrom: index.
↑oldObject

enumerating

do: aBlock

1 to: self basicSize do:
    [:index |
      (self basicAt: index) isNil
          ifFalse: [aBlock value: (self basicAt: index)]]

The private message find:ifAbsent: calls on findElementOrNil:; if the element, oldObject, is not found, the argument aBlock is evaluated. In order to guarantee that the hashing/probing technique works properly, remaining elements might need to be compacted whenever one is removed (fixCollisionsFrom:). These methods are good examples of when the accessing messages basicAt:, basicAt:put:, and basicSize must be used.

Class Dictionary

A Dictionary is a collection of Associations. Class Dictionary uses a hashing technique to locate its elements which is like that of its superclass, Set, but hashes on the keys in the Associations instead of on the Associations themselves. Most of the accessing messages for Dictionary are reimplemented to treat the values of the Associations as the elements, not the Associations themselves.

Dictionary implements at: and at:put:, but redefines the argument associated with the keyword at: to be any key in the Dictionary (not necessarily an Integer index). The argument of includes: is the value of one of the Associations in the Dictionary, not one of the Associations themselves. The message do: enumerates the values, not the Associations. The argument to remove: is also a value, but this is an inappropriate way to delete from a Dictionary because elements are referenced with keys. Either removeAssociation: or removeKey: should be used. Thus the messages remove: and remove:ifAbsent: should not be implemented for Dictionary.

Much of the work in the accessing protocol is done in private messages, either those inherited from Set or similar ones for finding a key (findKeyOrNil:).

class name	Dictionary
superclass	Set
instance methods	

accessing

at: key
    ↑self at: key ifAbsent: [self errorKeyNotFound]
at: key put: anObject
    | index element |
    index ← self findKeyOrNil: key.
    element ← self basicAt: index.
    element isNil
        ifTrue:
            [self basicAt: index put: (Association key: key value: anObject).
            tally ← tally + 1]
            "element is an Association. The key already exists, change its
                value."
        ifFalse:
            [element value: anObject].
    ↑anObject
at: key ifAbsent: aBlock
    | index |
    index ← self findKey: key ifAbsent: [↑aBlock value].
    ↑(self basicAt: index) value

testing

includes: anObject

"Revert to the method used in Collection."
self do: [:each | anObject = each ifTrue: [↑true]].
↑false

adding

add: anAssociation

| index element |
index ← self findKeyOrNil: anAssociation key.
element ← self basicAt: index.
element isNil
    ifTrue: [self basicAt: index put: anAssociation.
        tally ← tally + 1]
    ifFalse: [element value: anAssociation value].
↑anAssociation

removing

remove: anObject ifAbsent: aBlock

self shouldNotImplement

enumerating

do: aBlock

self associationsDo: [:assoc | aBlock value: assoc value]

private

errorKeyNotFound

self error: 'key not found'

Notice the similarity between at:put: and add:. The difference is in the action taken if the element is not found—in the case of at:put:, a new Association is created and stored in the Dictionary; in the case of add:, the argument, anAssociation, is stored so that any shared reference to the Association is preserved.

The message collect: is reimplemented in order to avoid the problems of collecting possibly identical values into a Set which would result in throwing away duplications. The message select: is reimplemented in order to select Associations by applying their values as the arguments to the block.

enumerating

collect: aBlock

| newCollection |
newCollection ← Bag new.
self do: [:each | newCollection add: (aBlock value: each)].
↑newCollection

select: aBlock
   | newCollection |
   newCollection ← self species new.
   self associationsDo:
     [:each |
      (aBlock value: each value) ifTrue: [newCollection add: each]].
   ↑newCollection

IdentityDictionary overrides at:, at:put:, and add: in order to implement checking for identical keys instead of equal keys. An IdentityDictionary is implemented as two parallel ordered collections of keys and values, rather than as a single collection of Associations. Thus do: must also be reimplemented. The implementation is not shown.

Sequenceable-Collections

SequenceableCollection is the superclass for all collections whose elements are ordered. Of the messages we are examining, remove:ifAbsent: is specified as being inappropriate for SequenceableCollections in general, since the order of elements might have been externally specified and it is assumed that they should be removed in order. Because SequenceableCollections are ordered, elements are accessed using at:; the implementation is provided in class Object. The message do: is implemented by accessing each element at index 1 through the size of the collection. SequenceableCollections are created using the message new:. Therefore, collect: and select: must be reimplemented to create the new collection using new: rather than new. The methods for collect: and select: shown next use a WriteStream in order to access the new collection, and the message at: in order to access elements of the original collection.

class name	SequenceableCollection
superclass	Collection
instance methods	

accessing

   size
     self subclassResponsibility

removing

   remove: oldObject ifAbsent: anExceptionBlock
     self shouldNotImplement

enumerating

   do: aBlock
     | index length |
     index ← 0.
     length ← self size.

```
        [(index ← index + 1) < = length]
            whileTrue: [aBlock value: (self at: index)]
```

collect: aBlock
```
    | aStream index length |
    aStream ← WriteStream on: (self species new: self size).
    index ← 0.
    length ← self size.
    [(index ← index + 1) < = length]
        whileTrue: [aStream nextPut: (aBlock value: (self at: index))].
    ↑aStream contents
```

select: aBlock
```
    | aStream index length |
    aStream ← WriteStream on: (self species new: self size).
    index ← 0.
    length ← self size.
    [(index ← index + 1) < = length]
        whileTrue:
            [(aBlock value: (self at: index))
                ifTrue: [aStream nextPut: (self at: index)]].
    ↑aStream contents
```

Notice that size is declared as a subclass responsibility in SequenceableCollection. The method inherited from the superclass Collection uses do: to enumerate and thereby count each element. But the method for do: as specified in SequenceableCollection determines the limit for indexing by requesting the size of the collection. Therefore, size must be reimplemented in order not to be stated in terms of do:.

Subclasses of
Sequenceable-
Collection

☐ *Class* LinkedList   Elements of LinkedList are instances of Link or of one of its subclasses. Each LinkedList has two instance variables, a reference to the first and to the last elements. Adding an element is assumed to be interpreted as adding to the end (addLast:); the method for addLast: is to make the element the next link of the current last link. Removing an element means that the element's preceding link must reference the element's succeeding link (or nil). If the element to be removed is the first one, then its succeeding link becomes the first one.

class name	LinkedList
superclass	SequenceableCollection
instance variable names	firstLink
	lastLink

instance methods

accessing

at: index
```
    | count element size |
    count ← 1.
```

```
              element ← self first.
              size ← self size.
          [count > size] whileFalse:
              [count = index
                 ifTrue: [↑element]
                 ifFalse: [count ← count + 1.
                           element ← element nextLink]].
          ↑self errorSubscriptBounds: index
```

at: index put: element
```
          self error: 'Do not store into a LinkedList using at:put: '
```

adding

add: aLink
```
          ↑self addLast: aLink
```
addLast: aLink
```
          self isEmpty
             ifTrue: [firstLink ← aLink]
             ifFalse: [lastLink nextLink: aLink].
          lastLink ← aLink.
          ↑aLink
```

removing

remove: aLink ifAbsent: aBlock
```
          | tempLink |
          aLink == firstLink
             ifTrue:
                [firstLink ← aLink nextLink.
                 aLink == lastLink ifTrue: [lastLink ←nil]]
             ifFalse:
                [tempLink ← firstLink.
                 [tempLink isNil ifTrue: [↑aBlock value].
                 tempLink nextLink == aLink]
                     whileFalse: [tempLink ← tempLink nextLink].
                 tempLink nextLink: aLink nextLink.
                 aLink == lastLink ifTrue: [lastLink ← tempLink]].
          aLink nextLink: nil.
          ↑aLink
```

enumerating

do: aBlock
```
          | aLink |
          aLink ← firstLink.
          [aLink isNil] whileFalse:
             [aBlock value: aLink.
              aLink ← aLink nextLink]
```

A nil link signals the end of the LinkedList. Thus the enumerating message do: is implemented as a simple loop that continues until a nil is encountered in the collection.

☐ *Class* Interval Intervals are SequenceableCollections whose elements are computed. Therefore, messages for adding and removing cannot be supported. Since elements are not explicitly stored, all accessing (at:, size, and do:) requires a computation. Each method checks to see if the last element computed is to be incremented (positive step) or decremented (negative step) in order to determine whether the limit (stop) has been reached.

class name	Interval
superclass	SequenceableCollection
instance variable names	start
	stop
	step

class methods

instance creation

from: startInteger to: stopInteger
↑self new
    setFrom: startInteger
    to: stopInteger
    by: 1

from: startInteger to: stopInteger by: stepInteger
↑self new
    setFrom: startInteger
    to: stopInteger
    by: stepInteger

instance methods

accessing

size
step < 0
    ifTrue: [start < stop
                ifTrue: [↑0]
                ifFalse: [↑stop − start // step + 1]]
    ifFalse: [stop < start
                ifTrue: [↑0]
                ifFalse: [↑stop − start // step + 1]]
at: index
(index > = 1 and: [index < = self size])
    ifTrue: [↑start + (step * (index − 1))]
    ifFalse: [self errorSubscriptBounds: index]

Implementation of the Basic Collection Protocol

at: index put: anObject
> self error: 'you cannot store into an Interval'

adding

add: newObject
> self error: 'elements cannot be added to an Interval'

removing

remove: newObject
> self error: 'elements cannot be removed from an Interval'

enumerating

do: aBlock
> | aValue |
> aValue ← start.
> step < 0
>   ifTrue: [[stop < = aValue]
>   whileTrue: [aBlock value: aValue.
>   aValue ← aValue + step]]
>   ifFalse: [[stop > = aValue]
>   whileTrue: [aBlock value: aValue.
>   aValue ← aValue + step]]

collect: aBlock
> | nextValue i result |
> result ← self species new: self size.
> nextValue ← start.
> i ← 1.
> step < 0
>   ifTrue: [[stop < = nextValue]
>   whileTrue:
>   [result at: i put: (aBlock value: nextValue).
>   nextValue ← nextValue + step.
>   i ← i + 1]]
>   ifFalse: [[stop > = nextValue]
>   whileTrue:
>   [result at: i put: (aBlock value: nextValue).
>   nextValue ← nextValue + step.
>   i ← i + 1]].
> ↑result

private

setFrom: startInteger to: stopInteger by: stepInteger
> start ← startInteger.
> stop ← stopInteger.
> step ← stepInteger

☐ ArrayedCollections—Array, ByteArray, String, Text, *and* Symbol
ArrayedCollection is a subclass of SequenceableCollection; each
ArrayedCollection is a variable-length object. All instance creation
methods are reimplemented to use new:, not new. ArrayedCollections are
fixed-length so add: is disallowed; in its superclass, remove: was already
disallowed and do: was implemented. Only size, therefore, is
implemented in ArrayedCollection—it is a system primitive that reports
the number of indexed instance variables.

Of the subclasses of ArrayedCollection, Array, and ByteArray do not
reimplement any of the messages we are examining in this chapter.
Accessing messages for String—at:, at:put:, and size—are system primitives; in Text, all accessing messages are passed as messages to the instance variable string (which is an instance of String). Symbol disallows
at:put: and returns String as its species.

☐ OrderedCollections *and* SortedCollections   OrderedCollection stores
an ordered, contiguous sequence of elements. Since OrderedCollections
are expandable, some efficiency is gained by allocating extra space for
the sequence. Two instance variables, firstIndex and lastIndex, point to
the first and the last actual elements in the sequence.

The index into OrderedCollection is converted to be within the range
of firstIndex to lastIndex for accessing messages (at: and at:put:) and the
size is simply one more than the difference between the two indices.
Adding an element is interpreted to be adding to the end; if there is no
room at the end, the collection is copied with additional space allocated
(makeRoomAtLast is the private message that does this work). The actual location for storing an element is the computed index position after
lastIndex. If an element is removed, then the remaining elements must
be moved up so that elements remain contiguous (removeIndex:).

class name	OrderedCollection
superclass	SequenceableCollection
instance variable names	firstIndex
	lastIndex

class methods
instance creation

new
↑self new: 10
new: anInteger
↑(super new: anInteger) setIndices

instance methods

accessing

size
↑lastIndex − firstIndex + 1

Implementation of the Basic Collection Protocol

at: anInteger
  (anInteger < 1 or: [anInteger + firstIndex − 1 > lastIndex])
    ifTrue: [self errorNoSuchElement]
    ifFalse: [↑super at: anInteger + firstIndex − 1]

at: anInteger put: anObject
  | index |
  index ← anInteger truncated.
  (index < 1 or: [index + firstIndex − 1 > lastIndex])
    ifTrue: [self errorNoSuchElement]
    ifFalse: [↑super at: index + firstIndex − 1 put: anObject]

adding

add: newObject
  ↑self addLast: aLink

addLast: newObject
  lastIndex = self basicSize ifTrue: [self makeRoomAtLast].
  lastIndex ← lastIndex˙+ 1.
  self basicAt: lastIndex put: newObject.
  ↑newObject

removing

remove: oldObject ifAbsent: absentBlock
  | index |
  index ← firstIndex.
  [index <= lastIndex]
    whileTrue:
      [oldObject = (self basicAt: index)
        ifTrue: [self removeIndex: index.
          ↑oldObject]
        ifFalse: [index ← index + 1]].
  ↑absentBlock value

private

setIndices
  firstIndex ← self basicSize // 2 max: 1.
  lastIndex ← firstIndex − 1 max: 0

errorNoSuchElement
  self error:
    ' attempt to index non-existent element in an ordered collection '

The enumerating messages do:, collect:, and select: are each reimplemented—do: in order to provide better performance than the method provided in SequenceableCollection.

enumerating

do: aBlock

```
| index |
index ← firstIndex.
[index < = lastIndex]
    whileTrue:
        [aBlock value: (self basicAt: index).
        index ← index + 1]
```

collect: aBlock

```
| newCollection |
newCollection ← self species new.
self do: [ :each | newCollection add: (aBlock value: each)].
↑newCollection
```

select: aBlock

```
| newCollection |
newCollection ← self copyEmpty.
self do: [ :each | (aBlock value: each) ifTrue: [newCollection add: each]].
↑newCollection
```

In the method for select:, the new collection is created by sending the original collection the message copyEmpty. This message creates a new collection with enough space allocated to hold all the elements of the original, although all the elements might not be stored. In this way, time taken in expanding the new collection is avoided.

SortedCollection is a subclass of OrderedCollection. The message at:put: reports an error, requesting the programmer to use add:; add: inserts the new element according to the value of the instance variable sortBlock. The determination of the position for insertion is done as a "bubble sort." collect: is also reimplemented to create an OrderedCollection rather than a SortedCollection for collecting the values of the block. The code is not shown; a bubble sort looks the same in Smalltalk-80 as it would in most programming languages.

Class
MappedCollection

Instances of MappedCollection have two instance variables—domain and map. The value of domain is either a Dictionary or a SequenceableCollection; its elements are accessed indirectly through map. The message add: is disallowed. Both at: and at:put: are reimplemented in MappedCollection in order to support the indirect access from map to the elements of domain. The size of a MappedCollection is the size of its domain.

class name	MappedCollection
superclass	Collection
instance variable names	domain
	map

class methods

instance creation

collection: domainCollection map: mapCollection
↑super new setCollection: domainCollection map: mapCollection
new
self error: ' use collection:map: to create a MappedCollection'

instance methods

accessing

at: anIndex
↑domain at: (map at: anIndex)
at: anIndex put: anObject
↑domain at: (map at: anIndex) put: anObject
size
↑map size

adding

add: newObject
self shouldNotImplement

enumerating

do: aBlock
map do:
   [:mapValue | aBlock value: (domain at: mapValue)]
collect: aBlock
| aStream |
aStream ← WriteStream on: (self species new: self size).
self do: [:domainValue |
     aStream nextPut: (aBlock value: domainValue)].
↑aStream contents
select: aBlock
| aStream |
aStream ← WriteStream on: (self species new: self size).
self do:
   [:domainValue |
    (aBlock value: domainValue)
       ifTrue: [aStream nextPut: domainValue]].
↑aStream contents

private

setCollection: domainCollection map: mapCollection
domain ← domainCollection.
map ← mapCollection
species
↑domain species

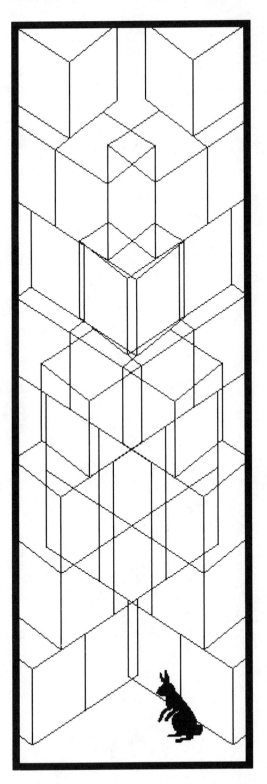

14

Kernel Support Classes

Class UndefinedObject

Classes Boolean, True, **and** False

Additional Protocol for Class Object
Dependence Relationships Among Objects
Message Handling
System Primitive Messages

```
Object

    Magnitude                                  Stream
        Character                                  PositionableStream
        Date                                           ReadStream
        Time                                           WriteStream
                                                           ReadWriteStream
        Number                                                 ExternalStream
            Float                                                  FileStream
            Fraction
            Integer                                Random
                LargeNegativeInteger
                LargePositiveInteger           File
                SmallInteger                   FileDirectory
                                               FilePage

        LookupKey                              UndefinedObject
            Association                        Boolean
                                                   False
Link                                               True

    Process
                                               ProcessorScheduler
Collection                                     Delay
                                               SharedQueue
    SequenceableCollection
        LinkedList                             Behavior
                                                   ClassDescription
            Semaphore                                  Class
                                                       MetaClass
        ArrayedCollection
            Array                              Point
                                               Rectangle
            Bitmap                             BitBlt
                DisplayBitmap                      CharacterScanner

            RunArray                               Pen
            String
                Symbol                         DisplayObject
            Text                                   DisplayMedium
            ByteArray                                  Form
                                                           Cursor
        Interval                                           DisplayScreen
        OrderedCollection                          InfiniteForm
            SortedCollection                       OpaqueForm
        Bag                                        Path
        MappedCollection                               Arc
        Set                                                Circle
            Dictionary                                 Curve
                IdentityDictionary                     Line
                                                       LinearFit
                                                       Spline
```

Class UndefinedObject

The object nil represents a value for uninitialized variables. It also represents meaningless results. It is the only instance of class UndefinedObject.

The purpose of including class UndefinedObject in the system is to handle error messages. The typical error in evaluating Smalltalk-80 expressions is that some object is sent a message it does not understand. Often this occurs because a variable is not properly initialized—in many cases, the variable name that should refer to some other object refers to nil instead. The error message is of the form

className does not understand messageSelector

where className mentions the class of the receiver and messageSelector is the selector of the erroneously-sent message.

Note, if nil were an instance of Object, then a message sent to it in error would state

Object does not understand messageSelector

which is less explicit than stating that an undefined object does not understand the message. At the price of a class description, it was possible to improve on the error message.

Tests to see if an object is nil are handled in class Object, but reimplemented in UndefinedObject. In class Object, messages isNil and notNil are implemented as

isNil
↑false
notNil
↑true

In class UndefinedObject, messages isNil and notNil are implemented as

isNil
↑true
notNil
↑false

so that no conditional test in Object is required.

Classes Boolean, True, and False

Protocol for logical values is provided by the class Boolean; logical values are represented by subclasses of Boolean—True and False. The subclasses add no new protocol; they reimplement many messages to have better performance than the methods in the superclass. The idea is similar to that in testing for nil in Object and UndefinedObject; true knows that it represents logical truth and false knows that it represents logical falsehood. We show the implementation of some of the controlling protocol to illustrate this idea.

The logical operations are

Boolean instance protocol

logical operations

& aBoolean	Evaluating conjunction. Answer true if both the receiver and the argument are true.
| aBoolean	Evaluating disjunction. Answer true if either the receiver or the argument is true.
not	Negation. Answer true if the receiver is false, answer false if the receiver is true.
eqv: aBoolean	Answer true if the receiver is equivalent to the argument, aBoolean.
xor: aBoolean	Exclusive OR. Answer true if the receiver is not equivalent to aBoolean.

These conjunction and disjunction operations are "evaluating"—this means that the argument is evaluated regardless of the value of the receiver. This is in contrast to and: and or: in which the receiver determines whether to evaluate the argument.

Boolean instance protocol

controlling

and: alternativeBlock	Nonevaluating conjunction. If the receiver is true, answer the value of the argument; otherwise, answer false without evaluating the argument.
or: alternativeBlock	Nonevaluating disjunction. If the receiver is false, answer the value of the argument; otherwise, answer true without evaluating the argument.
ifTrue: trueAlternativeBlock ifFalse: falseAlternativeBlock	Conditional statement. If the receiver is true, answer the result of evaluating trueAlternativeBlock; otherwise answer the result of evaluating falseAlternativeBlock.
ifFalse: falseAlternativeBlock ifTrue: trueAlternativeBlock	Conditional statement. If the receiver is true, answer the result of evaluating trueAlternativeBlock; otherwise answer the result of evaluating falseAlternativeBlock.
ifTrue: trueAlternativeBlock	Conditional statement. If the receiver is true, answer the result of evaluating trueAlternativeBlock; otherwise answer nil.
ifFalse: falseAlternativeBlock	Conditional statement. If the receiver is false, answer the result of evaluating falseAlternativeBlock; otherwise answer nil.

The arguments to and: and or: must be blocks in order to defer evaluation. Conditional statements are provided as messages ifTrue:ifFalse:, ifFalse:ifTrue:, ifTrue:, and ifFalse:, as already specified and exemplified throughout the previous chapters. The messages are implemented in the subclasses of class Boolean so that the appropriate argument block is evaluated.

In class True, the methods are

ifTrue: trueAlternativeBlock ifFalse: falseAlternativeBlock
↑trueAlternativeBlock value
ifFalse: falseAlternativeBlock ifTrue: trueAlternativeBlock
↑trueAlternativeBlock value
ifTrue: trueAlternativeBlock
↑trueAlternativeBlock value
ifFalse: falseAlternativeBlock
↑nil

In class False, the methods are

ifTrue: trueAlternativeBlock ifFalse: falseAlternativeBlock
↑falseAlternativeBlock value
ifFalse: falseAlternativeBlock ifTrue: trueAlternativeBlock
↑falseAlternativeBlock value
ifTrue: trueAlternativeBlock
↑nil
ifFalse: falseAlternativeBlock
↑falseAlternativeBlock value

If x is 3, then

$$x > 0 \text{ ifTrue: } [x \leftarrow x - 1] \text{ ifFalse: } [x \leftarrow x + 1]$$

is interpreted as $x > 0$ evaluates to true, the sole instance of class True; the method for ifTrue:ifFalse: is found in class True, so the block $[x \leftarrow x - 1]$ is evaluated without further testing.

In this way, the message lookup mechanism provides an effective implementation of conditional control with no additional primitive operations or circular definitions.

Additional Protocol for Class Object

Protocol for class Object, shared by all objects, was introduced in Chapter 6. Several categories of messages were not included in that early discussion. Most of these are part of Object's protocol to provide system support for message handling, dependence relationships, primitive message handling, and system primitives.

*Dependence
Relationships
Among Objects*

Information in the Smalltalk-80 system is represented by objects. The variables of objects themselves refer to objects; in this sense, objects are explicitly related or dependent on one another. Classes are related to their superclasses and metaclasses; these classes share external and internal descriptions and are thereby dependent on one another. These forms of dependency are central to the semantics of the Smalltalk-80 language. They coordinate descriptive information among objects.

An additional kind of dependency is supported in class Object. Its purpose is to *coordinate* activities among different objects. Specifically, its purpose is to be able to link one object, say A, to one or more other objects, say B, so B can be informed if A changes in any way. Upon being informed when A changes and the nature of the change, B can decide to take some action such as updating its own status. The concept of *change* and *update*, therefore, are integral to the support of this third kind of object dependence relationship.

The protocol in class Object is

Object instance protocol

---

dependents access

    addDependent: anObject — Add the argument, anObject, as one of the receiver's dependents.

    removeDependent: anObject — Remove the argument, anObject, as one of the receiver's dependents.

    dependents — Answer an OrderedCollection of the objects that are dependent on the receiver, that is, the objects that should be notified if the receiver changes.

    release — Remove references to objects that may refer back to the receiver. This message is reimplemented by any subclass that creates references to dependents; the expression super release is included in any such reimplementation.

change and update

    changed — The receiver changed in some general way; inform all the dependents by sending each dependent an update: message.

    changed: aParameter — The receiver changed; the change is denoted by the argument, aParameter. Usually the argument is a Symbol that is part of the dependent's change protocol; the default behavior is to use the receiver itself as the argument. Inform all of the dependents.

    update: aParameter — An object on whom the receiver is dependent has changed. The receiver updates its status accordingly (the default behavior is to do nothing).

    broadcast: aSymbol — Send the argument, aSymbol, as a unary message to all of the receiver's dependents.

broadcast: aSymbol with: anObject

> Send the argument, aSymbol, as a keyword
> message with argument, anObject, to all of the
> receiver's dependents.

Take, as an example, the objects that model traffic lights. A typical traffic light at a street corner is an object with three lights, each a different color. Only one of these lights can be ON at a given moment. In this sense, the ON-OFF status of each of the three lights is dependent on the status of the other two. There are a number of ways to create this relationship. Suppose we create the class Light as follows.

class name	Light
superclass	Object
instance variable names	status
class methods	

instance creation

setOn
    ↑self new setOn
setOff
    ↑self new setOff

instance methods

status

turnOn
    self isOff
      ifTrue: [status ← true. self changed]
turnOff
    self isOn
      ifTrue: [status ← false]

testing

isOn
    ↑status
isOff
    ↑status not

change and update

update: aLight
    aLight == self ifFalse: [self turnOff]

private

setOn
    status ← true
setOff
    status ← false

The model is very simple. A Light is either on or off, so a status flag is kept as an instance variable; it is true if the Light is on, false if the Light is off. Whenever a Light is turned on (turnOn), it sends itself the changed message. Any other status change is not broadcast to the dependents on the assumption that a Light is turned off in reaction to turning on another Light. The default response to changed is to send all dependents the message update: self (i.e., the object that changed is the argument to the update: message). Then update: is implemented in Light to mean turn off. If the parameter is the receiver, then, of course, the update: is ignored.

The class TrafficLight is defined to set up any number of coordinated lights. The instance creation message with: takes as its argument the number of Lights to be created. Each Light is dependent on all other Lights. When the TrafficLight is demolished, the dependencies among its Lights are disconnected (the message inherited from class Object for disconnecting dependents is release; it is implemented in TrafficLight in order to broadcast the message to all Lights).

class name	TrafficLight
superclass	Object
instance variable names	lights
class methods	

instance creation

with: numberOfLights
↑self new lights: numberOfLights

instance methods

operate

turnOn: lightNumber
(lights at: lightNumber) turnOn

initialize-release

release
super release.
lights do: [:eachLight | eachLight release].
lights ← nil

private

lights: numberOfLights
lights ← Array new: (numberOfLights max: 1).
lights at: 1 put: Light setOn.
2 to: numberOfLights do:
    [:index | lights at: index put: Light setOff].

```
lights do:
   [ :eachLight |
     lights do:
       [ :dependentLight |
         eachLight ~~ dependentLight
           ifTrue: [eachLight addDependent: dependentLight]]]
```

The private initialization method is lights: numberOfLights. Each light is created turned off except for the first light. Then each light is connected to all the other lights (using the message addDependent:). The simulated TrafficLight operates by some round robin, perhaps timed, sequencing through each light, turning it on. A simple example shown below creates the TrafficLight with the first light on, and then turns on each of the other lights, one at a time. A simulation of a traffic corner might include different models for controlling the lights.

```
trafficLight ← TrafficLight with: 3.
trafficLight turnOn: 2.
trafficLight turnOn: 3
```

The message turnOn: to a TrafficLight sends the message turnOn to the designated Light. If the Light is currently off, then it is set on and the message changed sent. The message changed sends update: to each dependent Light; if a dependent light is on, it is turned off.

A particularly important use of this dependency protocol is to support having multiple graphical images of an object. Each image is dependent on the object in the sense that, if the object changes, the image must be informed so that it can decide whether the change affects the displayed information. The user interface to the Smalltalk-80 system makes liberal use of this support for broadcasting notices that an object has changed; this is used to coordinate the contents of a sequence of menus of possible actions that the user can take with respect to the contents of information displayed on the screen. Menus themselves can be created by linking possible actions together, in a way similar to the way we linked together the traffic lights.

Message Handling

All processing in the Smalltalk-80 system is carried out by sending messages to objects. For reasons of efficiency, instances of class Message are only created when an error occurs and the message state must be stored in an accessible structure. Most messages in the system, therefore, do not take the form of directly creating an instance of Message and transmitting it to an object.

In some circumstances, it is useful to compute the message selector of a message transmission. For example, suppose that a list of possible message selectors is kept by an object and, based on a computation, one of these selectors is chosen. Suppose it is assigned as a value of a variable selector. Now we wish to transmit the message to some object, say, to receiver. We can not simply write the expression as

receiver selector

because this means—send the object referred to by receiver the unary message selector. We could, however, write

receiver perform: selector

The result is to transmit the value of the argument, selector, as the message to receiver. Protocol to support this ability to send a computed message to an object is provided in class Object. This protocol includes methods for transmitting computed keyword as well as unary messages.

Object instance protocol

message handling

perform: aSymbol

Send the receiver the unary message indicated by the argument, aSymbol. The argument is the selector of the message. Report an error if the number of arguments expected by the selector is not zero.

perform: aSymbol with: anObject

Send the receiver the keyword message indicated by the arguments. The first argument, aSymbol, is the selector of the message. The other argument, anObject, is the argument of the message to be sent. Report an error if the number of arguments expected by the selector is not one.

perform: aSymbol with: firstObject with: secondObject

Send the receiver the keyword message indicated by the arguments. The first argument, aSymbol, is the selector of the message. The other arguments, firstObject and secondObject, are the arguments of the message to be sent. Report an error if the number of arguments expected by the selector is not two.

perform: aSymbol with: firstObject with: secondObject with: thirdObject

Send the receiver the keyword message indicated by the arguments. The first argument, aSymbol, is the selector of the message. The other arguments, firstObject, secondObject, and thirdObject, are the arguments of the message to be sent. Report an error if the number of arguments expected by the selector is not three.

perform: selector withArguments: anArray

Send the receiver the keyword message indicated by the arguments. The argument, selector, is the selector of the message. The arguments of the message are the elements of anArray. Report an error if the number of arguments expected by the selector is not the same as the size of anArray.

One way in which this protocol can be used is as a decoder of user commands. Suppose for example that we want to model a very simple calculator in which operands precede operators. A possible implementation represents the calculator as having (1) the current result, which is also the first operand, and (2) a possibly undefined second operand. Each operator is a message selector understood by the result. Sending the message clear, once, resets the operand; sending the message clear when the operand is reset will reset the result.

class name	Calculator
superclass	Object
instance variable names	result
	operand

class methods

instance creation

new
   ↑super new initialize

instance methods

accessing

result
   ↑result

calculating

apply: operator
   (self respondsTo: operator)
      ifFalse: [self error: 'operation not understood'].
   operand isNil
      ifTrue: [result ← result perform: operator]
      ifFalse: [result ← result perform: operator with: operand]

clear
   operand isNil
      ifTrue: [result ← 0]
      ifFalse: [operand ← nil]

operand: aNumber
   operand ← aNumber

private

initialize
   result ← 0

An example illustrates the use of the class Calculator.

   hp ← Calculator new

Create hp as a Calculator. The instance variables are initialized with result 0 and operand nil.

hp operand: 3

Imagine the user has pressed the key labeled 3 and set the operand.

hp apply: # +

The user selects addition. The method for apply determines that the operator is understood and that the operand is not nil; therefore, the result is set by the expression

result perform: operator with: operand

which is equivalent to

0 + 3

The method sets result to 3; operand remains 3 so that

hp apply: # +

again adds 3, so the result is now 6.

hp operand: 1.
hp apply: # −.
hp clear.
hp apply: #squared

The result was 6, subtract 1, and compute the square; result is now 25.

System Primitive Messages

There are a number of messages specified in class Object whose purpose is to support the needs of the overall system implementation. They are categorized as system primitives. These are messages that provide direct access to the state of an instance and, to some extent, violate the principle that each object has sovereign control over storing values into its variables. However, this access is needed by the language interpreter. It is useful in providing class description/development utilities for the programming environment. Examples of these messages are instVarAt: anInteger and instVarAt: anInteger put: anObject which retrieve and store the values of named instance variables, respectively.

Object instance protocol

system primitives
    become: otherObject
        Swap the instance pointers of the receiver and the argument, otherObject. All variables in the entire system that pointed to the receiver

	will now point to the argument and vice versa. Report an error if either object is a SmallInteger.
instVarAt: index	Answer a named variable in the receiver. The numbering of the variables corresponds to the order in which the named instance variables were defined.
instVarAt: index put: value	Store the argument, value, into a named variable in the receiver. The number of variables corresponds to the order in which the named instance variables were defined. Answer value.
nextInstance	Answer the next instance after the receiver in the enumeration of all instances of this class. Answer nil if all instances have been enumerated.
numberOfPointers	Answer the number of objects to which the receiver refers.
refct	Answer the number of object pointers in the system that point at the receiver. Answer 0 if the receiver is a SmallInteger.

Probably the most unusual and effective of the system primitive messages is the message become: otherObject. The response to this message is to swap the instance pointer of the receiver with that of the argument, otherObject. An example of the use of this message is found in the implementation of the message grow in several of the collection classes. The message grow is sent when the number of elements that can be stored in a (fixed-length) collection have to be increased without copying the collection; copying is undesirable because all shared references to the collection must be preserved. Thus a new collection is created, its elements stored, and then the original collection transforms into (becomes) the new one. All pointers to the original collection are replaced by pointers to the new one.

The following is the method for grow as specified in class SequenceableCollection.

```
grow
    | newCollection |
    newCollection ← self species new: self size + self growSize.
    newCollection replaceFrom: 1 to: self size with: self.
    ↑self become: newCollection
growSize
    ↑ 10
```

Subclasses can redefine the response to the message growSize in order to specify alternative numbers of elements by which to expand.

15

Multiple Independent Processes

Processes
Scheduling
Priorities

Semaphores
Mutual Exclusion
Resource Sharing
Hardware Interrupts

Class SharedQueue

Class Delay

```
Object

    Magnitude                                    Stream
        Character                                    PositionableStream
        Date                                             ReadStream
        Time                                             WriteStream
                                                             ReadWriteStream
        Number                                                   ExternalStream
            Float                                                    FileStream
            Fraction
            Integer                                  Random
                LargeNegativeInteger
                LargePositiveInteger             File
                SmallInteger                     FileDirectory
                                                 FilePage

        LookupKey                                UndefinedObject
            Association                          Boolean
                                                     False
    Link                                             True

        Process

    Collection                               ProcessorScheduler
                                             Delay
        SequenceableCollection               SharedQueue
            LinkedList
                                             Behavior
                Semaphore                        ClassDescription
                                                     Class
        ArrayedCollection                            MetaClass
            Array
                                             Point
            Bitmap                           Rectangle
                DisplayBitmap                BitBlt
                                                 CharacterScanner
            RunArray
            String                               Pen
                Symbol
            Text                             DisplayObject
            ByteArray                            DisplayMedium
                                                     Form
        Interval                                         Cursor
        OrderedCollection                                DisplayScreen
            SortedCollection                     InfiniteForm
        Bag                                      OpaqueForm
        MappedCollection                         Path
        Set                                          Arc
            Dictionary                                Circle
                IdentityDictionary                   Curve
                                                     Line
                                                     LinearFit
                                                     Spline
```

The Smalltalk-80 system provides support for multiple independent processes with three classes named Process, ProcessorScheduler, and Semaphore. A Process represents a sequence of actions that can be carried out independently of the actions represented by other Processes. A ProcessorScheduler schedules the use of the Smalltalk-80 virtual machine that actually carries out the actions represented by the Processes in the system. There may be many Processes whose actions are ready to be carried out and ProcessorScheduler determines which of these the virtual machine will carry out at any particular time. A Semaphore allows otherwise independent processes to synchronize their actions with each other. Semaphores provide a simple form of synchronous communication that can be used to create more complicated synchronized interactions. Semaphores also provide synchronous communication with asynchronous hardware devices such as the user input devices and realtime clock.

Semaphores are often not the most useful synchronization mechanism. Instances of SharedQueue and Delay use Semaphores to satisfy the two most common needs for synchronization. A SharedQueue provides safe transfer of objects between independent processes and a Delay allows a process to be synchronized with the real time clock.

Processes

A *process* is a sequence of actions described by expressions and performed by the Smalltalk-80 virtual machine. Several of the processes in the system monitor asynchronous hardware devices. For example, there are processes monitoring the keyboard, the pointing device, and the realtime clock. There is also a process monitoring the available memory in the system. The most important process to the user is the one that performs the actions directly specified by the user, for example, editing text, graphics, or class definitions. This user interface process must communicate with the processes monitoring the keyboard and pointing device to find out what the user is doing. Processes might be added that update a clock or a view of a user-defined object.

A new process can be created by sending the unary message fork to a block. For example, the following expression creates a new process to display three clocks named EasternTime, MountainTime, and PacificTime on the screen.

```
[EasternTime display.
 MountainTime display.
 PacificTime display] fork
```

The actions that make up the new process are described by the block's expressions. The message fork has the same effect on these expressions as does the message value, but it differs in the way the result of the message is returned. When a block receives value, it waits to return until all of its expressions have been executed. For example, the following expression does not produce a value until all three clocks have been completely displayed.

```
[EasternTime display.
 MountainTime display.
 PacificTime display] value
```

The value returned from sending a block value is the value of the last expression in the block. When a block receives fork, it returns immediately, usually before its expressions have been executed. This allows the expressions following the fork message to be executed independently of the expressions in the block. For example, the following two expressions would result in the contents of the collection nameList being sorted independently of the three clocks being displayed.

```
[EasternTime display.
 MountainTime display.
 PacificTime display] fork.
 alphabeticalList ← nameList sort
```

The entire collection may be sorted before any of the clocks are displayed or all of the clocks may be displayed before the collection begins sorting. The occurrence of either one of these extreme cases or an intermediate case in which some sorting and some clock display are interspersed is determined by the way that display and sort are written. The two processes, the one that sends the messages fork and sort, and the one that sends display, are executed independently. Since a block's expressions may not have been evaluated when it returns from fork, the value of fork must be independent of the value of the block's expressions. A block returns itself as the value of fork.

Each process in the system is represented by an instance of class Process. A block's response to fork is to create a new instance of Process and schedule the processor to execute the expressions it contains. Blocks also respond to the message newProcess by creating and returning a new instance of Process, but the virtual machine is not scheduled to execute its expressions. This is useful because, unlike fork, it provides a reference to the Process itself. A Process created by newProcess is called *suspended* since its expressions are not being executed. For example, the following expression creates two new Processes but does not result in either display or sort being sent.

clockDisplayProcess ← [EasternTime display] newProcess.
sortingProcess ← [alphabeticalList ← nameList sort] newProcess

The actions represented by one of these suspended Processes can actually be carried out by sending the Process the message resume. The following two expressions would result in display being sent to EasternTime and sort being sent to nameList.

clockDisplayProcess resume.
sortingProcess resume

Since display and sort would be sent from different Processes, their execution may be interleaved. Another example of the use of resume is the implementation of fork in BlockContext.

fork
self newProcess resume

A complementary message, suspend, returns a Process to the suspended state in which the processor is no longer executing its expressions. The message terminate prevents a Process from ever running again, whether it was suspended or not.

Process instance protocol
changing process state	
resume	Allow the receiver to be advanced.
suspend	Stop the advancement of the receiver in such a way that it can resume its progress later (by sending it the message resume).
terminate	Stop the advancement of the receiver forever.

Blocks also understand a message with selector newProcessWith: that creates and returns a new Process supplying values for block arguments. The argument of newProcessWith: is an Array whose elements are used as the values of the block arguments. The size of the Array should be equal to the number of block arguments the receiver takes. For example,

displayProcess ← [:clock | clock display]
                    newProcessWith: (Array with: MountainTime)

The protocol of BlockContext that allows new Processes to be created is shown on the following page.

BlockContext instance protocol	
scheduling	
fork	Create and schedule a new Process for the execution of the expressions the receiver contains.
newProcess	Answer a new suspended Process for the execution of the expressions the receiver contains. The new Process is not scheduled.
newProcessWith: argumentArray	Answer a new suspended Process for the execution of the expressions the receiver contains supplying the elements of argumentArray as the values of the receiver's block arguments.

Scheduling

The Smalltalk-80 virtual machine has only one processor capable of carrying out the sequence of actions a Process represents. So when a Process receives the message resume, its actions may not be carried out immediately. The Process whose actions are currently being carried out is called *active*. Whenever the active Process receives the message suspend or terminate, a new active Process is chosen from those that have received resume. The single instance of class ProcessorScheduler keeps track of all of the Processes that have received resume. This instance of ProcessorScheduler has the global name Processor. The active Process can be found by sending Processor the message activeProcess. For example, the active Process can be terminated by the expression

Processor activeProcess terminate

This will be the last expression executed in that Process. Any expressions following it in a method would never be executed. Processor will also terminate the active Process in response to the message terminateActive.

Processor terminateActive

Priorities

Ordinarily, Processes are scheduled for the use of the processor on a simple first-come first-served basis. Whenever the active Process receives suspend or terminate, the Process that has been waiting the longest will become the new active Process. In order to provide more control of when a Process will run, Processor uses a very simple priority mechanism. There are a fixed number of priority levels numbered by ascending integers. A Process with a higher priority will gain the use of the processor before a Process with a lower priority, independent of the order of their requests. When a Process is created (with either fork or newProcess), it will receive the same priority as the Process that created it. The priority of a Process can be changed by sending it the message priority: with the priority as an argument. Or the priority of a Process can be specified when it is forked by using the message forkAt: with the priority as an argument. For example, consider the following expressions executed in a Process at priority 4.

```
wordProcess ← [['now' displayAt: 50@100] forkAt: 6.
               ['is' displayAt: 100@100] forkAt: 5.
                'the' displayAt: 150@100]
                          newProcess.
wordProcess priority: 7.
'time' displayAt: 200@100.
wordProcess resume.
'for' displayAt: 250@100
```

The sequence of displays on the screen would be as follows.

			time	
		the	time	
now		the	time	
now	is	the	time	
now	is	the	time	for

Priorities are manipulated with a message to Processes and a message to BlockContexts.

Process instance protocol

accessing

    priority: anInteger   Set the receiver's priority to be anInteger.

BlockContext instance protocol

scheduling

    forkAt: priority   Create a new process for the execution of the expressions the receiver contains. Schedule the new process at the priority level priority.

The methods in the Smalltalk-80 system do not actually specify priorities with literal integers. The appropriate priority to use is always obtained by sending a message to Processor. The messages used to obtain priorities are shown in the protocol for class ProcessorScheduler.

One other message to Processor allows other Processes with the same priority as the active Process to gain access to the processor. The ProcessorScheduler responds to the message yield by suspending the active Process and placing it on the end of the list of Processes waiting at its priority. The first Process on the list then becomes the active Process. If there are no other Processes at the same priority, yield has no effect.

ProcessorScheduler instance protocol

accessing
activePriority | Answer the priority of the currently running process.
activeProcess | Answer the currently running process.

process state change
terminateActive | Terminate the currently running process.
yield | Give other processes at the priority of the currently running process a chance to run.

priority names
highIOPriority | Answer the priority at which the most time critical input/output processes should run.
lowIOPriority | Answer the priority at which most input/output processes should run.
systemBackgroundPriority | Answer the priority at which system background processes should run.
timingPriority | Answer the priority at which the system processes keeping track of real time should run.
userBackgroundPriority | Answer the priority at which background processes created by the user should run.
userInterruptPriority | Answer the priority at which processes created by the user and desiring immediate service should run.
userSchedulingPriority | Answer the priority at which the user interface processes should run.

The messages to ProcessorScheduler requesting priorities were listed in alphabetical order above since this is the standard for protocol descriptions. The same messages are listed below from highest priority to lowest priority along with some examples of Processes that might have that priority.

timingPriority | The Process monitoring the real time clock (see description of class Wakeup later in this chapter).
highIOPriority | The Process monitoring the local network communication device.
lowIOPriority | The Process monitoring the user input devices and the Process distributing packets from the local network.
userInterruptPriority | Any Process forked by the user interface that should be executed immediately.
userSchedulingPriority | The Process performing actions specified through the user interface (editing, viewing, programming, and debugging).

| userBackgroundPriority | Any Process forked by the user interface that should be executed only when nothing else is happening. |
| systemBackgroundPriority | A system Process that should be executed when nothing else is happening. |

Semaphores

The sequence of actions represented by a Process is carried out asynchronously with the actions represented by other Processes. The function of one Process is independent of the function of another. This is appropriate for Processes that never need to interact. For example, the two Processes shown below that display clocks and sort a collection probably do not need to interact with each other at all.

```
[EasternTime display.
 MountainTime display.
 PacificTime display ] fork.
alphabeticalList ← nameList sort
```

However, some Processes that are substantially independent must interact occasionally. The actions of these loosely dependent Processes must be synchronized while they interact. Instances of Semaphore provide a simple form of synchronized communication between otherwise independent Processes. A Semaphore provides for the synchronized communication of a simple (∼1 bit of information) signal from one process to another. A Semaphore provides a nonbusy wait for a Process that attempts to consume a signal that has not been produced yet. Semaphores are the only safe mechanism provided for interaction between Processes. Any other mechanisms for interaction should use Semaphores to insure their synchronization.

Communication with a Semaphore is initiated in one Process by sending it the message signal. On the other end of the communication, another Process waits to receive the simple communication by sending wait to the same Semaphore. It does not matter in which order the two messages are sent, the Process waiting for a signal will not proceed until one is sent. A Semaphore will only return from as many wait messages as it has received signal messages. If a signal and two waits are sent to a Semaphore, it will not return from one of the wait messages. When a Semaphore receives a wait message for which no corresponding signal was sent, it suspends the process from which the wait was sent.

Semaphore instance protocol

communication

signal   Send a signal through the receiver. If one or more Processes have been suspended trying to receive a signal, allow the one that has been waiting the longest to proceed. If no Process is waiting, remember the excess signal.

wait   The active Process must receive a signal through the receiver before proceeding. If no signal has been sent, the active Process will be suspended until one is sent.

The processes that have been suspended will be resumed in the same order in which they were suspended. A Process's priority is only taken into account by Processor when scheduling it for the use of the processor. Each Process waiting for a Semaphore will be resumed on a first-come first-served basis, independent of its priority. A Semaphore allows a Process to wait for a signal that has not been sent without using processor capacity. The Semaphore does not return from wait until signal has been sent. One of the main advantages of creating an independent process for a particular activity is that, if the process requires something that is not available, other processes can proceed while the first process waits for it to become available. Examples of things that a process may require and that may or may not be available are hardware devices, user events (keystrokes or pointing device movements), and shared data structures. A specific time of day can also be thought of as something that might be required for a process to proceed.

Mutual Exclusion

Semaphores can be used to ensure mutually exclusive use of certain facilities by separate Processes. For example, a Semaphore might be used to provide a data structure that can be safely accessed by separate Processes. The following definition of a simple first-in first-out data structure does not have any provision for mutual exclusion.

class name	SimpleQueue
superclass	Object
instance variable names	contentsArray
	readPosition
	writePosition

class methods

instance creation

new
    ↑self new: 10

new: size
    ↑super new init: size

instance methods

accessing

next
```
| value |
readPosition = writePosition
    ifTrue: [self error: 'empty queue']
    ifFalse: [value ← contentsArray at: readPosition.
            contentsArray at: readPosition put: nil.
            readPosition ← readPosition + 1.
            ↑value]
```

nextPut: value
```
writePosition > contentsArray size
    ifTrue: [self makeRoomForWrite].
contentsArray at: writePosition put: value.
writePosition ← writePosition + 1.
↑value
```

size
```
↑writePosition - readPosition
```

testing

isEmpty
```
↑writePosition = readPosition
```

private

init: size
```
contentsArray ← Array new: size.
readPosition ← 1.
writePosition ← 1
```

makeRoomForWrite
```
| contentsSize |
readPosition = 1
    ifTrue: [contentsArray grow]
    ifFalse:
        [contentsSize ← writePosition − readPosition.
        1 to: contentsSize do:
            [ :index |
            contentsArray
                at: index
                put: (contentsArray at: index + readPosition − 1)].
        readPosition ← 1.
        writePosition ← contentsSize + 1]
```

A SimpleQueue remembers its contents in an Array named contentsArray and maintains two indices into the contentsArray named readPosition and writePosition. New contents are added at writePosition and removed at readPosition. The private message makeRoomForWrite is sent when there is no room at the end of contentsArray for remembering a new object. If contentsArray is completely full, its size is increased. Otherwise, the contents are moved to the first of contentsArray.

The problem with sending to a SimpleQueue from different Processes is that more than one Process at a time may be executing the method for next or nextPut:. Suppose a SimpleQueue were sent the message next from one Process, and had just executed the expression

value ← contentsArray at: readPosition

when a higher priority Process woke up and sent another next message to the same SimpleQueue. Since readPosition has not been incremented, the second execution of the expresson above will bind the same object to value. The higher priority Process will remove the reference to the object from contentsArray, increment the readPosition and return the object it removed. When the lower priority Process gets control back, readPosition has been incremented so it removes the reference to the next object from contentsArray. This object should have been the value of one of the next messages, but it is discarded and both next messages return the same object.

To ensure mutual exclusion, each Process must wait for the same Semaphore before using a resource and then signal the Semaphore when it is finished. The following subclass of SimpleQueue provides mutual exclusion so that its instances can be used from separate Processes.

class name	SimpleSharedQueue
superclass	SimpleQueue
instance variable names	accessProtect
instance methods	

accessing

next
```
| value |
accessProtect wait.
value ← super next.
accessProtect signal.
↑value
```

nextPut: value
```
accessProtect wait.
super nextPut: value.
accessProtect signal.
↑value
```

private

init: size

super init: size.
accessProtect ← Semaphore new.
accessProtect signal

Since mutual exclusion is a common use of Semaphores, they include a message for it. The selector of this message is critical:. The implementation of critical: is as follows.

critical: aBlock

| value |
self wait.
value ← aBlock value.
self signal.
↑value

A Semaphore used for mutual exclusion must start out with one excess signal so the first Process may enter the critical section. Class Semaphore provides a special initialization message, forMutualExclusion, that signals the new instance once.

Semaphore instance protocol

---

mutual exclusion
    critical: aBlock   Execute aBlock when no other critical blocks are executing.

Semaphore class protocol

---

instance creation
    forMutualExclusion   Answer a new Semaphore with one excess signal.

The implementation of SimpleSharedQueue could be changed to read as follows.

class name	SimpleSharedQueue
superclass	SimpleQueue
instance variable names	accessProtect
instance methods	

accessing

next

| value |
accessProtect critical: [value ← super next].
↑value

nextPut: value

accessProtect critical: [super nextPut: value.].
↑value

private

init: size
> super init: size.
> accessProtect ← Semaphore forMutualExclusion

Resource Sharing

In order for two Processes to share a resource, mutually exclusive access to it is not enough. The Processes must also be able to communicate about the availability of the resource. SimpleSharedQueue will not get confused by simultaneous accesses, but if an attempt is made to remove an object from an empty SimpleSharedQueue, an error occurs. In an environment with asynchronous Processes, it is inconvenient to guarantee that attempts to remove objects (by sending next) will be made only after they have been added (by sending nextPut:). Therefore, Semaphores are also used to signal the availability of shared resources. A Semaphore representing a resource is signalled after each unit of the resource is made available and waited for before consuming each unit. Therefore, if an attempt is made to consume a resource before it has been produced, the consumer simply waits.

Class SafeSharedQueue is an example of how Semaphores can be used to communicate about the availability of resources. SafeSharedQueue is similar to SimpleSharedQueue, but it uses another Semaphore named valueAvailable to represent the availability of the contents of the queue. SafeSharedQueue is not in the Smalltalk-80 system, it is described here only as an example. SharedQueue is the class that is actually used to communicate between processes in the system. SharedQueue provides functionality similar to SafeSharedQueue's. The protocol specification for SharedQueue will be given later in this chapter.

class name	SafeSharedQueue
superclass	SimpleQueue
instance variable names	accessProtect
	valueAvailable

instance methods

accessing

next
> | value |
> valueAvailable wait.
> accessProtect critical: [value ← super next].
> ↑value

nextPut: value
> accessProtect critical: [super nextPut: value].
> valueAvailable signal.
> ↑value

private

init: size
> super init: size.
> accessProtect ← Semaphore forMutualExclusion.
> valueAvailable ← Semaphore new

Hardware
Interrupts

Instances of Semaphore are also used to communicate between hardware devices and Processes. In this capacity, they take the place of interrupts as a means of communicating about the changes of state that hardware devices go through. The Smalltalk-80 virtual machine is specified to signal Semaphores on three conditions.

- user event: a key has been pressed on the keyboard, a button has been pressed on the pointing device, or the pointing device has moved.

- timeout: a specific value of the millisecond clock has been reached.

- low space: available object memory has fallen below certain limits.

These three Semaphores correspond to three Processes monitoring user events, the millisecond clock and memory utilization. Each monitoring Process sends wait to the appropriate Semaphore suspending itself until something of interest happens. Whenever the Semaphore is signalled, the Process will resume. The virtual machine is notified about these three types of monitoring by primitive methods. For example, the timeout signal can be requested by a primitive method associated with the message signal:atTime: to Processor.

Class Wakeup is an example of how one of these Semaphores can be used. Wakeup provides an alarm clock service to Processes by monitoring the millisecond clock. Wakeup is not in the Smalltalk-80 system; it is described here only as an example. Delay is the class that actually monitors the millisecond clock in the Smalltalk-80 system. Delay provides functionality similar to Wakeup's. The protocol specification for Delay will be given later in this chapter.

Wakeup provides a message that suspends the sending Process for a specified number of milliseconds. The following expression suspends its Process for three quarters of a second.

Wakeup after: 750

When Wakeup receives an after: message, it allocates a new instance which remembers the value of the clock at which the wakeup should occur. The new instance contains a Semaphore on which the active Process will be suspended until the wakeup time is reached. Wakeup keeps all of its instances in a list sorted by their wakeup times. A Process monitors the virtual machine's millisecond clock for the earliest of these wakeup times and allows the appropriate suspended Process to proceed. This Process is created in the class method for initializeTimingProcess. The Semaphore used to monitor the clock is referred to by a class variable named TimingSemaphore. The virtual machine is informed that the clock should be monitored with the following message found in the instance method for nextWakeup.

Processor signal: TimingSemaphore atTime: resumptionTime

The list of instances waiting for resumption is referred to by a class variable named PendingWakeups. There is another Semaphore named AccessProtect that provides mutually exclusive access to PendingWakeups.

class name	Wakeup
superclass	Object
instance variable names	alarmTime
	alarmSemaphore
class variable names	PendingWakeups
	AccessProtect
	TimingSemaphore

class methods

alarm clock service

after: millisecondCount
    (self new sleepDuration: millisecondCount) waitForWakeup

class initialization

initialize
    TimingSemaphore ← Semaphore new.
    AccessProtect ← Semaphore forMutualExclusion.
    PendingWakeups ← SortedCollection new.
    self initializeTimingProcess
initializeTimingProcess
    [[true]
      whileTrue:
        [TimingSemaphore wait.
        AccessProtect wait.
        PendingWakeups removeFirst wakeup.
        PendingWakeups isEmpty
          ifFalse: [PendingWakeups first nextWakeup].
        AccessProtect signal]]
            forkAt: Processor timingPriority

instance methods

process delay

waitForWakeup
>   AccessProtect wait.
>   PendingWakeups add: self.
>   PendingWakeups first == self
>   ifTrue: [self nextWakeup].
>   AccessProtect signal.
>   alarmSemaphore wait

comparison

< otherWakeup
>   ↑alarmTime < otherWakeup wakeupTlme

accessing

wakeupTime
>   ↑alarmTime

private

nextWakeup
>   Processor signal: TimingSemaphore atTime: resumptionTime
sleepDuration: millisecondCount
>   alarmTime ← Time millisecondClockValue + millisecondCount.
>   alarmSemaphore ← Semaphore new
wakeup
>   alarmSemaphore signal

**Class
SharedQueue**

Class SharedQueue is the system class whose instances provide safe communication of objects between Processes. Both its protocol and its implementation are similar to the SafeSharedQueue example shown earlier in this chapter.

SharedQueue instance protocol

---

accessing

next	Answer with the first object added to the receiver that has not yet been removed. If the receiver is empty, suspend the active Process until an object is added to it.
nextPut: value	Add value to the contents of the receiver. If a Process has been suspended waiting for an object, allow it to proceed.

Class Delay

A Delay allows a Process to be suspended for a specified amount of time. A Delay is created by specifying how long it will suspend the active Process.

halfMinuteDelay ← Delay forSeconds: 30.
shortDelay ← Delay forMilliseconds: 50

Simply creating a Delay has no effect on the progress of the active Process. It is in response to the message wait that a Delay suspends the active Process. The following expressions would both suspend the active Process for 30 seconds.

halfMinuteDelay wait.
(Delay forSeconds: 30) wait

Delay class protocol

instance creation
forMilliseconds: millisecondCount   Answer with a new instance that will suspend the active Process for millisecondCount milliseconds when sent the message wait.

forSeconds: secondCount   Answer with a new instance that will suspend the active Process for secondCount seconds when sent the message wait.

untilMilliseconds: millisecondCount
  Answer with a new instance that will suspend the active Process until the millisecond clock reaches the value millisecondCount.

general inquiries
millisecondClockValue   Answer with the current value of the millisecond clock.

Delay instance protocol

accessing
resumptionTime   Answer with the value of the millisecond clock at which the delayed Process will be resumed.

process delay
wait   Suspend the active Process until the millisecond clock reaches the appropriate value.

A trivial clock can be implemented with the following expression.

[[true] whileTrue:
    [Time now printString displayAt: 100@100.
    (Delay forSeconds: 1) wait]] fork

The current time would be displayed on the screen once a second.

16

Protocol for Classes

Class Behavior

Class ClassDescription

Class Metaclass

Class Class

Object

Magnitude
    Character
    Date
    Time

    Number
        Float
        Fraction
        Integer
            LargeNegativeInteger
            LargePositiveInteger
            SmallInteger

    LookupKey
        Association

Link

    Process

Collection

    SequenceableCollection
        LinkedList

            Semaphore

        ArrayedCollection
            Array

            Bitmap
                DisplayBitmap

            RunArray
            String
                Symbol
            Text
            ByteArray

        Interval
        OrderedCollection
            SortedCollection
        Bag
        MappedCollection
        Set
        Dictionary
            IdentityDictionary

Stream
    PositionableStream
        ReadStream
        WriteStream
            ReadWriteStream
                ExternalStream
                    FileStream

    Random

File
FileDirectory
FilePage

UndefinedObject
Boolean
    False
    True

ProcessorScheduler
Delay
SharedQueue

Behavior
    ClassDescription
        Class
        MetaClass

Point
Rectangle
BitBlt
    CharacterScanner

    Pen

DisplayObject
    DisplayMedium
        Form
            Cursor
            DisplayScreen
    InfiniteForm
    OpaqueForm
    Path
        Arc
            Circle
        Curve
        Line
        LinearFit
        Spline

We have now introduced the protocol for most of the classes that describe the basic components of the Smalltalk-80 system. One notable exception is the protocol for the classes themselves. Four classes—Behavior, ClassDescription, Metaclass, and Class—interact to provide the facilities needed to describe new classes. Creating a new class involves compiling methods and specifying names for instance variables, class variables, pool variables, and the class itself.

Chapters 3, 4, and 5 introduced the basic concepts represented by these classes. To summarize from that discussion, the Smalltalk-80 programmer specifies a new class by creating a subclass of another class. For example, class Collection is a subclass of Object; class Array is a subclass of ArrayedCollection (whose superclass chain terminates with Object).

> 1. Every class is ultimately a subclass of class Object, except for Object itself, which has no superclass. In particular, Class is a subclass of ClassDescription, which is a subclass of Behavior which is a subclass of Object.

There are two kinds of objects in the system, ones that can create instances of themselves (classes) and ones that can not.

> 2. Every object is an instance of a class.

Each class is itself an instance of a class. We call the class of a class, its metaclass.

> 3. Every class is an instance of a metaclass.

Metaclasses are not referenced by class names as are other classes. Instead, they are referred to by a message expression sending the unary message class to the instance of the metaclass. For example, the metaclass of Collection is referred to as Collection class; the metaclass of Class is referred to as Class class.

In the Smalltalk-80 system, a metaclass is created automatically whenever a new class is created. A metaclass has only one instance. The messages categorized as "class methods" in the class descriptions are found in the metaclass of the class. This follows from the way in which methods are found; when a message is sent to an object, the search for the corresponding method begins in the class of the object. When a message is sent to Dictionary, for example, the search begins in the metaclass of Dictionary. If the method is not found in the metaclass, then the search proceeds to the superclass of the metaclass. In this case, the superclass is Set class, the metaclass for Dictionary's superclass. If necessary, the search follows the superclass chain to Object class.

In the diagrams in this chapter, all arrows with solid lines denote a subclass relationship; arrows with dashed lines an instance relationship. A ---> B means A is an instance of B. Solid gray lines indicate the class hierarchy; solid black lines indicate the metaclass hierarchy.

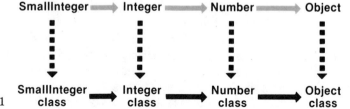

Figure 16.1

Since the superclass chain of all objects ends at Object as shown in Figure 16.1, and Object has no superclass, the superclass of Object's metaclass is not determined by the rule of maintaining a parallel hierarchy. It is at this point that Class is found. The superclass of Object class is Class.

4. All metaclasses are (ultimately) subclasses of Class (Figure 16.2).

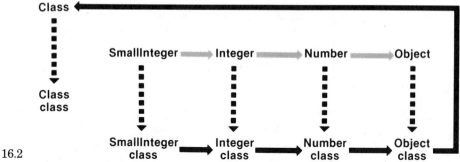

Figure 16.2

Since metaclasses are objects, they too must be instances of a class. Every metaclass is an instance of Metaclass. Metaclass itself is an instance of a metaclass. This is a point of circularity in the system—the metaclass of Metaclass must be an instance of Metaclass.

5. Every metaclass is an instance of Metaclass (Figure 16.3).

Figure 16.4 shows the relationships among Class, ClassDescription, Behavior, and Object, and their respective metaclasses. The class hierarchy follows a chain to Object, and the metaclass hierarchy follows a chain through Object class to Class and on to Object. While the methods of

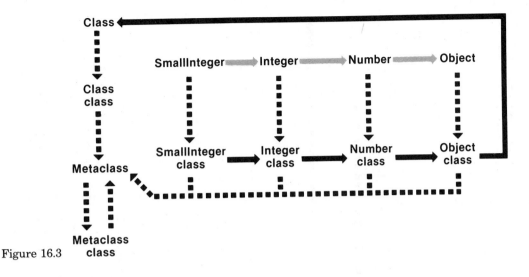

Figure 16.3

Object support the behavior common to all objects, the methods of Class and Metaclass support the behavior common to all classes.

6. The methods of Class and its superclasses support the behavior common to those objects that are classes.

7. The methods of instances of Metaclass add the behavior specific to particular classes.

The correspondence between the class and metaclass hierarchies is shown in Figure 16.5, in which the part of the number hierarchy and the behavior hierarchy of the last two figures are combined.

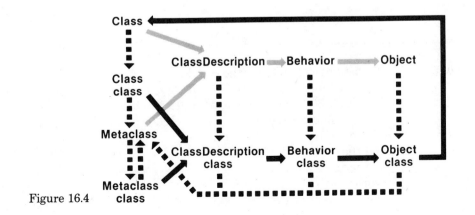

Figure 16.4

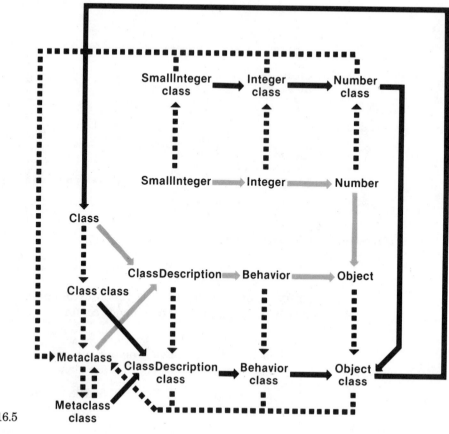

Figure 16.5

Class Behavior

Class Behavior defines the minimum state necessary for objects that have instances. In particular, Behavior defines the state used by the Smalltalk-80 interpreter. It provides the basic interface to the compiler. The state described by Behavior includes a class hierarchy link, a method dictionary, and a description of instances in terms of the number and the representation of their variables.

The message protocol for class Behavior will be described in four categories—*creating, accessing, testing,* and *enumerating.* These categories and their subcategories, as outlined below, provide a model for thinking about the functionality of classes in the Smalltalk-80 system.

Outline of Protocol for All Classes

creating
- creating a method dictionary
- creating instances
- creating a class hierarchy

accessing
- accessing the contents of the method dictionary
- accessing instances and variables: instance, class, and pool
- accessing the class hierarchy

testing
- testing the contents of the method dictionary
- testing the form of the instances
- testing the class hierarchy

enumerating
- enumerating subclasses and instances

☐ Behavior's *Creating Protocol* The methods in a class description are stored in a dictionary we refer to as the *method dictionary*. It is also sometimes called a message dictionary. The keys in this dictionary are message selectors; the values are the compiled form of methods (instances of CompiledMethod). The protocol for creating the method dictionary supports compiling methods as well as adding the association between a selector and a compiled method. It also supports accessing both the compiled and noncompiled (source) versions of the method.

Behavior instance protocol

creating method dictionary

methodDictionary: aDictionary	Store the argument, aDictionary, as the method dictionary of the receiver.
addSelector: selector withMethod: compiledMethod	
	Add the message selector, selector, with the corresponding compiled method, compiled-Method, to the receiver's method dictionary.
removeSelector: selector	Remove the argument, selector (which is a Symbol representing a message selector), from the receiver's method dictionary. If the selector is not in the method dictionary, report an error.
compile: code	The argument, code, is either a String or an object that converts to a String or it is a PositionableStream accessing an object that is or converts to a String. Compile code as the source code in the context of the receiver's variables. Report an error if the code can not be compiled.

compile: code notifying: requestor	Compile the argument, code, and enter the result in the receiver's method dictionary. If an error occurs, send an appropriate message to the argument, requestor.
recompile: selector	Compile the method associated with the message selector, selector.
decompile: selector	Find the compiled code associated with the argument, selector, and decompile it. Answer the resulting source code as a String. If the selector is not in the method dictionary, report an error.
compileAll	Compile all the methods in the receiver's method dictionary.
compileAllSubclasses	Compile all the methods in the receiver's subclasses' method dictionaries.

Instances of classes are created by sending the message new or new:. These two messages can be overridden in the method dictionary of a metaclass in order to supply special initialization behavior. The purpose of any special initialization is to guarantee that an instance is created with variables that are themselves appropriate instances. We have demonstrated this idea in many previous chapters. Look, for example, at the definition of class Random in Chapter 12; the method dictionary of Random class (the class methods) contains an implementation for new in which a new instance is sent the message setSeed; this initialization guarantees that the random number generation algorithm refers to a variable that is an appropriate kind of number.

Suppose a class overrides the method for new and then one of its subclasses wishes to do the same in order to avoid the behavior created by its superclass's change. The method for the first class might be

new
    ↑super new setVariables

where the message setVariables is provided in the protocol for instances of the class. By sending the message new to the pseudo-variable super, the method for creating an instance as specified in class Behavior is evaluated; the result, the new instance, is then sent the message setVariables. In the subclass, it is not possible to utilize the message super new because this will invoke the method of the first class—precisely the method to be avoided. In order to obtain the basic method in Behavior for creating an instance, the subclass must use the expression self basicNew. The message basicNew is the primitive instance creation message that should not be reimplemented in any subclass. In Behavior, new and basicNew are identical. A similar pair for creating variable-length objects, new: and basicNew:, are also provided in the protocol of class Behavior. (Note, this technique of dual messages is also used in class Object for accessing messages such as at: and at:put:.)

Behavior instance protocol

instance creation

new	Answer an instance of the receiver with no indexed variables. Send the receiver the message new: 0 if the receiver is indexable.
basicNew	Same as new, except this method should not be overridden in a subclass.
new: anInteger	Answer an instance of the receiver with anInteger number of indexed variables. Report an error if the receiver is not indexable.
basicNew: anInteger	Same as basicNew, except this method should not be overridden in a subclass.

The protocol for creating classes includes messages for placing the class within the hierarchy of classes in the system. Since this hierarchy is linear, there is only a need to set the superclass and to add or remove subclasses.

Behavior instance protocol

creating a class hierarchy

superclass: aClass	Set the superclass of the receiver to be the argument, aClass.
addSubclass: aClass	Make the argument, aClass, be a subclass of the receiver.
removeSubclass: aClass	Remove the argument, aClass, from the subclasses of the receiver.

Although the creating protocol for Behavior makes it possible to write expressions for creating a new class description, the usual approach is to take advantage of the graphical environment in which the Smalltalk-80 language is embedded, and to provide an interface in which the user fills out graphically-presented forms to specify information about the various parts of a class.

☐ Behavior's *Accessing Protocol*   The messages that access the contents of a method dictionary distinguish among the selectors in the class's locally specified method dictionary, and those in the method dictionaries of the class and each of its superclasses.

Behavior instance protocol

accessing the method dictionary

selectors	Answer a Set of all the message selectors specified in the receiver's local method dictionary.
allSelectors	Answer a Set of all the message selectors that instances of the receiver can understand. This consists of all message selectors in the receiver's method dictionary and in the dictionaries of each of the receiver's superclasses.

compiledMethodAt: selector	Answer the compiled method associated with the argument, selector, a message selector in the receiver's local method dictionary. Report an error if the selector can not be found.
sourceCodeAt: selector	Answer a String that is the source code associated with the argument, selector, a message selector in the receiver's local method dictionary. Report an error if the selector can not be found.
sourceMethodAt: selector	Answer a Text for the source code associated with the argument, selector, a message selector in the receiver's local method dictionary. This Text provides boldface emphasis for the message pattern part of the method. Report an error if the selector can not be found.

An instance can have named instance variables, indexed instance variables, class variables, and dictionaries of pool variables. Again, the distinction between locally specified variables and variables inherited from superclasses is made in the accessing protocol.

Behavior instance protocol

accessing instances and variables

allInstances	Answer a Set of all direct instances of the receiver.
someInstance	Answer an existing instance of the receiver.
instanceCount	Answer the number of instances of the receiver that currently exist.
instVarNames	Answer an Array of the instance variable names specified in the receiver.
subclassInstVarNames	Answer a Set of the instance variable names specified in the receiver's subclasses.
allInstVarNames	Answer an Array of the names of the receiver's instance variables, those specified in the receiver and in all of its superclasses. The Array ordering is the order in which the variables are stored and accessed by the Smalltalk-80 interpreter.
classVarNames	Answer a Set of the class variable names specified locally in the receiver.
allClassVarNames	Answer a Set of the names of the receiver's and the receiver's superclasses' class variables.
sharedPools	Answer a Set of the names of the pools (dictionaries) that are specified locally in the receiver.
allSharedPools	Answer a Set of the names of the pools (dictionaries) that are specified in the receiver and each of its superclasses.

Thus, for example,

expression	result
OrderedCollection instVarNames	('firstIndex' 'lastIndex')
OrderedCollection subclassInstVarNames	Set ('sortBlock')
SortedCollection allInstVarNames	('firstIndex' 'lastIndex' 'sortBlock')
String classVarNames	Set (StringBlter)
String allClassVarNames	Set (StringBlter DependentsFields ErrorRecursion)
Text sharedPools	a Set containing one element, TextConstants, a Dictionary

The accessing protocol includes messages for obtaining collections of the superclasses and subclasses of a class. These messages distinguish between a class's immediate superclass and subclasses, and all classes in the class's superclass chain.

Behavior instance protocol

accessing class hierarchy

subclasses	Answer a Set containing the receiver's immediate subclasses.
allSubclasses	Answer a Set of the receiver's subclasses and the receiver's descendent's subclasses.
withAllSubclasses	Answer a Set of the receiver, the receiver's subclasses and the receiver's descendent's subclasses.
superclass	Answer the receiver's immediate superclass.
allSuperclasses	Answer an OrderedCollection of the receiver's superclass and the receiver's ancestor's superclasses. The first element is the receiver's immediate superclass, followed by its superclass, and so on; the last element is always Object.

Thus, for example

expression	result
String superclass	ArrayedCollection
ArrayedCollection subclasses	Set (Array ByteArray RunArray Bitmap String Text)

ArrayedCollection allSubclasses	Set (Array ByteArray RunArray Bitmap String Text DisplayBitmap Symbol CompiledMethod)
ArrayedCollection withAllSubclasses	Set (ArrayedCollection Array ByteArray RunArray Bitmap String Text DisplayBitmap Symbol CompiledMethod)
ArrayedCollection allSuperclasses	OrderedCollection (SequenceableCollection Collection Object)
ArrayedCollection class allSuperclasses	OrderedCollection (SequenceableCollection class Collection class Object class Class ClassDescription Behavior Object)

☐ Behavior's *Testing Protocol*   Testing protocol provides the messages needed to find out information about the structure of a class and the form of its instances. The structure of a class consists of its relationship to other classes, its ability to respond to messages, the class in which a message is specified, and so on.

The contents of a method dictionary can be tested to find out which class, if any, implements a particular message selector, whether a class can respond to a message, and which methods reference particular variables or literals. These messages are all useful in creating a programming environment in which the programmer can explore the structure and functionality of objects in the system.

Behavior instance protocol

testing the method dictionary

hasMethods	Answer whether the receiver has any methods in its (local) method dictionary.
includesSelector: selector	Answer whether the message whose selector is the argument, selector, is in the local method dictionary of the receiver's class.
canUnderstand: selector	Answer whether the receiver can respond to the message whose selector is the argument.

The selector can be in the method dictionary of the receiver's class or any of its superclasses.

whichClassIncludesSelector: selector
Answer the first class on the receiver's superclass chain where the argument, selector, can be found as a message selector. Answer nil if no class includes the selector.

whichSelectorsAccess: instVarName
Answer a Set of selectors from the receiver's local method dictionary whose methods access the argument, instVarName, as a named instance variable.

whichSelectorsReferTo: anObject Answer a Set of selectors whose methods access the argument, anObject.

scopeHas: name ifTrue: aBlock Determine whether the variable name, name, is within the scope of the receiver, i.e., it is specified as a variable in the receiver or in one of its superclasses. If so, evalaute the argument, aBlock.

Thus, for example

expression	result
OrderedCollection includesSelector: #addFirst:	true
SortedCollection includesSelector: #size	false
SortedCollection canUnderstand: #size	true
SortedCollection whichClassIncludesSelector: #size	OrderedCollection
OrderedCollection whichSelectorsAccess: #firstIndex	Set (makeRoomAtFirst before: size makeRoomAtLast insert:before: remove:ifAbsent: addFirst: first removeFirst find: removeAllSuchThat: at: at:put: reverseDo: do: setIndices:)

The last example expression is useful in determining which methods must be changed if an instance variable is renamed or deleted. In addition to the messages intended for external access, the Set includes all messages implemented in support of the implementation of the external messages.

The testing protocol includes messages to a class that test how its variables are stored, whether the number of variables is fixed-length or variable-length, and the number of named instance variables.

Behavior instance protocol

---

testing the form of the instances

isPointers	Answer whether the variables of instances of the receiver are stored as pointers (words).
isBits	Answer whether the variables of instances of the receiver are stored as bits (i.e., not pointers).
isBytes	Answer whether the variables of instances of the receiver are stored as bytes (8-bit integers).
isWords	Answer whether the variables of instances of the receiver are stored as words.
isFixed	Answer true if instances of the receiver do not have indexed instance variables; answer false otherwise.
isVariable	Answer true if instances of the receiver do have indexed instance variables; answer false otherwise.
instSize	Answer the number of named instance variables of the receiver.

So we have

---

expression	*result*
LinkedList isFixed	true
String isBytes	true
Integer isBits	false
Float isWords	true
OrderedCollection isFixed	false
OrderedCollection instSize	2

oc ← OrderedCollection
    with: $a
    with: $b
    with: $c
	OrderedCollection
	    ($a $b $c)

oc size	3

The last four example lines show that instances of OrderedCollection are variable-length; the instance oc has three elements. In addition, instances of OrderedCollection have two named instance variables.

There are four kinds of classes in the system. Classes that have indexed instance variables are called *variable-length* and classes that do not are called *fixed-length*. The variables of all fixed-length classes are stored as pointers (word-sized references). The variables of variable-length classes can contain pointers, bytes, or words. Since a pointer is a word-sized reference, an object that contains pointers will answer true when asked whether it contains words, but the inverse is not always the case. Initialization messages specified in Class and itemized in a later section support creation of each kind of class.

Behavior instance protocol
_____

testing the class hierarchy

    inheritsFrom: aClass   Answer whether the argument, aClass, is on the receiver's superclass chain.

    kindOfSubclass   Answer a String that is the keyword that describes the receiver as a class: either a regular (fixed length) subclass, a variableSubclass, a variableByteSubclass, or a variableWordSubclass.

Thus

---

expression	*result*
String inheritsFrom: Collection	true
String kindOfSubclass	' variableByteSubclass: '
Array kindOfSubclass	' variableSubclass: '
Float kindOfSubclass	' variableWordSubclass: '
Integer kindOfSubclass	' subclass: '

☐ Behavior's *Enumerating Protocol* Messages specified in class Behavior also support listing out particular sets of objects associated with a class and applying each as the argument of a block. This enumeration of objects is similar to that provided in the collection classes, and consists of enumerating over all subclasses, superclasses, instances, and instances of subclasses. In addition, two messages support selecting those subclasses or superclasses for which a block evaluates to true.

Behavior instance protocol
_____

enumerating

    allSubclassesDo: aBlock   Evaluate the argument, aBlock, for each of the receiver's subclasses.

    allSuperclassesDo: aBlock   Evaluate the argument, aBlock, for each of the receiver's superclasses.

    allInstancesDo: aBlock   Evaluate the argument, aBlock, for each of the current instances of the receiver.

allSubinstancesDo: aBlock	Evaluate the argument, aBlock, for each of the current instances of the receiver's subclasses.
selectSubclasses: aBlock	Evaluate the argument, aBlock, for each of the receiver's subclasses. Collect into a Set only those subclasses for which aBlock evaluates to true. Answer the resulting Set.
selectSuperclasses: aBlock	Evaluate the argument, aBlock, with each of the receiver's superclasses. Collect into a Set only those superclasses for which aBlock evaluates to true. Answer the resulting Set.

As an example, in order to understand the behavior of an instance of the collection classes, it might be useful to know which subclasses of Collection implement the adding message addFirst:. With this information, the programmer can track down which method is actually evaluated when the message addFirst: is sent to a collection. The following expression collects each such class into a Set named subs.

```
subs ← Set new.
Collection allSubclassesDo:
        [ :class |
        (class includesSelector: #addFirst:)
                ifTrue: [subs add: class]]
```

The same information is accessible from

```
Collection selectSubclasses:
                [ :class | class includesSelector: #addFirst:]
```

Both create a Set of the three subclasses LinkedList, OrderedCollection, and RunArray.

The following expression returns a collection of the superclasses of SmallInteger that implement the message =.

```
SmallInteger selectSuperclasses:
                [ :class | class includesSelector: #=]
```

The response is

```
Set (Integer Magnitude Object )
```

Several subclasses of Collection implement the message first. Suppose we wish to see a list of the code for each implementation. The following expressions print the code on the file whose name is 'classMethods.first'.

```
| aStream |
aStream ← Disk file: 'classMethods.first'.
Collection allSubclassesDo:
        [ :class |
          (class includesSelector: #first)
           ifTrue:
               [class name printOn: aStream.
                aStream cr.
                (class sourceCodeAt: #first) printOn: aStream.
                aStream cr; cr]].
    aStream close
```

The resulting contents of the file is

```
SequenceableCollection
'first
    self emptyCheck.
    ↑self at: 1'
OrderedCollection
'first
    self emptyCheck.
    ↑self basicAt: firstIndex'
Interval
'first
    ↑start'
LinkedList
'first
    self emptyCheck.
    ↑firstLink'
```

The protocol described in the next sections is not generally used by programmers, but may be of interest to system developers. The messages described are typically accessed in the programming environment by selecting items from a menu presented in a graphically-oriented interface.

Although most of the facilities of a class are specified in the protocol of Behavior, a number of the messages can not be implemented because Behavior does not provide a complete representation for a class. In particular, Behavior does not provide a representation for instance variable names and class variable names, nor for a class name and a comment about the class.

Representations for a class name, class comment, and instance variable names are provided in ClassDescription, a subclass of Behavior. ClassDescription has two subclasses, Class and Metaclass. Class describes the representation for class variable names and pool variables. A metaclass shares the class and pool variables of its sole instance. Class adds additional protocol for adding and removing class variables and pool variables, and for creating the various kinds of subclasses. Metaclass adds an initialization message for creating a subclass of itself, that is, a message for creating a metaclass for a new class.

Class
ClassDescription

ClassDescription represents class naming, class commenting, and naming instance variables. This is reflected in additional protocol for accessing the name and comment, and for adding and removing instance variables.

ClassDescription instance protocol

accessing class description

name	Answer a String that is the name of the receiver.
comment	Answer a String that is the comment for the receiver.
comment: aString	Set the receiver's comment to be the argument, aString.
addInstVarName: aString	Add the argument, aString, as one of the receiver's instance variables.
removeInstVarName: aString	Remove the argument, aString, as one of the receiver's instance variables. Report an error if aString is not found.

ClassDescription was provided as a common superclass for Class and Metaclass in order to provide further structuring to the description of a class. This helps support a general program development environment. Specifically, ClassDescription adds structure for organizing the selector/method pairs of the method dictionary. This organization is a simple categorization scheme by which the subsets of the dictionary are grouped and named, precisely the way we have been grouping and naming messages throughout the chapters of this book. ClassDescription also provides the mechanisms for storing a full class description on an external stream (a file), and the mechanisms by which any changes to the class description are logged.

The classes themselves are also grouped into system category classifications. The organization of the chapters of this part of the book parallels that of the system class categories, for example, magnitudes, numbers, collections, kernel objects, kernel classes, and kernel support. Protocol for message and class categorization includes the following messages.

organization of messages and classes

category	Answer the system organization category for the receiver.
category: aString	Categorize the receiver under the system category, aString, removing the receiver from any previous category.
removeCategory: aString	Remove each of the messages categorized under the name aString and then remove the category itself.
whichCategoryIncludesSelector: selector	
	Answer the category of the argument, selector, in the organization of the receiver's method dictionary, or answer nil if the selector can not be found.

Given a categorization of the messages, ClassDescription is able to support a set of messages for copying messages from one method dictionary to another, retaining or changing the category name. Messages to support copying consists of

copy: selector from: aClass
copy: selector from: aClass classified: categoryName
copyAll: arrayOfSelectors from: class
copyAll: arrayOfSelectors from: class classified: categoryName
copyAllCategoriesFrom: aClass
copyCategory: categoryName from: aClass
copyCategory: categoryName
    from: aClass
    classified: newCategoryName

The categorization scheme has an impact on protocol for compiling since a compiled method must be placed in a particular category. Two messages are provided: compile: code classified: categoryName and compile: code classified: categoryName notifying: requestor.

We also note, for the next example, that Behavior supports special printing protocol so that arguments to the compiling messages can be computed. These are

printing

classVariableString	Answer a String that contains the names of each class variable in the receiver's variable declaration.
instanceVariableString	Answer a String that contains the names of each instance variable in the receiver's variable declaration.

sharedVariableString	Answer a String that contains the names of each pool dictionary in the receiver's variable declaration.

Take as an example the creation of a class named AuditTrail. This class should be just like LinkedList, except that removing elements should not be supported. Therefore, the class can be created by copying the accessing, testing, adding, and enumerating protocol of LinkedList. We assume that the elements of an AuditTrail are instances of a subclass of Link that supports storing the audit information. First, let's create the class. We assume that we do not know internal information about LinkedList so that the superclass name and variables must be accessed by sending messages to LinkedList.

```
LinkedList superclass
        subclass: #AuditTrail
        instanceVariableNames: LinkedList instanceVariableString
        classVariableNames: LinkedList classVariableString
        poolDictionaries: LinkedList sharedPoolString
        category: 'Record Keeping'.
```

AuditTrail is created as a subclass of whichever class is the superclass for LinkedList (LinkedList superclass). Now we copy the categories we are interested in from class LinkedList.

```
AuditTrail copyCategory: #accessing from: LinkedList.
AuditTrail copyCategory: #testing from: LinkedList.
AuditTrail copyCategory: #adding from: LinkedList.
AuditTrail copyCategory: #enumerating from: LinkedList.
AuditTrail copyCategory: #private from: LinkedList.
```

AuditTrail declared two instance variable names, firstLink and lastLink, and copied messages first, last, size, isEmpty, add:, addFirst:, and addLast:. We also copied all the messages in the category private on the assumption that at least one of them is needed in the implementation of the external messages.

Some messages in ClassDescription that support storing the class description on an external stream are

ClassDescription instance protocol

filing

fileOutOn: aFileStream	Store a description of the receiver on the file accessed by the argument, aFileStream.
fileOutCategory: categoryName	Create a file whose name is the name of the receiver concatenated by an extension, '.st'. Store on it a description of the messages categorized as categoryName.

fileOutChangedMessages: setOfChanges on: aFileStream
> The argument, setOfChanges, is a collection of class/message pairs that were changed. Store a description of each of these pairs on the file accessed by the argument, aFileStream.

We can write a description of class AuditTrail on the file 'AuditTrail.st' by evaluating the expression

AuditTrail fileOutOn: (Disk file: 'AuditTrail.st')

Class Metaclass

The primary role of a metaclass in the Smalltalk-80 system is to provide protocol for initializing class variables and for creating initialized instances of the metaclass's sole instance. Thus the key messages added by Metaclass are themselves initialization messages—one is sent to Metaclass itself in order to create a subclass of it, and one is sent to an instance of Metaclass in order to create its sole instance.

Metaclass class protocol

instance creation
    subclassOf: superMeta
> Answer an instance of Metaclass that is a subclass of the metaclass, superMeta.

    name: newName
        environment: aSystemDictionary
        subclassOf: superClass
        instanceVariableNames: stringOfInstVarNames
        variable: variableBoolean
        words: wordBoolean
        pointers: pointerBoolean
        classVariableNames: stringOfClassVarNames
        poolDictionaries: stringOfPoolNames
        category: categoryName
        comment: commentString
        changed: changed
> Each of these arguments, of course, is needed in order to create a fully initialized class.

The Smalltalk-80 programming environment provides a simplified way, using graphical interface techniques, in which the user specifies the information to create new classes.

Class Class

Instances of Class describe the representation and behavior of objects. Class adds more comprehensive programming support facilities to the basic ones provided in Behavior and more descriptive facilities to the ones provided in ClassDescription. In particular, Class adds the representation for class variable names and shared (pool) variables.

Class instance protocol

accessing instances and variables

addClassVarName: aString
Add the argument, aString, as a class variable of the receiver. The first character of aString must be capitalized; aString can not already be a class variable name.

removeClassVarName: aString
Remove the receiver's class variable whose name is the argument, aString. Report an error if it is not a class variable or if it is still being used in a method of the class.

addSharedPool: aDictionary
Add the argument, aDictionary, as a pool of shared variables. Report an error if the dictionary is already a shared pool in the receiver.

removeSharedPool: aDictionary
Remove the argument, aDictionary, as one of the receiver's pool dictionaries. Report an error if the dictionary is not one of the receiver's pools.

classPool
Answer the dictionary of class variables of the receiver.

initialize
Initialize class variables.

Additional accessing messages store a description of the class on a file, where the file has the same name as that of the class (fileOut), and remove the class from the system (removeFromSystem).

A variety of messages for creating one of the four kinds of subclasses in the system are specified in the method dictionary of Class. In addition, Class provides a message for renaming a class (rename: aString); this message is provided in Class rather than in ClassDescription because it is not an appropriate message to send to a metaclass.

Class instance protocol

instance creation

subclass: classNameString
 instanceVariableNames: stringInstVarNames
 classVariableNames: stringOfClassVarNames
 poolDictionaries: stringOfPoolNames
 category: categoryNameString
Create a new class that is a fixed-length (regular) subclass of the receiver. Each of the arguments provides the information needed to initialize the new class and categorize it.

Three other messages, like the one above except that the first keyword is variableSubclass:, variableByteSubclass:, or variableWordSubclass, support the creation of the other kinds of classes. Note also that the system requires that a subclass of a variable-length class be a variable-length class. When possible, the system makes the appropriate conversion; otherwise, an error is reported to the programmer.

Suppose that every time we created a new subclass, we wanted to install messages for storing and retrieving the instance variables of that class. For example, if we create a class Record with instance variable names name and address, we wish to provide messages name and address, to respond with the values of these variables, and name: argument and address: argument, to set the values of these variables to the value of the message argument. One way to accomplish this is to add the following method to the instance creation protocol of class Class.

```
accessingSubclass: className
        instanceVariableNames: instVarString
        classVariableNames: classVarString
        poolDictionaries: stringOfPoolNames
        category: categoryName
    | newClass |
    newClass ← self subclass: className
                instanceVariableNames: instVarString
                classVariableNames: classVarString
                poolDictionaries: stringOfPoolNames
                category: categoryName.
    newClass instVarNames do:
        [ :aName |
          newClass compile: (aName , '
        ↑', aName) classified: #accessing.
          newClass compile: (aName , ': argument
        ', aName, ' ← argument.
        ↑argument') classified: #accessing].
    ↑newClass
```

The method creates the class as usual, then, for each instance variable name, compiles two methods. The first is of the form

```
name
    ↑name
```

and the second is of the form

```
name: argument
    name ← argument.
    ↑argument
```

So, if we create the class Record, we can do so by sending Object the following message.

```
Object accessingSubclass: #Record
        instanceVariableNames: 'name address'
        classVariableNames: ''
        poolDictionaries: ''
        category: 'Example'.
```

The message is found in the method dictionary of Class, and creates the following four messages in the category accessing of class Record.

accessing

name
↑name
name: argument
name ← argument.
↑argument
address
↑address
address: argument
address ← argument.
↑argument

17

The Programming Interface

This chapter shows how a programmer adds new classes to the system and then tests and debugs their behavior using the Smalltalk-80 programming environment. The chapter presents a scenario of how a programmer might add class FinancialHistory to the system. FinancialHistory was used in the first part of this book as an example class. Its protocol and implementation descriptions can be found inside the front cover of this book. This example scenario is not intended as an exhaustive survey of the Smalltalk-80 programming interface. It is intended as an overview that provides motivation for the kinds of graphics support described in subsequent chapters.

A user and the Smalltalk-80 programming environment interact through a *bitmap display screen*, a *keyboard*, and a *pointing device*. The display is used to present graphical and textual views of information to the user. The keyboard is used to present textual information to the system. The pointing device is used to select information on the display screen. Smalltalk-80 uses an indirect pointing device called a *mouse*. A *cursor* on the screen shows the location currently being pointed to by the mouse. The cursor is moved by moving the mouse over a flat surface. The mouse has three buttons, which are used to make different kinds of selection.

Views

The display screen contains one or more rectangular areas called *views*. The views are displayed on a gray background and may overlap. Each view has a title shown at its upper left corner. Figure 17.1 shows the Smalltalk screen with two overlapping views on it. Their titles are Workspace and System Browser. These two views contain only text; other views might contain pictures or both text and pictures.

The view toward the top of the figure is a *workspace*. It contains text that can be edited or evaluated. The view towards the bottom of the figure is a *system browser*. It allows the class descriptions in the system to be viewed and edited. The arrow in the lower right part of the browser is the cursor. It shows the current location of the mouse. At the lower right corner of each figure in this chapter will be a small rectangle containing three ovals arranged side by side. These ovals represent the three mouse buttons. When one of the buttons is pressed, the corresponding oval will be filled in. The buttons will be referred to as the *left*, *middle*, and *right* buttons, even though they may not be arranged side by side on some mice.

A variety of information is typically visible on the Smalltalk-80 display screen. In order to take some action, the user indicates what part of the visible information should be affected. The general activity of directing attention to a particular piece of information is called *selec-

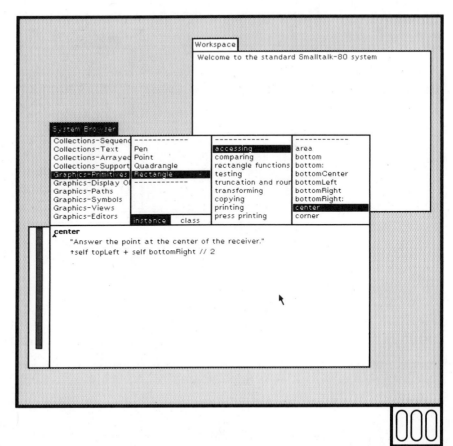

Figure 17.1

tion. The system gives visual feedback to indicate the current selection. The most common feedback mechanism is to complement a rectangular area of the screen, changing black to white and white to black. To begin using the system, one of the views is selected. The selected view is indicated by complementing only its title. The selected view will be completely displayed, obscuring the overlapping parts of any other views. In Figure 17.1, the browser is the selected view.

A different view can be selected by moving the cursor into part of its rectangular frame that hasn't been overlapped by other views, and then pressing the left button on the mouse. In Figure 17.2, the workspace has been selected. Note that the left mouse button is pressed. The workspace now obscures the overlapped part of the browser.

Text Selections

The Smalltalk-80 text editor provides the ability to select text and to perform editing operations on that selected text. For example, to replace the sequence of characters the standard with my special in the workspace, the old characters are selected and then the new characters are typed.

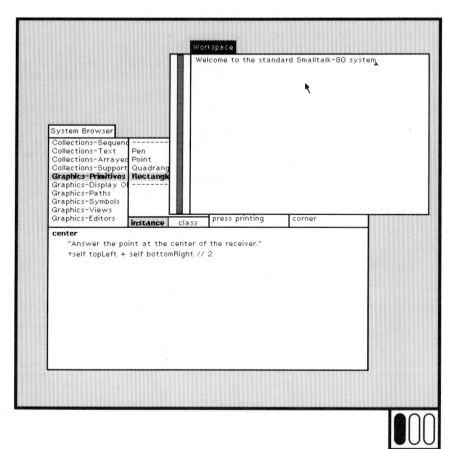

Figure 17.2

Characters are selected using the left mouse button. The cursor is positioned at one end of the selection and the mouse button is pressed (Figure 17.3).

The text selection is now empty—it contains no characters. The position of an empty selection is shown with a carat (an inverted "v"). The

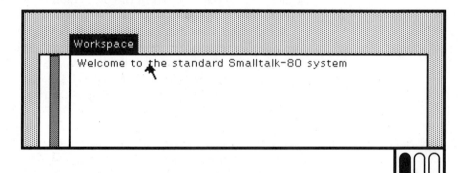

Figure 17.3

carat is partially obscured by the cursor in Figure 17.3. While the mouse button remains pressed, the cursor is moved to the other end of the characters to be selected. The selected characters are shown in a complemented rectangle (Figure 17.4).

When the button is released, the selection is complete (Figure 17.5). When characters are typed on the keyboard, they replace the selected characters. After typing the new characters, the selection is empty and positioned at the end of the new characters (Figure 17.6).

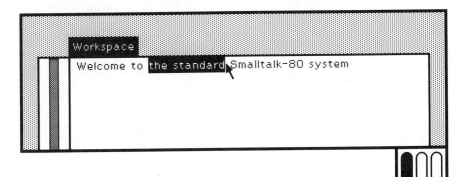

Figure 17.4

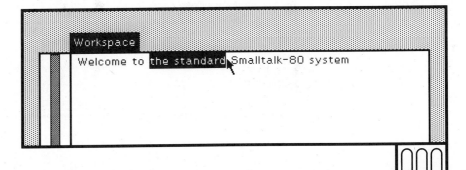

Figure 17.5

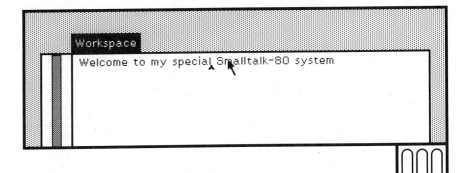

Figure 17.6

Another kind of selection used in the user interface is called *menu selection*. The middle and right mouse buttons are used to select commands from one of two menus. When one of these buttons is pressed, a menu appears at the location of the cursor. The menu obtained by pressing the middle button contains commands relevant to the contents of the selected view. When the view contains editable text, as does the workspace, these commands relate to text manipulation. The menu obtained by pressing the right button contains commands relevant to the selected view itself. The middle-button menu may be different in different views, but the right-button menu is always the same.

Characters can be deleted from a piece of text by selecting the characters and then invoking the *cut* command from the middle-button menu. In the next picture, the characters special have been selected and the middle button has been pressed. The menu of commands relevant to the contents of the view has appeared. While the button is held down, the cursor is moved to select the *cut* command in the menu (Figure 17.7). When the button is released, the selected command is carried out. In this example, the selected text is removed (Figure 17.8).

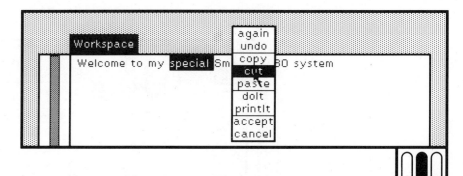

Figure 17.7

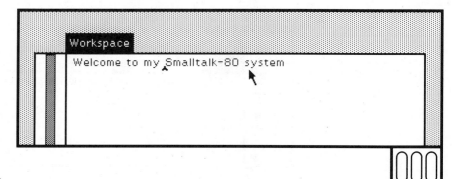

Figure 17.8

A text selection can be treated as a Smalltalk-80 expression and evaluated. There are two commands in the middle-button menu to carry out such an operation, doIt and printIt. Selecting doIt simply evaluates the selected expression and discards the resulting value. Selecting printIt evaluates the selected expression and prints its value after the expression. For example, after typing and selecting the expression Time now, printIt will print out the resulting new instance of Time (Figure 17.9). The printed result becomes the current text selection (Figure 17.10).

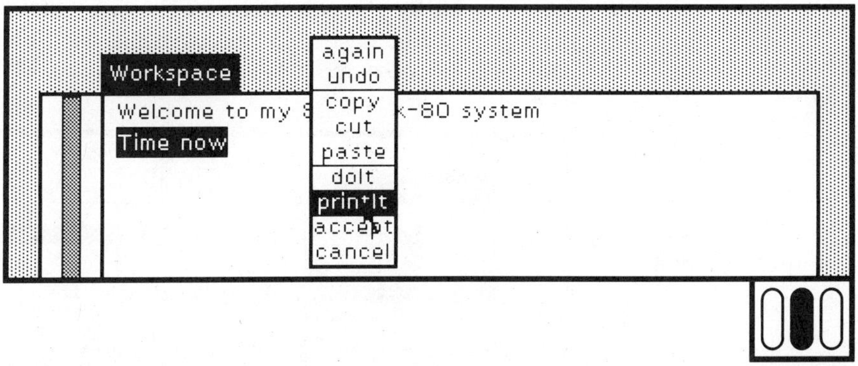

Figure 17.9

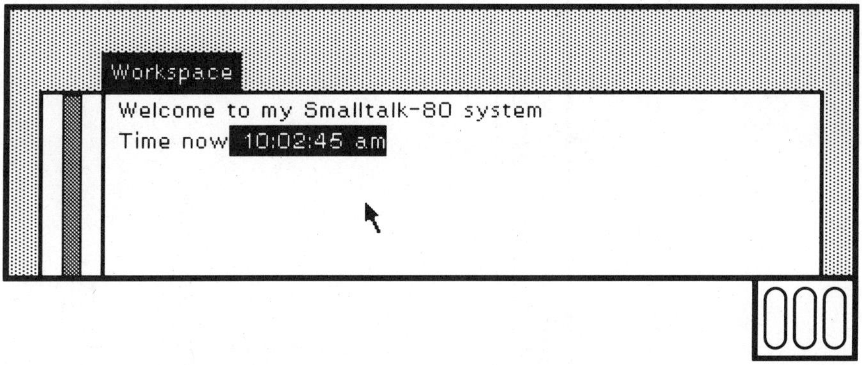

Figure 17.10

If the cursor is moved outside the menu before the button is released, no command is carried out.

Browsers

A browser is a view of the classes in the Smalltalk-80 system. Existing classes are examined and changed using a browser. New classes are added to the system using a browser. A browser consists of five rectangular subviews. Along the top are four subviews showing lists. Each list may or may not have one of its items selected. The selected item in each list is complemented. The contents of the list cannot be edited through the view, they can only be selected. Below the four list subviews is a subview showing some text. That subview is similar to the workspace, allowing the text to be edited. The selections in the four lists determine what text is visible in the lower subview. When a selection has been made in all four lists, the lower subview shows a Smalltalk-80 method. The method is found in a class determined by the selections in the two lists on the left. The method within that class is determined by the selections in the two lists on the right. The browser in Figure 17.11 is showing the method used by Rectangles to respond to the message center.

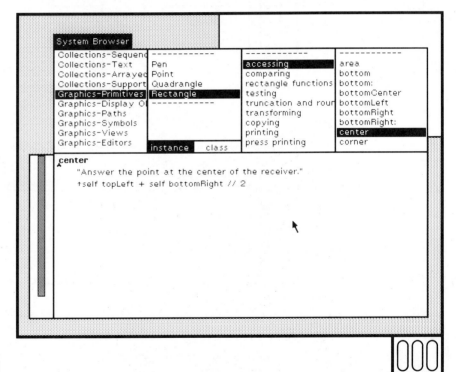

Figure 17.11

The classes in the system are organized into categories. The leftmost list in the browser shows the categories of classes in the system. When a category is selected, the classes in that category are shown in the next list to the right. In the example, the category Graphics-Primitives is selected. That category has four classes in it. When one of these classes is selected, its message categories are shown in the next list to its right.

Since Rectangle is selected, the categories in its instance protocol are displayed. At the bottom of the second list, two rectangular areas are labeled instance and class. One of these will be selected at all times. If class is selected, then the next list to the right shows the categories of class messages; if instance is selected, the list shows the categories of instance messages. When a message category is selected, the selectors of messages in that category are shown in the rightmost list. When one of these message selectors is selected, the corresponding method is displayed in the subview at the bottom of the browser. The method displayed can be edited and the old version can be replaced by the edited version, if desired.

List Selections

A selection is made in a list by placing the cursor over an item and then pressing and releasing the left mouse button. In Figure 17.12, another item is selected in the browser's rightmost list. Therefore, another method is presented in the lower text subview.

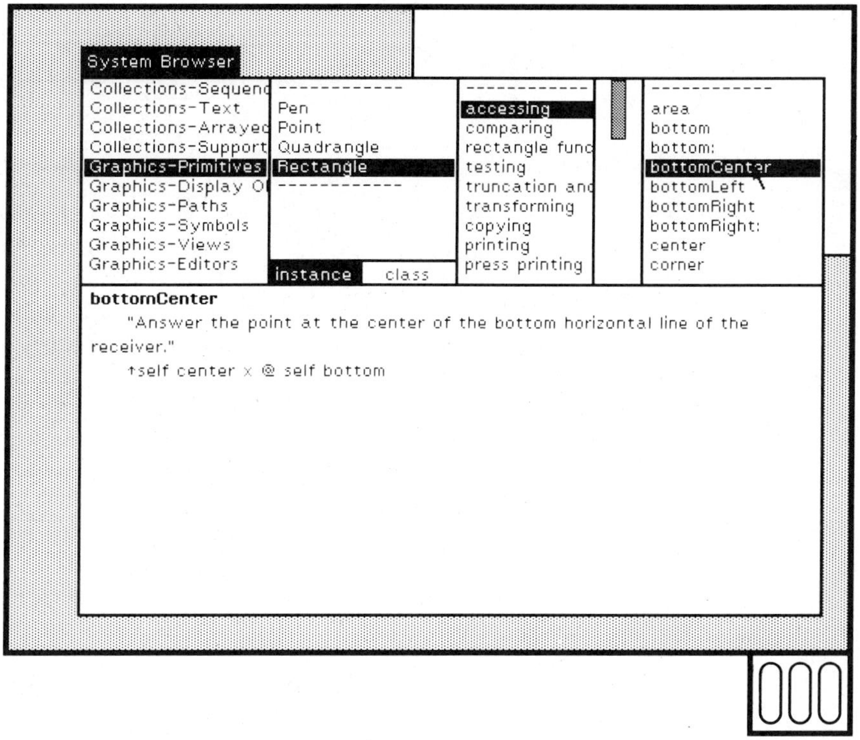

Figure 17.12

If the left button is pressed and released while the cursor is over the item already selected, that item is deselected (Figure 17.13).

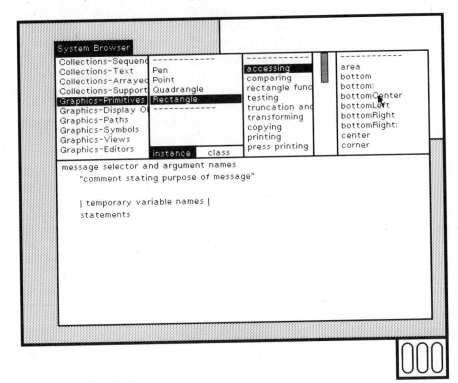

Figure 17.13

When a message category is selected, but none of its message selectors have been selected in the rightmost list, the lower subview contains some text describing the various syntactic parts of a method. This text can be replaced with a new method to be added to the system. The new method will be added to the selected category.

If a class category has been selected, but none of its classes has been selected, the lower subview contains some text describing the various parts of a class definition. This text is in the form of a message to a class (Object, in this case) asking it to create a new subclass of itself (Figure 17.14).

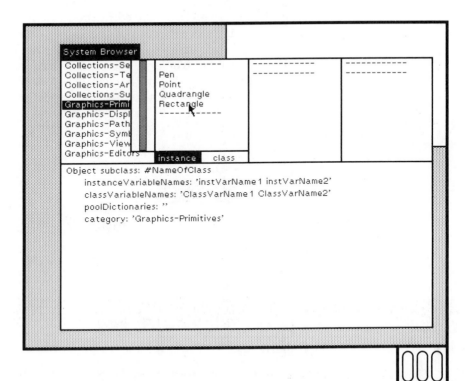

Figure 17.14

Scrolling

A view may not be large enough to show all of the information it might. For example, many of the lists viewed by the browser are too long to be completely displayed in the space available. The view can be positioned on different parts of the list by using a *scroll bar*. A scroll bar is a rectangular area that appears to the left of the subview containing the cursor. The gray box in the scroll bar indicates which part of the total list is visible in the view. The height of the scroll bar represents the length of the entire list. The part of the scroll bar occupied by the gray box indicates the part of the list that is visible.

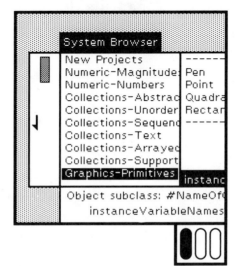

Figure 17.15

By moving the mouse into the scroll bar, another part of the list can be shown. This is called *scrolling*. When the cursor is in the right half of the scroll bar, it takes the shape of an upward pointing arrow. If the left mouse button is pressed, the items in the list appears to move up in the subview and new items become visible at the bottom. When the cursor is in the left half of the scroll bar, its shape is a downward pointing arrow; pressing the left button makes an earlier part of the list visible. For example, the browser's leftmost list can be scrolled to show categories earlier in the list (Figure 17.15).

Views containing text can also be scrolled if the view is too small to show all the text.

Class Definitions

A new class can be added to the system by selecting a class category and editing the text describing the parts of a class definition. The FinancialHistory example will be added to the category named New Projects.

While text is being changed in the lower subview, it may not accurately represent a class definition or a method. The accept command in the middle-button menu is used to indicate that the editing has been completed and the class definition or method should be added to the system (Figures 17.16 and 17.17).

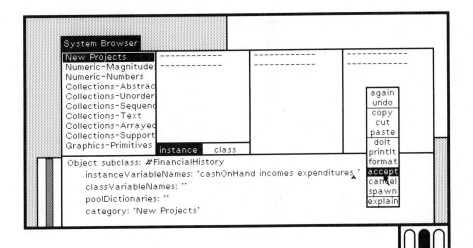

Figure 17.16

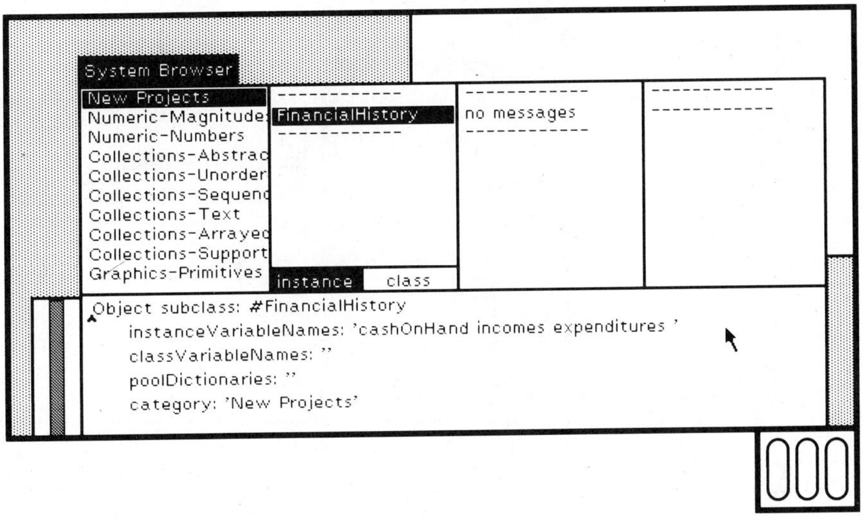

Figure 17.17

The menu that appears when the middle button is pressed is different in each of the browser's subviews. In the subview showing the classes in a category, the menu includes an item called definition. This command causes the class definition of an existing class to be displayed (Figures 17.18 and 17.19).

This class definition can then be modified with the standard text editing operations. After changing the text, accept must be selected again in the middle-button menu. For example, an instance variable could be added to all Rectangles by adding its name to the appropriate place in the class definition.

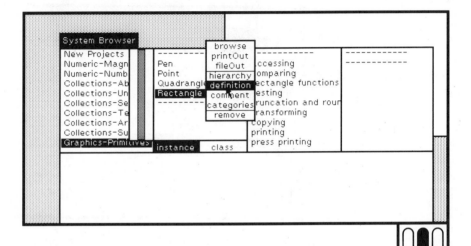

Figure 17.18

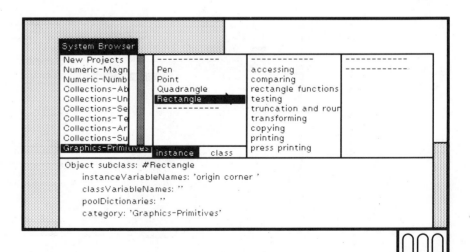

Figure 17.19

Another item in the middle-button menu for the class list is
categories. When it is selected, the message categorization is shown in
the bottom subview (Figures 17.20 and 17.21).

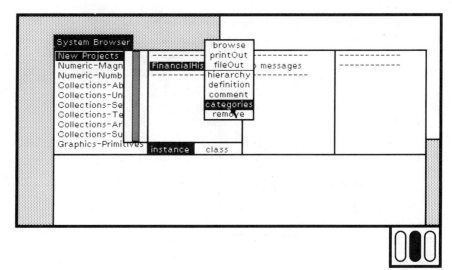

Figure 17.20

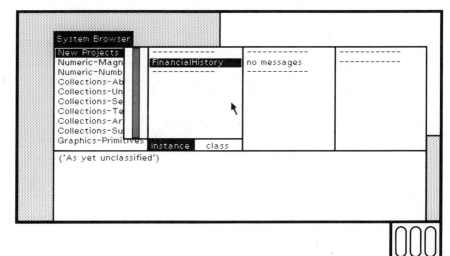

Figure 17.21

The new class has a single, empty message category called As yet
unclassified.

The categorization can be changed by editing the text and selecting accept (Figures 17.22 and 17.23). Notice the change in the third subview from the left of Figure 17.23. There are now three categories, transaction recording, inquiries, and private.

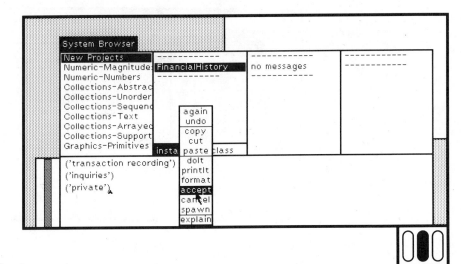

Figure 17.22

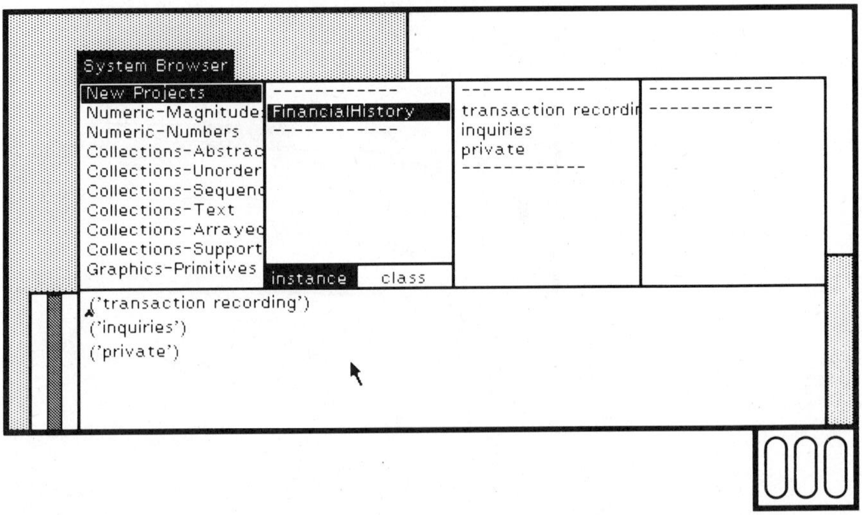

Figure 17.23

After a new class has been added to the system, methods can be added by selecting categories and editing method templates (Figures 17.24 and 17.25).

Notice the change in the rightmost subview of Figure 17.25. The selector of the new method is added to the (previously empty) list and becomes the current selection.

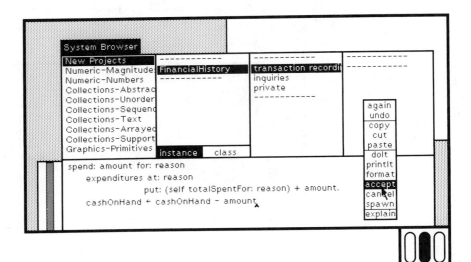

Figure 17.24

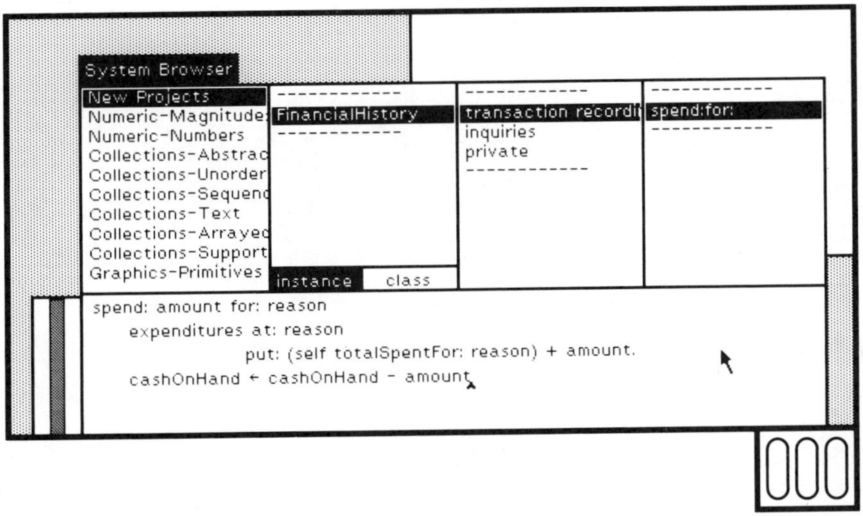

Figure 17.25

Testing

After the methods shown in Chapter 5 have been added to FinancialHistory, instances can be created and tested by sending them messages. First, a new global variable will be added to the system by sending the message at:put: to the dictionary of global variables whose name is Smalltalk. The first argument of at:put: is the name of the global variable and the second is the initial value. This global variable will be used to refer to the instance being tested (Figure 17.26).

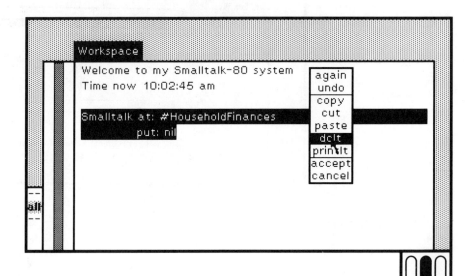

Figure 17.26

Messages are sent to HouseholdFinances by typing expressions in the workspace and evaluating them by invoking the commands doIt or printIt (Figure 17.27). Several expressions can be selected and evaluated at one time. The expressions are separated by periods (Figure 17.28).

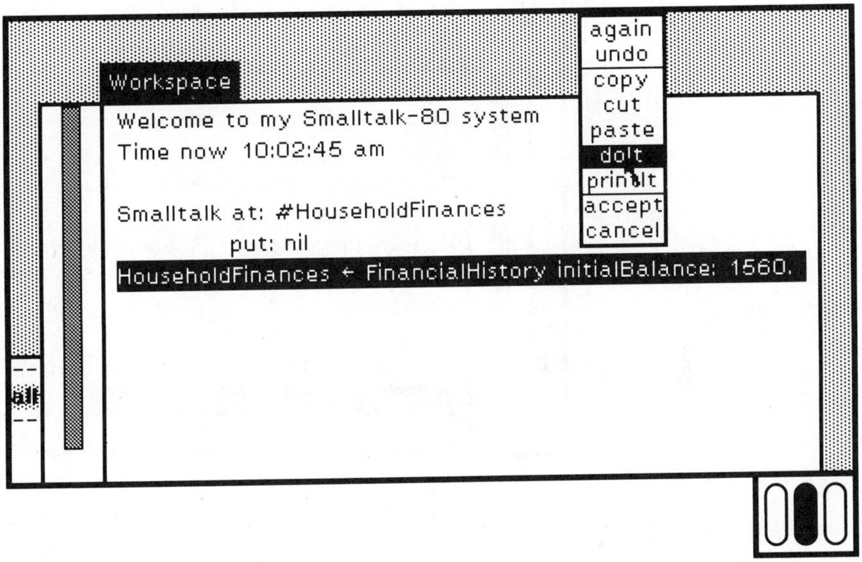

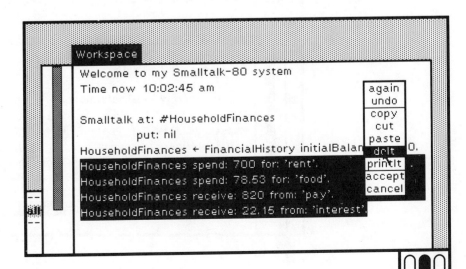

Figure 17.27

Figure 17.28

Selecting printIt instead of doIt displays the result following the expression (Figures 17.29 and 17.30).

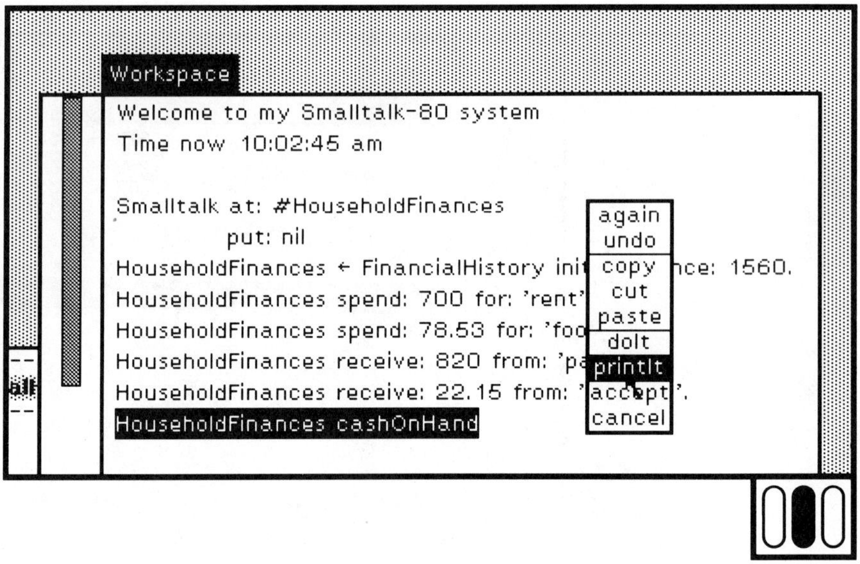

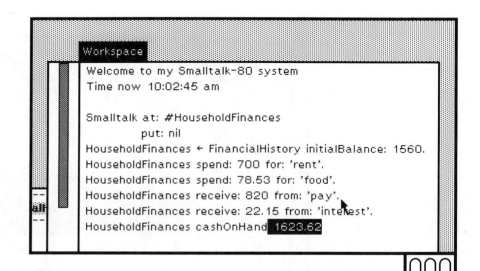

Figure 17.29

Figure 17.30

Inspectors

An inspector is a view of an object's instance variables. An inspector is created by sending inspect to the object whose instance variables are to be viewed (Figure 17.31).

After inspect has been sent, the user is prompted for a rectangular area in which to display the inspector. The shape of the cursor is changed to indicate that the upper left corner of the rectangular area should be specified (Figure 17.32).

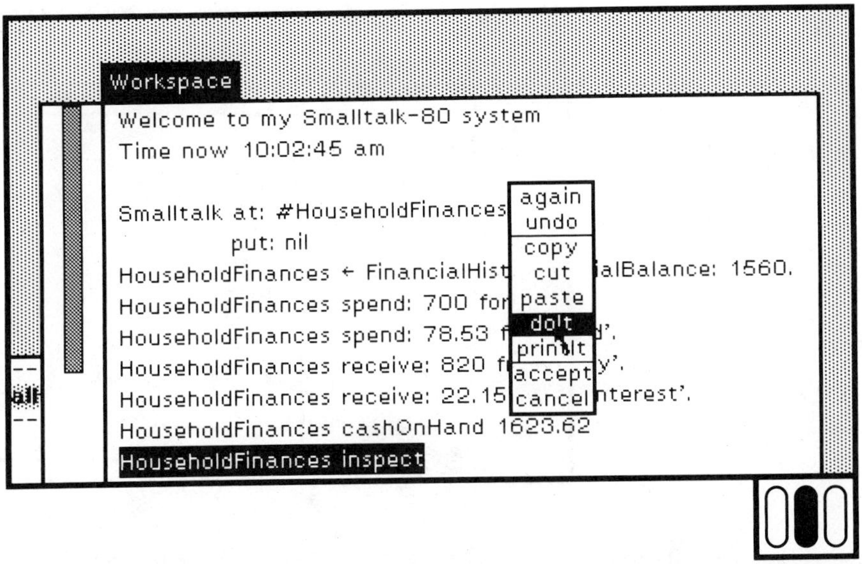

Workspace

Welcome to my Smalltalk-80 system
Time now 10:02:45 am

Smalltalk at: #HouseholdFinances
        put: nil
HouseholdFinances ← FinancialHist   alBalance: 1560.
HouseholdFinances spend: 700 for paste
HouseholdFinances spend: 78.53 f   d'.
HouseholdFinances receive: 820 f   y'.
HouseholdFinances receive: 22.15 nterest'.
HouseholdFinances cashOnHand 1623.62
HouseholdFinances inspect

again
undo
copy
cut
paste
do it
print it
accept
cancel

Figure 17.31

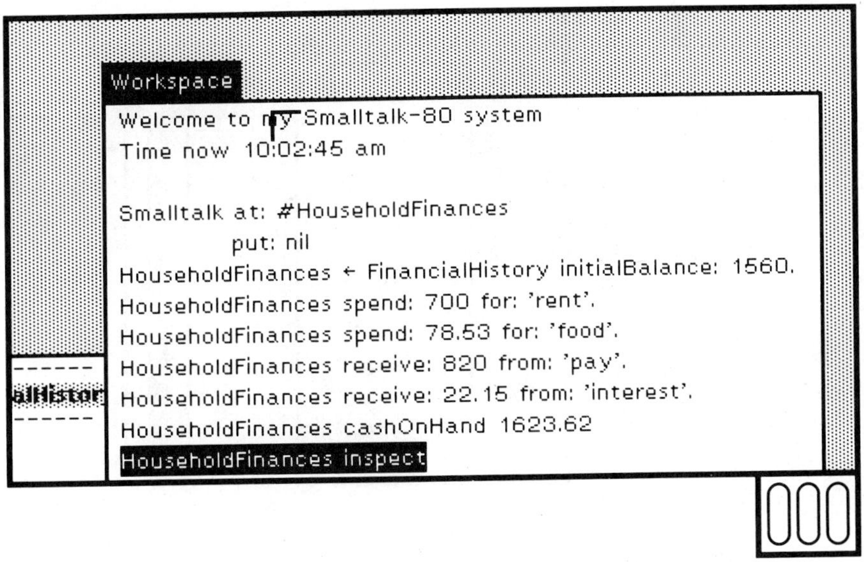

Workspace

Welcome to my Smalltalk-80 system
Time now 10:02:45 am

Smalltalk at: #HouseholdFinances
        put: nil
HouseholdFinances ← FinancialHistory initialBalance: 1560.
HouseholdFinances spend: 700 for: 'rent'.
HouseholdFinances spend: 78.53 for: 'food'.
HouseholdFinances receive: 820 from: 'pay'.
HouseholdFinances receive: 22.15 from: 'interest'.
HouseholdFinances cashOnHand 1623.62
HouseholdFinances inspect

Figure 17.32

The cursor is moved to the desired location and the left mouse button is pressed and held down. The shape of the cursor is changed again to indicate that the lower right corner of the rectangular area should now be specified. As long as the left mouse button remains pressed, the prospective new rectangular frame is displayed (Figure 17.33).

When the button is released, the inspector is displayed in the selected area (Figure 17.34).

The title of the inspector is the name of the inspected object's class.

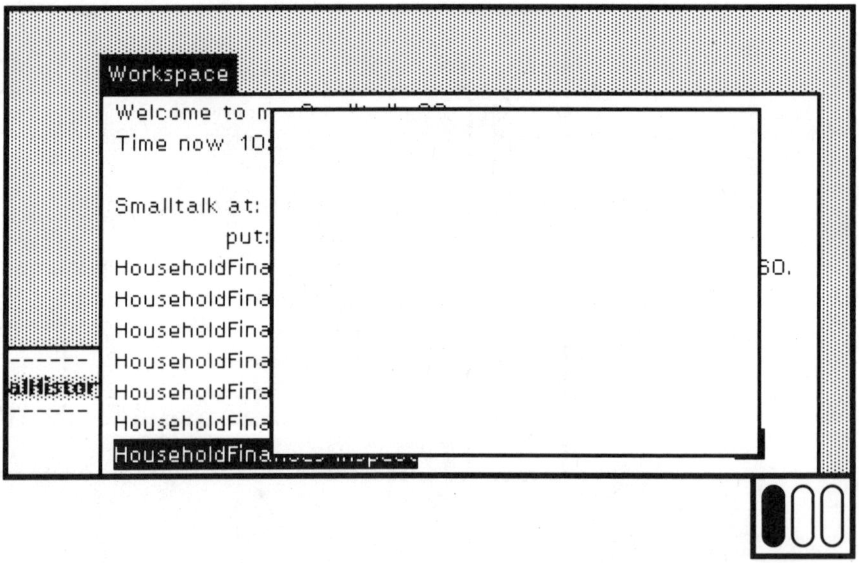

Figure 17.33

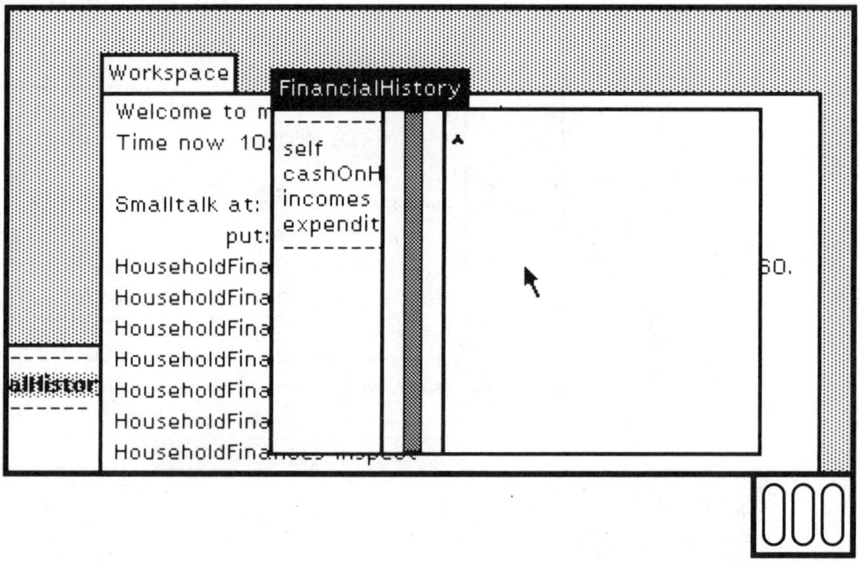

Figure 17.34

An inspector has two subviews. The left subview shows a list containing self and the names of the object's instance variables. When one of the elements of the list is selected, the corresponding value is printed in the subview to the right (Figures 17.35 and 17.36). The text that appears in the righthand subview is obtained as a result of sending printString to the selected object. Selecting the element self at the top of the list, prints the object being inspected (Figure 17.37).

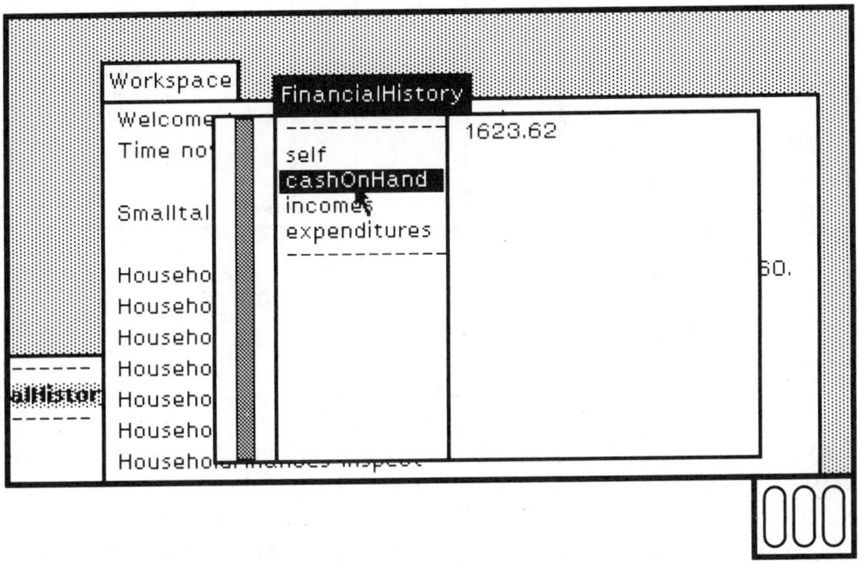

Figure 17.35

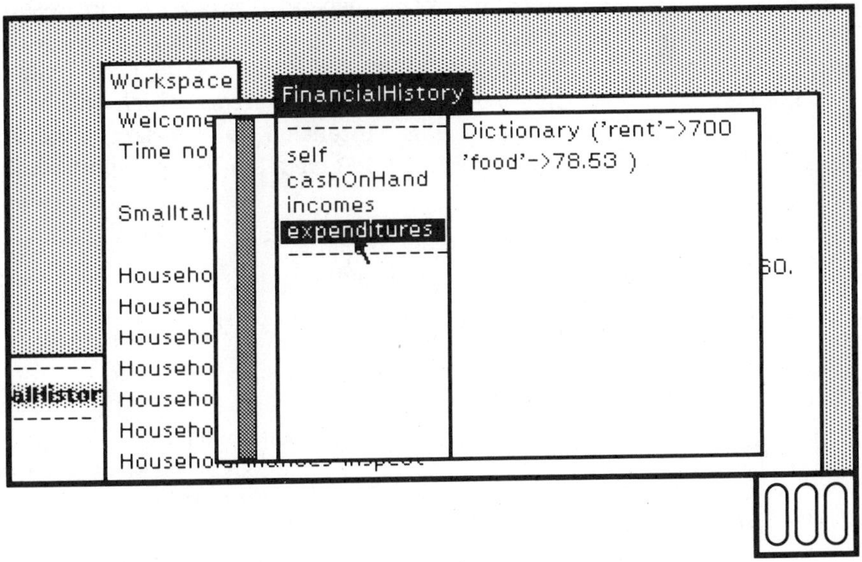

Figure 17.36

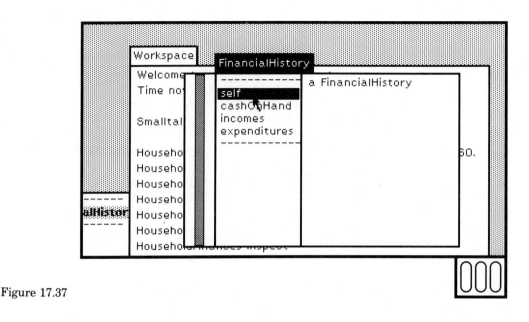

Figure 17.37

Error Reporting

When an error is encountered, the process in which the error occurred is suspended and a view of that process is created. Suspended processes can be viewed in two ways, with *notifiers* and with *debuggers*. A notifier provides a simple description of the process at the time of the error. A debugger provides a more detailed view and also the ability to change the state of the suspended process before resuming it.

As an example of error reporting, we will follow the addition and debugging of several new methods in FinancialHistory. The following methods contain several errors which will be "discovered" in the testing process. The intention of these new methods is to allow a FinancialHistory to give a summary report of its state.

```
report
    | reportStream |
    reportStream ← WriteStream on: (String new: 10).
    reportStream cr.
    reportStream nextPutAll: 'Expenses'.
    reportStream cr.
    self expenseReasons do:
        [ :reason | reportStream tab.
                reportStream nextPutAll: reason.
                reportStream tab.
                reportStream nextPutAll: (self totalSpentFor: reason).
                reportStream cr].
```

```
reportStream nextPutAll: ' Incomes' .
reportStream cr.
self incomeSources do:
    [ :source | reportStream tab.
            reportStream nextPutAll: source.
            reportStream tab.
            reportStream nextPutAll: (self totalReceivedFrom: source).
            reportStream cr].
↑reportStream contents
```

incomeSources
```
    ↑incomes keys
```
expenditureReasons
```
    ↑expenditures keys
```

A new category is added and the new methods typed in and accepted (Figure 17.38).

After adding the new methods, the instance of FinancialHistory can be asked for a report by evaluating an expression in the workspace (Figure 17.39). Instead of printing the report, a notifier appears on the screen (Figure 17.40).

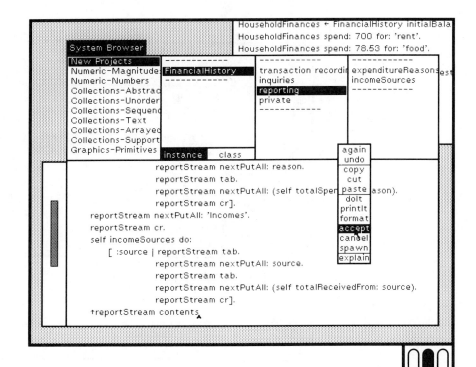

Figure 17.38

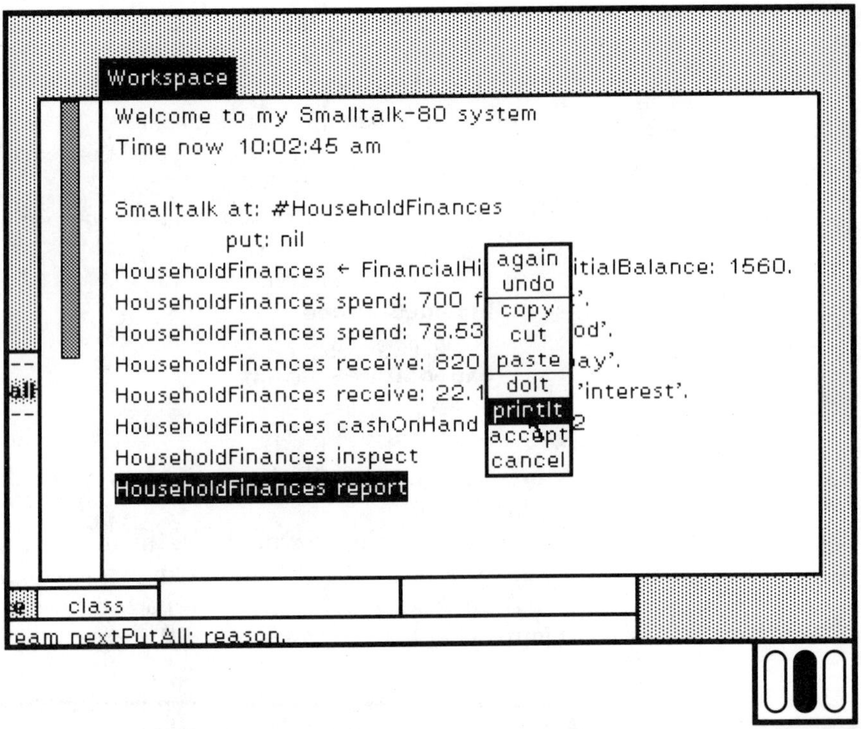

Workspace

Welcome to my Smalltalk-80 system
Time now 10:02:45 am

Smalltalk at: #HouseholdFinances
          put: nil
HouseholdFinances ← FinancialHi| again |itialBalance: 1560.
HouseholdFinances spend: 700 f| undo |',
                                 | copy |
HouseholdFinances spend: 78.53| cut |od'.
                                | paste |
HouseholdFinances receive: 820| dolt |ay'.
HouseholdFinances receive: 22.1| printlt |'interest'.
HouseholdFinances cashOnHand| accept |2
HouseholdFinances inspect | cancel |
HouseholdFinances report

class

ream nextPutAll: reason.

Figure 17.39

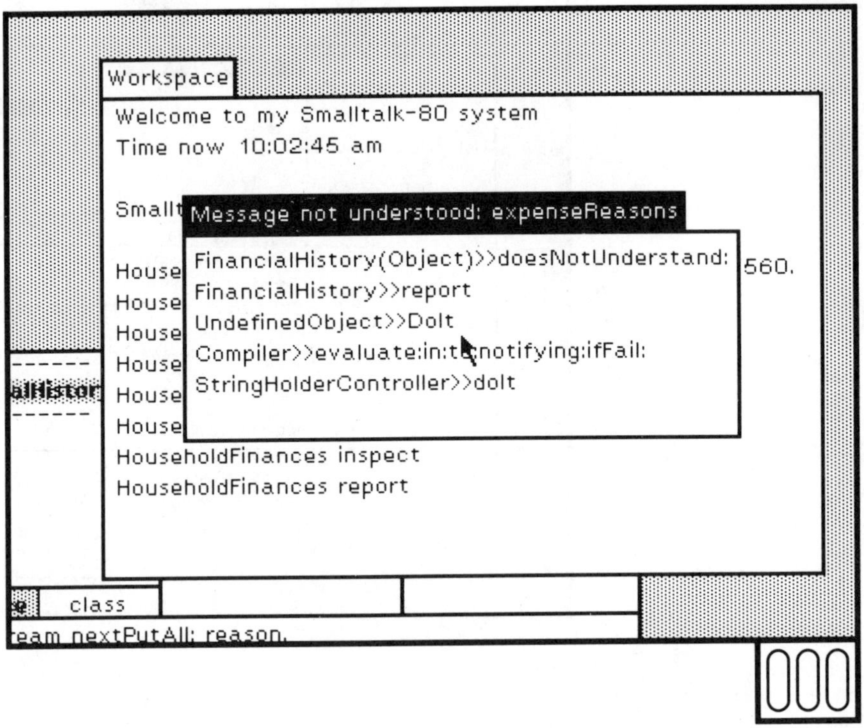

Workspace

Welcome to my Smalltalk-80 system
Time now 10:02:45 am

Smallt| Message not understood: expenseReasons
House| FinancialHistory(Object)>>doesNotUnderstand: |560.
House| FinancialHistory>>report
House| UndefinedObject>>Dolt
House| Compiler>>evaluate:in:to:notifying:ifFail:
alHistor| House| StringHolderController>>dolt
House
HouseholdFinances inspect
HouseholdFinances report

class

ream nextPutAll: reason.

Figure 17.40

Notifiers

A notifier is a simple view of a process suspended after an error. The notifier's title indicates the nature of the error. Notifiers are created by sending an object the message error:. The argument of the message becomes the title of the notifier. The notifier shown in Figure 17.40 indicates that the message expenseReasons was sent to an object that did not understand it. The list visible in the notifier shows part of the state of the suspended process.

The cause of this error is evident from the title of the notifier. The message added to FinancialHistory was expenditureReasons not expenseReasons. The notifier and the erroneous process can be discarded by selecting the command close in the right mouse-button menu (Figure 17.41).

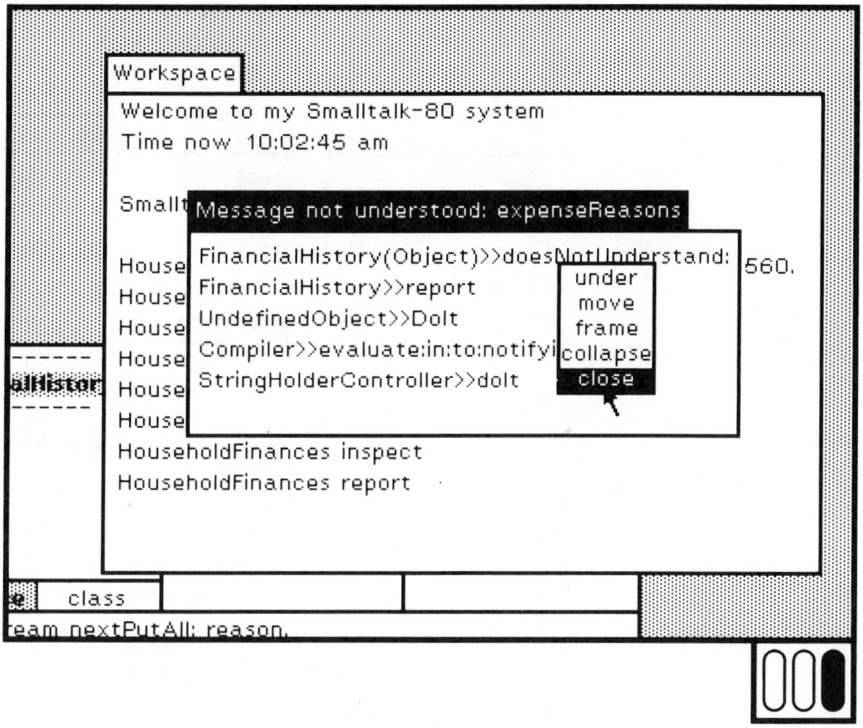

Workspace

Welcome to my Smalltalk-80 system
Time now 10:02:45 am

Smallt Message not understood: expenseReasons

House FinancialHistory(Object)>>doesNotUnderstand: 560.
House FinancialHistory>>report   under
House UndefinedObject>>DoIt   move
House Compiler>>evaluate:in:to:notifyi   frame
alHistor House StringHolderController>>doIt   collapse
House   close
House
HouseholdFinances inspect
HouseholdFinances report

class

eam nextPutAll: reason.

Figure 17.41

The misspelling in report can be corrected in the browser (Figures 17.42 and 17.43).

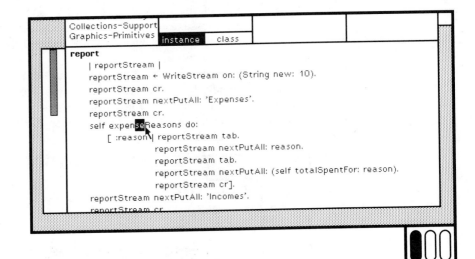

Figure 17.42

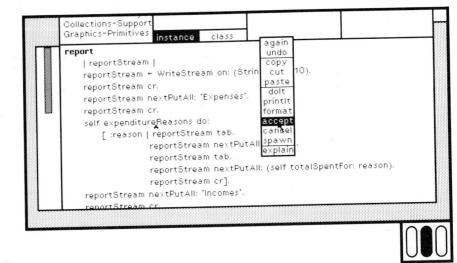

Figure 17.43

After fixing the misspelling in the browser, the original expression can be evaluated in the workspace again (Figures 17.44 and 17.45).

This creates another notifier. The cause of this error is not as obvious. The message do: was sent to an object that did not understand it. In order to learn more about the error, a more detailed view of the suspended process can be obtained by selecting the command debug in the middle-button menu.

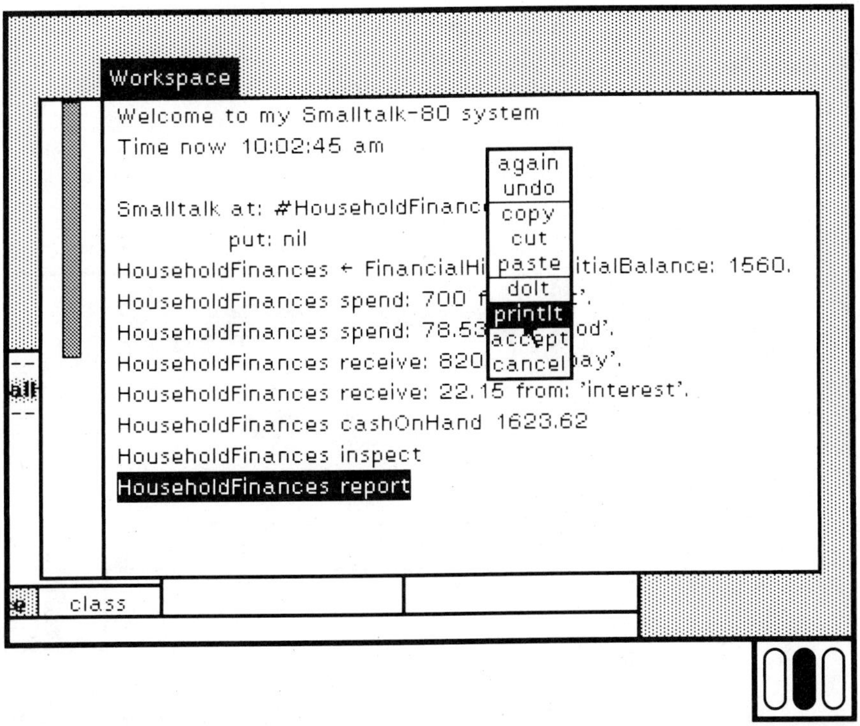

Figure 17.44

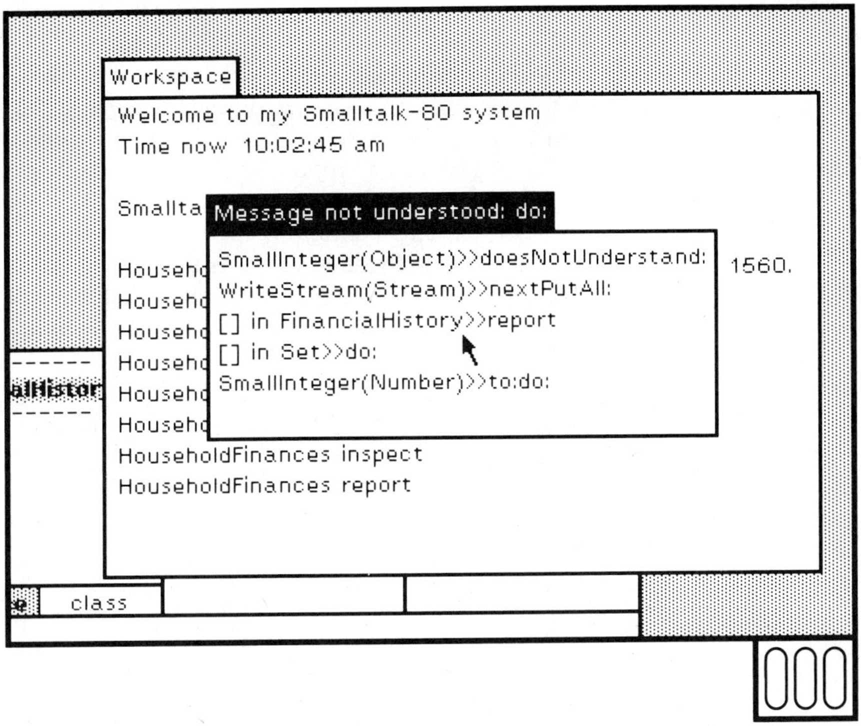

Figure 17.45

A debugger is a view of a suspended process that reveals more details than a notifier reveals. When debug is selected in a notifier's middle-button menu, a debugger is created viewing the same process the notifier viewed (Figure 17.46). After selecting debug, the user is prompted to supply a rectangular area in which to display the debugger. The rectangle is specified in the same way that the rectangular frame for a new inspector is specified (Figure 17.47).

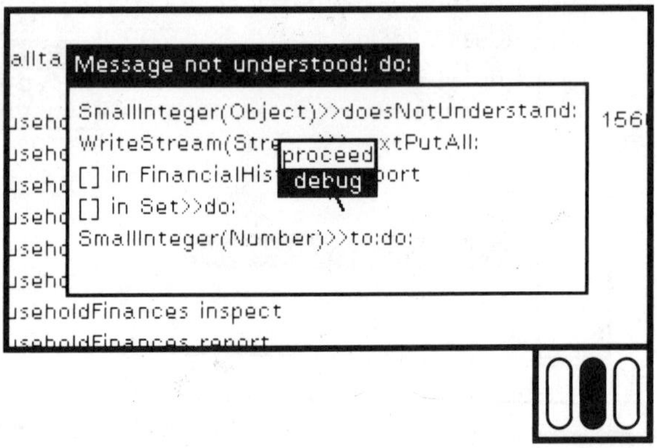

allta Message not understood: do:

usehd SmallInteger(Object)>>doesNotUnderstand: 156
usehd WriteStream(Str   xtPutAll:
usehd [] in FinancialHis proceed ort
usehd [] in Set>>do: debug
usehd SmallInteger(Number)>>to:do:
usehd
usehd
useholdFinances inspect
useholdFinances report

Figure 17.46

The debugger has six subviews. The top subview shows the same list that was visible through the notifier. This list gives a partial history of the process in which the error occurred. Each item corresponds to a message that was sent and whose response is not yet completed. The item contains the name of the receiver's class and the selector of the message, separated by " >> ". The last item visible in the list, FinancialHistory >> report, indicates that an instance of FinancialHistory received the message report. This message was sent when the middle-button menu command printIt was selected while the expression HouseholdFinances report was the text selection. When one of the items in the debugger's upper list is selected, the method invoked by the corresponding message is displayed in the subview immediately below.

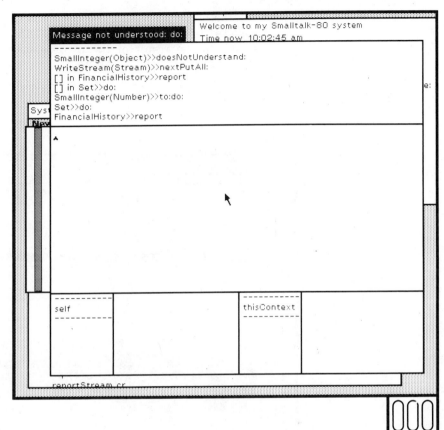

Figure 17.47

When a method is displayed, the last message sent before the process was suspended is complemented. Figure 17.48 shows that the message do: was sent to the result of the expression self expenditureReasons. The next item up on the list, Set>>do:, indicates that the receiver of do: was an instance of Set. The method invoked can be seen by selecting Set>>do: in the list.

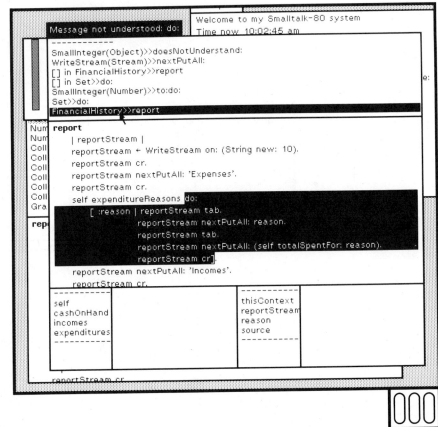

Figure 17.48

Figure 17.49 shows that this method sent a message to the object 1. The next item up on the list, SmallInteger(Number)>>to:do: shows that the receiver was an instance of SmallInteger. When the method invoked by a message was found in a superclass of the receiver's class, the name of that superclass is included in parentheses after the receiver's direct class. In the example, the method for to:do: was found in class Number.

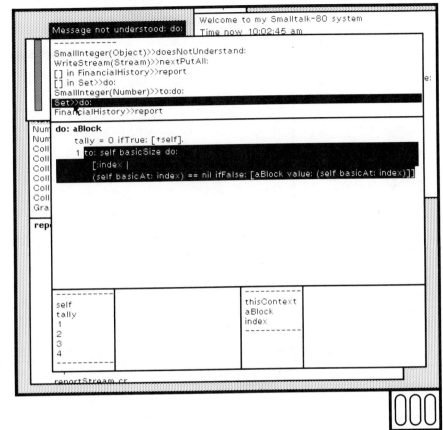

Figure 17.49

The top item on the list, SmallInteger(Object) >> doesNotUnderstand:, shows the last thing that happened before the process was suspended— an instance of SmallInteger received the message doesNotUnderstand:. This message was sent by the system when the do: message was not found in SmallInteger or in any of its superclasses. The doesNotUnderstand: message invoked a method that suspended the process and created the notifier viewing it. The second item from the top of the list, WriteStream(Stream) >> nextPutAll:, indicates that the misunderstood do: message was sent from the method for nextPutAll: in class Stream. Figure 17.50 shows the debugger with that item selected. The method displayed shows that do: was sent to the object named aCollection, which was provided as the argument of nextPutAll:.

The lower four subviews of a debugger are used to find the value of the variables used in the method. They function like two inspectors. The leftmost subview shows a list of the receiver (self) and its instance variable names. The third subview from the left shows the argument

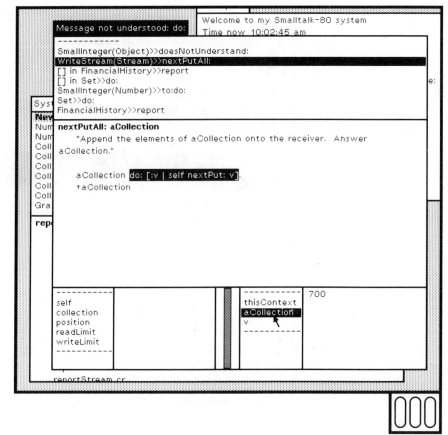

Figure 17.50

names and temporary variable names. When a name is selected in either one of these lists, the value of the associated variable is shown in the subview to its right. To display the receiver of the do: message, aCollection is selected in Figure 17.50.

The source of this error appears to be that the Stream was expecting a collection of elements as the argument of nextPutAll: and it got a number, 700, instead. Selecting the next item down from the top list shows where the argument came from. The argument was the result of evaluating the expression (self totalSpentFor: reason). In Figure 17.51, selections have been made in the bottom subviews to display the values of the instance variable, expenditures, and the argument, reason.

When text is selected and evaluated in the method displayed in the browser, the variable names are interpreted in that context. So the argument to nextPutAll: can be found by re-executing the expression (self totalSpentFor: reason) and printing the result (Figure 17.52).

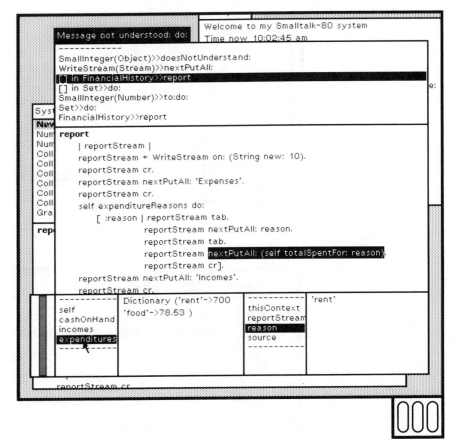

Figure 17.51

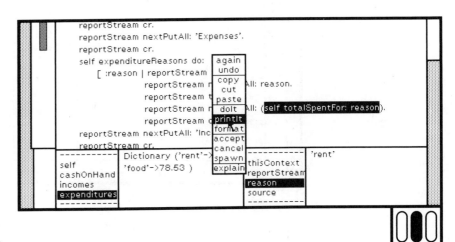

Figure 17.52

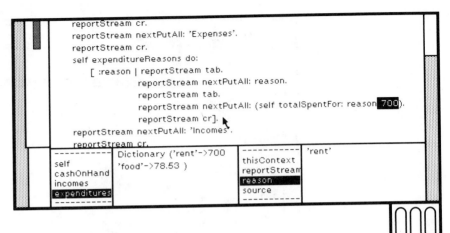

Figure 17.53

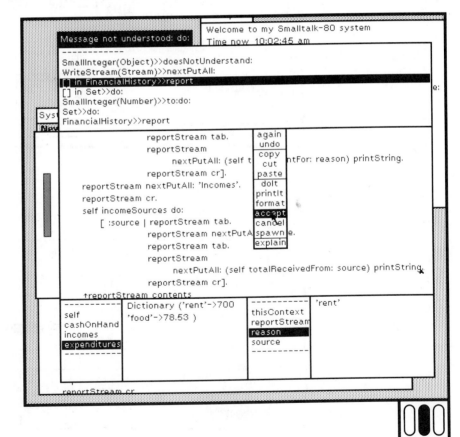

Figure 17.54

The result is 700, as expected (Figure 17.53).

The report method had intended that the character representation of 700 be appended to reportStream, but it appended the number itself instead. This bug is fixed by sending the number the message printString. The correction can be made in the debugger (Figure 17.54). Now the expression can be evaluated again. The report is now successfully printed in the workspace (Figure 17.55).

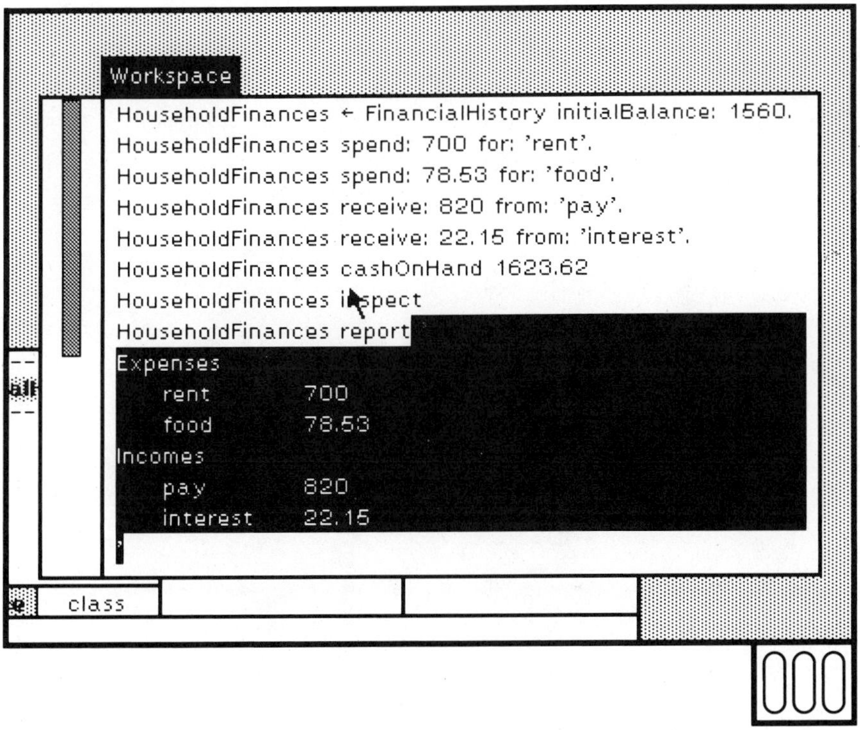

Figure 17.55

This completes the overview of the Smalltalk-80 programming interface. The ability to support this type of interaction with the user motivates the nature of many of the graphics classes discussed in subsequent chapters.

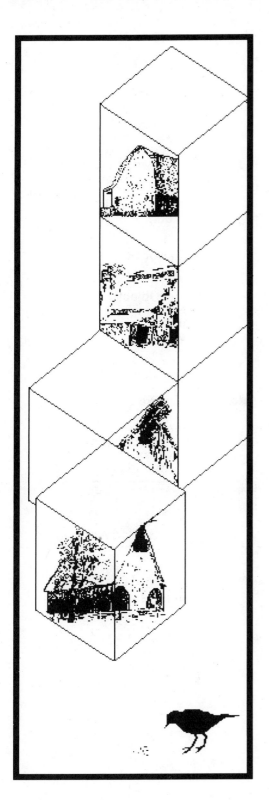

Object

Magnitude
    Character
    Date
    Time

    Number
      Float
      Fraction
      Integer
        LargeNegativeInteger
        LargePositiveInteger
        SmallInteger

    LookupKey
      Association

Link

    Process

Collection

    SequenceableCollection
      LinkedList

        Semaphore

      ArrayedCollection
        Array
        Bitmap
          DisplayBitmap
        RunArray
        String
          Symbol
        Text
        ByteArray

      Interval
      OrderedCollection
        SortedCollection
    Bag
    MappedCollection
    Set
      Dictionary
        IdentityDictionary

Stream
    PositionableStream
      ReadStream
      WriteStream
        ReadWriteStream
          ExternalStream
            FileStream

    Random

File
FileDirectory
FilePage

UndefinedObject
Boolean
    False
    True

ProcessorScheduler
Delay
SharedQueue

Behavior
    ClassDescription
      Class
      MetaClass

Point
Rectangle
BitBlt
    CharacterScanner
Pen

DisplayObject
    DisplayMedium
      Form
        Cursor
        DisplayScreen
    InfiniteForm
    OpaqueForm
    Path
      Arc
        Circle
      Curve
      Line
      LinearFit
      Spline

Graphical Representation

Figure 18.1 shows a view of the display screen for a Smalltalk-80 system. It illustrates the wide range of graphical idiom available to the system. Rectangular areas of arbitrary size are filled with white, black, and halftone patterns. Text, in various typefaces, is placed on the screen from stored images of the individual characters. Halftone shades are "brushed" by the user to create freehand paintings. Moreover, although not shown on the printed page, images on the display can be moved or sequenced in time to provide animation.

The example interaction with the system given in the previous chapter illustrated some of the ways in which objects can be observed and manipulated graphically. Meaningful presentation of objects in the system demands maximum control over the display medium. One approach that provides the necessary flexibility is to allow the brightness of every discernible point in the displayed image to be independently controlled. An implementation of this approach is a contiguous block of storage in which the setting of each *bit* is mapped into the illumination of a corresponding picture element, or *pixel*, when displaying the image. The block of storage is referred to as a *bitmap*. This type of display is called a *bitmapped display*. The simplest form of bitmap allows only two brightness levels, white and black, corresponding to the stored bit values 0 or 1 respectively. The Smalltalk-80 graphics system is built around this model of a display medium.

Graphical Storage

Images are represented by instances of class Form. A Form has height and width, and a bitmap, which indicates the white and black regions of the particular image being represented. Consider, for example, the man-shape in Figure 18.2. The height of the Form is 40, its width is 14, and its appearance is described by the pattern of ones and zeros (shown as light and dark squares) in its bitmap. The height and width of the Form serve to impose the appropriate two-dimensional ordering on the otherwise unstructured data in the bitmap. We shall return to the representation of Forms in more detail later in this chapter.

New Forms are created by combining several Forms. The freehand drawing in the center of Figure 18.1 is an example of a large Form that was created by combining and repeating several Forms that serve as "paint brushes" in a Smalltalk-80 application system. The text in Figure 18.1 is a structured combination of Forms representing characters.

A Form can be presented to the display hardware as a buffer in memory of the actual data or of the image to be shown on a display

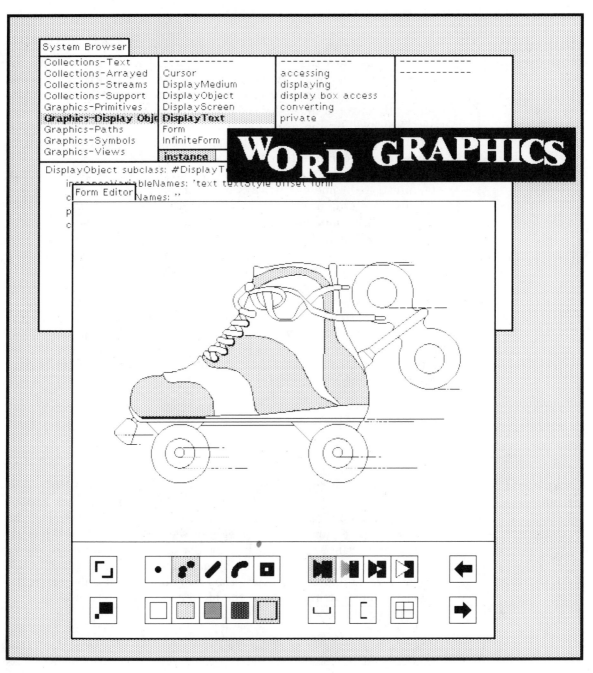

Figure 18.1

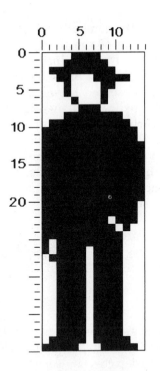

Figure 18.2

screen. Since the interface to the hardware is through a Form, there is no difference between combining images internally and displaying them on the screen. Animation can be displayed smoothly by using one Form as the display Form while the next image to be displayed is prepared in a second Form. As each image is completed, the two Forms exchange roles, causing the new image to be displayed and making the Form with the old image available for building yet another image in the sequence.

The Forms used as buffers for data to be shown on the display screen are instances of class DisplayScreen, a subclass of Form. Contiguous storage of bits is provided by instances of class Bitmap. DisplayScreen's bitmap is an instance of DisplayBitmap, a subclass of Bitmap. DisplayScreen and DisplayBitmap provide protocol specific to the actual hardware and to the fact that the Form represents the whole display screen rather than potential parts of it.

Graphical Manipulation

A basic operation on Forms, referred to as *BitBlt*, supports a wide range of graphical presentation. All text and graphic objects in the system are created and modified using this single graphical operation. The name

"BitBlt" derives from the generalization of data transfer to arbitrary bit locations, or pixels. One of the first computers on which a Smalltalk system was implemented had an instruction called BLT for *block transfer* of 16-bit words, and so "bit block transfer" became known as BitBlt.

Operations are represented by messages to objects. So BitBlt could have been implemented with a message to class Form. However, because BitBlts are fairly complicated operations to specify, they are represented by objects. These objects are instances of the class named BitBlt. The basic operation is performed by sending an appropriately initialized instance of BitBlt the message copyBits. The BitBlt operation is intentionally a very general operation, although most applications of it are graphically simple, such as "move this rectangle of pixels from here to there."

Figure 18.3 illustrates the process of copying a character of text into a region on the display. This operation will serve to illustrate most of the characteristics of BitBlt that are introduced in the remainder of this section.

Source and Destination Forms

The BitBlt copy operation involves two Forms, a source and a destination. The source in the example in Figure 18.3 is a *font* containing a set of character glyphs depicted in some uniform style and scale, and packed together horizontally. The destination in the example is assumed to be a Form that is used as the display buffer. Pixels are copied out of the source and stored into the destination. The width and height of the transfer correspond to the character size. The source x and y coordinates give the character's location in the font, and the destination coordinates specify the position on the display where its copy will appear.

Clipping Rectangle

BitBlt includes in its specification a rectangular area which limits the region of the destination that can be affected by its operation, independent of the other destination parameters. We call this area the *clipping rectangle*. Often it is desirable to display a partial *window* onto larger scenes, and the clipping rectangle ensures that all picture elements fall inside the bounds of the window. By its inclusion in the BitBlt primitive, the clipping function can be done efficiently and in one place, rather than being replicated in all application programs.

Figure 18.4 illustrates the result of imposing a clipping rectangle on the example of Figure 18.3. Pixels that would have been placed outside the clipping rectangle (the left edge of the "N" and half of the word "the") have not been transferred. Had there been other characters that fell above or below this rectangle, they would have been similarly clipped.

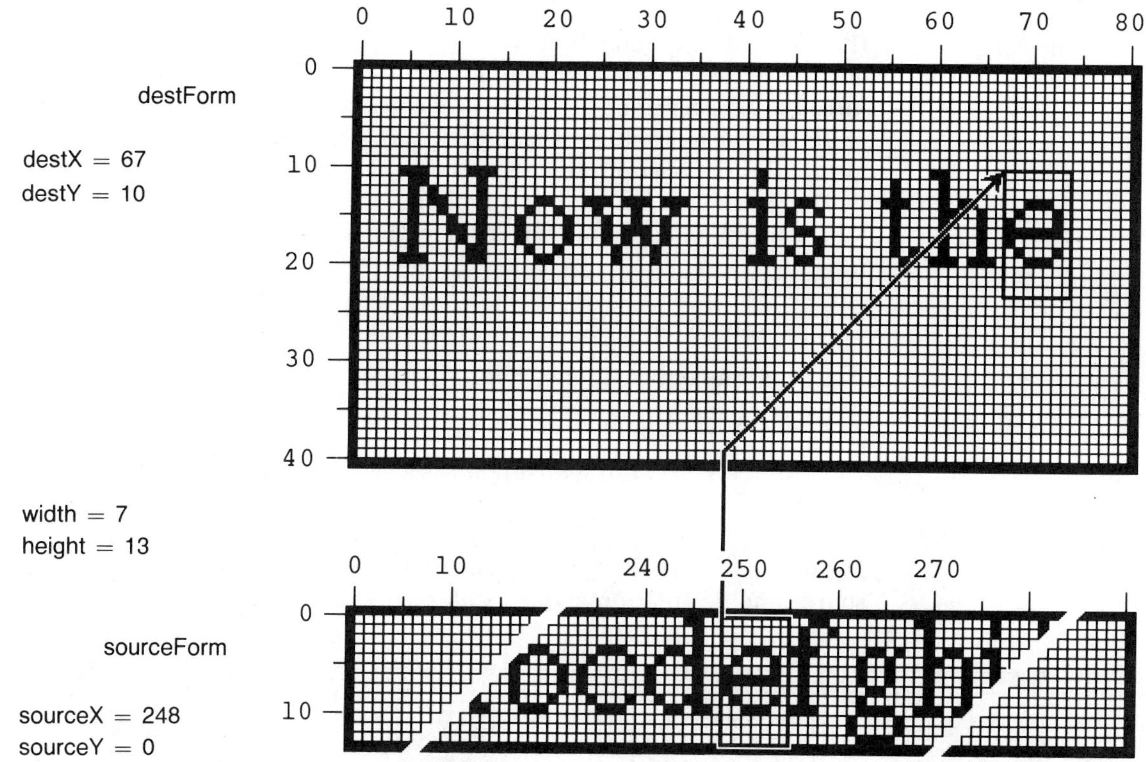
destForm
destX = 67
destY = 10
width = 7
height = 13
sourceForm
sourceX = 248
sourceY = 0
0 10 20 30 40 50 60 70 80
0 10 20 30 40
Now is the
0 10 240 250 260 270
0 10

Figure 18.3

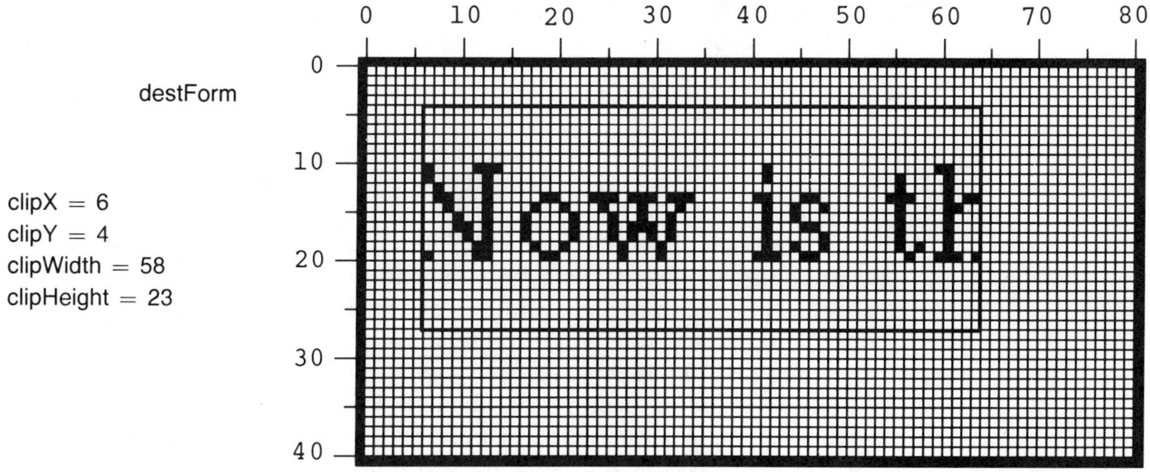
destForm
clipX = 6
clipY = 4
clipWidth = 58
clipHeight = 23
0 10 20 30 40 50 60 70 80
0 10 20 30 40
Now is th

Figure 18.4

Halftone Form

Often it is desirable to fill areas with a regular pattern that provides the effect of gray tone or texture. To this end, BitBlt provides for reference to a third Form containing the desired pattern. This Form is referred to as a halftone or *mask*. It is restricted to have height and width of 16. When halftoning is specified, this pattern is effectively repeated every 16 units horizontally and vertically over the entire destination.

There are four "modes" of supplying pixels from the source and halftone controlled by supplying nil for the source form or the halftone form:

0. no source, no halftone (supplies solid black)

1. halftone only (supplies halftone pattern)

2. source only (supplies source pixels)

3. source AND halftone (supplies source bits masked by halftone pattern)

Figure 18.5 illustrates the effect of these four modes with the same source and destination and a regular gray halftone.

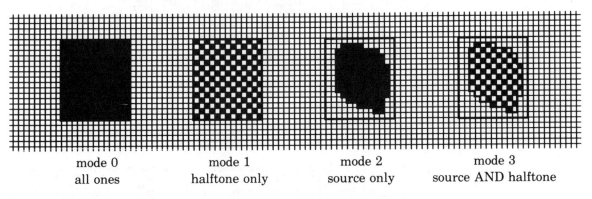

| mode 0 | mode 1 | mode 2 | mode 3 |
| all ones | halftone only | source only | source AND halftone |

Figure 18.5

Combination Rule

The examples above have all determined the new contents of the destination based only on the source and halftone, storing directly into the destination. The previous contents of the destination can also be taken into account in determining the result of the copying.

There are 16 possible rules for combining each source element **S** with the corresponding destination element **D** to produce the new destination element **D'**. Each rule must specify a white or black result for each of the four cases of source being white or black, and destination being white or black.

Figure 18.6 shows a box with four cells corresponding to the four cases encountered when combining source **S** and destination **D**. For instance, the cell numbered 2 corresponds to the case where the source was black and the destination was white. By appropriately filling the four cells with white or black, the box can be made to depict any combination rule. The numbers in the four cells map the rule as depicted graphically to the integer value which selects that rule. For example, to specify that the result should be black wherever the source or destination (or both) was black, we would blacken the cells numbered 4, 2, and 1. The associated integer for specifying that rule is the sum of the blackened cell numbers, or $4 + 2 + 1 = 7$.

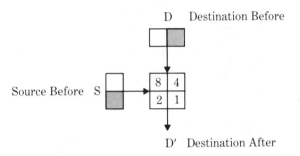

Figure 18.6

Figure 18.7 illustrates four common combination rules graphically. In addition, each is described by a combination diagram, its integer rule number, and the actual logical function being applied. The full set of 16 combination rules appears later in the chapter as part of the detailed simulation of BitBlt.

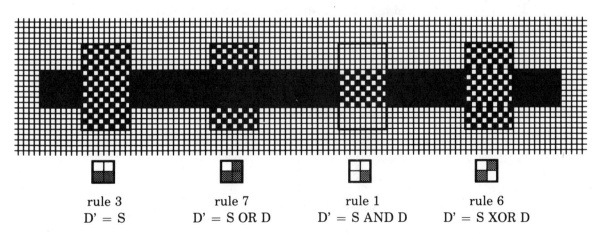

| rule 3 | rule 7 | rule 1 | rule 6 |
| D' = S | D' = S OR D | D' = S AND D | D' = S XOR D |

Figure 18.7

Classes Form and Bitmap

Figure 18.8 shows further information about the Form shown in Figure 18.2. The width and height are stored as Integers. The actual pixels are stored in a separate object which is an instance of class Bitmap. Bitmaps have almost no protocol, since their sole purpose is to provide storage for Forms. They also have no intrinsic width and height, apart from that laid on by their owning Form, although the figure retains this structure for clarity. It can be seen that space has been provided in the Bitmap for a width of 16; this is a manifestation of the hardware organization of storage and processing into 16-bit *words*. Bitmaps are allocated with an integral number of words for each row of pixels. This row size is referred to as the *raster* size. The integral word constraint on raster size facilitates movement from one row to the next within the operation of BitBlt, and during the scanning of the display screen by the hardware. While this division of memory into words is significant at the primitive level, it is encapsulated in such a way that none of the higher-level graphical components in the system need consider the issue of word size.

Two classes, Rectangle and Point, are used extensively in working with stored images. A Point contains x and y coordinate values and is used to refer to a pixel location in a Form; a Rectangle contains two Points—the top left corner and the bottom right corner—and is used to define a rectangular area of a Form.

Class Form includes protocol for managing a rectangular pattern of black and white dots. The bitmap of a Form can be (re)set by copying bits from a rectangular area of the display screen (fromDisplay:), and the extent and offset of the Form can be set (extent:, extent:offset:). Two messages provide access to the individual bits (valueAt: and valueAt:put:). Constants for modes and masks are known to class Form and can be obtained by the following class messages of Form.

Form instance protocol	
initialize-release	
fromDisplay: aRectangle	Copy the bits from the display screen within the boundaries defined by the argument, aRectangle, into the receiver's bitmap.
accessing	
extent: aPoint	Set the width and height of the receiver to be the coordinates of the argument, aPoint.
extent: extentPoint offset: offsetPoint	Set the width and height of the receiver to be the coordinates of the argument, extentPoint, and the offset to be offsetPoint.

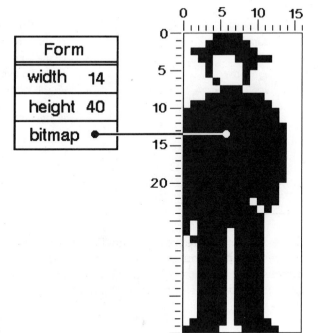

Figure 18.8

pattern
    valueAt: aPoint   Answer the bit, 0 or 1, at location aPoint within the receiver's bitmap.

    valueAt: aPoint put: bitCode   Set the bit at location aPoint within the receiver's bitmap to be bitCode, either 0 or 1.

Form class protocol

instance creation
    fromDisplay: aRectangle   Answer a new Form whose bits are copied from the display screen within the boundaries defined by the argument, aRectangle, into the receiver's bitmap.

mode constants
    erase   Answer the Integer denoting mode erase.
    over   Answer the Integer denoting mode over.
    reverse   Answer the Integer denoting mode reverse.
    under   Answer the Integer denoting mode under.

mask constants
black	Answer the Form denoting a black mask.
darkGray	Answer the Form denoting a dark gray mask.
gray	Answer the Form denoting a gray mask.
lightGray	Answer the Form denoting a light gray mask.
veryLightGray	Answer the Form denoting a very light gray mask.
white	Answer the Form denoting a white mask.

Spatial Reference

Since the images represented by Forms are inherently two-dimensional, image manipulation is simplified by providing objects representing two-dimensional locations and areas. Instances of class Point represent locations and instances of class Rectangle represent areas.

Class Point

A Point represents an x–y pair of numbers usually designating a pixel in a Form. Points refer to pixel locations relative to the top left corner of a Form (or other point of reference). By convention, x increases to the right and y down, consistent with the layout of text on a page and the direction of display scanning. This is in contrast to the "right-handed" coordinate system in which y increases in the upward direction.

A Point is typically created using the binary message @ to a Number. For example, the result of evaluating the expression

200 @ 150

is a Point with x and y coordinates 200 and 150. In addition, the class protocol of Point supports the instance creation message x: xInteger y: yInteger.

Point x: 200 y: 150

represents the same location as 200@150. The instance protocol for Point supports accessing messages and messages for comparing two Points.

Point instance protocol

accessing

x	Answer the x coordinate.
x: aNumber	Set the x coordinate to be the argument, aNumber.
y	Answer the y coordinate.
y: aNumber	Set the y coordinate to be the argument, aNumber.

comparing

< aPoint	Answer whether the receiver is above and to the left of the argument, aPoint.
< = aPoint	Answer whether the receiver is neither below nor to the right of the argument, aPoint.
> aPoint	Answer whether the receiver is below and to the right of the argument, aPoint.
> = aPoint	Answer whether the receiver is neither above nor to the left of the argument, aPoint.
max: aPoint	Answer the lower right corner of the rectangle uniquely defined by the receiver and the argument, aPoint.
min: aPoint	Answer the upper left corner of the rectangle uniquely defined by the receiver and the argument, aPoint.

With respect to the coordinates labeled in Figure 18.9, example expressions are

expression	result
(45@230) < (175@270)	true
(45@230) < (175@200)	false
(45@230) > (175@200)	false
(175@270) > (45@230)	true
(45@230) max: (175@200)	175@230
(45@230) min: (175@200)	45@200

Arithmetic can be carried out between two Points or between a Point and a Number (a scaling factor). Each of the arithmetic messages takes either a Point or a Number (a scalar) as an argument, and returns a new Point as the result. Truncation and round off messages, similar to those for Numbers, are also provided in the instance protocol of Point.

Point instance protocol

arithmetic

* scale	Answer a new Point that is the product of the receiver and the argument, scale.

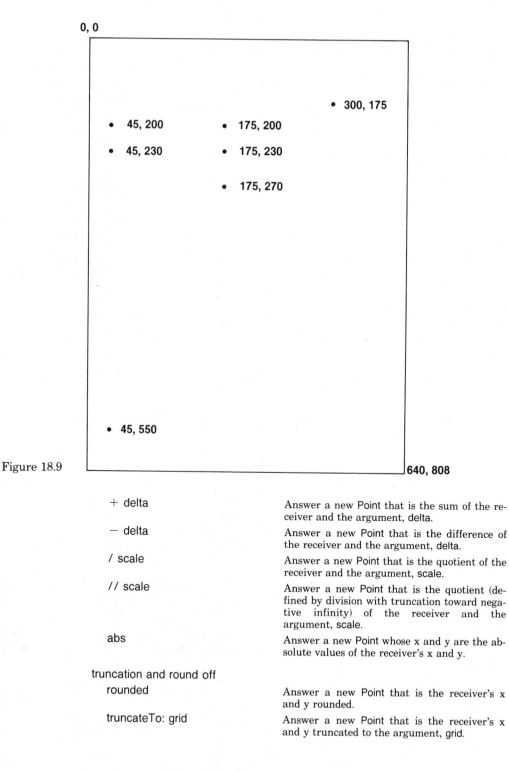

Figure 18.9

+ delta	Answer a new Point that is the sum of the receiver and the argument, delta.
− delta	Answer a new Point that is the difference of the receiver and the argument, delta.
/ scale	Answer a new Point that is the quotient of the receiver and the argument, scale.
// scale	Answer a new Point that is the quotient (defined by division with truncation toward negative infinity) of the receiver and the argument, scale.
abs	Answer a new Point whose x and y are the absolute values of the receiver's x and y.
truncation and round off	
rounded	Answer a new Point that is the receiver's x and y rounded.
truncateTo: grid	Answer a new Point that is the receiver's x and y truncated to the argument, grid.

Thus

expression	result
(45@230) + (175@300)	220@530
(45@230) + 175	220@405
(45@230) − (175@300)	−130@−70
(160@240) / 50	(16/5)@(24/5)
(160@240) // 50	3@4
(160@240) // (50@50)	3@4
((45@230) − (175@300)) abs	130@70
(120.5 @ 220.7) rounded	121@221
(160 @ 240) truncateTo: 50	150@200

Various other operations can be performed on Points including computing the distance between two Points, computing the dot product of two Points, transposing a point, and determining Points within some gridded range.

Point instance protocol

point functions

dist: aPoint	Answer the distance between the argument, aPoint, and the receiver.
dotProduct: aPoint	Answer a Number that is the dot product of the receiver and the argument, aPoint.
grid: aPoint	Answer a Point to the nearest rounded grid modules specified by the argument, aPoint.
normal	Answer a Point representing the unit vector rotated 90 deg clockwise.
transpose	Answer a Point whose x is the receiver's y and whose y is the receiver's x.
truncatedGrid: aPoint	Answer a Point to the nearest truncated grid modules specified by the argument, aPoint.

Examples are

expression	result
(45@230) dist: 175@270	136.015
(160@240) dotProduct: 50@50	20000
(160@240) grid: 50@50	150@250
(160@240) normal	−0.83105 @ 0.5547
(160@240) truncatedGrid: 50@50	150@200
(175@300) transpose	300@175

Points and Rectangles are used together as support for graphical manipulation. A Rectangle contains two Points—origin, which specifies the top left corner, and corner, which indicates the bottom right corner of the region described. Class Rectangle provides protocol for access to all the coordinates involved, and other operations such as intersection with other rectangles. Messages to a Point provide an infix way to create a Rectangle with the Point as the origin.

Point instance protocol	
converting	
corner: aPoint	Answer a Rectangle whose origin is the receiver and whose corner is the argument, aPoint.
extent: aPoint	Answer a Rectangle whose origin is the receiver and whose extent is the argument, aPoint.

Thus (45@200) corner: (175@270) represents the rectangular area shown earlier in the image of display coordinates.

Class Rectangle

Instances of Rectangle represent rectangular areas of pixels. Arithmetic operations take points as arguments and carry out scaling and translating operations to create new Rectangles. Rectangle functions create new Rectangles by determining intersections of Rectangles with Rectangles.

In addition to the messages to Point by which Rectangles can be created, class protocol for Rectangle supports three messages for creating instances. These messages specify either the boundaries of the rectangular area, the origin and corner coordinates, or the origin and width and height of the area.

Rectangle class protocol	
instance creation	
left: leftNumber right: rightNumber top: topNumber bottom: bottomNumber	
	Answer a Rectangle whose left, right, top, and bottom coordinates are determined by the arguments.
origin: originPoint corner: cornerPoint	
	Answer a Rectangle whose top left and bottom right corners are determined by the arguments, originPoint and cornerPoint.
origin: originPoint extent: extentPoint	
	Answer a Rectangle whose top left corner is originPoint and width by height is extentPoint.

The accessing protocol for Rectangle is quite extensive. It supports detailed ways of referencing eight significant locations on the boundary of the Rectangle. These points are shown in Figure 18.10.

Messages for accessing these positions have selectors with names like those shown in the diagram.

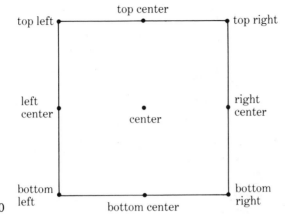

Figure 18.10

Rectangle instance protocol

---

accessing

topLeft	Answer the Point at the top left corner of the receiver.
topCenter	Answer the Point at the center of the receiver's top horizontal line.
topRight	Answer the Point at the top right corner of the receiver.
rightCenter	Answer the Point at the center of the receiver's right vertical line.
bottomRight	Answer the Point at the bottom right corner of the receiver.
bottomCenter	Answer the Point at the center of the receiver's bottom horizontal line.
bottomLeft	Answer the Point at the bottom left corner of the receiver.
leftCenter	Answer the Point at the center of the receiver's left vertical line.
center	Answer the Point at the center of the receiver.
area	Answer the receiver's area, the product of width and height.
width	Answer the receiver's width.
height	Answer the receiver's height.
extent	Answer the Point receiver's width @ receiver's height.
top	Answer the position of the receiver's top horizontal line.
right	Answer the position of the receiver's right vertical line.
bottom	Answer the position of the receiver's bottom horizontal line.
left	Answer the position of the receiver's left vertical line.

origin	Answer the Point at the top left corner of the receiver.
corner	Answer the Point at the bottom right corner of the receiver.

Suppose the Rectangle referred to as frame is created by the expression

frame ← Rectangle origin: 100 @ 100 extent: 150 @ 150

then

expression	result
frame topLeft	100 @ 100
frame top	100
frame rightCenter	250 @ 175
frame bottom	250
frame center	175 @ 175
frame extent	150 @ 150
frame area	22500

Each of the Rectangle's locations can be modified by an accessing message whose keyword is one of the positions named in Figure 18.10. In addition, the width and height can be set with the messages width: and height:, respectively. Two messages are listed below that are commonly used in the implementation of the system programming interface in order to reset the variables of a Rectangle.

Rectangle instance protocol
_____

accessing
    origin: originPoint corner: cornerPoint

> Set the points at the top left corner and the bottom right corner of the receiver.

    origin: originPoint extent: extentPoint

> Set the point at the top left corner of the receiver to be originPoint and set the width and height of the receiver to be extentPoint.

Rectangle functions create new Rectangles and compute relationships between two Rectangles.

Rectangle instance protocol
_____

rectangle functions
    amountToTranslateWithin: aRectangle

> Answer a Point, delta, such that the receiver, when moved by delta, will force the receiver to lie within the argument, aRectangle.

areasOutside: aRectangle	Answer a collection of Rectangles comprising the parts of the receiver which do not lie within the argument, aRectangle.
expandBy: delta	Answer a Rectangle that is outset from the receiver by delta, where delta is a Rectangle, Point, or scalar.
insetBy: delta	Answer a Rectangle that is inset from the receiver by delta, where delta is a Rectangle, Point, or scalar.
insetOriginBy: originDeltaPoint cornerBy: cornerDeltaPoint	
	Answer a Rectangle that is inset from the receiver by originDeltaPoint at the origin and cornerDeltaPoint at the corner.
intersect: aRectangle	Answer a Rectangle that is the area in which the receiver overlaps with the argument, aRectangle.
merge: aRectangle	Answer the smallest Rectangle that contains both the receiver and the argument, aRectangle.

Figure 18.11 shows three Rectangles, A, B, and C, created as follows.

```
A ← 50@50 corner: 200@200.
B ← 120@120 corner: 260@240.
C ← 100@300 corner: 300@400
```

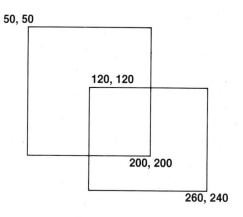

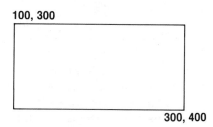

Figure 18.11

Then expressions using these three Rectangles are listed below. Notice that Rectangles print in the form originPoint corner: cornerPoint.

expression	result
A amountToTranslateWithin: C	50@250
A areasOutside: B	OrderedCollection ((50@50 corner: 200 @120) (50@120 corner: 120@200))
C expandBy: 10	90@290 corner: 310@410
C insetBy: 10@20	110@320 corner: 290@380
A intersect: B	120@120 corner: 200@200
B merge: C	100@120 corner: 300@400

The testing protocol for Rectangles includes messages to determine whether a Point or other Rectangle is contained within the boundaries of a Rectangle, or whether two Rectangles intersect.

Rectangle instance protocol

testing

contains: aRectangle	Answer whether the receiver contains all Points contained by the argument, aRectangle.
containsPoint: aPoint	Answer whether the argument, aPoint, is within the receiver.
intersects: aRectangle	Answer whether the receiver contains any Point contained by the argument, aRectangle.

Continuing the above example

expression	result
A contains: B	false
C containsPoint: 200@320	true
A intersects: B	true

Like the messages for a Point, the coordinates of a Rectangle can be rounded to the nearest integer. A Rectangle can be moved by some amount, translated to a particular location, and the coordinates can be scaled or translated by some amount. Rectangles also respond to scaling and translating messages; they are part of the protocol for any object that can display itself on a display medium.

Rectangle instance protocol
___

truncation and round off
  rounded   Answer a Rectangle whose origin and corner co-
                                     ordinates are rounded to the nearest integer.

transforming
  moveBy: aPoint   Change the corner positions of the receiver so
                                     that its area translates by the amount defined
                                     by the argument, aPoint.

  moveTo: aPoint   Change the corners of the receiver so that its
                                     top left position is the argument, aPoint.

  scaleBy: scale   Answer a Rectangle scaled by the argument,
                                     scale, where scale is either a Point or a scalar.

  translateBy: factor   Answer a Rectangle translated by the argu-
                                     ment, factor, where factor is either a Point or a
                                     scalar.

For example

expression	result
A moveBy: 50@50	100@100 corner: 250@250
A moveTo: 200@300	200@300 corner: 350@450
A scaleBy: 2	400@600 corner: 700@900
A translateBy: −100	100@200 corner: 250@350

Class BitBlt

The most basic interface to BitBlt is through a class of the same name. Each instance of BitBlt contains the variables necessary to specify a BitBlt operation. A specific application of BitBlt is governed by a list of parameters, which includes:

destForm   (destination form) a Form into which pixels will be stored

sourceForm   a Form from which pixels will be copied

halftoneForm   a Form containing a spatial halftone pattern

combinationRule	an Integer specifying the rule for combining corresponding pixels of the sourceForm and destForm
destX, destY, width, height	(destination area x, y, width, and height) Integers which specify the rectangular subregion to be filled in the destination
clipX, clipY, clipWidth, clipHeight	(clipping rectangular area x, y, width, and height) Integers which specify a rectangular area which restricts the affected region of the destination
sourceX, sourceY	Integers which specify the location (top left corner) of the subregion to be copied from the source

The BitBlt class protocol consists of one message for creating instances; this message contains a keyword and argument for each BitBlt variable. The BitBlt instance protocol includes messages for initializing the variables and a message, copyBits, which causes the primitive operation to take place. It also contains a message, drawFrom: startPoint to: stopPoint, for drawing a line defined by two Points.

BitBlt class protocol
_____

instance creation
    destForm: destination
        sourceForm: source
        halftoneForm: halftone
        combinationRule: rule
        destOrigin: destOrigin
        sourceOrigin: sourceOrigin
        extent: extent
        clipRect: clipRect   Answer a BitBlt with values set according to each of the arguments, where rule is an Integer; destination, source, and halftone are Forms; destOrigin, sourceOrigin, and extent are Points; and clipRect is a Rectangle.

BitBlt instance protocol
_____

accessing
    sourceForm: aForm   Set the receiver's source form to be the argument, aForm.

    destForm: aForm   Set the receiver's destination form to be the argument, aForm.

    mask: aForm   Set the receiver's halftone mask form to be the argument, aForm.

    combinationRule: anInteger   Set the receiver's combination rule to be the argument, anInteger, which must be an integer between 0 and 15.

    clipHeight: anInteger   Set the receiver's clipping area height to be the argument, anInteger.

    clipWidth: anInteger   Set the receiver's clipping area width to be the argument, anInteger.

clipRect	Answer the receiver's clipping rectangle.
clipRect: aRectangle	Set the receiver's clipping rectangle to be the argument, aRectangle.
clipX: anInteger	Set the receiver's clipping rectangle top left x coordinate to be the argument, anInteger.
clipY: anInteger	Set the receiver's clipping rectangle top left y coordinate to be the argument, anInteger.
sourceRect: aRectangle	Set the receiver's source form rectangular area to be the argument, aRectangle.
sourceOrigin: aPoint	Set the receiver's source form top left coordinates to be the argument, aPoint.
sourceX: anInteger	Set the receiver's source form top left x coordinate to be the argument, anInteger.
sourceY: anInteger	Set the receiver's source form top left y coordinate to be the argument, anInteger.
destRect: aRectangle	Set the receiver's destination form rectangular area to be the argument, aRectangle.
destOrigin: aPoint	Set the receiver's destination form top left coordinates to be the argument, aPoint.
destX: anInteger	Set the receiver's destination form top left x coordinate to be the argument, anInteger.
destY: anInteger	Set the receiver's destination form top left y coordinate to be the argument, anInteger.
height: anInteger	Set the receiver's destination form height to be the argument, anInteger.
width: anInteger	Set the receiver's destination form width to be the argument, anInteger.
copying	
copyBits	Perform the movement of bits from the source form to the destination form. Report an error if any variables are not of the right type (Integer or Form), or if the combination rule is not between 0 and 15 inclusive. Try to reset the variables and try again.

The state held in an instance of BitBlt allows multiple operations in a related context to be performed without the need to repeat all the initialization. For example, when displaying a scene in a display window, the destination form and clipping rectangle will not change from one operation to the next. Thus the instance protocol for modifying individual variables can be used to gain efficiency.

Line Drawing

Much of the graphics in the Smalltalk-80 system consists of lines and text. These entities are synthesized by repeated invocation of BitBlt.

The BitBlt protocol includes the messages drawFrom: startPoint to: stopPoint to draw a line whose end points are the arguments, startPoint and stopPoint.

line drawing

drawFrom: startPoint to: stopPoint

> Draw a line whose end points are the arguments, startPoint and stopPoint. The line is formed by displaying copies of the current source form according to the receiver's halftone mask and combination rule.

By using BitBlt, one algorithm can draw lines of varying widths, different halftones, and any combination rule. To draw a line, an instance of BitBlt is initialized with the appropriate destination Form and clipping rectangle, and with a source that can be any Form to be applied as a pen or "brush" shape along the line. The message drawFrom:to: with Points as the two arguments is then sent to the instance. Figure 18.12 shows a number of different pen shapes and the lines they form when the BitBlt combination rule is 6 or 7.

The message drawFrom: startPoint to: stopPoint stores the destX and destY values. Starting from these stored values, the line-drawing loop, drawLoopX: xDelta Y: yDelta, shown next, accepts x and y delta values and calculates x and y step values to determine points along the line, and then calls copyBits in order to display the appropriate image at each point. The method used is the Bresenham plotting algorithm (*IBM Systems Journal*, Volume 4, Number 1, 1965). It chooses a principal direction and maintains a variable, p. When p's sign changes, it is time to move in the minor direction as well. This method is a natural unit to be implemented as a primitive method, since the computation is trivial and the setup in copyBits is almost all constant from one invocation to the next.

The method for drawLoopX: xDelta Y: yDelta in class BitBlt is

drawLoopX: xDelta Y: yDelta

```
| dx dy px py p |
dx ← xDelta sign.
dy ← yDelta sign.
px ← yDelta abs.
py ← xDelta abs.
self copyBits. "first point"
```

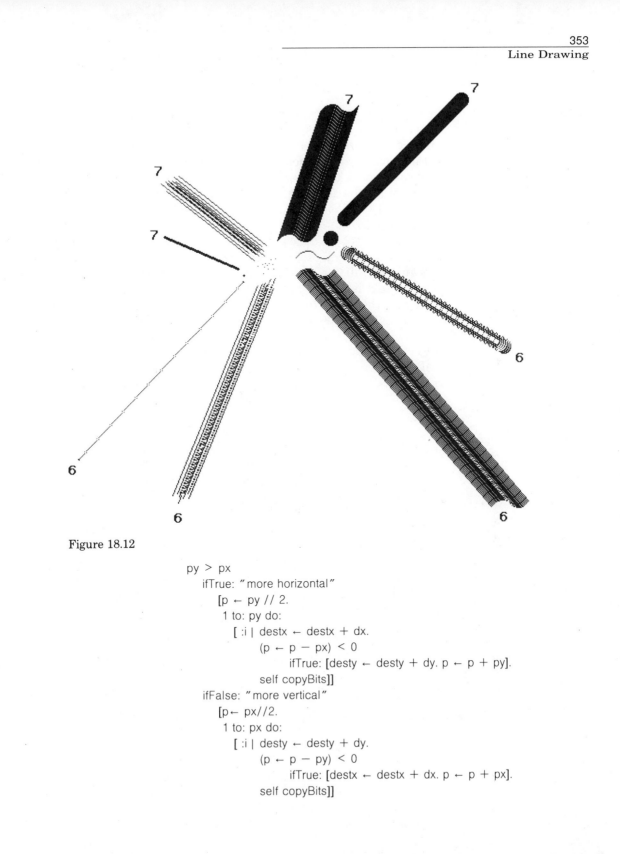

Figure 18.12

```
py > px
    ifTrue: "more horizontal"
        [p ← py // 2.
          1 to: py do:
            [ :i | destx ← destx + dx.
                (p ← p − px) < 0
                    ifTrue: [desty ← desty + dy. p ← p + py].
                self copyBits]]
    ifFalse: "more vertical"
        [p ← px//2.
          1 to: px do:
            [ :i | desty ← desty + dy.
                (p ← p − py) < 0
                    ifTrue: [destx ← destx + dx. p ← p + px].
                self copyBits]]
```

Text Display

One of the advantages derived from BitBlt is the ability to store fonts compactly and to display them using various combination rules. The compact storage arises from the possibility of packing characters horizontally one next to another (as shown earlier in Figure 18.3), since BitBlt can extract the relevant bits if supplied with a table of left x coordinates of all the characters. This is called a *strike* format from the typographical term meaning a contiguous display of all the characters in a font.

The scanning and display of text are performed in the Smalltalk-80 system by a subclass of BitBlt referred to as CharacterScanner. This subclass inherits all the normal state, with destForm indicating the Form in which text is to be displayed and sourceForm indicating a Form containing all the character glyphs side by side (as in Figure 18.3). In addition CharacterScanner defines further state including:

text	a String of Characters to be displayed
textPos	an Integer giving the current position in text
xTable	an Array of Integers giving the left x location of each character in sourceForm
stopX	an Integer that sets a right boundary past which the inner loop should stop scanning
exceptions	an Array of Symbols that, if non-nil, indicate messages for handling the corresponding characters specially
printing	a Boolean indicating whether characters are to be printed

Once an instance has been initialized with a given font and text location, the scanWord: loop below will scan or print text until some horizontal position (stopX) is passed, until a special character (determined from exceptions) is found, or until the end of this range of text (endRun) is reached. Each of these conditions is denoted by a symbolic code referred to as stopXCode, exceptions (an Array of Symbols) and endRunCode.

```
scanword: endRun
    | charIndex |
    [textPos < endRun] whileTrue:
        ["pick character" charIndex ← text at: textPos.
        "check exceptions"
        (exceptions at: charIndex) > 0
            ifTrue: [↑exceptions at: charIndex].
        "left x of character in font" sourceX ← xTable at: charIndex.
        "up to left of next char"
        width ← (xTable at: charIndex+ 1) − sourceX.
        "print the character" printing ifTrue: [self copyBits].
```

```
"advance by width of character" destX ← destX + width.
destX > stopX ifTrue: [↑stopXCode]. "passed right boundary"
"advance to next character"
textPos ← textPos + 1].
textPos ← textPos − 1.
↑endRunCode
```

The check on exceptions handles many possibilities in one operation. The space character may have to be handled exceptionally in the case of text that is padded to achieve a flush right margin. Tabs usually require a computation or table lookup to determine their width. Carriage return is also identified in the check for exceptions. Character codes beyond the range given in the font are detected similarly, and are usually handled by showing an exceptional character, such as a little lightning bolt, so that they can be seen and corrected.

The printing flag can be set false to allow the same code to measure a line (break at a word boundary) or to find to which character the cursor points. While this provision may seem over-general, two benefits (besides compactness) are derived from that generality. First, if one makes a change to the basic scanning algorithm, the parallel functions of measuring, printing, and cursor tracking are synchronized by definition. Second, if a primitive implementation is provided for the loop, it exerts a threefold leverage on the system performance.

The scanword: loop is designed to be amenable to such primitive implementation; that is, the interpreter may intercept it and execute primitive code instead of the Smalltalk-80 code shown. In this way, much of the setup overhead for copyBits can be avoided at each character and an entire word or more can be displayed directly. Conversely, the Smalltalk text and graphics system requires implementation of only the one primitive operation (BitBlt) to provide full functionality.

Simulation of BitBlt

We provide here a simulation of an implementation of copyBits in a subclass of BitBlt referred to as BitBltSimulation. The methods in this simulation are intentionally written in the style of machine code in order to serve as a guide to implementors. No attempt is made to hide the choice of 16-bit word size. Although the copyBits method is presented as a Smalltalk-80 method in BitBltSimulation, it is actually implemented in machine-code as a primitive method in class BitBlt; the simulation does the same thing, albeit slower.

The Graphics Kernel

class name	BitBltSimulation
superclass	BitBlt
instance variable names	sourceBits sourceRaster
	destBits destRaster
	halftoneBits
	skew skewMask
	mask1 mask2
	preload nWords
	hDir vDir
	sourceIndex sourceDelta
	destIndex destDelta
	sx sy dx dy w h
class variable names	AllOnes RightMasks
class methods	

initialize

```
"Initialize a table of bit masks"
RightMasks ←
    #(0 16r1 16r3 16r7 16rF
        16r1F 16r3F 16r7F 16rFF
        16r1FF 16r3FF 16r7FF 16rFFF
        16r1FFF 16r3FFF 16r7FFF 16rFFFF).
AllOnes ← 16rFFFF
```

instance methods

operations

copyBits

```
"sets w and h"
self clipRange.
(w < =0 or: [h < =0]) ifTrue: [↑self]. "null range"
self computeMasks.
self checkOverlap.
self calculateOffsets.
self copyLoop
```

private

clipRange

```
"clip and adjust source origin and extent appropriately"
"first in x"
destX > = clipX
    ifTrue: [sx ← sourceX. dx ← destX. w ← width]
    ifFalse: [sx ← sourceX + (clipX − destX).
            w ← width − (clipX − destX).
            dx ← clipX].
(dx + w) > (clipX + clipWidth)
    ifTrue: [w ← w − ((dx + w) − (clipX + clipWidth))].
```

```
"then in y"
destY > = clipY
    ifTrue: [sy ← sourceY. dy ← destY. h ← height]
    ifFalse: [sy ← sourceY + clipY − destY.
            h ← height − clipY + destY.
            dy ← clipY].
(dy + h) > (clipY + clipHeight)
    ifTrue: [h ← h − ((dy + h) − (clipY + clipHeight))].
sx < 0
    ifTrue: [dx ← dx − sx. w ← w + sx. sx ← 0].
sx + w > sourceForm width
    ifTrue: [w ← w − (sx + w − sourceForm width)].
sy < 0
    ifTrue: [dy ← dy − sy. h ← h + sy. sy ← 0].
sy + h > sourceForm height
    ifTrue: [h ← h − (sy + h − sourceForm height)]
```

Clipping first checks whether the destination x lies to the left of the clipping rectangle and, if so, adjusts both destination x and width. As mentioned previously, the data to be copied into this adjusted rectangle comes from a shifted region of the source, so that the source x must also be adjusted. Next, the rightmost destination x is compared to the clipping rectangle and the width is decreased again if necessary. This whole process is then repeated for y and height. Then the height and width are clipped to the size of the source form. The adjusted parameters are stored in variables sx, sy, dx, dy, w, and h. If either width or height is reduced to zero, the entire call to BitBlt can return immediately.

computeMasks

```
| startBits endBits |
"calculate skew and edge masks"
destBits ← destForm bits.
destRaster ← destForm width −1 // 16 + 1.
sourceForm notNil
    ifTrue: [sourceBits ← sourceForm bits.
            sourceRaster← sourceForm width − 1//16 + 1].
halftoneForm notNil
    ifTrue: [halftoneBits ← halftoneForm bits].
skew ← (sx − dx) bitAnd: 15.
"how many bits source gets skewed to right"
startBits ← 16 − (dx bitAnd: 15).
"how many bits in first word"
mask1 ← RightMasks at: startBits + 1.
endBits ← 15 − ((dx + w−1) bitAnd: 15).
"how many bits in last word"
mask2 ← (RightMasks at: endBits + 1) bitInvert.
```

```
skewMask ←
    (skew=0
        ifTrue: [0]
        ifFalse: [RightMasks at: 16 − skew + 1]).
    "determine number of words stored per line; merge masks if necessary"
w < startBits
    ifTrue: [mask1 ← mask1 bitAnd: mask2.
             mask2 ← 0.
             nWords ← 1]
    ifFalse: [nWords ← (w − startBits − 1) // 16 + 2].
```

In preparation for the actual transfer of data, several parameters are computed. First is skew, the horizontal offset of data from source to destination. This represents the number of bits by which the data will have to be rotated after being loaded from the source in order to line up with the final position in the destination. In the example of Figure 18.3, skew would be 5 because the glyph for the character "e" must be shifted left by 5 bits prior to being stored into the destination. From skew, skewMask is saved for use in rotating (this is unnecessary for machines with a rotate word instruction). Then mask1 and mask2 are computed for selecting the bits of the first and last partial words of each scan line in the destination. These masks would be 16r1FFF and 16rFFC0 respectively in the example of Figure 18.3 since startBits=13 and endBits=6. In cases such as this where only one word of each destination line is affected, the masks are merged to select the range within that word, here 16r1FC0.

checkOverlap

```
| t |
"check for possible overlap of source and destination"
hDir ← vDir ← 1. "defaults for no overlap"
(sourceForm = = destForm and: [dy > = sy])
    ifTrue:
        [dy > sy "have to start at bottom"
        ifTrue: [vDir ← −1. sy ← sy + h − 1. dy ← dy + h − 1]
        ifFalse: [dx > sx "y's are equal, but x's are backward "
                ifTrue: [hDir ← −1.
                        sx ← sx + w − 1.
                        "start at right"
                        dx ← dx + w − 1.
                        "and fix up masks"
                        skewMask ← skewMask bitInvert.
                        t ← mask1.
                        mask1 ← mask2.
                        mask2 ← t]]]
```

A check must be made for overlapping source and destination. When source and destination lie in the same bitmap, there is the possibility of the copy operation destroying the data as it is moved. Thus when the data is being moved downward, the copy must start at the bottom and proceed upward. Similarly when there is no vertical movement, if the horizontal movement is to the right, the copy must start at the right and work back to the left. In all other cases the copy can proceed from top to bottom and left to right.

calculateOffsets
```
"check if need to preload buffer
(i.e., two words of source needed for first word of destination)"
preload ← (sourceForm notNil) and:
            [skew ~= 0 and: [skew < = (sx bitAnd: 15)]].
hDir < 0 ifTrue: [preload ← preload = = false].
"calculate starting offsets"
sourceIndex ← sy * sourceRaster + (sx // 16).
destIndex ← dy * destRaster + (dx // 16).
"calculate increments from end of 1 line to start of next"
sourceDelta ←
    (sourceRaster * vDir) −
        (nWords + (preload ifTrue: [1] ifFalse: [0]) * hDir).
destDelta ← (destRaster * vDir) − (nWords * hDir)
```

In cases where two words of source are needed to store the first word into the destination, a flag preload is set indicating the need to preload a 32-bit shifter prior to the inner loop of the copy (this is an optimization; one could simply always load an extra word initially). The offsets needed for the inner loop are the starting offset in words from the source and destination bases; deltas are also computed for jumping from the end of the data in one scanline to the start of data in the next.

inner loop

copyLoop
```
| prevWord thisWord skewWord mergeMask
  halftoneWord mergeWord word |
1 to: h do: "here is the vertical loop:"
    [ :i |
    (halftoneForm notNil)
      ifTrue:
        [halftoneWord ← halftoneBits at: (1 + (dy bitAnd: 15)).
        dy ← dy + vDir]
      ifFalse: [halftoneWord ← AllOnes].
    skewWord ← halftoneWord.
```

```
                                preload
                                    ifTrue: [prevWord ← sourceBits at: sourceIndex + 1.
                                            "load the 32-bit shifter"
                                            sourceIndex ← sourceIndex + hDir]
                                    ifFalse: [prevWord ← 0].
                                mergeMask ← mask1.
                                1 to to: nWords do: "here is the inner horizontal loop"
                                [ :word |
                                  sourceForm notNil "if source is used"
                                    ifTrue:
                                        [prevWord ← prevWord bitAnd: skewMask.
                                        thisWord ← sourceBits at: sourceIndex + 1.
                                                                "pick up next word"
                                        skewWord ←
                                            prevWord bitOr: (thisWord bitAnd: skewMask bitInvert).
                                        prevWord ← thisWord.
                                        skewWord ← (skewWord bitShift: skew) bitOr:
                                                        (skewWord bitShift: skew − 16)].
                                                            "16-bit rotate"
                                    mergeWord ← self merge: (skewWord bitAnd: halftoneWord)
                                                    with: (destBits at: destIndex + 1).
                                destBits
                                    at: destIndex + 1
                                    put: ((mergeMask bitAnd: mergeWord)
                                                bitOr: (mergeMask bitInvert
                                                    bitAnd: (destBits at: destIndex + 1))).
                                sourceIndex ← sourceIndex + hDir.
                                destIndex ← destIndex + hDir.
                                word = (nWords − 1)
                                    ifTrue: [mergeMask ← mask2]
                                    ifFalse: [mergeMask ← AllOnes]].
                            sourceIndex ← sourceIndex + sourceDelta.
                            destIndex ← destIndex + destDelta]
```

The outer, or vertical, loop includes the overhead for each line, selecting the appropriate line of halftone gray, preloading the shifter if necessary, and stepping source and destination pointers to the next scanline after the inner loop. It should be noted here that the reason for indexing the halftone pattern by the destination y is to eliminate "seams" which would occur if the halftones in all operations were not coordinated this way.

The inner, or horizontal, loop picks up a new word of source, rotates it with the previous, and merges the result with a word of the destination. The store into the destination must be masked for the first and last partial words on each scanline, but in the middle, no masking is really necessary.

merge: sourceWord with: destinationWord
```
"These are the 16 combination rules:"
combinationRule=0
    ifTrue: [↑0].
combinationRule=1
    ifTrue: [↑sourceWord bitAnd: destinationWord].
combinationRule=2
    ifTrue: [↑sourceWord bitAnd: destinationWord bitInvert].
combinationRule=3
    ifTrue: [↑sourceWord].
combinationRule=4
    ifTrue: [↑sourceWord bitInvert bitAnd: destinationWord].
combinationRule=5
    ifTrue: [↑destinationWord].
combinationRule=6
    ifTrue:[↑sourceWord bitXor: destinationWord].
combinationRule=7
    ifTrue: [↑sourceWord bitOr: destinationWord].
combinationRule=8
    ifTrue: [↑sourceWord bitInvert bitAnd: destinationWord bitInvert].
combinationRule=9
    ifTrue: [↑sourceWord bitInvert bitXor: destinationWord].
combinationRule=10
    ifTrue: [↑destinationWord bitInvert].
combinationRule=11
    ifTrue: [↑sourceWord bitOr: destinationWord bitInvert].
combinationRule=12
    ifTrue: [↑sourceWord bitInvert].
combinationRule=13
    ifTrue: [↑sourceWord bitInvert bitOr: destinationWord].
combinationRule=14
    ifTrue: [↑sourceWord bitInvert bitOr: destinationWord bitInvert].
combinationRule=15
    ifTrue: [↑AllOnes]
```

Efficiency Considerations

Our experience has demonstrated the value of BitBlt's generality. This one primitive is so central to the programming interface that any improvement in its performance has considerable effect on the interactive quality of the system as a whole. In normal use of the Smalltalk-80 system, most invocations of BitBlt are either in the extreme microscopic or macroscopic range.

In the macroscopic range, the width of transfer spans many words. The inner loop across a horizontal scan line gets executed many times, and the operations requested tend to be simple moves or constant stores. Examples of these are:

clearing a line of text to white

clearing an entire window to white

scrolling a block of text up or down

Most processors provide a fast means for block moves and stores, and these can be made to serve the applications above. Suppose we structure the horizontal loop of BitBlt as

1. move left partial word,

2. move many whole words (or none),

3. move right partial word (or none).

Special cases can be provided for 2 if the operation is a simple store or a simple copy with no skew (horizontal bit offset) from source to destination. In this way, most macroscopic applications of BitBlt can be made fast, even on processors of modest power.

The microscopic range of BitBlt is characterized by a zero count for the inner loop. The work on each scanline involves at most two partial words, and both overall setup and vertical loop overhead can be considerably reduced for these cases. Because characters tend to be less than a word wide and lines tend to be less than a word thick, nearly all text and line drawing falls into this category. A convenient way to provide such efficiency is to write a special case of BitBlt which assumes the microscopic parameters, but goes to the general BitBlt whenever these are not met. Because of the statistics (many small operations and a few very large ones), it does not hurt to pay the penalty of a false assumption on infrequent calls. One can play the same trick with clipping by assuming no clipping will occur and running the general code only when this assumption fails.

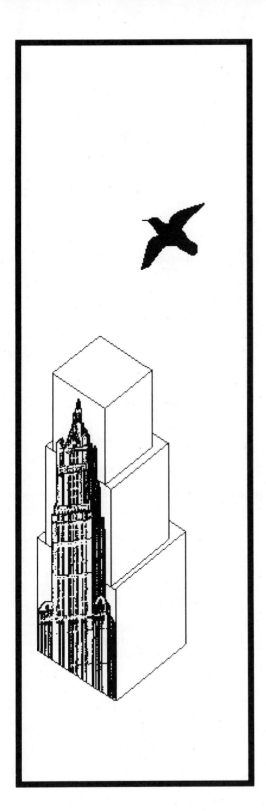

19

Pens

Class Pen

Geometric Designs
Spirals
Dragon Curve
Hilbert Curve

Commander Pen

Object

    Magnitude
        Character
        Date
        Time

        Number
           Float
           Fraction
           Integer
               LargeNegativeInteger
               LargePositiveInteger
               SmallInteger

        LookupKey
           Association

Link

    Process

Collection

    SequenceableCollection
        LinkedList

           Semaphore

        ArrayedCollection
           Array

           Bitmap
               DisplayBitmap

           RunArray
           String
               Symbol
           Text
           ByteArray

        Interval
        OrderedCollection
           SortedCollection
    Bag
    MappedCollection
    Set
        Dictionary
           IdentityDictionary

Stream
    PositionableStream
        ReadStream
        WriteStream
           ReadWriteStream
               ExternalStream
                   FileStream

    Random

File
FileDirectory
FilePage

UndefinedObject
Boolean
    False
    True

ProcessorScheduler
Delay
SharedQueue

Behavior
    ClassDescription
        Class
        MetaClass

Point
Rectangle
BitBlt
    CharacterScanner

Pen

DisplayObject
    DisplayMedium
        Form
           Cursor
           DisplayScreen
    InfiniteForm
    OpaqueForm
    Path
        Arc
           Circle
        Curve
        Line
        LinearFit
        Spline

As explained in the previous chapter, Forms represent images. Lines can be created by copying a Form to several locations in another Form at incremental distances between two designated points. Higher-level access to line drawing is provided by instances of class Pen.

Pen is a subclass of BitBlt. As such, it is a holder for source and destination Forms. The source Form can be colored black or white or different tones of gray, and copied into the destination Form with different combination rules, different halftone masks, and with respect to different clipping rectangles. The source Form is the Pen's writing tool or nib. The destination Form is the Pen's writing surface; it is usually the Form representing the display screen.

In addition to the implementations inherited from BitBlt, a Pen has a Point that indicates a position on the display screen and a Number that indicates a direction in which the Pen moves. A Pen understands messages that cause it to change its position or direction. When its position changes, the Pen can leave a copy of its Form at its former position. By moving the Pen to different screen positions and copying its Form to one or more of these positions, graphic designs are created.

Several programming systems provide this kind of access to line drawing. In these systems, the line drawer is typically called a "turtle" after the one first provided in the MIT/BBN Logo language (Seymour Papert, *MindStorms: Children, Computers and Powerful Ideas*, Basic Books, 1980; Harold Abelson and Andrea diSessa, *Turtle Geometry: The Computer as a Medium for Exploring Mathematics*, MIT Press, 1981). The protocol for Pens supports messages that are like the turtle commands provided in Logo. These consist of commands for telling the turtle to go some distance, turn some amount, to place a pen in a down position, and to place a pen in an up position. When the pen is down and it moves, a trace of the turtle's path is created. The corresponding Pen messages are go: distance, turn: amount, down, and up.

Multiple Pens can be created and their movement on the screen coordinated so that the process of creating a graphical design can itself be graphically pleasing. The next section contains the protocol that is provided in class Pen. Subsequent sections give examples of designs that can be created by sending messages to Pens.

Class Pen

Instances of class Pen are created by sending Pen the message new. A Pen created this way can draw anywhere on the display screen; its initial position is the center of the screen, facing in a direction towards the top of the screen. The Pen is set to draw (i.e., it is down) with a source Form or nib that is a 1 by 1 black dot.

There are two ways to change the source Form of a Pen. One way is to send the Pen the message defaultNib: widthInteger. The other way is to reset the source Form by sending the Pen the messages it inherits from its superclass, BitBlt. For example, the message sourceForm: changes the source form, or the message mask: changes the halftone form (the mask) used in displaying the source form. (Note that the default mask for displaying is black.)

Pen instance protocol

---

initialize-release

> defaultNib: shape

A "nib" is the tip of a pen. This is an easy way to set up a default pen. The Form for the receiver is a rectangular shape with height and width equal to (1) the argument, shape, if shape is an Integer; or (2) the coordinates of shape if shape is a Point.

Thus

> bic ← Pen new defaultNib: 2

creates a Pen with a black Form that is 2 bits wide by 2 bits high.

The accessing protocol for a Pen provides access to the Pen's current direction, location, and drawing region. The drawing region is referred to as the Pen's *frame*.

Pen instance protocol

---

accessing

> direction

Answer the receiver's current direction. 270 is towards the top of the screen.

> location

Answer the receiver's current location.

> frame

Answer the Rectangle in which the receiver can draw.

> frame: aRectangle

Set the Rectangle in which the receiver can draw to be the argument, aRectangle.

Continuing to use the example, bic, and assuming that the display screen is 600 bits wide and 800 bits high, we have

expression	result
bic direction	270
bic location	300 @ 400
bic frame: (50 @ 50 extent: 200 @ 200)	
bic location	300 @ 400

Notice that when the Pen direction is towards the top of the display screen, the angle is 270 degrees. Notice also that the Pen is currently outside its drawing region and would have to be placed within the Rectangle, 50@50 corner: 250@250, before any of its marks could be seen.

The "turtle" drawing commands alter the Pen's drawing state, orient its drawing direction, and reposition it.

Pen instance protocol

moving

down	Set the state of the receiver to "down" so that it leaves marks when it moves.
up	Set the state of the receiver to "up" so that it does not leave marks when it moves.
turn: degrees	Change the direction that the receiver faces by an amount equal to the argument, degrees.
north	Set the receiver's direction to facing toward the top of the display screen.
go: distance	Move the receiver in its current direction a number of bits equal to the argument, distance. If the receiver status is "down," a line will be drawn using the receiver's Form as the shape of the drawing brush.
goto: aPoint	Move the receiver to position aPoint. If the receiver status is "down", a line will be drawn from the current position to the new one using the receiver's Form as the shape of the drawing brush. The receiver's direction does not change.
place: aPoint	Set the receiver at position aPoint. No lines are drawn.
home	Place the receiver at the center of the region in which it can draw.

Thus we can place bic in the center of its frame by evaluating the expression

    bic home

If we then ask

    bic location

the response would be 150@150.

Suppose that we drew a line with a Pen and then decided that we wanted to erase it. If the line had been drawn with a black Form, then we can erase it by drawing over it with a white Form of at least the same size. Thus

    bic go: 100

draws the black line. Then

bic white

sets the drawing mask to be all white (the message white is inherited from the protocol of BitBlt), and then

bic go: −100

draws over the original line, erasing it.

An exercise that is common in the Logo examples is to create various polygon shapes, such as a square.

4 timesRepeat: [bic go: 100. bic turn: 90]

The following expression creates any polygon shape by computing the angle of turning as a function of the number of sides. If nSides is the number of sides of the desired polygon, then

nSides timesRepeat: [bic go: 100. bic turn: 360 // nSides]

will draw the polygon. We can create a class Polygon whose instances refer to the number of sides and length of each side. In addition, each Polygon has its own Pen for drawing. In the definition that follows, we specify that a Polygon can be told to draw on the display screen; the method is the one described earlier.

class name	Polygon
superclass	Object
instance variable names	drawingPen
	nSides
	length

class methods

instance creation

new
    ↑super new default

instance methods

drawing

draw
    drawingPen black.
    nSides timesRepeat: [drawingPen go: length; turn: 360 // nSides]

accessing

length: n
    length ← n
sides: n
    nSides ← n

private

default
    drawingPen ← Pen new.
    self length: 100.
    self sides: 4

Then a Polygon can be created and a sequence of polygons drawn by evaluating the expressions

poly ← Polygon new.
3 to: 10 do: [:sides | poly sides: sides. poly draw]

The result is shown in Figure 19.1.

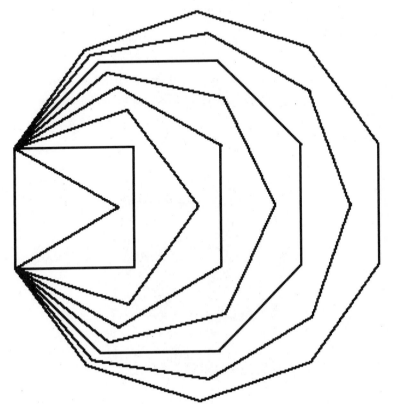

Figure 19.1

Geometric Designs

The Logo books mentioned earlier provide extensive examples of how to use this kind of access to line drawing in order to create images on a computer display screen. We provide several examples of methods that can be added to a Pen so that any Pen can draw a geometric design such as those shown in Figures 19.2 - 19.5. (Note: These methods are in the system as part of the description of Pen so that users can play with creating geometric designs.)

Spirals

The first design is called a *spiral*. A spiral is created by having the Pen draw incrementally longer lines; after each line is drawn, the Pen turns some amount. The lines drawn begin at length 1 and increase by 1 each time until reaching a length equal to the first argument of the message spiral:angle:. The second argument of the message is the amount the Pen turns after drawing each line.

```
spiral: n angle: a
    1 to: n do:
        [ :i | self go: i. self turn: a]
```

Each of the lines in Figure 19.2 was drawn by sending bic the message spiral:angle:, as follows.

```
bic spiral: 150 angle: 89
```

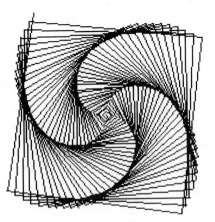

Figure 19.2a

bic spiral: 150 angle: 91

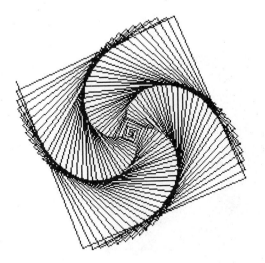

Figure 19.2b

bic spiral: 150 angle: 121

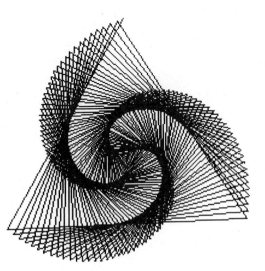

Figure 19.2c

bic home.
bic spiral: 150 angle: 89.
bic home.
bic spiral: 150 angle: 91

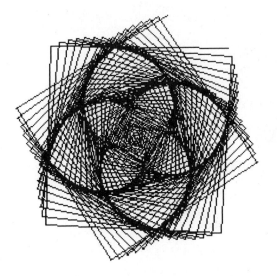

Figure 19.2d

Dragon Curve

Figure 19.3 is an image of a "dragon curve" of order 8 which was drawn in the middle of the screen by evaluating the expression

bic ← Pen new defaultNib: 4.
bic dragon: 9

The method associated with the message dragon: in class Pen is

```
dragon: n
    n = 0
        ifTrue: [self go: 10]
        ifFalse:
            [n > 0
                ifTrue:
                    [self dragon: n — 1.
                    self turn: 90.
                    self dragon: 1 — n]
                ifFalse:
                    [self dragon: —1 — n.
                    self turn: —90.
                    self dragon: 1 + n]]
```

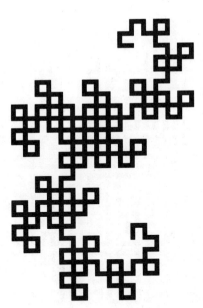

Figure 19.3

Dragon curves were discussed by Martin Gardner in his mathematical games column in *Scientific American* (March 1967, p. 124, and April 1967, p. 119). Another discussion of dragon curves appears in Donald Knuth and Chandler Davis, "Number Representations and Dragon Curves," *Journal of Recreation Mathematics*, Vol. 3, 1970, pp. 66-81 and 133-149.

Hilbert Curve

Figure 19.4 is a space-filling curve attributed to the mathematician David Hilbert. A space-filling curve has an index; as the index increases to infinity, the curve tends to cover the points in a plane. The example is the result of evaluating the expression

    Pen new hilbert: 5 side: 8

The index for the example is 5; at each point, a line 8 pixels long is drawn. The corresponding method for the message hilbert:side is

```
hilbert: n side: s
    | a m |
    n = 0 ifTrue: [↑self turn: 180].
    n > 0 ifTrue: [a ← 90.
                   m ← n − 1]
        ifFalse: [a ← −90.
                   m ← n + 1].
```

Figure 19.4

```
self turn: a.
self hilbert: 0 — m side: s.
self turn: a.
self go: s.
self hilbert: m side: s.
self turn: 0 — a.
self go: s.
self turn: 0 — a.
self hilbert: m side: s.
self go: s.
self turn: a.
self hilbert: 0 — m side: s.
self turn: a
```

A Hilbert curve, where the source form is a different shape, creates a nice effect. Suppose the Form is three dots in a row; this is a system cursor referred to as wait. The image in Figure 19.5 was created by evaluating the expressions

```
bic ← Pen new sourceForm: Cursor wait.
bic combinationRule: Form under.
bic hilbert: 4 side: 16
```

Figure 19.5

Expressions Cursor wait and Form under access a Form and a combination rule, respectively, that are constants in the system and that are known to the named classes. Other such constants are listed in a section of the next chapter. The messages sourceForm: and combinationRule: are inherited by Pens from their superclass BitBlt.

Commander Pen

The next example is shown in Figure 19.6. Although we can not show the process by which the design was created, it is a nice example for the reader to try. The basic idea is to create an object that controls several Pens and coordinates their drawing a design. We call the class of this kind of object, Commander. A Commander is an array of Pens. Pens controlled by a Commander can be given directions by having the Commander enumerate each Pen and evaluate a block containing Pen commands. So if a Commander's Pens should each go: 100, for example, then the Commander can be sent the message

    do: [:eachPen | eachPen go: 100]

A Commander also responds to messages to arrange its Pens so that interesting designs based on symmetries can be created. The two messages given in the description of Commander shown next are fanOut and lineUpFrom: startPoint to: endPoint. The first message arranges the Pens so that their angles are evenly distributed around 360 degrees. A Commander's Pens can be positioned evenly along a line using the message lineUpFrom:to:, where the arguments define the end points of the line.

A description for Commander follows. The message new: is redefined so that Pens are stored in each element of the Array.

class name	Commander
superclass	Array
class methods	

instance creation

new: numberOfPens
```
    | newCommander |
    newCommander ← super new: numberOfPens.
    1 to: numberOfPens do:
        [ :index | newCommander at: index put: Pen new].
    ↑newCommander
```

instance methods

distributing

fanOut
```
    1 to: self size do:
      [ :index |
        (self at: index) turn: (index − 1) * (360 / self size)]
```
lineUpFrom: startPoint to: endPoint
```
    1 to: self size do:
      [ :index |
        (self at: index)
          place: startPoint + (stopPoint−startPoint*(index−1) / (self size−1))]
```

The methods are useful examples of sending messages to instances of class Point. The image in Figure 19.6 was drawn by evaluating the expressions

```
    bic ← Commander new: 4.
    bic fanOut.
    bic do: [ :eachPen | eachPen up. eachPen go: 100. eachPen down].
    bic do: [ :eachPen | eachPen spiral: 200 angle: 121]
```

The message do: to a Commander is inherited from its Collection superclass.

Figure 19.6

Another example of the use of a Commander is given in Figure 19.7. This image was created by using the message lineUpFrom:to:. It is a simple sequence of spirals arranged along a line at an angle, created by evaluating the expressions

```
bic ← Commander new: 6.
bic lineUpFrom: (300 @ 150) to: (300 @ 500).
bic do: [ :eachPen | eachPen spiral: 200 angle: 121]
```

☐ *Additional Protocol for Commander* Pen An expanded description of Commander adds to Commander each message of the protocol of class Pen whose behavior changes position or orientation. This additional protocol supports the ability to send messages that are part of Pen's

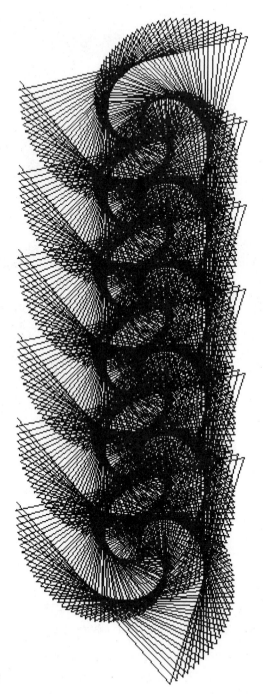

Figure 19.7

protocol to the Commander. Each such message is implemented as broadcasting the message to the elements of the collection. In this way, messages to Commander take the same form as messages to any Pen, rather than that of a do: message. With the class defined in this way, drawing sequences to a Commander appear more like drawing sequences to a Pen. Moreover, all the Pens commanded by a Commander draw in parallel; for example, all the spirals of Figures 19.6 or 19.7 would grow at once.

```
down
    self do: [ :each | each down]
up
    self do: [ :each | each up]
turn: degrees
    self do: [ :each | each turn: degrees]
north
    self do: [ :each | each north]
go: distance
    self do: [ :each | each go: distance]
goto: aPoint
    self do: [ :each | each goto: aPoint]
place: aPoint
    self do: [ :each | each place: aPoint]
home
    self do: [ :each | each home]
spiral: n angle: a
    1 to: n do:
        [ :i | self go: i. self turn: a]
```

With this additional protocol, Figure 19.6 can be drawn by evaluating the expressions

```
bic ← Commander new: 4.
bic fanOut.
bic up.
bic go: 100.
bic down.
bic spiral: 200 angle: 121
```

and Figure 19.7 by the expressions

```
bic ← Commander new: 6.
bic lineUpFrom: (300 @ 150) to: (300 @ 500).
bic spiral: 200 angle: 121
```

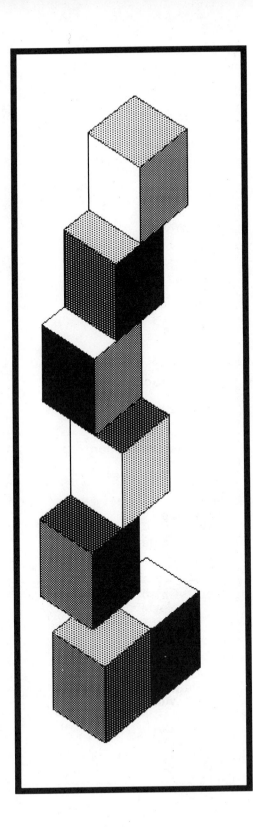

20

Display Objects

```
Object

    Magnitude                           Stream
        Character                           PositionableStream
        Date                                    ReadStream
        Time                                    WriteStream
                                                    ReadWriteStream
        Number                                      ExternalStream
            Float                                       FileStream
            Fraction
            Integer                         Random
                LargeNegativeInteger
                LargePositiveInteger    File
                SmallInteger            FileDirectory
                                        FilePage

        LookupKey                       UndefinedObject
            Association                 Boolean
                                            False
    Link                                    True

        Process
                                        ProcessorScheduler
    Collection                          Delay
                                        SharedQueue
        SequenceableCollection
            LinkedList                  Behavior
                                            ClassDescription
                Semaphore                       Class
                                                MetaClass
            ArrayedCollection
                Array                   Point
                                        Rectangle
                Bitmap                  BitBlt
                    DisplayBitmap           CharacterScanner

                RunArray                    Pen
                String
                    Symbol
                Text
                ByteArray

            Interval
            OrderedCollection
                SortedCollection
        Bag
        MappedCollection
        Set
            Dictionary
                IdentityDictionary
```

DisplayObject
    DisplayMedium
        Form
            Cursor
            DisplayScreen
    InfiniteForm
    OpaqueForm
    Path
        Arc
            Circle
        Curve
        Line
        LinearFit
        Spline

Graphics in the Smalltalk-80 system begin with the specification of BitBlt. Supported by Points, Rectangles, Forms, Pens, and Text, a wide variety of imagery can be created. The images in Figure 20.1 illustrate some of the graphical entities made possible by extending the use of these five kinds of objects.

The more artistic images in Figures 20.2 and 20.3 were created using the additional display objects available in the Smalltalk-80 system. The methods used in creating these images are described later. This chapter describes the available kinds of display objects and the various ways to manipulate them.

Class DisplayObject

A Form is a kind of display object. There are others in the system. The way in which these objects are implemented is as a hierarchy of classes whose superclass is named DisplayObject. Form is a subclass in this hierarchy.

A display object represents an image that has a width, a height, an assumed origin at 0@0, and an offset from this origin relative to which the image is to be displayed. All display objects are similar in their ability to copy their image into another image, to be scaled, and to be translated. They differ in how their image is created.

There are three primary subclasses of DisplayObject. They are DisplayMedium, DisplayText, and Path.

- DisplayMedium represents images that can be "colored" (that is, filled with a gray tone) and bordered (that is, their rectangular outline is colored).

- DisplayText represents textual images.

- Path represents images composed as collections of images.

A Form is a subclass of DisplayMedium; it adds the bitmap representation of the image. All DisplayObjects provide source information for images; Forms provide both the source and the destination information.

Class DisplayObject supports accessing messages for manipulating the various aspects of the image.

DisplayObject instance protocol

accessing	
width	Answer the width of the receiver's bounding box, a rectangle that represents the boundaries of the receiver's image.
height	Answer the height of the receiver's bounding box.
extent	Answer a Point representing the width and height of the receiver's bounding box.

TONES

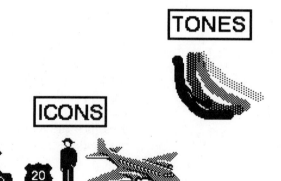

ICONS

FONT

ABCDEFGHIJKLMNOPQRST
abcdefghijklmnopqrstuvwxyz
1234567890

SYMBOL

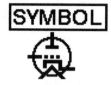

POINTS

TEXT

The modern age has brought to
Ikebana the concepts of individual
expression and abstract design
divorced from established rules.

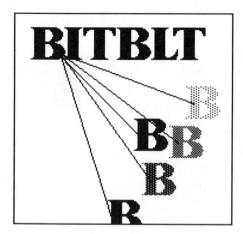

LINE

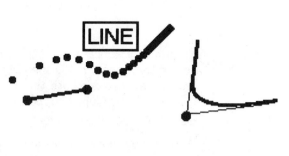

Figure 20.1

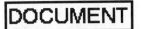

DOCUMENT

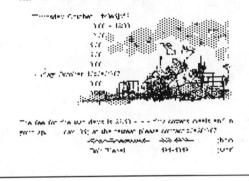

IMAGE

BRUSHES

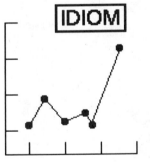

IDIOM

Figure 20.2

Figure 20.3

offset	Answer a Point representing the amount by which the receiver should be offset when it is displayed or its position is tested.
offset: aPoint	Set the receiver's offset.
rounded	Set the receiver's offset to the nearest integral amount.

DisplayObject also provides three kinds of messages that support *transforming* an image, *displaying* the image, and computing the *display box*, that is, a rectangular area that represents the boundaries of the area for displaying the image.

DisplayObject instance protocol

transforming

scaleBy: aPoint	Scale the receiver's offset by aPoint.
translateBy: aPoint	Translate the receiver's offset by aPoint.
align: alignmentPoint with: relativePoint	
	Translate the receiver's offset such that alignmentPoint aligns with relativePoint.

display box access

boundingBox	Answer the rectangular area that represents the boundaries of the receiver's space of information.

displaying

displayOn: aDisplayMedium at: aDisplayPoint clippingBox: clipRectangle rule: ruleInteger mask: aForm	
	Display the receiver at location aDisplayPoint with rule, ruleInteger, and halftone mask, aForm. Information to be displayed must be confined to the area that intersects with clipRectangle.

There are actually several displaying messages not shown above. Alternative displaying messages progressively omit a keyword (starting from the last one) and provide default masks, rules, clipping rectangles, and positions, when needed. Basically the display screen itself is the default clipping rectangle, 0@0 is the default display position, and the object that represents the system display screen, Display, (a global variable) is the default display medium.

The message displayAt: aDisplayPoint provides a generally useful message when the only parameter not defaulted is the location at which the image is to be placed. The message display assumes that the display location is 0@0.

DisplayObject instance protocol

displayAt: aDisplayPoint	Display the receiver at location aDisplayPoint with rule "over" or "storing"; halftone mask, a black Form; clipping rectangle the whose display screen; onto the display screen (Display).
display	Display the receiver at location 0@0.

These last two displaying messages are provided for textual objects such as String and Text as well, so that the programmer can place characters on the screen by evaluating an expression such as

'This is text to be displayed' displayAt: 100@100

Suppose locomotive is the Form that looks like

then it can be displayed on the screen with top left corner at location 50@150 by evaluating the expression

locomotive displayAt: 50@150

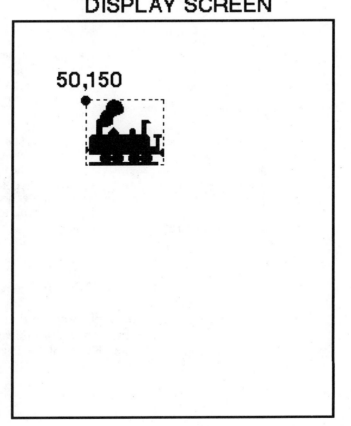

Class DisplayMedium

DisplayMedium is a subclass of DisplayObject that represents an object onto which images can be copied. In addition to those messages inherited from its superclass, DisplayMedium provides protocol for coloring the interior of images and placing borders around the display boxes of images. The "colors" are Forms that are already available in the system. These are black (the bitmap is all ones), white (all zeros), and various gray tones, either gray, veryLightGray, lightGray, or darkGray (mixtures of ones and zeros). Images of these colors are given below. All or portions of the DisplayMedium's area can be changed to one of these colors using the following messages.

DisplayMedium instance protocol

coloring

black	Change all of the receiver's area to black.
black: aRectangle	Change the area of the receiver defined by the argument, aRectangle, to black.
white	Change all of the receiver's area to white.
white: aRectangle	Change the area of the receiver defined by the argument, aRectangle, to white.
gray	Change all of the receiver's area to gray.
gray: aRectangle	Change the area of the receiver defined by the argument, aRectangle, to gray.
veryLightGray	Change all of the receiver's area to very light gray.
veryLightGray: aRectangle	Change the area of the receiver defined by the argument, aRectangle, to very light gray.
lightGray	Change all of the receiver's area to light gray.
lightGray: aRectangle	Change the area of the receiver defined by the argument, aRectangle, to light gray.
darkGray	Change all of the receiver's area to dark gray.
darkGray: aRectangle	Change the area of the receiver defined by the argument, aRectangle, to dark gray.

In the above messages, the origin of the argument, aRectangle, is in the coordinate system of the receiver.

Suppose picture is a kind of DisplayMedium that is 100 pixels in width and 100 pixels in height, and that box is an instance of Rectangle with origin at 30 @ 30 and width and height of 40. Then the protocol for filling the subarea of picture represented by box is illustrated by the following sequence.

expression	*result*
picture black: box	
picture white: box	
picture gray: box	
picture lightGray: box	
picture veryLightGray: box	

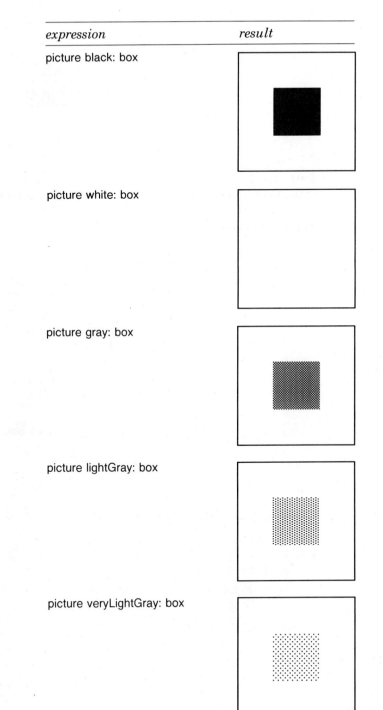

picture darkGray: box

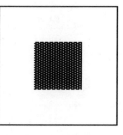

Part of an image can be filled with a pattern by sending a DisplayMedium a message to fill a particular sub-area with a halftone pattern. The other coloring messages use these filling messages in their implementation.

DisplayMedium instance protocol

fill: aRectangle mask: aHalftoneForm

> Change the area of the receiver defined by the argument, aRectangle, to white, by filling it with the 16 x 16-bit pattern, aHalftoneForm. The combination rule for copying the mask to the receiver is 3 (Form over).

fill: aRectangle rule: anInteger mask: aHalftoneForm

> Change the area of the receiver defined by the argument, aRectangle, to white, by filling it with the 16 x 16 bit pattern, aHalftoneForm. The combination rule for copying the mask to the receiver is anInteger.

As an example, the result of evaluating the expressions

    box ← 16@16 extent: 64@64.
    picture fill: box mask: locomotive

where locomotive is a 16x16-bit Form, is

The result of evaluating the sequence of two expressions

    picture lightGray: box.
    picture fill: box rule: Form under mask: locomotive

is

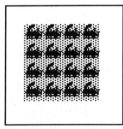

Note that in the above, the rule Form under refers to an Integer combination rule. Messages to Form to access combination rules and halftone masks were defined in Chapter 18.

Reversing an image means changing all the bits in the area that are white to black and those that are black to white. Either all or part of an image can be reversed.

DisplayMedium instance Protocol

reverse: aRectangle mask: aHalftoneForm	Change the area in the receiver defined by the argument, aRectangle, so that, in only those bits in which the mask, aHalftoneForm, is black, white bits in the receiver become black and black become white.
reverse: aRectangle	Change the area in the receiver defined by the argument, aRectangle, so that white is black and black is white. The default mask is Form black.
reverse	Change all of the receiver's area so that white is black and black is white.

The result of

picture reverse: box

on the last image is

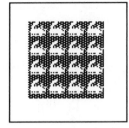

Bordering means coloring the outline of a rectangle. Bordering is done using a source Form and mask. Three messages provide methods for bordering an image.

DisplayMedium instance protocol

bordering

   border: aRectangle widthRectangle: insets mask: aHalftoneForm

Color an outline around the area within the receiver defined by the argument, aRectangle. The color is determined by the mask, aHalftoneForm. The width of the outline is determined by the Rectangle, insets, such that, origin x is the width of the left side, origin y is the width of the top side, corner x is the width of the right side, and corner y is the width of the bottom side.

   border: aRectangle width: borderWidth mask: aHalftoneForm

Color an outline around the area within the receiver defined by the argument, aRectangle. The color is determined by the mask, aHalftoneForm. The width of all the sides is borderWidth.

   border: aRectangle width: borderWidth

Color an outline around the area within the receiver defined by the argument, aRectangle. The color is Form black. The width of all the sides is borderWidth.

Examples are

expression	*result*

picture
   border: box
   width: 8
	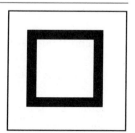

picture
   border: box
   width: 8
   mask: Form gray
	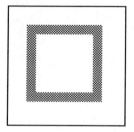

picture
  border: box
  widthRectangle:
     (4@16 corner: 4@16)
  mask: Form darkGray

picture
  border: box
  width: 16
  mask: locomotive

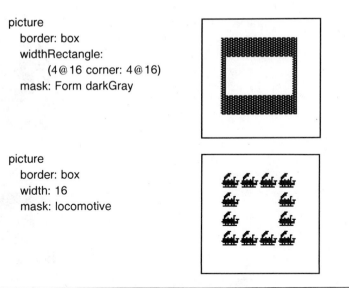

The next sequence of images shows how bordering can be done by manipulating the size of the rectangle used to designate which area within picture should be changed.

expression	*result*
frame ← 48@48 extent: 16@16. picture white. picture reverse: frame	

frame ← frame expandBy: 16.
picture
  fill: frame
  rule: Form reverse
  mask: Form black.	

```
frame ← frame expandBy: 16.
picture
    border: frame
    width: 16
    mask: locomotive
```

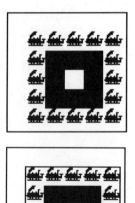

```
picture
    border: frame
    width: 1
```

Forms

Class Form is the only subclass of DisplayMedium in the standard Smalltalk-80 system. It was introduced in Chapter 18 in which we defined messages that provide access to constants representing masks and combination rules (modes). As an illustration of the use of Forms in creating complex images, the following sequence of expressions creates the image shown at the beginning of this chapter as Figure 20.2.

Suppose we have two Forms available, each 120 bits wide and 180 bits high. We name them face25 and face75. These images were created using a scanner to digitize photographs of a gentleman when he was in his 20's and on the occasion of his 75th birthday.

The scanned images were scaled to the desired size and then combined with halftone masks in the following way. Two Arrays, each size 8, contain references to the halftone masks (masks) and the Forms (forms) used in creating each part of the final image.

```
masks ← Array new: 8.
masks at: 1 put: Form black.
masks at: 2 put: Form darkGray.
masks at: 3 put: Form gray.
masks at: 4 put: Form lightGray.
masks at: 5 put: Form veryLightGray.
masks at: 6 put: Form lightGray.
masks at: 7 put: Form gray.
masks at: 8 put: Form black.
forms ← Array new: 8.
forms at: 1 put: face25.
forms at: 2 put: face25.
forms at: 3 put: face25.
forms at: 4 put: face25.
forms at: 5 put: face75.
forms at: 6 put: face75.
forms at: 7 put: face75.
forms at: 8 put: face75
```

The variable i is the initial index into the first halftone and first Form used in forming the first sub-image of each row. Each time a complete row is displayed, i is incremented by 1. Each row consists of 5 elements. The variable index is used to index 5 halftones and five Forms; index is set to i at the outset of each row. Thus the first row is made up by combining elements 1, 2, 3, 4, and 5 of masks and forms; the second row is made up by combining elements 2, 3, 4, 5, and 6 of masks and forms; and so on. The y coordinate of each row changes by 180 pixels each time; the x coordinate of each column changes by 120 pixels.

```
i ← 1.
0 to: 540 by: 180 do:
      [ :y |   index ← i.
            0 to: 480 by: 120 do:
                  [ :x |  (forms at: index)
                        displayOn: Display
                        at: x@y
                        clippingBox: Display boundingBox
                        rule: Form over
                        mask: (masks at: index).
                   index ← index + 1].
            i ← i + 1]
```

Other Forms

Two other kinds of forms exist in the system, InfiniteForm and OpaqueForm. These two classes are subclasses of DisplayObject, rather than of DisplayMedium. They therefore do not share Form's inherited ability to be colored and bordered. InfiniteForm represents a Form obtained by replicating a pattern Form indefinitely in all directions. Typically the overlapping views displayed in the Smalltalk-80 programming interface (as shown in Chapter 17) are placed over a light gray background; this background is defined by an InfiniteForm whose replicated pattern is Form gray. OpaqueForms represent a shape as well as a figure Form. The shape indicates what part of the background should be occluded in displaying the image, so that patterns other than black in the figure will still appear opaque. Instances of OpaqueForm support creating animations. Neither InfiniteForm nor OpaqueForm adds new protocol.

Cursors

Form has two subclasses of interest, class Cursor and class DisplayScreen. The Smalltalk-80 system makes extensive use of Forms to indicate both the current location of the hardware pointing device and the current status of the system. A Form used in this way is referred to as a *cursor* since its primary purpose is to move over the screen in order to locate screen coordinates.

Instances of class Cursor are Forms that are 16 pixels wide and 16 pixels high. Class Cursor adds three new messages to the displaying protocol that it inherits from DisplayObject.

Cursor instance protocol

displaying

show	Make the receiver be the current cursor shape.
showGridded: gridPoint	Make the receiver be the current cursor shape, forcing the location of cursor to the point nearest the location, gridPoint.
showWhile: aBlock	While evaluating the argument, aBlock, make the receiver be the cursor shape.

Several different cursors are supplied with the standard Smalltalk-80 system. They are shown in Figure 20.4 both small and enlarged in order to illustrate their bitmaps. The name of each cursor, given below its image, is the same as the message to class Cursor which accesses that particular Cursor. For example, the following expression shows a cursor that looks like eyeglasses on the screen while the system computes the factorial of 50. It then reverts to showing the original cursor shape.

normal

execute

up

down

origin

corner

read

write

crosshair

move

marker

wait

Figure 20.4

Cursor read showWhile: [50 factorial]

Changing the cursor shape is a very effective way of communicating with the user. Attention is always on the cursor, and changing its shape does not alter the appearance of the display.

DisplayScreen is another subclass of Form. There is usually only one instance of DisplayScreen in the system. It is referred to as Display, a global variable used to handle general user requests to deal with the whole display screen. In addition to the messages it inherits from its superclasses, DisplayObject, DisplayMedium, and Form, DisplayScreen provides class protocol for resetting the width, height, and displayed image of the screen.

The one case when multiple instances of DisplayScreen may exist is when (double-buffered) full screen animation is being done by alternating which instance of DisplayScreen supplies bits to the display hardware. Typically, full screen animation is not used, rather, animation is done within a smaller rectangular area. A hidden buffer of bits is used to form the next image. Each new image is displayed by copying the bits to the rectangular area using the copyBits: message of a BitBlt.

DisplayText

The second subclass of DisplayObject is class DisplayText. An instance of Text provides a font index (1 through 10) and an emphasis (italic, bold, underline) for each character of an instance of String. DisplayText consists of a Text and a TextStyle. A TextStyle associates each font index with an actual font (set of glyphs). In addition to representing this mapping to the set of fonts, a DisplayText supports the ability to display the characters on the screen. It does not support the protocol needed to create a user interface for editing either the characters or the choice of fonts and emphasis; this protocol must be supplied by subclasses of DisplayText.

Paths

A third subclass of DisplayObject is class Path. A Path is an OrderedCollection of Points and a Form that should be displayed at each Point. Complex images can be created by copying the Form along the trajectory represented by the Points.

Class Path is the basic superclass of the graphic display objects that represent trajectories. Instances of Path refer to an OrderedCollection and to a Form. The elements of the collection are Points. They can be added to the Path (add:); all Points that are described by some criterion can be removed from the Path (removeAllSuchThat:); and the Points can be enumerated, collected, and selected (do:, collect, and select:).

Path instance protocol	
accessing	
form	Answer the Form referred to by the receiver.
form: aForm	Set the Form referred to by the receiver to be aForm.
at: index	Answer the Point that is the indexth element of the receiver's collection.
at: index put: aPoint	Set the argument, aPoint, to be the indexth element of the receiver's collection.
size	Answer the number of Points in the receiver's collection.
testing	
isEmpty	Answer whether the receiver contains any Points.
adding	
add: aPoint	Add the argument, aPoint, as the last element of the receiver's collection of Points.
removing	
removeAllSuchThat: aBlock	Evaluate the argument, aBlock, for each Point in the receiver. Remove those Points for which aBlock evaluates to true.
enumerating	
do: aBlock	Evaluate the argument, aBlock, for each Point in the receiver.
collect: aBlock	Evaluate the argument, aBlock, for each Point in the receiver. Collect the resulting values into an OrderedCollection and answer the new collection.
select: aBlock	Evaluate the argument, aBlock, for each Point in the receiver. Collect into an Ordered-Collection those Points for which aBlock evaluates to true. Answer the new collection.

As an example, we create a "star" Path, and display a dot-shaped Form, referred to by the name dot, at each point on that Path.

```
aPath ← Path new form: dot.
aPath add: 150 @ 285.
aPath add: 400 @ 285.
aPath add: 185 @ 430.
aPath add: 280 @ 200.
aPath add: 375 @ 430.
```

```
aPath add: 150 @ 285.
aPath display
```

The resulting image is shown as the first path in Figure 20.5.

Figure 20.5

There are three paths in Figure 20.5.

- an instance of Path, created as indicated above
- an instance of LinearFit, using the same collection of Points
- an instance of Spline, using the same collection of Points

A LinearFit is displayed by connecting the Points in the collection, in order.

```
aPath ← LinearFit new form: dot.
aPath add: 150 @ 285.
aPath add: 400 @ 285.
aPath add: 185 @ 430.
aPath add: 280 @ 200.
aPath add: 375 @ 430.
aPath add: 150 @ 285.
aPath display
```

The Spline is obtained by fitting a cubic spline curve through the Points, again, in order. The order in which the Points are added to the Path significantly affects the outcome.

```
aPath ← Spline new form: dot.
aPath add: 150 @ 285.
aPath add: 400 @ 285.
aPath add: 185 @ 430.
aPath add: 280 @ 200.
aPath add: 375 @ 430.
aPath add: 150 @ 285.
aPath computeCurve.
aPath display
```

LinearFit and Spline are defined as subclasses of Path. In order to support the protocol of DisplayObject, each of these subclasses implements the message displayOn:at:clippingBox:rule:mask:.

Straight lines can be defined in terms of Paths. A Line is a Path specified by two points. An Arc is defined as a quarter of a circle. Instances of class Arc are specified to be one of the four possible quarters; they know their center Point and the radius of the circle. A Circle, then, is a kind of Arc that represents all four quarters. Again, in order to support the protocol of DisplayObject, each of these three classes (Line, Arc, and Circle) implements the messages displayOn:at:clippingBox:rule:mask:.

Class Curve is a subclass of Path. It represents a hyperbola that is tangent to lines determined by Points p1, p2 and p2, p3, and that passes through Points p1 and p3. The displaying message for Curve is defined as shown in the method below.

displayOn: aDisplayMedium
    at: aPoint
    clippingBox: aRectangle
    rule: anInteger
    mask: aForm

```
| pa pb k s p1 p2 p3 line |
line ← Line new.
line form: self form.
self size < 3 ifTrue: [self error: 'Curves are defined by three points'].
p1 ← self at: 1.
p2 ← self at: 2.
p3 ← self at: 3.
s ← Path new.
s add: p1.
pa ← p2 − p1.
pb ← p3 − p2.
k ← 5 max: pa x abs + pa y abs + pb x abs + pb y abs // 20.
"k is a guess as to how many line segments to use to approximate the
curve."
1 to: k do:
   [ :i | s add:
                pa∗i//k + p1∗(k−i) + (pb∗(i−1)//k + p2∗(i−1))//(k−1)].
s add: p3.
1 to: s size do:
   [ :i |
      line at: 1 put: (s at: i).
      line at: 2 put: (s at: i + 1).
      line displayOn: aDisplayMedium
         at: aPoint
         clippingBox: aRectangle
         rule: anInteger
         mask: aForm]
```

The algorithm was devised by Ted Kaehler. Basically the idea is to divide the line segments p1, p2 and p2, p3 into 10 sections. Numbering the sections as shown in the diagram, draw a line connecting point 1 on p1, p2 to point 1 on p2, p3; draw a line connecting point 2 on p1, p2 to point 2 on p2, p3; and so on. The hyperbola is the path formed from p1 to p3 by interpolating along the line segments formed on the outer shell.

Several curves are shown in Figure 20.6. The curves are the black lines; the gray lines indicate the lines connecting the points that were used to define the curves.

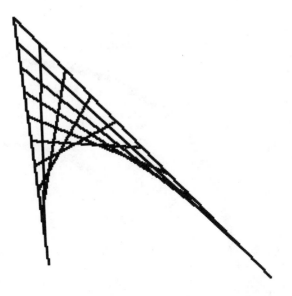

Two Curves were used to create the image shown in Figure 20.3. The Form was one of the images of the gentleman used in Figure 20.2.

Image Manipulation with Forms

We have shown in Chapter 18 how BitBlt can copy shapes and how repeated invocation can synthesize more complex images such as text and lines. BitBlt is also useful in the manipulation of existing images. For example, text can be made to look bold by ORing over itself, shifted right by one pixel. Just as complex images can be built from simple ones, complex processing can be achieved by repeated application of simple operations. In addition to its obvious manisfestation in the DisplayObject protocol, the power of BitBlt is made available for manipulating images through such messages as copy:from:in:rule:.

We present here four examples of such structural manipulation: magnification, rotation, area filling, and the Game of Life.

Magnification

A simple way to magnify a stored Form would be to copy it to a larger Form, making a big dot for every little dot in the original. For a height h and width w, this would take h*w operations. The algorithm presented here (as two messages to class Form) uses only a few more than h + w operations.

```
magnify: aRectangle by: scale
    | wideForm bigForm spacing |
    spacing ← 0 @ 0.
```

Display Objects

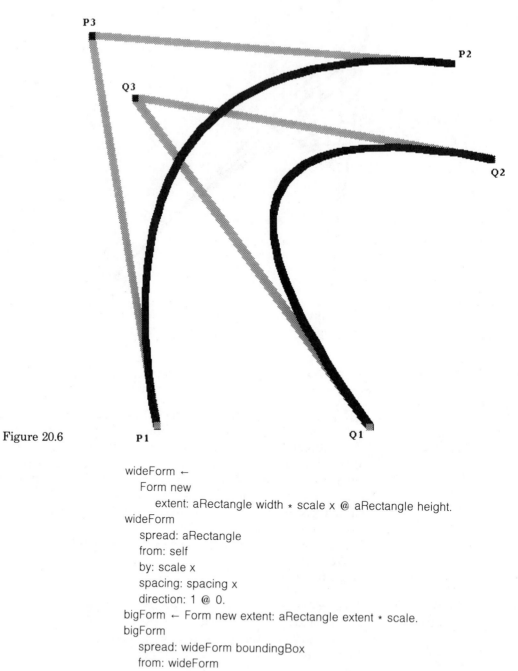

Figure 20.6

```
wideForm ←
    Form new
        extent: aRectangle width * scale x @ aRectangle height.
wideForm
    spread: aRectangle
    from: self
    by: scale x
    spacing: spacing x
    direction: 1 @ 0.
bigForm ← Form new extent: aRectangle extent * scale.
bigForm
    spread: wideForm boundingBox
    from: wideForm
    by: scale y
    spacing: spacing y
    direction: 0 @ 1.
↑bigForm
```

spread: rectangle
    from: aForm
    by: scale
    spacing: spacing
    direction: dir

```
| slice sourcePt |
slice ← 0@0 corner: dir transpose * self extent + dir.
sourcePt ← rectangle origin.
1 to: (rectangle extent dotProduct: dir) do:
    [ :i |
      "slice up original area"
      self copy: slice
          from: sourcePt
          in: aForm
          rule: 3.
      sourcePt ← sourcePt + dir.
      slice moveBy: dir * scale].
1 to: scale - spacing − 1 do:
    [ :i |
      "smear out the slices, leave white space"
      self copy: (dir corner: self extent)
          from: 0 @ 0
          in: self
          rule: 7]
```

The magnification proceeds in two steps. First, it slices up the image into vertical strips in wideForm separated by a space equal to the magnification factor. These are then smeared, using the ORing function, over the intervening area to achieve the horizontal magnification. The process is then repeated from wideForm into bigForm, with horizontal slices separated and smeared in the vertical direction, achieving the desired magnification. Figure 20.7 illustrates the progress of the above algorithm in producing the magnified "7".

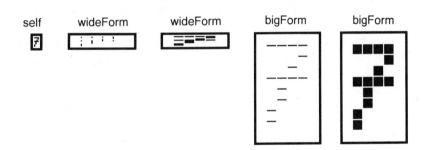

Figure 20.7

Rotation

Another useful operation on images is rotation by a multiple of 90 degrees. Rotation is often thought to be a fundamentally different operation from translation, and this point of view would dismiss the possibility of using BitBlt to rotate an image. However, the first transformation shown in Figure 20.8 is definitely a step toward rotating the image shown; all that remains is to rotate the insides of the four cells that have been permuted. The remainder of the figure shows each of these cells being further subdivided, its cells being similarly permuted, and so on. Eventually each cell being considered contains only a single pixel. At this point, no further subdivision is required, and the image has been faithfully rotated.

Each transformation shown in Figure 20.8 would appear to require successively greater amounts of computation, with the last one requiring several times more than h*w operations. The tricky aspect of the algorithm below is to permute the subparts of every subdivided cell at once, thus performing the entire rotation in a constant times $\log_2(h)$ operations. The parallel permutation of many cells is accomplished with the aid of two auxiliary Forms. The first, mask, carries a mask that selects the upper left quadrant of every cell; the second, temp, is used for temporary storage. A series of operations exchanges the right and left halves of every cell, and then another series exchanges the diagonal quadrants, achieving the desired permutation.

rotate

```
| mask temp quad all |
all ← self boundingBox.
mask ← Form extent: self extent.
temp ← Form extent: self extent.
mask white. "set up the first mask"
mask black: (0@0 extent: mask extent // 2).
quad ← self width // 2.
[quad > = 1] whileTrue:
    ["First exchange left and right halves"
    temp copy: all from: 0@0 in: mask rule: 3.
    temp copy: all from: 0@quad negated in: mask rule: 7.
    temp copy: all from: 0@0 in: self rule: 1.
    self copy: all from: 0@0 in: temp rule: 6.
    temp copy: all from: quad@0 in: self rule: 6.
    self copy: all from: quad@0 in: self rule: 7.
    self copy: all from: quad negated@0 in: temp rule: 6.
    "then flip the diagonals"
    temp copy: all from: 0@0 in: self rule: 3.
    temp copy: all from: quad@quad in: self rule: 6.
    temp copy: all from: 0@0 in: mask rule: 1.
```

Figure 20.8

```
self copy: all from: 0@0 in: temp rule: 6.
self copy: all from: quad negated@quad negated in: temp rule: 6.
"Now refine the mask"
mask copy: all from: (quad//2)@(quad//2) in: mask rule: 1.
mask copy: all from: 0@quad negated in: mask rule: 7.
mask copy: all from: quad negated@0 in: mask rule: 7.
quad ← quad // 2]
```

Figure 20.9 traces the state of temp and self after each successive operation.

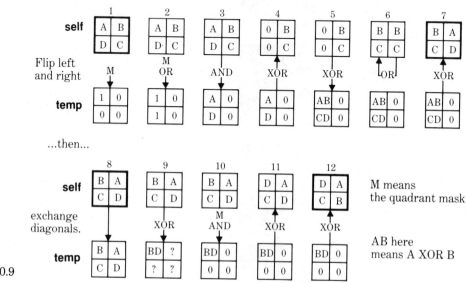

Figure 20.9

In the Figure 20.9, the offsets of each operation are not shown, though they are given in the program listing. After twelve operations, the desired permutation has been achieved. At this point the mask evolves to a finer grain, and the process is repeated for more smaller cells. Figure 20.10 shows the evolution of the mask from the first to the second stage of refinement.

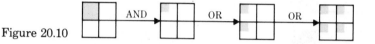

Figure 20.10

The algorithm presented here for rotation is applicable only to square forms whose size is a power of two. The extension of this technique to arbitrary rectangles is more involved. A somewhat simpler exercise is to apply the above technique to horizontal and vertical reflections about the center of a rectangle.

Area Filling

A useful operation on Forms is to be able to fill the interior of an outlined region with a halftone mask. The method given here takes as one argument a Point that marks a location in the interior of the region. A mark is placed at this location as a *seed*, and then the seed is smeared (in all four directions) into a larger blob until it extends to the region boundary. At each stage of the smearing process, the original Form is copied over the blob using the "erase" rule. This has the effect of trimming any growth which would have crossed the region borders. In addition, after every ten smear cycles, the resulting smear is compared with its previous version. When there is no change, the smear has filled the region and halftoning is applied throughout.

```
shapeFill: aMask interiorPoint: interiorPoint
    | dirs smearForm previousSmear all cycle noChange |
    all ← self boundingBox.
    smearForm ← Form extent: self extent.
    "Place a seed in the interior"
    smearForm valueAt: interiorPoint put: 1.
    previousSmear ← smearForm deepCopy.
    dirs ← Array with: 1@0 with: −1@0 with: 0@1 with: 0@−1.
    cycle ← 0.
    ["check for no change every 10 smears"
    (cycle ← cycle + 1)\\10 = 0 and:
       [previousSmear copy: all
                 from: 0@0
                 in: smearForm
                 rule: Form reverse.
      noChange ← previousSmear isAllWhite.
      previousSmear copy: all from: 0@0 in: smearForm rule: Form over.
      noChange]]
           whileFalse:
           [dirs do:
              [ :dir |
                 "smear in each of the four directions"
                 smearForm copy: all
                          from: dir
                          in: smearForm
                          rule: Form under.
                 "After each smear, trim around the region border"
                 smearForm copy: all from: 0@0 in: self rule: Form erase]].
    "Now paint the filled region in me with aMask"
    smearForm displayOn: self
              at: 0@0
              clippingBox: self boundingBox
              rule: Form under
              mask: aMask
```

Figure 20.11 shows a Form with a flower-shaped region to be filled. Successive smears appear below, along with the final result.

Figure 20.11

The Game of Life

Conway's Game of Life is a simple rule for successive populations of a bitmap. The rule involves the neighbor count for each cell—how many of the eight adjacent cells are occupied. Each cell will be occupied in the next generation if it has exactly three neighbors, or if it was occupied and has exactly two neighbors. This is explained as follows: three neighboring organisms can give birth in an empty cell, and an existing organism will die of exposure with less than two neighbors or from overpopulation with more than three neighbors. Since BitBlt cannot add, it would seem to be of no use in this application. However BitBlt's combination rules, available in the Form operations, do include the rules for partial sum (XOR) and carry (AND). With some ingenuity and a fair amount of extra storage, the next generation of any size of bitmap can be computed using a *constant* number of BitBlt operations.

```
nextLifeGeneration
    | nbr1 nbr2 nbr4 carry2 carry4 all delta |
    nbr1 ← Form extent: self extent.
    nbr2 ← Form extent: self extent.
    nbr4 ← Form extent: self extent.
    carry2 ← Form extent: self extent.
    carry4 ← Form extent: self extent.
    all ← self boundingBox.
    1 to: 8 do:
        [ :i |
        "delta is the offset of the eight neighboring cells"
        delta ← ((#(−1 0 1 1 1 0 −1 −1) at: i)
                    @ (#(−1 −1 −1 0 1 1 1 0) at: i)).
        carry2 copy: all from: 0@0 in: nbr1 rule: 3.
        carry2 copy: all from: delta in: self rule: 1. "AND for carry into 2"
```

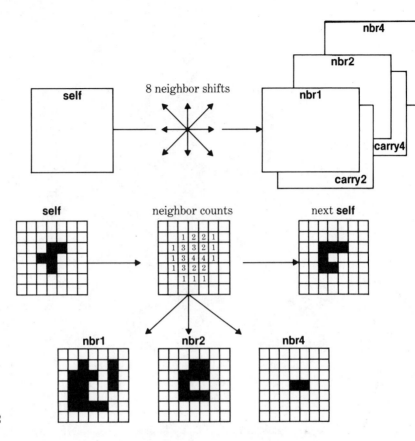

Figure 20.12

```
    nbr1 copy: all from: delta in: self rule: 6. "XOR for sum 1"
    carry4 copy: all from: 0@0 in: nbr2 rule: 3.
    carry4 copy: all from: 0@0 in: carry2 rule: 1. "AND for carry into 4"
    nbr2 copy: all from: 0@0 in: carry2 rule: 6. "XOR for sum 2"
    nbr4 copy: all from: 0@0 in: carry4 rule: 6].
 "XOR for sum 4 (ignore carry into 8)"
 self copy: all from: 0@0 in: nbr2 rule: 1.
 nbr1 copy: all from: 0@0 in: nbr2 rule: 1.
 self copy: all from: 0@0 in: nbr1 rule: 7.
 self copy: all from: 0@0 in: nbr4 rule: 4
 "compute next generation"
```

As shown in Figure 20.12, the number of neighbors is represented using three image planes for the 1's bit, 2's bit and 4's bit of the count in binary. The 8's bit can be ignored, since there are no survivors in that case, which is equivalent to zero (the result of ignoring the 8's bit). This Smalltalk-80 method is somewhat wasteful, as it performs the full carry propagation for each new neighbor, even though nothing will propagate into the 4-plane until at least the fourth neighbor.

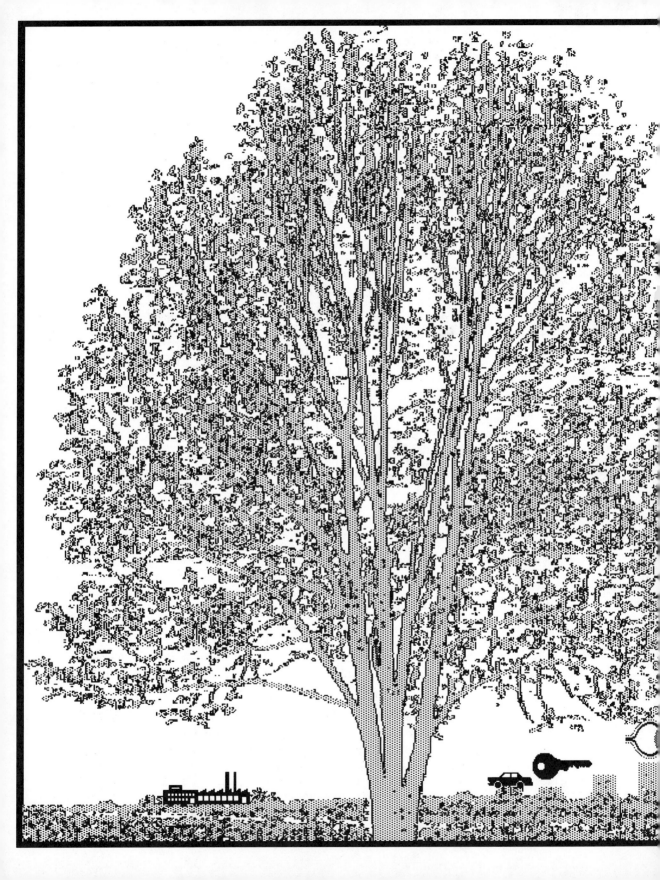

PART THREE

Part Three is an example of modeling discrete, event-driven simulations in the Smalltalk-80 system. A simulation is a representation of a system of objects in a real or fantasy world. The purpose of creating a computer simulation is to provide a framework in which to understand the simulation situation. In order to create the Smalltalk-80 simulations, we first describe a hierarchy of classes that represent probability distributions. Various kinds of probability distributions are used to determine arrival times of objects, such as customers, into a simulation; they are also used to randomly select response or service times for workers in a simulation. The example class SimulationObject represents any kind of object that enters into a simulation in order to carry out one or more tasks; class Simulation represents the simulation itself and provides the control structures for admitting and assigning tasks to new SimulationObjects.

The objects that participate in event-driven simulations operate more or less independently of one another. So it is necessary to consider the problem of coordinating and synchronizing their activities. The Smalltalk-80 system classes, Process, Semaphore, and SharedQueue, provide synchronization facilities for otherwise independent simulation events. The framework of classes defined in this part support the creation of simulations that use consumable, nonconsumable, and/or renewable resources. They also provide a number of ways in which a programmer can gather statistics about a running simulation.

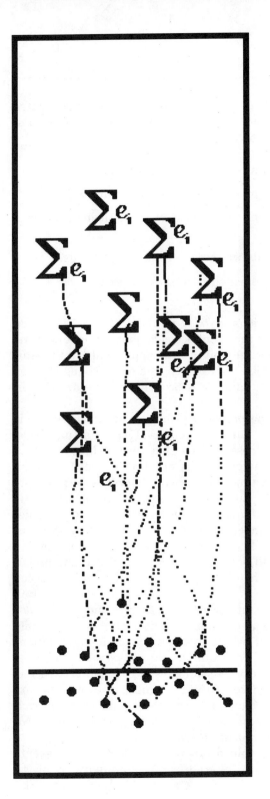

21

Probability Distributions

Probability Distribution Framework
Definitions
Introductory Examples
Class ProbabilityDistribution
Class DiscreteProbability
Class ContinuousProbability

Discrete Probability Distributions
The Bernoulli Distribution
The Binomial Distribution
The Geometric Distribution
The Poisson Distribution

Continuous Probability Distributions
The Uniform Distribution
The Exponential Distribution
The Gamma Distribution
The Normal Distribution

Probability Distribution Framework

Applications, such as simulations, often wish to obtain values associated with the outcomes of chance experiments. In such experiments, a number of possible questions might be asked, such as:

- What is the probability of a certain event occurring?
- What is the probability of one of several events occurring?
- What is the probability that, in the next N trials, at least one successful event will occur?
- How many successful events will occur in the next N trials?
- How many trials until the next successful event occurs?

Definitions

In the terminology of simulations, a *trial* is a tick of the simulated clock (where a clock tick might represent seconds, minutes, hours, days, months, or years, depending on the unit of time appropriate to the situation). An *event* or *success* is a job arrival such as a car arriving to a car wash, a customer arriving in a bank, or a broken machine arriving in the repair shop.

In the realm of statistics, the probability that an event will occur is typically obtained from a large number of observations of actual trials. For example, a long series of observations of a repair shop would be needed in order to determine the probability of a broken machine arriving in the shop during a fixed time interval. In general, several events might occur during that time interval. The set of possible events is called a *sample space*. A *probability function* on a sample space is defined as an association of a number between 0 and 1 with each event in the sample space. The probability or chance that at least one of the events in the sample space will occur is defined as 1; if p is the probability that event E will occur, then the probability that E will not occur is defined as $1 - p$.

Sample spaces are classified into two types: *discrete* and *continuous*. A sample space is discrete if it contains a finite number of possible events or an infinite number of events that have a one-to-one relationship with the positive integers. For example, the six possible outcomes of a throw of a die constitute a discrete sample space. A sample space is continuous if it contains an ordered, infinite number of events, for example, any number between 1.0 and 4.0. Probability functions on each of these types of sample spaces are appropriately named *discrete probability functions* and *continuous probability functions*.

A *random variable* is a real-valued function defined over the events in a sample space. The adjectives "discrete" and "continuous" apply to random variables according to the characteristic of their range. The probability function of a random variable is called a *probability distribution*; the values in the range of the function are the probabilities of occurrence of the possible values of the random variable. The *density* is a function that assigns probabilities to allowed ranges of the random variable. Any function can be a *density* function (discrete or continuous) if it has only positive values and its integral is 1.

Another useful function that plays an important role in simulations is called the *cumulative distribution function*. It gives the probability that the value of the random variable is within a designated range. For example, the cumulative distribution function answers the question: what is the probability that, in the throw of a die, the side is 4 or less?

The *mean* is defined as the average value that the random variable takes on. The *variance* is a measure of the spread of the distribution. It is defined as the average of the square of the deviations from the mean.

Introductory Examples

Two examples of sample spaces are given here before entering into a detailed description of the Smalltalk-80 classes. Suppose the sample space is the possible outcomes of a toss of a die. The sample space consists of

event 1: 1 is thrown
event 2: 2 is thrown
event 3: 3 is thrown
event 4: 4 is thrown
event 5: 5 is thrown
event 6: 6 is thrown

Then, for this discrete probability distribution, the probability function for any event is

f(event) = 1/6

If X is a random variable over the sample space, then the probability distribution of X is g(X) such that

$g(X=1) = f(event1) = 1/6, \ldots , g(X=6) = f(event6) = 1/6.$

The density of X is 1/6 for any value of X.

The cumulative distribution function of X is

$c(a, b) = \Sigma_a^b g(X)$

For example,

$c(2,4) = g(X=2) + g(X=3) + g(X=4) = 1/6 + 1/6 + 1/6 = 1/2$

As an example of a continuous probability distribution, let the sample space be the time of day where the start of the day is time = 12:00 a.m. and the end of the day is time = 11:59:59.99... p.m. The sample space is the interval between these two times.

The probability function is

$$f(event) = probability \ (event_i \leq time < event_j)$$

where $event_i < event_j$. The density of X is

$$g(X = any \ specified \ time) = 0$$

Suppose this is a 24-hour clock. Then the probability that, upon looking at a clock, the time is between 1:00 p.m. and 3:00 p.m., is defined by the cumulative distribution function

$$c(1:00, 3:00) = \int_{1:00}^{3:00} g(X)$$

$g(X)$ is uniform over 24 hours. So

$$c(1:00, 3:00) = c(1:00, 2:00) + c(2:00, 3:00) = 1/24 + 1/24 = 1/12.$$

Class
ProbabilityDistribution

The superclass for probability distributions provides protocol for obtaining one or more random samplings from the distribution, and for computing the density and cumulative distribution functions. It has a class variable U which is an instance of class Random. Class Random provides a simple way in which to obtain a value with uniform probability distribution over the interval [0,1].

Like class Random, ProbabilityDistribution is a Stream that accesses elements generated algorithmically. Whenever a random sampling is required, the message next is sent to the distribution. ProbabilityDistribution implements next by returning the result of the message inverseDistribution: var, where the argument var is a random number between 0 and 1. Subclasses of ProbabilityDistribution must implement inverseDistribution: in order to map [0,1] onto their sample space, or else they must override the definition of next. The message next: is inherited from the superclass Stream.

class name	ProbabilityDistribution
superclass	Stream
class variable names	U
class methods	

class initialization

initialize
"Uniformly distributed random numbers in the range [0,1]."
U ← Random new

instance creation

new
　↑self basicNew

instance methods

random sampling

next
　" This is a general random number generation method for any probability
　law; use the (0, 1) uniformly distributed random variable U as the val-
　ue of the law's distribution function. Obtain the next random value and
　then solve for the inverse. The inverse solution is defined by the sub-
　class."
　↑self inverseDistribution: U next

probability functions

density: x
　" This is the density function."
　self subclassResponsibility

distribution: aCollection
　" This is the cumulative distribution function. The argument is a range of
　contiguous values of the random variable. The distribution is mathemati-
　cally the area under the probability curve within the specified interval."
　self subclassResponsibility

private

inverseDistribution: x
　self subclassResponsibility

computeSample: m outOf: n
　" Compute the number of ways one can draw a sample without replace-
　ment of size m from a set of size n."
　m > n ifTrue: [↑0.0].
　↑n factorial / (n−m) factorial

In order to initialize the class variable U, evaluate the expression

ProbabilityDistribution initialize

Computing the number of ways one can draw a sample without replacement of size m from a set of size n will prove a useful method shared by
the subclass implementations that follow.

Class
DiscreteProbability

The two types of probability distributions, discrete and continuous, are
specified as subclasses of class ProbabilityDistribution; each provides an
implementation of the cumulative distribution function which depends

on the density function. These implementations assume that the density function will be provided in subclasses.

class name	DiscreteProbability
superclass	ProbabilityDistribution
instance methods	

probability functions

distribution: aCollection

"Answer the sum of the discrete values of the density function for each element in the collection."
| t |
t ← 0.0.
aCollection do: [:i | t ← t + (self density: i)].
↑t

Class
ContinuousProbability

class name	ContinuousProbability
superclass	ProbabilityDistribution
instance methods	

probability functions

distribution: aCollection

"This is a slow and dirty trapezoidal integration to determine the area under the probability function curve y=density(x) for x in the specified collection. The method assumes that the collection contains numerically-ordered elements."
| t aStream x1 x2 y1 y2 |
t ← 0.0.
aStream ← ReadStream on: aCollection.
x2 ← aStream next.
y2 ← self density: x2.
[x1 ← x2. x2 ← aStream next]
   whileTrue:
      [y1 ← y2.
      y2 ← self density: x2.
      t ← t + ((x2−x1)*(y2+y1))].
↑t*0.5

In order to implement the various kinds of probability distributions as subclasses of class DiscreteProbability or ContinuousProbability, both the density function and the inverse distribution function (or a different response to next) must be implemented.

Discrete Probability Distributions

As an example of a discrete probability distribution, take the heights of a class of 20 students and arrange a table indicating the frequency of students having the same heights (the representation of height is given in inches). The table might be

measured height	number of students
60″	3
62″	2
64″	4
66″	3
68″	5
70″	3

Given this information, we might ask the question: what is the probability of randomly selecting a student who is 5′4″ tall? This question is answered by computing the density function of the discrete probability associated with the observed information. In particular, we can define the density function in terms of the following table.

height	density
60″	3/20
62″	2/20
64″	4/20
66″	3/20
68″	5/20
70″	3/20

Suppose we define a subclass of DiscreteProbability which we name SampleSpace, and provide the above table as the value of an instance variable of SampleSpace. The response to the message density: x is the value associated with x in the table (in the example, the value of x is one of the possible heights); the value of the density of x, where x is not in the table, is 0. The probability of sampling each element of the collection is equally likely, so the density function is the reciprocal of the size of the collection. Since there may be several occurrences of a data element, the probability must be the appropriate sum of the probability for each occurrence. The implementation of the cumulative distribution function is inherited from the superclass.

class name	SampleSpace
superclass	DiscreteProbability
instance variable names	data
class methods	

instance creation

data: aCollection
    ↑self new setData: aCollection

instance methods

probability functions

density: x
    "x must be in the sample space; the probability must sum over all occur-
    rences of x in the sample space"
    (data includes: x)
      ifTrue: [↑(data occurrencesOf: x) / data size]
      ifFalse: [↑0]

private

inverseDistribution: x
    ↑data at: (x∗data size) truncated + 1
setData: aCollection
    data ← aCollection

Suppose heights is an instance of SampleSpace. The data is an array of 20 elements, the height of each student in the example.

heights ← SampleSpace data:
        #(60 60 60 62 62 64 64 64 64 66 66 66 68 68 68 68
        68 70 70 70)

Then we can ask heights the question, what is the probability of randomly selecting a student with height 64, or what is the probability of randomly selecting a student whose height is between 60″ and 64″? The answer to the first question is the density function, that is, the response to the message density: 64. The answer to the second is the cumulative distribution function; that is, the answer is the response to the message distribution: (60 to: 64 by: 2).

SampleSpace, in many ways, resembles a discrete uniform distribution. In general, a discrete uniform distribution is defined over a finite range of values. For example, we might specify a uniform distribution defined for six values: 1, 2, 3, 4, 5, 6, representing the sides of a die. The density function, as the constant 1/6, indicates that the die is "fair," i.e., the probability that each of the sides will be selected is the same.

We define four kinds of discrete probability distributions that are useful in simulation studies. They are Bernoulli, Binomial, Geometric, and Poisson. A Bernoulli distribution answers the question, will a success occur in the next trial? A binomial distribution represents N repeated, independent Bernoulli distributions, where N is greater than or equal to one. It answers the question, how many successes are there in N trials? Taking a slightly different point of view, the geometric distribution answers the question, how many repeated, independent Bernoulli trials are needed before the first success is obtained? A Poisson distribution is used to answer the question, how many events occur in a particular time interval? In particular, the Poisson determines the probability that K events will occur in a particular time interval, where K is greater than or equal to 0.

The Bernoulli Distribution

A Bernoulli distribution is used in the case of a sample space of two possibilities, each with a given probability of occurrence. Examples of sample spaces consisting of two possibilities are

- The throw of a die, in which I ask, did I get die side 4? The probability of success if the die is fair is 1/6; the probability of failure is 5/6.

- The toss of a coin, in which I ask, did I get heads? The probability of success if the coin is fair is 1/2; the probability of failure is 1/2.

- The draw of a playing card, in which I ask, is the playing card the queen of hearts? The probability of success if the card deck is standard is 1/52; the probability of failure is 51/52.

According to the specification of class Bernoulli, we create a Bernoulli distribution using expressions of the form

Bernoulli parameter: 0.17

In this example, we have created a Bernoulli distribution with a probability of success equal to 0.17. The probability of success is also referred to as the mean of the Bernoulli distribution.

The parameter, prob, of a Bernoulli distribution is the probability that one of the two possible outcomes will occur. This outcome is typically referred to as the successful one. The parameter prob is a number between 0.0 and 1.0. The density function maps the two possible outcomes, 1 or 0, onto the parameter prob or its inverse. The cumulative distribution, inherited from the superclass, can only return values prob or 1.

class name	Bernoulli
superclass	DiscreteProbability
instance variable names	prob

class methods

instance creation

parameter: aNumber
    (aNumber between: 0.0 and: 1.0)
        ifTrue: [↑self new setParameter: aNumber]
        ifFalse: [self error: 'The probability must be between 0.0 and 1.0']

instance methods

accessing

mean
    ↑prob
variance
    ↑prob * (1.0 − prob)

probability functions

density: x
    "let 1 denote success"
    x = 1 ifTrue: [↑prob].
    "let 0 denote failure"
    x = 0 ifTrue: [↑1.0−prob].
    self error: 'outcomes of a Bernoulli can only be 1 or 0'

private

inverseDistribution: x
    "Depending on the random variable x, the random sample is 1 or 0, denoting success or failure of the Bernoulli trial."
    x <= prob
      ifTrue: [↑1]
      ifFalse: [↑0]
setParameter: aNumber
    prob ← aNumber

Suppose, at some stage of playing a card game, we wish to determine whether or not the first draw of a card is an ace. Then a possible (randomly determined) answer is obtained by sampling from a Bernoulli distribution with mean of 4/52.

    (Bernoulli parameter: 4/52) next

Let's trace how the response to the message next is carried out.

    The method associated with the unary selector next is found in the method dictionary of class ProbabilityDistribution. The method returns the value of the expression self inverseDistribution: U next. That is, a uniformly distributed number between 0 and 1 is obtained (U next) in order to be the argument of inverseDistribution:. The method associated with the selector inverseDistribution: is found in the method dictionary of class Bernoulli. This is the inverse distribution function, a mapping from a value prob of the cumulative distribution function onto a value, x, such that prob is the probability that the random variable is less than or equal to x. In a Bernoulli distribution, x can only be one of two values; these are denoted by the integers 1 and 0.

The Binomial Distribution

In simulations, we use a Bernoulli distribution to tell us whether or not an event occurs, for example, does a car arrive in the next second or will a machine break down today? The binomial distribution answers how many successes occurred in N trials. The density function of a Bernoulli distribution tells us the probability of occurrence of one of two events. In contrast, the density function of a binomial answers the question, what is the probability that x successes will occur in the next N trials?

The binomial distribution represents N repeated, independent Bernoulli trials. It is the same as Bernoulli for N = 1. In the description of class Binomial, a subclass of class Bernoulli, the additional instance variable, N, represents the number of trials. That is, given an instance of Binomial, the response to the message next answers the question, how many successes are there in N trials?

The probability function for the binomial is

$$\frac{N!}{x!(N-x)!} \, p^x (1-p)^{N-x}$$

where x is the number of successes and p is the probability of success on each trial. The notation "!" represents the mathematical factorial operation. The first terms can be reduced to computing the number of ways to obtain x successes out of N trials, divided by the number of ways to obtain x successes out of x trials. Thus the implementation given below makes use of the method computeSample: a outOf: b provided in the superclass ProbabilityDistribution.

class name	Binomial
superclass	Bernoulli
instance variable names	N
class methods	

instance creation

events: n mean: m
    n truncated < = 0 ifTrue: [self error: 'number of events must be > 0'].
    ↑self new events: n mean: m

instance methods

random sampling

next
|t|
"A surefire but slow method is to sample a Bernoulli N times. Since the Bernoulli returns 0 or 1, the sum will be between 0 and N."
t ← 0.
N timesRepeat: [t ← t + super next].
↑t

probability functions

density: x
(x between: 0 and: N)
  ifTrue: [↑((self computeSample: x outOf: N)
        / (self computeSample: x outOf: x))
                 * (prob raisedTo: x) * ((1.0−prob) raisedTo: N−x)]
    ifFalse: [↑0.0]

private

events: n mean: m
N ← n truncated.
self setParameter: m/N
"setParameter: is implemented in my superclass"

Let's use flipping coins as our example. In five trials of a coin flip, where the probability of heads is 0.5, the Bernoulli distribution with parameter 0.5 represents one trial, i.e., one coin flip.

sampleA ← Bernoulli parameter: 0.5

The result of

sampleA next

is either 1 or 0, answering the question, did I get heads?
Suppose instead we create

sampleB ← Binomial events: 5 mean: 2.5

The result of

sampleB next

is a number between 0 and 5, answering the question, how many heads did I get in 5 trials?

The message

sampleB density: 3

is a number between 0 and 1, answering the question, what is the probability of getting heads 3 times in 5 trials?

The Geometric Distribution

Suppose we wish to answer the question, how many repeated, independent Bernoulli trials are needed before the first success is obtained? This new perspective on a Bernoulli distribution is the geometric distribution. As in the Bernoulli and binomial cases, the probability of a success is between 0.0 and 1.0; the mean of the geometric is the reciprocal of the success probability. Thus if we create a geometric distribution as

Geometric mean: 5

then the mean is 5 and the probability of a success is 1/5. The mean must be greater than or equal to 1.

A geometric distribution is more suitable for an event-driven simulation design than a Bernoulli or binomial. Instead of asking how many cars arrive in the next 20 seconds (a binomial question), the geometric distribution asks, how many seconds before the next car arrives. In event-driven simulations, the (simulated) clock jumps to the time of the next event. Using a geometric distribution, we can determine when the next event will occur, set the clock accordingly, and then carry out the event, potentially "saving" a great deal of real time.

The probability distribution function is

$$p(1-p)^{x-1}$$

where x is the number of trials required and p is the probability of success on a single trial.

class name	Geometric
superclass	Bernoulli
class methods	

instance creation

mean: m
    ↑self parameter: 1/m
    "Note that the message parameter: is implemented in the superclass"

instance methods

accessing

mean
   ↑ 1.0 / prob
variance
   ↑ (1.0−prob) / prob squared

probability functions

density: x
   x > 0 ifTrue: [↑prob ∗ ((1.0−prob) raisedTo: x−1)]
      ifFalse: [↑0.0]

private

inverseDistribution: x
   "Method is from Knuth, Vol. 2, pp.116–117"
   ↑(x ln / (1.0−prob) ln) ceiling

Suppose, on the average, two cars arrive at a ferry landing every minute. We can express this statistical information as

   sample ← Geometric mean: 2/60

The density function can be used to answer the question, what is the probability that it will take N trials before the next success? For example, what is the probability that it will take 30 seconds before the next car arrives?

   sample density: 30

The cumulative distribution function can be used to answer the question, did the next car arrive in 30 to 40 seconds?

   sample distribution: (30 to: 40)

*The Poisson
Distribution*

Suppose the question we wish to ask is, how many events occur in a unit time (or space interval)? The binomial distribution considers the occurrence of two independent events, such as drawing a king of hearts or a king of spades from a full deck of cards. There are random events, however, that occur at random points in time or space. These events do not occur as the outcomes of trials. In these circumstances, it does not make sense to consider the probability of an event happening or not happening. One does not ask how many cars did not arrive at a ferry or how many airplanes did not land at the airport; the appropriate questions are how many cars did arrive at the ferry and how many airplanes did land at the airport, in the next unit of time?

In simulations, the Poisson distribution is useful for sampling potential demands by customers for service, say, of cashiers, salesmen, technicians, or Xerox copiers. Experience has shown that the rate at which the service is provided often approximates a Poisson probability law.

The Poisson law describes the probability that exactly x events occur in a unit time interval, when the mean rate of occurrence per unit time is the variable mu. For a time interval of dt, the probability is mu*dt; mu must be greater than 0.0.

The probability function is

$$\frac{a^x e^{-a}}{x!}$$

where a is the mean rate (or mu), e the base of natural logarithms, x is the number of occurrences, and ! the factorial notation.

class name	Poisson
superclass	DiscreteProbability
instance variable names	mu
class methods	

instance creation

mean: p
"p is the average number of events happening per unit interval."
p > 0.0
    ifTrue: [↑self new setMean: p]
    ifFalse: [self error: 'mean must be greater than 0.0']

instance methods

accessing

mean
    ↑mu
variance
    ↑mu

random sampling

next
"how many events occur in the next unit interval?"
| p n q |
p ← mu negated exp.
n ← 0.
q ← 1.0.
[q ← q * U next.
 q >= p]
    whileTrue: [n ← n+ 1].
↑n

probability functions

density: x
  "the probability that in a unit interval, x events will occur"
  x > = 0
    ifTrue: [↑((mu raisedTo: x) * (mu negated exp)) / x factorial]
    ifFalse: [↑0.0]

private

setMean: p
  mu ← p

The response to the message next answers the question, how many events occur in the next unit of time or space? The density function of x determines the probability that, in a unit interval (of time or space), x events will occur. The cumulative distribution function of x determines the probability that, in a unit interval, x events or fewer will occur.

Continuous Probability Distributions

A continuous random variable can assume any value in an interval or collection of intervals. In the continuous case, questions similar to those asked in the discrete case are asked and the continuous probability distributions show strong correspondence to the discrete ones. An example of a question one asks of a continuous probability distribution is, what is the probability of obtaining a temperature at some moment of time. Temperature is a physical property which is measured on a continuous scale.

We define four kinds of continuous probability distributions; they are uniform, exponential, gamma, and normal distributions. The uniform distribution answers the question, given a set of equally likely events, which one occurs? Given that the underlying events are Poisson distributed, the exponential distribution is used to answer the question, how long before the first (next) event occurs? The gamma distribution is related in that it answers the question, how long before the Nth event occurs? The normal or Gaussian distribution is useful for approximating limiting forms of other distributions. It plays a significant role in statistics because it is simple to use; symmetrical about the mean; completely determined by two parameters, the mean and the variance; and reflects the distribution of everyday events.

The Uniform Distribution

We have already examined the uniform distribution from the perspective of selecting discrete elements from a finite sample space. The question we asked was, given a set of equally likely descriptions, which one to pick? In the continuous case, the sample space is a continuum, such as time or the interval between 0 and 1. The class Uniform provided here extends the capabilities of class Random by generating a random variable within any interval as a response to the message next.

class name	Uniform
superclass	ContinuousProbability
instance variable names	startNumber
	stopNumber

class methods

instance creation

from: begin to: end
    begin > end
        ifTrue: [self error: 'illegal interval']
        ifFalse: [↑self new setStart: begin toEnd: end]

instance methods

accessing

mean
    ↑(startNumber + stopNumber)/2
variance
    ↑(stopNumber − startNumber) squared / 12

probability functions

density: x
    (x between: startNumber and: stopNumber)
        ifTrue: [↑1.0 / (stopNumber − startNumber)]
        ifFalse: [↑0]

private

inverseDistribution: x
    "x is a random number between 0 and 1"
    ↑startNumber + (x * (stopNumber − startNumber))
setStart: begin toEnd: end
    startNumber ← begin.
    stopNumber ← end

The Exponential Distribution

Given that the underlying events are Poisson distributed, the exponential distribution determines how long before the next event occurs. This is more suitable for a simulation design than is Poisson in the same sense that the geometric distribution was more suitable than the binomial, because we can jump the simulated clock setting to the next occurrence of an event, rather than stepping sequentially through each time unit.

As an example of sampling with an exponential, we might ask, when will the next car arrive? The density function of x is the probability that the next event will occur in the time interval x, for example, what is the probability of the next car arriving in the next 10 minutes?

Exponential is typically used in situations in which the sample deteriorates with time. For example, an exponential is used to determine the probability that a light bulb or a piece of electronic equipment will fail prior to some time x. Exponential is useful in these cases because the longer the piece of equipment is used, the less likely it is to keep running.

As in the case of a Poisson, the parameter of the exponential distribution, mu, is in terms of events per unit time, although the domain of this distribution is time (not events).

The probability function for the exponential distribution is

$$\frac{e^{-\frac{x}{a}}}{a}$$

where a is the mean rate (mu = 1/a) between occurrences.

class name	Exponential
superclass	ContinuousProbability
instance variable names	mu
class methods	

instance creation

mean: p
    "Since the exponential parameter mu is the same as Poisson mu, if we are given the mean of the exponential, we take reciprocal to get the probability parameter"
    ↑self parameter: 1.0/p
parameter: p
    p > 0.0
      ifTrue: [↑self new setParameter: p]
      ifFalse: [self error:
          'The probability parameter must be greater than 0.0']

instance methods

accessing

mean
    ↑1.0/mu
variance
    ↑1.0/(mu * mu)

probability functions

density: x
   x > 0.0
      ifTrue: [↑mu * (mu*x) negated exp]
      ifFalse: [↑0.0]
distribution: anInterval
   anInterval stop < = 0.0
      ifTrue: [↑0.0]
      ifFalse: [↑1.0 − (mu * anInterval stop) negated exp −
                      (anInterval start > 0.0
                          ifTrue: [self distribution:
                                        (0.0 to: anInterval start)]
                        ifFalse: [0.0])]

private

inverseDistribution: x
   "implementation according to Knuth, Vol. 2, p. 114"
   ↑x ln negated / mu
setParameter: p
   mu ← p

The Gamma Distribution

A distribution related to the exponential is gamma, which answers the question, how long before the Nth event occurs? For example, we use a gamma distribution to sample how long before the Nth car arrives at the ferry landing. Each instance of class Gamma represents an Nth event and the probability of occurrence of that Nth event (inherited from the superclass Exponential). The variable N specified in class Gamma must be a positive integer.

The probability function is

$$\frac{x^{k-1} e^{-\frac{x}{a}}}{a^k (k-1)!}$$

where k is greater than zero and the probability parameter mu is 1/a. The second term of the denominator, (k-1)!, is the gamma function when it is known that k is greater than 0. The implementation given below does not make this assumption.

class name	Gamma
superclass	Exponential
instance variable names	N

class methods

instance creation

events: k mean: p
>   k ← k truncated.
>   k > 0
>   ifTrue: [↑(self parameter: k/p) setEvents: k]
>   ifFalse: [self error: 'the number of events must be greater than 0']

instance methods

accessing

mean
>   ↑super mean * N
variance
>   ↑super variance * N

probability functions

density: x
> | t |
>   x > 0.0
>   ifTrue: [t ← mu * x.
>   ↑(mu raisedTo: N) / (self gamma: N)
>   * (x raisedTo: N−1)
>   * t negated exp]
>   ifFalse: [↑0.0]

private

gamma: n
> | t |
>   t ← n − 1.0.
>   ↑self computeSample: t outOf: t
setEvents: events
>   N ← events

The Normal Distribution

The normal distribution, also called the Gaussian, is useful for summarizing or approximating other distributions. Using the normal distribution, we can ask questions such as how long before a success occurs (similar to the discrete binomial distribution) or how many events occur in a certain time interval (similar to the Poisson). Indeed, the normal can be used to approximate a binomial when the number of events is very large or a Poisson when the mean is large. However, the approximation is only accurate in the regions near the mean; the errors in approximation increase towards the tail.

A normal distribution is used when there is a central dominating value (the mean), and the probability of obtaining a value decreases with a deviation from the mean. If we plot a curve with the possible values on the x-axis and the probabilities on the y-axis, the curve will look like a bell shape. This bell shape is due to the requirements that the probabilities are symmetric about the mean, the possible values from the sample space are infinite, and yet the probabilities of all of these infinite values must sum to 1. The normal distribution is useful when determining the probability of a measurement, for example, when measuring the size of ball bearings. The measurements will result in values that cluster about a central mean value, off by a small amount.

The parameters of a normal distribution are the mean (mu) and a standard deviation (sigma). The standard deviation must be greater than 0. The probability function is

$$\frac{e^{\frac{1}{2}\left(\frac{x-a}{b}\right)^2}}{b\sqrt{2\pi}}$$

where a is the parameter mu and b is the standard deviation sigma.

class name	Normal
superclass	ContinuousProbability
instance variable names	mu
	sigma

class methods

instance creation

mean: a deviation: b
    b > 0.0
        ifTrue: [↑self new setMean: a standardDeviation: b]
        ifFalse: [self error: 'standard deviation must be greater than 0.0']

instance methods

accessing

mean
    ↑mu
variance
    ↑sigma squared

random sampling

next
    "Polar method for normal deviates, Knuth vol. 2, pp. 104, 113"
    | v1 v2 s rand u |
    rand ← Uniform from: −1.0 to: 1.0.
    [v1 ← rand next.
    v2 ← rand next.
    s ← v1 squared + v2 squared.
    s >= 1] whileTrue.
    u ← (−2.0 ∗ s ln / s) sqrt.
    ↑mu + (sigma ∗ v1 ∗ u)

probability functions

density: x

```
|  twoPi t  |
twoPi ← 2 * 3.1415926536.
t ← x − mu / sigma.
↑(−0.5 * t squared) exp / (sigma * twoPi sqrt)
```

private

setMean: m standardDeviation: s

```
mu ← m.
sigma ← s
```

In subsequent chapters, we define and provide examples of using class descriptions that support discrete, event-driven simulation. The probability distributions defined in the current chapter will be used throughout the example simulations.

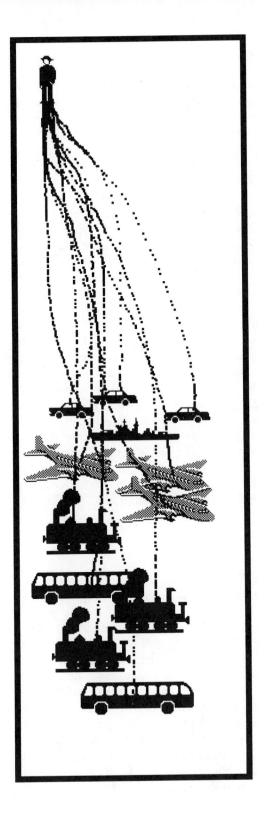

22

Event-Driven Simulations

A simulation is a representation of a system of objects in a real or fantasy world. The purpose of creating a computer simulation is to provide a framework in which to understand the simulated situation, for example, to understand the behavior of a waiting line, the workload of clerks, or the timeliness of service to customers. Certain kinds of simulations are referred to as "counter simulations." They represent situations for which there are places or counters in which clerks work. Customers arrive at a place in order to get service from a clerk. If a clerk is not available, the customer enters a waiting line. The first customer in the line is serviced by the next available clerk. Often a given simulation has several kinds of places and several customers, each with an agenda of places to visit. There are many examples of such situations: banks, car washes, barber shops, hospitals, cafeterias, airports, post offices, amusement parks, and factories. A computer simulation makes it possible to collect statistics about these situations, and to test out new ideas about their organization.

The objects that participate in a counter simulation operate more or less independently of one another. So, it is necessary to consider the problem of coordinating or synchronizing the activities of the various simulated objects. They typically coordinate their actions through the mechanism of message passing. Some objects, however, must synchronize their actions at certain critical moments; some objects can not proceed to carry out their desired actions without access to specific resources that may be unavailable at a given moment. The Smalltalk-80 system classes, Process, Semaphore, and SharedQueue, provide synchronization facilities for otherwise independent activities. To support a general description of counter simulations, mechanisms are needed for coordinating

- the use of fixed-size resources,
- the use of fluctuating resources, and
- the appearance of simultaneity in the actions of two objects.

Fixed resources can either be *consumable* or *nonconsumable*. For example, jelly beans are consumable, fixed resources of a candy store; books are non-consumable resources of a library. Fluctuating resources are typically referred to as *renewable* or producer/consumer synchronized. A store can model its supply of jelly beans as a fluctuating resource because the supply can be renewed. One can also imagine a resource that is both renewable and nonconsumable. Such a resource might be modeled in a simulation of car rentals: cars are renewable resources since new ones are manufactured and added to the available supply of cars to rent; the cars are also nonconsumable because a rented car is returned to the dealer for use by other customers. Actually, most nonconsumable resources are consumable, for example, library books eventually become too tattered for continued circulation; the rental cars eventually get junked. "Nonconsumable" means, minimally, that they are not consumed during the period of interest in the simulation.

When the actions of two objects in a simulation must be synchronized to give the appearance of carrying out a task together, the two objects are said to be in a server/client relationship. For example, a doctor needs the cooperation of the patient in order to carry out an examination. The server is a *coordinated* resource; it is a simulation object whose tasks can only be carried out when one or more clients request the resource.

An important aspect of simulations is that they model situations that change over time; customers enter and leave a bank; cars enter, get washed, get dried, and leave a car wash; airplanes land, unload passengers, load passengers, and take off from airports. It is often the case that these activities are time-related; at certain times or with certain intervals of time, events occur. Therefore, actions have to be synchronized with some notion of time. Often this notion of time is itself simulated.

There are a number of ways in which to represent the actions of simulated objects with respect to real or simulated time. In one approach, the clock runs in its usual manner. At each tick of the clock, all objects are given the opportunity to take any desired action. The clock acts as a synchronization device for the simulation, providing the opportunity to give the appearance of parallelism since the clock waits until all actions appropriate at the given time are completed. Often, no actions will take place at a given tick of the clock.

Alternatively, the clock can be moved forward according to the time at which the next action will take place. In this case, the system is driven by the next discrete action or event scheduled to occur. The implementation of a simulation using this approach depends on maintaining a queue of events, ordered with respect to simulated time. Each time an event is completed, the next one is taken from the queue and the clock is moved to the designated time.

The simulations presented in this chapter are based on this *event-driven* approach. They include simulations in which a collection of independent objects exist, each with a set of tasks to do (services or resources to obtain), and each needing to coordinate its activity's times with other objects in the simulated situation.

This chapter describes a framework in which such simulations can be developed. The class SimulationObject describes a general kind of object that might appear in a simulation, that is, one with a set of tasks to do. The message protocol of the class provides a framework in which the tasks are carried out. An instance of class Simulation maintains the simulated clock and the queue of events. The specification of the arrival of new objects into the system (objects such as customers) and the specification of resources (such as the clerks) are coordinated in this class.

The next chapter, Chapter 23, deals with ways to collect the data generated in running a simulation. Statistics gathering can be handled by providing a general mechanism in subclasses of class Simulation and/or class SimulationObject. Alternatively, each example simulation can provide its own mechanism for collecting information about its behavior.

Chapter 24 describes example simulations that make use of two kinds of synchronizations, shared use of fixed resources and shared use of fluctuating resources; Chapter 25 introduces additional support for coordination between two simulation objects—those wanting service and those providing service.

A Framework for Simulations

This section contains a description of the classes that provide the basic protocol for classes SimulationObject and Simulation. These classes are presented twice. First, a description of the protocol is given with an explanation of how to create a default example; second, an implementation of these classes is given.

Simulation Objects

Consider simulating a car wash. Major components of a car wash are washing places, drying places, paying places, washers, dryers, cashiers, and vehicles of different sorts such as trucks and cars. We can classify these components according to behavior. Major classifications are: places, where workers are located and work is performed; workers, such as washers, dryers, and cashiers; and the vehicles that are the customers of the places. These classifications might be translated into three classes of Smalltalk objects: Place, Worker, and Customer. But each of these classes of objects is similar in that each describes objects that have tasks to do—a Customer requests service, a Worker gives service, and a Place provides resources. In particular, a Place provides a waiting queue for the times when there are more customers than its workers can handle. These similarities are modeled in the superclass SimulationObject, which describes objects that appear in a simulated situation; a SimulationObject is any object that can be given a sequence of tasks to do. Each object defines a main sequence of activity that is initiated when the object enters the simulation. For example, the activities of a car in a car wash are to request a washer, wait while being washed, request a dryer, wait while being dried, pay for the service, and leave.

Class SimulationObject specifies a general control sequence by which the object enters, carries out its tasks, and leaves the simulation. This sequence consists of sending the object the messages startUp, tasks, and finishUp. Initialization of descriptive variables is specified as the response to message initialize. These messages are invoked by the method associated with startUp. Response to the messages tasks and initialize are implemented by subclasses of SimulationObject.

SimulationObject instance protocol

initialization
    initialize   Initialize instance variables, if any.

simulation control
    startUp   Initialize instance variables. Inform the simulation that the receiver is entering it, and then initiate the receiver's tasks.

    tasks   Define the sequence of activities that the receiver must carry out.

    finishUp   The receiver's tasks are completed. Inform the simulation.

There are several messages that any SimulationObject can use in order to describe its tasks. One is holdFor: aTimeDelay, where the argument aTimeDelay is some amount of simulated time for which the object delays further action. The idea of this delay is to create a period of time in which the object is presumably carrying out some activity.

We call the category of these messages, the modeler's task language to indicate that these are the messages sent to a SimulationObject as part of the implementation of the message tasks.

A simulation can contain simple or *static* resources, like "jelly beans," that can be acquired by a simulation object. Or a simulation can consist of *coordinated* resources, that is, simulation objects whose tasks must be synchronized with the tasks of other simulation objects. The task language includes messages for accessing each kind of resource, either to get or to give the resource.

There are 3 kinds of messages for static resources. There are 2 messages for getting an amount of the resource named resourceName. They are

    acquire: amount ofResource: resourceName
    acquire: amount ofResource: resourceName withPriority: priorityInteger

There is one for giving an amount of the resource named resourceName,

    produce: amount ofResource: resourceName

and one for giving up an acquired static resource,

    release: aStaticResource

There are also 3 kinds of messages for coordinated resources. The message for getting the resource named resourceName (here, the resource is a SimulationObject that models a kind of customer, and the asker is a server such as a clerk) is

acquireResource: resourceName

To produce the resource named resourceName (the asker is a customer), the message is

produceResource: resourceName

and to give up an acquired resource (which is a SimulationObject whose task events can now be resumed), the message is

resume: anEvent

When a SimulationObject makes a static resource request (acquire:ofResource: or request:), it can do so by stating the level of importance of the request. The number 0 represents the least important request, successively higher numbers represent successively higher levels of importance. The message acquire:ofResource: assumes a priority level of 0; acquire:ofResource:withPriority: specifies particular levels in its third argument.

Two queries check whether a static resource is in the simulation and how much of the resource is available. These are resourceAvailable: resourceName, which answers whether or not the simulation has a resource referred to by the String, resourceName; and inquireFor: amount ofResource: resourceName, which answers whether there is at least amount of the resource remaining.

When a SimulationObject is synchronizing its tasks with that of another SimulationObject, it might be useful to know whether such an object is available. Two additional inquiry messages support finding out whether a provider or requester of a coordinated task is available— numberOfProvidersOfResource: resourceName and numberOf- RequestersOfResource: resourceName.

In addition, a message to a SimulationObject can request that the Simulation it is in stop running. This is the message stopSimulation.

SimulationObject instance protocol
_____

task language
    holdFor: aTimeDelay   Delay carrying out the receiver's next task
                                        until aTimeDelay amount of simulated time
                                        has passed.

acquire: amount ofResource: resourceName

Ask the simulation to provide a simple resource that is referred to by the String, resourceName. If one exists, ask it to give the receiver amount of resources. If one does not exist, notify the simulation user (programmer) that an error has occurred.

acquire: amount ofResource: resourceName withPriority: priorityNumber

Ask the simulation to provide a simple resource that is referred to by the String, resourceName. If one exists, ask it to give the receiver amount of resources, taking into account that the priority for acquiring the resource is to be set as priorityNumber. If one does not exist, notify the simulation user (programmer) that an error has occurred.

produce: amount ofResource: resourceName

Ask the simulation to provide a simple resource that is referred to by the String, resourceName. If one exists, add to it amount more of its resources. If one does not exist, create it.

release: aStaticResource

The receiver has been using the resource referred to by the argument, aStaticResource. It is no longer needed and can be recycled.

inquireFor: amount ofResource: resourceName

Answer whether or not the simulation has at least a quantity, amount, of a resource referred to by the String, resourceName.

resourceAvailable: resourceName

Answer whether or not the simulation has a resource referred to by the String, resourceName.

acquireResource: resourceName Ask the simulation to provide a resource simulation object that is referred to by the String, resourceName. If one exists, ask it to give the receiver its services. If one does not exist, notify the simulation user (programmer) that an error has occurred.

produceResource: resourceName

Have the receiver act as a resource that is referred to by the String, resourceName. Wait for another SimulationObject that provides service to (acquires) this resource.

resume: anEvent

The receiver has been giving service to the resource referred to by the argument, anEvent. The service is completed so that the resource, a SimulationObject, can continue its tasks.

numberOfProvidersOfResource: resourceName

Answer the number of SimulationObjects waiting to coordinate its tasks by acting as the resource referred to by the String, resourceName.

numberOfRequestersOfResource: resourceName

Answer the number of SimulationObjects waiting to coordinate its tasks by acquiring the resource referred to by the String, resourceName.

stopSimulation	Tell the simulation in which the receiver is running to stop. All scheduled events are removed and nothing more can happen in the simulation.

The examples we present in subsequent chapters illustrate each message in the modeler's task language.

Simulations

The purpose of class Simulation is to manage the topology of simulation objects and to schedule actions to occur according to simulated time. Instances of class Simulation maintain a reference to a collection of SimulationObjects, to the current simulated time, and to a queue of events waiting to be invoked.

The unit of time appropriate to the simulation is saved in an instance variable and represented as a floating-point number. The unit might be milliseconds, minutes, days, etc. A simulation advances time by checking the queue to determine when the next event is scheduled to take place, and by setting its instance variable to the time associated with that next event. If the queue of events is empty, then the simulation terminates.

Simulation objects enter a simulation in response to one of several scheduling messages such as

scheduleArrivalOf: aSimulationObjectClass
     accordingTo: aProbabilityDistribution or
scheduleArrivalOf: aSimulationObject at: aTimeInteger.

These messages are sent to the simulation either at the time that the simulation is first initialized, in response to the message defineArrivalSchedule, or as part of the sequence of tasks that a SimulationObject carries out. The second argument of the first message, aProbabilityDistribution, is an instance of a probability distribution such as those defined in Chapter 21. In this chapter, we assume the availability of the definitions given in Chapter 21. The probability distribution defines the interval at which an instance of the first argument, aSimulationObjectClass, is to be created and sent the message startUp.

In addition, Simulation supports messages having to do with scheduling a particular sequence of actions. These are schedule: actionBlock at: timeInteger and schedule: actionBlock after: amountOfTime.

In order to define the resources in the simulation, the modeler can send the simulation one or more of two possible messages. Either

self produce: amount of: resourceName

where the second argument, resourceName, is a String that names a simple quantifiable resource available in the simulation; the first argument is the (additional) quantity of this resource to be made available.

Or

  self coordinate: resourceName

The argument, resourceName, is a String that names a resource that is to be provided by some objects in the simulation and requested by other objects. For example, the resource is car washing, the provider is a washer object and the requestor is a car object.

Simulation instance protocol
_____

initialization
    initialize   Initialize the receiver's instance variables.

modeler's initialization language
    defineArrivalSchedule   Schedule simulation objects to enter the simulation at specified time intervals, typically based on probability distribution functions. This method is implemented by subclasses. It involves a sequence of messages to the receiver (i.e., to self) that are of the form
                              schedule:at:, scheduleArrivalOf:at:,
                              scheduleArrivalOf:accordingTo:, or
                              scheduleArrivalOf:accordingTo:startingAt:.
                        See the next category of messages for descriptions of these.

    defineResources   Specify the resources that are initially entered into the simulation. These typically act as resources to be acquired. This method is implemented by subclasses and involves a sequence of messages to the receiver (i.e., to self) of the form produce: amount of: resourceName.

modeler's task language
    produce: amount of: resourceName
                        An additional quantity of amount of a resource referred to by the String, resourceName, is to be part of the receiver. If the resource does not as yet exist in the receiver, add it; if it already exists, increase its available quantity.

    coordinate: resourceName   Use of a resource referred to by the String, resourceName, is to be coordinated by the receiver.

    schedule: actionBlock after: timeDelayInteger
                        Set up a program, actionBlock, that will be evaluated after a simulated amount of time, timeDelayInteger, passes.

    schedule: actionBlock at: timeInteger
                        Schedule the sequence of actions (actionBlock) to occur at a particular simulated time, timeInteger.

    scheduleArrivalOf: aSimulationObject at: timeInteger
                        Schedule the simulation object, aSimulationObject, to enter the simulation at a specified time, timeInteger.

scheduleArrivalOf: aSimulationObjectClass
accordingTo: aProbabilityDistribution

> Schedule simulation objects that are instances of aSimulationObjectClass to enter the simulation at specified time intervals, based on the probability distribution aProbabilityDistribution. The first such instance should be scheduled to enter now. See Chapter 21 for definitions of possible probability distributions.

scheduleArrivalOf: aSimulationObjectClass
accordingTo: aProbabilityDistribution
startingAt: timeInteger

> Schedule simulation objects that are instances of aSimulationObjectClass to enter the simulation at specified time intervals, based on the probability distribution aProbabilityDistribution. The first such instance should be scheduled to enter at time timeInteger.

Notice that in the above scheduling messages, scheduleArrivalOf:at: takes a SimulationObject instance as its first argument, while scheduleArrivalOf:accordingTo: takes a SimulationObject class. These messages are used differently; the first one can be used by the SimulationObject itself to reschedule itself, while the second is used to initiate the arrival of SimulationObjects into the system.

The protocol for Simulation includes several accessing messages. One, the message includesResourceFor: resourceName, can be sent by a SimulationObject in order to determine whether or not a resource having a given name exists in the simulation.

Simulation instance protocol
___

accessing

includesResourceFor: resourceName

> Answer if the receiver has a resource that is referred to by the String, resourceName. If such a resource does not exist, then report an error.

provideResourceFor: resourceName

> Answer a resource that is referred to by the String, resourceName.

time

> Answer the receiver's current time.

The simulation control framework is like that of class SimulationObject. Initialization is handled by creating the Simulation and sending it the message startUp. Simulation objects and the scheduling of new objects create events that are placed in the event queue. Once initialized, the Simulation is made to run by sending it the message proceed until there are no longer any events in the queue.

In the course of running the simulation, objects will enter and exit. As part of the protocol for scheduling a simulation object, the object informs its simulation that it is entering or exiting. The corresponding messages are enter: anObject and exit: anObject. In response to these messages, statistics might be collected about simulation objects upon their entrance and their exit to the simulation. Or a subclass might choose to deny an object entrance to the simulation; or a subclass might choose to reschedule an object rather than let it leave the simulation.

Simulation instance protocol

simulation control

startUp	Specify the initial simulation objects and the arrival schedule of new objects.
proceed	This is a single event execution. The first event in the queue, if any, is removed, time is updated to the time of the event, and the event is initiated.
finishUp	Release references to any remaining simulation objects.
enter: anObject	The argument, anObject, is informing the receiver that it is entering.
exit: anObject	The argument, anObject, is informing the receiver that it is exiting.

Of the above messages, the default responses in class Simulation are mostly to do nothing. In particular, the response to messages enter: and exit: are to do nothing. Messages defineArrivalSchedule and defineResources also do nothing. As a result, the message startUp accomplishes nothing. These messages provide the framework that subclasses are to use—a subclass is created that overrides these messages in order to add simulation-specific behavior.

A "Default" Example: NothingAtAll

Unlike many of the system class examples of earlier chapters, the superclasses Simulation and SimulationObject typically do not implement their basic messages as

    self subclassResponsibility

By not doing so, instances of either of these classes can be successfully created. These instances can then be used as part of a basic or a "default" simulation that serves as a skeletal example. As we have seen, such simulation objects are scheduled to do nothing and consist of no events. Development of more substantive simulations can proceed by gradual refinement of these defaults. With a running, default example, the designer/programmer can incrementally modify and test the simulation, replacing the uninteresting instances of the superclasses with instances of appropriate subclasses. The example simulation NothingAtAll illustrates the idea of a "default" simulation.

Suppose we literally do nothing other than to declare the class NothingAtAll as a subclass of Simulation. A NothingAtAll has no initial resources since it does nothing in response to the message defineResources. And it has no simulation objects arriving at various intervals, because it does nothing in response to the message defineArrivalSchedule. Now we execute the following statement.

NothingAtAll new startUp proceed

The result is that an instance of NothingAtAll is created and sent the message startUp. It is a simulation with no resources and no objects scheduled, so the queue of events is empty. In response to the message proceed, the simulation determines that the queue is empty and does nothing.

As a modification of the description of NothingAtAll, we specify a response to the message defineArrivalSchedule. In it, the objects scheduled for arrival are instances of class DoNothing. DoNothing is created simply as a subclass of SimulationObject. A DoNothing has no tasks to carry out, so as soon as it enters the simulation, it leaves.

class name	DoNothing
superclass	SimulationObject
instance methods	

no new methods

class name	NothingAtAll
superclass	Simulation
instance methods	

initialization

defineArrivalSchedule
    self scheduleArrivalOf: DoNothing
        accordingTo: (Uniform from: 1 to: 5)

This version of NothingAtAll might represent a series of visitors entering an empty room, looking around without taking time to do so, and leaving. The probability distribution, Uniform, in the example in this chapter is assumed to be the one specified in Chapter 21. According to the above specification, new instances of class DoNothing should arrive in the simulation every 1 to 5 units of simulated time starting at time 0. The following expressions, when evaluated, create the simulation, send it the message startUp, and then iteratively send it the message proceed.

aSimulation ← NothingAtAll new startUp.
[aSimulation proceed] whileTrue

The message startUp invokes the message defineArrivalSchedule which schedules instances of DoNothing. Each time the message proceed is sent to the simulation, a DoNothing enters or exits. Evaluation might result in the following sequence of events. The time of each event is shown on the left and a description of the event is shown on the right.

0.0	a DoNothing enters
0.0	a DoNothing exits
3.21	a DoNothing enters
3.21	a DoNothing exits
7.76	a DoNothing enters
7.76	a DoNothing exits

and so on.

We can now make the simulation more interesting by scheduling the arrival of more kinds of simulation objects, ones that have tasks to do. We define Visitor to be a SimulationObject whose task is to enter the empty room and look around, taking between 4 and 10 simulated units to do so, that is, a random amount determined by evaluating the expression (Uniform from: 4 to: 10) next.

class name	Visitor
superclass	SimulationObject
instance methods	

simulation control

tasks
    self holdFor: (Uniform from: 4.0 to: 10.0) next

NothingAtAll is now defined as

class name	NothingAtAll
superclass	Simulation
instance methods	

initialization

defineArrivalSchedule
    self scheduleArrivalOf: DoNothing
        accordingTo: (Uniform from: 1 to: 5).
    self scheduleArrivalOf: Visitor
        accordingTo: (Uniform from: 4 to: 8)
        startingAt: 3

Two kinds of objects enter the simulation, one that takes no time to look around (a DoNothing) and one that visits a short while (a Visitor). Execution of

aSimulation ← NothingAtAll new startUp.
[aSimulation proceed] whileTrue

might result in the following sequence of events.

0.0	a DoNothing enters
0.0	a DoNothing exits
3.0	a Visitor enters
3.21	a DoNothing enters
3.21	a DoNothing exits
7.76	a DoNothing enters
7.76	a DoNothing exits
8.23	a (the first) Visitor exits after 5.23 seconds

and so on.

Implementation of the Simulation Classes

In order to trace the way in which the sequence of events occurs in the examples provided so far, it is necessary to show an implementation of the two classes. The implementations illustrate the control of multiple independent processes in the Smalltalk-80 system that were described in Chapter 15.

Class SimulationObject

Every SimulationObject created in the system needs access to the Simulation in which it is functioning. Such access is necessary, for example, in order to send messages that inform the simulation that an object is entering or exiting. In order to support such access, SimulationObject has a class variable, ActiveSimulation, that is initialized by each instance of Simulation when that instance is activated (that is, sent the message startUp). This approach assumes only one Simulation will be active at one time. It means that the tasks for any subclass of SimulationObject can send messages directly to its simulation, for example, to determine the current time. SimulationObject specifies no instance variables.

class name	SimulationObject
superclass	Object
class variable names	ActiveSimulation
class methods	

class initialization

activeSimulation: existingSimulation
    ActiveSimulation ← existingSimulation

instance creation

new
    ↑super new initialize

The simulation control framework, sometimes referred to as the "life cycle" of the object, involves the sequence startUp—tasks—finishUp. When the SimulationObject first arrives at the simulation, it is sent the message startUp.

instance methods

simulation control

initialize
"Do nothing. Subclasses will initialize instance variables."
↑self

startUp
ActiveSimulation enter: self.
"First tell the simulation that the receiver is beginning to do my tasks."
self tasks.
self finishUp

tasks
"Do nothing. Subclasses will schedule activities."
↑self

finishUp
"Tell the simulation that the receiver is done with its tasks."
ActiveSimulation exit: self

The category task language consists of messages the modeler can use in specifying the SimulationObject's sequence of actions. The object might hold for an increment of simulated time (holdFor:). The object might try to acquire access to another simulation object that is playing the role of a resource (acquire:ofResource:). Or the object might determine whether a resource is available (resourceAvailable:).

task language

holdFor: aTimeDelay
ActiveSimulation delayFor: aTimeDelay

acquire: amount ofResource: resourceName
"Get the resource and then tell it to acquire amount of it. Answers an instance of StaticResource"
↑(ActiveSimulation provideResourceFor: resourceName)
    acquire: amount
    withPriority: 0

acquire: amount
ofResource: resourceName
withPriority: priority
↑(ActiveSimulation provideResourceFor: resourceName)
    acquire: amount
    withPriority: priority

produce: amount ofResource: resourceName
ActiveSimulation produce: amount of: resourceName

release: aStaticResource

↑aStaticResource release

inquireFor: amount ofResource: resourceName

↑(ActiveSimulation provideResourceFor: resourceName)

amountAvailable > = amount

resourceAvailable: resourceName

"Does the active simulation have a resource with this attribute available?"

↑ActiveSimulation includesResourceFor: resourceName

acquireResource: resourceName

↑(ActiveSimulation provideResourceFor: resourceName)

acquire

produceResource: resourceName

↑(ActiveSimulation provideResourceFor: resourceName)

producedBy: self

resume: anEvent

↑anEvent resume

numberOfProvidersOfResource: resourceName

| resource |

resource ← ActiveSimulation provideResourceFor: resourceName.

resource serversWaiting

ifTrue: [↑resource queueLength]

ifFalse: [↑0]

numberOfRequestersOfResource: resourceName

| resource |

resource ← ActiveSimulation provideResourceFor: resourceName.

resource customersWaiting

ifTrue: [↑resource queueLength]

ifFalse: [↑0]

stopSimulation

ActiveSimulation finishUp

A Simulation stores a Set of resources. In the case of static resources, instances of class ResourceProvider are stored; in the case of resources that consist of tasks coordinated among two or more simulation objects, instances of ResourceCoordinator are stored.

When a SimulationObject requests a static resource (acquire:ofResource:) and that request succeeds, then the SimulationObject is given an instance of class StaticResource. A StaticResource refers to the resource that created it and the quantity of the resource it represents. Given the methods shown for class SimulationObject, we can see that a resource responds to the message amountAvailable to return the currently available quantity of the resource that the SimulationObject might acquire. This message is sent in the method associated with inquireFor:ofResource:.

In the methods associated with SimulationObject messages acquire:ofResource: and acquire:ofResource:withPriority:, a ResourceProvider is obtained and sent the message acquire: amount withPriority: priorityNumber. The result of this message is an instance of class StaticResource. However, if the amount is not available, the process in which the request was made will be suspended until the necessary resources become available. A StaticResource is sent the message release in order to recycle the acquired resource.

When a SimulationObject requests a coordinated resource (acquireResource:), and that request succeeds, then the object co-opts another simulation object acting as the resource (the object in need of service) until some tasks (services) are completed. If such a resource is not available, the process in which the request was made will be suspended until the necessary resources become available. Instances of class ResourceCoordinator understand messages acquire in order to make the request to coordinate service tasks and producedBy: aSimulationObject in order to specify that the argument is to be co-opted by another object in order to synchronize activities. As indicated by the implementation of SimulationObject, a ResourceCoordinator can answer queries such as customersWaiting or serversWaiting to determine if resources (customers) or service givers (servers) are waiting to coordinate their activities, and queueLength to say how many are waiting.

Explanations of the implementations of classes ResourceProvider and ResourceCoordinator are provided in Chapters 24 and 25.

Class
DelayedEvent

The implementation of a scheduling mechanism for class Simulation makes extensive use of the Smalltalk-80 processor scheduler classes presented in the chapter on multiple processes (Chapter 15). There are several problems that have to be solved in the design of class Simulation. First, how do we store an event that must be delayed for some increment of simulated time? Second, how do we make certain that all processes initiated at a particular time are completed before changing the clock? And third, in terms of the solutions to the first two problems, how do we implement the request to repeatedly schedule a sequence of actions, in particular, instantiation and initiation of a particular kind of SimulationObject?

In order to solve the first problem, the Simulation maintains a queue of all the scheduled events. This queue is a SortedCollection whose elements are the events, sorted with respect to the simulated time in which they must be invoked. Each event on the queue is placed there within a package that is an instance of class DelayedEvent. At the time the package is created, the event is the system's active process. As such, it can be stored with its needed running context by creating a Semaphore. When the event is put on the queue, the DelayedEvent is sent the message pause which sends its Semaphore the message wait; when the event is taken off the queue, it is continued by sending it the message resume. The method associated with resume sends the DelayedEvent's Semaphore the message signal.

The protocol for instances of class DelayedEvent consists of five messages.

DelayedEvent instance protocol

---

accessing

 condition   Answer a condition under which the event should be sequenced.

 condition: anObject   Set the argument, anObject, to be the condition under which the event should be sequenced.

scheduling

 pause   Suspend the current active process, that is, the current event that is running.

 resume   Resume the suspended process.

comparing

 < = aDelayedEvent   Answer whether the receiver should be sequenced before the argument, aDelayedEvent.

A DelayedEvent is created by sending the class the message new or onCondition: anObject. The implementation of class DelayedEvent is given next.

class name	DelayedEvent
superclass	Object
instance variable names	resumptionSemaphore resumptionCondition
class methods	

instance creation

 new
  ↑super new initialize
 onCondition: anObject
  ↑super new setCondition: anObject

instance methods

accessing

 condition
  ↑resumptionCondition
 condition: anObject
  resumptionCondition ← anObject

comparing

 < = aDelayedEvent
  resumptionCondition isNil
   ifTrue: [↑true]
   ifFalse: [↑resumptionCondition < = aDelayedEvent condition]

scheduling

pause
>   resumptionSemaphore wait
resume
>   resumptionSemaphore signal.
>   ↑resumptionCondition

private

initialize
>   resumptionSemaphore ← Semaphore new
setCondition: anObject
>   self initialize.
>   resumptionCondition ← anObject

According to the above specification, any object used as a resumption condition must respond to the message $<=$; SimulationObject is, in general, such a condition.

Class Simulation

Instances of class Simulation own four instance variables: a Set of objects that act as resources of the simulation (resources), a Number representing the current time (currentTime), a SortedCollection representing a queue of delayed events (eventQueue), and an Integer denoting the number of processes active at the current time (processCount).

Initialization of a Simulation sets the instance variables to initial values. When the instance is sent the scheduling message startUp, it sends itself the message activate which informs interested other classes which Simulation is now the active one.

class name	Simulation
superclass	Object
instance variable names	resources currentTime
	eventQueue processCount

class methods

instance creation

new
>   ↑super new initialize

instance methods

initialization

initialize
>   resources ← Set new.
>   currentTime ← 0.0.
>   processCount ← 0.
>   eventQueue ← SortedCollection new

activate

"This instance is now the active simulation. Inform class SimulationObject."
SimulationObject activeSimulation: self.
"Resource is the superclass for ResourceProvider and ResourceCoordinator"
Resource activeSimulation: self

Initialization messages are also needed by the subclasses. The messages provided for the modeler to use in specifying arrival schedules and resource objects provides an interface to the process scheduling messages.

initialization

defineArrivalSchedule

"A subclass specifies the schedule by which simulation objects dynamically enter into the simulation."
↑self

defineResources

"A subclass specifies the simulation objects that are initially entered into the simulation."
↑self

task language

produce: amount of: resourceName

(self includesResourceFor: resourceName)
ifTrue: [(self provideResourceFor: resourceName) produce: amount]
ifFalse: [resources add:
(ResourceProvider named: resourceName with: amount)]

coordinate: resourceName

(self includesResourceFor: resourceName)
ifFalse: [resources add:
(ResourceCoordinator named: resourceName)]

schedule: actionBlock after: timeDelay

self schedule: actionBlock at: currentTime + timeDelay

schedule: aBlock at: timeInteger

"This is the mechanism for scheduling a single action"
self newProcessFor:
[self delayUntil: timeInteger.
aBlock value]

scheduleArrivalOf: aSimulationObject at: timeInteger

self schedule: [aSimulationObject startUp] at: timeInteger

scheduleArrivalOf: aSimulationObjectClass
accordingTo: aProbabilityDistribution

"This means start now"
self scheduleArrivalOf: aSimulationObjectClass
accordingTo: aProbabilityDistribution
startingAt: currentTime

scheduleArrivalOf: aSimulationObjectClass
accordingTo: aProbabilityDistribution
startingAt: timeInteger

"Note that aClass is the class SimulationObject or one of its subclasses. The real work is done in the private message schedule:startingAt:andThenEvery:"
self schedule: [aSimulationObjectClass new startUp]
    startingAt: timeInteger
    andThenEvery: aProbabilityDistribution

The scheduling messages of the task language implement a reference-counting solution to keeping track of initiated processes. This is the technique used to solve the second problem cited earlier, that is, how to make certain that all processes initiated for a particular time are carried out by the single Smalltalk-80 processor scheduler before a different process gets the opportunity to change the clock. Using reference counting, we guarantee that simulated time does not change unless the reference count is zero.

The key methods are the ones associated with schedule: aBlock at: timeInteger and schedule: aBlock startingAt: timeInteger andThenEvery: aProbabilityDistribution. This second message is a private one called by the method associated with scheduleArrivalOf: aSimulationObjectClass accordingTo: aProbabilityDistribution startingAt: timeInteger. It provides a general mechanism for scheduling repeated actions and therefore represents a solution to the third design problem mentioned earlier, how we implement the request to repeatedly schedule a sequence of actions.

The basic idea for the schedule: aBlock at: timeInteger is to create a process in which to delay the evaluation of the sequence of actions (aBlock) until the simulation reaches the appropriate simulated time (timeInteger). The delay is performed by the message delayUntil: delayedTime. The associated method creates a DelayedEvent to be added to the simulation's event queue. The process associated with this DelayedEvent is then suspended (by sending it the message pause). When this instance of DelayedEvent is the first in the queue, it will be removed and the time will be bumped to the stored (delayed) time. Then this instance of DelayedEvent will be sent the message resume which will cause the evaluation of the block; the action of this block is to schedule some simulation activity.

A process that was active is suspended when the DelayedEvent is signaled to wait. Therefore, the count of the number of processes must be decremented (stopProcess). When the DelayedEvent resumes, the process continues evaluation with the last expression in the method delayedUntil:; therefore at this time, the count of the number of processes must be incremented (startProcess).

scheduling

delayUntil: aTime
```
    | delayEvent |
    delayEvent ← DelayedEvent onCondition: timeInteger.
    eventQueue add: delayEvent.
    self stopProcess.
    delayEvent pause.
    self startProcess
```
delayFor: timeDelay
```
    self delayUntil: currentTime + timeDelay
```
startProcess
```
    processCount ← processCount + 1
```
stopProcess
```
    processCount ← processCount − 1
```

Reference counting of processes is also handled in the method associated with class Simulation's scheduling message newProcessFor: aBlock. It is implemented as follows.

newProcessFor: aBlock
```
    self startProcess.
    [aBlock value.
     self stopProcess] fork
```

The first expression increments the count of processes. The second expression is a block that is forked. When the Smalltalk processor scheduler evaluates this block, the simulation sequence of actions, aBlock, is evaluated. The completion of evaluating aBlock signals the need to decrement the count of processes. In this way, a single sequence of actions is scheduled in the event queue of the Simulation and delayed until the correct simulated time. In summary, the reference count of processes increments whenever a new sequence of actions is initiated, decrements whenever a sequence completes, decrements whenever a DelayedEvent is created, and increments whenever the DelayedEvent is continued.

The method for the private message schedule: aBlock startingAt: timeInteger andThenEvery: aProbabilityDistribution forks a process that repeatedly schedules actions. The algorithm consists of iterations of two messages,

```
    self delayUntil: timeInteger.
    self newProcessFor: aBlock
```

Repetition of the two messages delayUntil: and newProcessFor: depends on a probability distribution function. The number of repetitions equals the number of times the distribution can be sampled. The number that is sampled represents the next time that the sequence of actions (aBlock)

should be invoked. Elements of the distribution are enumerated by sending the distribution the message do:.

private

schedule: aBlock
    startingAt: timeInteger
    andThenEvery: aProbabilityDistribution
    self newProcessFor:
        ["This is the first time to do the action."
        self delayUntil: timeInteger.
        "Do the action."
        self newProcessFor: aBlock copy.
        aProbabilityDistribution
          do: [:nextTimeDelay |
                "For each sample from the distribution,
                delay the amount sampled,"
                self delayFor: nextTimeDelay.
                "then do the action"
                self newProcessFor: aBlock copy]]

Simulation itself has a control framework similar to that of SimulationObject. The response to startUp is to make the simulation the currently active one and then to define the simulation objects and arrival schedule. The inner loop of scheduled activity is given as the response to the message proceed. Whenever the Simulation receives the message proceed, it checks the reference count of processes (by sending the message readyToContinue). If the reference count is not zero, then there are still processes active for the current simulated time. So, the system-wide processor, Processor, is asked to yield control and let these processes proceed. If the reference count is zero, then the event queue is checked. If it is not empty, the next event is removed from the event queue, time is changed, and the delayed process is resumed.

simulation control

startUp
    self activate.
    self defineResources.
    self defineArrivalSchedule
proceed
    | eventProcess |
    [self readyToContinue] whileFalse: [Processor yield].
    eventQueue isEmpty
        ifTrue: [↑self finishUp]
        ifFalse: [eventProcess ← eventQueue removeFirst.
               currentTime ← eventProcess time.
               eventProcess resume]

finishUp
"We need to empty out the event queue"
eventQueue ← SortedCollection new.
↑false
enter: anObject
↑self
exit: anObject
↑self

private

readyToContinue
↑processCount = 0

In addition to these various modeler's languages and simulation control messages, several accessing messages are provided in the protocol of Simulation.

accessing

includesResourceFor: resourceName
| test |
test ← resources
detect: [:each | each name = resourceName]
ifNone: [nil].
↑test notNil
provideResourceFor: resourceName
↑resources detect: [:each | each name = resourceName]
time
↑currentTime

The implementations of Simulation and SimulationObject illustrate the use of messages fork to a BlockContext, yield to a ProcessorScheduler, and signal and wait to a Semaphore.

Tracing the Example NothingAtAll

We can now trace the execution of the first example of the simulation, NothingAtAll, in which DoNothings only were scheduled. After sending the message

NothingAtAll new

the instance variables of the new simulation consist of

resources = Set ()
currentTime = 0.0
processCount = 0
eventQueue = SortedCollection ()

We then send this simulation the message startUp, which invokes the message scheduleArrivalOf: DoNothing accordingTo: (Uniform from: 1 to: 5). This is identical to sending the simulation the message

```
schedule: [DoNothing new startUp]
startingAt: 0.0
andThenEvery: (Uniform from: 1 to: 5)
```

The response is to call on newProcessFor:.

Step 1. newProcessFor: increments the processCount (self startProcess) and then creates a new Process that evaluates the following block, which will be referred to as block A.

```
[self delayUntil: timeInteger.
 self newProcessFor: block copy.
 aProbabilityDistribution do:
        [ :nextTimeDelay |
          self delayFor: nextTimeDelay.
          self newProcessFor: block copy]
```

where the variable block is

```
[DoNothing new startUp]
```

which will be referred to as block B.

Step 2. When the process returns to the second expression of the method newProcessFor:, execution continues by evaluating block A. Its first expression decrements the process count and suspends an activity until time is 0.0 (i.e., create a DelayedEvent for the active simulation scheduler to tell the DoNothing to startUp at time 0.0; put it on the event queue).

```
resources = Set ()
currentTime = 0.0
processCount = 0
eventQueue = SortedCollection (a DelayedEvent 0.0)
```

Now we send the simulation the message proceed. The process count is 0 so readyToContinue returns true; the event queue is not empty so the first DelayedEvent is removed, time is set to 0.0, and the delayed process is resumed (this was the scheduler block A). The next action increments the process count and evaluates block B. This lets a DoNothing enter and do its task, which is nothing, so it leaves immediately. The new processFor: message decrements the process count to 0, gets a number from the probability distribution, delays for this number of time units, and schedules a new process for some time later. The sequence continues indefinitely, as long as the message proceed is re-sent to the simulation.

Other tasks will enter the event queue depending on the method associated with the message tasks in a subclass of SimulationObject. Thus if Visitor is scheduled in NothingAtAll, then the expresson self holdFor: someTime will enter an event on the queue, intermingled with events that schedule new arrivals of Visitors and DoNothings.

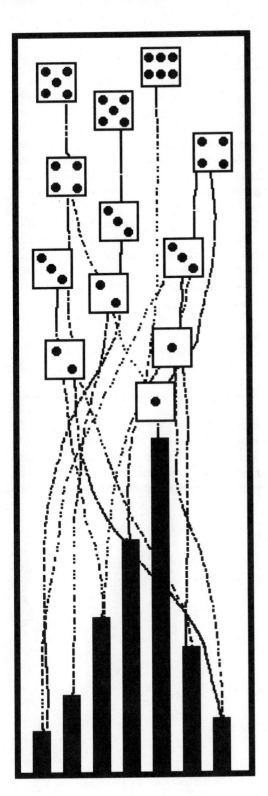

23

Statistics Gathering in Event-Driven Simulations

Duration Statistics

Throughput Histograms

Tallying Events

Event Monitoring

A framework for specifying event-driven simulations was presented in the previous chapter. This framework did not include methods for gathering statistics about a simulation as it is running. Statistics might consist of the amount of time each simulation object spends in the simulation (and, therefore, how well the model supports carrying out the kinds of tasks specified by the objects); information about the length of the queues such as the maximum, minimum and average lengths and amount of time spent in each queue; and information about the utilization of the simulation's resources.

There are a number of ways to add statistics gathering to class Simulation or class SimulationObject. In this chapter, we provide four examples of statistics gathering: duration statistics, throughput histograms, event tallying, and event monitoring. Each of these examples involves creating a subclass of Simulation or SimulationObject in order to provide a dictionary in which data can be stored or a file into which data can be written, and, in that subclass, modifying the appropriate methods in order to store the appropriate data.

Duration Statistics

For the first example of statistics gathering, we create a general subclass of Simulation that simply stores the time an object enters and exits the simulation. The times are kept in a special record whose fields are the time at which the object entered the simulation (entranceTime) and the length of time the object spent in the simulation (duration). Records are described as follows.

class name	SimulationObjectRecord
superclass	Object
instance variable names	entranceTime
	duration

instance methods

accessing

entrance: currentTime
    entranceTime ← currentTime
exit: currentTime
    duration ← entranceTime − currentTime
entrance
    ↑entranceTime
exit
    ↑entranceTime + duration
duration
    ↑duration

printing

printOn: aStream
entranceTime printOn: aStream.
aStream tab.
duration printOn: aStream

An example subclass of Simulation which uses SimulationObjectRecords for gathering statistics is StatisticsWithSimulation. It is defined as follows.

class name	StatisticsWithSimulation
superclass	Simulation
instance variable names	statistics
instance methods	

initialization

initialize
super initialize.
statistics ← Dictionary new

simulation scheduling

enter: anObject
statistics at: anObject
        put: (SimulationObjectRecord new entrance: currentTime)
exit: anObject
(statistics at: anObject) exit: currentTime

statistics

printStatisticsOn: aStream
| stat |
aStream cr.
aStream nextPutAll: 'Object'.
aStream tab.
aStream nextPutAll: 'Entrance Time'.
aStream tab.
aStream nextPutAll: 'Duration'.
aStream cr.
"Sort with respect to the time the object entered the simulation. Because the keys as well as the values are needed, it is necessary to first obtain the set of associations and then sort them."
stat ← SortedCollection
        sortBlock: [:i :j | i value entrance <= j value entrance].
statistics associationsDo: [:each | stat add: each].

```
stat do:
    [ :anAssociation |
    aStream cr.
    anAssociation key printOn: aStream.
    aStream tab.
    anAssociation value printOn: aStream
    "The value is a SimulationObjectRecord which prints the entrance
    time and duration"]
```

Suppose we created NothingAtAll as a subclass of StatisticsWithSimulation. In this example, NothingAtAll schedules two simulation objects: one that does nothing (a DoNothing), arriving according to a uniform distribution from 3 to 5 units of time starting at 0; and one that looks around for 5 units of simulated time (a Visitor), arriving according to a uniform distribution from 5 to 10 units of time starting at 1. Whenever one of these objects enters the simulation, an entry is put in the statistics dictionary. The key is the object itself; the equals (=) test is the default (==), so each object is a unique key. The value is an instance of SimulationObjectRecord with entrance data initialized. When the object exits, the record associated with it is retrieved and a message is sent to it in order to set the exit data.

class name	DoNothing
superclass	SimulationObject
instance methods	

no new methods

class name	Visitor
superclass	SimulationObject
instance methods	

simulation control

tasks
```
    self holdFor: 5
```

class name	NothingAtAll
superclass	StatisticsWithSimulation
instance methods	

initialization

defineArrivalSchedule
```
    self scheduleArrivalOf: DoNothing
        accordingTo: (Uniform from: 3 to: 5).
    self scheduleArrivalOf: Visitor
        accordingTo: (Uniform from: 5 to: 10)
        startingAt: 1
```

Whenever we halt the simulation, we can send the message printStatisticsOn: aFile (where aFile is a kind of FileStream). The result might look like:

Object	Entrance Time	Duration
a DoNothing	0.0	0.0
a Visitor	1.0	5.0
a DoNothing	4.58728	0.0
a Visitor	6.71938	5.0
a DoNothing	9.3493	0.0
a DoNothing	13.9047	0.0
a Visitor	16.7068	5.0
a DoNothing	17.1963	0.0
a DoNothing	21.7292	0.0
a Visitor	23.2563	5.0
a DoNothing	25.6805	0.0
a DoNothing	29.3202	0.0
a Visitor	32.1147	5.0
a DoNothing	32.686	0.0
a DoNothing	36.698	0.0
a DoNothing	41.1135	0.0
a Visitor	41.1614	5.0
a DoNothing	44.3258	0.0
a Visitor	48.4145	5.0
a DoNothing	48.492	0.0
a DoNothing	51.7833	0.0
a Visitor	53.5166	5.0
a DoNothing	56.4262	0.0
a DoNothing	60.5357	0.0
a Visitor	63.4532	5.0
a DoNothing	64.8572	0.0
a DoNothing	68.7634	0.0
a Visitor	68.921	5.0
a DoNothing	72.4788	0.0
a DoNothing	75.8567	0.0

Throughput Histograms

A common statistic gathered in simulations is the throughput of objects, that is, how many objects pass through the simulation in some amount of time; this is proportional to how much time each object spends in the simulation. Gathering such statistics involves keeping track of the number of objects that spend time within predetermined intervals of time. Reporting the results involves displaying the number of objects, the minimum time, maximum time, and the number of objects whose times fall within each specified interval. Such statistics are especially useful in simulations involving resources in order to determine whether or not there are sufficient resources to handle requests— if objects have to wait a long time to get a resource, then they must spend more time in the simulation.

In order to support the gathering of throughput statistics, we provide class Histogram. Histograms maintain a tally of values within prespecified ranges. For example, we might tally the number of times various values fall between 1 and 5, 5 and 10, 10 and 20, 20 and 25, 25 and 30, 30 and 35, 35 and 40, and 40 and 45. That is, we divide the interval 5 to 45 into bins of size 5 and keep a running count of the number of times a value is stored into each bin.

Class Histogram is created by specifying the lower bound, the upper bound, and the bin size. To obtain a Histogram for the above example, evaluate

Histogram from: 5 to: 45 by: 5

Besides data on the bins, a Histogram keeps track of minimum, maximum, and total values entered. An entry might not fit within the bounds of the interval; an additional variable is used to store all such entries (extraEntries). The bins are stored as elements of an array; the array size equals the number of bins (that is, upper bound - lower bound // bin size). The message store: aValue is used to put values in the Histogram. The index of the array element to be incremented is 1 + (aValue - lower bound // bins size). Most of the methods shown support printing the collected information.

class name	Histogram
superclass	Object
instance variable names	tallyArray
	lowerBound upperBound
	step
	minValue maxValue
	totalValues
	extraEntries
class methods	

class initialization

from: lowerNum to: upperNum by: step

↑self new newLower: lowerNum upper: upperNum by: step

instance methods

accessing

contains: aValue

↑lowerBound < = aValue and: [aValue < upperBound]

store: aValue

| index |
minValue isNil
    ifTrue: [minValue ← maxValue ← aValue]
    ifFalse: [minValue ← minValue min: aValue.
            maxValue ← maxValue max: aValue].
totalValues ← totalValues + aValue.
(self contains: aValue)
    ifTrue: [index ← (aValue - lowerBound // step) + 1.
            tallyArray at: index put: (tallyArray at: index) + 1]
    ifFalse: [extraEntries ← extraEntries + 1]

printing

printStatisticsOn: aStream

| totalObjs pos |
self firstHeader: aStream.
aStream cr; tab.
totalObjs ← extraEntries.
"count the number of entries the throughput records know"
tallyArray do: [:each | totalObjs ← totalObjs + each].
totalObjs printOn: aStream.
aStream tab.
minValue printOn: aStream.
aStream tab.
maxValue printOn: aStream.
aStream tab.
(totalValues / totalObjs) asFloat printOn: aStream.
aStream cr.
self secondHeader: aStream.
aStream cr.
pos ← lowerBound.
tallyArray do:
    [:entry |
    pos printOn: aStream.
    aStream nextPut: $—.
    (pos ← pos + step) printOn: aStream.
    aStream tab.
    entry printOn: aStream.
    aStream tab.
    (entry / totalObjs) asFloat printOn: aStream.

```
        aStream tab.
        aStream nextPut: $| .
        "print the X's"
        entry rounded timesRepeat: [aStream nextPut: $X].
        aStream cr]
```

firstHeader: aStream
```
    aStream cr; tab.
    aStream nextPutAll: 'Number of'.
    aStream tab.
    aStream nextPutAll: 'Minimum'.
    aStream tab.
    aStream nextPutAll: 'Maximum'.
    aStream tab.
    aStream nextPutAll: 'Average'.
    aStream cr; tab.
    aStream nextPutAll: 'Objects'.
    aStream tab.
    aStream nextPutAll: 'Value'.
    aStream tab.
    aStream nextPutAll: 'Value'.
    aStream tab.
    aStream nextPutAll: 'Value'
```

secondHeader: aStream
```
    aStream cr; tab.
    aStream nextPutAll: 'Number of'.
    aStream cr.
    aStream nextPutAll: 'Entry'.
    aStream tab.
    aStream nextPutAll: 'Objects'.
    aStream tab.
    aStream nextPutAll: 'Frequency'.
```

private

newLower: lowerNum upper: upperNum by: stepAmount
```
    tallyArray ← Array new: (upperNum − lowerNum // stepAmount).
    tallyArray atAllPut: 0.
    lowerBound ← lowerNum.
    upperBound ← upperNum.
    step ← stepAmount.
    minValue ← maxValue ← nil.
    totalValues ← 0.
    extraEntries ← 0
```

A simulation of visitors to a museum serves as an example of the use of a Histogram. Museum is like NothingAtAll in that Visitors arrive and look around. The Visitors take a varying amount of time to look around, depending on their interest in the museum artifacts. We assume that this time is normally distributed with a mean of 20 and a standard deviation of 5. Visitors come to the museum throughout the day, one every 5 to 10 units of simulated time.

class name	Museum
superclass	Simulation
instance variable names	statistics
instance methods	

initialization

initialize
```
    super initialize.
    statistics ← Histogram from: 5 to: 45 by: 5
```
defineArrivalSchedule
```
    self scheduleArrivalOf: Visitor
        accordingTo: (Uniform from: 5 to: 10)
```

scheduling

exit: aSimulationObject
```
    super exit: aSimulationObject.
    statistics store: currentTime - aSimulationObject entryTime
```
printStatisticsOn: aStream
```
    statistics printStatisticsOn: aStream
```

In order for class Museum to update the statistics, Visitors must keep track of when they entered the museum and be able to respond to an inquiry as to their time of entry.

class name	Visitor
superclass	SimulationObject
instance variable names	entryTime
instance methods	

initialization

initialize
```
    super initialize.
    entryTime ← ActiveSimulation time
```

accessing

entryTime
```
    ↑entryTime
```

simulation control

tasks
```
    self holdFor: (Normal mean: 20 deviation: 5) next
```

To create and run the simulation, we evaluate

```
aSimulation ← Museum new startUp.
[aSimulation time < 50] whileTrue: [aSimulation proceed]
```

When the Museum was created, a Histogram for statistics was created. Each time a Visitor left the Museum, data was stored in the Histogram. The data consists of the duration of the visit.

After running the simulation until time 50, we ask the Museum for a report.

```
aSimulation printStatisticsOn: (Disk file: 'museum.report')
```

The method associated with printStatisticsOn: sends the same message, printStatisticsOn:, to the Histogram, which prints the following information on the file museum.report.

Number of Objects	Minimum Value	Maximum Value	Average Value
64	10.0202	31.2791	20.152

Entry	Number of Objects	Frequency	
5-10	0	0	|
10-15	14	0.21875	| XXXXXXXXXXXXXX
15-20	16	0.25	| XXXXXXXXXXXXXXXX
20-25	20	0.3125	| XXXXXXXXXXXXXXXXXXXX
25-30	13	0.203125	| XXXXXXXXXXXXX
30-35	1	0.015625	| X
35-40	0	0	|
40-45	0	0	|

Tallying Events

As another example of tallying the events in a simulation, we present a commonly-used example of a simulation of Traffic. In this simulation, we tally the number of cars that enter an intersection, distinguishing those that drive straight through the intersection from those that turn left and those that turn right. By observation, we note that twice as many cars go straight as turn right or left, but twice as many turn left as right. A new car arrives at the intersection according to a uniform distribution every 0.5 to 2 units of time (self scheduleArrivalOf: Car accordingTo: (Uniform from: 0.5 to: 2)). We will run the simulation until simulated time exceeds 100.

class name	Traffic
superclass	Simulation
instance variable names	statistics
instance methods	

initialization

initialize
super initialize.
statistics ← Dictionary new: 3.
statistics at: #straight put: 0.
statistics at: #right put: 0.
statistics at: #left put: 0

defineArrivalSchedule
self scheduleArrivalOf: Car accordingTo: (Uniform from: 0.5 to: 2).
self schedule: [self finishUp] at: 100

statistics

update: key
statistics at: key put: (statistics at: key) + 1

printStatisticsOn: aStream
aStream cr.
aStream nextPutAll: ' Car Direction   Tally '
statistics associationsDo:
  [:assoc |
   aStream cr.
   assoc key printOn: aStream.
   aStream tab.
   assoc value printOn: aStream]

Note that in the method associated with defineArrivalSchedule, the action self finishUp is scheduled to occur at simulated time 100. This event will terminate the simulation as desired.

class name	Car
superclass	SimulationObject
instance methods	

simulation control

tasks
"Sample, without replacement, the direction through the intersection that the car will travel."
| sample |
sample ← SampleSpace data:
        #(left left right straight straight straight
         straight straight straight)
ActiveSimulation update: sample next

SampleSpace was a class we introduced in Chapter 21. Cars are scheduled to enter the simulation with the sole task of picking a direction to tell the simulation. After running the simulation, we ask the Traffic simulation to report the tallies by sending it the printStatisticsOn: message. A possible outcome of evaluating

aSimulation ← Traffic new startUp.
[aSimulation proceed] whileTrue.
aSimulation printStatisticsOn: (Disk file: 'traffic.data')

is the following information written on the file traffic.data.

Car Direction	Tally
straight	57
right	8
left	15

Event Monitoring

Another possible technique for gathering data from a simulation is to note the occurrence of each (major) event, including the entering and exiting of simulation objects. This is accomplished by creating a subclass of SimulationObject that we call EventMonitor. In this example, a class variable refers to a file onto which notations about their events can be stored. Each message that represents an event to be monitored must be overridden in the subclass to include the instructions for storing information on the file. The method in the superclass is still executed by distributing the message to the pseudo-variable super.

Basically, the notations consist of the time and identification of the receiver (a kind of SimulationObject), and an annotation such as "enters" or "requests" or "releases."

class name	EventMonitor
superclass	SimulationObject
class variable names	DataFile
class methods	

class initialization

file: aFile
    DataFile ← aFile

instance methods

scheduling

startUp
> self timeStamp.
> DataFile nextPutAll: ' enters '.
> super startUp

finishUp
> super finishUp.
> self timeStamp.
> DataFile nextPutAll: ' exits '

task language

holdFor: aTimeDelay
> self timeStamp.
> DataFile nextPutAll: ' holds for '.
> aTimeDelay printOn: DataFile.
> super holdFor: aTimeDelay

acquire: amount ofResource: resourceName
> | aStaticResource |
> "Store fact that resource is being requested."
> self timeStamp.
> DataFile nextPutAll: ' requests '.
> amount printOn: DataFile.
> DataFile nextPutAll: ' of ', resourceName.
> "Now try to get the resource."
> aStaticResource ← super acquire: amount
> > ofResource: resourceName.
> "Returns here when resource is obtained; store the fact."
> self timeStamp.
> DataFile nextPutAll: ' obtained '.
> amount printOn: DataFile.
> DataFile nextPutAll: ' of ', resourceName.
> ↑aStaticResource

acquire: amount
> **ofResource: resourceName**
> **withPriority: priorityNumber**
> | aStaticResource |
> "Store fact that resource is being requested"
> self timeStamp.
> DataFile nextPutAll: ' requests '.
> amount printOn: DataFile.
> DataFile nextPutAll: ' at priority '.
> priorityNumber printOn: DataFile.
> DataFile nextPutAll: ' of ', resourceName.

"Now try to get the resource."
aStaticResource ←
    super acquire: amount
            ofResource: resourceName
            withPriority: priorityNumber.
"Returns here when resource is obtained; store the fact."
self timeStamp.
DataFile nextPutAll: ' obtained '.
amount printOn: DataFile.
DataFile nextPutAll: ' of ', resourceName.
↑aStaticResource

produce: amount ofResource: resourceName
self timeStamp.
DataFile nextPutAll: ' produces '.
amount printOn: DataFile.
DataFile nextPutAll: ' of ', resourceName.
super produce: amount ofResource: resourceName

release: aStaticResource
self timeStamp.
DataFile nextPutAll: ' releases '.
aStaticResource amount printOn: DataFile.
DataFile nextPutAll: ' of ', aStaticResource name.
super release: aStaticResource

acquireResource: resourceName
| anEvent |
"Store fact that resource is being requested"
self timeStamp.
DataFile nextPutAll: ' wants to serve for '.
DataFile nextPutAll: resourceName.
"Now try to get the resource."
anEvent ← super acquireResource: resourceName.
"Returns here when resource is obtained; store the fact."
self timeStamp.
DataFile nextPutAll: ' can serve '.
anEvent condition printOn: DataFile.
↑anEvent

produceResource: resourceName
self timeStamp.
DataFile nextPutAll: ' wants to get service as '.
DataFile nextPutAll: resourceName.
super produce: amount ofResource: resourceName

resume: anEvent
self timeStamp.
DataFile nextPutAll: ' resumes '.

```
    anEvent condition printOn: DataFile.
    super resume: anEvent
```

private

timeStamp
```
    DataFile cr.
    ActiveSimulation time printOn: DataFile.
    DataFile tab.
    self printOn: DataFile.
```

We can monitor the events of the NothingAtAll simulation consisting of arrivals of Visitors and default simulations (DoNothings). Except for creating Visitor and DoNothing as subclassses of EventMonitor rather than of SimulationObject, the class definitions are the same.

class name	DoNothing
superclass	EventMonitor
instance methods	

no new methods

class name	Visitor
superclass	EventMonitor
instance methods	

simulation control

tasks
```
    self holdFor: (Uniform from: 4.0 to: 10.0) next
```

NothingAtAll is redefined so that the default simulation is an EventMonitor.

class name	NothingAtAll
superclass	Simulation
instance methods	

initialization

defineArrivalSchedule
```
    self scheduleArrivalOf: DoNothing
        accordingTo: (Uniform from: 1 to: 5).
    self scheduleArrivalOf: Visitor
        accordingTo: (Uniform from: 4 to: 8)
        startingAt: 3
```

After executing

Visitor file: (Disk file: 'NothingAtAll.events').
                      "This informs DoNothing too"
aSimulation ← NothingAtAll new startUp.
[aSimulation time < 25] whileTrue: [aSimulation proceed]

the file 'NothingAtAll.events' contains the following information

0.0	a DoNothing enters
0.0	a DoNothing exits
3.0	a Visitor enters
3.0	a Visitor holds for 7.5885
4.32703	a DoNothing enters
4.32703	a DoNothing exits
7.74896	a Visitor enters
7.74896	a Visitor holds for 4.14163
8.20233	a DoNothing enters
8.20233	a DoNothing exits
10.5885	a Visitor exits
11.8906	a Visitor exits
12.5153	a DoNothing enters
12.5153	a DoNothing exits
14.2642	a Visitor enters
14.2642	a Visitor holds for 4.51334
16.6951	a DoNothing enters
16.6951	a DoNothing exits
18.7776	a Visitor exits
19.8544	a Visitor enters
19.8544	a Visitor holds for 5.10907
20.5342	a DoNothing enters
20.5342	a DoNothing exits
23.464	a DoNothing enters
23.464	a DoNothing exits
24.9635	a Visitor exits

Distinctively labeling each arriving SimulationObject might improve the ability to follow the sequence of events. The goal is to have a trace for an execution of the NothingAtAll simulation look like the following.

0.0	DoNothing 1 enters
0.0	DoNothing 1 exits
3.0	Visitor 1 enters
3.0	Visitor 1 holds for 7.5885
4.32703	DoNothing 2 enters
4.32703	DoNothing 2 exits
7.74896	Visitor 2 enters

7.74896	Visitor 2 holds for 4.14163
8.20233	DoNothing 3 enters
8.20233	DoNothing 3 exits
10.5885	Visitor 1 exits
11.8906	Visitor 2 exits
12.5153	DoNothing 4 enters
12.5153	DoNothing 4 exits
14.2642	Visitor 3 enters
14.2642	Visitor 3 holds for 4.51334
16.6951	DoNothing 5 enters
16.6951	DoNothing 5 exits
18.7776	Visitor 3 exits
19.8544	Visitor 4 enters
19.8544	Visitor 4 holds for 5.10907
20.5342	DoNothing 6 enters
20.5342	DoNothing 6 exits
23.464	DoNothing 7 enters
23.464	DoNothing 7 exits
24.9635	Visitor 4 exits

Each subclass of EventMonitor must create its own sequence of labels. EventMonitor sets up a label framework in which the subclass can implement a way of distinguishing its instances. EventMonitor itself provides a model that the subclasses can duplicate; in this way, a default simulation using instances of EventMonitor can be used to produce the trace shown above. In addition to the scheduling, task language and private, messages shown in the earlier implementation of EventMonitor, the class description has the following messages.

class name	EventMonitor
superclass	SimulationObject
instance variable names	label
class variable names	DataFile
	Counter

class methods

class initialization

file: aFile
    DataFile ← aFile.
    Counter ← 0

instance methods

initialization

initialize
    super initialize.
    self setLabel

accessing

setLabel
        Counter ← Counter + 1.
        label ← Counter printString
label
        ↑label

printing

printOn: aStream
        self class name printOn: aStream.
        aStream space.
        aStream nextPutAll: self label

Visitor, as a subclass of EventMonitor, has to have an independent class variable to act as the counter of its instances. The class description of Visitor is now

class name	Visitor
superclass	EventMonitor
class variable names	MyCounter
class methods	

class initialization

file: aFile
        super file: aFile.
        MyCounter ← 0

instance methods

accessing

setLabel
        MyCounter ← MyCounter + 1.
        label ← MyCounter printString

simulation control

tasks
        self holdFor: (Uniform from: 4.0 to: 10.0) next

MyCounter is set to 0 when the instance is told initialize; the method is found in class EventMonitor. Printing retrieves the label that Visitor redefines with respect to MyCounter. We let DoNothing use the class variable, Counter, of its superclass. Then the desired trace will be produced using these definitions.

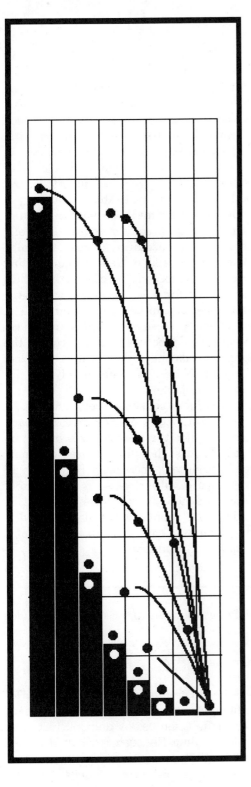

24

The Use of Resources in Event-Driven Simulations

Implementing Classes ResourceProvider
  and StaticResource

Consumable Resources

Nonconsumable Resources
Example of a File System

Renewable Resources
Example of a Ferry Service

In the previous chapters, we introduced a framework in which to specify event-driven simulations and to gather statistics about such simulations. Without resources to contend for and use, the only real task that an object can perform in a simulation is to hold (wait) for some specified amount of simulated time. Two kinds of resources are illustrated in this chapter: fixed resources and fluctuating resources. These kinds of resources were introduced in Chapter 22; the example in that chapter of classes Simulation and SimulationObject defined a support for resources coordination that will be further described in this chapter.

A fixed resource can be *consumable*. The simulation with a consumable resource begins with a given quantity of some resource, say, jelly beans. As the simulation proceeds, objects acquire the resource, ultimately using up all that were originally available. New objects needing the resource either terminate without successfully completing their tasks, or are indefinitely delayed waiting for a resource that will never be provided. Alternatively, a fixed resource can be *nonconsumable*. The simulation begins with a given quantity of some nonconsumable resource, say, glass jars. As the simulation proceeds, objects acquire the resource. When an object no longer needs the resource, it is recycled. Objects needing the resource either obtain it immediately or are delayed until a recycled one becomes available.

A fluctuating resource models producer/consumer relationships. A simulation can begin with a given quantity of some resource, say cars. As the simulation proceeds, objects acquire the resource; when they no longer need the resource, they recycle it (such as in the used car market). New resources can be added (produced), increasing the supply of the resource. Objects needing the resource either obtain it immediately or must wait until a recycled one or a new one becomes available. A fluctuating resource for which additional quantities can be produced is called a *renewable* resource. The example of the car is an example of a resource that is both renewable and nonconsumable.

Implementing ResourceProvider and StaticResource

The modeler's language for specifying resources in a Simulation includes expressions of the form

    self produce: amount of: resourceName

The response to this message is either to create an instance of class Resource with amount as its available quantity of resources, or to retrieve an existing Resource and increment its resources by amount. Instances of ResourceProvider are created by sending ResourceProvider the message named: aString or named: aString with: amount.

When a SimulationObject requests a resource (acquire: amount ofResource: resourceName), the currently active simulation

(ActiveSimulation) is asked to provide the corresponding resource (provideResourceFor:). Presumably the resource exists in the simulation as a result of the initialization of the Simulation; the Simulation refers to a Set of instances of ResourceProvider and can enumerate this Set in order to find one whose name is resourceName.

Once the SimulationObject has access to a ResourceProvider it can

ask how many resources it has available,
ask its name,
ask to acquire some amount (and with a particular access priority),
ask to produce some amount.

When a SimulationObject asks to acquire some resources, this request is added to a queue of such requests, ordered with respect to priority and, within identical priority levels, on a first-come first-served basis. Each time a request is made or more resources are produced, the ResourceProvider checks to see if one or more of its pending requests can be satisfied.

Each request is stored as an instance of class DelayedEvent. DelayedEvent was described in Chapter 22. Each DelayedEvent refers to a condition. In the case of delayed tasks, the condition is the time at which the tasks should be resumed; in the case of resource requests, the condition is an instance of StaticResource which is a representation of the requested resource and desired amount. Whenever a request is made, the request is stored on the waiting queue, pending, and then an attempt is made to provide the resource.

Class ResourceProvider is a subclass of class Resource. Class ResourceCoordinator, to be presented in the next chapter, is also a subclass of Resource. Resource represents the resource in terms of its name and the queue of requests that must be satisfied. A class variable refers to the currently active simulation (ActiveSimulation) for access to the time and process reference counting.

class name	Resource
superclass	Object
instance variable names	pending
	resourceName
class variable names	ActiveSimulation
class methods	

class initialization

activeSimulation: existingSimulation
ActiveSimulation ← existingSimulation

instance creation
named: resourceName
↑self new setName: resourceName

instance methods

accessing

addRequest: aDelayedEvent
pending add: aDelayedEvent.
self provideResources.
ActiveSimulation stopProcess.
aDelayedEvent pause.
ActiveSimulation startProcess

name
↑resourceName

private

provideResources
↑self
setName: aString
resourceName ← aString.
pending ← SortedCollection new

Notice that the mechanism used for storing requests on the SortedCollection, pending, is similar to that used for storing delayed events on the eventQueue of a Simulation. That is, a process that was running is suspended so that the reference count for processes in the Simulation is decremented. At the point that the process continues again, the reference count is incremented. A Semaphore is used in order to synchronize pausing and resuming the simulation process.

Class ResourceProvider represents resources as simple quantifiable items that have no tasks to do and are, therefore, not created as actual SimulationObjects. Rather, a numerical count is kept of the number of the items. When a SimulationObject successfully acquires this kind of resource, the SimulationObject is given access to an instance of StaticResource. The last expression of the method in ResourceProvider associated with acquire:withPriority: creates and returns a StaticResource. Prior to evaluating this expression, a DelayedEvent is removed from the collection of pending requests and the amount requested decremented from the amount currently available.

class name	ResourceProvider
superclass	Resource
instance variable names	amountAvailable
class methods	

instance creation

named: resourceName with: amount
↑self new setName: resourceName with: amount

named: resourceName
    ↑self new setName: resourceName with: 0

instance methods

accessing

amountAvailable
    ↑amountAvailable

task language

acquire: amountNeeded withPriority: priorityNumber
    | anEvent |
    anEvent ← DelayedEvent onCondition: (StaticResource
                                 for: amountNeeded
                                 of: self
                                 withPriority: priorityNumber).
    self addRequest: anEvent.
    ↑anEvent condition
produce: amount
    amountAvailable ← amountAvailable + amount.
    self provideResources

private

provideResources
    | anEvent |
    [pending isEmpty not
       and: [pending first condition amount < = amountAvailable]]
       whileTrue:
          [anEvent ← pending removeFirst.
          amountAvailable ← amountAvailable − anEvent condition amount.
          anEvent resume]
setName: resourceName with: amount
    super setName: aString.
    amountAvailable ← amount

A StaticResource represents a SimulationObject with no tasks to do other than to hold quantities of items for some other SimulationObject.

class name	StaticResource
superclass	SimulationObject
instance variable names	amount
	resource
	priority

class methods

instance creation

for: amount of: aResource withPriority: aNumber
    ↑self new setAmount: amount resource: aResource withPriority: aNumber

instance methods

accessing

amount
>↑amount

name
>↑resource name

priority
>↑priority

comparing

< = aStaticResource
>↑priority < = aStaticResource priority

task language

consume: aNumber
>amount ← (amount − aNumber) max: 0

release
>resource produce: amount.
>amount ← 0

private

setAmount: aNumber
  resource: aResource
  withPriority: priorityNumber
>amount ← aNumber.
>resource ← aResource.
>priority ← priorityNumber

Since a SimulationObject can hold on to a reference to a StaticResource, the messages consume: and release are part of the task language of a SimulationObject. When a SimulationObject acquires a resource, it is presumably consuming that resource, until that resource is returned to the simulation. The amount of resource held in the StaticResource is returned to the simulation by sending the StaticResource the message release. (Typically, however, the SimulationObject sends itself the message release: aStaticResource so that a uniform style of sending messages to self is maintained in the method associated with the object's tasks. This uniformity simplifies the design of a method for tracing or monitoring the events of a simulation. Because all task messages are sent as messages to self and therefore to a SimulationObject, it is possible to create a subclass of SimulationObject (EventMonitor was the example we presented in Chapter 23) in which all task messages are intercepted in order to store a notation that the task is being done.

Using acquire:ofResource: and release:, the resource is treated as a nonconsumable resource. A mixture is possible. The SimulationObject can acquire some amount of a resource, say 10, consume 5, and return 5. The message consume: is used to remove resources from the simulation. Thus the example would be accomplished by sending a StaticResource, acquired with 10 resources, the message consume: 5, and then the message release (or sending release: aStaticResource to self).

Consumable Resources

A simple jelly bean example illustrates the idea of a consumable resource. Recall the simulation example, NothingAtAll, introduced in Chapter 22. Suppose that whenever a Visitor enters the simulation and looks around, it has a task to acquire 2 jelly beans, take 2 units of time eating the beans, and leave. The simulation is initialized with one resource consisting of 15 jelly beans. The definition of this version of NothingAtAll is

class name	NothingAtAll
superclass	Simulation
instance methods	

initialization

defineResources
    self produce: 15 of: ' jelly beans '
defineArrivalSchedule
    self scheduleArrivalOf: Visitor accordingTo: (Uniform from: 1 to: 3)

The Visitor's tasks are expressed in two messages to self found in its method for tasks.

tasks
    self acquire: 2 ofResource: ' jelly beans ' .
    self holdFor: 2

An example execution of this simulation, in which only exits and entries are monitored, is

0.0	Visitor 1 enters
2.0	Visitor 1 exits
2.03671	Visitor 2 enters

The Use of Resources in Event-Driven Simulations

4.03671	Visitor 2 exits
4.34579	Visitor 3 enters
5.92712	Visitor 4 enters
6.34579	Visitor 3 exits
7.92712	Visitor 4 exits
8.46271	Visitor 5 enters
10.4627	Visitor 5 exits
10.5804	Visitor 6 enters
12.5804	Visitor 6 exits
12.7189	Visitor 7 enters
14.7189	Visitor 7 exits
15.0638	Visitor 8 enters
17.6466	Visitor 9 enters
19.8276	Visitor 10 enters

14.7189   Visitor 7 exits   *last visitor to get jelly beans*

15.0638   Visitor 8 enters   *endless waiting from now on*

After the seventh Visitor enters, there are no more jelly beans, so all the subsequent Visitors are endlessly delayed waiting for resources that will never be made available. Alternatively, the Visitor could check to see if any jelly beans remain available (inquireFor:ofResource:). If none remain, the Visitor can leave rather than getting caught in the queue. This corresponds to the following method for tasks.

tasks

```
(self inquireFor: 2 ofResource: ' jelly beans ' )
    ifTrue: [self acquire: 2 ofResource: ' jelly beans ' .
        self holdFor: 2]
```

One additional refinement might be to inform the simulation that all resources are used up and that it is time to "close the store." This is done by sending the Visitor the message stopSimulation. If we were to send this message the first time a Visitor enters who can not acquire enough jelly beans, then it is possible that a Visitor who has entered the store will get locked in. We have to make certain that a Visitor who acquires the last jelly beans, closes the store upon exit; in this way, a later Visitor will not lock this last successful one into the store. This corresponds to the following method for tasks.

tasks

```
| flag |
(self inquireFor: 2 ofResource: ' jelly beans ' )
    ifTrue: [self acquire: 2 ofResource: ' jelly beans ' .
            flag ← self inquireFor: 2 ofResource: ' jelly beans ' .
            "Are there still 2 left so that the next Visitor can be served?"
            self holdFor: 2.
            flag ifFalse: [self stopSimulation]]
```

Here is another example execution of the simulation NothingAtAll, in which only exits and entries are monitored.

0.0	Visitor 1 enters	
2.0	Visitor 1 exits	
2.26004	Visitor 2 enters	
4.26004	Visitor 2 exits	
4.83762	Visitor 3 enters	
6.34491	Visitor 4 enters	
6.83762	Visitor 3 exits	
8.34491	Visitor 4 exits	
8.51764	Visitor 5 enters	
9.9006	Visitor 6 enters	
10.5176	Visitor 5 exits	
11.9006	Visitor 6 exits	
12.6973	Visitor 7 enters	last successful requestor
14.0023	Visitor 8 enters	nothing available for this Visitor
14.0023	Visitor 8 exits	
14.6973	Visitor 7 exits	last successful requestor closes shop on exit

The EventMonitor class described in the previous chapter also monitors the use of resources. So, a trace of NothingAtAll would include the times at which jelly beans were requested and obtained.

0.0	Visitor 1 enters
0.0	Visitor 1 requests 2 of jelly beans
0.0	Visitor 1 obtained 2 of jelly beans
0.0	Visitor 1 holds for 2
1.40527	Visitor 2 enters
1.40527	Visitor 2 requests 2 of jelly beans
1.40527	Visitor 2 obtained 2 of jelly beans
1.40527	Visitor 2 holds for 2
2.0	Visitor 1 exits
2.56522	Visitor 3 enters
2.56522	Visitor 3 requests 2 of jelly beans
2.56522	Visitor 3 obtained 2 of jelly beans
2.56522	Visitor 3 holds for 2
3.40527	Visitor 2 exits
4.56522	Visitor 3 exits
5.3884	Visitor 4 enters
5.3884	Visitor 4 requests 2 of jelly beans
5.3884	Visitor 4 obtained 2 of jelly beans
5.3884	Visitor 4 holds for 2
6.69794	Visitor 5 enters
6.69794	Visitor 5 requests 2 of jelly beans
6.69794	Visitor 5 obtained 2 of jelly beans
6.69794	Visitor 5 holds for 2

7.3884	Visitor 4 exits
7.72174	Visitor 6 enters
7.72174	Visitor 6 requests 2 of jelly beans
7.72174	Visitor 6 obtained 2 of jelly beans
7.72174	Visitor 6 holds for 2
8.69794	Visitor 5 exits
9.72174	Visitor 6 exits
10.153	Visitor 7 enters
10.153	Visitor 7 requests 2 of jelly beans
10.153	Visitor 7 obtained 2 of jelly beans
10.153	Visitor 7 holds for 2
11.875	Visitor 8 enters
11.875	Visitor 8 exits
12.153	

At time 11.875, all but one jelly bean has been consumed. At time 12.153 Visitor number 7 stops the simulation.

Nonconsumable Resources

A car rental simulation serves to illustrate the use of a nonconsumable resource. The example simulation is a short-term car rental agency that opens up with 15 cars and 3 trucks available. Renters of cars arrive with a mean rate of one every 30 minutes, and those requiring trucks one every 120 minutes. The first car renter arrives when the shop opens, and the first truck renter arrives 10 minutes later. Classes CarRenter and TruckRenter represent these simulation objects.

RentalAgency is specified as a subclass of Simulation. It implements the two initialization messages, defineArrivalSchedule and defineResources.

class name	RentalAgency
superclass	Simulation
instance methods	

initialization

defineArrivalSchedule
    self scheduleArrivalOf: CarRenter
        accordingTo: (Exponential mean: 30).
    self scheduleArrivalOf: TruckRenter
        accordingTo: (Exponential mean: 120)
        startingAt: 10
defineResources
    self produce: 15 of: 'car'.
    self produce: 3 of: 'truck'

The tasks for CarRenter and TruckRenter are similar. First acquire a car or truck; if none are available, wait. Once the vehicle is obtained, use it. A CarRenter keeps the car between 4 and 8 hours (uniformly distributed); a TruckRenter keeps the truck between 1 and 4 hours (uniformly distributed). These usage times are indicated by having the renter hold for the appropriate amount of time before returning the vehicle (i.e., releasing the resource).

In order to monitor the two kinds of SimulationObject, and to have labels that separately identify each kind, the implementations of CarRenter and TruckRenter duplicate the labeling technique demonstrated earlier for class Visitor.

class name	CarRenter
superclass	EventMonitor
class variable names	CarCounter
	Hour

class methods

class initialization

file: file
> super file: file.
> CarCounter ← 0.
> Hour ← 60

instance methods

accessing

setLabel
> CarCounter ← CarCounter + 1.
> label ← CarCounter printString

simulation control

tasks
> | car |
> car ← self acquire: 1 ofResource: 'car'.
> self holdFor: (Uniform from: 4∗Hour to: 8∗Hour) next.
> self release: car

class name	TruckRenter
superclass	EventMonitor
class variable names	TruckCounter
	Hour

class methods

class initialization

file: file
> super file: file.
> TruckCounter ← 0
> Hour ← 60

accessing

setLabel
>   TruckCounter ← TruckCounter + 1.
>   label ← TruckCounter printString

instance methods

simulation control

tasks
> | truck |
>   truck ← self acquire: 1 ofResource: ' truck ' .
>   self holdFor: (Uniform from: Hour to: 4∗Hour) next.
>   self release: truck

The rental agency simulation is run by invoking

>   aFile ← Disk file: 'rental.events'.
>   CarRenter file: aFile.
>   TruckRenter file: aFile.
>   anAgency ← RentalAgency new startUp.
>   [anAgency time < 600] whileTrue: [anAgency proceed]

The trace on file rental.events after 10 hours (600 minutes) shows the following sequence of events.

0	CarRenter 1 enters
0	CarRenter 1 requests 1 of Car
0	CarRenter 1 obtained 1 of Car
0	CarRenter 1 holds for 460.426
10	TruckRenter 1 enters
10	TruckRenter 1 requests 1 of Truck
10	TruckRenter 1 obtained 1 of Truck
10	TruckRenter 1 holds for 87.2159
26.2079	CarRenter 2 enters
26.2079	CarRenter 2 requests 1 of Car
26.2079	CarRenter 2 obtained 1 of Car
26.2079	CarRenter 2 holds for 318.966
27.4147	CarRenter 3 enters
27.4147	CarRenter 3 requests 1 of Car
27.4147	CarRenter 3 obtained 1 of Car
27.4147	CarRenter 3 holds for 244.867
51.5614	CarRenter 4 enters
51.5614	CarRenter 4 requests 1 of Car
51.5614	CarRenter 4 obtained 1 of Car
51.5614	CarRenter 4 holds for 276.647
78.0957	CarRenter 5 enters

78.0957	CarRenter 5 requests 1 of Car
78.0957	CarRenter 5 obtained 1 of Car
78.0957	CarRenter 5 holds for 333.212
93.121	CarRenter 6 enters
93.121	CarRenter 6 requests 1 of Car
93.121	CarRenter 6 obtained 1 of Car
93.121	CarRenter 6 holds for 359.718
97.2159	TruckRenter 1 releases 1 of Truck
97.2159	TruckRenter 1 exits
99.0265	CarRenter 7 enters
99.0265	CarRenter 7 requests 1 of Car
99.0265	CarRenter 7 obtained 1 of Car
99.0265	CarRenter 7 holds for 417.572
106.649	CarRenter 8 enters
106.649	CarRenter 8 requests 1 of Car
106.649	CarRenter 8 obtained 1 of Car
106.649	CarRenter 8 holds for 294.43
107.175	CarRenter 9 enters
107.175	CarRenter 9 requests 1 of Car
107.175	CarRenter 9 obtained 1 of Car
107.175	CarRenter 9 holds for 314.198
121.138	CarRenter 10 enters
121.138	CarRenter 10 requests 1 of Car
121.138	CarRenter 10 obtained 1 of Car
121.138	CarRenter 10 holds for 467.032
127.018	TruckRenter 2 enters
127.018	TruckRenter 2 requests 1 of Truck
127.018	TruckRenter 2 obtained 1 of Truck
127.018	TruckRenter 2 holds for 74.5047
145.513	CarRenter 11 enters
145.513	CarRenter 11 requests 1 of Car
145.513	CarRenter 11 obtained 1 of Car
145.513	CarRenter 11 holds for 243.776
166.214	CarRenter 12 enters
166.214	CarRenter 12 requests 1 of Car
166.214	CarRenter 12 obtained 1 of Car
166.214	CarRenter 12 holds for 429.247
172.253	CarRenter 13 enters
172.253	CarRenter 13 requests 1 of Car
172.253	CarRenter 13 obtained 1 of Car
172.253	CarRenter 13 holds for 370.909
191.438	TruckRenter 3 enters
191.438	TruckRenter 3 requests 1 of Truck
191.438	TruckRenter 3 obtained 1 of Truck
191.438	TruckRenter 3 holds for 225.127

201.523	TruckRenter 2 releases 1 of Truck
201.523	TruckRenter 2 exits
220.102	CarRenter 14 enters
220.102	CarRenter 14 requests 1 of Car
220.102	CarRenter 14 obtained 1 of Car
220.102	CarRenter 14 holds for 334.684
252.055	CarRenter 15 enters
252.055	CarRenter 15 requests 1 of Car
252.055	CarRenter 15 obtained 1 of Car
252.055	CarRenter 15 holds for 408.358
269.964	CarRenter 16 enters
269.964	CarRenter 16 requests 1 of Car
272.282	CarRenter 3 releases 1 of Car
272.282	CarRenter 3 exits
272.282	CarRenter 16 obtained 1 of Car
272.282	CarRenter 16 holds for 281.349
292.375	CarRenter 17 enters
292.375	CarRenter 17 requests 1 of Car
328.208	CarRenter 4 releases 1 of Car
328.208	CarRenter 4 exits
328.208	CarRenter 17 obtained 1 of Car
328.208	CarRenter 17 holds for 270.062
345.174	CarRenter 2 releases 1 of Car
345.174	CarRenter 2 exits
350.53	CarRenter 18 enters
350.53	CarRenter 18 requests 1 of Car
350.53	CarRenter 18 obtained 1 of Car
350.53	CarRenter 18 holds for 297.154
354.126	CarRenter 19 enters
354.126	CarRenter 19 requests 1 of Car
358.269	TruckRenter 4 enters
358.269	TruckRenter 4 requests 1 of Truck
358.269	TruckRenter 4 obtained 1 of Truck
358.269	TruckRenter 4 holds for 173.648
367.88	TruckRenter 5 enters
367.88	TruckRenter 5 requests 1 of Truck
367.88	TruckRenter 5 obtained 1 of Truck
367.88	TruckRenter 5 holds for 175.972
389.289	CarRenter 11 releases 1 of Car
389.289	CarRenter 11 exits
389.289	CarRenter 19 obtained 1 of Car
389.289	CarRenter 19 holds for 379.017
401.079	CarRenter 8 releases 1 of Car
401.079	CarRenter 8 exits
402.224	CarRenter 20 enters

402.224	CarRenter 20 requests 1 of Car
402.224	CarRenter 20 obtained 1 of Car
402.224	CarRenter 20 holds for 341.188
410.431	TruckRenter 6 enters
410.431	TruckRenter 6 requests 1 of Truck
411.307	CarRenter 5 releases 1 of Car
411.307	CarRenter 5 exits
416.566	TruckRenter 3 releases 1 of Truck
416.566	TruckRenter 3 exits
416.566	TruckRenter 6 obtained 1 of Truck
416.566	TruckRenter 6 holds for 119.076
421.373	CarRenter 9 releases 1 of Car
421.373	CarRenter 9 exits
422.802	CarRenter 21 enters
422.802	CarRenter 21 requests 1 of Car
422.802	CarRenter 21 obtained 1 of Car
422.802	CarRenter 21 holds for 241.915
452.839	CarRenter 6 releases 1 of Car
452.839	CarRenter 6 exits
460.426	CarRenter 1 releases 1 of Car
460.426	CarRenter 1 exits
512.263	CarRenter 22 enters
512.263	CarRenter 22 requests 1 of Car
512.263	CarRenter 22 obtained 1 of Car
512.263	CarRenter 22 holds for 277.035
516.598	CarRenter 7 releases 1 of Car
516.598	CarRenter 7 exits
531.917	TruckRenter 4 releases 1 of Truck
531.917	TruckRenter 4 exits
535.642	TruckRenter 6 releases 1 of Truck
535.642	TruckRenter 6 exits
543.162	CarRenter 13 releases 1 of Car
543.162	CarRenter 13 exits
543.852	TruckRenter 5 releases 1 of Truck
543.852	TruckRenter 5 exits
553.631	CarRenter 16 releases 1 of Car
553.631	CarRenter 16 exits
554.786	CarRenter 14 releases 1 of Car
554.786	CarRenter 14 exits
574.617	CarRenter 23 enters
574.617	CarRenter 23 requests 1 of Car
574.617	CarRenter 23 obtained 1 of Car
574.617	CarRenter 23 holds for 436.783
588.171	CarRenter 10 releases 1 of Car
588.171	CarRenter 10 exits

591.51	CarRenter 24 enters
591.51	CarRenter 24 requests 1 of Car
591.51	CarRenter 24 obtained 1 of Car
591.51	CarRenter 24 holds for 430.067
595.461	CarRenter 12 releases 1 of Car
595.461	CarRenter 12 exits
598.27	CarRenter 17 releases 1 of Car
598.27	CarRenter 17 exits
599.876	CarRenter 25 enters
599.876	CarRenter 25 requests 1 of Car
599.876	CarRenter 25 obtained 1 of Car
599.876	CarRenter 25 holds for 472.042
642.188	TruckRenter 7 enters
642.188	TruckRenter 7 requests 1 of Truck
642.188	TruckRenter 7 obtained 1 of Truck
642.188	TruckRenter 7 holds for 190.586

A snapshot of the simulation shows that, at time 642.188, the following events are queued in anAgency and the following resources are available.

```
Resource (car) no pending requests; 6 available
Resource (truck) no pending requests; 2 available
Event Queue
        CarRenter for creation and start up
        TruckRenter for creation and start up
        9 CarRenters holding
        1 TruckRenter holding
```

Note that a nonconsumable resource differs from the description of a consumable resource only in the SimulationObject's sending the message release: in order to recycle acquired resources.

Example of a File System

The car rental is an open simulation in which objects (car renters and truck renters) arrive, do their tasks, and leave again. A closed simulation is one in which the same objects remain in the simulation for the duration of the simulation run. The next example is of a file system; it was adopted from a book by Graham Birtwistle that presents a Simula-based system named Demos [*A System for Discrete Event Modelling on Simula*, Graham M. Birtwistle, MacMillan, London, England, 1979]. The purpose of Demos is to support teaching about the kinds of event-driven simulations discussed in this chapter. The book is a thorough introduction to this class of simulations and to their implementation in Simula. There are many useful examples, each of which could be implemented in the context of the Smalltalk-80 simulation framework provided in this and in the previous chapter. We use variations of a Demos file system, a car ferry, and an information system example for illustration in this chapter so that, after seeing how we approach the Smalltalk-80 implementations, the interested reader can try out more of Birtwistle's examples.

In the example file system, "writer" processes update a file, and "reader" processes read it. Any number of readers may access the file at the same time, but writers must have sole access to the file. Moreover, writers have priority over readers. The individual sequencing of events is shown in the programs below. The example illustrates the use of priority queueing for resources as well as another approach to collecting statistics. In this case, the statistics gathered is a tally of the number of reads and the number of writes.

Suppose there are three system file readers and two file writers, and only three (nonconsumable) file resources. The initialization method specifies a statistics dictionary with two zero-valued entries, reads and writes. The simulation is to run for 25 simulated units of time; it schedules itself to receive the message finishUp at time 25.

Note in the implementation of defineArrivalSchedule that the FileSystemReaders and FileSystemWriters are given attributes so that they can be identified in the event traces.

class name	FileSystem
superclass	Simulation
instance variable names	statistics
instance methods	

initialize-release

initialize
```
    super initialize.
    statistics ← Dictionary new: 2.
    statistics at: #reads put: 0.
    statistics at: #writes put: 0
```
defineArrivalSchedule
```
    self scheduleArrivalOf: (FileSystemReader new label: 'first')
        at: 0.0.
    self scheduleArrivalOf: (FileSystemWriter new label: 'first')
        at: 0.0.
    self scheduleArrivalOf: (FileSystemReader new label: 'second')
        at: 0.0.
    self scheduleArrivalOf: (FileSystemWriter new label: 'second')
        at: 1.0.
    self scheduleArrivalOf: (FileSystemReader new label: 'third')
        at: 2.0.
    self schedule: [self finishUp] at: 25
```
defineResources
```
    self produce: 3 of: 'File'
```

statistics

statisticsAt: aKey changeBy: anInteger
statistics at: aKey
put: (statistics at: aKey) + anInteger
printStatisticsOn: aStream
statistics printOn: aStream

The FileSystemReader repeatedly carries out a sequence of five tasks: acquire one File resource, hold for an amount of time appropriate to reading the file, release the resource, update the tally of read statistics, and then hold for an amount of time appropriate to using the information read from the file. FileSystemWriters acquire three file resources, hold in order to write on the file, release the resources, and update the write statistics. The priority of a FileSystemReader is set to 1; the priority of a FileSystemWriter is 2. In this way, the nonconsumable ResourceProvider 'File' will give attention to FileSystemWriters before FileSystemReaders.

In order to obtain a trace of the events, the two simulation objects are created as subclasses of EventMonitor. Since each has a single label that will serve to identify it, only the response to printOn: aStream is reimplemented.

class name	FileSystemReader
superclass	EventMonitor
instance methods	

accessing

label: aString
label ← aString

simulation control

tasks
| file |
"The repeated sequence of tasks is as follows"
[true]
    whileTrue:
        [file ← self acquire: 1 ofResource: 'File' withPriority: 1.
        self holdFor: 2.0.
        self release: file.
        ActiveSimulation statisticsAt: #reads changeBy: 1.
        self holdFor: 5.0]

printing

printOn: aStream
aStream nextPutAll: label.
aStream space.
self class name printOn: aStream

class name	FileSystemWriter
superclass	EventMonitor
instance methods	

accessing

label: aString
>   label ← aString

simulation control

tasks
> | file |
>   "The repeated sequence of tasks is as follows"
>   [true]
>   whileTrue:
>   ["Gather information"
>   self holdFor: 5.0.
>   file ← self acquire: 3 ofResource: 'File' withPriority: 2.
>   self holdFor: 3.0.
>   self release: file.
>   ActiveSimulation statisticsAt: #writes changeBy: 1]

printing

printOn: aStream
>   aStream nextPutAll: label.
>   aStream space.
>   self class name printOn: aStream

The five simulation objects carry out their tasks, until the simulation stops itself at time 25. In specifying the tasks of a SimulationObject, the modeler has available all the control structures of the Smalltalk-80 language. A trace of the events shows how FileSystemReaders are held up because of the higher priority and larger resource needs of the FileSystemWriters. For example, the first and second FileSystemReaders are held up at time 7.0; the third at time 9.0; and all until time 11.0, the time at which no FileSystemWriter requires resources.

0.0	first FileSystemReader enters
0.0	first FileSystemReader requests 1 of File
0.0	first FileSystemReader obtained 1 of File
0.0	first FileSystemReader holds for 2.0
0.0	first FileSystemWriter enters
0.0	first FileSystemWriter holds for 5.0
0.0	second FileSystemReader enters
0.0	second FileSystemReader requests 1 of File
0.0	second FileSystemReader obtained 1 of File
0.0	second FileSystemReader holds for 2.0

1.0	second FileSystemWriter enters
1.0	second FileSystemWriter holds for 5.0
2.0	second FileSystemReader releases 1 of File
2.0	second FileSystemReader holds for 5.0
2.0	first FileSystemReader releases 1 of File
2.0	first FileSystemReader holds for 5.0
2.0	third FileSystemReader enters
2.0	third FileSystemReader requests 1 of File
2.0	third FileSystemReader obtained 1 of File
2.0	third FileSystemReader holds for 2.0
4.0	third FileSystemReader releases 1 of File
4.0	third FileSystemReader holds for 5.0
5.0	first FileSystemWriter requests 3 of File
5.0	first FileSystemWriter obtained 3 of File
5.0	first FileSystemWriter holds for 3.0
6.0	second FileSystemWriter requests 3 of File
7.0	first FileSystemReader requests 1 of File
7.0	second FileSystemReader requests 1 of File
8.0	first FileSystemWriter releases 3 of File
8.0	first FileSystemWriter holds for 5.0
8.0	second FileSystemWriter obtained 3 of File
8.0	second FileSystemWriter holds for 3.0
9.0	third FileSystemReader requests 1 of File
11.0	second FileSystemWriter releases 3 of File
11.0	second FileSystemWriter holds for 5.0
11.0	first FileSystemReader obtained 1 of File
11.0	first FileSystemReader holds for 2.0
11.0	second FileSystemReader obtained 1 of File
11.0	second FileSystemReader holds for 2.0
11.0	third FileSystemReader obtained 1 of File
11.0	third FileSystemReader holds for 2.0
13.0	third FileSystemReader releases 1 of File
13.0	third FileSystemReader holds for 5.0
13.0	second FileSystemReader releases 1 of File
13.0	second FileSystemReader holds for 5.0
13.0	first FileSystemReader releases 1 of File
13.0	first FileSystemReader holds for 5.0
13.0	first FileSystemWriter requests 3 of File
13.0	first FileSystemWriter obtained 3 of File
13.0	first FileSystemWriter holds for 3.0
16.0	first FileSystemWriter releases 3 of File
16.0	first FileSystemWriter holds for 5.0
16.0	second FileSystemWriter requests 3 of File
16.0	second FileSystemWriter obtained 3 of File
16.0	second FileSystemWriter holds for 3.0

18.0	first FileSystemReader requests 1 of File
18.0	second FileSystemReader requests 1 of File
18.0	third FileSystemReader requests 1 of File
19.0	second FileSystemWriter releases 3 of File
19.0	second FileSystemWriter holds for 5.0
19.0	first FileSystemReader obtained 1 of File
19.0	first FileSystemReader holds for 2.0
19.0	second FileSystemReader obtained 1 of File
19.0	second FileSystemReader holds for 2.0
19.0	third FileSystemReader obtained 1 of File
19.0	third FileSystemReader holds for 2.0
21.0	third FileSystemReader releases 1 of File
21.0	third FileSystemReader holds for 5.0
21.0	second FileSystemReader releases 1 of File
21.0	second FileSystemReader holds for 5.0
21.0	first FileSystemReader releases 1 of File
21.0	first FileSystemReader holds for 5.0
21.0	first FileSystemWriter requests 3 of File
21.0	first FileSystemWriter obtained 3 of File
21.0	first FileSystemWriter holds for 3.0
24.0	first FileSystemWriter releases 3 of File
24.0	first FileSystemWriter holds for 5.0
24.0	second FileSystemWriter requests 3 of File
24.0	second FileSystemWriter obtained 3 of File
24.0	second FileSystemWriter holds for 3.0

At this point, the current time is 25 and the statistics gathered is printed by sending the FileSystem the message printStatisticsOn: aStream where the Stream is, for example, a FileStream. The result is

reads	9
writes	5

Note that if the FileSystemReaders were not held up by lack of resources and lower priority, there would have been 12 reads during this timeframe.

Renewable Resources

In simulations involving producer/consumer synchronizations, simulation objects acting as producers make resources available to other objects acting as consumers. The simulation starts out with some fixed amount of resource, perhaps 0. Producer objects increase the available

The Use of Resources in Event-Driven Simulations

resources, consumer objects decrease them. This type of resource differs from a nonconsumable resource in that there is no limit to the amounts of resource that can be made available. Such resources are called *renewable* resources. Note that the limit in the nonconsumable case is enforced indirectly by the SimulationObject's returning resources through the StaticResource.

A simulation of a car dealership provides a simple example of a renewable resource. Suppose a customer comes in to buy a car every two to six days. The car dealer starts out with 12 cars on the lot; when these are sold, orders must wait until new cars are delivered. Ten to twelve new cars are shipped to the dealer every 90 days. We assume that all the cars are the same and that every customer is willing to wait so that no sales are lost if a car is not immediately available. The car dealer is interested in giving good service, but he is also unwilling to keep too large an inventory. By examining the average length of the queue of waiting customers, the dealer can modify his quarterly order of cars in order to minimize customer dissatisfaction and still maintain a small inventory of new cars.

Statistics on the amount of time that car buyers have to wait to get a car are kept by the simulation. The method used is the same as the method demonstrated in Chapter 23 for collecting information on Visitors to a Museum; a Histogram is maintained by the CarDealer. Each CarBuyer remembers its entry time; when it exists the simulation, the length of time the CarBuyer spent in the simulation is logged in the Histogram. This length of time is equivalent to the amount of time the CarBuyer had to wait to get a car because the CarBuyer's only task is to acquire a car.

class name	CarDealer
superclass	Simulation
instance variable names	statistics
instance methods	

initialize-release

initialize
    super initialize.
    statistics ← Histogram from: 1 to: 365 by: 7

defineArrivalSchedule
    self scheduleArrivalOf: CarBuyer
        accordingTo: (Uniform from: 2 to: 6)
        startingAt: 1.0.
    self scheduleArrivalOf: (CarDelivery new) at: 90.0
    "only one delivery is scheduled; the instance of CarDelivery will reschedule itself as the last of its tasks"

defineResources
    self produce: 12 of: 'Car'

accessing

exit: aSimulationObject
    super exit: aSimulationObject.
    "A CarDelivery could be exiting—ignore it"
    (aSimulationObject isKindOf: CarBuyer)
        ifTrue: [statistics store: currentTime − aSimulationObject entryTime]

printStatistics: aStream
    statistics printStatisticsOn: aStream

All the CarBuyer wants to do is get a car; the CarBuyer only waits if a car is not immediately available.

class name	CarBuyer
superclass	SimulationObject
instance variable names	entryTime
instance methods	

accessing

entryTime
    ↑entryTime

simulation control

initialize
    super initialize.
    entryTime ← ActiveSimulation time

tasks
    self acquire: 1 ofResource: 'Car'

The CarDelivery produces 10 to 12 new cars. After producing the new cars, the CarDelivery object schedules itself to return in 90 days. An alternative implementation would have the CarDelivery hold for 90 days and then repeat its task.

class name	CarDelivery
superclass	SimulationObject
instance methods	

simulation control

tasks
    "Get access to the Car resource and produce 10, 11, or 12 new cars"
    self produce: ((SampleSpace data: #(10 11 12)) next)
        ofResource: 'Car'.
    "Schedule a new delivery in 90 days"
    ActiveSimulation scheduleArrivalOf: self
                at: ActiveSimulation time + 90

The statistics give us the number of buyers, minimum, maximum, and average wait times for the buyers, and the number of buyers within each wait-time interval. No one waited longer than 204 days. 91 car buyers came to the dealer; 12 did not have to wait because the dealer had cars already. Of the 43 that waited and were served, they waited on the average of 78.5 days.

At time 360.0 the statistics indicates the following information.

Number of Objects	Minimum Value	Maximum Value	Average Value
55	0.0	197.168	78.5476

Entry	Number of Objects	Frequency	
1-8	2	0.0363636	| XX
8-15	3	0.0545454	| XXX
15-22	2	0.0363636	| XX
22-29	1	0.0181818	| X
29-36	2	0.0363636	| XX
36-43	1	0.0181818	| X
43-50	0	0.0	|
50-57	1	0.0181818	| X
57-64	2	0.0363636	| XX
64-71	1	0.0181818	| X
71-78	2	0.0363636	| XX
78-85	2	0.0363636	| XX
85-92	2	0.0363636	| XX
92-99	0	0.0	|
99-106	0	0.0	|
106-113	1	0.0181818	| X
113-120	3	0.0545454	| XXX
120-127	2	0.0363636	| XX
127-134	2	0.0363636	| XX
134-141	2	0.0363636	| XX
141-148	1	0.0181818	| X
148-155	0	0.0	|
155-162	1	0.0181818	| X
162-169	2	0.0363636	| XX
169-176	2	0.0363636	| XX
176-183	1	0.0181818	| X
183-190	2	0.0363636	| XX
190-197	2	0.0363636	| XX
197-204	1	0.0181818	| X
204-211	0	0.0	|

Pending Requests 36 buyers waiting for a car

From the above information, we can estimate that the number of cars delivered could safely be increased, even doubled, to meet the consumer demand.

<table>
<tr><td>Example of a
Ferry Service</td><td>This next example is like one in the Birtwistle book. The example is of a ferry shuttling between an island and the mainland, carrying cars back and forth. The ferry starts service at 7:00 a.m. (420 minutes into the day) and stops at 10:45 p.m. (1365 minutes into the day) once it has reached one of its docking locations. The ferry has a capacity of only six cars.</td></tr>
</table>

The ferry's task is to load no more than six of the waiting cars and then to cross over the waterway. The crossing takes about eight minutes with a standard deviation of 0.5 minutes. The activity of crossing from one side to the other continues until the time is 1365 minutes. The FerrySimulation described next simulates one day's ferry service. Note in the definition of Ferry the use of the Smalltalk-80 whileFalse: control structure to repetitively send the Ferry from one side to another; also note the use of messages to split up the task description into parts load, holdFor: (cross over), unload, and changeSide.

class name	Ferry
superclass	SimulationObject
instance variable names	carsOnBoard
	currentSide

instance methods

simulation control

initialize
    super initialize.
    carsOnBoard ← 0.
    currentSide ← 'Mainland'

tasks
    "Initialize the count of loaded cars and then keep loading until at most 6 are on board. Stop loading if no more cars are waiting at the dock."
    [ActiveSimulation time > 1365.0] whileFalse:
       [carsOnBoard ← 0.
      self load.
      self holdFor: (Normal mean: 8 deviation: 0.5) next.
      self unload.
      self changeSide]

load
    "It takes 0.5 minutes to load each car. Only try to acquire a resource, a car from this side's dock, if it is there. The conditional for the repetition checks remaining resources and only continues if a car is waiting."

The Use of Resources in Event-Driven Simulations

```
        [carsOnBoard < 6
            and: [self inquireFor: 1 of: currentSide]]
                whileTrue:
                    [self acquire: 1 ofResource: currentSide.
                    self holdFor: 0.5.
                    carsOnBoard ← carsOnBoard + 1]
```

changeSide
```
    currentSide ← currentSide = ' Mainland '
                            ifTrue: [' Island ']
                            ifFalse: [' Mainland ']
```

unload
```
    " It takes 0.5 minutes to unload each car. "
    self holdFor: carsOnBoard*0.5.
```

We will need two **SimulationObjects** in order to simulate the cars arriving at the dock of the Mainland or at the Island, that is, to produce a car at these locations.

class name	IslandArrival
superclass	SimulationObject
instance methods	

simulation control

    tasks

        self produce: 1 ofResource: ' Island '

class name	MainlandArrival
superclass	SimulationObject
instance methods	

simulation control

    tasks

        self produce: 1 ofResource: ' Mainland '

The ferry simulation has two kinds of **Resources**, one for the mainland and one for the island, in which to queue the arriving cars. When these resources are first created, i.e., the day begins, there are three cars already waiting at the mainland dock and no cars waiting at the island dock. The arrival schedule says that cars arrive with a mean rate of 0.15 every minute.

class name	FerrySimulation
superclass	Simulation

instance methods

initialization

defineArrivalSchedule
```
self scheduleArrivalOf: MainlandArrival
    accordingTo: (Exponential parameter: 0.15)
    startingAt: 420.0.
self scheduleArrivalOf: IslandArrival
    accordingTo: (Exponential parameter: 0.15)
    startingAt: 420.0.
self scheduleArrivalOf: Ferry new at: 420.0
```
defineResources
```
self produce: 3 of: 'Mainland'
self produce: 0 of: 'Island'
```

There is some data that the simulation should collect while it is accumulating. First, the Ferry should count the total number of trips it takes, the total cars it carries, and the number of trips it takes carrying no cars. This data is obtained by adding three instance variables (trips, totalCars, and emptyTrips) in the definition of class Ferry and modifying three methods.

class name	Ferry
superclass	SimulationObject
instance variable names	emptyTrips
	carsOnBoard
	currentSide
	trips
	totalCars
	emptyTrips

instance methods

initialize
```
super initialize.
carsOnBoard ← 0.
currentSide ← 'Mainland'
trips ← 0.
totalCars ← 0.
emptyTrips ← 0
```
load
```
"Keep a running tally of the cars carried"
[carsOnBoard < 6
    and: [self inquireFor: 1 ofResource: currentSide]]
        whileTrue:
            [self acquire: 1 ofResource: currentSide.
             self holdFor: 0.5.
             carsOnBoard ← carsOnBoard + 1.
             totalCars ← totalCars + 1]
```

The Use of Resources in Event-Driven Simulations

tasks
    "Check for an empty trip and keep a tally of trips"
    [ActiveSimulation time > 1365.0] whileFalse:
     [carsOnBoard ← 0.
     self load.
     carsOnBoard = 0 ifTrue: [emptyTrips ← emptyTrips + 1].
     self holdFor: (Normal mean: 8 deviation: 0.5) next.
     self unload.
     self changeSide.
     trips ← trips + 1]

In addition, we would like to know the maximum size of the number of Mainland and Island arrivals, that is, the maximum queue waiting for the Ferry. The FerrySimulation can determine this information by adding two instance variables, maxMainland and maxIsland; each time the message produce: amount of: resourceName is sent to the simulation and a resource amount is increased, the corresponding variable can be reset to the maximum of its current value and that of the resource.

The trace we provide shows the beginning and the ending sequence of events. The arrival of cars at the Island and the Mainland is listed separately from the repetitive tasks of the Ferry.

420.000	IslandArrival 1
420.000	MainlandArrival 1
425.290	MainlandArrival 2
429.380	MainlandArrival 3
430.830	IslandArrival 2
431.302	IslandArrival 3
434.209	IslandArrival 4
438.267	IslandArrival 5
440.864	IslandArrival 6
441.193	MainlandArrival 4
448.044	IslandArrival 7
448.827	IslandArrival 8
453.811	IslandArrival 9
458.804	MainlandArrival 5
467.860	IslandArrival 10
470.800	IslandArrival 11
473.957	MainlandArrival 6
475.508	IslandArrival 12

This continues until ...

1300.87	IslandArrival 169
1301.11	MainlandArrival 124
1301.19	IslandArrival 170

1306.75	IslandArrival 171
1309.30	IslandArrival 172
1315.24	MainlandArrival 125
1319.65	MainlandArrival 126
1321.80	MainlandArrival 127
1322.39	MainlandArrival 128
1328.45	IslandArrival 173
1328.99	IslandArrival 174
1329.77	MainlandArrival 129
1331.63	IslandArrival 175
1335.43	MainlandArrival 130
1338.93	IslandArrival 176
1342.46	MainlandArrival 131
1348.11	IslandArrival 177
1358.63	MainlandArrival 132
1359.10	IslandArrival 178
1360.79	MainlandArrival 133

The Ferry starts at the Mainland where there were three cars waiting; no cars are at the Island. Immediately a car arrives at each place.

420.0	Ferry 1 enters
	load at Mainland: there are now 4 cars waiting at Mainland and 1 car waiting at Island
420.0	Ferry 1 obtained 1 of Mainland, holds for 0.5
420.5	Ferry 1 obtained 1 of Mainland, holds for 0.5
421.0	Ferry 1 obtained 1 of Mainland, holds for 0.5
421.5	Ferry 1 obtained 1 of Mainland, holds for 0.5
	cross over
422.0	Ferry 1 holds for 8.56369
	unload 4 cars at Island: there are now 2 cars waiting at Mainland and 1 car waiting at Island
430.564	Ferry 1 holds for 2.0
	load at Island: there are now 2 cars at Mainland and 3 cars at Island
432.564	Ferry 1 obtained 1 of Island, holds for 0.5
433.064	Ferry 1 obtained 1 of Island, holds for 0.5
433.564	Ferry 1 obtained 1 of Island, holds for 0.5
	cross over
434.064	Ferry 1 holds for 8.55344
	unload 3 cars at Mainland: there are now 3 cars waiting at Mainland and 3 cars waiting at Island
442.617	Ferry 1 holds for 1.5
	load at Mainland: there is now 3 cars waiting at Mainland and 0 cars waiting at Island

444.117   Ferry 1 obtained 1 of Mainland, holds for 0.5
444.617   Ferry 1 obtained 1 of Mainland, holds for 0.5
445.117   Ferry 1 obtained 1 of Mainland, holds for 0.5
           cross over
445.617   Ferry 1 holds for 8.98081
           unload 3 cars at Island: there are now 0 cars waiting
           at Mainland and 6 cars waiting at Island
454.598   Ferry 1 holds for 1.5
           load at Island: there are now 0 cars waiting at Main-
           land and 6 cars waiting at Island
456.098   Ferry 1 obtained 1 of Island, holds for 0.5
456.598   Ferry 1 obtained 1 of Island, holds for 0.5
457.098   Ferry 1 obtained 1 of Island, holds for 0.5
457.598   Ferry 1 obtained 1 of Island, holds for 0.5
458.098   Ferry 1 obtained 1 of Island, holds for 0.5
458.598   Ferry 1 obtained 1 of Island, holds for 0.5

           cross over
459.098   Ferry 1 holds for 7.96448
           unload 6 cars at Mainland: there is now 1 car waiting
           at Mainland and 0 cars waiting at Island
467.062   Ferry 1 holds for 3.0
           load at Mainland: there is now 1 car waiting at Main-
           land and 1 car waiting at Island
470.062   Ferry 1 obtained 1 of Mainland, holds for 0.5
           continues until
           load at Island
1299.52   Ferry 1 obtained 1 of Island, holds for 0.5
1300.02   Ferry 1 obtained 1 of Island, holds for 0.5
           cross over
1300.52   Ferry 1 holds for 7.23914
           unload 2 cars at Mainland
1307.76   Ferry 1 holds for 1.0
           load at Mainland: there is now 1 car waiting at Main-
           land and 3 cars waiting at Island
1308.76   Ferry 1 obtained 1 of Mainland, holds for 0.5
           cross over
1309.26   Ferry 1 holds for 7.78433
           load at Island: there are now 2 cars waiting at
           Mainland and 4 cars waiting at Island
1317.54   Ferry 1 obtained 1 of Island, holds for 0.5
1318.04   Ferry 1 obtained 1 of Island, holds for 0.5
1318.54   Ferry 1 obtained 1 of Island, holds for 0.5
1319.04   Ferry 1 obtained 1 of Island, holds for 0.5
           cross over

1319.54	Ferry 1 holds for 8.51123
	unload 4 cars at Mainland: there are now 3 cars waiting at Mainland and 0 cars waiting at Island
1328.05	Ferry 1 holds for 2.0
	load at Mainland: there are now 5 cars waiting at Mainland and 2 cars waiting at Island
1330.05	Ferry 1 obtained 1 of Mainland, holds for 0.5
1330.55	Ferry 1 obtained 1 of Mainland, holds for 0.5
1331.05	Ferry 1 obtained 1 of Mainland, holds for 0.5
1331.55	Ferry 1 obtained 1 of Mainland, holds for 0.5
1332.05	Ferry 1 obtained 1 of Mainland, holds for 0.5
	cross over
1332.55	Ferry 1 holds for 8.17247
	unload 5 cars at Island: there is now 1 car waiting at Mainland and 4 cars waiting at Island
1340.72	Ferry 1 holds for 2.5
	load at Island: there are now 2 cars waiting at Mainland and 4 cars waiting at Island
1343.22	Ferry 1 obtained 1 of Island, holds for 0.5
1343.72	Ferry 1 obtained 1 of Island, holds for 0.5
1344.22	Ferry 1 obtained 1 of Island, holds for 0.5
1344.72	Ferry 1 obtained 1 of Island, holds for 0.5
	cross over
1345.22	Ferry 1 holds for 7.75318
	unload at Mainland: there are 2 cars waiting at Mainland and 1 car waiting at Island
1352.98	Ferry 1 holds for 2.0
	load at Mainland: there are 2 cars waiting at Mainland and 1 car waiting at Island
1354.98	Ferry 1 obtained 1 of Mainland, holds for 0.5
1355.48	Ferry 1 obtained 1 of Mainland, holds for 0.5
	cross over
1355.98	Ferry 1 holds for 8.54321
	unload 2 cars at Island: there are 2 cars waiting at Mainland and 2 cars waiting at Island
1364.52	Ferry 1 holds for 1.0
	quitting time
1365.52	Ferry 1 exits

The data collected shows that the Ferry took 79 trips, carrying a total of 310 cars (an average of 3.9 cars per trip). None of the trips was done with an empty load. The Mainland waiting line had a maximum of 7 cars while the Island had a maximum of 18. At the time that the Ferry closed, two cars were left at each location.

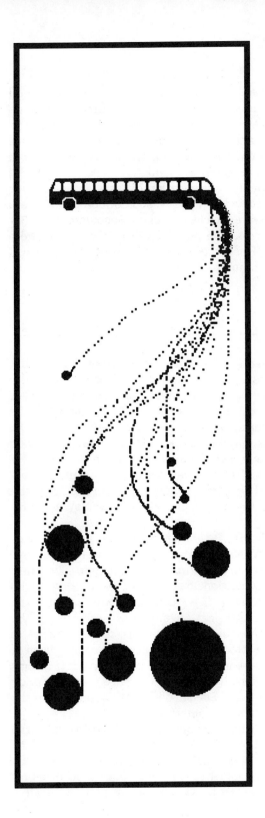

25

Coordinated Resources for Event-Driven Simulations

The three kinds of simulation objects, consumable, nonconsumable, and renewable, coordinate access to quantifiable static resources. Coordination is also needed in order to synchronize the tasks of two or more simulation objects. For example, a car washer only carries out its tasks when a vehicle appears in the car wash; a bank teller gives service to a customer when the customer appears in the bank.

The mechanism for providing synchronization of tasks among two or more SimulationObjects is supported by class ResourceCoordinator. Class ResourceCoordinator is a concrete subclass of class Resource; class Resource was defined in Chapter 24. The purpose of this chapter is to describe the implementation of ResourceCoordinator and to give several examples using this synchronization technique.

The Implementation of Class Resource-Coordinator

A ResourceCoordinator represents a SimulationObject whose tasks must be synchronized with the tasks of another SimulationObject. One of the objects is considered the resource or the "customer"; the other object acquires this resource in order to give it service and can, therefore, be thought of as a "server" or clerk. At any given time, customers may be waiting for a server or servers may be waiting for customers, or no one may be waiting. Only one queue has to be maintained; a variable of a ResourceCoordinator keeps track of whether that queue contains customers, servers, or is empty. The variable pending, inherited from the superclass Resource, refers to the queue; the variable whoIsWaiting refers to the status of the queue.

Three inquiries can be made of a ResourceCoordinator, are there customers waiting? (customersWaiting), are there servers waiting? (serversWaiting), and how many are waiting? (queueLength). The message acquire comes from a SimulationObject acting as a server who wants to acquire a customer to serve. If a customer is waiting, then the SimulationObject can give it service (giveService); otherwise, the SimulationObject is added to the queue which is set to be a queue of servers waiting. The message producedBy: aCustomer comes from a SimulationObject acting as a customer who wants to be served. If a server is waiting, then the SimulationObject can get service (getServiceFor: aCustomerRequest); otherwise, the SimulationObject is added to the queue which is set to be a queue of customers waiting.

In all cases, the queue consists of instances of DelayedEvent. If the queue consists of customers, then the DelayedEvent condition is the SimulationObject waiting to get service. If the queue consists of servers, then the DelayedEvent condition is nil until a customer is acquired, at which point the condition is set to be the customer request (itself a

DelayedEvent that was stored when the customer request was first made). When the DelayedEvent is resumed, the condition is returned to the requestor; in this way, a server gains access to a customer request. Once the synchronized tasks are completed, the server can resume the customer's activities by resuming the request.

class name	ResourceCoordinator
superclass	Resource
instance variable names	whoIsWaiting
instance methods	

accessing

customersWaiting
 ↑whoIsWaiting == #customer
serversWaiting
 ↑whoIsWaiting == #server
queueLength
 ↑pending size

task language
acquire
 | anEvent |
 self customersWaiting ifTrue: [↑self giveService].
 anEvent ← DelayedEvent new.
 whoIsWaiting ← #server.
 self addRequest: anEvent.
 "At this point, the condition of anEvent has been set to the customer request."
 ↑anEvent condition
producedBy: aCustomer
 | anEvent |
 anEvent ← DelayedEvent onCondition: aCustomer.
 self serversWaiting ifTrue: [↑self getServiceFor: anEvent].
 whoIsWaiting ← #customer.
 self addRequest: anEvent

private

getServiceFor: aCustomerRequest
 | aServerRequest |
 aServerRequest ← pending removeFirst.
 pending isEmpty ifTrue: [whoIsWaiting ← #none].
 aServerRequest condition: aCustomerRequest.
 aServerRequest resume.
 ActiveSimulation stopProcess.
 aCustomerRequest pause.
 ActiveSimulation startProcess

giveService
> | aCustomerRequest |
> aCustomerRequest ← pending removeFirst.
> pending isEmpty ifTrue: [whoIsWaiting ← #none].
> ↑aCustomerRequest

setName: aString
> super setName: aString.
> whoIsWaiting ← #none

Notice that when a server gives service to a customer, the customer request is suspended (pause) in which case the simulation process reference count must be decremented until the service task is resumed.

Example: A Car Wash Simulation

The example of a CarWash simulation consists of cars that arrive and ask to be washed or washed and waxed. Washers are available to do the washing and waxing; when there are no cars to service, the Washers are idle. The definition of the simulation CarWash follows. There is one resource coordinator for the various car customers. Cars arrive for washing about one every 20 minutes; cars arrive for washing and waxing about one every 30 minutes. The Washer arrives when the CarWash first starts and stays as long as the simulation proceeds.

class name	CarWash
superclass	Simulation

instance methods

initialization

defineArrivalSchedule
> self scheduleArrivalOf: Wash
>   accordingTo: (Exponential mean: 20).
> self scheduleArrivalOf: WashAndWax
>   accordingTo: (Exponential mean: 30).
> self scheduleArrivalOf: Washer new at: 0.0

defineResources
> self coordinate: 'CarCustomer'

Each kind of car customer can report the service it requires. The Washer tasks depend on the kind of service each car customer wants. First a customer is obtained. Then it is given service (wash, wax, or both) and then the customer's own activities are continued.

class name	Washer
superclass	SimulationObject

instance methods

simulation control

tasks

| carRequest |
[true] whileTrue:
  [carRequest ← self acquireResource: 'CarCustomer'.
  (carRequest condition wants: 'wash')
    ifTrue: [self holdFor: (Uniform from: 12.0 to: 26.0) next].
  (carRequest condition wants: 'wax')
    ifTrue: [self holdFor: (Uniform from: 8.0 to: 12.0) next].
  self resume: carRequest]

The vehicles Wash and WashAndWax are defined next. Each contains an attribute which defines the kinds of service they require. The tasks of these vehicles are simply to ask for service and, after getting the service, to leave.

class name	Wash
superclass	SimulationObject
instance variable names	service
instance methods	

accessing

wants: aService

↑service includes: aService

simulation control

initialize

super initialize.
service ← #('wash')

tasks

self produceResource: 'CarCustomer'

class name	WashAndWax
superclass	Wash
instance methods	

simulation control

initialize

super initialize.
service ← #('wash' 'wax')

WashAndWax is defined as a subclass of Wash since the only difference between the two is setting the service attributes. The following trace was produced by making Wash a subclass of EventMonitor.

0	Wash 1 enters
0	Wash 1 wants to get service as CarCustomer

0	WashAndWax 1 enters
0	WashAndWax 1 wants to get service as CarCustomer
0	Washer 1 enters
0	Washer 1 wants to serve for CarCustomer
0	Washer 1 can serve Wash 1
0	Washer 1 holds for 14.2509
7.95236	WashAndWax 2 enters
7.95236	WashAndWax 2 wants to get service as CarCustomer
8.42388	Wash 2 enters
8.42388	Wash 2 wants to get service as CarCustomer
12.9404	Wash 3 enters
12.9404	Wash 3 wants to get service as CarCustomer
14.2509	Washer 1 resumes Wash 1
14.2509	Washer 1 wants to serve for CarCustomer
14.2509	Washer 1 can serve WashAndWax 1
14.2509	Washer 1 holds for 25.502 (wash part)
14.2509	Wash 1 exits
26.6023	WashAndWax 3 enters
26.6023	WashAndWax 3 wants to get service as CarCustomer
26.8851	Wash 4 enters
26.8851	Wash 4 wants to get service as CarCustomer
29.5632	Wash 5 enters
29.5632	Wash 5 wants to get service as CarCustomer
32.1979	Wash 6 enters
32.1979	Wash 6 wants to get service as CarCustomer
38.7616	Wash 7 enters
38.7616	Wash 7 wants to get service as CarCustomer
39.753	Washer 1 holds for 9.21527 (wax part)
43.5843	Wash 8 enters
43.5843	Wash 8 wants to get service as CarCustomer
48.9683	Washer 1 resumes WashAndWax 1
48.9683	Washer 1 wants to serve for CarCustomer
48.9683	Washer 1 can serve WashAndWax 2
48.9683	Washer 1 holds for 14.2757 (wash part)
48.9683	WashAndWax 1 exits
51.8478	WashAndWax 4 enters
51.8478	WashAndWax 4 wants to get service as CarCustomer
63.244	Washer 1 holds for 11.7717 (wax part)
68.9328	Wash 9 enters
68.9328	Wash 9 wants to get service as CarCustomer
70.6705	WashAndWax 5 enters
70.6705	WashAndWax 5 wants to get service as CarCustomer
75.0157	Washer 1 resumes WashAndWax 2
75.0157	Washer 1 wants to serve for CarCustomer
75.0157	Washer 1 can serve Wash 2
75.0157	Washer 1 holds for 18.6168

75.0157	WashAndWax 2 exits
78.0228	Wash 10 enters
78.0228	Wash 10 wants to get service as CarCustomer
78.2874	WashAndWax 6 enters
78.2874	WashAndWax 6 wants to get service as CarCustomer

At 78.2874, there are 12 customers waiting—8 are Wash and 4 are WashAndWax; 2 Wash and 2 WashAndWax have been served.

From this trace one can see that more Washers are needed to service the demand in this CarWash. It is also possible to collect specific data on the amount of time customers wait (using the duration statistics gathering technique and throughput histogram from the previous chapter) and the percentage of time a worker is busy or idle.

Example: A Ferry Service for a Special Truck

The last example in Chapter 24 was of a ferry service in which a ferry crosses between an island and the mainland carrying cars. The cars were modeled as static resources that a ferry could acquire. The ferry's task was to load as many as six cars, cross over the water, unload the cars it carried, and repeat the process. The example was like one provided in the book on Demos by Graham Birtwistle. In that book, Birtwistle describes the ferry service as coordinating the ferry service with the travels of a truck. A truck goes from the mainland to the island in order to make deliveries, returns to the mainland to get more supplies, and then goes to the island again, etc. The ferry only crosses from one side to the other if it is carrying the truck. This version of the ferry simulation requires a coordination of SimulationObjects representing the ferry and the truck; each has its own tasks to do, but the truck can not do its tasks without the assistance of the ferry and the ferry has no tasks to do in the absence of a truck to carry.

Ferry service starts at 7:00 a.m. (420.0 minutes into the day) and ends at 7:00 p.m. (1140 minutes into the day).

class name	FerrySimulation
superclass	Simulation
instance methods	

initialization

defineArrivalSchedule
    self scheduleArrivalOf: Truck new at: 420.0.
    self scheduleArrivalOf: Ferry new at: 420.0.
defineResources
    self coordinate: 'TruckCrossing'

The Truck and the Ferry are defined in terms of producing and acquiring the resource 'TruckCrossing'.

class name	Ferry
superclass	SimulationObject
instance methods	

simulation control

tasks
```
| truckRequest |
[ActiveSimulation time > 1140.0] whileFalse:
    [truckRequest ← self acquireResource: 'TruckCrossing'.
    self load.
    self crossOver.
    self unload.
    self resume: truckRequest]
```
load
```
self holdFor: 5.0
```
unload
```
self holdFor: 3.0
```
crossOver
```
self holdFor: (Normal mean: 8 deviation: 0.5) next
```

The Truck delivers supplies on the island and picks up supplies on the mainland.

class name	Truck
superclass	SimulationObject
instance methods	

simulation control

tasks
```
[true]
    whileTrue:
        [self produceResource: 'TruckCrossing'.
        self deliverSupplies.
        self produceResource: 'TruckCrossing'.
        self pickUpSupplies]
```
deliverSupplies
```
self holdFor: (Uniform from: 15 to: 30) next
```
pickUpSupplies
```
self holdFor: (Uniform from: 30 to: 45) next
```

There is no check in the definition of Truck or Ferry for a particular side, mainland or island, because we assume that both simulations objects start on the same side (the mainland) and their synchronization for crossing over guarantees that they stay on the same side. A trace of the events for running FerrySimulation is

Start at the mainland

420.0	Ferry enters
420.0	Ferry wants to serve for TruckCrossing
420.0	Truck enters
420.0	Truck wants to get service as TruckCrossing
420.0	Ferry can serve Truck
420.0	Ferry load truck
420.0	Ferry holds for 5.0
425.0	Ferry cross over
425.0	Ferry holds for 7.84272

unload the truck at the island side

432.843	Ferry unload truck
432.843	Ferry holds for 3.0
435.843	Ferry resumes Truck
435.843	Ferry wants to serve for TruckCrossing
435.843	Truck deliver supplies
435.843	Truck holds for 21.1949
457.038	Truck wants to get service as TruckCrossing
457.038	Ferry can serve Truck
457.038	Ferry load truck
457.038	Ferry holds for 5.0

cross over back to the mainland

462.038	Ferry cross over
462.038	Ferry holds for 8.28948
470.327	Ferry unload truck
470.327	Ferry holds for 3.0
473.327	Ferry resumes Truck
473.327	Ferry wants to serve for TruckCrossing
473.327	Truck pick up supplies
473.327	Truck holds for 40.0344
513.361	Truck wants to get service as TruckCrossing
513.361	Ferry can serve Truck
513.361	Ferry load truck
513.361	Ferry holds for 5.0

back to the island

518.361	Ferry cross over
518.361	Ferry holds for 8.05166
526.413	Ferry unload truck
526.413	Ferry holds for 3.0
529.413	Ferry resumes Truck
529.413	Ferry wants to serve for TruckCrossing
529.413	Truck delivers supplies
529.413	Truck holds for 27.1916
556.605	Truck wants to get service as TruckCrossing
556.605	Ferry can serve Truck
556.605	Ferry load truck

556.605	Ferry holds for 5.0
	back to mainland, etc.
561.605	Ferry cross over
561.605	Ferry holds for 7.53188
569.137	Ferry unload truck
569.137	Ferry holds for 3.0
572.136	Ferry resumes Truck
572.136	Ferry wants to serve for TruckCrossing
572.136	Truck pick up supplies
572.136	Truck holds for 36.8832

The ferry tasks do not guarantee that the resting place for the evening is the mainland side. This can be done by monitoring which side the ferry is on and then stopping only after returning to the mainland. Only the definition of Ferry must change since the Truck side is synchronized with it.

class name	Ferry
superclass	SimulationObject
instance variable names	currentSide
instance methods	

simulation control

initialize
```
super initialize.
currentSide ← 'Mainland'
```
tasks
```
| truckRequest finished |
finished ← false
[finished] whileFalse:
    [truckRequest ← self acquireResource: 'TruckCrossing'.
    self load.
    self crossOver.
    self unload.
    self resume: truckRequest.
    finished ←
        ActiveSimulation time > 1140.0 and: [currentSide = 'Mainland']]
```
load
```
self holdFor: 5.0
```
unload
```
self holdFor: 3.0
```
crossOver
```
self holdFor: (Normal mean: 8 deviation: 0.5) next.
currentSide ←
    currentSide = 'Mainland'
        ifTrue: ['Island']
        ifFalse: ['Mainland']
```

Suppose now that cars can arrive at the ferry ramp in order to be carried across. The ferry can carry as many as 4 cars in addition to the truck, but the ferry will not cross over unless there is a truck to carry. Then the definition of the simulation changes by the addition of cars arriving at the mainland or the island; we introduce cars in the same way we did in Chapter 24—as static resources.

class name	FerrySimulation
superclass	Simulation
instance methods	

initialization

defineArrivalSchedule
    self scheduleArrivalOf: Truck new at: 420.0.
    self scheduleArrivalOf: Ferry new at: 420.0.
    self scheduleArrivalOf: MainlandArrival
        accordingTo: (Exponential parameter: 0.15)
        startingAt: 420.0.
    self scheduleArrivalOf: IslandArrival
        accordingTo: (Exponential parameter: 0.15)
        startingAt: 420.0

defineResources
    self coordinate: 'TruckCrossing'.
    self produce: 3 ofResource: 'Mainland'.
    self produce: 0 ofResource: 'Island'

The definitions for MainlandArrival and IslandArrival are the same as those given in Chapter 24.

class name	MainlandArrival
superclass	SimulationObject
instance methods	

simulation control

tasks
    self produce: 1 ofResource: 'Mainland'

class name	IslandArrival
superclass	SimulationObject
instance methods	

simulation control

tasks
    self produce: 1 ofResource: 'Island'

The Ferry now must take into consideration loading and unloading any cars waiting at the ramp of the current side.

class name	Ferry
superclass	SimulationObject
instance variable names	currentSide
	carsOnBoard

instance methods

simulation control

initialize
    super initialize.
    currentSide ← 'Mainland'.
    carsOnBoard ← 0

tasks
    | truckRequest finished |
    finished ← false.
    [finished] whileFalse:
        [truckRequest ← self acquireResource: 'TruckCrossing'.
        self load.
        self crossOver.
        self unload.
        self resume: truckRequest.
        finished ←
            ActiveSimulation time > 1140.0 and: [currentSide = 'Mainland']]

load
    "load the truck first"
    self holdFor: 5.0
    "now load any cars that are waiting on the current side"
    [carsOnBoard < 4
        and: [self inquireFor: 1 ofResource: currentSide]]
                whileTrue:
                    [self acquire: 1 ofResource: currentSide.
                    self holdFor: 0.5.
                    carsOnBoard ← carsOnBoard + 1]

unload
    "unload the cars and the truck"
    self holdFor: (carsOnBoard * 0.5) + 3.0

crossOver
    self holdFor: (Normal mean: 8 deviation: 0.5) next.
    currentSide ←
        currentSide = 'Mainland'
            ifTrue: ['Island']
            ifFalse: ['Mainland']

Example: A Bank

A bank teller only carries out tasks when a customer appears at the teller's window and asks for service. Since the teller's services are dependent on the needs of the customer, the specification of the teller's tasks includes requests for information from the customer.

Suppose the bank assigns two bank tellers to work all day. The bank opens at 9:00 a.m. and closes at 3:00 p.m. Throughout the day, customers arrive every 10 minutes with a standard deviation of 5 minutes. At the noon lunch hour, the number of customers increases dramatically, averaging one every three minutes. Two additional bank tellers are added to handle the increased demand for service. When a regular bank teller is not serving a customer, the teller has desk work to do.

The arrival of customers and regular workers into the bank is scheduled in the response to the message defineArrivalSchedule to BankSimulation. The lunchtime increase is represented by a discrete probability distribution that is a sample space of twenty 3's, representing a total of the 60 minutes during which lunchtime customers appear. Mixed with the normal load of customers, this means that 20 or more customers appear in that busiest hour.

We define simulation objects BankTeller, LunchtimeTeller, BankCustomer, as well as the BankSimulation.

class name	BankSimulation
superclass	Simulation
class variable names	Hour
instance methods	

initialization

defineArrivalSchedule
    self scheduleArrivalOf: BankCustomer
        accordingTo: (Normal mean: 10 deviation: 5)
        startingAt: 9*Hour.
    self scheduleArrivalOf: (BankTeller name: 'first') at: 9*Hour
    self scheduleArrivalOf: (BankTeller name: 'second') at: 9*Hour.
    self scheduleArrivalOf: BankCustomer
        accordingTo:
          (SampleSpaceWithoutReplacement
                data: ((1 to: 20) collect: [:i | 3]))
        startingAt: 12*Hour.
    self schedule: [self hireMoreTellers] at: 12*Hour.
    self schedule: [self finishUp] at: 15*Hour

defineResources
    self coordinate: 'TellerCustomer'

simulation control

hireMoreTellers
    self schedule: [(LunchtimeTeller name: 'first') startUp] after: 0.0.
    self schedule: [(LunchtimeTeller name: 'second') startUp] after: 0.0

The ResourceCoordinator is responsible for matching customers (takers of service) with bank tellers (givers of service). The bank customer's task is simple. After entering the bank, the customer gets the attention of a bank teller and asks for service. After obtaining service, the customer leaves. The amount of time the customer spends in the bank depends on how long the customer must wait for a teller and how long the teller takes giving service.

class name	BankCustomer
superclass	SimulationObject
instance methods	

simulation control

tasks

```
    self produceResource: 'TellerCustomer'
```

The bank teller's tasks depend on the needs of the customer. To keep this example simple, we will assume that a BankTeller does about the same work for each customer, taking between 2 and 15 minutes. Another alternative would be to give each BankCustomer a list of desired services as was done in the car wash example; the BankTeller would enumerate over the set, taking times appropriate to each kind of service. Whenever a customer is not available, the teller does other tasks. These tasks are small and take a short amount of time; however, the teller can not be interrupted. When one of these background desk tasks is completed, the teller checks to see if a customer has arrived and is waiting for service.

class name	BankTeller
superclass	SimulationObject
instance methods	

simulation control

tasks

```
    | customerRequest |
    [true] whileTrue:
        [(self numberOfProvidersOfResource: 'TellerCustomer') > 0
            ifTrue: [self counterWork]
            ifFalse: [self deskWork]]
```

counterWork

```
    | customerRequest |
    customerRequest ← self acquireResource: 'TellerCustomer'.
    self holdFor: (Uniform from: 2 to: 15) next.
    self resume: customerRequest
```

deskWork

```
    self holdFor: (Uniform from: 1 to: 5) next
```

A LunchtimeTeller has to schedule itself to leave the bank after an hour.

This scheduling can be specified in the response to initialize. When it is time to leave, the LunchtimeTeller has to make certain that all its tasks are completed before leaving. Therefore, a signal (getDone) is set to true the first time the message finishUp is sent; this signal is checked each time the teller's counter work completes. The second time finishUp is sent, the signal is true and the teller can exit. The LunchtimeTeller, unlike the regular BankTeller, does not do any desk work when customers are not available.

class name	LunchtimeTeller
superclass	BankTeller
instance variable names	getDone
instance methods	

initialization

initialize
    super initialize.
    getDone ← false.
    ActiveSimulation schedule: [self finishUp] after: 60

simulation control

finishUp
    getDone
        ifTrue: [super finishUp]
        ifFalse: [getDone ← true]
tasks
    [getDone] whileFalse: [self counterWork].
    self finishUp

A partial trace of the events follows.

540	BankCustomer 1 enters
540	BankCustomer 1 wants to get service as TellerCustomer
540	BankTeller first enters
540	BankTeller first wants to serve for TellerCustomer
540	BankTeller first can serve BankCustomer 1
540	BankTeller first holds for 9.33214
540	BankTeller second enters
540	BankTeller second does desk work
540	BankTeller second holds for 3.33594
543.336	BankTeller second does desk work
543.336	BankTeller second holds for 2.96246
546.298	BankTeller second does desk work
546.298	BankTeller second holds for 3.56238
549.332	BankTeller first resumes BankCustomer 1
549.332	BankTeller first does desk work

549.332	BankTeller first holds for 1.83978
549.332	BankCustomer 1 exits
549.819	BankCustomer 2 enters
549.819	BankCustomer 2 wants to get service as TellerCustomer
549.861	BankTeller second wants to serve for TellerCustomer
549.861	BankTeller second can serve BankCustomer 2
549.861	BankTeller second holds for 14.3192
551.172	BankTeller first does desk work
551.172	BankTeller first holds for 4.16901
555.341	BankTeller first does desk work
555.341	BankTeller first holds for 2.60681
557.948	BankTeller first does desk work
557.948	BankTeller first holds for 4.58929
559.063	BankCustomer 3 enters
559.063	BankCustomer 3 wants to get service as TellerCustomer
562.537	BankTeller first wants to serve for TellerCustomer
562.537	BankTeller first can serve BankCustomer 3
562.537	BankTeller first holds for 13.4452
564.18	BankTeller second resumes BankCustomer 2
564.18	BankTeller second does desk work
564.18	BankTeller second holds for 2.63007
564.18	BankCustomer 2 exits
565.721	BankCustomer 4 enters
565.721	BankCustomer 4 wants to get service as TellerCustomer
566.81	BankTeller second wants to serve for TellerCustomer
566.81	BankTeller second can serve BankCustomer 4
566.81	BankTeller second holds for 5.08139
571.891	BankTeller second resumes BankCustomer 4
571.891	BankTeller second does desk work
571.891	BankTeller second holds for 4.69818
571.891	BankCustomer 4 exits
575.982	BankTeller first resumes BankCustomer 3
575.982	BankTeller first does desk work
575.982	BankTeller first holds for 2.10718
575.982	BankCustomer 3 exits
576.59	BankTeller second does desk work
576.59	BankTeller second holds for 4.04327

... and so on until lunch hour when the extra help arrives; at this point, 18 customers have entered; BankTeller first is giving BankCustomer 18 service...

720	BankCustomer 19 enters
720	BankCustomer 19 wants to get service as TellerCustomer
720	LunchtimeTeller first enters
720	LunchtimeTeller first wants to serve for TellerCustomer
720	LunchtimeTeller first can serve BankCustomer 19
720	LunchtimeTeller first holds for 11.9505
720	LunchtimeTeller second enters
720	LunchtimeTeller second wants to serve for TellerCustomer
721.109	BankTeller second does desk work
721.109	BankTeller second holds for 2.09082
721.663	BankTeller first resumes BankCustomer 18
721.663	BankTeller first does desk work
721.663	BankTeller first holds for 3.43219
721.663	BankCustomer 18 exits
722.085	BankCustomer 20 enters
722.085	BankCustomer 20 wants to get service as TellerCustomer
722.085	LunchtimeTeller second can serve BankCustomer 20
722.085	LunchtimeTeller second holds for 9.51483
723	BankCustomer 21 enters
723	BankCustomer 21 wants to get service as TellerCustomer
723.2	BankTeller second wants to serve for TellerCustomer
723.2	BankTeller second can serve BankCustomer 21
723.2	BankTeller second holds for 9.66043
725.095	BankTeller first does desk work
725.095	BankTeller first holds for 4.97528
726	BankCustomer 22 enters
726	BankCustomer 22 wants to get service as TellerCustomer
729	BankCustomer 23 enters
729	BankCustomer 23 wants to get service as TellerCustomer
730.071	BankTeller first wants to serve for TellerCustomer
730.071	BankTeller first can serve BankCustomer 22
730.071	BankTeller first holds for 8.17746
731.6	LunchtimeTeller second resumes BankCustomer 20
731.6	LunchtimeTeller second wants to serve for TellerCustomer
731.6	LunchtimeTeller second can serve BankCustomer 23
731.6	LunchtimeTeller second holds for 6.27971
731.6	BankCustomer 20 exits

731.95	LunchtimeTeller first resumes BankCustomer 19
731.95	LunchtimeTeller first wants to serve for TellerCustomer
731.95	BankCustomer 19 exits
732	BankCustomer 24 enters
732	BankCustomer 24 wants to get service as TellerCustomer
732	LunchtimeTeller first can serve BankCustomer 24
732	LunchtimeTeller first holds for 9.52138

... BankCustomer 40 just left and lunch time is over; there are 3 other customers in the bank; as soon as they finish with their current customers, the LunchtimeTellers will leave...

780.0	BankCustomer 44 enters
780.0	BankCustomer 44 wants to get service as TellerCustomer
780.918	BankTeller first wants to serve for TellerCustomer
780.918	BankTeller first can serve BankCustomer 44
780.918	BankTeller first holds for 13.1566
781.968	BankCustomer 45 enters
781.968	BankCustomer 45 wants to get service as TellerCustomer
784.001	LunchtimeTeller second resumes BankCustomer 43
784.001	LunchtimeTeller second exits
784.001	BankCustomer 43 exits
787.879	LunchtimeTeller first resumes BankCustomer 42
787.879	LunchtimeTeller first exits
787.879	BankCustomer 42 exits
789.189	BankTeller second resumes BankCustomer 41
789.189	BankTeller second wants to serve for TellerCustomer
789.189	BankTeller second can serve BankCustomer 45
789.189	BankTeller second holds for 2.38364
789.189	BankCustomer 41 exits
791.572	BankTeller second resumes BankCustomer 45
791.572	BankTeller second does desk work
791.572	BankTeller second holds for 2.34467
791.572	BankCustomer 45 exits
793.917	BankTeller second does desk work
793.917	BankTeller second holds for 3.19897

and so on...

The data that would be collected here includes the busy/idle percentages of the tellers and the customers' average wait time.

Example: An Information System

Our last example is also in the Birtwistle book and, according to Birtwistle, is a popular example for simulation systems such as GPSS. The example is an information system simulation that describes remote terminals at which users can arrive and make retrieval requests. A customer with a query arrives at one or the other of the terminals and queues, if necessary, to use it. The system scanner rotates from terminal to terminal seeing if a request is waiting and, if so, provides service. Service means that the scanner copies the query to a buffer unit capable of holding three queries simultaneously; if no buffer position is available, the copying process must wait until one becomes available. Once copying to the buffer succeeds, the system processes the query and places the answer in the buffer to return to the terminal without need for the scanner again.

Using the data provided by Birtwistle, we will model a system with six terminals. Customers arrive at terminals with an exponential mean time of 5 minutes. The buffers are modeled as static resources; the terminals are also static resources; while the terminal services are objects whose tasks are coordinated with the tasks of the queries.

class name	InformationSystem
superclass	Simulation
instance methods	

initialization

defineArrivalSchedule
    "Schedule many queries and only one scanner"
    self scheduleArrivalOf: Query
        accordingTo: (Exponential parameter: 5)
        startingAt: 0.0.
    self scheduleArrivalOf: SystemScanner new at: 0.0

defineResources
    self produce: 3 ofResource: 'Buffer'.
    0 to: 5 do:
      [:n |
        self produce: 1 ofResource: 'Terminal', n printString.
        self coordinate: 'TerminalService', n printString]

In the above method, we use string concatenation to form the attribute names of six terminals as static resources and six terminal services as coordinated services; the names are Terminal0,...,Terminal5 and TerminalService0,...,TerminalService5.

The ResourceCoordinators for terminal service for each of the six terminals are being handled differently here than in the bank and car wash simulation examples. At any time, the queues of customers or servers will contain only one or no elements. During the simulation, a Query will enter a queue to wait for terminal service. A SystemScanner moves from coordinator to coordinator, round-robin fashion, to act as the giver of service if a Query is waiting.

The customer, a Query, must first access a terminal resource to get a reply. On accessing one of the six terminals, the customer keys in a request and awaits the reply. It takes between 0.3 and 0.5 minutes (uniformly distributed) to enter a query. Then terminal service is requested. The query now waits for the SystemScanner; when the SystemScanner notices the waiting query, it gives it the needed service. This means that the SystemScanner obtains a buffer slot for the query and copies the request into the buffer. It takes 0.0117 minutes to transfer a query to the buffer. Now the reply can be transferred to the terminal and read, the buffer can be freed up, and the terminal released. It takes between 0.05 and 0.10 (uniformly distributed) to process a query, and 0.0397 minutes to transfer the reply back to the terminal. Customers take between 0.6 and 0.8 minutes (uniformly distributed) to read a reply.

class name	Query
superclass	SimulationObject
instance methods	

scheduling

tasks

```
| terminal terminalNum |
"pick a terminal"
terminalNum ← (SampleSpace data: #('0' '1' '2' '3' '4' '5')) next.
"get a terminal resource"
terminal ← self acquire: 1 ofResource: 'Terminal', terminalNum.
"got the terminal, now enter the query"
self holdFor: (Uniform from: 0.3 to: 0.5) next.
"act as a resource for a terminal service in order to process the query"
self produceResource: 'TerminalService', terminalNum.
"the query is now processed; now read the reply"
self holdFor: (Uniform from: 0.6 to: 0.8) next.
"and release the terminal"
self release: terminal
```

The scanner's job is to rotate from terminal to terminal seeing if a request is pending and, if so, to wait to transfer a query into a buffer and then move on. Scanner rotation takes 0.0027 minutes and the same amount of time to test a terminal.

class name	SystemScanner
superclass	SimulationObject
instance variable names	n

instance methods

simulation control

initialize
>
> super initialize.
>
> n ← 5

tasks
>
> | terminalServiceRequest buffer test |
>
> [true]
>
>> whileTrue:
>>
>>> [n ← (n + 1) \\ 6.
>>> self holdFor: 0.0027.
>>> test ←
>>>> self numberOfProvidersOfResource:
>>>>> 'TerminalService', n printString.
>>>>
>>> self holdFor: 0.0027.
>>> test = 0 ifFalse:
>>>> [terminalServiceRequest ←
>>>>> self acquireResource: ('TerminalService', n printString).
>>>>
>>>> buffer ← self acquire: 1 ofResource: 'Buffer'.
>>>> "copy the request"
>>>> self holdFor: 0.0117.
>>>> "process the query"
>>>> self holdFor: (Uniform from: 0.05 to: 0.10) next.
>>>> "return the reply to the terminal"
>>>> self holdFor: 0.0397.
>>>> "done, release the resources"
>>>> self release: buffer.
>>>> self resume: terminalServiceRequest]]

The SystemScanner is not idle when no Query is waiting; it continually moves from terminal to terminal checking for a Query. This movement stops when a Query is found in order to provide service. When the service is completed, the SystemScanner returns to circulating around, looking for another Query.

Not much happens at first. The first Query enters but it holds for 0.360428 units of time in order to enter its query at Terminal1; meanwhile the SystemScanner moves around the terminals. A second Query enters at 0.0472472 and requests Terminal3; a third enters at 0.130608 and requests Terminal4. At 0.360428, the first Query requests service at Terminal1 which is given a short time later at time 0.367198. Between this time and time 0.478235, the SystemScanner gives service by getting a Buffer, copying the query to the Buffer, processing it, transferring the reply, and then releasing the Buffer and resuming the Query. In the meantime, the second Query requested service, and a fourth Query entered at Terminal4. The SystemScanner then rotates to Terminal3 to give service to the second Query waiting there.

0.0	Query 1 enters
0.0	Query 1 requests 1 of Terminal1
0.0	Query 1 obtained 1 of Terminal1
0.0	Query 1 holds for 0.360428
0.0	SystemScanner enters
0.0	SystemScanner holds for 0.0027
0.0027	SystemScanner holds for 0.0027
0.0054	SystemScanner holds for 0.0027

...etc...

0.0432	SystemScanner holds for 0.0027
0.0459	SystemScanner holds for 0.0027
0.0472472	Query 2 enters
0.0472472	Query 2 requests 1 of Terminal3
0.0472472	Query 2 obtained 1 of Terminal3
0.0472472	Query 2 holds for 0.363611
0.0486	SystemScanner holds for 0.0027
0.0513	SystemScanner holds for 0.0027

...etc...

0.1269	SystemScanner holds for 0.0027
0.1296	SystemScanner holds for 0.0027
0.130608	Query 3 enters
0.130608	Query 3 requests 1 of Terminal4
0.130608	Query 3 obtained 1 of Terminal4
0.130608	Query 3 holds for 0.445785
0.1323	SystemScanner holds for 0.0027
0.135	SystemScanner holds for 0.0027

...etc...

0.356398	SystemScanner holds for 0.0027
0.359098	SystemScanner holds for 0.0027
0.360428	Query 1 wants to get service as TerminalService1
0.361798	SystemScanner holds for 0.0027
0.364498	SystemScanner holds for 0.0027
0.367198	SystemScanner wants to give service as TerminalService1
0.367198	SystemScanner can serve as TerminalService1
0.367198	SystemScanner requests 1 of Buffer
0.367198	SystemScanner obtained 1 of Buffer
0.367198	SystemScanner holds for 0.0117
0.378898	SystemScanner holds for 0.0596374

0.410858	Query 2 wants to get service as TerminalService3
0.41396	Query 4 enters
0.41396	Query 4 requests 1 of Terminal4
0.438535	SystemScanner holds for 0.0397
0.478235	SystemScanner releases 1 of Buffer
0.478235	SystemScanner resumes Query 1
0.478235	SystemScanner holds for 0.0027
0.478235	Query 1 got served as TerminalService1
0.478235	Query 1 holds for 0.740207
0.480935	SystemScanner holds for 0.0027
0.483635	SystemScanner holds for 0.0027
0.486335	SystemScanner holds for 0.0027
0.489035	SystemScanner wants to give service as TerminalService3
0.489035	SystemScanner can serve as TerminalService3
0.489035	SystemScanner requests 1 of Buffer
0.489035	SystemScanner obtained 1 of Buffer
0.489035	SystemScanner holds for 0.0117
0.500735	SystemScanner holds for 0.0515655
0.552301	SystemScanner holds for 0.0397
0.576394	Query 3 wants to get service as TerminalService4
0.592001	SystemScanner releases 1 of Buffer
0.592001	SystemScanner resumes Query 2
0.592001	SystemScanner holds for 0.0027
0.592001	Query 2 got served as TerminalService3
0.592001	Query 2 holds for 0.655313

...etc...

For more examples to try, see the Birtwistle book.

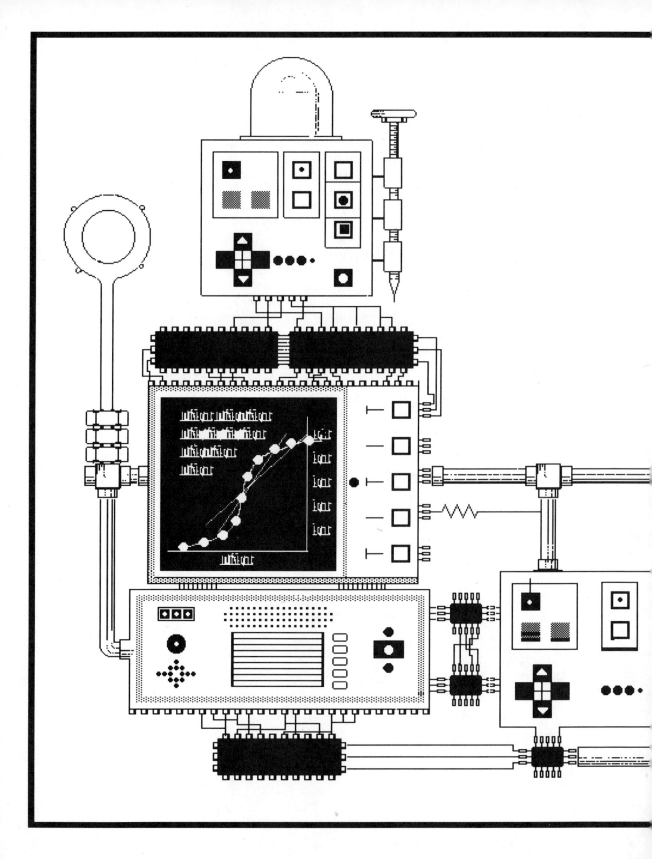

PART FOUR

The previous three parts of the book described the Smalltalk-80 system from the programmer's point of view. The five chapters in this part present the system from the implementer's point of view. Readers who are not interested in how the system is implemented may skip these chapters. Readers interested only in the flavor of the implementation can read Chapter 26 alone. Readers interested in the details of the implementation, including those actually implementing the system, will want to read the following four chapters as well.

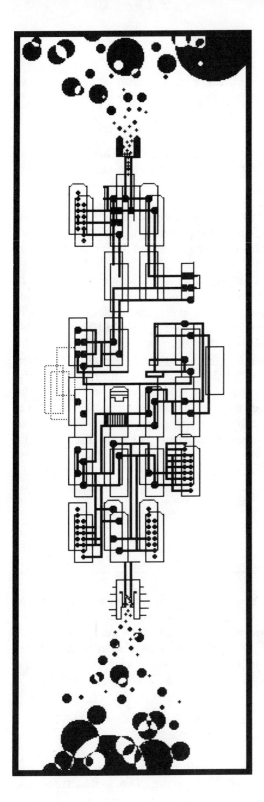

26

The Implementation

Two major components of the Smalltalk-80 system can be distinguished: the *virtual image* and the *virtual machine*.

1. The *virtual image* consists of all of the objects in the system.

2. The *virtual machine* consists of the hardware devices and machine language (or microcode) routines that give dynamics to the objects in the virtual image.

The system implementer's task is to create a virtual machine. A virtual image can then be loaded into the virtual machine and the Smalltalk-80 system becomes the interactive entity described in earlier chapters.

The overview of the Smalltalk-80 implementation given in this chapter is organized in a top-down fashion, starting with the source methods written by programmers. These methods are translated by a *compiler* into sequences of eight-bit instructions called *bytecodes*. The compiler and bytecodes are the subject of this chapter's first section. The bytecodes produced by the compiler are instructions for an *interpreter*, which is described in the second section. Below the interpreter in the implementation is an *object memory* that stores the objects that make up the virtual image. The object memory is described in the third section of this chapter. At the bottom of any implementation is the *hardware*. The fourth and final section of this chapter discusses the hardware required to implement the interpreter and object memory. Chapters 27 - 30 give a detailed specification of the virtual machine's interpreter and object memory.

The Compiler

Source methods written by programmers are represented in the Smalltalk-80 system as instances of String. The Strings contain sequences of characters that conform to the syntax introduced in the first part of this book. For example, the following source method might describe how instances of class Rectangle respond to the unary message center. The center message is used to find the Point equidistant from a Rectangle's four sides.

center
    ↑origin + corner / 2

Source methods are translated by the system's *compiler* into sequences of instructions for a stack-oriented interpreter. The instructions are eight-bit numbers called *bytecodes*. For example, the bytecodes corresponding to the source method shown above are,

0, 1, 176, 119, 185, 124

Since a bytecode's value gives us little indication of its meaning to the interpreter, this chapter will accompany lists of bytecodes with comments about their functions. Any part of a bytecode's comment that depends on the context of the method in which it appears will be parenthesized. The unparenthesized part of the comment describes its general function. For example, the bytecode 0 always instructs the interpreter to push the value of the receiver's first instance variable on its stack. The fact that the variable is named origin depends on the fact that this method is used by Rectangles, so origin is parenthesized. The commented form of the bytecodes for Rectangle center is shown below.

Rectangle center

0	push the value of the receiver's first instance variable (origin) onto the stack
1	push the value of the receiver's second instance variable (corner) onto the stack
176	send a binary message with the selector +
119	push the SmallInteger 2 onto the stack
185	send a binary message with the selector /
124	return the object on top of the stack as the value of the message (center)

The stack mentioned in some of the bytecodes is used for several purposes. In this method, it is used to hold the receiver, arguments, and results of the two messages that are sent. The stack is also used as the source of the result to be returned from the center method. The stack is maintained by the interpreter and will be described in greater detail in the next section. A description of all the types of bytecodes will appear at the end of this section.

A programmer does not interact directly with the compiler. When a new source method is added to a class (Rectangle in this example), the class asks the compiler for an instance of CompiledMethod containing the bytecode translation of the source method. The class provides the compiler with some necessary information not given in the source method, including the names of the receiver's instance variables and the dictionaries containing accessible shared variables (global, class, and pool variables). The compiler translates the source text into a CompiledMethod and the class stores the method in its message dictionary. For example, the CompiledMethod shown above is stored in Rectangle's message dictionary associated with the selector center.

Another example of the bytecodes compiled from a source method illustrates the use of a store bytecode. The message extent: to a Rectangle changes the receiver's width and height to be equal to the x and y coordinates of the argument (a Point). The receiver's upper left corner (origin) is kept the same and the lower right corner (corner) is moved.

extent: newExtent
corner ← origin + newExtent

Rectangle extent:

0	push the value of the receiver's first instance variable (origin) onto the stack
16	push the argument (newExtent) onto the stack
176	send a binary message with the selector +
97	pop the top object off of the stack and store it in the receiver's second instance variable (corner)
120	return the receiver as the value of the message (extent:)

The forms of source methods and compiled bytecodes are different in several respects. The variable names in a source method are converted into instructions to push objects on the stack, the selectors are converted into instructions to send messages, and the uparrow is converted into an instruction to return a result. The order of the corresponding components is also different in a source method and compiled bytecodes. Despite these differences in form, the source method and compiled bytecodes describe the same actions.

Compiled Methods

The compiler creates an instance of CompiledMethod to hold the bytecode translation of a source method. In addition to the bytecodes themselves, a CompiledMethod contains a set of objects called its *literal frame*. The literal frame contains any objects that could not be referred to directly by bytecodes. All of the objects in Rectangle center and Rectangle extent: were referred to directly by bytecodes, so the CompiledMethods for these methods do not need literal frames. As an example of a CompiledMethod with a literal frame, consider the method for Rectangle intersects:. The intersects: message inquires whether one Rectangle (the receiver) overlaps another Rectangle (the argument).

intersects: aRectangle
↑(origin max: aRectangle origin) < (corner min: aRectangle corner)

The four message selectors, max:, origin, min:, and corner are not in the set that can be directly referenced by bytecodes. These selectors are included in the CompiledMethod's literal frame and the send bytecodes refer to the selectors by their position in the literal frame. A CompiledMethod's literal frame will be shown after its bytecodes.

Rectangle intersects:

0	push the value of the receiver's first instance variable (origin) onto the stack
16	push the argument (aRectangle)

209	send a unary message with the selector in the second literal frame location (origin)
224	send a single argument message with the selector in the first literal frame location (max:)
1	push the value of the receiver's second instance variable (corner) onto the stack
16	push the argument (aRectangle) onto the stack
211	send a unary message with the selector in the fourth literal frame location (corner)
226	send a single argument message with the selector in the third literal frame location (min:)
178	send a binary message with the selector <
124	return the object on top of the stack as the value of the message (intersects:)

literal frame
#max:
#origin
#min:
#corner

The categories of objects that can be referred to directly by bytecodes are:

- the receiver and arguments of the invoking message
- the values of the receiver's instance variables
- the values of any temporary variables required by the method
- seven special constants (true, false, nil, −1, 0, 1, and 2)
- 32 special message selectors

The 32 special message selectors are listed below.

+	−	<	>
< =	> =	=	~=
*	/	\	@
bitShift:	\\	bitAnd:	bitOr:
(at:)	(at:put:)	(size)	(next)
(nextPut:)	(atEnd)	==	class
blockCopy:	value	value:	(do:)
(new)	(new:)	(x)	(y)

The selectors in parentheses may be replaced with other selectors by modifying the compiler and recompiling all methods in the system. The other selectors are built into the virtual machine.

Any objects referred to in a CompiledMethod's bytecodes that do not fall into one of the categories above must appear in its literal frame. The objects ordinarily contained in a literal frame are

- shared variables (global, class, and pool)

- most literal constants (numbers, characters, strings, arrays, and symbols)

- most message selectors (those that are not special)

Objects of these three types may be intermixed in the literal frame. If an object in the literal frame is referenced twice in the same method, it need only appear in the literal frame once. The two bytecodes that refer to the object will refer to the same location in the literal frame.

Two types of object that were referred to above, temporary variables and shared variables, have not been used in the example methods. The following example method for Rectangle merge: uses both types. The merge: message is used to find a Rectangle that includes the areas in both the receiver and the argument.

merge: aRectangle
> | minPoint maxPoint |
> minPoint ← origin min: aRectangle origin.
> maxPoint ← corner max: aRectangle corner.
> ↑Rectangle origin: minPoint
> corner: maxPoint

When a CompiledMethod uses temporary variables (maxPoint and minPoint in this example), the number required is specified in the first line of its printed form. When a CompiledMethod uses a shared variable (Rectangle in this example) an instance of Association is included in its literal frame. All CompiledMethods that refer to a particular shared variable's name include the same Association in their literal frames.

Rectangle merge: requires 2 temporary variables

0	push the value of the receiver's first instance variable (origin) onto the stack
16	push the contents of the first temporary frame location (the argument aRectangle) onto the stack
209	send a unary message with the selector in the second literal frame location (origin)
224	send the single argument message with the selector in the first literal frame location (min:)
105	pop the top object off of the stack and store in the second temporary frame location (minPoint)
1	push the value of the receiver's second instance variable (corner) onto the stack
16	push the contents of the first temporary frame location (the argument aRectangle) onto the stack

211	send a unary message with the selector in the fourth literal frame location (corner)
226	send a single argument message with the selector in the third literal frame location (max:)
106	pop the top object off of the stack and store it in the third temporary frame location (maxPoint)
69	push the value of the shared variable in the sixth literal frame location (Rectangle) onto the stack
17	push the contents of the second temporary frame location (minPoint) onto the stack
18	push the contents of the third temporary frame location (maxPoint) onto the stack
244	send the two argument message with the selector in the fifth literal frame location (origin:corner:)
124	return the object on top of the stack as the value of the message (merge:)

literal frame

#min:
#origin
#max:
#corner
#origin:corner:
Association: #Rectangle ➤Rectangle

☐ *Temporary Variables*   Temporary variables are created for a particular execution of a CompiledMethod and cease to exist when the execution is complete. The CompiledMethod indicates to the interpreter how many temporary variables will be required. The arguments of the invoking message and the values of the temporary variables are stored together in the *temporary frame*. The arguments are stored first and the temporary variable values immediately after. They are accessed by the same type of bytecode (whose comments refer to a temporary frame location). Since merge: takes a single argument, its two temporary variables use the second and third locations in the temporary frame. The compiler enforces the fact that the values of the argument names cannot be changed by never issuing a store bytecode referring to the part of the temporary frame inhabited by the arguments.

☐ *Shared Variables*   Shared variables are found in dictionaries.

- *global variables* in a dictionary whose names can appear in any method

- *class variables* in a dictionary whose names can only appear in the methods of a single class and its subclasses

- *pool variables* in a dictionary whose names can appear in the methods of several classes

Shared variables are the individual associations that make up these dictionaries. The system represents associations in general, and shared variables in particular, with instances of Association. When the compiler encounters the name of a shared variable in a source method, the Association with the same name is included in the CompiledMethod's literal frame. The bytecodes that access shared variables indicate the location of an Association in the literal frame. The actual value of the variable is stored in an instance variable of the Association. In the CompiledMethod for Rectangle merge: shown above, class Rectangle is referenced by including the Association from the global dictionary whose name is the symbol #Rectangle and whose value is the class Rectangle.

The Bytecodes

The interpreter understands 256 bytecode instructions that fall into five categories: pushes, stores, sends, returns, and jumps. This section gives a general description of each type of bytecode without going into detail about which bytecode represents which instruction. Chapter 28 describes the exact meaning of each bytecode. Since more than 256 instructions for the interpreter are needed, some of the bytecodes take extensions. An extension is one or two bytes following the bytecode, that further specify the instruction. An extension is not an instruction on its own, it is only a part of an instruction.

□ *Push Bytecodes*   A push bytecode indicates the source of an object to be added to the top of the interpreter's stack. The sources include

- the receiver of the message that invoked the CompiledMethod

- the instance variables of the receiver

- the temporary frame (the arguments of the message and the temporary variables)

- the literal frame of the CompiledMethod

- the top of the stack (i.e., this bytecode duplicates the top of the stack)

Examples of most of the types of push bytecode have been included in the examples. The bytecode that duplicates the top of the stack is used to implement cascaded messages.

Two different types of push bytecode use the literal frame as their source. One is used to push literal constants and the other to push the value of shared variables. Literal constants are stored directly in the literal frame, but the values of shared variables are stored in an Association that is pointed to by the literal frame. The following example method uses one shared variable and one literal constant.

incrementIndex
↑Index ← Index + 4

ExampleClass incrementIndex

64	push the value of the shared variable in the first literal frame location (Index) onto the stack
33	push the constant in the second literal frame location (4) onto the stack
176	send a binary message with the selector +
129,192	store the object on top of the stack in the shared variable in the first literal frame location (Index)
124	return the object on top of the stack as the value of the message (incrementIndex)

literal frame
Association: #Index ⟶ 260
4

☐ *Store Bytecodes* The bytecodes compiled from an assignment expression end with a store bytecode. The bytecodes before the store bytecode compute the new value of a variable and leave it on top of the stack. A store bytecode indicates the variable whose value should be changed. The variables that can be changed are

- the instance variables of the receiver

- temporary variables

- shared variables

Some of the store bytecodes remove the object to be stored from the stack, and others leave the object on top of the stack, after storing it.

☐ *Send Bytecodes* A send bytecode specifies the selector of a message to be sent and how many arguments it should have. The receiver and arguments of the message are taken off the interpreter's stack, the receiver from below the arguments. By the time the bytecode following the send is executed, the message's result will have replaced its receiver and arguments on the top of the stack. The details of sending messages and returning results is the subject of the next sections of this chapter. A set of 32 send bytecodes refer directly to the special selectors listed earlier. The other send bytecodes refer to their selectors in the literal frame.

☐ *Return Bytecodes* When a return bytecode is encountered, the CompiledMethod in which it was found has been completely executed. Therefore a value is returned for the message that invoked that CompiledMethod. The value is usually found on top of the stack. Four special return bytecodes return the message receiver (self), true, false, and nil.

☐ *Jump Bytecodes*   Ordinarily, the interpreter executes the bytecodes sequentially in the order they appear in a CompiledMethod. The jump bytecodes indicate that the next bytecode to execute is not the one following the jump. There are two varieties of jump, *unconditional* and *conditional*. The unconditional jumps transfer control whenever they are encountered. The conditional jumps will only transfer control if the top of the stack is a specified value. Some of the conditional jumps transfer if the top object on the stack is true and others if it is false. The jump bytecodes are used to implement efficient control structures.

The control structures that are so optimized by the compiler are the conditional selection messages to Booleans (ifTrue:, ifFalse:, and ifTrue:ifFalse:), some of the logical operation messages to Booleans (and: and or:), and the conditional repetition messages to blocks (whileTrue: and whileFalse:). The jump bytecodes indicate the next bytecode to be executed relative to the position of the jump. In other words, they tell the interpreter how many bytecodes to skip. The following method for Rectangle includesPoint: uses a conditional jump.

includesPoint: aPoint
> origin < = aPoint
>> ifTrue: [↑aPoint < corner]
>> ifFalse: [↑false]

Rectangle includesPoint:

0	push the value of the receiver's first instance variable (origin) onto the stack
16	push the contents of the first temporary frame location (the argument aPoint) onto the stack
180	send a binary message with the selector < =
155	jump ahead 4 bytecodes if the object on top of the stack is false
16	push the contents of the first temporary frame location (the argument aPoint) onto the stack
1	push the value of the receiver's second instance variable (corner) onto the stack
178	send a binary message with the selector <
124	return the object on top of the stack as the value of the message (includesPoint:)
122	return false as the value of the message (includesPoint:)

The Interpreter

The Smalltalk-80 interpreter executes the bytecode instructions found in CompiledMethods. The interpreter uses five pieces of information and repeatedly performs a three-step cycle.

The State of the Interpreter

1. The CompiledMethod whose bytecodes are being executed.

2. The location of the next bytecode to be executed in that CompiledMethod. This is the interpreter's *instruction pointer*.

3. The receiver and arguments of the message that invoked the CompiledMethod.

4. Any temporary variables needed by the CompiledMethod.

5. A stack.

The execution of most bytecodes involves the interpreter's stack. Push bytecodes tell where to find objects to add to the stack. Store bytecodes tell where to put objects found on the stack. Send bytecodes remove the receiver and arguments of messages from the stack. When the result of a message is computed, it is pushed onto the stack.

The Cycle of the Interpreter

1. Fetch the bytecode from the CompiledMethod indicated by the instruction pointer.

2. Increment the instruction pointer.

3. Perform the function specified by the bytecode.

As an example of the interpreter's function, we will trace its execution of the CompiledMethod for Rectangle center. The state of the interpreter will be displayed after each of its cycles. The instruction pointer will be indicated by an arrow pointing at the next bytecode in the CompiledMethod to be executed.

> ▶ 0   push the value of the receiver's first instance variable (origin) onto the stack

The receiver, arguments, temporary variables, and objects on the stack will be shown as normally printed (their responses to printString). For example, if a message is sent to a Rectangle, the receiver will be shown as

Receiver   100@100 corner: 200@200

At the start of execution, the stack is empty and the instruction pointer indicates the first bytecode in the CompiledMethod. This CompiledMethod does not require temporaries and the invoking message did not have arguments, so these two categories are also empty.

Method for Rectangle center

▶ **0**   push the value of the receiver's first instance variable (origin) onto the stack

  1   push the value of the receiver's second instance variable (corner) onto the stack

176   send a binary message with the selector +

119   push the SmallInteger 2 onto the stack

185   send a binary message with the selector /

124   return the object on top of the stack as the value of the message (center)

Receiver   100@100 corner: 200@200

Arguments

Temporary Variables

Stack

Following one cycle of the interpreter, the instruction pointer has been advanced and the value of the receiver's first instance variable has been copied onto the stack.

Method for Rectangle center

  0   push the value of the receiver's first instance variable (origin) onto the stack

▶ **1**   push the value of the receiver's second instance variable (corner) onto the stack

176   send a binary message with the selector +

119   push the SmallInteger 2 onto the stack

185   send a binary message with the selector /

124   return the object on top of the stack as the value of the message (center)

Receiver   100@100 corner: 200@200

Arguments

Temporary Variables

Stack   100@100

The interpreter's second cycle has an effect similar to the first. The top of the stack is shown toward the bottom of the page. This corresponds to the commonly used convention that memory locations are shown with addresses increasing toward the bottom of the page.

Method for Rectangle center

0	push the value of the receiver's first instance variable (origin) onto the stack
1	push the value of the receiver's second instance variable (corner) onto the stack
▸ 176	send a binary message with the selector +
119	push the SmallInteger 2 onto the stack
185	send a binary message with the selector /
124	return the object on top of the stack as the value of the message (center)

Receiver   100@100 corner: 200@200

Arguments

Temporary Variables

Stack   100@100
                                200@200

The interpreter's third cycle encounters a send bytecode. It removes two objects from the stack and uses them as the receiver and argument of a message with selector + . The procedure for sending the message will not be described in detail here. For the moment, it is only necessary to know that eventually the result of the + message will be pushed onto the stack. Sending messages will be described in later sections.

Method for Rectangle center

0	push the value of the receiver's first instance variable (origin) onto the stack
1	push the value of the receiver's second instance variable (corner) onto the stack
176	send a binary message with the selector +
▸ 119	push the SmallInteger 2 onto the stack
185	send a binary message with the selector /
124	return the object on top of the stack as the value of the message (center)

Receiver   100@100 corner: 200@200

Arguments

Temporary Variables

Stack   300@300

The interpreter's next cycle pushes the constant 2 onto the stack.

Method for Rectangle center

0	push the value of the receiver's first instance variable (origin) onto the stack
1	push the value of the receiver's second instance variable (corner) onto the stack
176	send a binary message with the selector +
119	push the SmallInteger 2 onto the stack
▶ **185**	send a binary message with the selector /
124	return the object on top of the stack as the value of the message (center)

Receiver	100@100 corner: 200@200
Arguments	
Temporary Variables	
Stack	300@300
	2

The interpreter's next cycle sends another message whose result replaces its receiver and arguments on the stack.

Method for Rectangle center

0	push the value of the receiver's first instance variable (origin) onto the stack
1	push the value of the receiver's second instance variable (corner) onto the stack
176	send a binary message with the selector +
119	push the SmallInteger 2 onto the stack
185	send a binary message with the selector /
▶ **124**	return the object on top of the stack as the value of the message (center)

Receiver	100@100 corner: 200@200
Arguments	
Temporary Variables	
Stack	150@150

The final bytecode returns a result to the center message. The result is found on the stack (150@150). It is clear by this point that a return bytecode must involve pushing the result onto another stack. The details of returning a value to a message will be described after the description of sending a message.

Contexts

Push, store, and jump bytecodes require only small changes to the state of the interpreter. Objects may be moved to or from the stack, and the instruction pointer is always changed; but most of the state remains the same. Send and return bytecodes may require much larger changes to the interpreter's state. When a message is sent, all five parts of the interpreter's state may have to be changed in order to execute a different CompiledMethod in response to this new message. The interpreter's old state must be remembered because the bytecodes after the send must be executed after the value of the message is returned.

The interpreter saves its state in objects called *contexts*. There will be many contexts in the system at any one time. The context that represents the current state of the interpreter is called the *active context*. When a send bytecode in the active context's CompiledMethod requires a new CompiledMethod to be executed, the active context becomes *suspended* and a new context is created and made active. The suspended context retains the state associated with the original CompiledMethod until that context becomes active again. A context must remember the context that it suspended so that the suspended context can be resumed when a result is returned. The suspended context is called the new context's *sender*.

The form used to show the interpreter's state in the last section will be used to show contexts as well. The active context will be indicated by the word Active in its top delimiter. Suspended contexts will say Suspended. For example, consider a context representing the execution of the CompiledMethod for Rectangle rightCenter with a receiver of 100@ 100 corner: 200@200. The source method for Rectangle rightCenter is

rightCenter
↑ self right @ self center y

The interpreter's state following execution of the first bytecode is shown below. The sender is some other context in the system.

———————————— **Active** ————————————

Method for Rectangle rightCenter

112	push the receiver (self) onto the stack
▶ **208**	send a unary message with the selector in the first literal (right)
112	push the receiver (self) onto the stack
209	send the unary message with the selector in the second literal (center)
207	send the unary message with the selector y
187	send the unary message with the selector @
124	return the object on top of the stack as the value of the message (rightCenter)

literal frame
#right
#center

Receiver	100@100 corner: 200@200
Arguments	
Temporary Variables	
Stack	100@100 corner: 200@200
Sender ⬇	

After the next bytecode is executed, that context will be suspended. The object pushed by the first bytecode has been removed to be used as the receiver of a new context, which becomes active. The new active context is shown above the suspended context.

-- **Active** --

Method for Rectangle right

▶ 1	push the value of the receiver's second instance variable (corner) onto the stack
206	send a unary message with the selector x
124	return the object on top of the stack as the value of the message (right)

Receiver   100@100 corner: 200@200

Arguments

Temporary Variables

Stack

Sender ⇩

-- **Suspended** --

Method for Rectangle rightCenter

112	push the receiver (self) onto the stack
208	send a unary message with the selector in the first literal (right)
▶ 112	push the receiver (self) onto the stack
209	send the unary message with the selector in the second literal (center)
207	send the unary message with the selector y
187	send the unary message with the selector @
124	return the object on top of the stack as the value of the message (rightCenter)

literal frame
    #right
    #center

Receiver   100@100 corner: 200@200

Arguments

Temporary Variables

Stack

Sender ⇩

The next cycle of the interpreter advances the new context instead of the previous one.

_____ Active _____

Method for Rectangle right

1	push the value of the receiver's second instance variable (corner) onto the stack
▶ 206	send a unary message with the selector x
124	return the object on top of the stack as the value of the message (right)

Receiver   100 @ 100 corner: 200 @ 200

Arguments

Temporary Variables

Stack   200 @ 200

Sender ⇩

_____ Suspended _____

Method for Rectangle rightCenter

112	push the receiver (self) onto the stack
208	send a unary message with the selector in the first literal (right)
▶ 112	push the receiver (self) onto the stack
209	send the unary message with the selector in the second literal (center)
207	send the unary message with the selector y
187	send the unary message with the selector @
124	return the object on top of the stack as the value of the message (rightCenter)

literal frame
 #right
 #center

Receiver   100 @ 100 corner: 200 @ 200

Arguments

Temporary Variables

Stack

Sender ⇩

In the next cycle, another message is sent, perhaps creating another context. Instead of following the response of this new message (x), we will skip to the point that this context returns a value (to right). When the result of x has been returned, the new context looks like this:

―――――――――――――――――――― **Active** ――――――――――――――――――――

Method for Rectangle right

    1   push the value of the receiver's second instance variable (corner) onto the stack

    206   send a unary message with the selector x

▶ **124**   return the object on top of the stack as the value of the message (right)

Receiver   100@100 corner: 200@200

Arguments

Temporary Variables

Stack   200

Sender ⇩

―――――――――――――――――――― **Suspended** ――――――――――――――――――――

Method for Rectangle rightCenter

    112   push the receiver (self) onto the stack

    208   send a unary message with the selector in the first literal (right)

▶ **112**   push the receiver (self) onto the stack

    209   send the unary message with the selector in the second literal (center)

    207   send the unary message with the selector y

    187   send the unary message with the selector @

    124   return the object on top of the stack as the value of the message (rightCenter)

    literal frame

       #right

       #center

Receiver   100@100 corner: 200@200

Arguments

Temporary Variables

Stack

Sender ⇩

The next bytecode returns the value on the top of the active context's stack (200) as the value of the message that created the context (right). The active context's sender becomes the active context again and the returned value is pushed on its stack.

_____ Active _____

Method for Rectangle rightCenter

	112	push the receiver (self) onto the stack
	208	send a unary message with the selector in the first literal (right)
▶	**112**	push the receiver (self) onto the stack
	209	send the unary message with the selector in the second literal (center)
	207	send the unary message with the selector y
	187	send the unary message with the selector @
	124	return the object on top of the stack as the value of the message (rightCenter)

literal frame
#right
#center

Receiver   100@100 corner: 200@200

Arguments

Temporary Variables

Stack   200

Sender ⬇

Block Contexts

The contexts illustrated in the last section are represented in the system by instances of MethodContext. A MethodContext represents the execution of a CompiledMethod in response to a message. There is another type of context in the system, which is represented by instances of BlockContext. A BlockContext represents a block in a source method that is not part of an optimized control structure. The compilation of the optimized control structures was described in the earlier section on jump bytecodes. The bytecodes compiled from a nonoptimized control structure are illustrated by the following hypothetical method in Collection. This method returns a collection of the classes of the receiver's elements.

classes
    ↑self collect: [:element | element class]

Collection classes requires 1 temporary variable

112	push the receiver (self) onto the stack
137	push the active context (thisContext) onto the stack
118	push the SmallInteger 1 onto the stack
200	send a single argument message with the selector blockCopy:
164,4	jump around the next 4 bytes
104	pop the top object off of the stack and store in the first temporary frame location (element)

16	push the contents of the first temporary frame location (element) onto the stack
199	send a unary message with the selector class
125	return the object on top of the stack as the value of the block
224	send a single argument message with the selector in the first literal frame location (collect:)
124	return the object on top of the stack as the value of the message (classes)

literal frame
#collect:

A new BlockContext is created by the blockCopy: message to the active context. The bytecode that pushes the active context was not described along with the rest of the push bytecodes since the function of contexts had not been described at that point. The argument to blockCopy: (1 in this example) indicates the number of block arguments the block requires. The BlockContext shares much of the state of the active context that creates it. The receiver, arguments, temporary variables, CompiledMethod, and sender are all the same. The BlockContext has its own instruction pointer and stack. Upon returning from the blockCopy: message, the newly created BlockContext is on the stack of the active context and the next instruction jumps around the bytecodes that describe the actions of the block. The active context gave the BlockContext an initial instruction pointer pointing to the bytecode after this jump. The compiler always uses an extended (two-byte) jump after a blockCopy: so that the BlockContext's initial instruction pointer is always two more than the active context's instruction pointer when it receives the blockCopy: message.

The method for Collection classes creates a BlockContext, but does not execute its bytecodes. When the collection receives the collect: message, it will repeatedly send value: messages to the BlockContext with the elements of the collection as arguments. A BlockContext responds to value: by becoming the active context, which causes its bytecodes to be executed by the interpreter. Before the BlockContext becomes active, the argument to value: is pushed onto the BlockContext's stack. The first bytecode executed by the BlockContext stores this value in a temporary variable used for the block argument.

A BlockContext can return a value in two ways. After the bytecodes in the block have been executed, the final value on the stack is returned as the value of the message value or value:. The block can also return a value to the message that invoked the CompiledMethod that created the BlockContext. This is done with the regular return bytecodes. The hypothetical method for Collection containsInstanceOf: uses both types of return from a BlockContext.

containsInstanceOf: aClass
self do: [:element | (element isKindOf: aClass) ifTrue: [↑true]].
↑false

Collection containsInstanceOf: requires 1 temporary variable

112	push the receiver (self) onto the stack
137	push the active context (thisContext) onto the stack
118	push the SmallInteger 1 onto the stack
200	send a single argument message with the selector blockCopy:
164,8	jump around the next 8 bytes
105	pop the top object off of the stack and store in the second temporary frame location (element)
17	push the contents of the second temporary frame location (element) onto the stack
16	push the contents of the first temporary frame location (aClass) onto the stack
224	send a single argument message with the selector in the first literal frame location (isKindOf:)
152	pop the top object off of the stack and jump around 1 byte if it is false
121	return true as the value of the message (containsInstanceOf:)
115	push nil onto the stack
125	return the object on top of the stack as the value of the block
203	send the single argument message with the selector do:
135	pop the top object off the stack
122	return false as the value of the message (containsInstanceOf:)

literal frame

    #isKindOf:

Messages

When a send bytecode is encountered, the interpreter finds the CompiledMethod indicated by the message as follows.

1. *Find the message receiver.* The receiver is below the arguments on the stack. The number of arguments is indicated in the send bytecode.

2. *Access a message dictionary.* The original message dictionary is found in the receiver's class.

3. *Look up the message selector in the message dictionary.* The selector is indicated in the send bytecode.

4. *If the selector is found,* the associated CompiledMethod describes the response to the message.

5. *If the selector is not found,* a new message dictionary must be searched (returning to step 3). The new message dictionary will be found in the superclass of the last class whose message dictionary was searched. This cycle may be repeated several times, traveling up the superclass chain.

If the selector is not found in the receiver's class nor in any of its superclasses, an error is reported, and execution of the bytecodes following the send is suspended.

☐ *Superclass Sends* A variation of the send bytecodes called *super-sends* uses a slightly different algorithm to find the CompiledMethod associated with a message. Everything is the same except for the second step, which specifies the original message dictionary to search. When a super-send is encountered, the following second step is substituted.

2. *Access a message dictionary.* The original message dictionary is found in the superclass of the class in which the currently executing CompiledMethod was found.

Super-send bytecodes are used when super is used as the receiver of a message in a source method. The bytecode used to push the receiver will be the same as if self had been used, but a super-send bytecode will be used to describe the selector.

As an example of the use of a super-send, imagine a subclass of Rectangle called ShadedRectangle that adds an instance variable named shade. A Rectangle might respond to the message shade: by producing a new ShadedRectangle. ShadedRectangle provides a new method for the message intersect:, returning a ShadedRectangle instead of a Rectangle. This method must use super to access its own ability to actually compute the intersection.

intersect: aRectangle
   ↑ (super intersect: aRectangle)
    shade: shade

ShadedRectangle intersect:

112	push the receiver (self) onto the stack
16	push the contents of the first temporary frame location (the argument aRectangle) onto the stack
133,33	send to super a single argument message with the selector in the second literal frame location (intersect:)
2	push the value of the receiver's third instance variable (shade) onto the stack
224	send a single argument message with the selector in the first literal frame location (shade:)
124	return the object on top of the stack as the value of the message (intersect:)

literal frame
   #shade:
   #intersect:
   Association: #ShadedRectangle → ShadedRectangle

It is important to note that the initial class searched in response to a super-send will be the superclass of the receiver's class only if the CompiledMethod containing the super-send was originally found the receiver's class. If the CompiledMethod was originally found in a super-class of the receiver's class, the search will start in *that* class's superclass. Since the interpreter's state does not include the class in which it found each CompiledMethod, that information is included in the CompiledMethod itself. Every CompiledMethod that includes a super-send bytecode refers to the class in whose message dictionary it is found. The last entry of the literal frame of those CompiledMethods contains an association referring to the class.

<table>
<tr><td>

Primitive Methods

</td><td>

The interpreter's actions after finding a CompiledMethod depend on whether or not the CompiledMethod indicates that a *primitive method* may be able to respond to the message. If no primitive method is indicated, a new MethodContext is created and made active as described in previous sections. If a primitive method is indicated in the CompiledMethod, the interpreter may be able to respond to the message without actually executing the bytecodes. For example, one of the primitive methods is associated with the + message to instances of SmallInteger.

</td></tr>
</table>

+ **addend**
    < primitive: 1 >
    ↑ super + addend

SmallInteger + associated with primitive #1

112	push the receiver (self) onto the stack
16	push the contents of the first temporary frame location (the argument addend) onto the stack
133,32	send to super a single argument message with the selector in the first literal frame location (+)
124	return the object on top of the stack as the value of the message (+)
literal frame	
#+	

Even if a primitive method is indicated for a CompiledMethod, the interpreter may not be able to respond successfully. For example, the argument of the + message might not be another instance of SmallInteger or the sum might not be representable by a SmallInteger. If the interpreter cannot execute the primitive for some reason, the primitive is said to *fail*. When a primitive fails, the bytecodes in the CompiledMethod are executed as if the primitive method had not been indicated. The method for SmallInteger + indicates that the + method in the superclass (Integer) will be used if the primitive fails.

There are about a hundred primitive methods in the system that perform four types of operation. The exact function of all of the primitives will be described in Chapter 29.

1. Arithmetic

2. Storage management

3. Control

4. Input-output

The Object Memory

The object memory provides the interpreter with an interface to the objects that make up the Smalltalk-80 virtual image. Each object is associated with a unique identifier called its *object pointer*. The object memory and interpreter communicate about objects with object pointers. The size of object pointers determines the maximum number of objects a Smalltalk-80 system can contain. This number is not fixed by anything about the language, but the implementation described in this book uses 16-bit object pointers, allowing 65536 objects to be referenced. Implementation of the Smalltalk-80 system with larger object references will require changing certain parts of the virtual machine specification. It is not within the scope of this book to detail the relevant changes.

The object memory associates each object pointer with a set of other object pointers. Every object pointer is associated with the object pointer of a class. If an object has instance variables, its object pointer is also associated with the object pointers of their values. The individual instance variables are referred to by zero-relative integer indices. The value of an instance variable can be changed, but the class associated with an object cannot be changed. The object memory provides the following five fundamental functions to the interpreter.

1. *Access* the value of an object's *instance variable*. The object pointer of the instance and the index of the instance variable must be supplied. The object pointer of the instance variable's value is returned.

2. *Change* the value of an object's *instance variable*. The object pointer of the instance and the index of the instance variable must be supplied. The object pointer of the new value must also be supplied.

3. *Access* an object's *class*. The object pointer of the instance must be supplied. The object pointer of the instance's class is returned.

4. *Create* a new *object*. The object pointer of the new object's class

and the number of instance variables it should have must be supplied. The object pointer of the new instance is returned.

5. Find the *number of instance variables* an object has. The object's pointer must be supplied. The number of instance variables is returned.

There is no explicit function of the object memory to remove an object no longer being used because these objects are reclaimed automatically. An object is reclaimed when there are no object pointers to it from other objects. This reclamation can be accomplished either by reference counting or garbage collection.

There are two additional features of the object memory that provide efficient representation of numerical information. The first of these sets aside certain object pointers for instances of class SmallInteger. The second allows objects to contain integer values instead of object pointers.

☐ *Representation of Small Integers* The instances of class SmallInteger represent the integers −16384 through 16383. Each of these instances is assigned a unique object pointer. These object pointers all have a 1 in the low-order bit position and the two's complement representation of their value in the high-order 15 bits. An instance of SmallInteger needs no instance storage since both its class and its value can be determined from its object pointer. Two additional functions are provided by the object memory to convert back and forth between SmallInteger object pointers and numerical values.

6. Find the numerical value represented by a SmallInteger. The object pointer of the SmallInteger must be supplied. The two's complement value is returned.

7. Find the SmallInteger representing a numerical value. The two's complement value must be supplied. A SmallInteger object pointer is returned.

This representation for SmallIntegers implies that there can be 32768 instances of the other classes in the system. It also implies that equality (=) and equivalence (==) will be the same for instances of SmallInteger. Integers outside the range −16384 through 16383 are represented by instances of class LargePositiveInteger or LargeNegativeInteger. There may be several instances representing the same value, so equality and equivalence are different.

☐ *Collections of Integer Values* Another special representation is included for objects representing collections of integers. Instead of storing the object pointers of the SmallIntegers representing the contents of the collection, the actual numerical values are stored. The values in these special collections are constrained to be positive. There are two varieties of collection, one limiting its values to be less than 256 and the other limiting its values to be less than 65536. The object memory provides functions analogous to the first five listed in this section, but for objects whose contents are numerical values instead of object pointers.

The distinction between objects that contain object pointers and those that contain integer values is never visible to the Smalltalk-80 programmer. When one of these special numerical collections is accessed by sending it a message, the object pointer of an object representing the value is returned. The nature of these special collections is only evident in that they may refuse to store objects that do not represent integers within the proper range.

The Hardware

The Smalltalk-80 implementation has been described as a virtual machine to avoid unnecessary hardware dependencies. It is naturally assumed that the hardware will include a processor and more than enough memory to store the virtual image and the machine language routines simulating the interpreter and object memory. The current size of the virtual image requires at least a half megabyte of memory.

The size of the processor and the organization of the memory are not actually constrained by the virtual machine specification. Since object pointers are 16 bits, the most convenient arrangement would be a 16-bit processor and a memory of 16-bit words. As with the processor and memory of any system, the faster the better.

The other hardware requirements are imposed by the primitives that the virtual image depends on. These input-output devices and clocks are listed below.

1. A bitmap display. It is most convenient if the bitmap being displayed can be located in the object memory, although this is not absolutely necessary.

2. A pointing device.

3. Three buttons associated with the pointing device. It is most convenient if these are physically located on the device.

4. A keyboard, either decoded ASCII or undecoded ALTO.

5. A disk. The standard Smalltalk-80 virtual image contains only a skeleton disk system that must be tailored to the actual disk used.

6. A millisecond timer.

7. A real time clock with one second resolution.

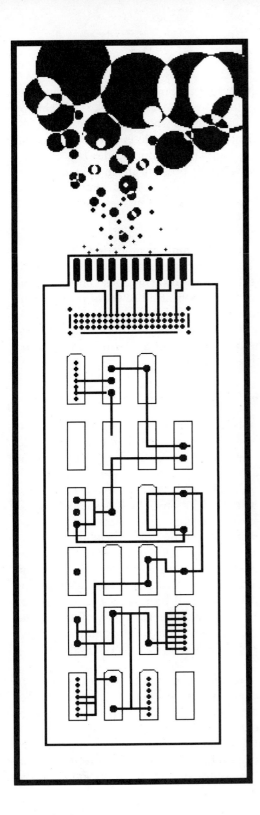

Specification
of the Virtual Machine

Chapter 26 described the function of the Smalltalk virtual machine, which consists of an interpreter and an object memory. This chapter and the next three present a more formal specification of these two parts of the virtual machine. Most implementations of the virtual machine will be written in machine language or microcode. However, for specification purposes, these chapters will present an implementation of the virtual machine in Smalltalk itself. While this is a somewhat circular proposition, every attempt has been made to ensure that no details are hidden as a result.

This chapter consists of three sections. The first describes the conventions and terminology used in the formal specification. It also provides some warnings of possible confusion resulting from the form of this specification. The second section describes the object memory routines used by the interpreter. The implementation of these routines will be described in Chapter 30. The third section describes the three main types of object that the interpreter manipulates, methods, contexts, and classes. Chapter 28 describes the bytecode set and how it is interpreted; Chapter 29 describes the primitive routines.

Form of the Specification

Two class descriptions named Interpreter and ObjectMemory make up the formal specification of the Smalltalk-80 virtual machine. The implementation of Interpreter will be presented in detail in this chapter and the following two; the implementation of ObjectMemory in Chapter 30.

A potential source of confusion in these chapters comes from the two Smalltalk systems involved in the descriptions, the system containing Interpreter and ObjectMemory and the system being interpreted. Interpreter and ObjectMemory have methods and instance variables and they also manipulate methods and instance variables in the system they interpret. To minimize the confusion, we will use a different set of terminology for each system. The methods of Interpreter and ObjectMemory will be called *routines*; the word *method* will be reserved for the methods being interpreted. Similarly, the instance variables of Interpreter and ObjectMemory will be called *registers*; the word *instance variable* will be reserved for the instance variables of objects in the system being interpreted.

The arguments of the routines and the contents of the registers of Interpreter and ObjectMemory will almost always be instances of Integer (SmallIntegers and LargePositiveIntegers). This can also be a source of confusion since there are Integers in the interpreted system. The Integers that are arguments to routines and contents of registers represent object pointers and numerical values of the interpreted system. Some of these will represent the object pointers or values of Integers in the interpreted system.

The interpreter routines in this specification will all be in the form of Smalltalk method definitions. For example

routineName: argumentName
| temporaryVariable |
temporaryVariable ← self anotherRoutine: argumentName.
↑temporaryVariable − 1

The routines in the specification will contain five types of expression.

1. *Calls on other routines of the interpreter.* Since both the invocation and definition of the routine are in Interpreter, they will appear as messages to self.

  - self headerOf: newMethod
  - self storeInstructionPointerValue: value
       inContext: contextPointer

2. *Calls on routines of the object memory.* An Interpreter uses the name memory to refer to its object memory, so these calls will appear as messages to memory.

  - memory fetchClassOf: newMethod
  - memory storePointer: senderIndex
       ofObject: contextPointer
       withValue: activeContext

3. *Arithmetic operations on object pointers and numerical values.* Arithmetic operations will be represented by standard Smalltalk arithmetic expressions, so they will appear as messages to the numbers themselves.

  - receiverValue + argumentValue
  - selectorPointer bitShift: −1

4. *Array accesses.* Certain tables maintained by the interpreter are represented in the formal specification by Arrays. Access to these will appear as at: and at:put: messages to the Arrays.

  - methodCache at: hash
  - semaphoreList at: semaphoreIndex put: semaphorePointer

5. *Conditional control structures.* The control structures of the virtual machine will be represented by standard Smalltalk conditional control structures. Conditional selections will appear as messages to Booleans. Conditional repetitions will appear as messages to blocks.

- index < length ifTrue: [...]
- sizeFlag = 1 ifTrue: [...]
  ifFalse: [...]
- [currentClass ~= NilPointer] whileTrue: [...]

The definition of Interpreter describes the function of the Smalltalk-80 bytecode interpreter; however, the form of a machine language implementation of the interpreter may be very different, particularly in the control structures it uses. The dispatch to the appropriate routine to execute a bytecode is an example of something a machine language interpreter might do differently. To find the right routine to execute, a machine language interpreter would probably do some kind of address arithmetic to calculate where to jump; whereas, as we will see, Interpreter does a series of conditionals and routine calls. In a machine language implementation, the routines that execute each bytecode would simply jump back to the beginning of the bytecode fetch routine when they were finished, instead of returning through the routine call structure.

Another difference between Interpreter and a machine language implementation is the degree of optimization of the code. For the sake of clarity, the routines specified in this chapter have not been optimized. For example, to perform a task, Interpreter may fetch a pointer from the object memory several times in different routines, when a more optimized interpreter might save the value in a register for later use. Many of the routines in the formal specification will not be subroutines in a machine language implementation, but will be written in-line instead.

Object Memory Interface

Chapter 26 gave an informal description of the object memory. Since the routines of Interpreter need to interact with the object memory, we need its formal functional specification. This will be presented as the protocol specification of class ObjectMemory. Chapter 30 will describe one way to implement this protocol specification.

The object memory associates a 16-bit object pointer with

1. the object pointer of a class-describing object and

2. a set of 8- or 16-bit fields that contain object pointers or numerical values.

The interface to the object memory uses zero-relative integer indices to indicate an object's fields. Instances of Integer are used for both object pointers and field indices in the interface between the interpreter and object memory.

The protocol of ObjectMemory contains pairs of messages for fetching and storing object pointers or numerical values in an object's fields.

object pointer access

fetchPointer: fieldIndex ofObject: objectPointer

> Return the object pointer found in the field numbered fieldIndex of the object associated with objectPointer.

storePointer: fieldIndex ofObject: objectPointer withValue: valuePointer

> Store the object pointer valuePointer in the field numbered fieldIndex of the object associated with objectPointer.

word access

fetchWord: fieldIndex ofObject: objectPointer

> Return the 16-bit numerical value found in the field numbered fieldIndex of the object associated with objectPointer.

storeWord: fieldIndex ofObject: objectPointer withValue: valueWord

> Store the 16-bit numerical value valueWord in the field numbered fieldIndex of the object associated with objectPointer.

byte access

fetchByte: byteIndex ofObject: objectPointer

> Return the 8-bit numerical value found in the byte numbered byteIndex of the object associated with objectPointer.

storeByte: byteIndex ofObject: objectPointer withValue: valueByte

> Store the 8-bit numerical value valueByte in the byte numbered byteIndex of the object associated with objectPointer.

Note that fetchPointer:ofObject: and fetchWord:ofObject: will probably be implemented in an identical fashion, since they both load a 16-bit quantity. However, the implementation of storePointer:ofObject: will be different from the implementation of storeWord:ofObject: since it will have to perform reference counting (see Chapter 30) if the object memory keeps dynamic reference counts. We have maintained a separate interface for fetchPointer:ofObject: and fetchWord:ofObject: for the sake of symmetry.

Even though most of the maintenance of reference counts can be done automatically in the storePointer:ofObject:withValue: routine, there are some points at which the interpreter routines must directly manipulate the reference counts. Therefore, the following two routines are included in the object memory interface. If an object memory uses only garbage collection to reclaim unreferenced objects, these routines are no-ops.

reference counting

increaseReferencesTo: objectPointer

> Add one to the reference count of the object whose object pointer is objectPointer.

decreaseReferencesTo: objectPointer

> Subtract one from the reference count of the object whose object pointer is objectPointer.

Since every object contains the object pointer of its class description, that pointer could be considered the contents of one of the object's fields. Unlike other fields, however, an object's class may be fetched, but its value may not be changed. Given the special nature of this pointer, it was decided not to access it in the same way. Therefore, there is a special protocol for fetching an object's class.

class pointer access

fetchClassOf: objectPointer

> Return the object pointer of the class-describing object for the object associated with objectPointer.

The length of an object might also be thought of as the contents of one of its fields. However, it is like the class field in that it may not be changed. There are two messages in the object memory protocol that ask for the number of words in an object and the number of bytes in an object. Note that we have not made a distinction between words and pointers in this case since we assume that they both fit in exactly one field.

length access

fetchWordLengthOf: objectPointer

> Return the number of fields in the object associated with objectPointer.

fetchByteLengthOf: objectPointer

> Return the number of byte fields in the object associated with objectPointer.

Another important service of the object memory is to create new objects. The object memory must be supplied with a class and a length and will respond with a new object pointer. Again, there are three versions for creating objects with pointers, words, or bytes.

object creation

instantiateClass: classPointer withPointers: instanceSize

> Create a new instance of the class whose object pointer is classPointer with instanceSize fields that will contain pointers. Return the object pointer of the new object.

instantiateClass: classPointer withWords: instanceSize

> Create a new instance of the class whose object pointer is classPointer with instanceSize fields that will contain 16-bit numerical values. Return the object pointer of the new object.

instantiateClass: classPointer withBytes: instanceByteSize

> Create a new instance of the class whose object pointer is classPointer with room for instanceByteSize 8-bit numerical values. Return the object pointer of the new object.

Two routines of the object memory allow the instances of a class to be enumerated. These follow an arbitrary ordering of object pointers. Using the numerical order of the pointers themselves is reasonable.

instance enumeration

initialInstanceOf: classPointer	Return the object pointer of the first instance of the class whose object pointer is classPointer in the defined ordering (e.g., the one with the smallest object pointer).
instanceAfter: objectPointer	Return the object pointer of the next instance of the same class as the object whose object pointer is objectPointer in the defined ordering (e.g., the one with the next larger object pointer).

Another routine of the object memory allows the object pointers of two objects to be interchanged.

pointer swapping

swapPointersOf: firstPointer and: secondPointer	Make firstPointer refer to the object whose object pointer was secondPointer and make secondPointer refer to the object whose object pointer was firstPointer.

As described in Chapter 26, integers between -16384 and 16383 are encoded directly as object pointers with a 1 in the low-order bit position and the appropriate 2's complement value stored in the high-order 15 bits. These objects are instances of class SmallInteger. A SmallInteger's value, which would ordinarily be stored in a field, is actually determined from its object pointer. So instead of storing a value into a SmallInteger's field, the interpreter must request the object pointer of a SmallInteger with the desired value (using the integerObjectOf: routine). And instead of fetching the value from a field, it must request the value associated with the object pointer (using the integerValueOf: routine). There are also two routines that determine whether an object pointer refers to a SmallInteger (isIntegerObject:) and whether a value is in the right range to be represented as a SmallInteger (isIntegerValue:). The function of the isIntegerObject: routine can also be performed by requesting the class of the object and seeing if it is SmallInteger.

integer access

integerValueOf: objectPointer	Return the value of the instance of SmallInteger whose pointer is objectPointer.
integerObjectOf: value	Return the object pointer for an instance of SmallInteger whose value is value.
isIntegerObject: objectPointer	Return true if objectPointer is an instance of SmallInteger, false if not.
isIntegerValue: value	Return true if value can be represented as an instance of SmallInteger, false if not.

The interpreter provides two special routines to access fields that contain SmallIntegers. The fetchInteger:ofObject: routine returns the value of a SmallInteger whose pointer is stored in the specified field. The check to make sure that the pointer is for a SmallInteger is made for uses of this routine when non-SmallIntegers can be tolerated. The primitiveFail routine will be described in the section on primitive routines.

fetchInteger: fieldIndex ofObject: objectPointer
```
| integerPointer |
integerPointer ← memory fetchPointer: fieldIndex
                        ofObject: objectPointer.
(memory isIntegerObject: integerPointer)
    ifTrue: [↑memory integerValueOf: integerPointer]
    ifFalse: [↑self primitiveFail]
```

The storeInteger:ofObject:withValue: routine stores the pointer of the SmallInteger with specified value in the specified field.

storeInteger: fieldIndex
  ofObject: objectPointer
  withValue: integerValue
```
| integerPointer |
(memory isIntegerValue: integerValue)
    ifTrue: [integerPointer ← memory integerObjectOf: integerValue.
        memory storePointer: fieldIndex
                ofObject: objectPointer
                withValue: integerPointer]
    ifFalse: [↑self primitiveFail]
```

The interpreter also provides a routine to perform a transfer of several pointers from one object to another. It takes the number of pointers to transfer, and the initial field index and object pointer of the source and destination objects as arguments.

transfer: count
  fromIndex: firstFrom
  ofObject: fromOop
  toIndex: firstTo
  ofObject: toOop
```
| fromIndex toIndex lastFrom oop |
fromIndex ← firstFrom.
lastFrom ← firstFrom + count.
toIndex ← firstTo.
[fromIndex < lastFrom] whileTrue:
    [oop ← memory fetchPointer: fromIndex
                ofObject: fromOop.
    memory storePointer: toIndex
            ofObject: toOop
            withValue: oop.
```

```
memory storePointer: fromIndex
        ofObject: fromOop
        withValue: NilPointer.
fromIndex ← fromIndex + 1.
toIndex ← toIndex + 1]
```

The interpreter also provides routines to extract bit fields from numerical values. These routines refer to the high-order bit with index 0 and the low-order bit with index 15.

extractBits: firstBitIndex to: lastBitIndex of: anInteger
↑(anInteger bitShift: lastBitIndex − 15)
    bitAnd: (2 raisedTo: lastBitIndex − firstBitIndex + 1) − 1
highByteOf: anInteger
↑self extractBits: 0 to: 7
        of: anInteger
lowByteOf: anInteger
↑self extractBits: 8 to: 15
        of: anInteger

Objects Used by the Interpreter

This section describes what might be called the data structures of the interpreter. Although they are objects, and therefore more than data structures, the interpreter treats these objects as data structures. The first two types of object correspond to data structures found in the interpreters for most languages. *Methods* correspond to programs, subroutines, or procedures. *Contexts* correspond to stack frames or activation records. The final structure described in this section, that of *classes*, is not used by the interpreter for most languages but only by the compiler. Classes correspond to aspects of the type declarations of some other languages. Because of the nature of Smalltalk messages, the classes must be used by the interpreter at runtime.

There are many constants included in the formal specification. They mostly represent object pointers of known objects or field indices for certain kinds of objects. Most of the constants will be named and a routine that initializes them will be included as a specification of their value. As an example, the following routines initialize the object pointers known to the interpreter.

initializeSmallIntegers
```
"SmallIntegers"
MinusOnePointer ← 65535.
ZeroPointer ← 1.
OnePointer ← 3.
TwoPointer ← 5
```

initializeGuaranteedPointers

"UndefinedObject and Booleans"
NilPointer ← 2.
FalsePointer ← 4.
TruePointer ← 6.
"Root"
SchedulerAssociationPointer ← 8.
"Classes"
ClassStringPointer ← 14.
ClassArrayPointer ← 16.
ClassMethodContextPointer ← 22.
ClassBlockContextPointer ← 24.
ClassPointPointer ← 26.
ClassLargePositiveIntegerPointer ← 28.
ClassMessagePointer ← 32.
ClassCharacterPointer ← 40.
"Selectors"
DoesNotUnderstandSelector ← 42.
CannotReturnSelector ← 44.
MustBeBooleanSelector ← 52.
"Tables"
SpecialSelectorsPointer ← 48.
CharacterTablePointer ← 50

Compiled Methods

The bytecodes executed by the interpreter are found in instances of CompiledMethod. The bytecodes are stored as 8-bit values, two to a word. In addition to the bytecodes, a CompiledMethod contains some object pointers. The first of these object pointers is called the *method header* and the rest of the object pointers make up the method's *literal frame*. Figure 27.1 shows the structure of a CompiledMethod and the following routine initializes the indices used to access fields of CompiledMethods.

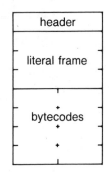

Figure 27.1

initializeMethodIndices
"Class CompiledMethod"
HeaderIndex ← 0.
LiteralStart ← 1

The header is a SmallInteger that encodes certain information about the CompiledMethod.

headerOf: methodPointer
↑memory fetchPointer: HeaderIndex
ofObject: methodPointer

The literal frame contains pointers to objects referred to by the bytecodes. These include the selectors of messages that the method sends, and shared variables and constants to which the method refers.

literal: offset ofMethod: methodPointer
↑memory fetchPointer: offset + LiteralStart
ofObject: methodPointer

Following the header and literals of a method are the bytecodes. Methods are the only objects in the Smalltalk system that store both object pointers (in the header and literal frame) and numerical values (in the bytecodes). The form of the bytecodes will be discussed in the next chapter.

☐ *Method Headers*   Since the method header is a SmallInteger, its value will be encoded in its pointer. The high-order 15 bits of the pointer are available to encode information; the low-order bit must be a one to indicate that the pointer is for a SmallInteger. The header includes four bit fields that encode information about the CompiledMethod. Figure 27.2 shows the bit fields of a header.

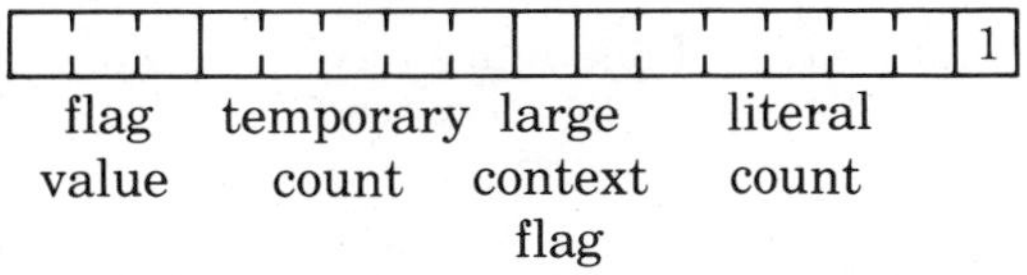

| flag value | temporary count | large context flag | literal count | 1 |

Figure 27.2

The temporary count indicates the number of temporary variables used by the CompiledMethod. This includes the number of arguments.

temporaryCountOf: methodPointer
↑self extractBits: 3 to: 7
of: (self headerOf: methodPointer)

The large context flag indicates which of two sizes of MethodContext are needed. The flag indicates whether the sum of the maximum stack depth and the number of temporary variables needed is greater than twelve. The smaller MethodContexts have room for 12 and the larger have room for 32.

largeContextFlagOf: methodPointer
↑self extractBits: 8 to: 8
    of: (self headerOf: methodPointer)

The literal count indicates the size of the MethodContext's literal frame. This, in turn, indicates where the MethodContext's bytecodes start.

literalCountOf: methodPointer
↑self literalCountOfHeader: (self headerOf: methodPointer)

literalCountOfHeader: headerPointer
↑self extractBits: 9 to: 14
    of: headerPointer

The object pointer count indicates the total number of object pointers in a MethodContext, including the header and literal frame.

objectPointerCountOf: methodPointer
↑(self literalCountOf: methodPointer) + LiteralStart

The following routine returns the byte index of the first bytecode of a CompiledMethod.

initialInstructionPointerOfMethod: methodPointer
↑((self literalCountOf: methodPointer) + LiteralStart) * 2 + 1

The flag value is used to encode the number of arguments a CompiledMethod takes and whether or not it has an associated primitive routine.

flagValueOf: methodPointer
↑self extractBits: 0 to: 2
    of: (self headerOf: methodPointer)

The eight possible flag values have the following meanings:

flag value	meaning
0-4	no primitive and 0 to 4 arguments
5	primitive return of self (0 arguments)
6	primitive return of an instance variable (0 arguments)

7	a header extension contains the number of arguments and a primitive index

Since the majority of CompiledMethods have four or fewer arguments and do not have an associated primitive routine, the flag value is usually simply the number of arguments.

☐ *Special Primitive Methods* Smalltalk methods that *only* return the receiver of the message (self) produce CompiledMethods that have no literals or bytecodes, only a header with a flag value of 5. In similar fashion, Smalltalk methods that only return the value of one of the receiver's instance variables produce CompiledMethods that contain only headers with a flag value of 6. All other methods produce CompiledMethods with bytecodes. When the flag value is 6, the index of the instance variable to return is found in the header in the bit field ordinarily used to indicate the number of temporary variables used by the CompiledMethod. Figure 27.3 shows a CompiledMethod for a Smalltalk method that only returns a receiver instance variable.

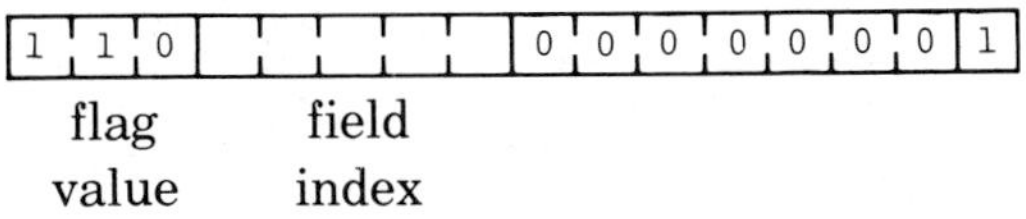

Figure 27.3

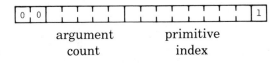

flag field
value index

The following routine returns the index of the field representing the instance variable to be returned in the case that the flag value is 6.

fieldIndexOf: methodPointer
 ↑self extractBits: 3 to: 7
  of: (self headerOf: methodPointer)

☐ *Method Header Extensions* If the flag value is 7, the next to last literal is a header extension, which is another SmallInteger. The header extension includes two bit fields that encode the argument count and primitive index of the CompiledMethod. Figure 27.4 shows the bit fields of a header extension.

Figure 27.4

argument primitive
count index

The following routines are used to access a header extension and its bit fields.

headerExtensionOf: methodPointer
 | literalCount |
 literalCount ← self literalCountOf: methodPointer.
 ↑self literal: literalCount−2
      ofMethod: methodPointer

argumentCountOf: methodPointer
 | flagValue |
 flagValue ← self flagValueOf: methodPointer.
 flagValue < 5
    ifTrue: [↑flagValue].
 flagValue < 7
   ifTrue: [↑0]
   ifFalse: [↑self extractBits: 2 to: 6
              of: (self headerExtensionOf: methodPointer)]

primitiveIndexOf: methodPointer
 | flagValue |
 flagValue ← self flagValueOf: methodPointer.
 flagValue = 7
   ifTrue: [↑self extractBits: 7 to: 14
              of: (self headerExtensionOf: methodPointer)]
   ifFalse: [↑0]

Any CompiledMethod that sends a superclass message (i.e., a message to super) or contains a header extension, will have as its last literal an Association whose value is the class in whose message dictionary the CompiledMethod is found. This is called the *method class* and is accessed by the following routine.

methodClassOf: methodPointer
 | literalCount association |
 literalCount ← self literalCountOf: methodPointer.
 association ← self literal: literalCount−1
               ofMethod: methodPointer.
 ↑memory fetchPointer: ValueIndex
       ofObject: association

An example of a CompiledMethod whose literal frame contained a method class was given in the last chapter. The CompiledMethod for the intersect: message to ShadedRectangle was shown in the section of the last chapter called Messages.

Contexts

The interpreter uses *contexts* to represent the state of its execution of CompiledMethods and blocks. A context can be a MethodContext or a BlockContext. A MethodContext represents the execution of a CompiledMethod that was invoked by a message. Figure 27.5 shows a MethodContext and its CompiledMethod.

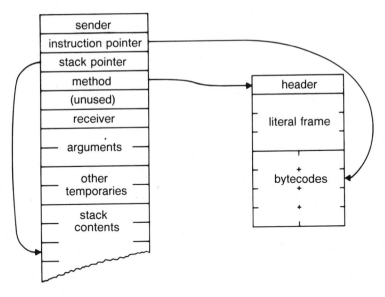

Figure 27.5

A BlockContext represents a block encountered in a CompiledMethod. A BlockContext refers to the MethodContext whose CompiledMethod contained the block it represents. This is called the BlockContext's *home*. Figure 27.6 shows a BlockContext and its home.

The indices used to access the fields of contexts are initialized by the following routine.

initializeContextIndices

```
"Class MethodContext"
SenderIndex ← 0.
InstructionPointerIndex ← 1.
StackPointerIndex ← 2.
MethodIndex ← 3.
ReceiverIndex ← 5.
TempFrameStart ← 6.
"Class BlockContext"
CallerIndex ← 0.
BlockArgumentCountIndex ← 3.
InitialIPIndex ← 4.
HomeIndex ← 5
```

Both kinds of context have six fixed fields corresponding to six named instance variables. These fixed fields are followed by some indexable fields. The indexable fields are used to store the temporary frame (arguments and temporary variables) followed by the contents of the evaluation stack. The following routines are used to fetch and store the instruction pointer and stack pointer stored in a context.

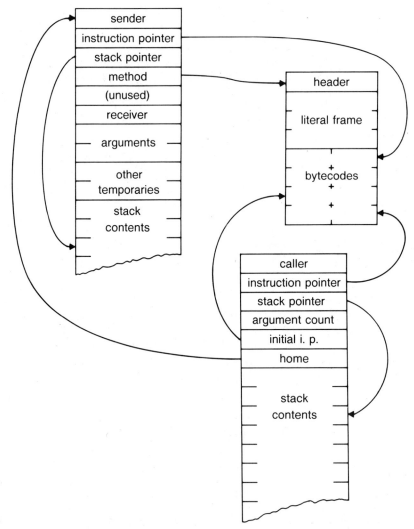

Figure 27.6

instructionPointerOfContext: contextPointer
    ↑self fetchInteger: InstructionPointerIndex
        ofObject: contextPointer

storeInstructionPointerValue: value inContext: contextPointer
    self storeInteger: InstructionPointerIndex
        ofObject: contextPointer
        withValue: value

stackPointerOfContext: contextPointer
    ↑self fetchInteger: StackPointerIndex
        ofObject: contextPointer

storeStackPointerValue: value inContext: contextPointer

    self storeInteger: StackPointerIndex
        ofObject: contextPointer
        withValue: value

A BlockContext stores the number of block arguments it expects in one of its fields.

argumentCountOfBlock: blockPointer

    ↑self fetchInteger: BlockArgumentCountIndex
        ofObject: blockPointer

The context that represents the CompiledMethod or block currently being executed is called the *active context*. The interpreter caches in its registers the contents of the parts of the active context it uses most often. These registers are:

Context-related Registers of the Interpreter

activeContext	This is the active context itself. It is either a MethodContext or a BlockContext.
homeContext	If the active context is a MethodContext, the home context is the same context. If the active context is a BlockContext, the home context is the contents of the home field of the active context. This will always be a MethodContext.
method	This is the CompiledMethod that contains the bytecodes the interpreter is executing.
receiver	This is the object that received the message that invoked the home context's method.
instructionPointer	This is the byte index of the next bytecode of the method to be executed.
stackPointer	This is the index of the field of the active context containing the top of the stack.

Whenever the active context changes (when a new CompiledMethod is invoked, when a CompiledMethod returns or when a process switch occurs), all of these registers must be updated using the following routine.

fetchContextRegisters

    (self isBlockContext: activeContext)
        ifTrue: [homeContext ← memory fetchPointer: HomeIndex
                             ofObject: activeContext]
        ifFalse: [homeContext ← activeContext].
    receiver ← memory fetchPointer: ReceiverIndex
                ofObject: homeContext.
    method ← memory fetchPointer: MethodIndex
               ofObject: homeContext.
    instructionPointer ← (self instructionPointerOfContext: activeContext) − 1.
    stackPointer ←
        (self stackPointerOfContext: activeContext) + TempFrameStart − 1

Note that the receiver and method are fetched from the homeContext and the instructionPointer and stackPointer are fetched from the activeContext. The interpreter tells the difference between MethodContexts and BlockContexts based on the fact that MethodContexts store the method pointer (an object pointer) and BlockContexts store the number of block arguments (an integer pointer) in the same field. If this location contains an integer pointer, the context is a BlockContext; otherwise, it is a MethodContext. The distinction could be made on the basis of the class of the context, but special provision would have to be made for subclasses of MethodContext and BlockContext.

isBlockContext: contextPointer

```
| methodOrArguments |
methodOrArguments ← memory fetchPointer: MethodIndex
                            ofObject: contextPointer.
↑memory isIntegerObject: methodOrArguments
```

Before a new context becomes the active context, the values of the instruction pointer and stack pointer must be stored into the active context with the following routine.

storeContextRegisters

```
self storeInstructionPointerValue: instructionPointer + 1
    inContext: activeContext.
self storeStackPointerValue: stackPointer − TempFrameStart + 1
    inContext: activeContext
```

The values of the other cached registers do not change so they do not need to be stored back into the context. The instruction pointer stored in a context is a one-relative index to the method's fields because subscripting in Smalltalk (i.e., the at: message) takes one-relative indices. The memory, however, uses zero-relative indices; so the fetchContextRegisters routine subtracts one to convert it to a memory index and the storeContextRegisters routine adds the one back in. The stack pointer stored in a context tells how far the top of the evaluation stack is beyond the fixed fields of the context (i.e., how far after the start of the temporary frame) because subscripting in Smalltalk takes fixed fields into account and fetches from the indexable fields after them. The memory, however, wants an index relative to the start of the object; so the fetchContextRegisters routine adds in the offset of the start of the temporary frame (a constant) and the storeContextRegisters routine subtracts the offset.

The following routines perform various operations on the stack of the active context.

push: object
    stackPointer ← stackPointer + 1.
    memory storePointer: stackPointer
        ofObject: activeContext
        withValue: object

popStack
    | stackTop |
    stackTop ← memory fetchPointer: stackPointer
                ofObject: activeContext.
    stackPointer ← stackPointer − 1.
    ↑stackTop

stackTop
    ↑memory fetchPointer: stackPointer
        ofObject: activeContext

stackValue: offset
    ↑memory fetchPointer: stackPointer-offset
        ofObject: activeContext

pop: number
    stackPointer ← stackPointer − number

unPop: number
    stackPointer ← stackPointer + number

The active context register must count as a reference to the part of the object memory that deallocates unreferenced objects. If the object memory maintains dynamic reference counts, the routine to change active contexts must perform the appropriate reference counting.

newActiveContext: aContext
    self storeContextRegisters.
    memory decreaseReferencesTo: activeContext.
    activeContext ← aContext.
    memory increaseReferencesTo: activeContext.
    self fetchContextRegisters

The following routines fetch fields of contexts needed by the interpreter infrequently enough that they are not cached in registers. The sender is the context to be returned to when a CompiledMethod returns a value (either because of a "↑" or at the end of the method). Since an explicit return from within a block should return from the CompiledMethod enclosing the block, the sender is fetched from the home context.

sender
    ↑memory fetchPointer: SenderIndex
        ofObject: homeContext

The caller is the context to be returned to when a BlockContext returns a value (at the end of the block).

caller
>   ↑memory fetchPointer: SenderIndex
>   ofObject: activeContext

Since temporaries referenced in a block are the same as those referenced in the CompiledMethod enclosing the block, the temporaries are fetched from the home context.

temporary: offset
>   ↑memory fetchPointer: offset + TempFrameStart
>   ofObject: homeContext

The following routine provides convenient access to the literals of the currently executing CompiledMethod.

literal: offset
>   ↑self literal: offset
>   ofMethod: method

Classes

The interpreter finds the appropriate CompiledMethod to execute in response to a message by searching a *message dictionary*. The message dictionary is found in the *class* of the message receiver or one of the *superclasses* of that class. The structure of a class and its associated message dictionary is shown in Figure 27.7. In addition to the message dictionary and superclass the interpreter uses the class's *instance specification* to determine its instances' memory requirements. The other fields of a class are used only by Smalltalk methods and ignored by the interpreter. The following routine initializes the indices used to access fields of classes and their message dictionaries.

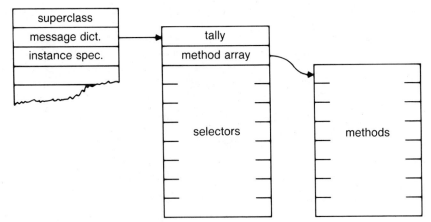

Figure 27.7

initializeClassIndices
"Class Class"
SuperclassIndex ← 0.
MessageDictionaryIndex ← 1.
InstanceSpecificationIndex ← 2.
"Fields of a message dictionary"
MethodArrayIndex ← 1.
SelectorStart ← 2

The interpreter uses several registers to cache the state of the message lookup process.

Class-related Registers of the Interpreter

messageSelector	This is the selector of the message being sent. It is always a Symbol.
argumentCount	This is the number of arguments in the message currently being sent. It indicates where the message receiver can be found on the stack since it is below the arguments.
newMethod	This is the method associated with the messageSelector.
primitiveIndex	This is the index of a primitive routine associated with newMethod if one exists.

A message dictionary is an IdentityDictionary. IdentityDictionary is a subclass of Set with an additional Array containing values associated with the contents of the Set. The message selectors are stored in the indexed instance variables inherited from Set. The CompiledMethods are stored in an Array added by IdentityDictionary. A CompiledMethod has the same index in that Array that its selector has in the indexable variables of the dictionary object itself. The index at which to store the selector and CompiledMethod are computed by a hash function.

The selectors are instances of Symbol, so they may be tested for equality by testing their object pointers for equality. Since the object pointers of Symbols determine equality, the hash function may be a function of the object pointer. Since object pointers are allocated quasi-randomly, the object pointer itself is a reasonable hash function. The pointer shifted right one bit will produce a better hash function, since all object pointers other than SmallIntegers are even.

hash: objectPointer
↑objectPointer bitShift: −1

The message selector lookup assumes that methods have been put into the dictionary using the same hashing function. The hashing algorithm reduces the original hash function modulo the number of indexable locations in the dictionary. This gives an index in the dictionary. To make the computation of the modulo reduction simple, message dictionaries have an exact power of two fields. Therefore the modulo calculation can be performed by masking off an appropriate number of bits. If the selector is not found at the initial hash location, successive fields are examined until the selector is found or a nil is encountered. If a nil is encountered in the search, the selector is not in the dictionary. If the end of the dictionary is encountered while searching, the search wraps around and continues with the first field.

The following routine looks in a dictionary for a CompiledMethod associated with the Symbol in the messageSelector register. If it finds the Symbol, it stores the associated CompiledMethod's pointer into the newMethod register, its primitive index into the primitiveIndex register and returns true. If the Symbol is not found in the dictionary, the routine returns false. Since finding a nil or an appropriate Symbol are the only exit conditions of the loop, the routine must check for a full dictionary (i.e., no nils). It does this by keeping track of whether it has wrapped around. If the search wraps around twice, the selector is not in the dictionary.

lookupMethodInDictionary: dictionary

```
| length index mask wrapAround nextSelector methodArray |
length ← memory fetchWordLengthOf: dictionary.
mask ← length−SelectorStart−1.
index ← (mask bitAnd: (self hash: messageSelector)) + SelectorStart.
wrapAround ← false.
[true] whileTrue:
    [nextSelector ← memory fetchPointer: index
                        ofObject: dictionary.
    nextSelector=NilPointer ifTrue: [↑false].
    nextSelector=messageSelector
        ifTrue: [methodArray ← memory fetchPointer: MethodArrayIndex
                            ofObject: dictionary.
                newMethod ← memory fetchPointer: index−SelectorStart
                            ofObject: methodArray.
                primitiveIndex ← self primitiveIndexOf: newMethod.
                ↑true].
    index ← index + 1.
    index=length
        ifTrue: [wrapAround ifTrue: [↑false].
                wrapAround ← true.
                index ← SelectorStart]]
```

This routine is used in the following routine to find the method a class associates with a selector. If the selector is not found in the initial class's dictionary, it is looked up in the next class on the superclass chain. The search continues up the superclass chain until a method is found or the superclass chain is exhausted.

lookupMethodInClass: class

```
| currentClass dictionary |
currentClass ← class.
[currentClass~=NilPointer] whileTrue:
    [dictionary ← memory fetchPointer: MessageDictionaryIndex
                            ofObject: currentClass.
    (self lookupMethodInDictionary: dictionary)
        ifTrue: [↑true].
    currentClass ← self superclassOf: currentClass].
messageSelector = DoesNotUnderstandSelector
    ifTrue: [self error: 'Recursive not understood error encountered'].
self createActualMessage.
messageSelector ← DoesNotUnderstandSelector.
↑self lookupMethodInClass: class
```

superclassOf: classPointer

```
↑memory fetchPointer: SuperclassIndex
            ofObject: classPointer
```

The interpreter needs to do something out of the ordinary when a message is sent to an object whose class and superclasses do not contain a CompiledMethod associated with the message selector. In keeping with the philosophy of Smalltalk, the interpreter sends a message. A CompiledMethod for this message is guaranteed to be found. The interpreter packages up the original message in an instance of class Message and then looks for a CompiledMethod associated with the selector doesNotUnderstand:. The Message becomes the single argument for the doesNotUnderstand: message. The doesNotUnderstand: message is defined in Object with a CompiledMethod that notifies the user. This CompiledMethod can be overridden in a user-defined class to do something else. Because of this, the lookupMethodInClass: routine will always complete by storing a pointer to a CompiledMethod in the newMethod register.

createActualMessage

```
| argumentArray message |
argumentArray ← memory instantiateClass: ClassArrayPointer
                        withPointers: argumentCount.
message ← memory instantiateClass: ClassMessagePointer
                    withPointers: self messageSize.
memory storePointer: MessageSelectorIndex
        ofObject: message
        withValue: messageSelector.
memory storePointer: MessageArgumentsIndex
        ofObject: message
        withValue: argumentArray.
```

```
self transfer: argumentCount
    fromField: stackPointer − (argumentCount − 1)
    ofObject: activeContext
    toField: 0
    ofObject: argumentArray.
self pop: argumentCount.
self push: message.
argumentCount ← 1
```

The following routine initializes the indices used to access fields of a Message.

initializeMessageIndices
```
    MessageSelectorIndex ← 0.
    MessageArgumentsIndex ← 1.
    MessageSize ← 2
```

The instance specification field of a class contains a SmallInteger pointer that encodes the following four pieces of information:

1. Whether the instances' fields contain object pointers or numerical values

2. Whether the instances' fields are addressed in word or byte quantities

3. Whether the instances have indexable fields beyond their fixed fields

4. The number of fixed fields the instances have

Figure 27.8 shows how this information is encoded in the instance specification.

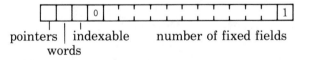

Figure 27.8

The four pieces of information are not independent. If the instances' fields contain object pointers, they will be addressed in word quantities. If the instances' fields contain numerical values, they will have indexable fields and no fixed fields.

instanceSpecificationOf: classPointer
```
    ↑memory fetchPointer: InstanceSpecificationIndex
        ofObject: classPointer
```

isPointers: classPointer

    | pointersFlag |

    pointersFlag ← self extractBits: 0 to: 0

                      of: (self instanceSpecificationOf: classPointer).

    ↑pointersFlag = 1

isWords: classPointer

    | wordsFlag |

    wordsFlag ← self extractBits: 1 to: 1

                  of: (self instanceSpecificationOf: classPointer).

    ↑wordsFlag = 1

isIndexable: classPointer

    | indexableFlag |

    indexableFlag ← self extractBits: 2 to: 2

                    of: (self instanceSpecificationOf: classPointer).

    ↑indexableFlag = 1

fixedFieldsOf: classPointer

    ↑self extractBits: 4 to: 14

        of: (self instanceSpecificationOf: classPointer)

Note: the instance specification of CompiledMethod does not accurately reflect the structure of its instances since CompiledMethods are not homogeneous. The instance specification says that the instances do not contain pointers and are addressed by bytes. This is true of the bytecode section of a CompiledMethod only. The storage manager needs to know that CompiledMethods are special and actually contain some pointers. For all other classes, the instance specification is accurate.

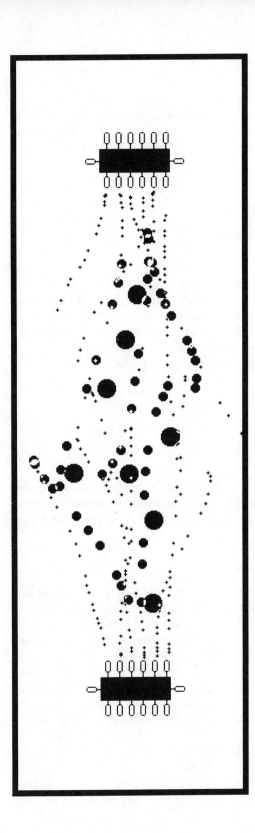

28

Formal Specification
of the Interpreter

Stack Bytecodes

Jump Bytecodes

Send Bytecodes

Return Bytecodes

The main loop of the Smalltalk-80 interpreter fetches bytecodes from a CompiledMethod sequentially and dispatches to routines that perform the operations the bytecodes indicate. The fetchByte routine fetches the byte indicated by the active context's instruction pointer and increments the instruction pointer.

fetchByte
```
| byte |
byte ← memory fetchByte: instructionPointer
              ofObject: method.
instructionPointer ← instructionPointer + 1.
↑byte
```

Since process switches are only allowed between bytecodes, the first action in the interpreter's main loop is to call a routine that switches processes if necessary. The checkProcessSwitch routine will be described with the process scheduling primitive routines in the next chapter. After checking for a process switch, a bytecode is fetched (perhaps from a new process), and a dispatch is made to the appropriate routine.

interpret
```
[true] whileTrue: [self cycle]
```
cycle
```
self checkProcessSwitch.
currentBytecode ← self fetchByte.
self dispatchOnThisBytecode
```

The table on page 595 lists the Smalltalk-80 bytecodes. The bytecodes are listed in ranges that have similar function. For example, the first range includes the bytecodes from 0 through 15 and its entry is shown below.

0-15   0000 i i i i   Push Receiver Variable # i i i i

Each range of bytecodes is listed with a bit pattern and a comment about the function of the bytecodes. The bit pattern shows the binary representation of the bytecodes in the range. 0s and 1s are used in bit locations that have the same value for all bytecodes in the range. Since all numbers from 0 through 15 have four zeros in their high order bits, these bits are shown as 0000. Lower case letters are used in bit locations whose values vary within the range. The value of each letter can be either 0 or 1. The letters used in the pattern can be included in the comment to refer to the value of those bits in a specific bytecode in the range. The comment for the first range of bytecodes indicates that the low-order four bits of the bytecode specify the index of one of the receiver's variables to be pushed on the stack.

The variable bits in a bit pattern are also sometimes used as a zero-relative index into a list included in the comment. For example, the entry

120-123   011110 i i   Return (receiver, true, false, nil) [i i] From Message

specifies that the bytecode 120 returns the receiver, bytecode 121 returns true, bytecode 122 returns false and bytecode 123 returns nil.

The entries for bytecodes that take extensions will include more than one bit pattern. For example,

131   10000011   Send Literal Selector #k k k k k With j j j Arguments
    j j j k k k k k

There are four basic types of bytecode.

- *stack bytecodes* move object pointers between the object memory and the active context's evaluation stack. These include both the push bytecodes and store bytecodes described in Chapter 26.

- *jump bytecodes* change the instruction pointer of the active context.

- *send bytecodes* invoke CompiledMethods or primitive routines.

- *return bytecodes* terminate the execution of CompiledMethods.

Not all of the bytecodes of one type are contiguous, so the main dispatch has seven branches each of which calls one of four routines (stackBytecode, jumpBytecode, sendBytecode, or returnBytecode). These four routines will be described in the next four subsections.

dispatchOnThisBytecode
    (currentBytecode between: 0 and: 119) ifTrue: [↑self stackBytecode].
    (currentBytecode between: 120 and: 127) ifTrue: [↑self returnBytecode].
    (currentBytecode between: 128 and: 130) ifTrue: [↑self stackBytecode].
    (currentBytecode between: 131 and: 134) ifTrue: [↑self sendBytecode].
    (currentBytecode between: 135 and: 137) ifTrue: [↑self stackBytecode].
    (currentBytecode between: 144 and: 175) ifTrue: [↑self jumpBytecode].
    (currentBytecode between: 176 and: 255) ifTrue: [↑self sendBytecode]

The bytecodes 176-191 refer to Arithmetic Messages. These are

    $+$, $-$, $<$, $>$, $<=$, $>=$, $=$, $\sim=$, $*$, $/$, $\backslash\backslash$, @, bitShift:, //, bitAnd:, bitOr:

The bytecodes 192-207 refer to Special Messages. These are

    at:*, at:put:*, size*, next*, nextPut:*, atEnd*, $==$, class, blockCopy:, value, value:, do:*, new*, new:*, x*, y*

Selectors indicated with an asterisk (*) can be changed by compiler modification.

The Smalltalk-80 Bytecodes

Range	Bits	Function
0-15	0 0 0 0 i i i i	Push Receiver Variable #i i i i
16-31	0 0 0 1 i i i i	Push Temporary Location #i i i i
32-63	0 0 1 i i i i i	Push Literal Constant #i i i i i
64-95	0 1 0 i i i i i	Push Literal Variable #i i i i i
96-103	0 1 1 0 0 i i i	Pop and Store Receiver Variable #i i i
104-111	0 1 1 0 1 i i i	Pop and Store Temporary Location #i i i
112-119	0 1 1 1 0 i i i	Push (receiver, true, false, nil, -1, 0, 1, 2) [i i i]
120-123	0 1 1 1 1 0 i i	Return (receiver, true, false, nil) [i i] From Message
124-125	0 1 1 1 1 1 0 i	Return Stack Top From (Message, Block) [i]
126-127	0 1 1 1 1 1 1 i	unused
128	10000000 jjkkkkkk	Push (Receiver Variable, Temporary Location, Literal Constant, Literal Variable) [jj] #k k k k k k
129	10000001 jjkkkkkk	Store (Receiver Variable, Temporary Location, Illegal, Literal Variable) [jj] #k k k k k k
130	10000010 jjkkkkkk	Pop and Store (Receiver Variable, Temporary Location, Illegal, Literal Variable) [jj] #k k k k k k
131	10000011 jjjkkkkk	Send Literal Selector #k k k k k With jjj Arguments
132	10000100 j j j j j j j j kkkkkkkk	Send Literal Selector #k k k k k k k k With jjjjjjjj Arguments
133	10000101 jjjkkkkk	Send Literal Selector #kkkkk To Superclass With jjj Arguments
134	10000110 j j j j j j j j kkkkkkkk	Send Literal Selector #kkkkkkkk To Superclass With jjjjjjjj Arguments
135	10000111	Pop Stack Top
136	10001000	Duplicate Stack Top
137	10001001	Push Active Context
138-143		unused
144-151	1 0 0 1 0 i i i	Jump i i i+1 (i.e., 1 through 8)
152-159	1 0 0 1 1 i i i	Pop and Jump On False i i i+1 (i.e., 1 through 8)
160-167	1 0 1 0 0 i i i j j j j j j j j	Jump (i i i-4)∗256+j j j j j j j j
168-171	1 0 1 0 1 0 i i j j j j j j j j	Pop and Jump On True i i∗256+j j j j j j j j
172-175	1 0 1 0 1 1 i i j j j j j j j j	Pop and Jump On False i i∗256+j j j j j j j j
176-191	1 0 1 1 i i i i	Send Arthmetic Message #i i i i
192-207	1 1 0 0 i i i i	Send Special Message #i i i i
208-223	1 1 0 1 i i i i	Send Literal Selector #i i i i With No Arguments
224-239	1 1 1 0 i i i i	Send Literal Selector #i i i i With 1 Argument
240-255	1 1 1 1 i i i i	Send Literal Selector #i i i i With 2 Arguments

Stack Bytecodes

The stack bytecodes all perform simple operations on the active context's evaluation stack.

- 107 bytecodes *push* an object pointer on the stack
  - 99 push an object pointer found in the object memory
  - 7 push a constant object pointer
  - 1 pushes the interpreter's active context register (activeContext)
- 18 bytecodes *store* an object pointer found on the stack into the object memory
  - 17 of these also remove it from the stack
  - 1 leaves it on the stack
- 1 bytecode *removes* an object pointer from the stack without storing it anywhere.

The routines used to manipulate the stack were described in the section of the previous chapter on contexts (push:, popStack, pop:). The stackBytecode routine dispatches to the appropriate routine for the current bytecode.

```
stackBytecode
    (currentBytecode between: 0 and: 15)
        ifTrue: [↑self pushReceiverVariableBytecode].
    (currentBytecode between: 16 and: 31)
        ifTrue: [↑self pushTemporaryVariableBytecode].
    (currentBytecode between: 32 and: 63)
        ifTrue: [↑self pushLiteralConstantBytecode].
    (currentBytecode between: 64 and: 95)
        ifTrue: [↑self pushLiteralVariableBytecode].
    (currentBytecode between: 96 and: 103)
        ifTrue: [↑self storeAndPopReceiverVariableBytecode].
    (currentBytecode between: 104 and: 111)
        ifTrue: [↑self storeAndPopTemporaryVariableBytecode].
    currentBytecode = 112
        ifTrue: [↑self pushReceiverBytecode].
    (currentBytecode between: 113 and: 119)
        ifTrue: [↑self pushConstantBytecode].
    currentBytecode = 128
        ifTrue: [↑self extendedPushBytecode].
    currentBytecode = 129
        ifTrue: [↑self extendedStoreBytecode].
    currentBytecode = 130
        ifTrue: [↑self extendedStoreAndPopBytecode].
```

```
currentBytecode = 135
    ifTrue: [↑self popStackBytecode].
currentBytecode = 136
    ifTrue: [↑self duplicateTopBytecode].
currentBytecode = 137
    ifTrue: [↑self pushActiveContextBytecode]
```

There are single byte instructions that push the first 16 instance variables of the receiver and the first 16 temporary frame locations. Recall that the temporary frame includes the arguments and the temporary variables.

pushReceiverVariableBytecode
```
| fieldIndex |
fieldIndex ← self extractBits: 12 to: 15
                of: currentBytecode.
self pushReceiverVariable: fieldIndex
```
pushReceiverVariable: fieldIndex
```
self push: (memory fetchPointer: fieldIndex
                ofObject: receiver)
```
pushTemporaryVariableBytecode
```
| fieldIndex |
fieldIndex ← self extractBits: 12 to: 15
                of: currentBytecode.
self pushTemporaryVariable: fieldIndex
```
pushTemporaryVariable: temporaryIndex
```
self push: (self temporary: temporaryIndex)
```

There are also single byte instructions that reference the first 32 locations in the literal frame of the active context's method. The contents of one of these locations can be pushed with pushLiteralConstantBytecode. The contents of the value field of an Association stored in one of these locations can be pushed with pushLiteralVariableBytecode.

pushLiteralConstantBytecode
```
| fieldIndex |
fieldIndex ← self extractBits: 11 to: 15
                of: currentBytecode.
self pushLiteralConstant: fieldIndex
```
pushLiteralConstant: literalIndex
```
self push: (self literal: literalIndex)
```
pushLiteralVariableBytecode
```
| fieldIndex |
fieldIndex ← self extractBits: 11 to: 15
                of: currentBytecode.
self pushLiteralVariable: fieldIndex
```

pushLiteralVariable: literalIndex
```
| association |
association ← self literal: literalIndex.
self push: (memory fetchPointer: ValueIndex
                    ofObject: association)
```

Associations are objects with two fields, one for a name and one for a value. They are used to implement shared variables (global variables, class variables, and pool variables). The following routine initializes the index used to fetch the value field of Associations.

initializeAssociationIndex
```
ValueIndex ← 1
```

The extended push bytecode can perform any of the four operations described above (receiver variable, temporary frame location, literal constant, or literal variable). However, instead of a limit of 16 or 32 variables accessible, it can access up to 64 instance variables, temporary locations, literal constants, or literal variables. The extended push bytecode is followed by a byte whose high order two bits determine which type of push is being done and whose low order six bits determine the offset to use.

extendedPushBytecode
```
| descriptor variableType variableIndex |
descriptor ← self fetchByte.
variableType ← self extractBits: 8 to: 9
                        of: descriptor.
variableIndex ← self extractBits: 10 to: 15
                        of: descriptor.
variableType=0 ifTrue: [↑self pushReceiverVariable: variableIndex].
variableType=1 ifTrue: [↑self pushTemporaryVariable: variableIndex].
variableType=2 ifTrue: [↑self pushLiteralConstant: variableIndex].
variableType=3 ifTrue: [↑self pushLiteralVariable: variableIndex]
```

The pushReceiverBytecode routine pushes a pointer to the active context's receiver. This corresponds to the use of self or super in a Smalltalk method.

pushReceiverBytecode
```
self push: receiver
```

The duplicateTopBytecode routine pushes another copy of the object pointer on the top of the stack.

duplicateTopBytecode
```
↑self push: self stackTop
```

The pushConstantBytecode routine pushes one of seven constant object pointers (true, false, nil, −1, 0, 1, or 2).

pushConstantBytecode

currentBytecode = 113 ifTrue: [↑self push: TruePointer].

currentBytecode = 114 ifTrue: [↑self push: FalsePointer].

currentBytecode = 115 ifTrue: [↑self push: NilPointer].

currentBytecode = 116 ifTrue: [↑self push: MinusOnePointer].

currentBytecode = 117 ifTrue: [↑self push: ZeroPointer].

currentBytecode = 118 ifTrue: [↑self push: OnePointer].

currentBytecode = 119 ifTrue: [↑self push: TwoPointer]

The pushActiveContextBytecode routine pushes a pointer to the active context itself. This corresponds to the use of thisContext in a Smalltalk method.

pushActiveContextBytecode

self push: activeContext

The store bytecodes transfer references in the opposite direction from the push bytecodes; from the top of the stack to the receiver's instance variables, the temporary frame, or the literal frame. There are single byte versions for storing into the first eight variables of the receiver or the temporary frame and then popping the stack.

storeAndPopReceiverVariableBytecode

| variableIndex |

variableIndex ← self extractBits: 13 to: 15
                          of: currentBytecode.

memory storePointer: variableIndex
        ofObject: receiver
        withValue: self popStack

storeAndPopTemporaryVariableBytecode

| variableIndex |

variableIndex ← self extractBits: 13 to: 15
                          of: currentBytecode.

memory storePointer: variableIndex + TempFrameStart
        ofObject: homeContext
        withValue: self popStack

Stores into variables other than those accessible by the single byte versions are accomplished by two extended store bytecodes. One pops the stack after storing and the other does not. Both extended stores take a following byte of the same form as the extended push. It is illegal, however, to follow an extended store with a byte of the form 10xxxxxx since this would mean changing the value of a literal constant.

extendedStoreAndPopBytecode

self extendedStoreBytecode.

self popStackBytecode

extendedStoreBytecode

| descriptor variableType variableIndex association |

```
descriptor ← self fetchByte.
variableType ← self extractBits: 8 to: 9
                        of: descriptor.
variableIndex ← self extractBits: 10 to: 15
                        of: descriptor.
variableType=0 ifTrue:
   [↑memory storePointer: variableIndex
            ofObject: receiver
            withValue: self stackTop].
variableType=1 ifTrue:
   [↑memory storePointer: variableIndex + TempFrameStart
            ofObject: homeContext
            withValue: self stackTop].
variableType=2 ifTrue:
   [↑self error: 'illegal store'].
variableType=3 ifTrue:
   [association ← self literal: variableIndex.
    ↑memory storePointer: ValueIndex
            ofObject: association
            withValue: self stackTop]
```

The last stack bytecode removes the top object pointer from the stack
without doing anything else with it.

popStackBytecode
```
self popStack
```

Jump Bytecodes

The jump bytecodes change the active context's instruction pointer by a
specified amount. Unconditional jumps change the instruction pointer
whenever they are encountered. Conditional jumps only change the instruction pointer if the object pointer on the top of the stack is a specified Boolean object (either true or false). Both unconditional and
conditional jumps have a short (single-byte) and a long (two-byte) form.

jumpBytecode
```
(currentBytecode between: 144 and: 151)
            ifTrue: [↑self shortUnconditionalJump].
(currentBytecode between: 152 and: 159)
            ifTrue: [↑self shortConditionalJump].
(currentBytecode between: 160 and: 167)
            ifTrue: [↑self longUnconditionalJump].
(currentBytecode between: 168 and: 175)
            ifTrue: [↑self longConditionalJump]
```

The jump bytecodes use the jump: routine to actually change the bytecode index.

jump: offset

    instructionPointer ← instructionPointer + offset

The eight short unconditional jumps advance the instruction pointer by 1 through 8.

shortUnconditionalJump

    | offset |
    offset ← self extractBits: 13 to: 15
                    of: currentBytecode.
    self jump: offset + 1

The eight long unconditional jumps are followed by another byte. The low order three bits of the jump bytecode provide the high order three bits of an 11-bit twos complement displacement to be added to the instruction pointer. The byte following the jump provides the low order eight bits of the displacement. So long unconditional jumps can jump up to 1023 forward and 1024 back.

longUnconditionalJump

    | offset |
    offset ← self extractBits: 13 to: 15
                    of: currentBytecode.
    self jump: offset − 4 * 256 + self fetchByte

The conditional jumps use the jumpIf:by: routine to test the top of the stack and decide whether to perform the jump. The top of stack is discarded after it is tested.

jumpIf: condition by: offset

    | boolean |
    boolean ← self popStack.
    boolean=condition
        ifTrue: [self jump: offset]
        ifFalse: [(boolean=TruePointer) | (boolean=FalsePointer)
                    ifFalse: [self unPop:1.
                                self sendMustBeBoolean]]

The conditional jumps are used in the compiled form of messages to booleans (e.g., ifTrue: and whileFalse:). If the top of the stack at the time of a conditional jump is not true or false it is an error since an object other than a boolean has been sent a message that only booleans understand. Instead of sending doesNotUnderstand:, the interpreter sends mustBeBoolean to it.

sendMustBeBoolean
> self sendSelector: MustBeBooleanSelector
> argumentCount: 0

The sendSelector:argumentCount: routine is described in the next section on send bytecodes.

The eight short conditional jumps advance the instruction pointer by 1 through 8 if the top of the stack is false.

shortConditionalJump
> | offset |
> offset ← self extractBits: 13 to: 15
>   of: currentBytecode.
> self jumpIf: FalsePointer
>   by: offset + 1

So, there are three possible outcomes to a short conditional jump:

- If the top of the stack is false, the jump is taken.

- If the top of the stack is true, the jump is not taken.

- If the top of the stack is neither, mustBeBoolean is sent to it.

Half of the long conditional jumps perform the jump if the top of the stack is false while the other half perform the jump if it is true. The low order two bits of the bytecode become the high order two bits of a 10-bit unsigned displacement. The byte following the jump provides the low order eight bits of the displacement. So long conditional jumps can jump up to 1023 forward.

longConditionalJump
> | offset |
> offset ← self extractBits: 14 to: 15
>   of: currentBytecode.
> offset ← offset * 256 + self fetchByte.
> (currentBytecode between: 168 and: 171)
>   ifTrue: [↑self jumpIf: TruePointer
>   by: offset].
> (currentBytecode between: 172 and: 175)
>   ifTrue: [↑self jumpIf: FalsePointer
>   by: offset]

Send Bytecodes

The send bytecodes cause a message to be sent. The object pointers for the receiver and the arguments of the message are found on the active context's evaluation stack. The send bytecode determines the selector of the message and how many arguments to take from the stack. The number of arguments is also indicated in the CompiledMethod invoked by the message. The compiler guarantees that this information is redundant except when a CompiledMethod is reached by a perform: message, in which case it is checked to make sure the CompiledMethod takes the right number of arguments. The perform: messages will be discussed in the next chapter in a section on control primitives.

The selectors of most messages are found in the literal frame of the CompiledMethod. The *literal-selector* bytecodes and the *extended-send* bytecodes specify the argument count of the message and the index of the selector in the literal frame. The 32 *special-selector* bytecodes specify the offset of the selector and argument count in an Array in the object memory. This Array is shared by all CompiledMethods in the system.

sendBytecode
```
(currentBytecode between: 131 and: 134)
            ifTrue: [↑self extendedSendBytecode].
(currentBytecode between: 176 and: 207)
            ifTrue: [↑self sendSpecialSelectorBytecode].
(currentBytecode between: 208 and: 255)
            ifTrue: [↑self sendLiteralSelectorBytecode]
```

The literal-selector bytecodes are single bytes that can specify 0, 1, or 2 arguments and a selector in any one of the first 16 locations of the literal frame. Both the selector index and the argument count are encoded in the bits of the bytecode.

sendLiteralSelectorBytecode
```
| selector |
selector ← self literal: (self extractBits: 12 to: 15
                            of: currentBytecode).
self sendSelector: selector
    argumentCount: (self extractBits: 10 to: 11
                        of: currentBytecode) − 1
```

Most of the send bytecodes call the sendSelector:argumentCount: routine after determining the appropriate selector and argument count. This routine sets up the variables messageSelector and argumentCount, which are available to the other routines in the interpreter that will lookup the message and perhaps activate a method.

sendSelector: selector argumentCount: count
```
| newReceiver |
messageSelector ← selector.
argumentCount ← count.
newReceiver ← self stackValue: argumentCount.
self sendSelectorToClass: (memory fetchClassOf: newReceiver)
```

sendSelectorToClass: classPointer

```
self findNewMethodInClass: classPointer.
self executeNewMethod
```

The interpreter uses a method cache to reduce the number of dictionary lookups necessary to find CompiledMethods associated with selectors. The method cache may be omitted by substituting a call on lookupMethodInClass: for the call on findNewMethodInClass: in sendSelectorToClass: above. The lookupMethodInClass: routine is described in the previous chapter in a section on classes. The cache may be implemented in various ways. The following routine uses four sequential locations in an Array for each entry. The four locations store the selector, class, CompiledMethod, and primitive index for the entry. This routine does not allow for reprobes.

findNewMethodInClass: class

```
| hash |
hash ← (((messageSelector bitAnd: class) bitAnd: 16rFF) bitShift: 2) + 1.
((methodCache at: hash) = messageSelector
                    and: [(methodCache at: hash + 1) = class])
    ifTrue: [newMethod ← methodCache at: hash + 2.
            primitiveIndex ← methodCache at: hash + 3]
    ifFalse: [self lookupMethodInClass: class.
            methodCache at: hash put: messageSelector.
            methodCache at: hash + 1 put: class.
            methodCache at: hash + 2 put: newMethod.
            methodCache at: hash + 3 put: primitiveIndex]
```

The method cache is initialized with the following routine.

initializeMethodCache

```
methodCacheSize ← 1024.
methodCache ← Array new: methodCacheSize
```

The executeNewMethod routine calls a primitive routine if one is associated with the CompiledMethod. The primitiveResponse routine returns false if no primitive is indicated or the primitive routine is unable to produce a result. In that case, the CompiledMethod is activated. Primitive routines and the primitiveResponse routine will be described in the next chapter.

executeNewMethod

```
self primitiveResponse
    ifFalse: [self activateNewMethod]
```

The routine that activates a method creates a MethodContext and transfers the receiver and arguments from the currently active context's stack to the new context's stack. It then makes this new context be the interpreter's active context.

activateNewMethod
| contextSize newContext newReceiver |
(self largeContextFlagOf: newMethod) = 1
 ifTrue: [contextSize ← 32 + TempFrameStart]
 ifFalse: [contextSize ← 12 + TempFrameStart].
newContext ← memory instantiateClass: ClassMethodContextPointer
     withPointers: contextSize.
memory storePointer: SenderIndex
  ofObject: newContext
  withValue: activeContext.
self storeInstructionPointerValue:
   (self initialInstructionPointerOfMethod: newMethod)
 inContext: newContext.
self storeStackPointerValue: (self temporaryCountOf: newMethod)
 inContext: newContext.
memory storePointer: MethodIndex
  ofObject: newContext
  withValue: newMethod.
self transfer: argumentCount + 1
 fromIndex: stackPointer − argumentCount
 ofObject: activeContext
 toIndex: ReceiverIndex
 ofObject: newContext.
self pop: argumentCount + 1.
self newActiveContext: newContext

There are four extended-send bytecodes. The first two have the same effect as the literal-selector bytecodes except that the selector index and argument count are found in one or two following bytes instead of in the bytecode itself. The other two extended-send bytecodes are used for superclass messages.

extendedSendBytecode
currentBytecode = 131 ifTrue: [↑self singleExtendedSendBytecode].
currentBytecode = 132 ifTrue: [↑self doubleExtendedSendBytecode].
currentBytecode = 133 ifTrue: [↑self singleExtendedSuperBytecode].
currentBytecode = 134 ifTrue: [↑self doubleExtendedSuperBytecode]

The first form of extended send is followed by a single byte specifying the number of arguments in its high order three bits and selector index in the low order five bits.

singleExtendedSendBytecode
| descriptor selectorIndex |
descriptor ← self fetchByte.
selectorIndex ← self extractBits: 11 to: 15
    of: descriptor.

```
self sendSelector: (self literal: selectorIndex)
    argumentCount: (self extractBits: 8 to: 10
                        of: descriptor)
```

The second form of extended send bytecode is followed by two bytes; the first is the number of arguments and the second is the index of the selector in the literal frame.

doubleExtendedSendBytecode

```
| count selector |
count ← self fetchByte.
selector ← self literal: self fetchByte.
self sendSelector: selector
    argumentCount: count
```

When the compiler encounters a message to **super** in a symbolic method, it uses the bytecode that pushes **self** for the receiver, but it uses an extended-super bytecode to indicate the selector instead of a regular send bytecode. The two extended-super bytecodes are similar to the two extended-send bytecodes. The first is followed by a single byte and the second by two bytes that are interpreted exactly as for the extended-send bytecodes. The only difference in what these bytecodes do is that they start the message lookup in the superclass of the class in which the current CompiledMethod was found. Note that this is not necessarily the immediate superclass of **self**. Specifically, it will not be the immediate superclass of **self** if the CompiledMethod containing the extended-super bytecode was found in a superclass of **self** originally. All CompiledMethods that contain extended-super bytecodes have the class in which they are found as their last literal variable.

singleExtendedSuperBytecode

```
| descriptor selectorIndex methodClass |
descriptor ← self fetchByte.
argumentCount ← self extractBits: 8 to: 10
                        of: descriptor.
selectorIndex ← self extractBits: 11 to: 15
                        of: descriptor.
messageSelector ← self literal: selectorIndex.
methodClass ← self methodClassOf: method.
self sendSelectorToClass: (self superclassOf: methodClass)
```

doubleExtendedSuperBytecode

```
| methodClass |
argumentCount ← self fetchByte.
messageSelector ← self literal: self fetchByte.
methodClass ← self methodClassOf: method.
self sendSelectorToClass: (self superclassOf: methodClass)
```

The set of special selectors can be used in a message without being included in the literal frame. An Array in the object memory contains the object pointers of the selectors in alternating locations. The argument count for each selector is stored in the location following the selector's object pointer. The specialSelectorPrimitiveResponse routine will be described in the next chapter.

sendSpecialSelectorBytecode

```
| selectorIndex selector count |
self specialSelectorPrimitiveResponse
    ifFalse: [selectorIndex ← (currentBytecode − 176) * 2.
        selector ← memory fetchPointer: selectorIndex
                        ofObject: SpecialSelectorsPointer.
        count ← self fetchInteger: selectorIndex + 1
                        ofObject: SpecialSelectorsPointer.
        self sendSelector: selector
            argumentCount: count]
```

Return Bytecodes

There are six bytecodes that return control and a value from a context; five return the value of a message (invoked explicitly by "↑" or implicitly at the end of a method) and the other one returns the value of a block (invoked implicitly at the end of a block). The distinction between the two types of return is that the former returns to the sender of the home context while the latter returns to the caller of the active context. The values returned from the five return bytecodes are: the receiver (self), true, false, nil, or the top of the stack. The last return bytecode returns the top of the stack as the value of a block.

returnBytecode

```
currentBytecode = 120
    ifTrue: [↑self returnValue: receiver
                to: self sender].
currentBytecode = 121
    ifTrue: [↑self returnValue: TruePointer
                to: self sender].
currentBytecode = 122
    ifTrue: [↑self returnValue: FalsePointer
                to: self sender].
currentBytecode = 123
    ifTrue: [↑self returnValue: NilPointer
                to: self sender].
```

```
currentBytecode = 124
    ifTrue: [↑self returnValue: self popStack
                to: self sender].
currentBytecode = 125
    ifTrue: [↑self returnValue: self popStack
                to: self caller]
```

The simple way to return a value to a context would be to simply make it the active context and push the value on its stack.

simpleReturnValue: resultPointer to: contextPointer

```
    self newActiveContext: contextPointer.
    self push: resultPointer
```

However, there are three situations in which this routine is too simple to work correctly. If the sender of the active context were nil; this routine would store a nil in the interpreter's active context pointer, bringing the system to an unpleasant halt. In order to prevent this, the actual returnValue:to: routine first checks to see if the sender is nil. The interpreter also prevents returns *to* a context that has already been returned *from*. It does this by storing nil in the instruction pointer of the active context on return and checking for a nil instruction pointer of the context being returned to. Both of these situations can arise since contexts are objects and can be manipulated by user programs as well as by the interpreter. If either situation arises, the interpreter sends a message to the active context informing it of the problem. The third situation will arise in systems that automatically deallocate objects based on their reference counts. The active context may be deallocated as it is returning. It, in turn, may contain the only reference to the result being returned. In this case, the result will be deallocated before it can be pushed on the new context's stack. Because of these considerations, the returnValue: routine must be somewhat more complicated.

returnValue: resultPointer to: contextPointer

```
    | sendersIP |
    contextPointer=NilPointer
        ifTrue: [self push: activeContext.
                self push: resultPointer.
                ↑self sendSelector: CannotReturnSelector
                    argumentCount: 1].
    sendersIP ← memory fetchPointer: InstructionPointerIndex
                    ofObject: contextPointer.
    sendersIP=NilPointer
        ifTrue: [self push: activeContext.
                self push: resultPointer.
                ↑self sendSelector: CannotReturnSelector
                    argumentCount: 1].
```

```
memory increaseReferencesTo: resultPointer.
self returnToActiveContext: contextPointer.
self push: resultPointer.
memory decreaseReferencesTo: resultPointer
```

This routine prevents the deallocation of the result being returned by raising the reference count until it is pushed on the new stack. It could also have pushed the result before switching active contexts. The returnToActiveContext: routine is basically the same as the newActiveContext: routine except that instead of restoring any cached fields of the context being returned from, it stores nil into the sender and instruction pointer fields.

returnToActiveContext: aContext

```
memory increaseReferencesTo: aContext.
self nilContextFields.
memory decreaseReferencesTo: activeContext.
activeContext ← aContext.
self fetchContextRegisters
```

nilContextFields

```
memory storePointer: SenderIndex
        ofObject: activeContext
        withValue: NilPointer.
memory storePointer: InstructionPointerIndex
        ofObject: activeContext
        withValue: NilPointer
```

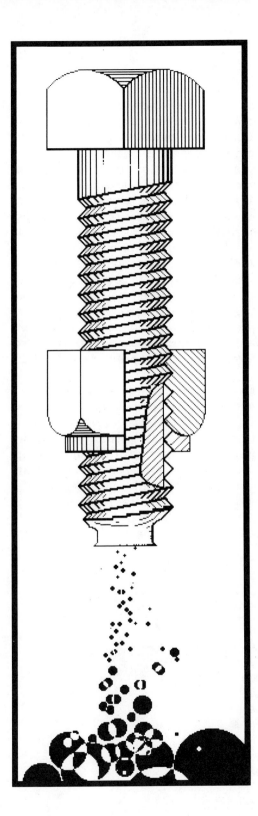

29

Formal Specification of the Primitive Methods

Arithmetic Primitives

Array and Stream Primitives

Storage Management Primitives

Control Primitives

Input/Output Primitives

System Primitives

When a message is sent, the interpreter usually responds by executing a Smalltalk CompiledMethod. This involves creating a new MethodContext for that CompiledMethod and executing its bytecodes until a return bytecode is encountered. Some messages, however, may be responded to *primitively*. A primitive response is performed directly by the interpreter without creating a new context or executing any other bytecodes. Each primitive response the interpreter can make is described by a *primitive routine*. A primitive routine removes the message receiver and arguments from the stack and replaces them with the appropriate result. Some primitive routines have other effects on the object memory or on some hardware devices. After a primitive response is completed, the interpreter proceeds with interpretation of the bytecode after the send bytecode that caused the primitive to be executed.

At any point in its execution, a primitive routine may determine that a primitive response cannot be made. This may, for example, be due to a message argument of the wrong class. This is called *primitive failure*. When a primitive fails, the Smalltalk method associated with the selector and receiver's class will be executed as if the primitive method did not exist.

The table below shows the class-selector pairs associated with each primitive routine. Some of these class-selector pairs have not appeared earlier in this book since they are part of the class's private protocol. Some of the primitive routines must meet their specification in order for the system to function properly. Other primitive routines are optional; the system will simply perform less efficiently if they always fail. The optional primitives are marked with an asterisk. The Smalltalk methods associated with optional primitive routines must do everything the primitive does. The Smalltalk methods associated with required primitive routines need only handle the cases for which the primitive fails.

The Smalltalk Primitives

Primitive Index	Class-Selector Pairs
1	SmallInteger +
2	SmallInteger −
3	SmallInteger <
4	SmallInteger >
5*	SmallInteger <=
6*	SmallInteger >=
7	SmallInteger =
8*	SmallInteger ~=
9	SmallInteger *
10*	SmallInteger /
11*	SmallInteger \\
12*	SmallInteger //

13	SmallInteger quo:	
14	SmallInteger bitAnd:	
15	SmallInteger bitOr:	
16	SmallInteger bitXor:	
17	SmallInteger bitShift:	
18*	Number @	
19		
20		
21*	Integer +	LargePositiveInteger +
22*	Integer −	LargePositiveInteger −
23*	Integer <	LargePositiveInteger <
24*	Integer >	LargePositiveInteger >
25*	Integer < =	LargePositiveInteger < =
26*	Integer > =	LargePositiveInteger > =
27*	Integer =	LargePositiveInteger =
28*	Integer ∼=	LargePositiveInteger ∼=
29*	Integer *	LargePositiveInteger *
30*	Integer /	LargePositiveInteger /
31*	Integer \\	LargePositiveInteger \\
32*	Integer //	LargePositiveInteger //
33*	Integer quo:	LargePositiveInteger quo:
34*	Integer bitAnd:	LargePositiveInteger bitAnd:
35*	Integer bitOr:	LargePositiveInteger bitOr:
36*	Integer bitXor:	LargePositiveInteger bitXor:
37*	Integer bitShift:	LargePositiveInteger bitShift:
38		
39		
40	SmallInteger asFloat	
41	Float +	
42	Float −	
43	Float <	
44	Float >	
45*	Float < =	
46*	Float > =	
47	Float =	
48*	Float ∼=	
49	Float *	
50	Float /	
51	Float truncated	
52*	Float fractionPart	
53*	Float exponent	
54*	Float timesTwoPower:	
55		
56		
57		
58		

59	
60	LargeNegativeInteger digitAt:
	LargePositiveInteger digitAt:
	Object at:
	Object basicAt:
61	LargeNegativeInteger digitAt:put:
	LargePositiveInteger digitAt:put:
	Object basicAt:put:
	Object at:put:
62	ArrayedCollection size
	LargeNegativeInteger digitLength
	LargePositiveInteger digitLength
	Object basicSize
	Object size
	String size
63	String at:
	String basicAt:
64	String basicAt:put:
	String at:put:
65*	ReadStream next ReadWriteStream next
66*	WriteStream nextPut:
67*	PositionableStream atEnd
68	CompiledMethod objectAt:
69	CompiledMethod objectAt:put:
70	Behavior basicNew Behavior new
	Interval class new
71	Behavior new:
	Behavior basicNew:
72	Object become:
73	Object instVarAt:
74	Object instVarAt:put:
75	Object asOop
	Object hash
	Symbol hash
76	SmallInteger asObject
	SmallInteger asObjectNoFail
77	Behavior someInstance
78	Object nextInstance
79	CompiledMethod class newMethod:header:
80*	ContextPart blockCopy:
81	BlockContext value:value:value:
	BlockContext value:
	BlockContext value:
	BlockContext value:value:
82	BlockContext valueWithArguments:
83*	Object perform:with:with:with:

	Object perform:with:
	Object perform:with:with:
	Object perform:
84	Object perform:withArguments:
85	Semaphore signal
86	Semaphore wait
87	Process resume
88	Process suspend
89	Behavior flushCache
90*	InputSensor primMousePt InputState primMousePt
91	InputState primCursorLocPut:
	InputState primCursorLocPutAgain:
92	Cursor class cursorLink:
93	InputState primInputSemaphore:
94	InputState primSampleInterval:
95	InputState primInputWord
96	BitBlt copyBitsAgain BitBlt copyBits
97	SystemDictionary snapshotPrimitive
98	Time class secondClockInto:
99	Time class millisecondClockInto:
100	ProcessorScheduler signal:atMilliseconds:
101	Cursor beCursor
102	DisplayScreen beDisplay
103*	CharacterScanner scanCharactersFrom:to:in: rightX:stopConditions:displaying:
104*	BitBlt drawLoopX:Y:
105*	ByteArray primReplaceFrom:to:with:startingAt:
	ByteArray replaceFrom:to:withString:startingAt:
	String replaceFrom:to:withByteArray:startingAt:
	String primReplaceFrom:to:with:startingAt:
106	
107	
108	
109	
110	Character =
	Object ==
111	Object class
112	SystemDictionary coreLeft
113	SystemDictionary quitPrimitive
114	SystemDictionary exitToDebugger
115	SystemDictionary oopsLeft
116	SystemDictionary signal:atOopsLeft:wordsLeft:
117	
118	
119	
120	

121
122
123
124
125
126
127

An example of a primitive method is the response of instances of SmallInteger to messages with selector +. If the argument is also an instance of SmallInteger, and the sum of the values of the receiver and argument is in the range that can be represented by SmallInteger, then the primitive method will remove the receiver and argument from the stack and replace them with an instance of SmallInteger whose value is the sum. If the argument is not a SmallInteger or the sum is out of range, the primitive will fail and the Smalltalk method associated with the selector + in SmallInteger will be executed.

The control structures used in the specification of the interpreter given in this book and the control structures used in a machine language implementation of the interpreter will probably use different mechanisms when primitive routines fail to complete. When a failure condition arises, a machine language primitive routine can decide not to return to its caller and simply jump to the appropriate place in the interpreter (usually the place that activates a CompiledMethod). However, since the formal specification is written in Smalltalk, all routines *must* return to their senders and Interpreter must keep track of primitive success or failure independently of the routine call structure. Part of the book specification, therefore, is a register called success that is initialized to true when a primitive is started and may be set to false if the routine fails. The following two routines set and test the state of the primitive success register.

success: successValue
    success ← successValue & success
success
    ↑success

The following routines set the state of the success flag in the two common cases of initialization before a primitive routine runs and discovery by a primitive routine that it cannot complete.

initPrimitive
    success ← true
primitiveFail
    success ← false

Many of the primitives manipulate integer quantities, so the interpreter includes several routines that perform common functions. The popInteger routine is used when a primitive expects a SmallInteger on the top of the stack. If it is a SmallInteger, its value is returned; if not, a primitive failure is signaled.

popInteger
```
    | integerPointer |
    integerPointer ← self popStack.
    self success: (memory isIntegerObject: integerPointer).
    self success
        ifTrue: [↑memory integerValueOf: integerPointer]
```

Recall that the fetchInteger:ofObject: routine signaled a primitive failure if the indicated field did not contain a SmallInteger. The pushInteger: routine converts a value to a SmallInteger and pushes it on the stack.

pushInteger: integerValue
```
    self push: (memory integerObjectOf: integerValue)
```

Since the largest indexable collections may have 65534 indexable elements, and SmallIntegers can only represent values up to 16383, primitive routines that deal with indices or sizes must be able to manipulate LargePositiveIntegers. The following two routines convert back and forth between 16-bit unsigned values and object pointers to SmallIntegers or LargePositiveIntegers.

positive16BitIntegerFor: integerValue
```
    | newLargeInteger |
    integerValue < 0
        ifTrue: [↑self primitiveFail].
    (memory isIntegerValue: integerValue)
        ifTrue: [↑memory integerObjectOf: integerValue].
    newLargeInteger ← memory instantiateClass:
                                ClassLargePositiveIntegerPointer
                            withBytes: 2.
    memory storeByte: 0
            ofObject: newLargeInteger
            withValue: (self lowByteOf: integerValue).
    memory storeByte: 1
            ofObject: newLargeInteger
            withValue: (self highByteOf: integerValue).
    ↑newLargeInteger
```
positive16BitValueOf: integerPointer
```
    | value |
    (memory isIntegerObject: integerPointer)
```

Formal Specification of the Primitive Methods

```
            ifTrue: [↑memory integerValueOf: integerPointer].
    (memory fetchClassOf: integerPointer) =
                            ClassLargePositiveIntegerPointer
        ifFalse: [↑self primitiveFail].
    (memory fetchByteLengthOf: integerPointer) = 2
        ifFalse: [↑self primitiveFail].
    value ← memory fetchByte: 1
                    ofObject: integerPointer.
    value ← value∗256 + (memory fetchByte: 0
                            ofObject: integerPointer).
↑value
```

There are three ways that a primitive routine can be reached in the process of interpreting a send-message bytecode.

1. Some primitive routines are associated with send-special-selector bytecodes for certain classes of receiver. These can be reached without a message lookup.

2. The two most common primitive routines (returning self or an instance variable) can be indicated in the flag value of the header of a CompiledMethod. These are only found after a message lookup has produced a CompiledMethod, but only the header need be examined.

3. Most primitive routines are indicated by a number in the header extension of a CompiledMethod. These are also found after a message lookup.

The first path to a primitive routine was represented by the call on specialSelectorPrimitiveResponse in the sendSpecialSelectorBytecode routine. The specialSelectorPrimitiveResponse routine selects an appropriate primitive routine and returns true if a primitive response was sucessfully made and false otherwise. Recall that the sendSpecialSelectorBytecode routine looks up the special selector if specialSelectorPrimitiveResponse returns false.

specialSelectorPrimitiveResponse
```
    self initPrimitive.
    (currentBytecode between: 176 and: 191)
        ifTrue: [self arithmeticSelectorPrimitive].
    (currentBytecode between: 192 and: 207)
        ifTrue: [self commonSelectorPrimitive].
    ↑self success
```

A primitive routine will be accessed by a special arithmetic selector only if the receiver is a SmallInteger. The actual primitive routines will be described in the section on arithmetic primitives.

arithmeticSelectorPrimitive

self success: (memory isIntegerObject: (self stackValue: 1)).
self success
   ifTrue: [currentBytecode = 176 ifTrue: [↑self primitiveAdd].
           currentBytecode = 177 ifTrue: [↑self primitiveSubtract].
           currentBytecode = 178 ifTrue: [↑self primitiveLessThan].
           currentBytecode = 179 ifTrue: [↑self primitiveGreaterThan].
           currentBytecode = 180 ifTrue: [↑self primitiveLessOrEqual].
           currentBytecode = 181 ifTrue: [↑self primitiveGreaterOrEqual].
           currentBytecode = 182 ifTrue: [↑self primitiveEqual].
           currentBytecode = 183 ifTrue: [↑self primitiveNotEqual].
           currentBytecode = 184 ifTrue: [↑self primitiveMultiply].
           currentBytecode = 185 ifTrue: [↑self primitiveDivide].
           currentBytecode = 186 ifTrue: [↑self primitiveMod].
           currentBytecode = 187 ifTrue: [↑self primitiveMakePoint].
           currentBytecode = 188 ifTrue: [↑self primitiveBitShift].
           currentBytecode = 189 ifTrue: [↑self primitiveDiv].
           currentBytecode = 190 ifTrue: [↑self primitiveBitAnd].
           currentBytecode = 191 ifTrue: [↑self primitiveBitOr]]

Only five of the non-arithmetic special selectors invoke primitives without a message lookup (= =, class, blockCopy:, value, and value:). The primitive routine for = = is found in the section on system primitives and the routine for class in storage management primitives. They are both invoked for any class of receiver. The routines for blockCopy:, value, and value: are found in the section on control primitives. The routine for blockCopy: will be invoked if the receiver is a MethodContext or a BlockContext. The routines for value and value: will only be invoked if the receiver is a BlockContext.

commonSelectorPrimitive

| receiverClass |
argumentCount ← self fetchInteger: (currentBytecode − 176)∗2 + 1
                     ofObject: SpecialSelectorsPointer.
receiverClass ←
      memory fetchClassOf: (self stackValue: argumentCount).
currentBytecode = 198 ifTrue: [↑self primitiveEquivalent].
currentBytecode = 199 ifTrue: [↑self primitiveClass].
currentBytecode = 200
   ifTrue: [self success:
              (receiverClass = ClassMethodContextPointer)
               | (receiverClass = ClassBlockContextPointer).
        ↑self success ifTrue: [self primitiveBlockCopy]].
(currentBytecode = 201) | (currentBytecode = 202)
   ifTrue: [self success: receiverClass = ClassBlockContextPointer.
        ↑self success ifTrue: [self primitiveValue]].
self primitiveFail

The second and third paths to primitive routines listed above are taken after a CompiledMethod for a message has been found. The presence of a primitive is detected by the primitiveResponse routine called in executeNewMethod. The primitiveResponse routine is similar to the specialSelectorPrimitiveResponse routine in that it returns true if a primitive response was successfully made and false otherwise. Recall that the executeNewMethod routine activates the CompiledMethod that has been looked up if primitiveResponse returns false.

primitiveResponse
```
| flagValue thisReceiver offset |
primitiveIndex=0
    ifTrue: [flagValue ← self flagValueOf: newMethod.
            flagValue = 5
                ifTrue: [self quickReturnSelf.
                        ↑true].
            flagValue = 6
                ifTrue: [self quickInstanceLoad.
                        ↑true].
            ↑false]
    ifFalse: [self initPrimitive.
            self dispatchPrimitives.
            ↑self success]
```

Flag values of 5 and 6 reach the two most commonly found primitives, a simple return of self and a simple return of one of the receiver's instance variables. Returning self is a no-op as far as the interpreter is concerned since self's object pointer occupies the same place on the stack as the message receiver that it should occupy as the message response.

quickReturnSelf

Returning an instance variable of the receiver is almost as easy.

quickInstanceLoad
```
| thisReceiver fieldIndex |
thisReceiver ← self popStack.
fieldIndex ← self fieldIndexOf: newMethod.
self push: (memory fetchPointer: fieldIndex
                    ofObject: thisReceiver)
```

The six types of primitives in the formal specification deal with arithmetic, subscripting and streaming, storage management, control structures, input/output, and general system access. These correspond to six ranges of primitive indices. A range of primitive indices has been reserved for implementation-private primitive routines. They may be assigned any meaning, but cannot be depended upon from interpreter to interpreter. Since these are not part of the specification, they cannot be described here.

dispatchPrimitives

> primitiveIndex < 60
>> ifTrue: [↑self dispatchArithmeticPrimitives].
> primitiveIndex < 68
>> ifTrue: [↑self dispatchSubscriptAndStreamPrimitives].
> primitiveIndex < 80
>> ifTrue: [↑self dispatchStorageManagementPrimitives].
> primitiveIndex < 90
>> ifTrue: [↑self dispatchControlPrimitives].
> primitiveIndex < 110
>> ifTrue: [↑self dispatchInputOutputPrimitives].
> primitiveIndex < 128
>> ifTrue: [↑self dispatchSystemPrimitives].
> primitiveIndex < 256
>> ifTrue: [↑self dispatchPrivatePrimitives]

Arithmetic Primitives

There are three sets of arithmetic primitive routines, one for SmallIntegers, one for large integers (LargePositiveIntegers and LargeNegativeIntegers), and one for Floats. The primitives for SmallIntegers and Floats must be implemented, the primitives for large integers are optional.

dispatchArithmeticPrimitives

> primitiveIndex < 20
>> ifTrue: [↑self dispatchIntegerPrimitives].
> primitiveIndex < 40
>> ifTrue: [↑self dispatchLargeIntegerPrimitives].
> primitiveIndex < 60
>> ifTrue: [↑self dispatchFloatPrimitives]

The first set of arithmetic primitive routines all pop a receiver and argument off the stack and fail if they are not both SmallIntegers. The routines then push on the stack either the integral result of a computation or the Boolean result of a comparison. The routines that produce an integral result fail if the value cannot be represented as a SmallInteger.

dispatchIntegerPrimitives

> primitiveIndex = 1 ifTrue: [↑self primitiveAdd].
> primitiveIndex = 2 ifTrue: [↑self primitiveSubtract].
> primitiveIndex = 3 ifTrue: [↑self primitiveLessThan].

```
primitiveIndex = 4 ifTrue: [↑self primitiveGreaterThan].
primitiveIndex = 5 ifTrue: [↑self primitiveLessOrEqual].
primitiveIndex = 6 ifTrue: [↑self primitiveGreaterOrEqual].
primitiveIndex = 7 ifTrue: [↑self primitiveEqual].
primitiveIndex = 8 ifTrue: [↑self primitiveNotEqual].
primitiveIndex = 9 ifTrue: [↑self primitiveMultiply].
primitiveIndex = 10 ifTrue: [↑self primitiveDivide].
primitiveIndex = 11 ifTrue: [↑self primitiveMod].
primitiveIndex = 12 ifTrue: [↑self primitiveDiv].
primitiveIndex = 13 ifTrue: [↑self primitiveQuo].
primitiveIndex = 14 ifTrue: [↑self primitiveBitAnd].
primitiveIndex = 15 ifTrue: [↑self primitiveBitOr].
primitiveIndex = 16 ifTrue: [↑self primitiveBitXor].
primitiveIndex = 17 ifTrue: [↑self primitiveBitShift].
primitiveIndex = 18 ifTrue: [↑self primitiveMakePoint]
```

The primitiveAdd, primitiveSubtract, and primitiveMultiply routines are all identical except for the arithmetic operation used, so only the primitiveAdd routine will be shown here.

primitiveAdd

```
| integerReceiver integerArgument integerResult |
integerArgument ← self popInteger.
integerReceiver ← self popInteger.
self success
    ifTrue: [integerResult ← integerReceiver + integerArgument.
            self success: (memory isIntegerValue: integerResult)].
self success
    ifTrue: [self pushInteger: integerResult]
    ifFalse: [self unPop: 2]
```

The primitive routine for division (associated with the selector /) is different than the other three arithmetic primitives since it only produces a result if the division is exact, otherwise the primitive fails. This primitive, and the next three that have to do with rounding division, all fail if their argument is 0.

primitiveDivide

```
| integerReceiver integerArgument integerResult |
integerArgument ← self popInteger.
integerReceiver ← self popInteger.
self success: integerArgument~=0.
self success: integerReceiver\\integerArgument=0.
self success
    ifTrue: [integerResult ← integerReceiver//integerArgument.
            self success: (memory isIntegerValue: integerResult)].
```

```
self success
    ifTrue: [self push: (memory integerObjectOf: integerResult)]
    ifFalse: [self unPop: 2]
```

The primitive routine for the modulo function (associated with the selector \\) gives the remainder of a division where the quotient is always rounded down (toward negative infinity).

primitiveMod

```
| integerReceiver integerArgument integerResult |
integerArgument ← self popInteger.
integerReceiver ← self popInteger.
self success: integerArgument~=0.
self success
    ifTrue: [integerResult ← integerReceiver\\integerArgument.
             self success: (memory isIntegerValue: integerResult)].
self success
    ifTrue: [self pushInteger: integerResult]
    ifFalse: [self unPop: 2]
```

There are two primitive routines for rounding division (associated with the selectors // and quo:). The result of // is always rounded down (toward negative infinity).

primitiveDiv

```
| integerReceiver integerArgument integerResult |
integerArgument ← self popInteger.
integerReceiver ← self popInteger.
self success: integerArgument~=0.
self success
    ifTrue: [integerResult ← integerReceiver//integerArgument.
             self success: (memory isIntegerValue: integerResult)].
self success
    ifTrue: [self pushInteger: integerResult]
    ifFalse: [self unPop: 2]
```

The result of quo: is truncated (rounded toward zero).

primitiveQuo

```
| integerReceiver integerArgument integerResult |
integerArgument ← self popInteger.
integerReceiver ← self popInteger.
self success: integerArgument~=0.
self success
    ifTrue: [integerResult ← integerReceiver quo: integerArgument.
             self success: (memory isIntegerValue: integerResult)].
```

Formal Specification of the Primitive Methods

```
self success
    ifTrue: [self pushInteger: integerResult]
    ifFalse: [self unPop: 2]
```

The primitiveEqual, primitiveNotEqual, primitiveLessThan, primitive-LessOrEqual, primitiveGreaterThan, and primitiveGreaterOrEqual routines are all identical except for the comparison operation used, so only the primitiveEqual routine will be shown here.

primitiveEqual

```
| integerReceiver integerArgument integerResult |
integerArgument ← self popInteger.
integerReceiver ← self popInteger.
self success
    ifTrue: [integerReceiver = integerArgument
                ifTrue: [self push: TruePointer]
                ifFalse: [self push: FalsePointer]]
    ifFalse: [self unPop: 2]
```

The primitiveBitAnd, primitiveBitOr, and primitiveBitXor routines perform logical operations on the two's-complement binary representations of SmallInteger values. They are identical except for the logical operation used, so only the primitiveBitAnd routine will be shown here.

primitiveBitAnd

```
| integerReceiver integerArgument integerResult |
integerArgument ← self popInteger.
integerReceiver ← self popInteger.
self success
    ifTrue: [integerResult ← integerReceiver bitAnd: integerArgument].
self success
    ifTrue: [self pushInteger: integerResult]
    ifFalse: [self unPop: 2]
```

The primitive routine for shifting (associated with the selector bitShift:) returns a SmallInteger whose value represented in two's-complement is the receiver's value represented in two's-complement shifted left by the number of bits indicated by the argument. Negative arguments shift right. Zeros are shifted in from the right in left shifts. The sign bit is extended in right shifts. This primitive fails if the correct result cannot be represented as a SmallInteger.

primitiveBitShift

```
| integerReceiver integerArgument integerResult |
integerArgument ← self popInteger.
integerReceiver ← self popInteger.
```

```
    self success
        ifTrue: [integerResult ← integerReceiver bitShift: integerArgument.
            self success: (memory isIntegerValue: integerResult)].
    self success
        ifTrue: [self pushInteger: integerResult]
        ifFalse: [self unPop: 2]
```

The primitive routine associated with the selector @ returns a new Point whose x value is the receiver and whose y value is the argument.

primitiveMakePoint
```
    | integerReceiver integerArgument pointResult |
    integerArgument ← self popStack.
    integerReceiver ← self popStack.
    self success: (memory isIntegerValue: integerReceiver).
    self success: (memory isIntegerValue: integerArgument).
    self success
        ifTrue: [pointResult ← memory instantiateClass: ClassPointPointer
                                        withPointers: ClassPointSize.
            memory storePointer: XIndex
                ofObject: pointResult
                withValue: integerReceiver.
            memory storePointer: YIndex
                ofObject: pointResult
                withValue: integerArgument.
            self push: pointResult]
        ifFalse: [self unPop: 2]
```

initializePointIndices
```
    XIndex ← 0.
    YIndex ← 1.
    ClassPointSize ← 2
```

The primitive indices 21 to 37 are the same as primitives 1 to 17 except that they perform their operations on large integers (instances of LargePositiveInteger and LargeNegativeInteger). There are adequate Smalltalk implementations for all of these operations so the primitive routines are optional and will not be specified in this chapter. To implement them, the corresponding Smalltalk methods should be translated into machine language routines.

dispatchLargeIntegerPrimitives
```
    self primitiveFail
```

Instances of Float are represented in IEEE single-precision (32-bit) format. This format represents a floating point quantity as a number between one and two, a power of two, and a sign. A Float is a word-size, nonpointer object. The most significant bit of the first field indicates the sign of the number (1 means negative). The next eight most significant bits of the first field are the 8-bit exponent of two biased by 127 (0 means an exponent of -127, 128 means an exponent of 1, and so on). The seven least significant bits of the first field are the seven most significant bits of the fractional part of the number between one and two. The fractional part is 23 bits long and its 16 least significant bits are the contents of the second field of the Float. So a Float whose fields are

SEEEEEEE EFFFFFFF
FFFFFFFF FFFFFFFF

represents the value

$$-1^S * 2^{E-127} * 1.F$$

0 is represented as both fields=0. The floating point primitives fail if the argument is not an instance of Float or if the result cannot be represented as a Float. This specification of the Smalltalk-80 virtual machine does not specifically include the parts of the IEEE standard other than the representation of floating point numbers. The implementation of routines that perform the necessary operations on floating point values is left to the implementer.

The primitiveAsFloat routine converts its SmallInteger receiver into a Float. The routines for primitives 41 through 50 perform the same operations as 1 through 10 or 21 through 30, except that they operate on Floats. The primitiveTruncated routine returns a SmallInteger equal to the value of the receiver without any fractional part. It fails if its truncated value cannot be represented as a SmallInteger. The primitiveFractionalPart returns the difference between the receiver and its truncated value. The primitiveExponent routine returns the exponent of the receiver and the primitiveTimesTwoPower routine increases the exponent by an amount specified by the argument.

dispatchFloatPrimitives
```
    primitiveIndex = 40 ifTrue: [↑self primitiveAsFloat].
    primitiveIndex = 41 ifTrue: [↑self primitiveFloatAdd].
    primitiveIndex = 42 ifTrue: [↑self primitiveFloatSubtract].
    primitiveIndex = 43 ifTrue: [↑self primitiveFloatLessThan].
    primitiveIndex = 44 ifTrue: [↑self primitiveFloatGreaterThan].
    primitiveIndex = 45 ifTrue: [↑self primitiveFloatLessOrEqual].
    primitiveIndex = 46 ifTrue: [↑self primitiveFloatGreaterOrEqual].
    primitiveIndex = 47 ifTrue: [↑self primitiveFloatEqual].
    primitiveIndex = 48 ifTrue: [↑self primitiveFloatNotEqual].
    primitiveIndex = 49 ifTrue: [↑self primitiveFloatMultiply].
    primitiveIndex = 50 ifTrue: [↑self primitiveFloatDivide].
    primitiveIndex = 51 ifTrue: [↑self primitiveTruncated].
```

primitiveIndex = 52 ifTrue: [↑self primitiveFractionalPart].
primitiveIndex = 53 ifTrue: [↑self primitiveExponent].
primitiveIndex = 54 ifTrue: [↑self primitiveTimesTwoPower]

Array and Stream Primitives

The second set of primitive routines are for manipulating the indexable fields of objects both directly, by subscripting, and indirectly, by streaming. These routines make use of the 16-bit positive integer routines, since the limit on indexable fields is 65534.

dispatchSubscriptAndStreamPrimitives
primitiveIndex = 60 ifTrue: [↑self primitiveAt].
primitiveIndex = 61 ifTrue: [↑self primitiveAtPut].
primitiveIndex = 62 ifTrue: [↑self primitiveSize].
primitiveIndex = 63 ifTrue: [↑self primitiveStringAt].
primitiveIndex = 64 ifTrue: [↑self primitiveStringAtPut].
primitiveIndex = 65 ifTrue: [↑self primitiveNext].
primitiveIndex = 66 ifTrue: [↑self primitiveNextPut].
primitiveIndex = 67 ifTrue: [↑self primitiveAtEnd]

The following routines are used to check the bounds on subscripting operations and to perform the subscripting accesses. They determine whether the object being indexed contains pointers, 16-bit integer values, or 8-bit integer values, in its indexable fields. The check-IndexableBoundsOf:in: routine takes a one-relative index and determines whether it is a legal subscript of an object. It must take into account any fixed fields.

checkIndexableBoundsOf: index in: array
| class |
class ← memory fetchClassOf: array.
self success: index > = 1.
self success: index + (self fixedFieldsOf: class) < = (self lengthOf: array)
lengthOf: array
(self isWords: (memory fetchClassOf: array))
ifTrue: [↑memory fetchWordLengthOf: array]
ifFalse: [↑memory fetchByteLengthOf: array]

The subscript:with: and subscript:with:storing: routines assume that the number of fixed fields has been added into the index, so they use it as a one-relative index into the object as a whole.

Formal Specification of the Primitive Methods

subscript: array with: index
```
| class value |
class ← memory fetchClassOf: array.
(self isWords: class)
    ifTrue: [(self isPointers: class)
                ifTrue: [↑memory fetchPointer: index−1
                                ofObject: array]
                ifFalse: [value ← memory fetchWord: index−1
                                ofObject: array.
                          ↑self positive16BitIntegerFor: value]]
    ifFalse: [value ← memory fetchByte: index−1
                ofObject: array.
              ↑memory integerObjectOf: value]
```

subscript: array with: index storing: value
```
| class |
class ← memory fetchClassOf: array.
(self isWords: class)
    ifTrue: [(self isPointers: class)
                ifTrue: [↑memory storePointer: index−1
                                ofObject: array
                                withValue: value]
                ifFalse: [self success: (memory isIntegerObject: value).
                          self success ifTrue:
                              [↑memory
                                  storeWord: index−1
                                  ofObject: array
                                  withValue: (self positive16BitValueOf:
                                                           value)]]]
    ifFalse: [self success: (memory isIntegerObject: value).
              self success ifTrue:
                  [↑memory storeByte: index−1
                          ofObject: array
                          withValue: (self lowByteOf:
                                          (memory integerValueOf:
                                                          value))]]
```

The primitiveAt and primitiveAtPut routines simply fetch or store one of the indexable fields of the receiver. They fail if the index is not a SmallInteger or if it is out of bounds.

primitiveAt
```
| index array arrayClass result |
index ← self positive16BitValueOf: self popStack.
array ← self popStack.
arrayClass ← memory fetchClassOf: array.
self checkIndexableBoundsOf: index
    in: array.
```

```
        self success
            ifTrue: [index ← index + (self fixedFieldsOf: arrayClass).
                    result ← self subscript: array
                                with: index].
        self success
            ifTrue: [self push: result]
            ifFalse: [self unPop: 2]
```

The primitiveAtPut routine also fails if the receiver is not a pointer type and the second argument is not an 8-bit (for byte-indexable objects) or 16-bit (for word-indexable objects) positive integer. The primitive routine returns the stored value as its value.

primitiveAtPut

```
        | array index arrayClass value result |
        value ← self popStack.
        index ← self positive16BitValueOf: self popStack.
        array ← self popStack.
        arrayClass ← memory fetchClassOf: array.
        self checkIndexableBoundsOf: index
            in: array.
        self success
            ifTrue: [index ← index + (self fixedFieldsOf: arrayClass).
                    self subscript: array
                        with: index
                        storing: value].
        self success
            ifTrue: [self push: value]
            ifFalse: [self unPop: 3]
```

The primitiveSize routine returns the number of indexable fields the receiver has (i.e., the largest legal subscript).

primitiveSize

```
        | array class length |
        array ← self popStack.
        class ← memory fetchClassOf: array.
        length ← self positive16BitIntegerFor:
                        (self lengthOf: array) − (self fixedFieldsOf: class).
        self success
            ifTrue: [self push: length]
            ifFalse: [self unPop: 1]
```

The primitiveStringAt and primitiveStringAtPut routines are special responses to the at: and at:put: messages by instances of String. A String actually stores 8-bit numbers in byte-indexable fields, but it communicates through the at: and at:put: messages with instances of Character. A Character has a single instance variable that holds a SmallInteger. The value of the SmallInteger returned from the at: message is the byte stored in the indicated field of the String. The primitiveStringAt routine always returns the same instance of Character for any particular value. It gets the Characters from an Array in the object memory that has a guaranteed object pointer called characterTablePointer.

primitiveStringAt

```
| index array ascii character |
index ← self positive16BitValueOf: self popStack.
array ← self popStack.
self checkIndexableBoundsOf: index
    in: array.
self success
    ifTrue: [ascii ← memory integerValueOf: (self subscript: array
                                                with: index).
            character ← memory fetchPointer: ascii
                            ofObject: CharacterTablePointer].
self success
    ifTrue: [self push: character]
    ifFalse: [self unPop: 2]
```

initializeCharacterIndex

```
CharacterValueIndex ← 0
```

The primitiveStringAtPut routine stores the value of a Character in one of the receiver's indexable bytes. It fails if the second argument of the at:put: message is not a Character.

primitiveStringAtPut

```
| index array ascii character |
character ← self popStack.
index ← self positive16BitValueOf: self popStack.
array ← self popStack.
self checkIndexableBoundsOf: index
    in: array.
self success: (memory fetchClassOf: character)=ClassCharacterPointer.
self success
    ifTrue: [ascii ← memory fetchPointer: CharacterValueIndex
                        ofObject: character.
            self subscript: array
                with: index
                storing: ascii].
self success
    ifTrue: [self push: character]
    ifFalse: [self unPop: 2]
```

The primitiveNext, primitiveNextPut, and primitiveAtEnd routines are optional primitive versions of the Smalltalk code for the next, nextPut:, and atEnd messages to streams. The primitiveNext and primitiveNextPut routines only work if the object being streamed is an Array or a String.

initializeStreamIndices
```
StreamArrayIndex ← 0.
StreamIndexIndex ← 1.
StreamReadLimitIndex ← 2.
StreamWriteLimitIndex ← 3
```

primitiveNext
```
| stream index limit array arrayClass result ascii |
stream ← self popStack.
array ← memory fetchPointer: StreamArrayIndex
                ofObject: stream.
arrayClass ← memory fetchClassOf: array.
index ← self fetchInteger: StreamIndexIndex
            ofObject: stream.
limit ← self fetchInteger: StreamReadLimitIndex
            ofObject: stream.
self success: index < limit.
self success:
    (arrayClass = ClassArrayPointer) | (arrayClass = ClassStringPointer).
self checkIndexableBoundsOf: index + 1
    in: array.
self success
    ifTrue: [index ← index + 1.
            result ← self subscript: array
                        with: index].
self success
    ifTrue: [self storeInteger: StreamIndexIndex
            ofObject: stream
            withValue: index].
self success
    ifTrue: [arrayClass = ClassArrayPointer
            ifTrue: [self push: result]
            ifFalse: [ascii ← memory integerValueOf: result.
                    self push: (memory fetchPointer: ascii
                                ofObject:
                                    CharacterTablePointer)]]
    ifFalse: [self unPop: 1]
```

primitiveNextPut
```
| value stream index limit array arrayClass result ascii |
value ← self popStack.
stream ← self popStack.
```

Formal Specification of the Primitive Methods

    array ← memory fetchPointer: StreamArrayIndex
            ofObject: stream.
    arrayClass ← memory fetchClassOf: array.
    index ← self fetchInteger: StreamIndexIndex
           ofObject: stream.
    limit ← self fetchInteger: StreamWriteLimitIndex
           ofObject: stream.
    self success: index < limit.
    self success:
      (arrayClass = ClassArrayPointer) | (arrayClass = ClassStringPointer).
    self checkIndexableBoundsOf: index + 1
      in: array.
    self success
      ifTrue: [index ← index + 1.
          arrayClass = ClassArrayPointer
            ifTrue: [self subscript: array
                with: index
                storing: value]
            ifFalse: [ascii ← memory fetchPointer:
                        CharacterValueIndex
                    ofObject: value.
               self subscript: array
                 with: index
                 storing: ascii]].
    self success
      ifTrue: [self storeInteger: StreamIndexIndex
            ofObject: stream
            withValue: index].
    self success
      ifTrue: [self push: value]
      ifFalse: [self unPop: 2]

primitiveAtEnd
    | stream array arrayClass length index limit |
    stream ← self popStack.
    array ← memory fetchPointer: StreamArrayIndex
            ofObject: stream.
    arrayClass ← memory fetchClassOf: array.
    length ← self lengthOf: array.
    index ← self fetchInteger: StreamIndexIndex
           ofObject: stream.
    limit ← self fetchInteger: StreamReadLimitIndex
           ofObject: stream.
    self success:
      (arrayClass = ClassArrayPointer) | (arrayClass = ClassStringPointer).

```
    self success
        ifTrue: [(index > =limit) | (index > =length)
                ifTrue: [self push: TruePointer]
                ifFalse: [self push: FalsePointer]]
        ifFalse: [self unPop: 1]
```

Storage Management Primitives

The storage management primitive routines manipulate the representation of objects. They include primitives for manipulating object pointers, accessing fields, creating new instances of a class, and enumerating the instances of a class.

dispatchStorageManagementPrimitives

```
    primitiveIndex = 68 ifTrue: [↑self primitiveObjectAt].
    primitiveIndex = 69 ifTrue: [↑self primitiveObjectAtPut].
    primitiveIndex = 70 ifTrue: [↑self primitiveNew].
    primitiveIndex = 71 ifTrue: [↑self primitiveNewWithArg].
    primitiveIndex = 72 ifTrue: [↑self primitiveBecome].
    primitiveIndex = 73 ifTrue: [↑self primitiveInstVarAt].
    primitiveIndex = 74 ifTrue: [↑self primitiveInstVarAtPut].
    primitiveIndex = 75 ifTrue: [↑self primitiveAsOop].
    primitiveIndex = 76 ifTrue: [↑self primitiveAsObject].
    primitiveIndex = 77 ifTrue: [↑self primitiveSomeInstance].
    primitiveIndex = 78 ifTrue: [↑self primitiveNextInstance].
    primitiveIndex = 79 ifTrue: [↑self primitiveNewMethod]
```

The primitiveObjectAt and primitiveObjectAtPut routines are associated with the objectAt: and objectAt:put: messages in CompiledMethod. They provide access to the object pointer fields of the receiver (the method header and the literals) from Smalltalk. The header is accessed with an index of 1 and the literals are accessed with indices 2 through the number of literals plus 1. These messages are used primarily by the compiler.

primitiveObjectAt

```
    | thisReceiver index |
    index ← self popInteger.
    thisReceiver ← self popStack.
    self success: index > 0.
    self success: index < =(self objectPointerCountOf: thisReceiver).
    self success
        ifTrue: [self push: (memory fetchPointer: index−1
                                        ofObject: thisReceiver)]
        ifFalse: [self unPop: 2]
```

primitiveObjectAtPut

```
| thisReceiver index newValue |
newValue ← self popStack.
index ← self popInteger.
thisReceiver ← self popStack.
self success: index > 0.
self success: index < =(self objectPointerCountOf: thisReceiver).
self success
    ifTrue: [memory storePointer: index−1
                    ofObject: thisReceiver
                    withValue: newValue.
            self push: newValue]
    ifFalse: [self unPop: 3]
```

The primitiveNew routine creates a new instance of the receiver (a class) without indexable fields. The primitive fails if the class is indexable.

primitiveNew

```
| class size |
class ← self popStack.
size ← self fixedFieldsOf: class.
self success: (self isIndexable: class) = =false.
self success
    ifTrue: [(self isPointers: class)
                    ifTrue: [self push: (memory instantiateClass: class
                                            withPointers: size)]
                    ifFalse: [self push: (memory instantiateClass: class
                                            withWords: size)]]
    ifFalse: [self unPop: 1]
```

The primitiveNewWithArg routine creates a new instance of the receiver (a class) with the number of indexable fields specified by the integer argument. The primitive fails if the class is not indexable.

primitiveNewWithArg

```
| size class |
size ← self positive16BitValueOf: self popStack.
class ← self popStack.
self success: (self isIndexable: class).
self success
    ifTrue: [size ← size + (self fixedFieldsOf: class).
            (self isPointers: class)
                    ifTrue: [self push: (memory instantiateClass: class
                                            withPointers: size)]
                    ifFalse: [(self isWords: class)
                                    ifTrue: [self push: (memory instantiateClass:
                                                            class
                                                            withWords: size)]
```

```
                    ifFalse: [self push: (memory instantiateClass:
                                                        class
                                                withBytes: size)]]]
```

```
    ifFalse: [self unPop: 2]
```

The primitiveBecome routine swaps the instance pointers of the receiver and argument. This means that all objects that used to point to the receiver now point to the argument and vice versa.

primitiveBecome
```
    | thisReceiver otherPointer |
    otherPointer ← self popStack.
    thisReceiver ← self popStack.
    self success: (memory isIntegerObject: otherPointer) not.
    self success: (memory isIntegerObject: thisReceiver) not.
    self success
        ifTrue: [memory swapPointersOf: thisReceiver and: otherPointer.
            self push: thisReceiver]
        ifFalse: [self unpop: 2]
```

The primitiveInstVarAt and primitiveInstVarAtPut routines are associated with the instVarAt: and instVarAt:put: messages in Object. They are similar to primitiveAt and primitiveAtPut except that the numbering of fields starts with the fixed fields (corresponding to named instance variables) instead of with the indexable fields. The indexable fields are numbered starting with one more than the number of fixed fields. These routines need a different routine to check the bounds of the subscript.

checkInstanceVariableBoundsOf: index in: object
```
    | class |
    class ← memory fetchClassOf: object.
    self success: index > = 1.
    self success: index < = (self lengthOf: object)
```
primitiveInstVarAt
```
    | thisReceiver index value |
    index ← self popInteger.
    thisReceiver ← self popStack.
    self checkInstanceVariableBoundsOf: index
        in: thisReceiver.
    self success
        ifTrue: [value ← self subscript: thisReceiver
                            with: index].
    self success
        ifTrue: [self push: value]
        ifFalse: [self unPop: 2]
```
primitiveInstVarAtPut
```
    | thisReceiver index newValue realValue |
    newValue ← self popStack.
```

```
index ← self popInteger.
thisReceiver ← self popStack.
self checkInstanceVariableBoundsOf: index
    in: thisReceiver.
self success
    ifTrue: [self subscript: thisReceiver
                  with: index
                  storing: newValue].
self success
    ifTrue: [self push: newValue]
    ifFalse: [self unPop: 3]
```

The primitiveAsOop routine produces a SmallInteger whose value is half of the receiver's object pointer (interpreting object pointers as 16-bit *signed* quantities). The primitive only works for non-SmallInteger receivers. Since non-SmallInteger object pointers are even, no information in the object pointer is lost. Because of the encoding of SmallIntegers, the halving operation can be performed by setting the least significant bit of the receiver's object pointer.

primitiveAsOop

```
| thisReceiver |
thisReceiver ← self popStack.
self success: (memory isIntegerObject: thisReceiver) = =false.
self success
    ifTrue: [self push: (thisReceiver bitOr: 1)]
    ifFalse: [self unPop: 1]
```

The primitiveAsObject routine performs the inverse operation of primitiveAsOop. It only works for SmallInteger receivers (it is associated with the asObject message in SmallInteger). It produces the object pointer that is twice the receiver's value. The primitive fails if there is no object for that pointer.

primitiveAsObject

```
| thisReceiver newOop |
thisReceiver ← self popStack.
newOop ← thisReceiver bitAnd: 16rFFFE.
self success: (memory hasObject: newOop).
self success
    ifTrue: [self push: newOop]
    ifFalse: [self unPop: 1]
```

The primitiveSomeInstance and primitiveNextInstance routines allow for the enumeration of the instances of a class. They rely on the ability of the object memory to define an ordering on object pointers, to find the first instance of a class in that ordering, and, given an object pointer, to find the next instance of the same class.

primitiveSomeInstance

```
| class |
class ← self popStack.
(memory instancesOf: class)
    ifTrue: [self push: (memory initialInstanceOf: class)]
    ifFalse: [self primitiveFail]
```

primitiveNextInstance

```
| object |
object ← self popStack.
(memory isLastInstance: object)
    ifTrue: [self primitiveFail]
    ifFalse: [self push: (memory instanceAfter: object)]
```

The primitiveNewMethod routine is associated with the newMethod:header: message in CompiledMethod class. Instances of CompiledMethod are created with a special message. Since the part of a CompiledMethod that contains pointers instead of bytes is indicated in the header, all CompiledMethods must have a valid header. Therefore, CompiledMethods are created with a message (newMethod:header:) that takes the number of bytes as the first argument and the header as the second argument. The header, in turn, indicates the number of pointer fields.

primitiveNewMethod

```
| header bytecodeCount class size |
header ← self popStack.
bytecodeCount ← self popInteger.
class ← self popStack.
size ← (self literalCountOfHeader: header) + 1 * 2 + bytecodeCount.
self push: (memory instantiateClass: class
                withBytes: size)
```

Control Primitives

The control primitives provide the control structures not provided by the bytecodes. They include support for the behavior of BlockContexts, Processes, and Semaphores. They also provide for messages with parameterized selectors.

dispatchControlPrimitives

```
primitiveIndex = 80 ifTrue: [↑self primitiveBlockCopy].
primitiveIndex = 81 ifTrue: [↑self primitiveValue].
primitiveIndex = 82 ifTrue: [↑self primitiveValueWithArgs].
primitiveIndex = 83 ifTrue: [↑self primitivePerform].
primitiveIndex = 84 ifTrue: [↑self primitivePerformWithArgs].
primitiveIndex = 85 ifTrue: [↑self primitiveSignal].
```

primitiveIndex = 86 ifTrue: [↑self primitiveWait].
primitiveIndex = 87 ifTrue: [↑self primitiveResume].
primitiveIndex = 88 ifTrue: [↑self primitiveSuspend].
primitiveIndex = 89 ifTrue: [↑self primitiveFlushCache]

The primitiveBlockCopy routine is associated with the blockCopy: message in both BlockContext and MethodContext. This message is only produced by the compiler. The number of block arguments the new BlockContext takes is passed as the argument. The primitiveBlockCopy routine creates a new instance of BlockContext. If the receiver is a MethodContext, it becomes the new BlockContext's home context. If the receiver is a BlockContext, its home context is used for the new BlockContext's home context.

primitiveBlockCopy

```
| context methodContext blockArgumentCount newContext initialIP
contextSize |
blockArgumentCount ← self popStack.
context ← self popStack.
(self isBlockContext: context)
    ifTrue: [methodContext ← memory fetchPointer: HomeIndex
                                        ofObject: context]
    ifFalse: [methodContext ← context].
contextSize ← memory fetchWordLengthOf: methodContext.
newContext ← memory instantiateClass: ClassBlockContextPointer
                        withPointers: contextSize.
initialIP ← memory integerObjectOf: instructionPointer + 3.
memory storePointer: InitialIPIndex
        ofObject: newContext
        withValue: initialIP.
memory storePointer: InstructionPointerIndex
        ofObject: newContext
        withValue: initialIP.
self storeStackPointerValue: 0
    inContext: newContext.
memory storePointer: BlockArgumentCountIndex
        ofObject: newContext
        withValue: blockArgumentCount.
memory storePointer: HomeIndex
        ofObject: newContext
        withValue: methodContext.
self push: newContext
```

The primitiveValue routine is associated with all "value" messages in BlockContext (value, value:, value:value:, and so on). It checks that the receiver takes the same number of block arguments that the "value" message did and then transfers them from the active context's stack to the receiver's stack. The primitive fails if the number of arguments do not match. The primitiveValue routine also stores the active context in the receiver's caller field and initializes the receiver's instruction pointer and stack pointer. After the receiver has been initialized, it becomes the active context.

primitiveValue

```
| blockContext blockArgumentCount initialIP |
blockContext ← self stackValue: argumentCount.
blockArgumentCount ← self argumentCountOfBlock: blockContext.
self success: argumentCount=blockArgumentCount.
self success
    ifTrue: [self transfer: argumentCount
                fromIndex: stackPointer-argumentCount + 1
                ofObject: activeContext
                toIndex: TempFrameStart
                ofObject: blockContext.
        self pop: argumentCount + 1.
        initialIP ← memory fetchPointer: InitialIPIndex
                        ofObject: blockContext.
        memory storePointer: InstructionPointerIndex
                ofObject: blockContext
                withValue: initialIP.
        self storeStackPointerValue: argumentCount
            inContext: blockContext.
        memory storePointer: CallerIndex
                ofObject: blockContext
                withValue: activeContext.
        self newActiveContext: blockContext]
```

The primitiveValueWithArgs routine is associated with the valueWithArguments: messages in BlockContext. It is basically the same as the primitiveValue routine except that the block arguments come in a single Array argument to the valueWithArguments: message instead of as multiple arguments to the "value" message.

primitiveValueWithArgs

```
| argumentArray blockContext blockArgumentCount
arrayClass arrayArgumentCount initialIP |
argumentArray ← self popStack.
blockContext ← self popStack.
blockArgumentCount ← self argumentCountOfBlock: blockContext.
arrayClass ← memory fetchClassOf: argumentArray.
self success: (arrayClass = ClassArrayPointer).
self success
    ifTrue: [arrayArgumentCount ← memory fetchWordLengthOf:
                                        argumentArray.
        self success: arrayArgumentCount=blockArgumentCount].
```

```
                      self success
                         ifTrue: [self transfer: arrayArgumentCount
                                     fromIndex: 0
                                     ofObject: argumentArray
                                     toIndex: TempFrameStart
                                     ofObject: blockContext.
                                  initialIP ← memory fetchPointer: InitialIPIndex
                                                    ofObject: blockContext.
                                  memory storePointer: InstructionPointerIndex
                                     ofObject: blockContext
                                     withValue: initialIP.
                                  self storeStackPointerValue: arrayArgumentCount
                                     inContext: blockContext.
                                  memory storePointer: CallerIndex
                                     ofObject: blockContext
                                     withValue: activeContext.
                                  self newActiveContext: blockContext]
                         ifFalse: [self unPop: 2]
```

The primitivePerform routine is associated with all "perform" messages in Object (perform:, perform:with:, perform:with:with:, and so on). It is equivalent to sending a message to the receiver whose selector is the first argument of and whose arguments are the remaining arguments. It is, therefore, similar to the sendSelector:argumentCount: routine except that it must get rid of the selector from the stack before calling executeNewMethod and it must check that the CompiledMethod it finds takes one less argument that the "perform" message did. The primitive fails if the number of arguments does not match.

primitivePerform
```
    | performSelector newReceiver selectorIndex |
    performSelector ← messageSelector.
    messageSelector ← self stackValue: argumentCount−1.
    newReceiver ← self stackValue: argumentCount.
    self lookupMethodInClass: (memory fetchClassOf: newReceiver).
    self success: (self argumentCountOf: newMethod)=(argumentCount−1).
    self success
        ifTrue: [selectorIndex ← stackPointer-argumentCount + 1.
                 self transfer: argumentCount−1
                     fromIndex: selectorIndex + 1
                     ofObject: activeContext
                     toIndex: selectorIndex
                     ofObject: activeContext.
                 self pop: 1.
                 argumentCount ← argumentCount−1.
                 self executeNewMethod]
        ifFalse: [messageSelector ← performSelector]
```

The primitivePerformWithArgs routine is associated with the performWithArguments: messages in Object. It is basically the same as the primitivePerform routine except that the message arguments come in a single Array argument to the performWithArguments: message instead of as multiple arguments to the "perform" message.

primitivePerformWithArgs
```
| thisReceiver performSelector argumentArray arrayClass arraySize
index |
argumentArray ← self popStack.
arraySize ← memory fetchWordLengthOf: argumentArray.
arrayClass ← memory fetchClassOf: argumentArray.
self success: (stackPointer + arraySize)
                    < (memory fetchWordLengthOf: activeContext).
self success: (arrayClass = ClassArrayPointer).
self success
    ifTrue: [performSelector ← messageSelector.
            messageSelector ← self popStack.
            thisReceiver ← self stackTop.
            argumentCount ← arraySize.
            index ← 1.
            [index < = argumentCount]
                    whileTrue: [self push: (memory fetchPointer: index − 1
                                            ofObject: argumentArray).
                            index ← index + 1].
            self lookupMethodInClass:
                    (memory fetchClassOf: thisReceiver).
            self success: (self argumentCountOf: newMethod)
                            = argumentCount.
            self success
                ifTrue: [self executeNewMethod]
                ifFalse: [self unPop: argumentCount.
                        self push: messageSelector.
                        self push: argumentArray.
                        argumentCount ← 2.
                        messageSelector ← performSelector]]
    ifFalse: [self unPop: 1]
```

The next four primitive routines (for primitive indices 85 through 88) are used for communication and scheduling of independent processes. The following routine initializes the indices used to access Processes, ProcessorSchedulers, and Semaphores.

initializeSchedulerIndices
```
"Class ProcessorScheduler"
ProcessListsIndex ← 0.
ActiveProcessIndex ← 1.
```

```
"Class LinkedList"
FirstLinkIndex ← 0.
LastLinkIndex ← 1.
"Class Semaphore"
ExcessSignalsIndex ← 2.
"Class Link"
NextLinkIndex ← 0.
"Class Process"
SuspendedContextIndex ← 1.
PriorityIndex ← 2.
MyListIndex ← 3
```

Process switching must be synchronized with the execution of bytecodes. This is done using the following four interpreter registers and the four routines: checkProcessSwitch, asynchronousSignal:, synchronousSignal:, and transferTo:.

Process-related Registers of the Interpreter

newProcessWaiting	The newProcessWaiting register will be true if a process switch is called for and false otherwise.
newProcess	If newProcessWaiting is true then the newProcess register will point to the Process to be transferred to.
semaphoreList	The semaphoreList register points to an Array used by the interpreter to buffer Semaphores that should be signaled. This is an Array in Interpreter, not in the object memory. It will be a table in a machine-language interpreter.
semaphoreIndex	The semaphoreIndex register holds the index of the last Semaphore in the semaphoreList buffer.

The asynchronousSignal: routine adds a Semaphore to the buffer.

asynchronousSignal: aSemaphore
```
semaphoreIndex ← semaphoreIndex + 1.
semaphoreList at: semaphoreIndex put: aSemaphore
```

The Semaphores will actually be signaled in the checkProcessSwitch routine which calls the synchronousSignal: routine once for each Semaphore in the buffer. If a Process is waiting for the Semaphore, the synchronousSignal: routine resumes it. If no Process is waiting, the synchronousSignal: routine increments the Semaphore's count of excess signals. The isEmptyList:, resume:, and removeFirstLinkOfList: routines are described later in this section.

synchronousSignal: aSemaphore

```
| excessSignals |
(self isEmptyList: aSemaphore)
    ifTrue: [excessSignals ← self fetchInteger: ExcessSignalsIndex
                                         ofObject: aSemaphore.
             self storeInteger: ExcessSignalsIndex
                 ofObject: aSemaphore
                 withValue: excessSignals + 1]
    ifFalse: [self resume: (self removeFirstLinkOfList: aSemaphore)]
```

The transferTo: routine is used whenever the need to switch processes is detected. It sets the newProcessWaiting and newProcess registers.

transferTo: aProcess

```
newProcessWaiting ← true.
newProcess ← aProcess
```

The checkProcessSwitch routine is called before each bytecode fetch (in the interpret routine) and performs the actual process switch if one has been called for. It stores the active context pointer in the old Process, stores the new Process in the ProcessorScheduler's active process field, and loads the new active context out of that Process.

checkProcessSwitch

```
| activeProcess |
[semaphoreIndex > 0]
    whileTrue:
        [self synchronousSignal: (semaphoreList at: semaphoreIndex).
         semaphoreIndex ← semaphoreIndex − 1].
newProcessWaiting
    ifTrue: [newProcessWaiting ← false.
             activeProcess ← self activeProcess.
             memory storePointer: SuspendedContextIndex
                 ofObject: activeProcess
                 withValue: activeContext.
             memory storePointer: ActiveProcessIndex
                 ofObject: self schedulerPointer
                 withValue: newProcess.
             self newActiveContext:
                     (memory fetchPointer: SuspendedContextIndex
                         ofObject: newProcess)]
```

Any routines desiring to know what the active process will be must take into account the newProcessWaiting and newProcess registers. Therefore, they use the following routine.

activeProcess

```
newProcessWaiting
    ifTrue: [↑newProcess]
    ifFalse: [↑memory fetchPointer: ActiveProcessIndex
                     ofObject: self schedulerPointer]
```

The instance of ProcessorScheduler responsible for scheduling the actual processor needs to be known globally so that the primitives will know where to resume and suspend Processes. This ProcessorScheduler is bound to the name Processor in the Smalltalk global dictionary. The association corresponding to Processor has a guaranteed object pointer, so the appropriate ProcessorScheduler can be found.

schedulerPointer

```
↑memory fetchPointer: ValueIndex
         ofObject: SchedulerAssociationPointer
```

When Smalltalk is started up, the initial active context is found through the scheduler's active Process.

firstContext

```
newProcessWaiting ← false.
↑memory fetchPointer: SuspendedContextIndex
         ofObject: self activeProcess
```

If the object memory automatically deallocates objects on the basis of reference counting, special consideration must be given to reference counting in the process scheduling routines. During the execution of some of these routines, there will be times at which there are no references to some object from the object memory (e.g., after a Process has been removed from a Semaphore but before it has been placed on one of the ProcessorScheduler's LinkedLists). If the object memory uses garbage collection, it simply must avoid doing a collection in the middle of a primitive routine. The routines listed here ignore the reference-counting problem in the interest of clarity. Implementations using reference counting will have to modify these routines in order to prevent premature deallocation of objects.

The following three routines are used to manipulate LinkedLists.

removeFirstLinkOfList: aLinkedList

```
| firstLink lastLink nextLink |
firstLink ← memory fetchPointer: FirstLinkIndex
                   ofObject: aLinkedList.
lastLink ← memory fetchPointer: LastLinkIndex
                   ofObject: aLinkedList.
lastLink = firstLink
    ifTrue: [memory storePointer: FirstLinkIndex
                    ofObject: aLinkedList
                    withValue: NilPointer.
```

```
                    memory storePointer: LastLinkIndex
                         ofObject: aLinkedList
                         withValue: NilPointer]
         ifFalse: [nextLink ← memory fetchPointer: NextLinkIndex
                                    ofObject: firstLink.
                       memory storePointer: FirstLinkIndex
                            ofObject: aLinkedList
                            withValue: nextLink].
       memory storePointer: NextLinkIndex
            ofObject: firstLink
            withValue: NilPointer.
       ↑firstLink
```

addLastLink: aLink toList: aLinkedList

```
       | lastLink |
       (self isEmptyList: aLinkedList)
          ifTrue: [memory storePointer: FirstLinkIndex
                          ofObject: aLinkedList
                          withValue: aLink]
          ifFalse: [lastLink ← memory fetchPointer: LastLinkIndex
                                     ofObject: aLinkedList.
                       memory storePointer: NextLinkIndex
                            ofObject: lastLink
                            withValue: aLink].
       memory storePointer: LastLinkIndex
            ofObject: aLinkedList
            withValue: aLink.
       memory storePointer: MyListIndex
            ofObject: aLink
            withValue: aLinkedList
```

isEmptyList: aLinkedList

```
       ↑(memory fetchPointer: FirstLinkIndex
              ofObject: aLinkedList)
                = NilPointer
```

These three LinkedList routines are used, in turn, to implement the following two routines that remove links from or add links to the ProcessorScheduler's LinkedLists of quiescent Processes.

wakeHighestPriority

```
       | priority processLists processList |
       processLists ← memory fetchPointer: ProcessListsIndex
                              ofObject: self schedulerPointer.
       priority ← memory fetchWordLengthOf: processLists.
       [processList ← memory fetchPointer: priority−1
                              ofObject: processLists.
       self is EmptyList: processList] whileTrue: [priority ← priority − 1].
```

Formal Specification of the Primitive Methods

```
            ↑self removeFirstLinkOfList: processList!
    sleep: aProcess
        | priority processLists processList |
        priority ← self fetchInteger: PriorityIndex
                    ofObject: aProcess.
        processLists ← memory fetchPointer: ProcessListsIndex
                        ofObject: self schedulerPointer.
        processList ← memory fetchPointer: priority−1
                        ofObject: processLists.
        self addLastLink: aProcess
            toList: processList
```

These two routines are used, in turn, to implement the following two routines that actually suspend and resume Processes.

```
    suspendActive
        self transferTo: self wakeHighestPriority
    resume: aProcess
        | activeProcess activePriority newPriority |
        activeProcess ← self activeProcess.
        activePriority ← self fetchInteger: PriorityIndex
                        ofObject: activeProcess.
        newPriority ← self fetchInteger: PriorityIndex
                        ofObject: aProcess.
        newPriority > activePriority
            ifTrue: [self sleep: activeProcess.
                    self transferTo: aProcess]
            ifFalse: [self sleep: aProcess]
```

The primitiveSignal routine is associated with the signal message in Semaphore. Since it is called in the process of interpreting a bytecode, it can use the synchronousSignal: routine. Any other signaling of Semaphores by the interpreter (for example, for timeouts and keystrokes) must use the asynchronousSignal: routine.

```
    primitiveSignal
        self synchronousSignal: self stackTop.
```

The primitiveWait routine is associated with the wait message in Semaphore. If the receiver has an excess signal count greater than 0, the primitiveWait routine decrements the count. If the excess signal count is 0, the primitiveWait suspends the active Process and adds it to the receiver's list of Processes.

```
    primitiveWait
        | thisReceiver excessSignals |
        thisReceiver ← self stackTop.
        excessSignals ← self fetchInteger: ExcessSignalsIndex
                        ofObject: thisReceiver.
```

```
            excessSignals > 0
                ifTrue: [self storeInteger: ExcessSignalsIndex
                        ofObject: thisReceiver
                        withValue: excessSignals — 1]
                ifFalse: [self addLastLink: self activeProcess
                        toList: thisReceiver.
                    self suspendActive]
```

The primitiveResume routine is associated with the resume message in Process. It simply calls the resume: routine with the receiver as argument.

primitiveResume
```
    self resume: self stackTop
```

The primitiveSuspend routine is associated with the suspend message in Process. The primitiveSuspend routine suspends the receiver if it is the active Process. If the receiver is not the active Process, the primitive fails.

primitiveSuspend
```
    self success: self stackTop=self activeProcess.
    self success
        ifTrue: [self popStack.
            self push: NilPointer.
            self suspendActive]
```

The primitiveFlushCache routine removes the contents of the method cache. Implementations that do not use a method cache can treat this as a no-op.

primitiveFlushCache
```
    self initializeMethodCache
```

Input/Output Primitives

The input/output primitive routines provide Smalltalk with access to the state of the hardware devices. Since the implementation of these routines will be dependent on the structure of the implementing machine, no routines will be given, just a specification of the behavior of the primitives.

dispatchInputOutputPrimitives
```
    primitiveIndex = 90 ifTrue: [↑self primitiveMousePoint].
    primitiveIndex = 91 ifTrue: [↑self primitiveCursorLocPut].
    primitiveIndex = 92 ifTrue: [↑self primitiveCursorLink].
```

```
primitiveIndex = 93 ifTrue: [↑self primitiveInputSemaphore].
primitiveIndex = 94 ifTrue: [↑self primitiveSampleInterval].
primitiveIndex = 95 ifTrue: [↑self primitiveInputWord].
primitiveIndex = 96 ifTrue: [↑self primitiveCopyBits].
primitiveIndex = 97 ifTrue: [↑self primitiveSnapshot].
primitiveIndex = 98 ifTrue: [↑self primitiveTimeWordsInto].
primitiveIndex = 99 ifTrue: [↑self primitiveTickWordsInto].
primitiveIndex = 100 ifTrue: [↑self primitiveSignalAtTick].
primitiveIndex = 101 ifTrue: [↑self primitiveBeCursor].
primitiveIndex = 102 ifTrue: [↑self primitiveBeDisplay].
primitiveIndex = 103 ifTrue: [↑self primitiveScanCharacters].
primitiveIndex = 104 ifTrue: [↑self primitiveDrawLoop].
primitiveIndex = 105 ifTrue: [↑self primitiveStringReplace]
```

Four of the primitive routines are used to detect actions by the user. The two types of user action the system can detect are changing the state of a bi-state device and moving the pointing device. The bi-state devices are the keys on the keyboard, three buttons associated with the pointing device and an optional five-paddle keyset. The buttons associated with the pointing device may or may not actually be on the physical pointing device. Three of the four input primitive routines (primitiveInputSemaphore, primitiveInputWord, and primitiveSampleInterval) provide an *active* or *event-initiated* mechanism to detect either state change or movement. The other primitive routine (primitiveMousePoint) provides a *passive* or *polling* mechanism to detect pointing device location.

The event-initiated mechanism provides a buffered stream of 16-bit words that encode changes to the bi-state devices or the pointing device location. Each time a word is placed in the buffer, a Semaphore is signaled (using the asynchronousSignal: routine). The Semaphore to signal is initialized by the primitiveInputSemaphore routine. This routine is associated with the primInputSemaphore: message in InputState and the argument of the message becomes the Semaphore to be signaled. The primitiveInputWord routine (associated with the primInputWord message in InputState) returns the next word in the buffer, removing it from the buffer. Since the Semaphore is signaled once for every word in the buffer, the Smalltalk process emptying the buffer should send the Semaphore a wait message before sending each primInputWord message. There are six types of 16-bit word placed in the buffer. Two types specify the time of an event, two types specify state change of a bi-state device, and two types specify pointing device movement. The type of the word is stored in its high order four bits. The low order 12-bits are referred to as the *parameter*.

The six type codes have the following meanings.

type code	meaning
0	Delta time (the parameter is the number of milliseconds since the last event of any type)
1	X location of the pointing device
2	Y location of the pointing device
3	Bi-state device turned on (the parameter indicates which device)
4	Bi-state device turned off (the parameter indicates which device)
5	Absolute time (the parameter is ignored, the next two words in the buffer contain a 32-bit unsigned number that is the absolute value of the millisecond clock)

Whenever a device state changes or the pointing device moves, a time word is put into the buffer. A type 0 word will be used if the number of milliseconds since the last event can be represented in 12 bits. Otherwise, a type 5 event is used followed by two words representing the absolute time. Note that the Semaphore will be signaled 3 times in the latter case. Following the time word(s) will be one or more words of type 1 through 4. Type 1 and 2 words will be generated whenever the pointing device moves at all. It should be remembered that Smalltalk uses a left-hand coordinate system to talk about the screen. The origin is the upper left corner of the screen, the x dimension increases toward the right, and the y dimension increases toward the bottom. The minimum time span between these events can be set by the primitiveSampleInterval routine which is associated with the primSampleInterval: message in InputState. The argument to primSampleInterval: specifies the number of milliseconds between movement events if the pointing device is moving constantly.

Type 3 and 4 words use the low-order eight bits of the parameter to specify which device changed state. The numbering scheme is set up to work with both decoded and undecoded keyboards. An undecoded keyboard is made up of independent keys with independent down and up transitions. A decoded keyboard consists of some independent keys and some "meta" keys (shift and escape) that cannot be detected on their own, but that change the value of the other keys. The keys on a decoded keyboard only indicate their down transition, not their up transition. On an undecoded keyboard, the standard keys produce parameters that are the ASCII code of the character on the keytop *without* shift or control information (i.e., the key with "A" on it produces the ASCII for "a" and the key with "2" and "@" on it produces the ASCII for "2"). The other standard keys produce the following parameters.

key	parameter
backspace	8
tab	9
line feed	10
return	13
escape	27
space	32
delete	127

For an undecoded keyboard, the meta keys have the following parameters.

key	parameter
left shift	136
right shift	137
control	138
alpha-lock	139

For a decoded keyboard, the full shifted and "controlled" ASCII should be used as a parameter and successive type 3 and 4 words should be produced for each keystroke.

The remaining bi-state devices have the following parameters.

key	parameter
left or top "pointing device" button	128
center "pointing device" button	129
right or bottom "pointing device" button	130
keyset paddles right to left	131 through 135

The primitiveMousePoint routine allows the location of the pointing device to be polled. It allocates a new Point and stores the location of the pointing device in its x and y fields.

The display screen is a rectangular set of pixels that can each be one of two colors. The colors of the pixels are determined by the individual bits in a specially designated instance of DisplayScreen. DisplayScreen is a subclass of Form. The instance of DisplayScreen that should be used to update the screen is designated by sending it the message beDisplay. This message invokes the primitiveBeDisplay primitive routine. The screen will be updated from the last recipient of beDisplay approximately 60 times a second.

Every time the screen is updated, a *cursor* is ORed into its pixels. The cursor image is determined by a specially designated instance of Cursor. Cursor is a subclass of Form whose instances always have both width and height of 16. The instance of Cursor that should be ORed into the screen is designated by sending it the message beCursor. This message invokes the primitiveBeCursor primitive routine.

The location at which the cursor image should appear is called the *cursor location*. The cursor location may be linked to the location of the pointing device or the two locations may be independent. Whether or not the two locations are linked is determined by sending a message to class Cursor with the selector cursorLink: and either true or false as the argument. If the argument is true, then the two locations will be the same; if it is false, they are independent. The cursorLink: message in Cursor's metaclass invokes the primitiveCursorLink primitive routine.

The cursor can be moved in two ways. If the cursor and pointing device have been linked, then moving the pointing device moves the cursor. The cursor can also be moved by sending the message primCursorLocPut: to an instance of InputState. This message takes a Point as an argument and invokes the primitiveCursorLocPut primitive routine. This routine moves the cursor to the location specified by the argument. If the cursor and pointing device are linked, the primitiveCursorLocPut routine also changes the location indicated by the pointing device.

The primitiveCopyBits routine is associated with the copyBits message in BitBlt and performs an operation on a bitmap specified by the receiver. This routine is described in Chapter 18.

The primitiveSnapshot routine writes the current state of the object memory on a file of the same format as the Smalltalk-80 release file. This file can be resumed in exactly the same way that the release file was originally started. Note that the pointer of the active context at the time of the primitive call must be stored in the active Process on the file.

The primitiveTimeWordsInto and primitiveTickWordsInto routines are associated with the timeWordsInto: and tickWordsInto: messages in Sensor. Both of these messages take a byte indexable object of at least four bytes as an argument. The primitiveTimeWordsInto routine stores the number of seconds since the midnight previous to January 1, 1901 as an unsigned 32-bit integer into the first four bytes of the argument. The primitiveTickWordsInto routine stores the number of ticks of the millisecond clock (since it last was reset or rolled over) as an unsigned 32-bit integer into the first four bytes of the argument.

The primitiveSignalAtTick routine is associated with the signal:atTick: messages in ProcessorScheduler. This message takes a Semaphore as the first argument and a byte indexable object of at least four bytes as the second argument. The first four bytes of the second argument are interpreted as an unsigned 32-bit integer of the type stored by the primitiveTickWordsInto routine. The interpreter should signal the Semaphore argument when the millisecond clock reaches the value specified by the second argument. If the specified time has passed, the Semaphore is signaled immediately. This primitive signals the last Semaphore to be passed to it. If a new call is made on it before the last timer value has been reached, the last Semaphore will not be signaled. If the first argument is not a Semaphore, any currently waiting Semaphore will be forgotten.

The primitiveScanCharacters routine is an optional primitive associated with the scanCharactersFrom:to:in:rightX:stopConditions:displaying message in CharacterScanner. If the function of the Smalltalk method is duplicated in the primitive routine, text display will go faster. The primitiveDrawLoop routine is similarly an optional primitive associated with the drawLoopX:Y: message in BitBlt. If the function of the Smalltalk method is duplicated in the primitive routine, drawing lines will go faster.

System Primitives

The seven final primitives are grouped together as system primitives.

dispatchSystemPrimitives

```
primitiveIndex = 110 ifTrue: [↑self primitiveEquivalent].
primitiveIndex = 111 ifTrue: [↑self primitiveClass].
primitiveIndex = 112 ifTrue: [↑self primitiveCoreLeft].
primitiveIndex = 113 ifTrue: [↑self primitiveQuit].
primitiveIndex = 114 ifTrue: [↑self primitiveExitToDebugger].
primitiveIndex = 115 ifTrue: [↑self primitiveOopsLeft].
primitiveIndex = 116 ifTrue: [↑self primitiveSignalAtOopsLeftWordsLeft]
```

The primitiveEquivalent routine is associated with the == message in Object. It returns true if the receiver and argument are the same object (have the same object pointer) and false otherwise.

primitiveEquivalent
```
| thisObject otherObject |
otherObject ← self popStack.
thisObject ← self popStack.
thisObject=otherObject
    ifTrue: [self push: TruePointer]
    ifFalse: [self push: FalsePointer]
```

The primitiveClass routine is associated with the class message in Object. It returns the object pointer of the receiver's class.

primitiveClass
```
| instance |
instance ← self popStack.
self push: (memory fetchClassOf: instance)
```

The primitiveCoreLeft routine returns the number of unallocated words in the object space. The primitiveQuit routine exits to another operating system for the host machine, if one exists. The primitiveExitToDebugger routine calls the machine language debugger, if one exists.

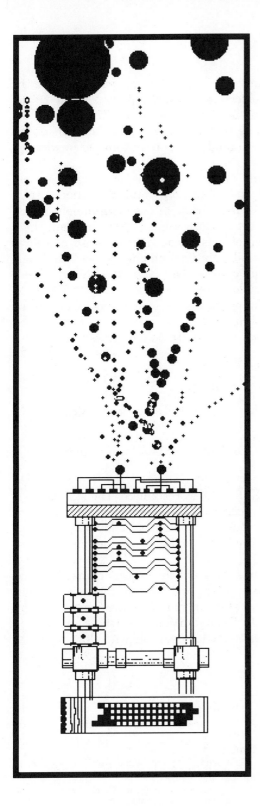

30

Formal Specification
of the Object Memory

The two major components of any Smalltalk-80 implementation are the bytecode interpreter and the object memory. Chapters 28 and 29 described an implementation of the bytecode interpreter. This chapter describes an implementation of the object memory. The function of the object memory is to create, store, and destroy objects, and to provide access to their fields.

Memory-management systems fall into two major categories, *real-memory* implementations and *virtual-memory* implementations. In a real-memory implementation, all the objects in the environment reside in primary memory that is directly addressable by the program. In a virtual-memory implementation, objects reside in more than one level of a memory hierarchy and must be shuffled among the various levels during execution. This chapter describes the design of RealObjectMemory, an object memory for a real-memory Smalltalk-80.

Although Smalltalk can be implemented on computers of any word size, this presentation will be simplified by several assumptions in the standard algorithms. The routines of RealObjectMemory assume

- that there are eight bits in a byte,

- that there are two bytes in a word,

- that the more significant byte of a word precedes the less significant byte, and

- that the target computer is word addressed and word indexed.

Moreover, the routines assume that the address space is partitioned into 16 or fewer *segments* of 64K (65,536) words apiece. The standard algorithms can be systematically changed to adapt them to hardware with different properties. The routines of RealObjectMemory deal almost exclusively with 16-bit integers, as would a machine-language implementation.

To access locations in the address space of the host machine, machine language implementations use load and store instructions. In RealObjectMemory, the load and store instructions are symbolized by messages to an instance of RealWordMemory whose name is wordMemory. The protocol of RealWordMemory is shown below

RealWordMemory instance protocol

segment: s word: w	Return word w of segment s
segment: s word: w put: value	Store value into word w of segment s; return value.
segment: s word: w byte: byteNumber	
	Return byte byteNumber of word w of segment s.
segment: s word: w byte: byteNumber put: value	
	Store value into byte byteNumber of word w of segment s; return value.

segment: s word: w bits: firstBitIndex to: lastBitIndex

> Return bits firstBitIndex to lastBitIndex of word
> w of segment s.

segment: s word: w bits: firstBitIndex to: lastBitIndex put: value

> Store value into bits firstBitIndex to lastBitIndex
> of word w of segment s; return value.

When it is necessary to distinguish the two bytes of a word, the left (more significant) byte will be referred to with the index 0 and the right (less significant) byte with the index 1. The most significant bit in a word will be referred to with the index 0 and the least significant with the index 15. Note that self is an instance of class RealObjectMemory in all routines of this chapter.

The most important thing about any implementation of the object memory is that it conform to the functional specification of the object memory interface given in Chapter 27. This chapter describes a range of possible implementations of that interface. In particular, simple versions of some routines are presented early in the chapter and refined versions are presented later as the need for those refinements becomes clear. These preliminary versions will be flagged by including the comment, "**Preliminary Version**", on the first line of the routine.

Heap Storage

In a real-memory implementation of Smalltalk, all objects are stored in an area called the *heap*. A new object is created by obtaining space to store its fields in a contiguous series of words in the heap. An object is destroyed by releasing the heap space it occupied. The format of an allocated object in the heap is shown in Figure 30.1. The actual data of the object are preceded by a two-word *header*. The size field of the header indicates the number of words of heap that the object occupies, including the header. It is an unsigned 16-bit number, and can range from 2 up to 65,536.

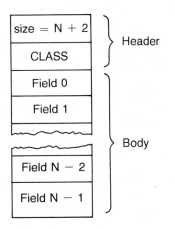

Figure 30.1

When memory is segmented, it is usually convenient for a Smalltalk-80 implementation to divide the heap into *heap segments*, each in a different memory segment. As stated earlier, the routines in this chapter assume that the target computer is segmented into address spaces of 65,536 words.

Heap Related Constants

HeapSegmentCount	The number of heap segments used in the implementation.
FirstHeapSegment	The index of the first memory segment used to store the heap.
LastHeapSegment	The index of the last memory segment used to store the heap (FirstHeapSegment + HeapSegmentCount − 1).
HeapSpaceStop	The address of the last location used in each heap segment.
HeaderSize	The number of words in an object header (2).

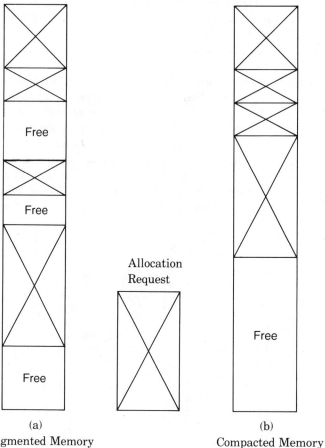

Figure 30.2 Fragmented Memory   Compacted Memory

Compaction

Suppose for a moment that an object once allocated never changes its location in the heap. To allocate a new object, a space between existing objects must be found that is large enough to hold the new object. After a while, the memory "fragments" or "checkerboards." That is, an allocation request is bound to arrive for an amount of space smaller than the total available memory but larger than any of the disjoint pieces (Figure 30.2a). This can occur even if there is a large amount of available space and a relatively small allocation request.

Fragmentation cannot be tolerated in an interactive system that is expected to preserve a dynamic environment for hundreds of hours or more without reinitialization. Therefore when memory fragments, it must be *compacted*. Memory is compacted by moving all objects that are still in use towards one end of the heap, squeezing out all the free space between them and leaving one large unallocated block at the other end (see Figure 30.2b).

Each heap segment is compacted separately. Even on a linearly-addressed machine it is preferable to segment a large heap to reduce the duration of each compaction.

The Object Table

When an object is moved during compaction, all pointers to its heap memory must be updated. If many other objects contain pointers directly to the old location, then it is time-consuming on a sequential computer to find and update those references to point to the new location. Therefore to make the pointer update inexpensive, only one pointer to an object's heap memory is allowed. That pointer is stored in a table called the *object table*. All references to an object must be indirected through the object table. Thus, the object pointers found in Smalltalk objects are really indices into the object table, in which pointers into the heap are in turn found (see Figure 30.3).

Indirection through the object table provides another benefit. The number of objects of average size Z addressable by an n-bit pointer is on the order of 2^n instead of $2^n/Z$. In our experience, objects average 10 words in size ($Z\sim10$), so a significant gain in address space can be realized by indirection.

Throughout the object table, abandoned entries can occur that are not associated with any space on the heap. These entries are called *free entries* and their object pointers are called *free pointers*. It is easy to recycle a free entry, because all object table entries are the same size. Compaction of the object table is difficult and generally unnecessary, so it is not supported.

Although the heap is segmented, the object table is stored in a single segment so that an object pointer can be 16 bits and thus fit in one

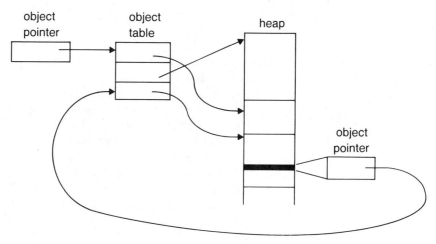

Figure 30.3

word. Consequently, the number of objects that can be addressed in real memory is limited to the number of object table entries that can fit in one segment. A common arrangement is for each object table entry to occupy two words and for the entire table to occupy 64K words or less, yielding a maximum capacity of 32K objects.

Object Pointers

An object pointer occupies 16 bits, apportioned as in Figure 30.4.

Object Table Index	0

Figure 30.4

Immediate Signed Integer	1

When the low-order bit of the object pointer is 0, the first 15 bits are an index into the object table. Up to 2^{15} (32K) objects can be addressed. When the low-order bit of the object pointer is 1, the first 15 bits are an immediate signed integer, and no additional space in the object table or the heap is utilized. The benefit of giving special treatment to integers in the range $\pm2^{14}$ is that they come and go with high frequency during arithmetic and many other operations. The cost of their efficient representation is the number of tests the interpreter must perform to distinguish object pointers of small integers from object pointers of other objects.

The isIntegerObject: routine tests the low order bit of objectPointer to determine whether the rest of the pointer is an immediate integer value rather than an object table index.

isIntegerObject: objectPointer
↑(objectPointer bitAnd: 1) = 1

Every other object-access routine requires that its object pointer argument really be an object table index. The cantBeIntegerObject: routine is used to trap erroneous calls. If the hardware, the bytecode interpreter, and the object memory manager are bug free, then this error condition is never encountered.

cantBeIntegerObject: objectPointer
(self isIntegerObject: objectPointer)
ifTrue: [Sensor notify: 'A small integer has no object table entry']

Object Table
Entries

The format of an object table entry is shown in Figure 30.5. If the free entry bit is on, then the entry is free. If the free entry bit is off, then the four segment bits select a heap segment and the 16 location bits locate the beginning of the space in that segment that is owned by the object table entry. The count field, the odd length bit (O), and the pointer fields bit will be explained later in the chapter.

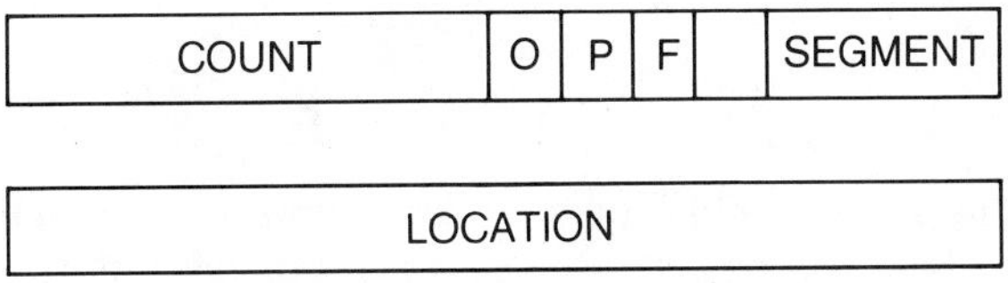

COUNT	O	P	F		SEGMENT

LOCATION

Figure 30.5

Object Table Related Constants

ObjectTableSegment	The number of the memory segment containing the object table.
ObjectTableStart	The location in objectTableSegment of the base of the object table.
ObjectTableSize	The number of words in the object table (an even number ≤ 64K).
HugeSize	The smallest number that is too large to represent in an eight-bit count field; that is, 256.
NilPointer	The object table index of the object nil

The following set of routines accesses the first word of object table entries in four different ways: loading the whole word, storing the whole word, loading a bit field, and storing a bit field. These routines in turn utilize routines of wordMemory, an instance of RealWordMemory. They assume that objectPointer is expressed as an even word offset relative to objectTableStart, the base of the object table in segment objectTableSegment. Note that ot is an abbreviation for "object table."

ot: objectPointer
self cantBeIntegerObject: objectPointer.
↑wordMemory segment: ObjectTableSegment
word: ObjectTableStart + objectPointer

ot: objectPointer put: value
　　self cantBeIntegerObject: objectPointer.
　　↑wordMemory segment: ObjectTableSegment
　　　　　　word: ObjectTableStart + objectPointer
　　　　　　put: value

ot: objectPointer bits: firstBitIndex to: lastBitIndex
　　self cantBeIntegerObject: objectPointer.
　　↑wordMemory segment: ObjectTableSegment
　　　　　　word: ObjectTableStart + objectPointer
　　　　　　bits: firstBitIndex
　　　　　　to: lastBitIndex

ot: objectPointer bits: firstBitIndex to: lastBitIndex put: value
　　self cantBeIntegerObject: objectPointer.
　　↑wordMemory segment: ObjectTableSegment
　　　　　　word: ObjectTableStart + objectPointer
　　　　　　bits: firstBitIndex
　　　　　　to: lastBitIndex
　　　　　　put: value

The following 12 object-access subroutines load or store the various
fields of the object table entry of objectPointer.

countBitsOf: objectPointer
　　↑self ot: objectPointer bits: 0 to: 7
countBitsOf: objectPointer put: value
　　↑self ot: objectPointer bits: 0 to: 7 put: value
oddBitOf: objectPointer
　　↑self ot: objectPointer bits: 8 to: 8
oddBitOf: objectPointer put: value
　　↑self ot: objectPointer bits: 8 to: 8 put: value
pointerBitOf: objectPointer
　　↑self ot: objectPointer bits: 9 to: 9
pointerBitOf: objectPointer put: value
　　↑self ot: objectPointer bits: 9 to: 9 put: value
freeBitOf: objectPointer
　　↑self ot: objectPointer bits: 10 to: 10
freeBitOf: objectPointer put: value
　　↑self ot: objectPointer bits: 10 to: 10 put: value
segmentBitsOf: objectPointer
　　↑self ot: objectPointer bits: 12 to: 15
segmentBitsOf: objectPointer put: value
　　↑self ot: objectPointer bits: 12 to: 15 put: value
locationBitsOf: objectPointer
　　self cantBeIntegerObject: objectPointer.
　　↑wordMemory segment: ObjectTableSegment
　　　　　　word: ObjectTableStart + objectPointer + 1

locationBitsOf: objectPointer put: value
    self cantBeIntegerObject: objectPointer.
    ↑wordMemory segment: ObjectTableSegment
              word: ObjectTableStart + objectPointer + 1
              put: value

For objects that occupy a chunk of heap storage (those whose free bit is 0), the following four object-access subroutines load or store words or bytes from the chunk.

heapChunkOf: objectPointer word: offset
    ↑wordMemory segment: (self segmentBitsOf: objectPointer)
              word: ((self locationBitsOf: objectPointer) + offset)
heapChunkOf: objectPointer word: offset put: value
    ↑wordMemory segment: (self segmentBitsOf: objectPointer)
              word: ((self locationBitsOf: objectPointer) + offset)
              put: value
heapChunkOf: objectPointer byte: offset
    ↑wordMemory segment: (self segmentBitsOf: objectPointer)
              word: ((self locationBitsOf: objectPointer) + (offset//2))
              byte: (offset\\2)
heapChunkOf: objectPointer byte: offset put: value
    ↑wordMemory segment: (self segmentBitsOf: objectPointer)
              word: ((self locationBitsOf: objectPointer) + (offset//2))
              byte: (offset\\2) put: value

The next four object-access subroutines are more specialized in that they load or store words of the object header.

sizeBitsOf: objectPointer
    ↑self heapChunkOf: objectPointer word: 0
sizeBitsOf: objectPointer put: value
    ↑self heapChunkOf: objectPointer word: 0 put: value
classBitsOf: objectPointer
    ↑self heapChunkOf: objectPointer word: 1
classBitsOf: objectPointer put: value
    ↑self heapChunkOf: objectPointer word: 1 put: value

The remaining two object-access subroutines are functionally identical to sizeBitsOf: in the versions shown below. Later in this chapter, refinements to the object-memory manager will require new versions of both of these subroutines that will return something different from the object size in certain cases. For that reason, these methods are marked "preliminary."

lastPointerOf: objectPointer ″**Preliminary Version**″
    ↑self sizeBitsOf: objectPointer
spaceOccupiedBy: objectPointer ″**Preliminary Version**″
    ↑self sizeBitsOf: objectPointer

Unallocated Space

All free entries in the object table are kept on a linked list headed at the location named freePointerList. The link from one free entry to the next is an object pointer in its location field (see Figure 30.6).

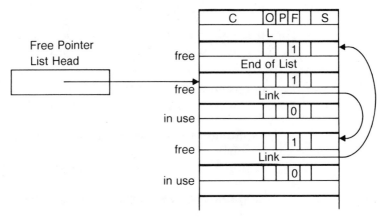

Figure 30.6

Unallocated space in the heap is grouped into *free chunks* (contiguous blocks) of assorted sizes and each of those free chunks is assigned an object table entry. Free chunks are linked together on lists, each containing chunks of the same size. The link from one free chunk to the next is in its class field (Figure 30.7). To keep the table of list heads small, all free chunks bigger than 20 words are linked onto a single list.

Free Space Related Constants

FreePointerList	The location of the head of the linked list of free object table entries.
BigSize	The smallest size of chunk that is not stored on a list whose chunks are the same size. (The index of the last free chunk list).
FirstFreeChunkList	The location of the head of the linked list of free chunks of size zero. Lists for chunks of larger sizes are stored in contiguous locations following FirstFreeChunkList. Note that the lists at FirstFreeChunkList and FirstFreeChunkList + 1 will always be empty since all chunks are at least two words long.
LastFreeChunkList	The location of the head of the linked list of free chunks of size BigSize or larger.
NonPointer	Any sixteen-bit value that cannot be an object table index, e.g., $2^{16} - 1$.

A separate set of free chunk lists is maintained for each heap segment, but only one free pointer list is maintained for the object table. Note that the object table entry associated with a "free chunk" is not a "free

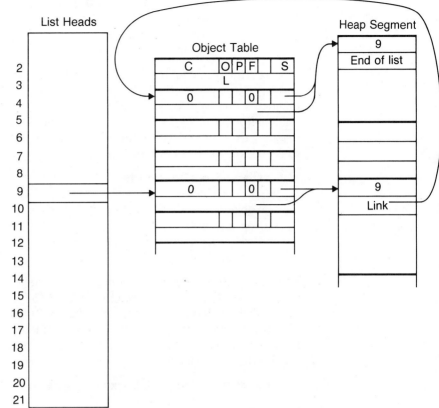

Figure 30.7

entry." It is not on the free pointer list, and its free entry bit is not set. The way a free chunk is distinguished from an allocated chunk is by setting the count field of the object table entry to zero for a free chunk and to nonzero for an allocated chunk.

The following four routines manage the free pointer list headed at freePointerList in segment objectTableSegment. The first two routines simply load and store the list head.

headOfFreePointerList
    ↑wordMemory segment: ObjectTableSegment
        word: FreePointerList
headOfFreePointerListPut: objectPointer
    ↑wordMemory segment: ObjectTableSegment
        word: FreePointerList
        put: objectPointer

The routine toFreePointerListAdd: adds a free entry to the head of the list.

toFreePointerListAdd: objectPointer

self locationBitsOf: objectPointer
   put: (self headOfFreePointerList).
self headOfFreePointerListPut: objectPointer

The routine removeFromFreePointerList removes the first entry from the list and returns it; if the list was empty, it returns nil. The distinguished value NonPointer signifies the end of a linked list. A good value for NonPointer is $2^{16}-1$, a value that is easily detected on most computers and that cannot be confused with an actual object table entry address because it is an odd number.

removeFromFreePointerList

| objectPointer |
objectPointer ← self headOfFreePointerList.
objectPointer = NonPointer ifTrue: [↑nil].
self headOfFreePointerListPut: (self locationBitsOf: objectPointer).
↑objectPointer

The following routines manage the free-chunk lists headed at FirstFreeChunkList + 2 through LastFreeChunkList of each heap segment. Their behavior is exactly analogous to that of the routines above. The first three routines work in the segment specified or implied by their second parameter. The fourth routine works in the segment specified by the register currentSegment.

headOfFreeChunkList: size inSegment: segment

↑wordMemory segment: segment
        word: FirstFreeChunkList + size

headOfFreeChunkList: size
inSegment: segment
put: objectPointer

↑wordMemory segment: segment
        word: FirstFreeChunkList + size
        put: objectPointer

toFreeChunkList: size add: objectPointer

| segment |
segment ← self segmentBitsOf: objectPointer.
self classBitsOf: objectPointer
   put: (self headOfFreeChunkList: size inSegment: segment).
self headOfFreeChunkList: size
  inSegment: segment
  put: objectPointer

removeFromFreeChunkList: size

| objectPointer secondChunk |
objectPointer ← self headOfFreeChunkList: size
           inSegment: currentSegment.
objectPointer = NonPointer ifTrue: [↑nil].

    secondChunk ← self classBitsOf: objectPointer.
  self headOfFreeChunkList: size
      inSegment: currentSegment
      put: secondChunk.
  ↑objectPointer

The routine resetFreeChunkList:inSegment: resets the specified free-chunk list to an empty list.

resetFreeChunkList: size inSegment: segment
  self headOfFreeChunkList: size
      inSegment: segment
      put: NonPointer

Allocation and Deallocation

To allocate an object, an entry is obtained from the object table and sufficient space for the header and data is obtained from some heap segment. The heap segment in which space is found is called the *current segment*. It becomes the first segment in which to look for space to allocate the next object. The only register required by the object memory holds the index of the current segment.

Registers of the Object Memory

currentSegment   The index of the heap segment currently being used for allocation.

To allocate a "large" object requiring n words of heap space (n >= BigSize), the list beginning at LastFreeChunkList in the current segment is searched for a free chunk whose size is either n words or at least n+ headerSize words. If the free chunk found is larger than n words, it is *subdivided* and only n of the words are used to satisfy the allocation request.

To allocate a "small" object requiring n words of heap space (headerSize <= n < BigSize), the list beginning at freeChunkLists+n is searched. If the list is nonempty, its first free chunk is removed and used for the new object. If the list is empty, the above algorithm for "large" objects is used.

If no chunk of sufficient size is found in the current segment, then the next segment is made current and the search continues there. The new current segment is compacted first to improve the chances of finding sufficient space. In a compacted segment, all the allocated objects are at one end and the (presumably large) space at the other end is all in one large chunk, the sole member of the list LastFreeChunkLists. If enough space is not found in any segment, execution is halted.

When an object is deallocated, its space is recycled on the list of free chunks of the appropriate size. However, to simplify the presentation in this chapter, the standard algorithms leave the unused part of any subdivided chunk on the list of big free chunks even if that part is small in size.

An Allocation Algorithm

The allocate:class: routine is presented below as an example of a simple allocation routine. It takes as parameters the size of the desired chunk (in words, including header) and the class of the object that chunk will represent. The actual allocation routine takes several other parameters and so the allocate:class: routine will be flagged as preliminary. A more complete routine, allocate:extra:class:, is presented in a later section and the actual routine used in the implementation, allocate:odd:pointer:-extra:class:, is presented after that.

```
allocate: size class: classPointer  "**Preliminary Version**"
    | objectPointer |
    objectPointer ← self allocateChunk: size.  "actually allocate"
    self classBitsOf: objectPointer put: classPointer.  "fill in class"
    "initialize all fields to the object table index of the object nil"
    (headerSize to: size−1) do:
        [ :i | self heapChunkOf: objectPointer word: i put: NilPointer].
    self sizeBitsOf: objectPointer put: size.
    "return the new object's pointer"
    ↑objectPointer
```

The routine allocateChunk: either succeeds in its allocation task, or it reports an unrecoverable error. It uses a subroutine, attempt-ToAllocateChunk:, that either completes the job or returns nil if no space can be found.

```
allocateChunk: size  "**Preliminary Version**"
    | objectPointer |
    objectPointer ← self attemptToAllocateChunk: size.
    objectPointer isNil ifFalse: [↑objectPointer].
    ↑self error: 'Out of memory'
```

The attemptToAllocateChunk: routine first tries to allocate in currentSegment, the segment currently targeted for allocations. It does so using the subroutine attemptToAllocateChunkInCurrentSegment:. If the subroutine fails (returns nil), then the routine compacts the next segment and retries the allocation there. This procedure continues until the original segment has been compacted and searched. If no space can be found anywhere, the routine returns nil. Note that it uses implementation-dependent constants: HeapSegmentCount, FirstHeapSegment, and LastHeapSegment.

attemptToAllocateChunk: size
```
| objectPointer |
objectPointer ← self attemptToAllocateChunkInCurrentSegment: size.
objectPointer isNil ifFalse: [↑objectPointer].
1 to: HeapSegmentCount do:
    [ :i |
    currentSegment ← currentSegment + 1.
    currentSegment > LastHeapSegment
        ifTrue: [currentSegment ← FirstHeapSegment].
    self compactCurrentSegment.
    objectPointer
            ← self attemptToAllocateChunkInCurrentSegment: size.
    objectPointer isNil ifFalse: [↑objectPointer]].
↑nil
```

The attemptToAllocateChunkInCurrentSegment: routine searches the current heap segment's free-chunk lists for the first chunk that is the right size or that can be subdivided to yield a chunk of the right size. Because most objects are smaller than BigSize and most allocation requests can be satisfied by recycling deallocated objects of the desired size, most allocations execute only the first four lines of the routine.

attemptToAllocateChunkInCurrentSegment: size
```
| objectPointer predecessor next availableSize excessSize newPointer |
size < BigSize
    ifTrue: [objectPointer ← self removeFromFreeChunkList: size].
objectPointer notNil
    ifTrue: [↑objectPointer]. "small chunk of exact size handy so use it"
predecessor ← NonPointer.
            "remember predecessor of chunk under consideration"
objectPointer ← self headOfFreeChunkList: LastFreeChunkList
                    inSegment: currentSegment.
"the search loop stops when the end of the linked list is encountered"
[objectPointer = NonPointer] whileFalse:
    [availableSize ← self sizeBitsOf: objectPointer.
    availableSize = size
        ifTrue: "exact fit —remove from free chunk list and return"
            [next ← self classBitsOf: objectPointer.
                    "the link to the next chunk"
            predecessor=NonPointer
                ifTrue: "it was the head of the list; make the next item the head"
                    [self headOfFreeChunkList: LastFreeChunkList
                        inSegment: currentSegment put: next]
                ifFalse: "it was between two chunks; link them together"
                    [self classBitsOf: predecessor
                        put: next].
            ↑objectPointer].
```

"this chunk was either too big or too small; inspect the amount of variance"
excessSize ← availableSize-size.
excessSize >= HeaderSize
  ifTrue: "can be broken into two usable parts: return the second part"
    ["obtain an object table entry for the second part"
     newPointer ← self obtainPointer: size
             location: (self locationBitsOf: objectPointer)
                        + excessSize.
     newPointer isNil ifTrue: [↑nil].
     "correct the size of the first part (which remains on the free list)"
     self sizeBitsOf: objectPointer put: excessSize.
     ↑newPointer]
  ifFalse: "not big enough to use; try the next chunk on the list"
    [predecessor ← objectPointer.
     objectPointer ← self classBitsOf: objectPointer]].
↑nil "the end of the linked list was reached and no fit was found"

The subroutine obtainPointer:location: used by the above routine obtains a free object table entry, zeroes its free entry bit as well as the rest of the first word of the entry, points the entry at the specified location, and sets the size field of the header to the specified size.

obtainPointer: size location: location
| objectPointer |
objectPointer ← self removeFromFreePointerList.
objectPointer isNil ifTrue: [↑nil].
self ot: objectPointer put: 0.
self segmentBitsOf: objectPointer put: currentSegment.
self locationBitsOf: objectPointer put: location.
self sizeBitsOf: objectPointer put: size.
↑objectPointer

*A Deallocation
Algorithm*

It is much simpler to deallocate an object than to allocate one. The chunk is recycled on a free-chunk list. The following routine expects the count field to have been reset to zero by a higher-level routine.

deallocate: objectPointer "**Preliminary Version**"
| space |
space ← self spaceOccupiedBy: objectPointer.
self toFreeChunkList: (space min: BigSize)
  add: objectPointer

Note that this routine computes the space occupied by the object using spaceOccupiedBy: instead of sizeBitsOf:. The reason will become clear later in the chapter when spaceOccupiedBy: is redefined.

A Compaction Algorithm

The compactCurrentSegment routine invoked above by attemptToAllocateChunk: sweeps through a heap segment, massing all allocated objects together and updating their object table entries. For the benefit of subsequent allocation, it also links the object table entries reclaimed from the free chunk lists onto the free pointer list and creates a single free chunk from the unused portion of the heap segment. The algorithm for compactCurrentSegment will be presented shortly, after some preparatory discussion.

After a heap segment is compacted a number of times, relatively permanent objects sift to the bottom of the segment and most allocation and deallocation activity occurs nearer to the top. The segment consists of a densely packed region of allocated chunks, followed by a region of both allocated and free chunks. During compaction, chunks in the densely packed region never move, because there is no space beneath them to eliminate. Therefore, the compacter expends effort only on chunks above the first free chunk, whose location is referred to as lowWaterMark.

The abandonFreeChunksInSegment: routine computes lowWaterMark. It also finds all deallocated chunks, recycles their object table entries onto the list of free pointers using the subroutine releasePointer:, and changes their class fields to the distinguished value nonPointer. During the subsequent sweep, when the compacter encounters objects so marked it can recognize them as deallocated chunks.

abandonFreeChunksInSegment: segment
    | lowWaterMark objectPointer nextPointer |
    lowWaterMark ← HeapSpaceStop. "first assume that no chunk is free"
    HeaderSize to: BigSize do: "for each free-chunk list"
       [:size |
         objectPointer ← self headOfFreeChunkList: size
                       inSegment: segment.
       [objectPointer = NonPointer] whileFalse:
        [lowWaterMark ← lowWaterMark
                    min: (self locationBitsOf: objectPointer).
        nextPointer ← self classBitsOf: objectPointer.
               "link to next free chunk"
        self classBitsOf: objectPointer put: NonPointer.
               "distinguish for sweep"
        self releasePointer: objectPointer.
               "add entry to free-pointer list"
        objectPointer ← nextPointer].
       self resetFreeChunkList: size inSegment: segment].
    ↑lowWaterMark
releasePointer: objectPointer
    self freeBitOf: objectPointer put: 1.
    self toFreePointerListAdd: objectPointer

A heap segment is compacted by sweeping through it from bottom to top. Each allocated object is moved as far down in the segment as possible without overwriting other allocated objects. For each object moved, the corresponding object table entry is found and its location field is updated to point to the new location of the object.

It is by no means trivial to find the object table entry of an object encountered during a sweep of the heap segment. The representation of the object in the heap does not include a pointer back to the object table entry. To avoid the cost of such a backpointer for every object or making the compacter search the object table after every object is moved, a trick called "reversing pointers" is employed. During compaction, instead of the usual arrangement in which the object table entry points to the header in the heap, the header points temporarily to the object table entry.

Pointers are reversed before starting to sweep through a heap segment. The object table is scanned to find every in-use entry whose segment field refers to the segment being compacted and whose location field is above lowWaterMark. Each such entry points to the header of an object that is to be moved (Figure 30.8a). The pointer is then reversed, i.e., the object's own object pointer is stored in the first word of its header. This causes the header to point to the object table entry. By doing this, the size field of the header is overwritten. To prevent losing the size, it is saved in the second word of the object table entry (Figure 30.8b). By doing that, the location field is overwritten, but that is of no

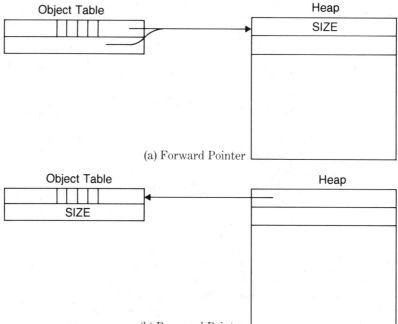

(a) Forward Pointer

(b) Reversed Pointer

Figure 30.8

consequence, because the compacter recomputes the object's heap location after the move.

reverseHeapPointersAbove: lowWaterMark

```
| size |
0 to: ObjectTableSize-2 by: 2 do:
    [ :objectPointer |
     (self freeBitOf: objectPointer)=0
        ifTrue: "the Object Table entry is in use"
            [(self segmentBitsOf: objectPointer) = currentSegment
                ifTrue: "the object is in this segment"
                    [(self locationBitsOf: objectPointer) < lowWaterMark
                        ifFalse: "the object will be swept"
                            [size ← self sizeBitsOf: objectPointer.
                                        "rescue the size"
                            self sizeBitsOf: objectPointer
                                put: objectPointer. "reverse the pointer"
                            self locationBitsOf: objectPointer
                                put: size "save the size"]]]]
```

After all preparations for compaction are complete, the current heap segment is swept using the sweepCurrentSegmentFrom: routine. It maintains two pointers into the segment, si (source index) and di (destination index). The pointer si points to the header of an object currently being considered for retention or elimination. The pointer di points to the location where that object will be moved if retained.

sweepCurrentSegmentFrom: lowWaterMark

```
| si di objectPointer size space |
si ← di ← lowWaterMark.
[si < HeapSpaceStop]
    whileTrue: "for each object, si"
        [(wordMemory segment: currentSegment word: si + 1) = NonPointer
            ifTrue: "unallocated, so skip it"
                [size ← wordMemory segment: currentSegment word: si.
                si ← si + size]
            ifFalse: "allocated, so keep it, but move it to compact storage"
                [objectPointer
                        ← wordMemory
                            segment: currentSegment word: si.
                size ← self locationBitsOf: objectPointer.
                        "the reversed size"
                self locationBitsOf: objectPointer
                    put: di. "point object table at new location"
                self sizeBitsOf: objectPointer
                    put: size. "restore the size to its proper place"
                si ← si + 1. "skip the size"
                di ← di + 1. "skip the size"
```

```
                                    2 to: (self spaceOccupiedBy: objectPointer) do:
                                      "move the rest of the object"
                                    [ :i |
                                      wordMemory segment: currentSegment
                                                 word: di
                                                 put: (wordMemory segment:
                                                                    currentSegment
                                                          word: si).
                                    si ← si + 1.
                                    di ← di + 1]]].
         ↑di
```

Note that while pointers are reversed, it is impossible to access the heap memory of an object from its object table entry. Therefore the Smalltalk interpreter cannot run during compaction.

The compactCurrentSegment routine invokes the above routines in the proper order and then creates the single free chunk at the top of the heap segment.

compactCurrentSegment

```
| lowWaterMark bigSpace |
lowWaterMark ← self abandonFreeChunksInSegment: currentSegment.
lowWaterMark < HeapSpaceStop
    ifTrue:
        [self reverseHeapPointersAbove: lowWaterMark.
        bigSpace ← self sweepCurrentSegmentFrom: lowWaterMark.
        self deallocate: (self obtainPointer:
                             (HeapSpaceStop + 1 − bigSpace)
                          location: bigSpace)]
```

If there are no free chunks within the segment when this routine is invoked, then it does not move any objects.

Garbage Collection

In Smalltalk, a new object is allocated explicitly (e.g., when the message new is sent to a class) but there is no explicit language construct that causes an object to be deallocated. Such a construct would be unsafe, because it could be used to deallocate an object even though "dangling" references to it still existed in other objects. An environment containing dangling references would be inconsistent and would be likely to exhibit unintended behavior and to suffer unrecoverable errors.

Most noninteractive programming systems require explicit deallocation. The burden of avoiding dangling references is placed on the programmer. If a dangling reference arises, the programmer is expected to find the bug that created it, fix that bug, and restart the program. In an interactive environment like Smalltalk (as well as most LISP and APL systems), to require a restart because of a common bug would be unacceptable, since it could require the user to redo a potentially large amount of work.

Because there is no explicit deallocation in Smalltalk, the memory manager must identify objects that have become *inaccessible* and deallocate them automatically. This task is traditionally known as *garbage collection*. As compared with explicit deallocation, garbage collection entails a large performance penalty. The penalty is incurred because the computer must manage deallocation at execution time instead of relying on the programmer to have done so during coding time. However, the cost is well worth the reliability it adds to an interactive system.

There are two traditional approaches to identifying inaccessible objects in an object memory: *marking* and *reference counting*. A marking garbage collector performs an exhaustive search of memory for accessible objects and marks them all. Then it scans memory in search of objects that are unmarked and thus inaccessible and deallocates them. A reference-counting garbage collector maintains a count of how many references there are to each object from other objects. When the count of references to some object reaches zero, that object is known to be inaccessible, and the space it occupies can be reclaimed.

Reference-counting systems do not deal properly with so-called "cyclic structures." Such a structure is said to occur when an object references itself directly or when an object references itself indirectly via other objects that reference it. In a reference-counting system, when a cyclic structure becomes inaccessible to the program, it will have nonzero reference counts due to the intrastructure references. Therefore the memory manager doesn't recognize that the structure should be deallocated, and the objects that constitute the structure are not deallocated. These inaccessible objects waste space; but, unlike dangling references, they do not cause inconsistency in the environment.

Both reference counting and marking involve performance penalties on conventional computers. In a reference-counting system, the frequently performed operation of storing a reference to an object involves overhead for reference-count maintenance, so programs run significantly more slowly. In a marking garbage collector, an extensive search of memory must be performed whenever space is entirely depleted. Therefore, program execution is subject to relatively lengthy interruptions that can be quite annoying in an interactive system. Both approaches incur space overhead. In a reference-counting system, space must be provided to store reference counts. In a marking system, extra space must be allotted in the heap to allow garbage to accumulate between collections. Otherwise, collections occur too frequently.

The approach to garbage collection that should be used in a particular implementation of Smalltalk depends in part on the capacity of the hardware. If a relatively small amount of memory (e.g., 100 kilobytes) is available, a reference counting system is intolerable, because it can waste precious space by leaving inaccessible cyclic structures allocated. On the other hand, a marking collector is quite acceptable in these circumstances, in spite of the interruption that occurs when it is invoked, because when memory is small, the duration of the interruption can be so brief as to be imperceptible. If an abundant supply of memory (e.g., two megabytes) is available, the time it takes to mark all accessible objects can be so long as to be intolerable. On the other hand, there is enough space available that a moderate number of inaccessible objects can be tolerated.

The contrast between the two approaches is accentuated in a large virtual-memory system. Marking is even more costly because so much time is spent in random accesses to secondary memory. Reference counting is even less costly because unreclaimed cyclic structures simply migrate to secondary memory where wasted space is less bothersome. When memory is abundant, a reference-counting garbage collector is appropriate. However, Smalltalk programmers should take precautions to avoid the accumulation of an excessive number of inaccessible cyclic structures, otherwise even a large memory will be depleted. To break a cyclic structure before it becomes inaccessible, the program can change any pointer that participates in the cycle to nil.

The two approaches to garbage collection can be combined. References can be counted during normal operation and marking collections performed periodically to reclaim inaccessible cyclic structures. A combined approach is suitable for all but the smallest real-memory implementations. If a small-to-medium-size memory is available, a marking collection can be performed whenever compaction fails to recover enough space. If an abundant memory is available, marking collections can be performed nightly or at other convenient intervals.

A Simple Reference-counting Collector

In the reference-counting collector described in this chapter, the reference count of an object is recorded in the count field of its object table entry. If an object pointer is an immediate integer, it is its own only reference, so its reference count is not recorded explicitly. Reference counts are updated during store operations. When an object pointer referencing object P is stored into a location that formerly contained an object pointer referencing object Q, the count field of P is incremented and the count field of Q is decremented. Because the count field of an object table entry has only eight bits, it is possible for an incremented count to overflow. To facilitate overflow detection on most computers, the high order bit of the count field serves as an overflow bit. Once the count field reaches 128, it remains at that value and it will not increase or decrease. The algorithm for incrementing a reference count is

countUp: objectPointer
```
    | count |
    (self isIntegerObject: objectPointer)
        ifFalse:
            [count ← (self countBitsOf: objectPointer) + 1.
             count < 129 ifTrue: [self countBitsOf: objectPointer put: count]].
    ↑objectPointer
```

If the decremented reference count of an object reaches zero, then that object is deallocated. Before doing so, the count field of every object referenced from that object is decremented, because once the object is deallocated it will no longer reference those other objects. Note that this procedure recurs if any of the latter counts reach zero. A recursive procedure that can traverse the original object plus all the objects it references is expressed below as the routine forAllObjectsAccessibleFrom:-suchThat:do:. This routine takes two procedural arguments represented by blocks, a predicate that decrements a count and tests for zero and an action that deallocates an object. Between evaluating the predicate and the action, the procedure's subroutine, forAllOtherObjectsAccessibleFrom:-suchThat:do:, recursively processes every pointer in the object. The procedure is allowed to alter the count as a side effect, so the action argument must restore the count to zero in preparation for deallocation.

countDown: rootObjectPointer
```
    | count |
    (self isIntegerObject: rootObjectPointer)
        ifTrue: [↑rootObjectPointer]
        ifFalse: "this is a pointer, so decrement its reference count"
            [↑self forAllObjectsAccessibleFrom: rootObjectPointer
                suchThat:
                    "the predicate decrements the count and tests for zero"
                    [ :objectPointer |
                      count ← (self countBitsOf: objectPointer) − 1.
                      count < 127
                          ifTrue: [self countBitsOf: objectPointer
                                       put: count].
                      count=0]
                do: "the action zeroes the count and deallocates the object"
                    [ :objectPointer |
                      self countBitsOf: objectPointer put: 0.
                      self deallocate: objectPointer]]
```

The traversal routine shown below first tests the predicate on the supplied object. It then invokes a subroutine that (1) recursively processes all objects referenced from within the supplied object that satisfy predicate, and (2) performs action on the supplied object.

forAllObjectsAccessibleFrom: objectPointer
suchThat: predicate
do: action
(predicate value: objectPointer)
    ifTrue:
        [↑self forAllOtherObjectsAccessibleFrom: objectPointer
            suchThat: predicate
            do: action]

forAllOtherObjectsAccessibleFrom: objectPointer
suchThat: predicate
do: action
| next |
1 to: (self lastPointerOf: objectPointer) − 1 do:
  [:offset |
    next ← self heapChunkOf: objectPointer word: offset.
    ((self isIntegerObject: next) = = false and: [predicate value: next])
        ifTrue: "it's a non-immediate object and it should be processed"
            [self forAllOtherObjectsAccessibleFrom: next
                suchThat: predicate
                do: action]].
  "all pointers have been followed; now perform the action"
  action value: objectPointer.
  ↑objectPointer

A Space-efficient
Reference-counting
Collector

The traversal algorithm outlined above is recursive and, therefore, must use a stack in its execution. To guard against stack overflow, the depth of the stack must be greater than the longest chain of pointers in memory. This requirement is difficult to satisfy when memory space is limited. To guarantee that enough space is available, the pointer chain itself can be used as the stack. If object A references object B from A's i^{th} field, and object B references object C from B's j^{th} field, and object C references another object from C's k^{th} field, and so on, the pointer chain can be represented as $A.i \rightarrow B.j \rightarrow C.k \rightarrow ...$ (Figure 30.9a). To use the pointer chain as a stack for the recursion of the traversal algorithm, the chain is temporarily reversed to $... \rightarrow C.k \rightarrow B.j \rightarrow A.i$ so that each field in the chain points to its predecessor instead of to its successor (Figure 30.9b).

Each step of the traversal algorithm's recursion must be completed by "popping the stack." After processing any object in the chain (e.g., C), its predecessor (e.g., B) is found by following the reversed pointer chain. The algorithm also needs to know which field of the predecessor was being worked on. To maintain this information, the algorithm must be changed at the earlier stage where it left B to process C. At that stage, the index of the field, j, is copied into the count field of the object table

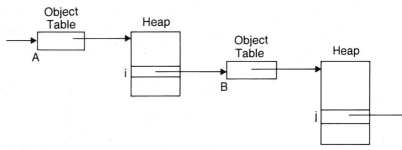

(a) Forward Chain

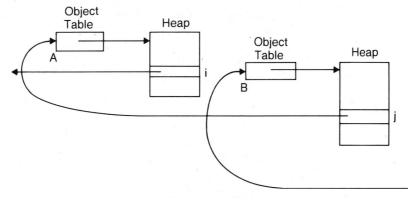

Figure 30.9

(b) Reversed Chain

entry of *B*. The count can be overwritten because the object is being deallocated. But if the size of *B* exceeds 255 words, then the count field will not be large enough to store every field index. Instead, the allocator is revised to over-allocate by one word any object that is HugeSize (256) words or more and to reserve that extra word for use by the traversal algorithm to store *offset*.

To accommodate over-allocation, the allocation routine is revised to accept an additional argument, extraWord, that is either 0 or 1. It is also necessary for the allocator to increment the reference count of the new object's class before storing the class into the header of the new object. (In fact, this must be accomplished even earlier, before calling allocateChunk:, to assure that the class is not deallocated accidentally by some side effect of that subroutine.)

allocate: size extra: extraWord class: classPointer
```
    "**Preliminary Version**"
    | objectPointer |
    self countUp: classPointer.
            "increment the reference count of the class"
    objectPointer ← self allocateChunk: size + extraWord.
            "allocate enough"
    self classBitsOf: objectPointer put: classPointer.
```

```
HeaderSize to: size-1 do:
    [ :i |   self heapChunkOf: objectPointer word: i put: NilPointer].
    "the next statement to correct the SIZE need only be executed if
        extraWord > 0"
self sizeBitsOf: objectPointer put: size.
↑objectPointer
```

The actual heap space occupied by an object with at least HugeSize fields is one greater than that stated in its size field, because of the extra word allocated. Therefore, the spaceOccupiedBy: routine must be changed to account for the difference.

spaceOccupiedBy: objectPointer "**Preliminary Version**"

```
| size |
size ← self sizeBitsOf: objectPointer.
size < HugeSize
    ifTrue: [↑size]
    ifFalse: [↑size + 1]
```

The deallocation algorithm must also be revised because deallocated objects have no provision for an extra word not counted in the size field.

deallocate: objectPointer

```
| space |
space ← self spaceOccupiedBy: objectPointer.
self sizeBitsOf: objectPointer put: space.
self toFreeChunkList: (space min: BigSize) add: objectPointer
```

The following routine implements the space-efficient traversal algorithm, with A, B, and C of the above example represented by the variables prior, current, and next. To simplify the loop test, the method scans the fields of each chunk in reverse order. Thus the class field is processed last.

Note that the last statement of the method restores the pointer chain to get $B.j$ again pointing to C instead of to A. It is easy to do so when returning to B from processing C, because object pointer of C can simply be stored in the jth field of B. One might think that step unnecessary, because B is being deallocated. However, the same traversal algorithm can be used by a marking collector in which B is not being deallocated.

forAllOtherObjectsAccessibleFrom: objectPointer
      suchThat: predicate
      do: action

```
| prior current offset size next |
"compute prior, current, offset, and size to begin processing
objectPointer"
prior ← NonPointer.
```

```
current ← objectPointer.
offset ← size ← self lastPointerOf: objectPointer.
[true] whileTrue: "for all pointers in all objects traversed"
    [(offset ← offset − 1) > 0 "decrement the field index"
        ifTrue: "the class field hasn't been passed yet"
            [next← self heapChunkOf: current word: offset.
                    "one of the pointers"
            ((self isIntegerObject: next)==false
                            and: [predicate value: next])
            ifTrue: "it's a non-immediate object and it should be pro-
                    cessed"
                ["reverse the pointer chain"
                self heapChunkOf: current word: offset put: prior.
                "save the offset either in the count field or in the extra
                    word"
                size < HugeSize
                    ifTrue: [self countBitsOf: current put: offset]
                    ifFalse: [self heapChunkOf: current
                                word: size + 1 put: offset].
                "compute prior, current, offset, and size to begin pro-
                    cessing next"
                prior ← current. current ← next.
                offset ← size ← self lastPointerOf: current]]
    ifFalse:
        ["all pointers have been followed; now perform the action"
        action value: current.
        "did we get here from another object?"
        prior=NonPointer
            ifTrue: "this was the root object, so we are done"
                [↑objectPointer].
        "restore next, current, and size to resume processing prior"
        next ← current. current ← prior.
        size ← self lastPointerOf: current.
        "restore offset either from the count field or from the extra word"
        size < HugeSize
            ifTrue: [offset ← self countBitsOf: current]
            ifFalse: [offset ← self heapChunkOf: current word: size + 1].
        "restore prior from the reversed pointer chain"
        prior ← self heapChunkOf: current word: offset.
        "restore (unreverse) the pointer chain"
        self heapChunkOf: current word: offset put: next]]
```

The machine-language implementation can deal with the procedural arguments either by passing a pair of subroutine addresses to be called
indirectly or by expanding the subroutines in line. If the hardware has
enough registers, it is possible to keep the variables next, current, prior,
size, and offset in registers for additional speed of execution.

*A Marking
Collector*

The job of the marking garbage collector is to mark all accessible objects so that the remaining inaccessible objects can be identified and added to the lists of free chunks. Accessible objects can be found most easily by a recursive search from the "roots of the world," namely, the interpreter's stacks and the table of global variables (the Dictionary named Smalltalk).

The following algorithm is performed on each root object. In the object table entry of the object, set the count field to 1 to mean "marked." Apply the algorithm of this paragraph to each unmarked object referenced by the object.

Note that the above *marking algorithm* is inherently recursive. In its implementation, the same traversal routine used for reference counting can be used, in either the simple or the space-efficient version. Before marking begins, the count fields of all objects are reset to 0 to mean "unmarked." After marking ends, all unmarked objects are deallocated and the reference counts of all marked objects are recomputed. The routine that performs all the necessary steps is called reclaimInaccessibleObjects.

reclaimInaccessibleObjects

```
self zeroReferenceCounts.
self markAccessibleObjects.
self rectifyCountsAndDeallocateGarbage
```

The subroutine that sets the count fields of all objects to 0 is called zeroReferenceCounts. It is superfluous to zero the count field of a free chunk or of a free entry. Nevertheless, the following version zeroes the count field of every entry, because on most computers, it takes less time to zero the first byte of an entry than it takes to test the status of that entry.

zeroReferenceCounts

```
0 to: ObjectTableSize-2 by: 2 do:
   [ :objectPointer |
     self countBitsOf: objectPointer put: 0]
```

The subroutine markAccessibleObjects invokes the marking algorithm markObjectsAccessibleFrom: for every object in the list rootObjectPointers. Typically, the list rootObjectPointers includes the object pointer of the current process and the object pointer of the global variable dictionary, from which all other accessible objects are referenced directly or indirectly.

markAccessibleObjects

```
rootObjectPointers do:
   [ :rootObjectPointer |
     self markObjectsAccessibleFrom: rootObjectPointer]
```

The marking algorithm markObjectsAccessibleFrom: calls the same traversal routine as the reference-counting collector did. Its predicate succeeds for unmarked objects and it marks them with a count of 1 as a side effect. Its action restores the count field to 1 because the space-efficient version of the traversal routine could have changed that field to any nonzero value as a side effect.

markObjectsAccessibleFrom: rootObjectPointer
```
| unmarked |
↑self forAllObjectsAccessibleFrom: rootObjectPointer
    suchThat: "the predicate tests for an unmarked object and marks it"
        [ :objectPointer |
            unmarked ← (self countBitsOf: objectPointer) = 0.
            unmarked ifTrue: [self countBitsOf: objectPointer put: 1].
            unmarked]
    do: "the action restores the mark to count=1"
        [ :objectPointer |
            self countBitsOf: objectPointer put: 1]
```

After the marking algorithm has been executed, every non-free object table entry is examined using the subroutine rectifyCountsAndDeallocateGarbage. If the entry is unmarked, then the entry and its heap chunk are added to the appropriate free lists. If the entry is marked, then the count is decremented by one to unmark it, and the counts of all objects that it references directly are incremented. Note that when a marked object is processed, its count may exceed 1 because objects previously processed may have referenced it. That is why it is unmarked by subtraction instead of by setting its count to 0.

During the examination of object table entries, chunks that were already free before the marking collection began will be encountered. The count field of an already-free chunk is zero just like an unmarked object, so it will be added to a free-chunk list. Doing so would cause a problem if the chunk were already on a free-chunk list. Therefore before the scan begins, all heads of free-chunk lists are reset.

As a final step, the reference count of each root object is incremented to assure that it is not deallocated accidentally.

rectifyCountsAndDeallocateGarbage
```
| count |
"reset heads of free-chunk lists"
FirstHeapSegment to: LastHeapSegment do: "for every segment"
    [ :segment |
        HeaderSize to: BigSize do: "for every free chunk list"
            [ :size |  "reset the list head"
                self resetFreeChunkList: size inSegment: segment]].
"rectify counts, and deallocate garbage"
```

```
                    0 to: ObjectTableSize−2 by: 2 do: "for every object table entry"
                    [ :objectPointer |
                      (self freeBitOf: objectPointer)=0
                        ifTrue: "if it is not a free entry"
                          [(count ← self countBitsOf: objectPointer) = 0
                            ifTrue: "it is unmarked, so deallocate it"
                              [self deallocate: objectPointer]
                            ifFalse: "it is marked, so rectify reference counts"
                              [count < 128 ifTrue: "subtract 1 to compensate for the mark"
                                [self countBitsOf: objectPointer put: count−1].
                              1 to: (self lastPointerOf: objectPointer)−1 do:
                                [ :offset | "increment the reference count of each
                                              pointer"
                                  self countUp: (self heapChunkOf: objectPointer
                                                       word: offset)]]]].
                              "be sure the root objects don't disappear"
                    rootObjectPointers do:
                      [ :rootObjectPointer | self countUp: rootObjectPointer].
                    self countBitsOf: NilPointer put: 128
```

The allocateChunk: routine can now be revised so that it attempts a marking collection if compaction of all segments has failed to yield enough space to satisfy an allocation request.

allocateChunk: size

```
| objectPointer |
objectPointer ← self attemptToAllocateChunk: size.
objectPointer isNil ifFalse: [↑objectPointer].
self reclaimInaccessibleObjects. "garbage collect and try again"
objectPointer ← self attemptToAllocateChunk: size.
objectPointer isNil ifFalse: [↑objectPointer].
self outOfMemoryError "give up"
```

Nonpointer Objects

The object format presented in this chapter is not particularly space efficient, but since its uniformity makes the system software small and simple, the inefficiency can generally be forgiven. There are two classes of object for which the inefficiency is intolerable, namely, character strings and bytecoded methods. There are usually many strings and methods in memory, and when stored one character or one bytecode per word, they are quite wasteful of space.

To store such objects more efficiently, an alternate memory format is used in which the data part of an object contains 8-bit or 16-bit values that are interpreted as unsigned integers rather than as object pointers. Such objects are distinguished by the setting of the pointer-fields bit of the object table entry: when that bit is 1, the data consist of object pointers; when that bit is 0, the data consist of positive 8- or 16-bit integers. When there are an odd number of bytes of data in a nonpointer object, the final byte of the last word is 0 (a slight waste of space), and the odd-length bit of the object table entry, which is normally 0, is set to 1. To support nonpointer objects, the allocator needs two additional parameters, pointerBit and oddBit. In the case of a nonpointer object (pointerBit=0), the default initial value of the elements is 0 instead of nil. The final version of the allocation routine is shown below.

allocate: size
      odd: oddBit
      pointer: pointerBit
      extra: extraWord
      class: classPointer
  | objectPointer default |
  self countUp: classPointer.
  objectPointer ← self allocateChunk: size + extraWord.
  self oddBitOf: objectPointer put: oddBit.
  self pointerBitOf: objectPointer put: pointerBit.
  self classBitsOf: objectPointer put: classPointer.
  default ← pointerBit=0 ifTrue: [0] ifFalse: [NilPointer].
  HeaderSize to: size-1 do:
    [:i | self heapChunkOf: objectPointer word: i put: default].
  self sizeBitsOf: objectPointer put: size.
  ↑objectPointer

The garbage-collecting traversal routines need only process the class field of each nonpointer object, because the data contain no pointers. To make this happen, the routine lastPointerOf: is changed as follows:

lastPointerOf: objectPointer ″**Preliminary Version**″
  (self pointerBitOf: objectPointer)=0
    ifTrue:
      [↑HeaderSize]
    ifFalse:
      [↑self sizeBitsOf: objectPointer]

The value of lastPointerOf: is never as large as 256 for a nonpointer object, so a nonpointer object never needs to be over-allocated. Therefore, spaceOccupiedBy: is revised again as follows:

spaceOccupiedBy: objectPointer
  | size |
  size ← self sizeBitsOf: objectPointer.
  (size < HugeSize or: [(self pointerBitOf: objectPointer) = 0])
    ifTrue: [↑size]
    ifFalse: [↑size + 1]

Formal Specification of the Object Memory

CompiledMethods

A CompiledMethod is an anomaly for the memory manager because its data are a mixture of 16-bit pointers and 8-bit unsigned integers. The only change needed to support CompiledMethods is to add to lastPointerOf: a computation similar to that in the bytecode interpreter's routine bytecodeIndexOf:. MethodClass is the object table index of CompiledMethod.

lastPointerOf: objectPointer
    | methodHeader |
    (self pointerBitOf: objectPointer)=0
        ifTrue:
            [↑HeaderSize]
        ifFalse:
            [(self classBitsOf: objectPointer)=MethodClass
                ifTrue: [methodHeader ← self heapChunkOf: objectPointer
                                            word: HeaderSize.
                        ↑HeaderSize + 1 + ((methodHeader bitAnd: 126)
                                                    bitShift: −1)]
                ifFalse: [↑self sizeBitsOf: objectPointer]]

Interface to the Bytecode Interpreter

The final step in the implementation of the object memory is to provide the interface routines required by the interpreter. Note that fetchClassOf: objectPointer returns IntegerClass (the object table index of SmallInteger) if its argument is an immediate integer.

object pointer access

fetchPointer: fieldIndex ofObject: objectPointer
    ↑self heapChunkOf: objectPointer word: HeaderSize + fieldIndex
storePointer: fieldIndex
        ofObject: objectPointer
        withValue: valuePointer
    | chunkIndex |
    chunkIndex ← HeaderSize + fieldIndex.
    self countUp: valuePointer.
    self countDown: (self heapChunkOf: objectPointer word: chunkIndex).
    ↑self heapChunkOf: objectPointer word: chunkIndex put: valuePointer

word access

fetchWord: wordIndex ofObject: objectPointer
    ↑self heapChunkOf: objectPointer word: HeaderSize + wordIndex
storeWord: wordIndex
        ofObject: objectPointer
        withValue: valueWord
    ↑self heapChunkOf: objectPointer word: HeaderSize + wordIndex
        put: valueWord

byte access

fetchByte: byteIndex ofObject: objectPointer
↑self heapChunkOf: objectPointer byte: (HeaderSize*2 + byteIndex)
storeByte: byteIndex
ofObject: objectPointer
withValue: valueByte
↑self heapChunkOf: objectPointer
byte: (HeaderSize*2 + byteIndex)
put: valueByte

reference counting

increaseReferencesTo: objectPointer
self countUp: objectPointer
decreaseReferencesTo: objectPointer
self countDown: objectPointer

class pointer access

fetchClassOf: objectPointer
(self isIntegerObject: objectPointer)
ifTrue: [↑IntegerClass]
ifFalse: [↑self classBitsOf: objectPointer]

length access

fetchWordLengthOf: objectPointer
↑(self sizeBitsOf: objectPointer)-HeaderSize
fetchByteLengthOf: objectPointer
↑(self loadWordLengthOf: objectPointer)*2 − (self oddBitOf: objectPointer)

object creation

instantiateClass: classPointer withPointers: length
| size extra |
size ← HeaderSize + length.
extra ← size < HugeSize ifTrue: [0] ifFalse: [1].
↑self allocate: size odd: 0 pointer: 1 extra: extra class: classPointer
instantiateClass: classPointer withWords: length
| size |
size ← HeaderSize + length.
↑self allocate: size odd: 0 pointer: 0 extra: 0 class: classPointer
instantiateClass: classPointer withBytes: length
| size |
size ← HeaderSize + ((length + 1)/2).
↑self allocate: size odd: length\\2 pointer: 0 extra: 0 class: classPointer

Formal Specification of the Object Memory

instance enumeration

initialInstanceOf: classPointer

0 to: ObjectTableSize−2 by: 2 do:
   [:pointer |
     (self freeBitOf: pointer)=0
         ifTrue: [(self fetchClassOf: pointer)=classPointer
                               ifTrue: [↑pointer]]].
↑NilPointer

instanceAfter: objectPointer

| classPointer |
objectPointer to: ObjectTableSize−2 by: 2 do:
   [:pointer |
     (self freeBitOf: pointer)=0
         ifTrue: [(self fetchClassOf: pointer)=classPointer
                               ifTrue: [↑pointer]]].
↑NilPointer

pointer swapping

swapPointersOf: firstPointer and: secondPointer

| firstSegment firstLocation firstPointer firstOdd |
firstSegment ← self segmentBitsOf: firstPointer.
firstLocation ← self locationBitsOf: firstPointer.
firstPointer ← self pointerBitOf: firstPointer.
firstOdd ← self oddBitOf: firstPointer.
self segmentBitsOf: firstPointer put: (self segmentBitsOf: secondPointer).
self locationBitsOf: firstPointer put: (self locationBitsOf: secondPointer).
self pointerBitOf: firstPointer put: (self pointerBitOf: secondPointer).
self oddBitOf: firstPointer put: (self oddBitOf: secondPointer).
self segmentBitsOf: secondPointer put: firstSegment.
self locationBitsOf: secondPointer put: firstLocation.
self pointerBitOf: secondPointer put: firstPointer.
self oddBitOf: secondPointer put: firstOdd

integer access

integerValueOf: objectPointer

↑objectPointer/2

integerObjectOf: value

↑(value bitShift: 1) + 1

isIntegerObject: objectPointer

↑(objectPointer bitAnd: 1) = 1

isIntegerValue: valueWord

↑valueWord <= −16384 and: [valueWord > 16834]

Indexes

Subject Index

There are four indexes to this book. The first is the type of index found in most books. It is called the *subject index* and includes the concepts discussed in the book. The other three indexes include the class names, variable names and message selectors referred to in the book. The *system index* includes names and selectors found in the actual Smalltalk-80 system. The *example class index* includes the names of classes introduced as examples but not found in the system. The *implementation index* includes the names and selectors used in the formal specification found in Part Four of the book.

System Index

Example Class Index

Implementation Index

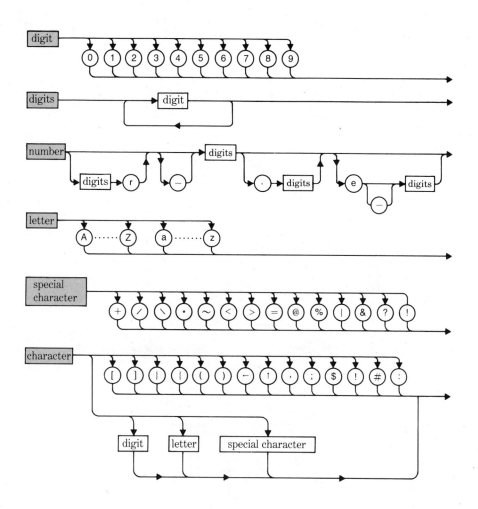

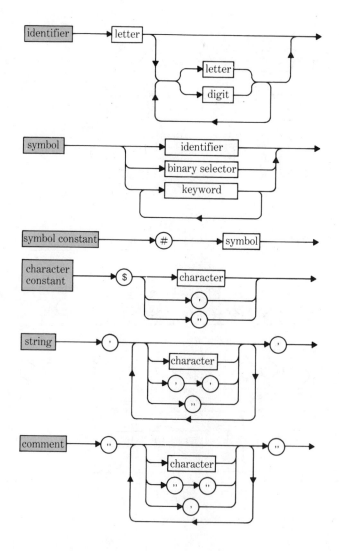

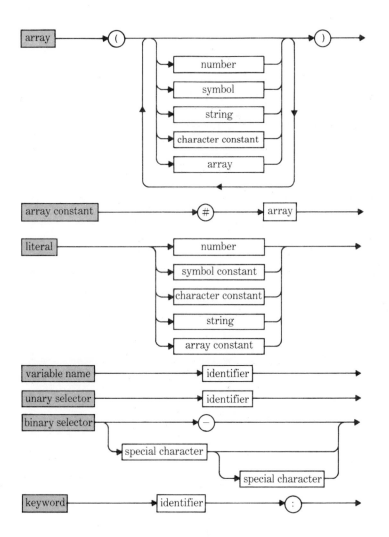

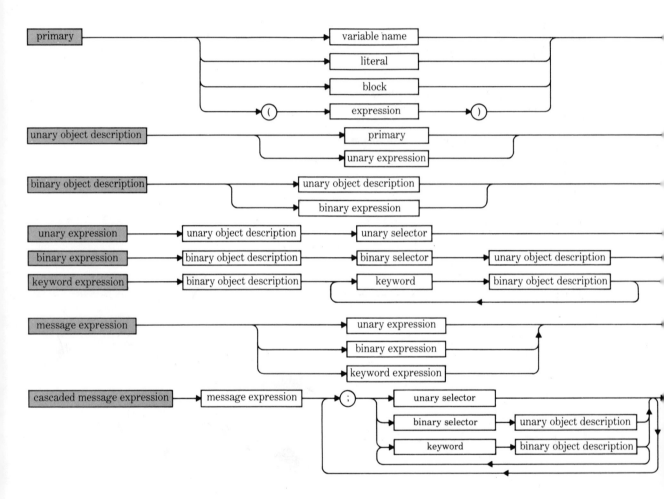